ALSO BY THE EDITORS OF COOK'S ILLUSTRATED,
HOME OF AMERICA'S TEST KITCHEN

The Best Recipe
The Best Recipe: American Classics
The Best Recipe: Italian Classics
The Best Recipe: Grilling and Barbecue
The Best Recipe: Soups and Stews

The America's Test Kitchen Cookbook
Here in America's Test Kitchen

The Best Kitchen Quick Tips

The Complete Book of Pasta and Noodles
The Cook's Illustrated Complete Book of Poultry

How to Barbecue and Roast on the Grill
How to Cook Chicken Breasts
How to Cook Chinese Favorites
How to Cook Garden Vegetables
How to Cook Shrimp and Other Shellfish
How to Grill
How to Make an American Layer Cake
How to Make Cookie Jar Favorites
How to Make Ice Cream
How to Make Muffins, Biscuits, and Scones
How to Make Pasta Sauces
How to Make Pot Pies and Casseroles
How to Make Salad
How to Make Sauces and Gravies
How to Make Simple Fruit Desserts
How to Make Soup
How to Make Stew
How to Sauté

To order any of our books, visit us at
http://www.cooksillustrated.com
or call 800-611-0759.

THE QUICK RECIPE

A BEST RECIPE CLASSIC

The Quick Recipe

BY THE EDITORS OF

COOK'S ILLUSTRATED

PHOTOGRAPHY BY CARL TREMBLAY AND DANIEL VAN ACKERE

FRONT COVER PHOTOGRAPH BY CHRISTOPHER HIRSHEIMER

ILLUSTRATIONS BY JOHN BURGOYNE

BOSTON COMMON PRESS

BROOKLINE, MASSACHUSETTS

Boston Common Press
17 Station Street
Brookline, MA 02445

ISBN 0-936184-66-3
Library of Congress Cataloging-in-Publication Data
The Editors of *Cook's Illustrated*
The Quick Recipe: Would you make 50 batches of cinnamon buns to figure out the simplest and the best version? We did.
Here are more than 300 exhaustively tested quick-from-scratch recipes—all ready in less than 60 minutes.
1st Edition

ISBN 0-936184-66-3 (hardback): $29.95
I. Cooking. I. Title
2003

10 9 8 7 6 5 4 3 2 1

Manufactured in the United States of America

Distributed by Boston Common Press, 17 Station Street, Brookline, MA 02445

Designed by Amy Klee
Edited by Jack Bishop

Pictured on front of jacket:	Fastest Cinnamon Buns (page 375)
Pictured on back of jacket:	30-Minute Chocolate Mousse (page 435)
	30-Minute Tarte Tatin (page 414)
	Breaded Chicken Fingers (page 200)

CONTENTS

PREFACE

I AM NO FAN OF MOST "QUICK" COOK- books because they tend to create artificial limits, allowing only so many ingredients or so much time for every recipe. This can lead to less than ideal results, as the cook is forced to sacrifice good sense and flavor for some elusive philosophical goal—fast food.

This all reminds me of 1991, when I came to Boston to take over the *East West Journal,* a magazine dedicated to the macrobiotic lifestyle. In terms of food, this meant no meat, no dairy, no sugar, and—after looking around at the first editorial meeting—not a lot of health, either. The assembled crowd was universally pale, enervated, and anything but robust. At first, I was impressed that many of them ate brown rice with steamed rutabaga, carrots, and kale for lunch, but then I noticed that the office was strangely silent come midafternoon. Where had the staff gone? To the ice cream parlor down the street! The leader of the macrobiotic movement, who founded the magazine, was equally proficient at philosophical dissembling. It turns out that he was often seen smoking cigarettes at the local pizza parlor.

I am not casting aspersions on the macrobiotic or the quick-cooking movements. A macrobiotic diet is a vastly better diet than what most Americans eat every day, and, because I am the father of four still-young children, quick cooking is a key element of my repertoire. I am, however, deeply suspicious of authors and leaders who promote a system that requires adherence to a strict code, whether it be "Four Ingredients" or "Eat No Sugar." A bit of flexibility seems to be in order, as any rigid system is probably doomed to failure.

What does all of this mean in terms of this "quick" cookbook? It means that some recipes are longer than others, that we actually count all of the preparation time (not just the cooking time), and that we set a reasonable limit of one hour per recipe, with many of the dishes in this book requiring much less time. We also discounted most convenience foods (other than a few basics such as frozen puff pastry, frozen blueberries, or instant polenta) and all prepared foods—shortcuts that are not worthy of any serious cookbook.

The other key ingredient was a healthy dose of skepticism. Could we make an authentic New Orleans jambalaya in just 45 minutes? Is 30-minute chocolate mousse worth eating? Can chicken soup become a simple Tuesday-night dinner? In most cases, the answer turned out to be yes. In fact, our own test cooks have turned to the recipes they developed for *The Quick Recipe* as their new bible of midweek cooking.

I am not promising you culinary nirvana. The recipes in this book still take time and careful preparation. You will not have dinner on the table 20 minutes from the moment you walk in the door. But you will have a collection of 300 recipes that work, that taste good, and that can be made in an hour or less. We think that is, on the face of it, a modest proposal but one worth investigating. Good food and good recipes, after all, are never easy to come by.

Christopher Kimball
Founder and Editor
Cook's Illustrated

ACKNOWLEDGMENTS

ALL OF THE PROJECTS UNDERTAKEN AT *Cook's Illustrated* are collective efforts, the combined experience and work of editors, test cooks, and writers, all joining in the search for the best cooking methods. This book is no exception.

Editor Jack Bishop spearheaded this project. Julia Collin supervised the recipe development process and organized the in-house photography shoots. Julia Collin, Matthew Card, Keith Dresser, and Raquel Pelzel were the researchers, recipe developers, and writers for the book.

Amy Klee created the design for the book, and Nina Madjid transformed computer files and digital scans into a book. Julia Sedykh designed the cover, and Christopher Hirsheimer photographed the front cover image. Carl Tremblay captured the food images that appear throughout the book as well as on the back cover. Daniel J. van Ackere took photographs of the equipment and ingredients, and John Burgoyne drew all of the illustrations.

The following individuals on the editorial, production, circulation, customer service, and office staffs also worked on the book: Ron Bilodeau, Barbara Bourassa, Rich Cassidy, Sharyn Chabot, Mary Connelly, Cathy Dorsey, Lenira DosReis, Freddy Flores, Lori Galvin-Frost, Robin Gilmore-Barnes, Larisa Greiner, Rebecca Hays, India Koopman, Jim McCormack, Jennifer McCreary, Nicole Morris, Henrietta Murray, Madeline Gutin Perri, Jessica Quirk, Jean Rogers, and Mandy Shito. And without help from members of the marketing staff, readers might never find our books. Special thanks to Deborah Broide, Steven Browall, Shekinah Cohn, Connie Forbes, Julie Gardner, Jason Geller, David Mack, Adam Perry, Steven Sussman, Jacqui Valerio, and Jonathan Venier; all contributed to our marketing and distribution efforts.

WHAT IS A QUICK RECIPE?

QUICK COOKING MEANS DIFFERENT THINGS TO DIFFERENT people. For many Americans, it means heating a frozen dinner in the microwave. Recipes that rely on multiple convenience products, such as canned soups, precooked meats, and instant potatoes, are the next step up in the quick hierarchy. Because many of these "convenience" recipes take 30 minutes to prepare, we don't understand the point. Why not just microwave a frozen dinner? The end result is pretty much the same.

This is not to say that all convenience foods are taboo. We regularly use canned chicken broth, canned beans, frozen vegetables, and canned tomatoes in the test kitchen. The trick is to pair high-quality convenience products with fresh ingredients. That was our goal in creating the recipes for this book. We wanted food that tasted good—very good—but we recognized the fact that most home cooks can't spend a lot of time in the kitchen.

So what is our definition of a quick recipe?

1. A quick recipe must be worth the effort. It should taste far better than you might expect, given the amount of work needed to prepare it. The sum should be greater than the individual parts.

2. A quick recipe is ready to serve in less than 60 minutes—often in less than 30. This timing begins when you walk into the kitchen and includes the time needed to assemble and prepare ingredients as well as that needed for cooking and/or cooling.

3. A quick recipe does not have a laundry list of ingredients. A 25-ingredient stir-fry does not fit the quick profile, even if the actual cooking time is just 10 minutes. Just as important, a four-ingredient recipe that would taste far better with a few more ingredients and 5 minutes of extra work doesn't make sense to us either. Most of the recipes in this book have 10 or fewer ingredients. Some recipes have one or two more ingredients, but in those cases many of the ingredients are spices or other pantry items that don't require any preparation.

How did we meet these requirements? Quick cooking techniques, such as grilling, sautéing, and stir-frying, are part of the answer. Quick-cooking foods—steaks and chops rather than huge roasts—are also essential. These techniques and foods are highlighted in Building-Block Recipes throughout the book. These recipes will teach you the quick-cooking basics—how to scramble eggs, sauté chicken cutlets, pan-sear steaks, and steam white rice.

In addition to quick cooking methods and foods, we have relied on ingredients with "big" flavors, such as chiles, fresh herbs, citrus zest and juices, and spices. Many recipes in this book call for the bold-flavored ethnic ingredients now widely available in supermarkets—everything from chipotle chiles and soy sauce to balsamic vinegar and curry powder. Last, we have employed sensible shortcuts to save on time and work. For example, we put the same skillet to multiple uses when preparing a meal. We add whole herb sprigs during cooking rather than stripping leaves from the stems and mincing them.

The 300 recipes in this book represent the way we cook at home on weeknights. We are willing to invest a modest amount of time and energy in order to produce food we can be proud of. We hope these quick recipes will do more than just quell your hunger. We hope they will satisfy your appetite.

1

APPETIZERS

A GOOD APPETIZER IS QUICK BY DEFINITION. Who wants to spend all day in the kitchen making food that will be consumed in a few bites and with little attention? Of course, you can serve cheese and crackers or good olives with drinks and be done with it, but there are times when you want to do something special. You may not bother with one for a casual weeknight supper, but the ideal appetizer is simple enough that you *could* whip it up for your family. Our goal for this chapter was clear: develop recipes that are not much harder than unwrapping a piece of cheese but somehow are much more interesting.

WHIPPED GOAT CHEESE

A QUICK WAY TO DRESS UP A LOG OF plain goat cheese is to whip it, which changes its texture from dry and crumbly to soft, silky, and spreadable. Although this technique is simple, it can yield goat cheese spreads that are too soft, too wet, or too crumbly. We knew there were tricks to discover.

First, we tried whipping the goat cheese on its own, but we wound up with a mixture that was far too dry. We then added liquid to the cheese and had better luck. Testing water, milk, heavy cream, sour cream, and mayonnaise, we found the luscious yet clean flavor of heavy cream worked best. Milk and water were too lightweight, turning the cheese into a wimpy-tasting spread, while the sour cream was simply too sour and the mayonnaise too oily. For an 8-ounce log of goat cheese, we found ⅓ cup heavy cream was needed to temper the cheese's harsh edges and to make the whipped texture light and airy. Although the final texture is spreadable, it is not wet, and the cream does not alter the goat cheese's natural character much.

Adding a few flavorings makes this quick goat cheese transformation not only incredibly easy but a refreshing change of pace from the same old plate of cheese and crackers. Tasters found that lemon zest and chives, plus the standard salt and pepper, yielded a mild spread that works with almost any meal. Mint, garlic, and hot red pepper flakes produced a zestier version that is right at home with Mediterranean dishes.

Whipped Goat Cheese with Chives and Lemon

MAKES ABOUT 1 CUP, SERVING 4

TIME: 5 MINUTES

Serve with pita chips (page 15), crostini (page 19), or any good crackers.

8	ounces fresh goat cheese
⅓	cup heavy cream
	Pinch salt
⅛	teaspoon ground black pepper
1	tablespoon minced fresh chives
½	teaspoon grated lemon zest

Whip all the ingredients with an electric mixer until the mixture is soft and uniform, about 1 minute. Transfer the cheese mixture to a serving bowl; serve. (The whipped cheese can be refrigerated in an airtight container for 1 day.)

> VARIATION

Whipped Goat Cheese with Garlic and Mint

Follow the recipe for Whipped Goat Cheese with Chives and Lemon, replacing the pepper, chives, and zest with ¼ teaspoon hot red pepper flakes, 2 teaspoons minced fresh mint leaves, and 1 small garlic clove minced with the pinch of salt to form a smooth paste.

CREAMY DIPS

DIPS MADE FROM DRIED SOUP MIXES are a guilty pleasure. However, dips made with fresh ingredients have more vibrant flavors. We wanted to find an easy way to make creamy dips using only a few ingredients and minimal effort—and no packaged mixes.

Our search began with the consistency of the dip. The word *creamy* can be variously interpreted, so we polled our tasters. None of them were fond of the thick consistency of supermarket tub dips. As one of them put it, "If a carrot can stand straight up without moving, you know the dip is loaded with unsavory ingredients." The tasters wanted dips that were substantial enough to coat their vegetables and chips without engulfing them.

To start, we tested every potential combination of creamy ingredients, from the standard mayonnaise, sour cream, and yogurt to the less obvious buttermilk, heavy cream, cottage cheese, and cream cheese. In the end, two combinations made it across the finish line: mayonnaise and sour cream, and mayonnaise and yogurt. Mayonnaise contributes the body, richness, and velvety texture that are perfect in a creamy dip. Both sour cream and yogurt heighten flavor; sour cream is refreshingly cool and tangy, while yogurt is bright and sharp. Yogurt has one problem, however. Right out of the container, it is too slack and requires draining to thicken it. Although we found that an overnight stay in the refrigerator in a fine-mesh sieve firms the yogurt, this takes too long. A combination of 2 parts mayonnaise and 1 part sour cream offered the best flavor and was ready in seconds.

Turning our attention to the flavorings, we gathered a battalion of ingredients—strong cheeses, fiery horseradish, spicy chiles, tangy citrus, and pungent herbs, to name a few— and got to work. Right off the bat, we discovered that boldness was required, as the flavorings were up against the deadening effects of rich dairy products. Yet we also wanted simplicity, not a laundry list of ingredients. After going through a fair amount of mayonnaise and sour cream, we came up with these vibrant, singular dips that offer just the right combinations of texture and flavor.

One final note: Although these recipes come together in moments, tasters found they taste best when refrigerated for at least 40 minutes before serving. The dips can be prepared up to two days in advance and pulled out of the refrigerator on a minute's notice.

~

Chipotle-Lime Dip with Scallions

MAKES ABOUT 1 1/2 CUPS, SERVING 8 TO 10

TIME: 50 MINUTES (INCLUDES 40 MINUTES IN THE REFRIGERATOR)

See pages 5, 6, and 7 for information about preparing vegetables to accompany this dip.

1	cup mayonnaise
1/2	cup sour cream
3	medium scallions, trimmed and sliced thin
2	medium cloves garlic, minced or pressed through a garlic press (about 2 teaspoons)
3	small chipotle chiles in adobo sauce, minced to paste (about 1 tablespoon), plus 1/2 teaspoon adobo sauce
1	teaspoon grated zest plus 1 tablespoon juice from 1 lime

Combine all the ingredients in a medium bowl and mix until smooth and creamy. Transfer the dip to a serving bowl, cover with plastic wrap, and refrigerate until the flavors are blended, at least 40 minutes; serve cold. (The dip can be refrigerated for up to 2 days.)

MINCING GARLIC TO A PASTE

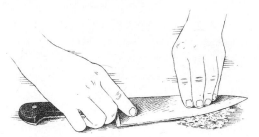

Mince the garlic as you normally would on a cutting board with a chef's knife. Sprinkle the minced garlic with a little salt, then drag the side of the knife over the garlic-salt mixture to form a fine puree. Continue to mince and drag the knife as necessary until the puree is smooth. If possible, use kosher or coarse salt; the larger crystals do a better job of breaking down the garlic than fine table salt does.

"Caesar" Dip with Parmesan and Anchovies

MAKES ABOUT 1 ½ CUPS,
SERVING 8 TO 10

TIME: 50 MINUTES (INCLUDES 40
MINUTES IN THE REFRIGERATOR)

See pages 5, 6, and 7 for information about preparing vegetables to accompany this dip.

1	cup mayonnaise
½	cup sour cream
½	cup grated Parmesan cheese
1	tablespoon juice from 1 lemon
1	tablespoon minced fresh parsley leaves
2	medium cloves garlic, minced or pressed through a garlic press (about 2 teaspoons)
2	anchovy fillets, minced to a paste (about 1 teaspoon)
⅛	teaspoon ground black pepper

Combine all the ingredients in a medium bowl and mix until smooth and creamy. Transfer the dip to a serving bowl, cover with plastic wrap, and refrigerate until the flavors are blended, at least 40 minutes; serve cold. (The dip can be refrigerated for up to 2 days.)

Green Goddess Dip

MAKES ABOUT 1 ½ CUPS,
SERVING 8 TO 10

TIME: 50 MINUTES (INCLUDES 40
MINUTES IN THE REFRIGERATOR)

See pages 5, 6, and 7 for information about preparing vegetables to accompany this dip.

¾	cup mayonnaise
¾	cup sour cream
2	medium cloves garlic, minced or pressed through a garlic press (about 2 teaspoons)
¼	cup minced fresh parsley leaves
¼	cup minced fresh chives
2	tablespoons minced fresh tarragon leaves
1	tablespoon juice from 1 lemon
⅛	teaspoon salt
⅛	teaspoon ground black pepper

Combine all the ingredients in a medium bowl and mix until smooth and creamy. Transfer the dip to a serving bowl, cover with plastic wrap, and refrigerate until the flavors are blended, at least 40 minutes; serve cold. (The dip can be refrigerated for up to 2 days.)

CRUDITÉS

WITH AN EXTENSIVE SELECTION OF vegetables now available year-round, crudités should be tempting, if not downright exotic, and offer a colorful variety of flavors and textures. But the key to good crudités doesn't lie only in the selection and arrangement of good-looking vegetables. If you want vegetables that actually taste good, they must be properly prepared.

Not all vegetables are meant to be eaten raw (unless you're a rabbit), and after extensive kitchen tests we concluded that many require a quick dunk in boiling, salted water (blanching) before being added to the platter. This crucial step is often overlooked for the sake of convenience, but we found it makes all the difference between mediocre and great crudités. Not only does blanching bring tough vegetables to a gentle crunch but also the salty water seasons the vegetables as they cook, enhancing their natural flavors.

Here are three keys to successfully blanched vegetables:

First, to prevent the carrots from tasting like asparagus or the cauliflower from turning green, blanch each vegetable separately. Being mindful of the order in which you blanch them, begin with the bland and pale and finish with the bold and dark (the vegetables listed in the cooking chart (below) are organized in the order in which they should be blanched).

Second, use a large pot that allows the vegetables ample room to cook and become seasoned. A large volume of water (we use 6 quarts) ensures quick cooking times and brightly colored vegetables.

Third, once the vegetables are crisp-tender, transfer them from the boiling water to an ice-water bath immediately. This process (called shocking) prevents residual heat in the vegetables from cooking them further, which compromises their final color, texture, and flavor.

BUILDING BLOCK RECIPE

Blanched Vegetables for Crudités

Celery, bell peppers, endive, jícama, tomatoes, and radishes taste best raw, but the vegetables listed below are best served by a quick blanch-and-shock before joining the rest on the platter. Blanch the vegetables in the order given, which starts with the mildest and ends with the strongest. See the illustrations on pages 6 and 7 for tips on preparing some of these vegetables. We found that 2 pounds of prepared vegetables and 1½ cups dip are sufficient for a group of 8 to 10 people.

CARROTS	15 seconds
SNOW/SNAP PEAS	15 seconds
CAULIFLOWER	1 to 1½ minutes
GREEN BEANS	1 minute
FENNEL	1 minute
BROCCOLI	1 to 1½ minutes
ASPARAGUS	30 to 60 seconds

KEY STEPS FOR BLANCHING VEGETABLES

1. Bring 6 quarts water to a boil in a large pot over high heat and season with 5 teaspoons salt. Cook the vegetables, one variety at a time, until slightly softened but still crunchy (crisp-tender), following the times recommended in the chart to the left.

2. Transfer the blanched vegetables to a bowl of ice water and allow to soak until completely cool, about 1 minute. Place the vegetables on several layers of paper towels and pat them completely dry.

PREPARING VEGETABLES FOR CRUDITÉS

We found a few tricks that make vegetables more palatable and a lot easier to swipe through a dip.

ASPARAGUS

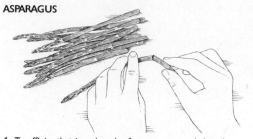

1. To efficiently trim a bunch of asparagus, gently bend one stalk until the tough portion of the stem breaks off.

2. Place this broken asparagus alongside the others, still untrimmed. Using it as a guide, cut the tough ends off the remaining asparagus.

BROCCOLI AND CAULIFLOWER

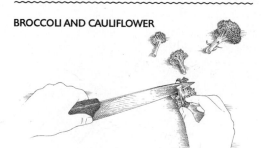

To cut attractive, bite-size florets, slice down through the main stem and out through the buds to produce 1-inch florets with 2-inch stems.

GREEN BEANS

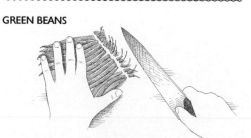

Instead of trimming the stem from one green bean at a time, line up the beans and trim all the ends with just one slice.

CARROTS

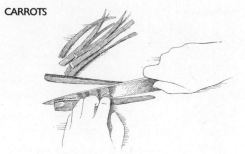

Although it is tempting to use bagged prewashed baby carrots, their stubby stature makes it all too easy for fingers or knuckles to graze the surface of the dip when swiping. For long, elegant lengths of carrot, slice peeled carrots in half lengthwise. Then, with the cut side flat to the board, slice each half into three long pieces.

CELERY

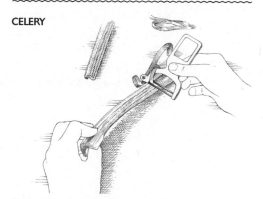

Celery often tastes harsh and vegetal, but its flavors can quickly turn sweet and mellow after its bitter skin and stringy fibers are removed with a vegetable peeler.

SNOW AND SNAP PEAS

Delicate snow and snap peas taste best when rid of the fibrous string that runs along the straight edge of the pod. Using a paring knife, carefully remove this string.

BELL PEPPER

1. Slice a ½-inch section off both the tip and stem ends. Make one slit in the trimmed shell, place it skin-side down, and press the flesh flat against the cutting board.

2. After removing the seeds and core, use a sharp knife to remove a ⅛-inch-thick piece of the tasteless inner membrane, then cut the pepper into ½-inch-wide lengths.

ENDIVE

Gently pull the leaves off one at a time, continuing to trim the root end as you work your way toward the center.

RADISHES

Halve radishes with their green tops still attached so each half has a leafy handle for grasping and dipping.

FENNEL

1. After trimming the base and removing the upper stalks and fronds, slice the oval bulb in half lengthwise.

2. Remove the layers of fennel from each half, then cut them into ½-inch-thick strips.

ZUCCHINI, SUMMER SQUASH, AND DAIKON RADISH

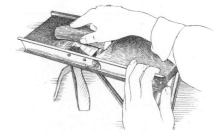

1. Though somewhat unusual for crudités, these vegetables can easily be added to the platter. Using a mandoline, cut them into ⅛-inch-thick slices.

2. To make the thin slices easy to dip and eat, roll them into tidy cylinders and secure with a toothpick.

SPINACH DIP

IN 1954, AMERICA WAS INTRODUCED to what would become our most popular party fare: Lipton's onion soup mix combined with sour cream. Spinach dip—made with vegetable soup mix, sour cream, and frozen spinach—was hot on its heels. Fifty years later, most spinach dips are still based on soup mixes, and the flavors are still flat, exorbitantly salty, and nowhere near fresh. Yet a good spinach dip can be made easily enough with just a few fresh ingredients, a couple of kitchen tools, and no more than 30 minutes of preparation. (A good onion dip takes much longer because the onions must be caramelized in a skillet for at least 45 minutes.) Spinach dip should be rich, thick, and creamy—perfectly dippable—and brimming with big, bold flavors, especially that of spinach. We set out to renovate spinach dip without compromising its quick and easy appeal.

To begin, we gathered five varieties of spinach: curly (or crinkly), flat (or smooth), semisavoy (a hybrid of the two), baby, and, for the sake of comparison, frozen spinach. We then trimmed, washed, chopped, and wilted the fresh spinaches in hot pots (we simply thawed the frozen spinach), made the dips, chilled them to set (cool and thicken), and let tasters dig in. The results were so surprising we had to tally them twice. Frozen spinach was the victor. Tasters liked its "familiar," "intense" flavor and even used the word "fresh" to describe it. The fresh varieties were too "meek," their flavor lost among the other ingredients. After a few more tests to determine consistency, we found that 20 to 30 seconds in the food processor chopped the thawed frozen spinach into small, manageable bits and made the dip smooth and creamy.

The 1950s were creeping their way back into the recipe—frozen spinach, no cooking (so far), and speedy preparation—but we weren't about to backtrack on flavor. Armed with a host of fresh herbs and other pungent ingredients, we began developing the flavor components for the dip sans soup mix. Among the herbs, parsley and dill were by and large the standards, and they worked appealingly well when combined. Onions and shallots were problematic, however, as they required cooking to mellow their astringency and soften their crunch. We weren't cooking the spinach and thought it would be a waste of time and effort to start pulling out pots and pans now. In the end, a combination of raw scallion whites and a single clove of garlic added the perfect amount of bite and pungency. With a dash of hot pepper sauce for a kick of heat and some salt and pepper, the dip came out of the processor light, fresh, and full of bold flavors—far better than the soup mix recipe and not much more work.

The only problem remaining was that the dip, which took only about 15 minutes to make, took almost 2 hours to chill. Wanting to skip this polar timeout, we found the solution was simple enough. Instead of thawing the spinach completely, we simply thawed it only partially. Before processing, we microwaved the frozen block for 3 minutes on low, broke it into icy chunks, and squeezed each to extract a surprising amount of liquid. The chunks were still ice cold and thoroughly cooled the dip as they broke down in the processor. Although our hands were slightly numb, the dip was quick, thick, creamy, and cool enough for immediate service.

Creamy Herbed Spinach Dip

MAKES ABOUT 1½ CUPS,
SERVING 8 TO 10

TIME: 10 MINUTES

Partial thawing of the spinach produces a cold dip that can be served without further chilling. If you don't own a microwave, thaw the frozen spinach at room temperature for 1½ hours, then squeeze out the excess liquid. The garlic must be minced or pressed before going into the food processor; otherwise, the dip will contain large chunks of garlic. See pages 5, 6, and 7 for information about preparing vegetables to accompany this dip.

10	ounces frozen chopped spinach
½	cup sour cream
½	cup mayonnaise
3	medium scallions, white parts only, sliced thin (about 2 tablespoons)
1	tablespoon chopped fresh dill leaves
½	cup packed fresh parsley leaves
1	small clove garlic, minced or pressed through a garlic press (about 1 teaspoon)
¼	teaspoon hot pepper sauce, such as Tabasco
½	teaspoon salt
¼	teaspoon ground black pepper
½	medium red bell pepper, diced fine (about ¼ cup)

1. Thaw the spinach in a microwave for 3 minutes at 40 percent power. (The edges should be thawed but not warm; the center should be soft enough to be broken into icy chunks.) Squeeze the partially frozen spinach of excess water.

2. In a food processor, process the spinach, sour cream, mayonnaise, scallions, dill, parsley, garlic, hot pepper sauce, salt, and pepper until smooth and creamy, about 30 seconds. Transfer the mixture to a serving bowl and stir in the bell pepper; serve. (The dip can be covered with plastic wrap and refrigerated for up to 2 days.)

SMOKED SALMON MOUSSE

POTENT, SALTY-SWEET SMOKED SALMON is perfect for an appetizer mousse. Its strong, perfumed flavor stands up to the creamy base that often overwhelms less flavorful ingredients. On the other hand, because that flavor is so pervasive, smoked salmon mousse often turns out tasting one-dimensional and unbalanced.

To start, we found that smoked salmon is now sold everywhere in vacuum-sealed packages. Most packages we found held 4 ounces, so we decided to base our recipe on this amount. Turning our attention to the base of the mousse, we tried a variety of ingredients, including cream cheese, sour cream, crème fraîche, yogurt, and mayonnaise. Tossing the yogurt aside as tasting awful with smoked salmon, we thought mayonnaise tasted like a sandwich spread with an unattractive, oily mouthfeel. Sour cream and crème fraîche both tasted fantastic, but they produced textures that were far too loose and diplike. Cream cheese produced a good, spreadable texture but tasted more like a bagel topping than a mousse. By mixing crème fraîche or sour cream with the cream cheese, however, we were able to get just the flavor and texture we were looking for. We found that, rounded out with shallot, lemon juice, and black pepper, the mousse required no additional salt due to the naturally salty character of the smoked salmon.

Up to this point, we had been chopping the salmon by hand and using a rubber spatula to mix it with the other ingredients in a large bowl. Wondering if we could streamline the technique, we were surprised when mousse prepared in a food processor not only tasted as good as the hand-mixed version but also had a better texture. However, neither the shallot nor the crème fraîche processed in the same amount of time the salmon did. Because the food-processed shallot didn't break down into small enough pieces, we had to mince it first. As for the crème fraîche, we noted that it turned loose and watery when processed for too long and found it best simply to pulse it into the mixture at the end.

Smoked Salmon Mousse

MAKES ABOUT 1 ¼ CUPS,
SERVING 4 TO 6

TIME: 5 MINUTES

Our favorite way to use this spread is as a canapé topping on small, thin squares of black bread. If you have more time, pipe the mousse onto endive leaves. Crème fraîche gives the mousse a slightly creamier, subtler flavor than sour cream does, but sour cream works admirably, too. To soften the cream cheese, cut it into chunks and leave it at room temperature for several minutes while you mince the shallot and measure the other ingredients.

4	ounces sliced smoked salmon
1	large shallot, minced
2	ounces cream cheese, softened
2	teaspoons juice from 1 lemon
¼	cup crème fraîche or sour cream
	Ground black pepper

1. Place the salmon and shallot in the workbowl of a food processor and process, scraping down the sides of the bowl as necessary, until the mixture is finely chopped, about 10 seconds. Add the cream cheese and lemon juice and process until the mixture forms a ball, scraping down the sides of the bowl as necessary. Add the crème fraîche and pulse just to incorporate, 5 seconds.

2. Scrape the mousse into a serving bowl and season with pepper to taste; serve. (The mousse can be refrigerated in an airtight container for up to 2 days.)

➤ VARIATION
Smoked Trout Mousse
Follow the recipe for Smoked Salmon Mousse, replacing the salmon with 8 ounces smoked trout fillets (about 2 fillets), skinned and broken into pieces. Substitute lime juice for the lemon juice and increase the crème fraîche to ⅓ cup. Add 2 tablespoons well-drained prepared horseradish along with the crème fraîche.

HUMMUS

ALTHOUGH HUMMUS IS RELATIVELY new to the American diet, this simple chickpea puree has been eaten since the time of Socrates and Plato. Tubs of prepared hummus are sold in supermarkets across the United States, but they don't taste very good. We wanted to make a much better hummus without expending too much effort.

We did some research and found that hummus actually has multiple interpretations. Across the Middle East and throughout the Mediterranean region, individual families each have their own recipe; these vary by texture and flavor. The only thing they have in common is the combination of chickpeas and *tahini* (sesame paste). Tasting several hummus interpretations side by side, tasters chose the American style as their favorite. Seasoned with lemon and garlic, this smooth version has a stiff, diplike texture and is far less oily than the other options we tested.

We were impressed by the results obtained with canned chickpeas. Most brands pack the beans in a slimy, water-based liquid, and we found the hummus tasted cleaner when we rinsed the chickpeas before pureeing them. Also, we noted that some of the thin skins would come off the beans if they were then quickly toweled dry, ensuring a smooth puree.

Finding that a 15-ounce can of chickpeas made a good-sized batch of hummus, we then moved our attention to the seasonings. We tried various amounts of tahini and found that ¼ cup yielded a good balance of flavors. One clove of garlic along with a pinch of cayenne added just the right bite. We fussed over the amount of lemon juice and eventually decided that 3 tablespoons added just the right level of brightness.

After adding these ingredients, we tried adjusting the final texture by adding extra-virgin olive oil. We found, however, that the amount of oil needed to achieve a smooth yet sturdy consistency was overpowering in flavor. We corrected this by replacing half the oil with water, bringing all the flavors into line. Last, we found that the hummus tasted better when allowed to sit for 30 minutes so the flavors could meld. Classically served with pita chips (see our recipe on page 15) or crackers, this zippy-quick hummus tastes far better than anything bought at the store.

INGREDIENTS: Jarred Roasted Red Peppers

Jarred peppers are convenient, but are all brands created equal? To find out, we collected six brands from local supermarkets. The contenders were Divina Roasted Sweet Peppers, Greek Gourmet Roasted Sweet Red Peppers, Lapas Sweet Roasted Peppers, Gaea Flame Roasted Red Peppers, and Peloponnese Roasted Florina Whole Sweet Peppers. Three of these brands identified the type of pepper used (Divina, Gaea, and Peloponnese all use Florina peppers), and we wondered if a company's willingness to identify the variety of pepper it was selling would be an indicator of the quality of the pepper. In other words, would tasters prefer the clearly named Florina peppers over the generic, whose main ingredient was identified only as "peppers"? To more easily identify their preferences, tasters tried the peppers straight from the jar.

Tasters did not necessarily prefer the peppers labeled Florina. What counted was the flavor and texture of the pepper itself as well as the flavor of the brine. The top two brands, Divina (roasted Florina pimento red peppers) and Greek Gourmet (fire-roasted peppers), were preferred for their "soft and tender texture" (the Divinas) and "refreshing," "piquant," "smoky" flavor (the Greek Gourmets). The other brands were marked down for their lack of "roasty flavor" and for the unpleasantly overpowering flavor of the brines. These peppers tasted as if they'd been "buried under brine and acid," or they had a "pepperoncini-like sourness" or a "sweet and acidic aftertaste."

The conclusion? Tasters preferred peppers with a full, smoky, roasted flavor, a brine that was spicy but not too sweet, and a tender texture.

THE BEST JARRED ROASTED RED PEPPERS

Divina peppers (left) were the top choice of tasters. Greek Gourmet peppers (right) were a close second.

Hummus

MAKES ABOUT 2 CUPS,
SERVING 8 TO 10

TIME: 40 MINUTES (INCLUDES 30
MINUTES IN THE REFRIGERATOR)

*Serve hummus with pita chips (page 15) or fresh
pita breads cut into wedges. If you like, serve with
crudités (pages 5, 6, and 7) as well.*

1	(15-ounce) can chickpeas, drained, rinsed, and toweled dry
1	medium clove garlic, minced
¾	teaspoon salt
	Pinch cayenne pepper
3	tablespoons juice from 1 large lemon
¼	cup tahini
¼	cup extra-virgin olive oil
¼	cup water

Process all the ingredients in a food processor
until smooth, about 40 seconds. Transfer the
hummus to a serving bowl, cover with plastic
wrap, and chill until the flavors meld, at least
30 minutes; serve cold. (The hummus can be
refrigerated for up to 2 days.)

ROASTED RED
PEPPER SPREAD

MUHAMMARA, MADE FROM ROASTED
red peppers, walnuts, and pomegranate
molasses, is a popular spread made throughout
the eastern Mediterranean. We wanted to
develop a quick version, based on pantry staples, without losing the sweet, smoky, savory
flavors that make this spread so popular.

The first hurdle was the roasted peppers.
Although roasting red peppers is fairly easy, we
found that good-quality jarred peppers could
be used (see page 11 for more information).
The trick is to rinse them of their brine before
using them. The next hurdle was finding a
replacement for the pomegranate molasses,
which is difficult to locate in typical American
supermarkets. Seeking its thick, syrupy texture
and sweet-sour flavor, we tested a variety of
pantry ingredients to come up with a substitute. In the end, we found that a combination
of lemon juice, honey, and mild molasses
worked well. Seasoned with cayenne, ground
cumin, and salt, the spread required only a
small amount of olive oil to help loosen its
consistency and toasted walnuts to enrich it.

At this point, our dip tasted pretty good,

CUTTING PITA BREADS

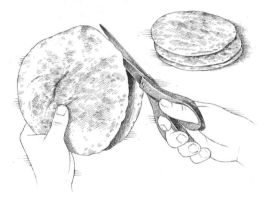

1. Using kitchen shears, cut around the perimeter of each
pita bread to yield 2 thin rounds.

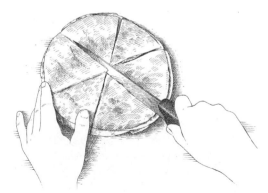

2. Stack the pita rounds and, using a chef's knife, cut them
into 6 wedges each.

but it was still missing something. Taking a look at Paula Wolfert's recipe for muhammara, we quickly realized what it was—crumbled wheat crackers. We added a generic brand of plain wheat crackers from the supermarket and found they contributed both flavor and substance to the mix, turning our roasted red pepper spread into a fair replication of authentic muhammara. Last, we noted that the flavors needed time to meld—at least 30 minutes—before serving.

Roasted Red Pepper Spread

MAKES ABOUT 2 CUPS,
ENOUGH FOR 8 TO 10

TIME: 40 MINUTES (INCLUDES 30 MINUTES IN THE REFRIGERATOR)

Serve this dip with pita chips (page 15), fresh pitas cut into wedges, or baguette slices. See page 11 for information on our testing of jarred roasted red peppers.

1	cup walnuts
12	ounces jarred roasted red peppers, drained, rinsed, and patted dry with paper towels
1/8	teaspoon cayenne pepper
1/4	cup plain wheat crackers, crumbled
3	tablespoons juice from 1 large lemon
1	tablespoon mild molasses
1	teaspoon honey
1/2	teaspoon ground cumin
3/4	teaspoon salt
2	tablespoons extra-virgin olive oil

1. Place the walnuts in a medium skillet over medium heat and toast, shaking the pan occasionally to turn the nuts, until they are fragrant, about 5 minutes. Cool the nuts on a plate.

2. Process the toasted walnuts with the remaining ingredients in a food processor until smooth, about ten 1-second pulses. Transfer the mixture to a serving bowl, cover with plastic wrap, and chill until the flavors meld, at least 30 minutes; serve cold. (The spread can be refrigerated for up to 2 days.)

PITA CHIPS

PITA CHIPS ARE A NATURAL ACCOMPANIMENT to hummus and roasted red pepper spread, and when made at home they taste far better than the expensive bags of broken chips available at the grocery store. Because pita chips are essentially pieces of toast made from pita bread, we figured that developing this recipe was going to be a breeze. Surprisingly, it took a few more tests than we figured on.

We took advantage of the pocket in the middle of each pita by first cutting the pitas into two thin, round layers. Thin one-layer chips not only baked more evenly than two-layered chips but also were easier to dip and eat. After a few tests, we realized that the most efficient way to prepare the pitas was to cut them around the edge with scissors. Then, using a chef's knife, it was easy to cut through a stack of the single-layered pitas into chips of the appropriate size.

Next, we tried baking two batches—one plain, the other brushed with a little olive oil. Hands down, we preferred the crisp, flavorful chips made with a little oil. The oil made all the difference between authentic pita chips and boring pita toast. Not only did the oil matter but, surprisingly, which side of the pita was oiled made a difference as well. After the pita is cut into layers, each chip has two distinct sides—one smooth (the exterior of the original pita bread), the other rough (from the inside of the original bread). When the oil was brushed onto the smooth side, tasters claimed the chips felt greasy. Not so

INGREDIENTS: Tortilla Chips

Most tortilla chips are made from just three basic ingredients—corn, oil, and salt—and processed similarly, yet our tasters found a wide range of textures and flavors in the 10 brands we sampled. How, we wondered, could such simple ingredients and a consistent manufacturing process yield such different results?

To answer this question, we began by examining the manufacturing process and the primary ingredient, corn. Tortilla chips begin with masa, or corn dough. Resembling cookie dough in texture, masa can be made from a number of corn products, including corn flour, which has the texture of fine sand; stone-ground corn flour, which has a rougher, grittier texture; and stone-ground corn (made from softened whole corn kernels), which is rough, like pebbly sand.

Many manufacturers make a big deal out of their chips being made from stone-ground masa. A stone-ground corn chip, they say, has better texture, is stronger, and absorbs less oil. While that all sounds good on paper, tasters preferred finer and more fragile chips made with corn flour, like second-place Miguel's, described as "delicate," or third-place Newman's Own, called "crisp." (Frito-Lay, which manufactures our top-rated chip, Doritos, would not comment on the ingredients in its masa. However, given the delicate texture of Doritos, it seems likely that corn flour is used here, too.) In contrast, two of the roughest, heartiest stone-ground chips, Nana's Cocina and Kettle Foods, ended at the bottom of the scorecard. Their textures were described as "stale" and "like cardboard," respectively.

In addition to the masa, salt has a big impact on tortilla chip flavor. Here the results of our tasting were quite clear. More salt makes a tastier chip. Among the top five brands, four had sodium levels between 110 and 120 milligrams per ounce. The sodium level in the five lowest-ranked brands ranged from 40 to 90 milligrams per ounce.

Now that we understood more about the inner workings of masa and the effect of salt levels on flavor, we moved on to the oil. We thought the success of our second-favorite brand, Miguel's, might be due, in part, to the corn/oil combination. Miguel's pairs canola oil with its white corn masa chip. Because canola oil has a neutral flavor, using it with the subtly flavored masa works well, as the flavor of the oil doesn't overwhelm that of the chip.

But then we came to Cape Cod chips, which were something of an anomaly. Like Miguel's, they were made with white corn masa and fried in canola oil. So why were Miguel's chips described as having a "toasted," "authentic" flavor, whereas Cape Cod chips were deemed "bland" and "unremarkable"? The most obvious difference, right off the bat, was in the packaging. Miguel's tortilla chips are packaged in a metallized bag, meaning the bag's surface is lined with a very thin film of aluminum.

Craig Mooney, vice president of sales for Miguel's, says the metal lining helps ward off oxidation of the oil by blocking light. "Light can oxidize the product and cause it to go bad," he explained; the foil-lined bag "also creates a moisture barrier to help the chips stay crunchy." In fact, we observed that all of our top three chips—Doritos, Miguel's, and Newman's Own—are packed in metallized bags. Could oxidation be a reason for the lack of flavor in Cape Cod chips and the off flavors in some of the other brands we tasted?

According to Theron Downes, a packaging professor with Michigan State University, "there are piles of evidence" that metallized bags improve the shelf life of fried foods. In fact, Dr. Downes refuses to purchase peanuts, a high-fat and light-susceptible food, packaged in clear bags because the oil in the peanuts goes rancid from oxidation within a couple of weeks.

In the end, the results of our tasting were unexpected. Doritos won over smaller boutique brands like Nana's Cocina and Kettle Foods. Although many boutique brands make a big deal about the organically raised stone-ground corn they use, it seems the secret to a great tortilla chip isn't all that complicated. Just use fine corn flour—not coarse stone-ground—add plenty of salt, and pack the chips in a foil-lined bag to keep the oil from oxidizing.

when the oil was brushed onto the rough side, which seemed to absorb it.

We also noted that it made a difference which side was facing up or down during baking. When baked rough-side down, the chips stuck to the cookie sheet, requiring a fair amount of prying to remove. But when they were baked smooth-side down, no such problem developed. Finding it necessary to flip the chips during baking for an even toasting, we found it best to begin with the smooth side down, giving the rough side a chance to toast so it wouldn't stick when flipped to the bottom.

Last, we tried baking the chips at various oven temperatures. Temperatures too high baked the chips unevenly, while temperatures too low dried the chips without really toasting them. We noted that a 350-degree oven worked best. Sprinkled with just a little bit of salt, these chips take only 12 minutes to bake and are worth the minimal amount of effort they require.

Pita Chips

MAKES 48 CHIPS,
ENOUGH TO ACCOMPANY 2 CUPS DIP

TIME: 30 MINUTES (INCLUDES 10
MINUTES COOLING TIME)

See the illustrations on page 12 for tips on cutting the pita breads.

4	(8-inch) pita breads, cut into wedges
¼	cup olive oil
1	teaspoon salt

1. Adjust the oven racks to the upper-middle and lower-middle positions and heat the oven to 350 degrees. Spread the pita triangles, smooth-side down, over 2 rimmed baking sheets. Brush the top of each chip lightly with oil and sprinkle with salt.

2. Bake the chips until they begin to crisp and brown lightly, about 6 minutes. Remove the baking sheets from the oven and flip the chips so their smooth side is up. Return the baking sheets to the oven, reversing their positions from top to bottom, and continue to bake until the chips are fully toasted, about 6 minutes longer. Remove the baking sheets from the oven and cool the chips before serving.

CLASSIC TOMATO SALSA

CHIPS AND SALSA ARE QUITE POSSIBLY the most popular party food today. Yet, for such a common item, we were disappointed with the quality of jarred salsas available in supermarkets. After sampling 12 jarred salsas side by side, we found they were watery and sweet, with mushy vegetables and processed flavorings. We wondered if we could make a quick salsa that tasted better than the jarred stuff without the hassle of chopping multiple vegetables and herbs.

Starting with our favorite recipe for red salsa, we quickly discovered that it could be made in the food processor. Processing the heartier ingredients, such as onion and jalapeños, first, we then added the tomatoes and pulsed until the mixture was a good consistency. To boot, we found this salsa tasted just fine when made with canned diced tomatoes, so it can be made year-round. Last but not least, we noted that quickly draining the salsa when it came out of the food processor helped remove excessive moisture. The result is a fresh, spicy, well-balanced salsa that takes just minutes to make and leaves the commercial jarred stuff in the dust.

Five-Minute Tomato Salsa

MAKES ABOUT 1 CUP, SERVING 4 TO 6
TIME: 5 MINUTES

If you want to use fresh tomatoes, core and cut 2 small ripe tomatoes (about ¾ pound) into eighths. Serve with tortilla chips.

½	small jalapeño chile or ½ chipotle chile in adobo sauce, minced
¼	small red onion, peeled and root end removed
1	small clove garlic, minced or pressed through a garlic press (about ½ teaspoon)
2	tablespoons packed fresh cilantro leaves
¼	teaspoon salt
	Pinch ground black pepper
2	teaspoons juice from 1 lime
1	(14 ½-ounce) can diced tomatoes, drained

Pulse all the ingredients except the tomatoes in the workbowl of a food processor until minced, about five 1-second pulses, scraping down the sides of the bowl as necessary. Add the tomatoes and pulse until roughly chopped, about two 1-second pulses. Transfer the mixture to a fine-mesh sieve and allow the excess moisture to drain, about 1 minute. Transfer the salsa to a serving bowl; serve. (The salsa can be covered with plastic wrap and refrigerated for up to 2 days.)

CHEESE STRAWS

CHEESE STRAWS ARE AN OLD-FASHIONED appetizer that never fails to impress. In fact, a recipe for them, called Parmesan Cheese Pastry Twists, is usually printed on the back of the Pepperidge Farm Puff Pastry box. Yet, after making this old standby as the box suggested, we knew we could do better.

First, we wanted more cheese flavor. While the back-of-the-box recipe called for only ¼ cup cheese, we found it took a full cup of grated Parmesan to produce cheese straws with a good, hearty flavor. We then tried a few other cheeses, including Asiago, smoked cheddar, and manchego. Although all the cheeses melted just fine, only the Parmesan and Asiago retained their full-flavored punch after baking. The other cheeses, although potent on their own, tasted bland against the rich dough. We also tried adding various herbs and spices, such as fresh thyme, smoked paprika, and chili powder; however, tasters preferred the batches seasoned with a little salt and black pepper only.

To form the straws, we found it much easier to work with pastry that wasn't

INGREDIENTS: Puff Pastry

Puff pastry is a super-flaky dough with hundreds of buttery layers. It is made by wrapping a simple pastry dough around a stick of cold butter, rolling the dough, folding the dough over itself at least four times, and chilling the dough for at least one hour after each fold. When baked, the water in the butter creates steam, which causes the dough to puff into flaky, delicate layers.

Almost no one—not even chefs at fine restaurants—makes puff pastry. Home cooks have one, maybe two commercial options in the freezer case. Pepperidge Farm Puff Pastry Sheets (made with vegetable oil, not butter) is available in almost every supermarket. Better supermarkets and gourmet shops might carry Classic Puff Pastry from Dufour Pastry Kitchens. When pitted in the test kitchen against Pepperidge Farm, the all-butter pastry was easy to pick out and was the clear favorite. That said, cheese straws made with Pepperidge Farm were still quite good. Our advice is to buy all-butter puff pastry if you can, but don't go without cheese straws if Pepperidge Farm is your only option.

completely thawed. When left just a bit icy, the dough came to room temperature as we rolled it out. The recipe on the box forms the straws by cutting the dough into two pieces and sandwiching the cheese between them. We tried pressing the cheese into just one side of a single piece of dough, but there was simply not enough surface area to hold a cup of cheese. In the end, we found it was better (and simpler) to press the grated cheese onto both sides of a single piece of dough. The exposed cheese was able to melt and toast as the pastry puffed in the oven.

Many recipes call for the dough to be put back into the freezer for several minutes before baking to maximize the height of the puff. We found this wasn't necessary, as the dough was still relatively cool after rolling it out with the cheese. At 425 degrees, the straws take only 10 minutes to bake through. They emerge from the oven with a crisp, airy texture and an undeniable cheese flavor that is a classic.

Cheese Straws

MAKES 14 STRAWS, SERVING 6
TIME: 30 MINUTES

See page 16 for information about buying frozen commercial puff pastry. Thaw the puff pastry on the counter as you preheat the oven and grate the cheese. Stand the baked cheese straws straight up in a tall glass and serve with drinks and olives. This recipe requires parchment paper; see page 18 for more information about this product. See the illustrations below for tips on shaping cheese straws.

1	sheet (9 by 9½ inches) frozen commercial puff pastry, thawed on the counter for 10 minutes
1	cup grated Parmesan or Asiago cheese
¼	teaspoon salt
¼	teaspoon ground black pepper

1. Adjust the oven racks to the upper-middle and lower-middle positions and heat the oven to 425 degrees. Line 2 baking sheets with parchment paper and set them aside. Lay the

MAKING CHEESE STRAWS

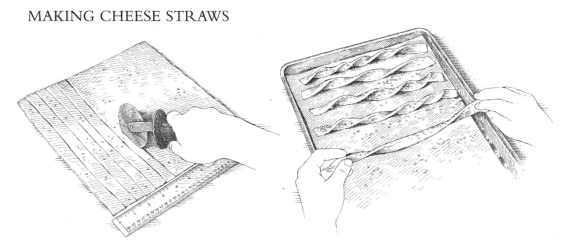

1. Using a sharp knife or pizza cutter, cut the dough into fourteen ¾-inch-wide strips.

2. Holding 1 strip of dough at each end, gently twist the dough in opposite directions and transfer it to a parchment-lined baking sheet. Repeat with the remaining pieces of dough, spacing the dough strips about 1 inch apart.

puff pastry on a sheet of parchment and sprinkle with ½ cup cheese, ⅛ teaspoon salt, and ⅛ teaspoon pepper. Place another sheet of parchment on top of the cheese, and, using a rolling pin, press the cheese into the dough by gently rolling the pin back and forth. Without removing the parchment, carefully flip the dough over, cheese-side down. Remove the top layer of parchment and sprinkle with the remaining cheese, salt, and pepper. Cover the pastry with the top sheet of parchment. Measure the piece of dough and continue to roll out, if necessary, to form a 10½-inch square.

2. Remove the top layer of parchment and, using a sharp knife or pizza cutter, cut the dough into fourteen ¾-inch-wide strips. Gently twist each strip of dough and transfer it to a parchment-lined baking sheet, spacing the strips about 1 inch apart.

3. Bake immediately until fully puffed and golden brown, about 10 minutes, reversing the positions of the baking sheets from top to bottom halfway through the baking time. Remove the straws from the oven and cool for 5 minutes before serving.

CROSTINI WITH WHITE BEAN SPREAD

SMALL TOASTS, CALLED CROSTINI IN Italian, served with a white bean spread are standard Tuscan fare. The crostini, which are also commonly served with soup or wedges of

EQUIPMENT: Parchment Paper

In the test kitchen, we use large commercial-grade sheets of parchment (16⅜ by 24⅜ inches) that we order by the case from professional kitchen supply stores. Because most home cooks use retail-grade parchment, we decided to compare a few popular brands. Included were Fox Run Craftsmen (flat sheets), Beyond Gourmet (unbleached roll), Reynolds (bleached roll), and a sheet of Super Parchment (a washable and reusable product). We tested these products using two of our recipes: Thin and Crispy Chocolate Chip Cookies and Thin-Crust Pizza.

For the cookie test, we lined baking sheets with each type of parchment paper. After 12 minutes in a 375-degree oven, all brands performed well, displaying little browning and no charring at all. Release was also not an issue; the cookies slid off their respective parchment sheets with ease. Beyond Gourmet and Reynolds—the two brands that come in a roll—tended to curl up at the edges, but this was easily solved by placing the sheets with the curled edges down. The weight of the dough kept the parchment paper flat.

With all brands performing well with cookies, we moved on to the more stressful test involving our recipe for Thin-Crust Pizza. (Pizza dough is rolled into a 14-inch circle between a floured sheet of parchment and plastic wrap. The plastic is removed, the dough is topped with sauce and cheese, and excess parchment is trimmed. The pizza, still on the parchment, is then slid onto a pre-heated pizza stone in a 500-degree oven and baked for 12 minutes.) Once again, none of the brands burned. However, size mattered. Reynolds was the only brand wide enough to handle a 14-inch pizza. (Using two sheets to make a larger area yielded a pizza with slightly undercooked dough. Of course, this wasn't even an option with the 17 by 13-inch sheet of Super Parchment.) Reynolds is available nationwide in 30-square-foot rolls that retail for approximately $2.50.

THE BEST PARCHMENT PAPER

Reynolds Parchment Paper was the test kitchen's top choice among leading retail brands.

cheese, are crusty, rustic pieces of toast lightly flavored with garlic and olive oil. For the spread, we wanted to make a simple, well-rounded puree from canned beans, avoiding the hassle and time it takes to soak and cook dried beans.

Making crostini is easy. Most Italian cookbooks offer similar directions whereby the bread is toasted and then rubbed lightly with a clove of raw garlic. The crisp texture of the toast acts like sandpaper against the garlic, releasing flavorful, perfumed oils. The dry, garlic-infused toast is then allowed to soak up a bit of olive oil, turning an otherwise ordinary piece of bread into a tasty morsel. We found that toasting technique is the most important part of this process. We discovered it is best to toast the bread for about 10 minutes in a 400-degree oven. Although this may seem like an inconvenient way to make toast, it dries the interior of the bread so the crostini are crunchy throughout.

Using canned beans for the puree, we immediately noticed that white navy beans did not work as well as cannellini. Navy beans are small, and their higher ratio of bean skin to creamy interior resulted in a starchy, lumpy spread that was difficult to fix. The larger cannellini beans, on the other hand, produced a silky, creamy puree that tasters liked. Flavored simply with a little lemon juice, a clove of garlic, and parsley, the puree was tasty—but too thick. We tried adjusting the texture of the final puree with extra-virgin olive oil. However, the amount of olive oil required to achieve a spreadable texture made the olive flavor overwhelming. Cannellini beans are fairly mild and easily overpowered by the fruity, slightly bitter characteristics of olive oil. To keep the flavors balanced, we wound up using a mixture of half oil and half water to attain the proper texture.

Last, tasters liked the puree left a bit chunky, but the ingredients did need to be processed to blend and meld flavors. We decided to leave one-third of the beans aside until the puree was nearly done, pulsing the reserved beans in only at the end.

Crostini with White Bean Spread

MAKES ABOUT 20 TOASTS,
SERVING 4 TO 6

TIME: 25 MINUTES

These crostini can be used as a base for almost any spread, including whipped goat cheese (page 2), hummus (page 12), and roasted red pepper spread (page 13).

CROSTINI

1   large baguette or thin Italian loaf, cut on the bias into ½-inch-thick slices (about 20 slices)

1   large clove garlic, peeled

2   tablespoons extra-virgin olive oil
     Salt and ground black pepper

WHITE BEAN PUREE

1   (15-ounce) can cannellini beans, drained, rinsed, and patted dry

2   tablespoons extra-virgin olive oil

2   tablespoons water

1   tablespoon juice from 1 lemon

1   medium clove garlic, crushed

1   tablespoon packed fresh parsley leaves

1. Adjust an oven rack to the middle position and heat the oven to 400 degrees. Arrange the bread in a single layer on a large baking sheet. Bake, turning the bread slices once, until the bread is dry and crisp, about 10 minutes. While they are still hot, gently rub the slices of bread with the raw garlic clove. Drizzle the olive oil over the slices and

sprinkle with salt and pepper to taste. (Crostini are best straight from the oven, but they can be set aside on a plate for several hours.)

2. Meanwhile, process two-thirds of the beans with the oil, water, lemon juice, garlic, and parsley in a food processor until smooth, about 10 seconds. Scrape down the sides of the work-bowl, add the remaining beans, and pulse to incorporate them, but do not make the puree perfectly smooth—about five 1-second pulses.

3. To serve, spread the dip onto the bread slices or serve it in a bowl alongside a plate of toasts.

QUESADILLAS

QUESADILLAS ARE NOT HARD TO PREPARE. Yet, all too often, they taste terrible, with bland, unmelted cheese sandwiched between flabby, floury tortillas. So although quesadillas appear to be effortless, we realized they need thoughtful attention.

Noting that flour tortillas come in a variety of sizes, we preferred those with an 8-inch diameter because they easily fit into a 10-inch pan. As for cheese, we tried a few varieties; although many tasted good, we found that Monterey Jack melted well and had an easy-going flavor that paired well with other quesadilla-friendly ingredients. We tried using preshredded cheese but were unimpressed with its artificial flavor and gummy texture. Take a couple of minutes to shred cheese yourself.

For a quick appetizer, we liked potent flavors, such as roasted red peppers, cilantro, and red onion, along with the spicy, smoky flavor of chipotle chiles in adobo sauce. We tried putting avocado inside the quesadilla, but tasters disliked its texture when warm; served on the side, however, it provided a smooth, cool, contrast to the hot, crisp tortilla that tasters really liked. To help prevent the filling from leaking out of the sides, we found it necessary to leave a 1-inch border of plain tortilla.

Cooking quesadillas is fairly straight-forward, but after making a few batches, we discovered a few little tricks. Although both regular and nonstick pans work, we liked the absolutely effortless release guaranteed by using a nonstick. The nonstick pan also allowed us to

PITTING AN AVOCADO

1. Start by slicing around both ends of the avocado with a chef's knife. With your hands, twist to separate the avocado into halves.

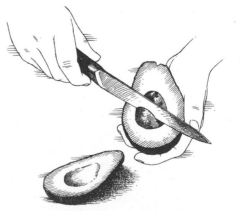

2. Stick the blade of the chef's knife sharply into the pit. Lift the knife, twisting the blade, if necessary, to loosen and remove the pit. Use a large spoon to pry the pit off the blade. Discard the pit.

use less oil, resulting in less greasy quesadillas. Wanting to use the smallest amount of oil possible, we found it easy to just brush the outside of the tortillas with oil rather than adding it to the pan. A hot pan is absolutely necessary to a well-toasted crust, but if the pan is too hot, the tortilla will burn in spots. Medium heat, we found, toasted both sides of the quesadilla and melted the cheese through without either burning the tortillas or requiring an oven finish.

DICING AN AVOCADO

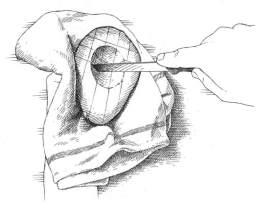

1. Use a dish towel to hold the avocado steady. Make ¹/₂-inch crosshatch incisions in the flesh of each avocado half with a dinner knife, cutting down to, but not through, the skin.

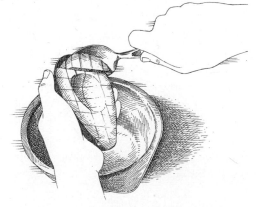

2. Using a soupspoon inserted between the skin and flesh, separate the diced flesh from the skin by gently scooping out the avocado cubes.

Last, we discovered that placing a small weight on the quesadilla as it cooked ensured a crisp, even crust. Using an empty saucepan with a diameter of roughly 8 inches, we found the weight flattened the nooks and crannies of the tortilla against the hot pan without forcing the filling out of the sides. The result was a crisp, toasty quesadilla with melted cheese throughout and a flavor that left tasters wanting more than just one slice.

Spicy Roasted
Red Pepper Quesadillas
MAKES 16 WEDGES, SERVING 4 TO 6
TIME: 30 MINUTES

The avocado salsa takes just 5 minutes to prepare and adds a pleasing contrast of flavors and textures to the quesadillas. However, if you are pressed for time, the salsa can be omitted; the quesadillas are tasty enough to serve as is. See page 11 for information about buying jarred roasted red peppers. Soft taco-size tortillas will work best in this recipe.

QUICK AVOCADO SALSA

1   medium avocado, pitted, peeled, and cut into ¹/₂-inch dice (see the illustrations at left)

1   tablespoon juice from 1 lime
Salt and ground black pepper

QUESADILLAS

8   ounces jarred roasted red peppers, drained and minced (about 1 cup)

1   small chipotle chile in adobo sauce, minced

¹/₂   small clove garlic, minced

2   tablespoons minced fresh cilantro leaves
Salt and ground black pepper

4   (8-inch) soft flour tortillas

3   thin slices red onion, rings separated

4   ounces Monterey Jack cheese, shredded (about 1 cup)

2   tablespoons vegetable oil

1. FOR THE SALSA: Gently toss the avocado with the lime juice and season to taste with salt and pepper in a small bowl; set aside.

2. FOR THE QUESADILLAS: Combine the roasted red peppers, chipotle, garlic, and cilantro in a small bowl and season to taste with salt and pepper. Spread half the mixture evenly over 1 tortilla, leaving a 1-inch border bare. Arrange half the onion slices over the pepper mixture and sprinkle with half the cheese, again leaving a 1-inch border. Place a second tortilla over the cheese and press slightly to position. Repeat with the remaining ingredients to make a second quesadilla.

3. Set a 10-inch nonstick skillet over medium heat for 2 minutes. Brush 1 side of 1 tortilla with 1½ teaspoons oil and place it, greased side down, in the heated pan. Place a clean saucepan on the quesadilla as a weight and cook until the bottom of the quesadilla is golden brown and crisp, 3 to 4 minutes. Remove the weight and brush the top with 1½ teaspoons oil. Using a wide metal spatula, flip the quesadilla over in the pan and replace the weight. Cook until the second side is golden brown and crisp, about 3 minutes more.

4. Transfer the quesadilla to a cutting board to cool slightly; return the skillet to medium heat. Cook the second quesadilla. Cut each quesadilla into 8 wedges and serve warm with the avocado salsa.

~~~~~~~~~~~~~~~~~~~~~~~~

MINI STEAK SANDWICHES

THE COMBINATION OF ROAST BEEF and horseradish sauce is a classic often found on the hors d'oeuvre table. Wanting to find a fast way to get this pair to the party, we focused on a few key issues. First, we tried simply serving toothpicked slices of beef alongside a horseradish dip, but we found the presentation was just a bit off. The skewered pieces of beef released some of their juices on the platter and wound up sitting in an unappetizing pool of red liquid. The toothpicks were also a bit awkward, as the beef often slid off them into the dip. Moving on to the idea of little, open-faced sandwiches, we found it easy to slice a baguette into small rounds, toast the slices, and top each with the horseradish dressing and the beef. To boot, these little morsels held up on the platter for some time, looking almost as good as they did when freshly made.

Having settled on sandwiches, we turned our attention morse specifically to the beef. We tried using sliced roast beef from the deli, but the results were disappointing. Although fast, the deli-sliced beef was much too dry and often came in shaggy, ragged pieces. Roasting a large piece of meat ourselves was out of the question, so we began to search for small, quick-cooking steaks that could be seared on the stove, then sliced. Flank steak turned out to be the answer. With a thin profile that cooks in less than 10 minutes, a 1½-pound flank steak yielded the perfect balance of economy and ease and offered a full, meaty flavor and handsome appearance when sliced.

After making a few sandwiches, we discovered a couple of tricks to cooking a flank steak on top of the stove. We noted the importance of using a heavy-bottomed pan that has been preheated for several minutes. The meat simply doesn't brown properly in pans that aren't sturdy enough or hot enough. Although many steaks have enough fat to pan-sear with little or no oil, we discovered that lean flank steak requires a tablespoon of vegetable oil in the pan. Once the steak is well browned on both sides, it is imperative to let the meat rest before slicing it; when cut too soon, the steak loses most of its natural juice and turns out dry. To make the sandwiches easy to eat, we found it important to slice the meat thinly across the grain. When sliced either thickly or with the grain, the beef was unpleasantly tough and chewy.

As for the horseradish sauce, we tried making it with sour cream, crème fraîche, and mayonnaise. In the end, we liked a simple mixture of mayonnaise, prepared horseradish, and a pinch of black pepper on the sandwiches. Rounded out with a spicy sprig of arugula and a sliver of red onion, these quick open-faced sandwiches look as good as they taste, leaving plenty of time to enjoy the party.

Mini Steak Sandwiches with Arugula and Horseradish

MAKES ABOUT 40 PIECES,
SERVING 10 TO 12

TIME: 40 MINUTES

This appetizer is a bit fancier than the other recipes in this chapter and appropriate for a larger and more formal gathering. If the baguettes look small, buy and slice two to ensure you'll have enough. If you can't find baby arugula (it is sold in packages or loose in many markets), simply tear regular arugula leaves into bite-size pieces.

I	large baguette, cut crosswise into ½-inch-thick slices (about 40 slices)
I	tablespoon vegetable oil
I ½	pounds flank steak, trimmed of excess fat and patted dry with paper towels
	Salt and ground black pepper
¾	cup mayonnaise
3	tablespoons prepared horseradish
3	cups packed baby arugula
I	small red onion, halved and sliced thin

1. Adjust an oven rack to the middle position and heat the oven to 400 degrees. Arrange the bread slices in a single layer on a large baking sheet. Bake, turning over the slices halfway through baking, until the bread is dry and crisp, about 10 minutes. Remove the baking sheet from the oven and cool for about 5 minutes.

2. Meanwhile, heat the oil in a heavy-bottomed 12-inch skillet over medium-high heat until it begins to smoke. Season the steak liberally with salt and pepper and lay it in the pan. Cook, not moving the steak until it is well browned, 4 to 5 minutes. Turn over the steak with tongs and reduce the heat to medium. Continue to cook until the second side is browned, about 5 minutes. Transfer the steak to a plate and let rest for 10 minutes. Slice the steak crosswise on the bias into ⅛-inch-thick slices. Halve the longer slices into roughly 3-inch lengths (you should have about 40 slices).

3. Mix together the mayonnaise, horseradish, and a pinch of pepper in a small bowl.

4. To assemble the sandwiches, spread 1 teaspoon horseradish mayonnaise on a piece of bread and curl a piece of steak on top. Place a piece of arugula and a sliver of onion within the curl of beef and serve.

KIELBASA WRAPPED IN PUFF PASTRY

THE FRENCH CALL IT SAUCISSON EN croûte, but in the test kitchen we know it as sausage wrapped in puff pastry. With only two ingredients, the recipe is as straightforward as you would expect. After making a few batches, however, we did uncover several helpful tricks.

After testing several types of sausage available in the supermarket, we narrowed our focus to kielbasa for several reasons. First, kielbasa is precooked and needs only to be heated through. This makes it a good match with the pastry, which puffs quickly in the oven.

Second, kielbasa has a well-rounded smoky flavor that all the tasters liked. Last, we noted that prepackaged kielbasa was easy to find in most of the supermarkets we visited.

When we used it straight out of the package, however, we found kielbasa was so juicy that it turned the pastry soggy. To avoid this problem, we had to rid the sausage of some of its natural juices and fat. When pricked with a fork and wrapped in layers of paper towel, the sausage needed just a minute or two in the microwave to release excess moisture. We found that giving the sausage a quick squeeze while it was still hot also helped this process along.

Most supermarket kielbasa comes in a long, curved link weighing about one pound. We cut the link in half, making two slightly curved pieces, and found that a single piece of commercial puff pastry was big enough to cover both halves. Puff pastry is commonly rolled out, and we found this necessary to avoid an overly puffy sausage. Further, we found it much easier to work with dough that was still partially frozen. As it was rolled out and manipulated over the sausage, the dough quickly came to room temperature. We used an egg wash to seal the edges of the pastry to prevent the seams from splitting in the oven. Pinching the edges closed with our fingers also helped. Last, we noted that a quick repose in the freezer before baking was beneficial. Otherwise, the sausage, which was still on the warm side from its stint in the microwave, tended to melt the pastry and make it a bit soggy before it reached the oven—and pastry that melts prior to baking loses the ability to puff. By letting it rechill in the freezer, we ensured the pastry would come out of the oven light and flaky.

With a quick egg wash brushed over the rechilled pastry dough for sheen, the sausage

took only 20 to 25 minutes in a 425-degree oven to puff, brown, and heat through. Although it is hard to let the pastry rest for 5 minutes after it comes out of the oven, the result is a perfect saucisson en croûte that easily slices into bite-size medallions that won't burn your mouth.

Kielbasa Wrapped in Puff Pastry

MAKES 12 TO 16 PIECES, SERVING 6
TIME: 60 MINUTES

The key to success with this recipe is rendering some of the sausage fat, which keeps the puff pastry from becoming soggy. See page 16 for information about buying puff pastry. Thaw the pastry on the counter as the oven heats. Pastries can be assembled and frozen for up to 2 weeks or refrigerated for several hours before baking.

1	pound kielbasa
1	sheet (9 by 9½ inches) frozen commercial puff pastry, thawed on the counter for 10 minutes
2	large eggs, beaten
¼	cup grainy mustard

1. Adjust an oven rack to the middle position and heat the oven to 425 degrees. Cut the kielbasa in half crosswise and pierce both pieces several times with a fork. Roll each half in several layers of paper towel and microwave on high power until hot, 1 to 2 minutes. Lightly squeeze the hot links in the towels to help release excess moisture and set them aside to cool.

2. Meanwhile, cut the sheet of puff pastry in half and place each piece between 2 sheets of parchment paper. Using a rolling pin, roll each piece of pastry into a rectangle that measures about 10 by 7 inches. Remove the top sheet of parchment paper and brush the pastry edges with beaten egg. Roll the pastry

MAKING SAUSAGE WRAPPED IN PUFF PASTRY

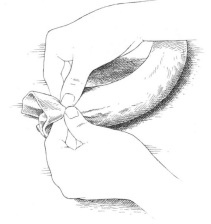

Place a piece of kielbasa on the longer edge of the puff pastry. Roll the kielbasa in the pastry, then pinch the seam and the ends to seal.

around the cooled sausage, pinching the seam and both ends closed (see the illustration below). Place the pastry, seam-side down, on a parchment-lined rimmed baking sheet. Repeat with the second piece of puff pastry and the second kielbasa, placing it on the same baking sheet. Put the baking sheet in the freezer for 10 minutes.

3. Remove the baking sheet from the freezer and brush each pastry with the remaining beaten egg. Bake until deep golden brown, 20 to 25 minutes. Remove the baking sheet from the oven and allow the pastry to rest for 5 minutes. Slice the pastry crosswise into ½-inch slices. Arrange the slices on a platter and serve immediately with the mustard in a separate small bowl.

SPICY CARIBBEAN– STYLE SHRIMP COCKTAIL

THE CLASSIC SHRIMP COCKTAIL—COLD poached shrimp accompanied by a spicy, ketchup-based sauce—probably will never fade in popularity. Yet, as with most classics, these flavors can easily become boring. We went looking for a new dipping sauce for a refreshing change of pace. We also wanted to streamline the cooking of the shrimp.

To start, we were immediately drawn to the spicy-sweet flavors of the Caribbean. Making a sauce with lime juice, hot chiles, and brown sugar, we noted this combination had sweet and spicy components similar to those of the classic ketchup-horseradish mixture, yet it was livelier. After a little fussing, we found an equal ratio of sugar to lime juice was necessary to balance the spicy nature of the hot chile. Supplemented with garlic, ginger, and scallion, this sauce was a welcome (and potent) break from the same old cocktail sauce.

Moving on to the shrimp, we tried poaching them quickly but were disappointed in the results. The poached shrimp tasted plain and seemed disconnected from the tropical-tasting sauce. Wanting to give the shrimp a little more life, we tried cooking them under the broiler. This also resulted in boring shrimp that seemed to have little to do with the sauce. Even when well seasoned or quickly marinated, the shrimp just tasted bland. Then someone suggested sautéing. Although it seemed odd to sauté shrimp for cocktail, we found this approach worked like a charm. When cooked in a preheated skillet, the shrimp browned in places and took on a little bit of charred flavor that worked well with the zesty sauce. Seasoning the shrimp liberally with black pepper and glazing them quickly off the heat with dipping sauce after they were cooked helped unite the flavors of the shrimp and the sauce. Although the glazed shrimp tails were a little sticky and dirtied our fingers as we tasted, no one in the test kitchen minded.

Last but not least, we found it necessary to spread the sautéed shrimp on a rimmed sheet pan to cool for about 5 minutes after cooking. Otherwise, the shrimp were just too hot to enjoy. Made in 20 minutes, this combination of spicy sautéed shrimp and a rejuvenating, sweet-hot dipping sauce is not only good but, as someone in the test kitchen aptly put it, "This isn't just shrimp cocktail; this is the kind of shrimp people will still be taking about the next day."

Caribbean-Style Shrimp Cocktail with Jalapeño-Lime Dipping Sauce

MAKES ABOUT 24 SHRIMP, SERVING 6
TIME: 20 MINUTES

The shrimp are served with tails on but can be sticky. Serve with ample cocktail napkins.

DIPPING SAUCE
1   medium clove garlic, peeled
    Salt
1   (1½-inch) piece fresh ginger, minced
    (about 1½ tablespoons)
2   medium scallions, white and green parts, minced
1   large jalapeño chile, stemmed, seeded, and minced
¼   cup juice from 2 limes
¼   cup packed brown sugar

SHRIMP
1   tablespoon vegetable oil
1   pound extra-large shrimp (21 to 25 count per pound), peeled, tails left on
¼   teaspoon salt
¼   teaspoon ground black pepper

1. FOR THE DIPPING SAUCE: Mince the garlic and ⅛ teaspoon salt to make a paste (see the illustration on page 4). Mix the garlic paste, ginger, scallions, chile, lime juice, and brown sugar in a small serving bowl and set the mixture aside.

2. FOR THE SHRIMP: Heat the oil in a large heavy-bottomed skillet over high heat until it begins to smoke. Season the shrimp with the salt and pepper. Add the shrimp to the hot pan and sauté until they are well colored and cooked through, about 2 minutes. Remove the pan from the heat, add 2 tablespoons jalapeño-lime sauce to the hot pan, and toss to coat the shrimp. Spread the shrimp on a rimmed baking sheet to cool, about 5 minutes.

3. Once the shrimp have cooled, arrange them on a platter around the bowl of sauce and serve immediately.

2

SALADS

CONSTRUCTING THE PERFECT SALAD is trickier than you might think. From battered greens to acidic vinaigrettes, simple salads can suffer from a variety of ills. Good salad begins with clean greens.

Unwashed greens should be stowed carefully in the crisper. The rubber band or twist tie should be removed from bound greens, as the constriction encourages rotting.

Nothing ruins a salad faster than gritty leaves. Our favorite way to wash small amounts of lettuce is in the bowl of the salad spinner; larger amounts require a sink. Make sure there is ample room to swish the leaves about and rid them of sand and dirt. Exceptionally dirty greens (spinach and arugula often fall into this category) may require at least two changes of water. Do not pour water directly from the spigot onto the greens, as the force of the water can bruise them. When you are satisfied the leaves are grit-free, spin them dry in a salad spinner (see

EQUIPMENT: Salad Spinners

The basic design of all salad spinners is similar. A perforated basket is fitted into a larger outer bowl, and gears connected to the mechanism in the lid spin the basket rapidly, creating centrifugal force that pulls the greens to the sides of the basket and the water on the leaves through the perforations into the outer bowl. Beyond this, however, models can differ in three important ways.

First is the lid. Some lids are solid, and some have a hole so you can run water directly into the basket while you spin. Second is the outer bowl. Some, like the lids, are solid, while others are perforated so water can flow through. The third major difference is the mechanism that makes the baskets spin—pull cord, turning crank, lever crank, or pump knob.

To be fair, all of the eight spinners we tested did a reasonably good job of drying wet lettuce leaves and parsley, though none dried the greens so thoroughly they wouldn't benefit from a quick blotting with paper towels before being dressed. Because the differences between them in terms of drying performance are not dramatic, what you really want is a spinner that is well designed, easy to use, and sturdy.

We didn't like the spinners with flow-through lids. The greens we cleaned by running water into the basket tended to bruise from the rushing water and never got clean enough. We also didn't like models with bowls that had holes in the bottom. Again, we did not consider this a benefit, in part because it assumes you have an empty sink in which to place the spinner. Second, we like to use the outer bowl of the spinner to soak the leaves clean, which obviously can't be done if it is full of holes.

As for the turning mechanism, the real standout in terms of design and ease of use was the spinner made by Oxo ($26). You can use the Oxo with just one hand because of its clever nonskid base and the pump knob by which it operates. Pushing the pump down both makes the basket spin and pushes the whole unit down onto the counter.

Among the other models tested, the pull cord on the Zyliss ($21) was the easiest to grip, and the Zyliss did, in fact, get the greens a tad drier than other spinners, including the Oxo. The Zyliss and the Oxo were also the sturdiest of the bunch.

THE BEST SALAD SPINNERS

With its nonskid base and push-button brake, the Oxo Good Grips spinner (left) requires just one hand to operate. The Zyliss Salad Spinner (right) is especially sturdy and dried green exceptionally well in our tests.

below for information on our testing of leading models). Greens must be quite dry; otherwise, the dressing will slide off.

With the greens cleaned and dried, you are ready to make salad. Of course, salad can be nothing more than a simple vinaigrette and a single kind of green, but it also can be a more involved affair with multiple greens, vegetables, meat, seafood, chicken, and/or cheese. The recipes in this chapter fall into four basic categories: basic salads with just greens and dressing; slightly more elaborate leafy salads, meant to be served as first courses; side-dish salads (many made with vegetables rather than leafy greens), meant to be served on the dinner plate with something from the grill or sauté pan; and main-course salads that combine leafy greens and protein.

STORING CLEAN SALAD GREENS

1. Line the empty salad spinner with paper towels, then layer in the greens, covering each layer with additional towels. In this manner, the greens will keep for at least 2 days in the refrigerator.

2. For longer-term storage—up to a week—loosely roll the greens in paper towels, then place the rolled greens inside a large zipper-lock bag, seal the bag, and refrigerate.

BASIC LEAFY SALADS

MOST SALAD GREENS FALL INTO ONE of three categories: mellow, spicy, or bitter. The following salads are representational pairings of each type of green and a vinaigrette that best matches its particular flavors. Feel free to mix and match greens from within each category to change the flavor, color, and texture of each salad.

The vinaigrette recipes yield ¼ cup dressing, or enough for 2 quarts of greens, about four servings. When making smaller or larger amounts of salad, figure on 2 tablespoons dressing per quart of greens.

Whole fresh herb leaves, like parsley, basil, thyme, oregano, marjoram, and chervil, may also be added to any of these salads for a burst of flavor.

Mellow Salad with Red Wine Vinaigrette

SERVES 4 AS A FIRST COURSE

TIME: 10 MINUTES

Mellow-flavored greens include Boston, Bibb, red and green leaf, red oak, lolla rossa, and iceberg lettuce as well as flat-leaf spinach. Their mild flavors are easily overpowered and are best complemented by a simple dressing, such as a classic red wine vinaigrette.

3	tablespoons extra-virgin olive oil
2	teaspoons red wine vinegar
⅛	teaspoon salt
	Pinch ground black pepper
2	quarts washed and dried mellow greens

29

Combine all the dressing ingredients in a jar, seal the lid, and shake vigorously until emulsified, about 20 seconds. Dress the greens according to the illustrations on page 31.

Spicy Salad with Mustard and Balsamic Vinaigrette

SERVES 4 AS A FIRST COURSE

TIME: 10 MINUTES

Spicy greens include arugula, watercress, mizuna, and baby mustard greens. They easily stand up to strong flavors, like mustard, shallots, and balsamic vinegar.

- 3 tablespoons extra-virgin olive oil
- 2 teaspoons balsamic vinegar
- 1 ½ teaspoons Dijon mustard
- ½ teaspoon finely minced shallot (see the illustrations on page 34)
- ⅛ teaspoon salt
  Pinch ground black pepper
- 2 quarts washed and dried spicy greens

Combine all the dressing ingredients in a jar, seal the lid, and shake vigorously until emulsified, about 20 seconds. Dress the greens according to the illustrations on page 31.

Bitter Salad with Creamy Garlic Vinaigrette

SERVES 4 AS A FIRST COURSE

TIME: 10 MINUTES

Escarole, chicory, Belgian endive, radicchio, frisée, and young dandelion greens all fall into this category. A creamy, assertive vinaigrette tempers the astringency of bitter greens.

- 2 tablespoons extra-virgin olive oil
- 1 tablespoon sour cream or yogurt
- 1 ½ teaspoons white wine vinegar
- 1 ½ teaspoons juice from 1 small lemon

- 1 teaspoon Dijon mustard
- ½ small garlic clove, minced to a paste with ⅛ teaspoon salt (see the illustration on page 4)
  Pinch ground black pepper
- 2 quarts washed and dried bitter greens

Combine all the dressing ingredients in a jar, seal the lid, and shake vigorously until emulsified, about 20 seconds. Dress the greens according to the illustrations on page 31.

ICEBERG LETTUCE WITH BLUE CHEESE DRESSING

ICEBERG LETTUCE HAS GOTTEN A BAD rap. Twenty years ago, iceberg was the only salad option in many markets. But with baby greens and mesclun so widely available today, many people turn up their noses at iceberg lettuce. Granted, iceberg on its own can be tasteless, but top a crisp wedge of this lettuce with a creamy and unctuous blue cheese dressing and you'll have a classic, quick, and delicious salad. While this salad is easy to prepare, you do face one potential hurdle: the perfect blue cheese dressing.

For this salad, you want an assertive dressing. Because of its high water content, iceberg lettuce tends to dilute the flavors of a dressing. That is why blue cheese dressing is such a good choice. However, most bottled blue cheese dressings are one-dimensional. They are either too sweet or tongue-numbingly tart—and, in general, they lack blue cheese punch. So we searched for a better alternative.

Most of the dressing recipes we uncovered in our research were similar—a combination of blue cheese and a creamy component, usually mayonnaise or sour cream, thinned with heavy cream or buttermilk. The richness of the dressings was normally offset with a little bit of vinegar or lemon juice. Our challenge was to find the right balance of ingredients.

We made many batches of blue cheese dressing by changing the proportions of various ingredients. We found dressings made with just mayonnaise and blue cheese were too heavy and greasy. On the other hand, dressings that used strictly sour cream tended to be tart, especially when thinned with buttermilk. After fiddling around with different ratios, we found that equal amounts of buttermilk and sour cream with a bit

TOSSING GREENS AND DRESSING

We found the ideal salad bowl is wide and relatively shallow, which helps the greens become evenly coated with vinaigrette quickly. A wide bowl also facilitates gentle handling of the greens. The bowl should be roughly 50 percent larger than the amount of greens to allow adequate room for tossing. For example, a salad with 2 quarts greens should be tossed in a 3-quart bowl.

1. For salads where only the mildest hint of garlic is desired (and where the dressing contains no garlic), rubbing the bowl with a cut garlic clove does the trick. The oils released from the clove impart a subtle bite and aroma as the greens are tossed. Peel and halve a clove of garlic. With the cut-side down, rub the interior of the salad bowl.

2. Measure the greens by loosely packing them into a large measuring cup, figuring on 2 cups per serving. Place the greens in the bowl.

3. If the greens are too large to eat neatly, gently tear them into manageable pieces with your hands. If torn ahead of time, they will discolor and wilt. Do not use a knife on anything but Belgian endive; the knife's cut encourages browning.

4. Just before dressing the greens, give the jar a quick shake to ensure the dressing is fully combined and the solid ingredients, like shallots, are evenly dispersed.

5. To prevent overdressed greens, add the dressing in small increments as you toss the salad.

6. Coat the greens by gently fluffing them with your hands, adding more vinaigrette only when you are certain the greens need it.

less mayonnaise yielded the best dressing. The mayonnaise gave the dressing body and richness, the sour cream balanced the mayonnaise and gave it tartness, and the buttermilk thinned the dressing and supported the role of the sour cream. With this perfect balance, our next decision was to determine how much cheese to add.

Starting with about ¾ cup of the sour cream, mayonnaise, and buttermilk combination, we added blue cheese in small amounts until we had a dressing that achieved a harmony among all the ingredients. In the end, we had added ¾ cup blue cheese to the initial ¾ cup base dressing. This one-to-one ratio of base to cheese ceded center stage to the blue cheese while maintaining the proper density of the dressing.

At this point, our dressing was good but just a bit dull. We added a smidgen of sugar for sweetness and white wine vinegar for a little zing. A pinch of garlic powder added a savory note. We had successfully created

CORING AND WASHING ICEBERG LETTUCE

1. Rap the bottom of the head of lettuce sharply on the counter to loosen the core. Turn over the head and pull out the core in one piece.

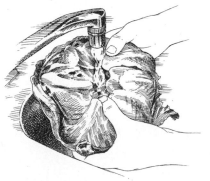

2. Fill the hole left by the core with water to rinse soil from the lettuce. Separate the leaves, wash again if necessary, and dry.

INGREDIENTS: Blue Cheese

Using our recipe, we prepared eight batches of blue cheese dressing, each containing a different blue cheese, and had our editorial staff engage in a blind taste test. While many tasters preferred the stronger cheeses when eaten alone, most preferred blue cheese dressing made with milder, less pungent cheeses.

Stella brand blue cheese (which is made in Wisconsin and is readily available in supermarkets) came out as our tasters' overall favorite for dressing because of its "nicely balanced flavor" and "nice sweetness." Danish Blue (also sold in many supermarkets) came in second; one taster described it as "bright," with a "good creamy and chunky balance."

While pricier blue cheeses, such as Stilton and Gorgonzola, also did well, the lower-priced versions scored higher, making them the logical choice for our dressing. Stronger, more intense cheeses, such as Cabrales, did not fare well in our dressing taste tests.

THE BEST BLUE CHEESE

Stella Blue from Wisconsin is our first choice when making dressing. This mild cheese is widely available in supermarkets and costs half as much as imported cheeses, which tasters felt were too pungent in our dressing recipe.

a creamy, tangy dressing with an assertive blue cheese bite—a perfect foil for our wedge of iceberg lettuce. Tomato wedges and sliced cucumber finished the salad by supplying contrasting colors, textures, and flavors. There's something comforting about this classic. That it can be made so quickly is another reason to try it again.

Iceberg Lettuce with Blue Cheese Dressing

SERVES 6 AS A FIRST COURSE

TIME: 15 MINUTES

Realizing that buttermilk isn't often at hand in most households, we tried cream instead, but the flavor of the dressing fell flat under its weight. Milk is a better substitute, though it makes a somewhat lighter dressing. See the illustration on page 190 for tips on seeding the cucumber.

1	medium head iceberg lettuce, cored and cut into 6 wedges
3	ounces blue cheese, crumbled (about ¾ cup)
5	tablespoons buttermilk
5	tablespoons sour cream
3	tablespoons mayonnaise
1	tablespoon white wine vinegar
¼	teaspoon sugar
⅛	teaspoon garlic powder
½	teaspoon salt
¼	teaspoon ground black pepper
1	large cucumber, peeled, seeded, and cut into ¼-inch slices
3	medium ripe tomatoes, cored and cut into 8 wedges each

1. Gently rinse the lettuce wedges under cold water. Place them on a cloth towel to dry.

2. Using a fork, mash the blue cheese and buttermilk together in a small bowl until the mixture resembles cottage cheese with small curds. Stir in the sour cream, mayonnaise, vinegar, sugar, garlic powder, salt, and pepper.

3. Place 1 lettuce wedge on each salad plate. Arrange the cucumber slices and tomato wedges around the lettuce. Spoon dressing over each wedge of lettuce. Serve immediately.

WARM LEAFY SALADS

SOMEWHERE AROUND COLUMBUS DAY, most cooks start to prepare fewer salads. What was once a refreshing dish on a hot summer night loses its appeal once the days get shorter and the temperatures start to fall. In addition, summer greens, tomatoes, and other ingredients are harder to come by. However, there's no reason to abandon salads just because the weather turns cooler. Salads that pair crisp, hearty greens with a flavorful warm dressing are the perfect winter starter, guaranteed to awaken your hibernating taste buds. In addition to being packed with flavor, the ingredients and the dressing for the salads can be easily prepared in several steps, ideal for those nights when you don't have a lot of time to spend in the kitchen.

These salads, however, are not without their pitfalls. In the course of testing, we had many disappointing results. The problems fit into two categories. The first problem was the tendency to overdress the salad, resulting in soggy and slimy greens. The second problem was that many of the dressings we tried were bland and flavorless. In recipe development, we strove to avoid both these disappointments.

Our first task was to determine which greens best stood up to a dousing of warm vinaigrette. We tried many combinations of greens, all with varying degrees of success. Leaf lettuces, like the familiar red leaf, and butterhead lettuces, like Bibb, didn't fare well with the warm vinaigrette treatment. Their light texture could not support the hearty dressing. We also tried romaine lettuce. While romaine fared better than the previous greens, romaine salads seemed too bland, most likely due to the high water content of the lettuce.

We shifted our focus to more substantial greens, such as escarole, watercress, and radicchio. These proved the best option. Their hearty texture withstood being tossed with the warm vinaigrette without overwilting, and the assertive flavor of the greens enlivened the salads, complementing the vinaigrette and other ingredients. As a bonus, many of these greens peak during the winter months, so availability and freshness are not a problem.

Turning our attention to the dressing, we tried to develop vinaigrettes that provided strong flavors as well as contrast to the slightly bitter greens. We also wanted a dressing easily prepared in one pan. Under these guidelines, we experimented with a wide variety of ingredients. Many tasters preferred a hint of sweetness in addition to the acidic aspect of the vinaigrette, hence the use of dried figs and slightly cooked fennel in the following recipes.

Now, all that was left was to add the finishing touches to the salads. A crumble of cheese over the completed salads added depth and richness, a plus for most tasters.

Radicchio, Watercress, and Goat Cheese Salad with Warm Fennel Dressing

SERVES 6 AS A FIRST COURSE

TIME: 20 MINUTES

Serve this salad before chicken or fish. See the illustrations on page 37 for tips on handling fennel.

1	large clove garlic, minced
3	tablespoons white wine vinegar
¼	teaspoon salt
⅛	teaspoon ground black pepper
⅓	cup plus 1 tablespoon extra-virgin olive oil
2	large bunches watercress, washed, dried, and large stems removed (about 6 cups lightly packed)
1	medium head radicchio, washed, dried, and torn into bite-size pieces (about 2 cups lightly packed)
1	medium fennel bulb, fronds and stems removed, cored, and sliced thin (about 2 cups)
6	ounces goat cheese, crumbled (about 1 ½ cups)

MINCING SHALLOTS

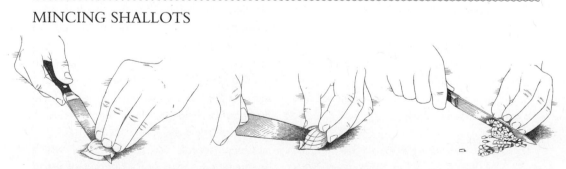

1. Place the peeled bulb, flat-side down, on a work surface and slice crosswise almost to (but not through) the root end with a paring knife.

2. Make a number of closely spaced parallel cuts through the top of the shallot down to the work surface.

3. Make very thin slices perpendicular to the lengthwise cuts.

1. Whisk the garlic, vinegar, salt, pepper, and ⅓ cup oil together in a small bowl until smooth; set the dressing aside. Place the watercress and radicchio in a large bowl; set the greens aside.

2. Heat the remaining 1 tablespoon oil in a medium nonstick skillet over medium heat until the oil begins to shimmer. Add the fennel and sauté until it begins to soften and turns light brown, about 3 minutes. Remove the pan from the heat, add the vinaigrette, and stir to coat the fennel evenly.

3. Toss the watercress and radicchio with the warm fennel dressing. Arrange the greens on individual plates and sprinkle with the goat cheese. Serve immediately.

Arugula, Escarole, and Fig Salad with Warm Port Dressing

SERVES 6 AS A FIRST COURSE

TIME: 25 MINUTES

This salad makes an excellent first course before beef.

I	cup walnuts, chopped coarse
⅓	cup port
4	ounces dried figs (6 large or 12 small), stems removed
2	tablespoons balsamic vinegar
2	medium shallots, minced (about 3 tablespoons)
¼	teaspoon salt
⅛	ground black pepper
¼	cup extra-virgin olive oil
2	large bunches arugula, washed, dried, stems trimmed, and leaves torn into bite-size pieces (about 3 cups lightly packed)
I	small head escarole, washed, dried, and torn into bite-size pieces (about 6 cups lightly packed)
4	ounces blue cheese, crumbled (about I cup)

1. Adjust an oven rack to the middle position and heat the oven to 325 degrees. Spread the walnuts on a rimmed baking sheet and toast until they are fragrant and lightly browned, about 15 minutes. Set aside to cool.

2. Meanwhile, bring the port and figs to a boil in a small saucepan over high heat. Cover the pan, reduce the heat to low, and simmer until the figs are soft but not mushy, about 15 minutes. Using a slotted spoon, transfer the figs to a clean plate, reserving the port in the saucepan. When the figs are cool enough to handle, cut them into quarters and set aside.

3. Whisk the vinegar, shallots, salt, pepper, and oil into the reserved port. Return the quartered figs to the saucepan and reheat over medium, stirring occasionally, until warm but not steaming, about 1½ minutes.

4. Toss the arugula and escarole with the warm dressing in a large bowl. Arrange the greens on individual plates and sprinkle with the blue cheese and walnuts. Serve immediately.

FENNEL SALAD

FENNEL IS ONE OF THE MOST UNDER-appreciated vegetables in the supermarket. Although this highly versatile bulb is used extensively in Europe, American cooks tend to overlook it. When fennel is cooked, it turns subtly sweet and can meld smoothly with other ingredients. It also adapts well to any cooking method, including grilling, roasting, and braising. But there is more to fennel than just cooking it. Its anise flavor and crunchy texture (when raw) make it a superb salad candidate. Fennel requires little in the way of preparation and can be turned quickly into a light, refreshing salad.

Surprisingly, our research turned up few recipes for fennel salad. Those we did find were more like vegetable side dishes meant to accompany fish. Most of these recipes were simply sliced fennel tossed with a little lemon juice and olive oil. We tried several of these recipes and found them overwhelming. A salad of straight fennel was too much in both flavor and texture. We were searching for a salad in which fennel was the focus but which included other ingredients that tempered the intense anise flavor and provided a softer mouthfeel.

It occurred to us that some sort of leafy green would help in our quest to tone down the anise flavor of the fennel and improve the overall texture of the salad. Following this thought, we tried several varieties of greens. Initially, we tried arugula, but it was soon clear that it would not do. While the texture of arugula was a good complement to the fennel, its peppery taste competed with the flavor of the fennel. Next up was romaine. Romaine had a milder flavor, for sure, but its texture was too watery, making the salad taste bland. We finally settled on Bibb lettuce. Its mildness complemented the fennel, and its

soft but toothsome texture lightened the salad perfectly.

Even with the greens, the salad needed an additional kick. Looking back at the recipes, it seemed likely that a protein, such as fish, would do the trick. We tried topping the salad with small pieces of poached salmon. Although the result was tasty, we worried that we were wandering away from the quick and easy concept. Canned salmon was out of the question, so we turned, instead, to smoked fish. Having already figured that the richness of fish would provide an appropriate contrast to the fennel, we guessed that the smokiness would add an interesting twist. We tried both smoked salmon and trout and unanimously settled on the smoked trout due to its drier texture and less insistent smoky flavor.

We opted for a lemon vinaigrette to finish the salad because the lemon provided a freshness that vinegar-based vinaigrettes lacked. The lemon vinaigrette was also tart without being overly acidic. A Granny Smith apple supplied a satisfying bit of sweetness, and a garnish of chopped tarragon added freshness.

CUTTING AN APPLE INTO THIN STRIPS

1. Cut around the core, removing the flesh in 4 pieces and leaving a square block containing the core and seeds; discard the core.

2. Lay each piece of apple flat-side down and cut into 1/8-inch-thick pieces.

3. Stack the apple slices and cut them into 1/8-inch-thick strips about 3 inches long.

✂ Fennel and Apple Salad with Smoked Trout

SERVES 4 TO 6 AS A FIRST COURSE

TIME: 20 MINUTES

The fennel should be thinly sliced, and the slicing disk of the food processor is the best tool for the job. See the illustration at right for tips on coring fennel.

2	tablespoons juice from 1 lemon
2	teaspoons minced fresh tarragon leaves
1/4	teaspoon salt
1/8	teaspoon ground black pepper
1/2	cup extra-virgin olive oil
2	medium fennel bulbs, fronds and stems removed, cored, halved, and sliced 1/16 inch thick with the slicing disk of a food processor
1	Granny Smith apple, peeled, cored, and cut into 1/8 by 1/8 by 3-inch strips (see the illustrations on page 36)
16	leaves Bibb lettuce, washed and dried
8	ounces smoked trout, skin and pin bones removed, flaked

1. Whisk the lemon juice, 1 teaspoon tarragon, salt, pepper, and oil together in a large bowl. Add the fennel and apple and toss to coat.

2. Arrange the lettuce on a large platter or individual plates. Arrange the fennel and apple over the lettuce, reserving any extra dressing left in the bowl. Sprinkle the trout and remaining 1 teaspoon tarragon over the salad and drizzle any extra vinaigrette over top. Serve immediately.

SUMMER SQUASH SALAD

IF YOU HAVE EVER KEPT A GARDEN, you know that summer squash magically multiply overnight. By the end of August, they have taken over your garden, and you are up to your ankles in squash and worrying about what to do with all of it. You just can't stomach another loaf of zucchini bread. Here's a solution: a salad that exploits the firm texture and mild flavor of summer squash.

Most salad recipes containing summer squash combine the squash with other summery ingredients, such as corn and tomatoes. Wanting to focus solely on squash, we limited our search to recipes in which squash was the main ingredient; the resulting search didn't turn up much.

Of the recipes we found, most called for cooking the squash before tossing it with vinaigrette. Cooking methods for the squash included steaming, grilling, sautéing, and roasting. We figured the best cooking method

PREPARING FENNEL

1. Cut off the stems and feathery fronds.

2. Trim a thin slice from the base of the bulb and remove any tough or blemished outer layers. Cut the bulb in half through the base and use a paring knife to remove the pyramid-shaped piece of the core in each half. The bulb can now be sliced or chopped as desired.

would be determined by the high water content of squash—almost 95 percent. We quickly ruled out steaming, being nearly positive that cooking a vegetable that is mostly water with moist heat would leave little in the way of flavor. This left us with dry heat methods. Grilling didn't make much sense. Why fire up the grill to cook only a couple of squash? So we tried making several salads with both roasted and sautéed squash. The results, however, were lackluster. The squash was bland and watery, and the texture was mushy.

In our initial research, we had found several recipes that called for raw squash. These salads were made by tossing thin slices of squash with lemon juice and olive oil. We tried this and were astonished by the results. The squash was crisp and subtly sweet, and the lemon juice and olive oil enhanced its natural flavor. We knew we were on the right track.

We next searched for contrasting flavors and textures, feeling that raw squash by itself was a little one-dimensional. Arugula, with its peppery bite and light texture, was a perfect complement to the mild, sturdy squash. For accent, minced shallots in the vinaigrette provided an assertive edge, and torn basil leaves enlivened the taste. We finished our salad by crumbling goat cheese over the top, which added richness and made the dish more substantial.

Summer Squash Salad

SERVES 6 AS A FIRST COURSE
TIME: 15 MINUTES

This light salad makes an especially good starter before a summer barbecue. It is important to slice the squash as thinly as possible. Our first choice for this task is the slicing disk on a food processor. If using a sharp chef's knife, start by halving the squash lengthwise. The flat surface will allow you to slice the squash thinly without its rolling around.

¼	cup extra-virgin olive oil
2	tablespoons juice from 1 lemon
1	medium shallot, minced (about 1 tablespoon)
¼	teaspoon salt
⅛	teaspoon ground black pepper
1	pound small green and yellow summer squash, sliced ¹⁄₁₆-inch thick with the slicing disk of a food processor
1	bunch arugula, washed, dried, and torn into bite-size pieces (about 4 cups lightly packed)
¼	cup packed fresh basil leaves, torn into small pieces
5	ounces goat cheese, crumbled (about 1¼ cups)

Whisk together the oil, lemon juice, shallot, salt, and pepper in a large bowl. Add the squash, toss to coat, and let stand for 3 minutes. Add the arugula and basil and toss to combine. Arrange the salad on a serving platter or individual plates and sprinkle with the goat cheese. Serve immediately.

FRENCH POTATO SALAD

FOR YEARS, AMERICAN POTATO SALAD has reigned supreme over the picnic table. This salad often suffers from being overdressed with mayonnaise, creating a sodden mess. While these salads can be just what you're craving, they can also be too heavy to eat on a hot summer day. So we went seeking an heir to the potato salad throne—and we think we've found one: French-style potato salad.

French potato salad is quite different from its American cousin. It is a delightful combination of warm slices of potato dressed lightly with fruity olive oil, white wine vinegar, and copious amounts of herbs. This salad is also a perfect fit with our quick cooking guidelines.

Most French potato salad recipes we consulted followed the same basic procedures. Normally, they called for boiling whole red potatoes, draining them, allowing them to cool slightly, and then slicing them thinly. After being sliced, the potatoes are tossed with vinaigrette made with olive oil, vinegar, and Dijon mustard. We tried several of these salads but found it almost impossible to slice the potatoes without tearing the skin, upon which the slices broke apart into an unappetizing mess. This only got worse when we tossed the potatoes with the vinaigrette. We were left with a ragged, sloppy mound of potatoes. Another problem we encountered with the recipes was that no matter how assertive we made the vinaigrette, the potatoes still seemed bland.

We first tackled the problem of the potatoes. Initially, we thought the problem was with the Red Bliss potato we were using, so we tried different varieties. Russets and Yukon Golds did not hold together any better, and neither rivaled the delicate flavor and texture of the Red Bliss. Realizing that most of the problem lay in slicing cooked potatoes, we considered slicing the potatoes before we cooked them. This was a revelation. The frustrating problem of cutting hot potatoes without breaking them was solved. In addition to not burning our hands, this technique allowed all the potatoes to cook at the same rate, so we no longer struggled with some potatoes being cooked through and others not. Finally, sliced potatoes cooked more quickly than whole potatoes.

We moved on to the dressing. We evaluated each ingredient of the vinaigrette to see where we could pump up the flavor. Up to this point, we had been using the standard test kitchen vinaigrette ratio (4 parts oil to 1 part vinegar), but we found the potatoes could stand up to a little more vinegar, so we increased the amount in the dressing. The extra vinegar added a little sharpness to the salad, which tasters overwhelmingly preferred. Shallot improved the salad in two ways: It provided extra assertiveness to the taste, and when sliced rather than minced it added a slight crunch to the texture. Some garlic and a healthy dose of Dijon mustard rounded out our list of flavor-boosting ingredients. As for the herbs, a combination of tarragon and parsley gave the salad a fresh taste with a hint of anise, a perfect complement to the earthy potatoes.

The last problem was how to toss the cooked, warm potatoes with the vinaigrette without damaging the slices. The solution was simple. We carefully laid the potatoes in a single layer on a baking sheet, then poured the vinaigrette over them. Spreading the potatoes in this way also allowed them to cool quickly (this salad should be served warm, but not hot). It was also easy to dress the potatoes evenly and quickly.

French Potato Salad

SERVES 6 AS A SIDE DISH

TIME: 35 MINUTES

It is important to save a little of the water from boiling the potatoes, for it serves several purposes. First, it adds a little extra moisture to the salad, helping each potato slice get a good dose of the dressing. Second, the generous amount of salt in the boiling water helps season the entire salad. While this potato salad is definitely a candidate to replace the traditional mayonnaise-based American potato salad at your next picnic, it's also a good companion to grilled fish and meat. This salad tastes best when served warm.

2 pounds small red potatoes (about 2 inches in diameter), scrubbed and cut into ¼-inch slices

2 tablespoons salt

1 medium clove garlic, peeled and threaded on skewer

2 medium shallots, sliced thin

1½ tablespoons white wine vinegar

2 teaspoons Dijon mustard

¼ cup extra-virgin olive oil

½ teaspoon ground black pepper

1½ tablespoons minced fresh parsley leaves

2 teaspoons minced fresh tarragon leaves

1. Bring the potatoes, 6 cups cold water, and salt to a boil in a large saucepan over high heat. Reduce the heat to medium, lower the skewered garlic into the simmering water, and partially blanch, about 45 seconds. Immediately run the garlic under cold water to stop cooking; remove the garlic from the skewer and set aside. Continue to simmer the potatoes, uncovered, until tender but still firm (a thin-bladed paring knife can be slipped into and out of the center of a potato slice with no resistance), about 5 minutes. Drain the potatoes, reserving ¼ cup cooking water. Arrange the hot potato slices close together in a single layer on a rimmed baking sheet.

2. Press the garlic through a garlic press or mince by hand. Whisk the garlic, shallots, reserved potato cooking water, vinegar, mustard, oil, and pepper together in a small bowl until combined. Drizzle the dressing evenly over the warm potatoes; let stand 10 minutes.

3. Transfer the potatoes to a large serving bowl. Add the parsley and tarragon and mix gently with a rubber spatula to combine. Serve immediately.

MOROCCAN-STYLE CARROT SALAD

WHEN CARROT SALADS WERE MENTIONED in the test kitchen, there was a collective groan. Everybody seemed to remember a slimy carrot and raisin salad from childhood—an overly sweet mix of shredded carrots and chewy raisins bound by a little too much mayonnaise. But not long ago, one of us had a carrot salad in a local Moroccan restaurant. The shredded carrots were the same, but this time they were tossed with slices of oranges and flavored with cumin, coriander, and cinnamon. This was not your mother's carrot salad.

In our research, we found a wide range of North African carrot salads. The ingredients and procedures for the salads were all similar. Most recipes called for grated carrots tossed with olive oil, lemon juice, and Moroccan spices. Many recipes specified additional flavors, such as olives, toasted almonds, orange-flower water—and, yes, even raisins. In the spirit of simple, quick cooking, however, we decide to stick to the basics.

Our first question was how to cut the carrots. Some recipes called for the carrots to be pared into thin ribbons with a vegetable peeler. While this made a pretty salad, the vinaigrette had nothing to cling to, so the carrots were rather bland. Remembering the positive aspects of Mom's carrot salad and figuring we shouldn't mess with a good thing, we turned to grating. We tried several methods of grating the carrots with a box grater and with a food processor. We found the large holes on the box grater worked the best. The food processor grated the carrots too finely; the resulting salad didn't have enough body or texture and was watery. The carrot pieces from the box grater were a little larger.

Considering that we were going to add

oranges to the salad, we decided to build a vinaigrette around orange juice. The orange juice didn't provide enough acidity, however, resulting in a salad that was too sweet. Adding a squeeze of lemon juice to the orange juice did the trick. As for the oil, extra-virgin olive oil worked best. A touch of honey added a pleasing floral note.

Moving to the spices in the vinaigrette, we initially tried ½ teaspoon each coriander, cumin, and cinnamon. This was entirely too overpowering; none of the spices dominated, and the total amount gave the salad a grainy mouthfeel. So we tried reducing the amount of spices and making one spice the dominant flavor. Tasters felt that both cinnamon and coriander were too sweet as dominant flavors and failed to provide enough contrast. Cumin, on the other hand, worked perfectly in the starring role. The musty aroma and the slight nuttiness of the cumin complemented the sweetness of the carrots. With a hint of cinnamon (the coriander seemed redundant and was dropped) and a little spiciness provided by cayenne pepper, we finally had our dressing. Now all we had to do was to dress the carrots—or so we thought.

Several minutes after we dressed the salad, a pool of juice—water being expelled by the carrots—developed in the bowl. We explored several ways of getting rid of this liquid. We tried salting the carrots as we would cucumbers to rid them of unwanted juices, but this process requires at least half an hour. We also tried squeezing the carrots in a towel after we grated them, but this resulted in a loss of intense carrot flavor. We then turned to the idea of letting the carrots sit in a strainer for several minutes after dressing. While this certainly got rid of the extra water, it also got rid of flavor. We finally settled on increasing the amount of spices in the vinaigrette; the carrots thus received an initial overdose of spices,

enough to give them intense flavor that was slightly tempered by inevitable excess liquid. By straining some of the liquid from the salad, we reached a proper level of seasoning.

~✂~

Moroccan-Style Carrot Salad

SERVES 6 AS A SIDE DISH

TIME: 15 MINUTES

Make sure to segment the oranges over a small bowl to catch their juices. You should have several tablespoons of juice in the bowl by the time you are done segmenting both oranges. The flavor combinations in this slaw-like salad make it a natural to serve with couscous or North African stews. It also works well with firm white fish, such as halibut.

1	pound carrots, grated on the large holes of a box grater
2	medium seedless oranges, segmented (see the illustrations on page 57)
1	teaspoon honey
1	tablespoon juice from one lemon
¼	cup extra-virgin olive oil
¾	teaspoon ground cumin
½	teaspoon salt
¼	teaspoon cayenne pepper
⅛	teaspoon ground cinnamon
3	tablespoons chopped fresh cilantro leaves

1. Place the grated carrots and orange segments in a large bowl. Set them aside.

2. Whisk the honey, lemon juice, oil, cumin, salt, cayenne, and cinnamon together with the reserved orange juice in a small bowl.

3. Pour the dressing over the carrots, add the cilantro, and toss to coat. Let stand until liquid starts to pool in the bottom of the bowl, about 3 minutes. Place the salad in a fine-mesh strainer and let it sit undisturbed for 2 minutes. Remove the salad from the strainer and serve immediately.

CELERY ROOT SALAD

LET'S ADMIT IT: CELERY ROOT IS THE ugly duckling of the supermarket produce aisle. Often overlooked, this fibrous, bumpy, softball-sized root has a crunchy texture and a refreshing flavor that resembles a cross between celery and radishes. More often than not, celery root is cooked into purees and gratins that often mask its unique flavor and texture. When used raw, however, its pure white flesh provides a good launch pad for flavorful coleslaw-like salads. One such salad is celery root rémoulade, a classic French bistro side dish consisting of raw celery root that has been grated or finely julienned and then dressed in a creamy dressing redolent of mustard. With further research, we found that celery root salads were easy to make and time-efficient, perfectly fitting our quick-cook guidelines.

The first problem that presented itself during development was how to prepare the celery root. Its thick, uneven surface and unwieldy size made peeling quite a challenge. We tried all sorts of knives and peelers in the test kitchen and found that most of them were ineffective. Finally, we were inspired by the method of paring the peel of citrus fruits in preparation for segmenting them. We trimmed both the top and bottom of the celery root, which made a stable flat surface to work with. Then, with a paring knife, we cut from top to bottom, slightly underneath the skin, following the contours of the root and rotating it until fully peeled.

Now that we had safely peeled the celery root, the question was how to cut it. We tried several ways of cutting and grating the celery root, all with varying degrees of success. First, we tried cutting the celery root by hand. This took considerable time and effort, and the result was not so good. Next, we tried a box

grater, but we found the fine side of the grater produced a watery salad when the celery root was mixed with the dressing. The coarse side of the grater was better, but not as good as the grating attachment of our food processor. Not only was the food processor extremely quick but also, when the celery root was mixed with the dressing, it developed contrasting flavors and textures, softening the outside but maintaining a good crunch.

With a bowl of grated celery root, we set out to find a suitable dressing—one that highlighted the vegetable without overpowering its subtle flavors. Because this salad was partially inspired by its French ancestor, the celery root rémoulade, we decided to try a mayonnaise-based dressing laced with mustard. Most tasters agreed that this was not the route to take. The salad was heavy and sodden, masking the nuances of the celery root. We then switched to a vinaigrette, which was a little better, but some felt it was greasy—that the salad ingredients did not blend well. Seeking the middle ground, we tried whisking a little sour cream into the vinaigrette. This turned out to be the perfect compromise. The creaminess of the vinaigrette complemented

PREPARING CELERY ROOT

Cut off about ³⁄₈ inch from the root end (where there is a mass of rootlets) and the stalk end (the opposite side). The celery root can now rest flat on a cutting board. To peel, simply cut from top to bottom, rotating the celery root as you remove wide strips of skin.

the celery root and lent the dish as a whole a fuller flavor.

Now that we had developed a dressing, the only remaining job was to apply the final touches. The addition of scallions and tarragon provided depth and contrasting flavors, giving the salad a boost. We also added apples to the recipe for a little extra crunch and a touch of sweetness.

Celery Root Salad with Apple and Tarragon
SERVES 6 AS A SIDE DISH
TIME: 35 MINUTES (INCLUDES 15 MINUTES IN THE REFRIGERATOR)

This classic bistro salad can be served with everything from steaks to poached fish. If tarragon is not available, use parsley instead.

1½	tablespoons juice from 1 lemon
1½	tablespoons Dijon mustard
	Salt and ground black pepper
3	tablespoons canola oil
2	tablespoons sour cream
1	medium celery root (13 to 14 ounces), peeled (see the illustration on page 42) and rinsed
½	medium tart apple (such as Granny Smith), peeled and cored
2	scallions, sliced thin
2	teaspoons chopped fresh tarragon leaves

1. Whisk together the lemon juice, mustard, ½ teaspoon salt, pepper to taste, and oil in a large bowl. Whisk in the sour cream and set the dressing aside.

2. If using a food processor, cut the celery root and apple into 1½-inch pieces and grate with the shredding disk. Alternatively, grate the celery root and apple on the large holes of a box grater. You should have 3 to 3½ cups total.

3. Add the celery root, apple, scallions, and tarragon to the bowl with the dressing and toss to coat. Adjust the seasonings with salt and pepper to taste. Refrigerate for 15 minutes. Serve lightly chilled.

PASTA SALAD
PASTA SALADS ARE CLASSIC SUMMER-time fare. They should be simple and light and full of bright flavors. They should also be able to stand by themselves as a light entrée on a hot summer evening. All too often, however, pasta salads are the exact opposite. They taste of bland pasta swimming in heavy dressing.

Our research turned up a dizzying number of recipes for pasta salad. We quickly decided to narrow our focus. Because pasta salad is a summery dish, recipes that featured tomatoes seemed a natural choice.

As we started making pasta salads with tomatoes, we repeatedly encountered the same problem. The tomatoes made the salad too watery and wouldn't allow the flavors of the salad to meld. We tried different sizes of pasta in hopes of capturing the tomatoes. We also tried cutting the tomatoes in different shapes and sizes, but the problem persisted. How to obtain a sweet tomato flavor in a cohesive pasta salad? The answer, surprisingly enough, was sun-dried tomatoes. Granted, we lost the freshness of garden tomatoes, but using sun-dried tomatoes had several benefits. First, the problem of watery salad was eliminated. Second, as we were using tomatoes packed in olive oil, we could use that oil in our vinaigrette, thus giving the salad a double shot of tomato flavor. Last, we did not need perfectly ripe summer tomatoes to make pasta salad.

One drawback of sun-dried tomatoes is that their concentrated flavor is sometimes too sweet. We tempered this sweetness by

INGREDIENTS: Red Wine Vinegar

The source of that notable edge you taste when sampling any red wine vinegar is acetic acid, the chief flavor component in all vinegar and the by-product of the bacterium *Acetobacter aceti*, which feeds on the alcohol in wine. The process of converting red wine to vinegar once took months, if not years, but now, with the help of an *acetator* (a machine that speeds the metabolism of the *Acetobacter aceti*), red wine vinegar can be made in less than 24 hours.

Does this faster, cheaper method—the one used to make most supermarket brands—produce inferior red wine vinegar? Or is this a case in which modern technology trumps Old World craftsmanship, which is still employed by makers of the more expensive red wine vinegars? To find out, we included in our tasting vinegars made using the fast process (acetator) and the slow process (often called the *Orleans method*, after the city in France where it was developed).

We first tasted 10 nationally available supermarket brands in two ways: by dipping sugar cubes in each brand and sucking out the vinegar (to cut down on palate fatigue) and by making a simple vinaigrette with each and tasting it on iceberg lettuce. We then pitted the winners of the supermarket tasting against four high-end red wine vinegars.

Although no single grape variety is thought to make the best red wine vinegar, we were curious to find out if our tasters were unwittingly fond of vinegars made from the same grape. We sent the vinegars to a food lab for an anthocyanin pigment profile, a test that can detect the 10 common pigments found in red grapes. Although the lab was unable to distinguish specific grape varieties (Cabernet, Merlot, Pinot Noir, Zinfandel, and the like), it did provide us with an interesting piece of information: Some of the vinegars weren't made with wine grapes (known as *Vitus vinifera*) but with less expensive Concord-type grapes, the kind used to make Welch's grape juice.

Did the vinegars made with grape juice fare poorly, as might be expected? Far from it. The taste-test results were both shocking and unambiguous: Concord-type grapes not only do just fine when it comes to making vinegar, they may be a key element in the success of the top-rated brands in our tasting. Spectrum, our overall winner, is made from a mix of wine grapes and Concord grapes. Pompeian, which came in second among the supermarket brands, is made entirely of Concord-type grapes.

What else might contribute to the flavor of these vinegars? One possibility, we thought, was the way in which the acetic acid is developed. Manufacturers that mass-produce vinegar generally prefer not to use the Orleans method because it's slow and expensive. Spectrum red wine vinegar is produced with the Orleans method, but Pompeian is made in an acetator in less than 24 hours.

What, then, can explain why Spectrum and Pompeian won the supermarket tasting and beat the gourmet vinegars? Oddly enough, for a food that defines *sourness*, the answer seems to lie in its *sweetness*. It turns out that Americans like their vinegar sweet (think balsamic vinegar).

The production of Spectrum is outsourced to a small manufacturer in Modena, Italy, that makes generous use of the Trebbiano grape, the same grape used to make balsamic vinegar. The Trebbiano, which is a white wine grape, gives Spectrum the sweetness our tasters admired. Pompeian vinegar is finished with a touch of sherry vinegar, added to give the red vinegar a more fruity, well-rounded flavor. Also, both Spectrum and Pompeian start with wines containing Concord grapes, which are sweet enough to be a common choice when making jams and jellies.

When pitted against gourmet vinegars, Spectrum and Pompeian still came out on top. Which red wine vinegar should you buy? Skip the specialty shop and head to the supermarket.

THE BEST RED WINE VINEGARS

Spectrum vinegar (left) and Pompeian vinegar (right) are available in supermarkets and bested gourmet brands costing eight times as much.

adding green olives to our salad; the pleasant brininess of the olives balanced the tastes in the dish.

There remained one small problem: how to integrate all the ingredients in the salad. As it was, all the flavorful stuff fell to the bottom of the salad bowl, leaving the pasta alone at the top. Thinking back to good pasta salads we've had, they all had one ingredient in common: a leafy green. Thus, we tried adding some arugula. It was a breakthrough. The leaves gave the flavorful ingredients something to stick to, and they were large enough so they didn't fall to the bottom of the bowl. Essentially, the arugula acted as a bridge between the pasta and the other ingredients in the salad. With our ingredients well balanced and evenly mixed, we finished the salad by tossing in cubed fresh mozzarella.

Pasta Salad with Arugula and Sun-Dried Tomato Vinaigrette

SERVES 6 AS A SIDE DISH

TIME: 30 MINUTES

We like the assertive flavor of red wine vinegar in this recipe. See page 44 for information about our testing of leading brands. This salad can also be served as a light entrée for four.

	Salt
I	pound fusilli
I	tablespoon extra-virgin olive oil
I	(8-ounce) jar sun-dried tomatoes packed in olive oil
2	tablespoons red wine vinegar
I	large clove garlic, minced to a paste (see the illustration on page 4)
⅛	teaspoon ground black pepper
I	bunch arugula, washed, dried, and torn into bite-size pieces (about 4 cups lightly packed)
½	cup green olives, pitted and sliced
6	ounces fresh mozzarella cheese, cut into ½-inch cubes

1. Bring 4 quarts water to a boil in a large pot over high heat. Add 1 tablespoon salt and the pasta to the boiling water. Cook until al dente. Drain, rinsing the pasta well with cold water. Drain the cold pasta well, transfer it to a large mixing bowl, and toss it with the olive oil. Set aside.

2. Drain the tomatoes, reserving the oil. (You should have ⅓ cup reserved oil. If necessary, make up the difference with extra-virgin olive oil.) Coarsely chop the tomatoes. Whisk the reserved oil from the tomatoes with the vinegar, garlic, ¼ teaspoon salt, and pepper in a small bowl.

3. Add the arugula, olives, mozzarella, and chopped tomatoes to the bowl with the pasta. Pour the tomato vinaigrette over the pasta, toss gently, and serve immediately.

COLD SESAME NOODLE SALAD

COLD SESAME NOODLES APPEAR ON almost every Chinese takeout menu. What you get when you order these noodles is usually a mass of yellow noodles in a thick sauce that tastes more like peanut butter than sesame seeds. Although it's not really a salad, we wondered if we could turn this takeout standard into a quick, refreshing salad.

Our research turned up a number of cold sesame noodle recipes. After we threw out the recipes with peanut butter as the main ingredient (we wanted sesame noodles, not peanut noodles), we still had a wide range of recipes, many of which included mixed vegetables, which made for more of a salad than a noodle dish. These recipes varied on type of noodle, how the sesame flavor was created, and the added ingredients.

We first tackled how to introduce the sesame flavor to the noodles. We tried using tahini for the dressing. But tahini, a sesame paste most commonly used in Middle Eastern cooking, did not fare well. The resulting salad didn't have much sesame flavor and was slightly bitter. We moved then to toasted sesame oil. Easily found in the supermarket, this dark brown oil made a salad that was the exact opposite of the tahini-based salad. The flavor was so strong, even when we used only a small amount of sesame oil, that no other ingredient could be tasted. The next option was Chinese sesame paste. Although similar to tahini in consistency, it has a deeper toasted sesame flavor. The salad made with this paste was just what we were looking for. One problem, however, was that Chinese sesame paste is hard to find outside communities with a large Chinese population. We wondered if we could achieve the same result by making our own.

We bought sesame seeds in bulk at a local natural foods store and toasted some in a small sauté pan until they were dark and fragrant. Transferring them to our blender with a little oil, we pureed them until they were smooth. To our pleasant surprise, the resulting puree was similar to Chinese sesame paste. Adding a little mirin (a sweet rice wine) to this mixture enhanced the nuttiness of the sesame. A dash of rice vinegar gave our dressing a slight acidic bite. After finishing with soy sauce, we had a good dressing, full of sesame nuttiness without being too strong. We could now shift our focus to the noodles.

The Asian noodle section in the international aisle of the local supermarket is daunting. The noodles generally fall into two types: those made with wheat and those made with rice (there are, of course, other variations, but normally these are found only in Asian markets or well-stocked international sections of supermarkets). Rice noodles didn't fit well in this salad; they work better in lighter salads, like those from Southeast Asia. So we concentrated mainly on wheat-based noodles.

We tried many brands and varieties of noodles, and some worked okay for our salad. One thing, however, we generally did not like about the wheat-based noodles was their high starch content. As a result of it, several minutes after the noodles had been mixed with our dressing, they turned into a big sticky mass that made it nearly impossible to mix in the vegetables. We thought we could rectify this by rinsing the cooked noodles well, but the rinsed noodles were bland and watery. We couldn't seem to find a middle ground—that is, until we tried soba noodles. Soba noodles are made with buckwheat flour and are less starchy when boiled. After a cursory rinse, the starch was removed, but the noodles did not become waterlogged. As a bonus, the buckwheat gives the soba noodles a slight nutty flavor, which complemented the sesame taste.

Now that we had a perfect match of noodle and dressing, all we had to do was complete the salad with the addition of vegetables. We chose a trio of radishes, bean sprouts, and scallions, which all lent pungency and crunch to the salad. How could we go back to takeout after this?

Cold Sesame Noodle Salad

SERVES 6 AS A SIDE DISH
TIME: 20 MINUTES

These noodles can be served with salmon, chicken, or tofu, especially if Asian flavors are used in the main course.

¼	cup sesame seeds
2	tablespoons vegetable oil
2	tablespoons soy sauce

2 tablespoons mirin

2 teaspoons rice vinegar

1 teaspoon salt

8 ounces soba noodles

3 medium radishes, cut into ⅛-inch rounds and then into ⅛-inch strips

2 medium scallions, trimmed and sliced thin on an angle

½ cup bean sprouts

1. Toast the sesame seeds in a small skillet over medium-high heat until lightly browned, about 2½ minutes. Set 1 tablespoon seeds aside. Place the remaining seeds in the jar of a blender. Add the oil and process on low speed for 10 seconds. Scrape down the sides of the blender and process for another 10 seconds. Add the soy sauce, mirin, and vinegar and process to combine, about 5 seconds. Set the dressing aside.

2. Bring 3 quarts water to a boil in a medium pot. Add the salt and soba noodles and boil until al dente, about 4 minutes. Drain the noodles in a colander and return them to the cooking pot. Add cold water to the pot, swishing the noodles around to wash away the starch. Drain well. Transfer the noodles to a large mixing bowl and toss with the dressing. Let stand 5 minutes. Add the radishes, scallions, sprouts, and reserved tablespoon sesame seeds and toss to combine. Serve immediately.

BREAD SALADS

THROUGHOUT HISTORY, BREAD HAS been among the most important foods. This is especially true in the countries that ring the Mediterranean, where throwing out bread would be an unspeakable act. So it is not surprising that cooks in these countries have found many uses for stale bread. One such use is to incorporate it into a salad. Panzanella, made by the Italians, is probably the most common bread salad. But the Italians are not alone in making salads. Fattoush, a bread salad with origins in Lebanon, is equally as good as its Italian cousin (see page 48 for details on this recipe).

All bread salads, of course, start with bread. The rule here is the better the bread, the better the salad. It's crucial that the bread be of the best quality, with no added flavors or sweeteners. It should also have a sturdy texture in order to stand up to the dressing and liquid ingredients. In our testing, we found it better to dry the bread pieces in the oven before mixing the salad. The reason is that not all bread is equal. We found that bread varies from brand to brand and loaf to loaf in the amount of moisture it contains. So a bread salad made with one loaf worked fine, but a salad made with another loaf ended up soggy.

To level the playing field, we decided to crisp the bread in an oven, avoiding any discrepancies in the loaves and their relative dryness. Another advantage to drying the bread in the oven is that you can make a salad at any time; you don't have to wait until you have stale bread (and who has enough stale bread on hand to make a large salad?). Finally, the salad made with our oven-dried bread held its shape admirably, even with a liberal quantity of wet ingredients.

Panzanella consists of rustic Italian bread with juicy ripe tomatoes and loads of fresh basil. For our panzanella, we wanted to focus on vegetables at their height of freshness in the later days of the summer. Tomatoes and corn were the obvious candidates. In addition to cubing the tomatoes, we simply cut the corn kernels from the ears and tossed them with our rustic bread. The corn, while not an authentic panzanella ingredient, provided a contrasting crunch and a dose of sweetness. To some tasters, in fact, the sweetness was overpowering, so we searched for an ingredient to temper it just a bit. We tried raw red onion, slicing it into thin pieces, but even in small amounts, the onion proved too strong. We then experimented with quick-pickled onion. Here was the perfect solution. The pickled onions keep their oniony flavor, but they are not harsh.

Bread Salad with Tomatoes, Corn, and Pickled Onions

SERVES 6 AS A SIDE DISH
TIME: 30 MINUTES

The corn kernels are a decidedly American addition to this Italian salad. Bread salad makes a nice companion to classic summer picnic fare or a meal from the grill.

QUICK PICKLED ONIONS

1/2	cup red wine vinegar
1	tablespoon sugar
1/4	teaspoon salt
1/2	medium red onion, sliced thin

BREAD SALAD

1	loaf rustic bread (about 1 pound), crust removed, remaining bread torn into 1-inch pieces
2	tablespoons red wine vinegar
1/2	cup extra-virgin olive oil
1/2	teaspoon salt
1/4	teaspoon ground black pepper
2	ears fresh corn, husks and silk discarded, kernels removed with a knife
2	medium tomatoes (about 1 pound), cored and cut into 3/4-inch dice
1/4	cup packed fresh basil leaves, torn into small pieces

1. FOR THE PICKLED ONIONS: Bring the vinegar, sugar, and salt to a boil in a small saucepan over high heat. Add the onion and return to a boil. Remove the pan from the heat and cool to room temperature. Drain when cool and set the onions aside.

2. FOR THE SALAD: Meanwhile, adjust an oven rack to the middle position and heat the oven to 375 degrees. Place the bread on a rimmed baking sheet and bake until dry but not browned, 13 to 15 minutes. Remove the bread from the oven and cool to room temperature.

3. Whisk the vinegar, oil, salt, and pepper together in a small bowl until smooth.

4. Place the cooled bread, corn, tomatoes, basil, and pickled onions in a large bowl. Pour the dressing over the salad and toss to coat. Serve immediately.

PITA BREAD SALAD

TRADITIONALLY, FATTOUSH CONSISTS of small bites of pita bread mixed with cucumbers and tomatoes and dressed with lemon juice and a fruity olive oil. But after making several of these traditional salads, we noticed several minor flaws. While the salads we tested were tasty, they lacked body and texture.

Wanting to create a more substantial salad—one that could be eaten as a light entrée—we decided that cheese would be one of the key ingredients. Feta cheese naturally came to mind, as it is one of the more popular cheeses consumed in countries in the eastern Mediterranean (the same countries where pita is the favored bread). Feta's bright, fresh flavor would also meld well in the salad without making it too heavy.

Continuing our ingredient search, we wanted to select items that would lend crispness to the salad without adding excess moisture. Romaine lettuce was perfect. It added crunch without making the other ingredients soggy. We wanted to avoid tomatoes, but tasters missed their sweetness, so we tried several varieties with less moisture than traditional vine-ripened tomatoes. We found halved cherry tomatoes contributed deep tomato flavor without the liquid. Some briny kalamata olives and thinly sliced red onion rounded out our ingredient list.

To finish our pita bread salad, we needed a dressing. We knew we wanted to stay with the traditional trio of olive oil, lemon, and mint, but we found our normal ratio of 4 parts oil to 1 part acid resulted in a boring salad, short on brightness. So we played with the ratio until settling on 2 parts oil to 1 part acid. While this seemed extreme, it gave the salad a tartness that tasters preferred. Finally, we added chopped mint. The only problem with the mint was that with one bite you might get intense mint flavor, and the next bite you might not get any. For some reason, the mint was not distributing evenly through the chunky salad. To solve this problem, we threw all the dressing ingredients in a blender and processed them until the mint was finely minced. The salad made with this dressing was just right; the mint flavor was evenly distributed and complemented the other ingredients without overpowering them.

Pita Bread Salad with Olives, Feta, and Mint

SERVES 6 AS A SIDE DISH

TIME: 30 MINUTES

Let the onions sit in the dressing for 5 minutes to remove some of their sting. This salad can also be served as a light entrée for four.

4	(8-inch) pita breads, torn into ½-inch pieces
¼	cup packed fresh mint leaves, torn into small pieces
¼	cup juice from 2 lemons
½	cup extra-virgin olive oil
½	small red onion, sliced thin
1	small head romaine lettuce, cut or torn into 1-inch pieces (about 6 cups lightly packed)
20	cherry tomatoes, halved
½	cup kalamata olives, pitted and sliced
6	ounces feta cheese, crumbled (about 1½ cups)

1. Adjust an oven rack to the middle position and heat the oven to 375 degrees. Place the pita pieces on a rimmed baking sheet and bake until crisp but not brown, 7 to 10 minutes. Remove the pita from the oven and cool to room temperature.

2. Meanwhile, process the mint, lemon juice, and oil in a blender until the mint is finely chopped, using a rubber spatula to scrape the sides of the blender as necessary, about twenty 1-second pulses. Combine the dressing and onion in a large bowl, toss to coat, and let stand for 5 minutes.

3. Add the pita, romaine, tomatoes, and olives to the bowl with the onion and toss to coat. Arrange the salad on a large serving platter or individual plates, sprinkle with the feta, and serve immediately.

BEAN SALAD

OUR COLLECTIVE MEMORIES OF BEAN salads involved overly sweet and soupy mixtures of canned green, yellow, and red kidney beans. The green and yellow beans were always mushy and never actually tasted like beans, and the kidney beans never had enough flavor. They seemed to have been added as an afterthought—one less can cluttering the cupboard. While it is possible to make an excellent version of the classic American bean salad, we thought we would explore other possibilities.

We were looking for a salad with fresh flavors unified by a dressing that did not overpower the beans' subtle flavor. With this in mind, we concentrated on several points: improving the texture and flavor of the beans and developing a tasty dressing.

Focusing first on green beans, our initial task was to determine the best way to cook them. Canned green beans were not an option. We wanted to preserve the texture of the beans, and canned beans are always mushy. Blanching and then shocking fresh beans in ice water was the best method. Although steaming was an alternative option, the blanch-and-shock approach resulted in beans with much more crunch. The blanched beans also kept their bright green color. We found that three minutes in boiling water was just enough time for the beans to lose their raw, waxy flavor without becoming mushy and unappetizing.

We next moved on to the canned beans. This proved the most challenging part. We tried many varieties of canned beans in our salad. Larger beans fared better than smaller beans because they were creamier and more substantial and had more bean flavor. One of our favorite larger beans was the cannellini, or white kidney bean. We nevertheless had one recurring problem with the cannellini: They tended to be bland. Try as we might, the cannellini never seemed to pick up much flavor. It then occurred to us that we might try cooking the beans. Inspired by warm salads we had developed in the past, we found a compromise between the cooking for flavor and the time constraint on our quick recipes.

We started by building a dressing in a sauté pan, which would be later used to heat the beans. The dressing would impart much-needed flavor to the vegetables. We began by quickly softening onions in olive oil, then adding the beans and allowing them to heat through. After removing the pan from the heat, we swirled in some vinegar (we learned

in earlier tests that it was better to add the vinegar off the heat to preserve its brightness). Although the warm vinaigrette greatly improved the taste of the beans, some tasters felt the dressing left something to be desired. We considered adding bacon to the pan but thought the smokiness might not blend well with the other flavors. It then occurred to us that because we were using cannellini beans, which are used heavily in Italian cuisine, pancetta might be a good match. Indeed it was. The pancetta (unsmoked Italian bacon) added a meaty depth to the salad, and its additional salt further boosted the flavor of the beans. We now turned to the finishing touches.

We needed an ingredient that would provide contrasting flavors and texture. Initially, we thought arugula would work well in this situation, but it didn't provide any texture because the warm dressing wilted it too much. Recalling an Italian salad that combined white beans with grilled radicchio, we decided to add small pieces of raw radicchio. This unusual (for us) combination worked surprisingly well. The radicchio lent a slight bitter flavor to the salad and also added crunch—exactly what we were looking for.

Green and White Bean Salad with Pancetta

SERVES 6 AS A SIDE DISH

TIME: 25 MINUTES

Serve this warm salad with grilled meats.

	Salt
½	pound green beans, cut into 1-inch pieces
½	head radicchio, torn into ½-inch pieces (about 1 cup)
3	tablespoons olive oil
2	ounces thinly sliced pancetta, cut into ⅛-inch pieces

½   medium white onion, diced fine
I   (15-ounce) can cannellini beans, drained
and rinsed
2   tablespoons red wine vinegar
Ground black pepper

1. Bring 2½ quarts water to a boil in a large saucepan over high heat. Add 1 teaspoon salt and the green beans, return to a boil, and cook until the beans are bright green and crisp-tender, about 3 minutes. Meanwhile, fill a medium bowl with ice water. Drain the beans in a colander and immediately transfer them to the ice water. When the beans no longer feel warm to the touch, drain well in a colander again. Place the beans in a large bowl with the radicchio and set the bowl aside.

2. Heat the oil and pancetta in a large skillet over medium heat. Cook until the pancetta has rendered its fat and become slightly crisp, about 6 minutes. Add the onion and cook, stirring occasionally, until slightly softened, about 3 minutes. Add the cannellini beans and cook, stirring occasionally, until heated through, about 3 minutes. Remove the pan from the heat and swirl in the vinegar.

3. Pour the white bean mixture over the green beans and radicchio and toss to combine. Adjust the seasonings with salt and pepper to taste. Serve immediately.

Lentil Salad

BECAUSE LENTILS CAN BE COOKED without soaking, they can be part of a quick bean salad that requires no canned products. We first needed to determine the kind of lentil to use in our salad. After some research, we found four main varieties of lentils on the market: green lentils du Puy from France, common brown lentils, peeled red lentils, and whole massor (red lentils with the brownish seed coat left on). To test the lentils, we cooked all four types using the same method: bringing the lentils to a boil in an abundant amount of water and then simmering them until tender.

As the water simmered, we found that not all the lentils cooked in the same fashion. The peeled red lentils almost immediately lost their shape and quickly turned to mush. The common brown and the massor lentils became tender and creamy, but by the time they were fully cooked they had started to lose their seed coats, which caused them to disintegrate. The French lentils turned out to be the best of the four for this purpose. Although it took the French lentils a little longer than the other types to become tender, when they were fully cooked they held their shape nicely, an essential trait for a good lentil salad.

Although we had settled on French green lentils, tasters felt they were a little bland. Many of us in the test kitchen had been warned against salting legumes during cooking because it supposedly toughened their skins. Because the lentils were definitely lacking in flavor, we decided to challenge this unwritten rule. Much to our surprise, it seemed this rule was meant to be broken. While the salted lentils took slightly longer to cook, the taste was markedly better. The salted lentils tasted more robust and earthier than the lentils cooked in plain water.

With the question of how to cook the lentils behind us, we next focused on developing the seasonings for the recipe. To do this, we consulted numerous cookbooks. Because lentils are popular around the world (especially in Europe, the Middle East, and India), the recipes we found varied widely. Traditionally, as one would expect, the different lentil types are prepared and flavored in the style of their region of origin. Given that we were using French lentils, we narrowed our search to primarily French cookbooks.

Many of the recipes we found employed similar cooking methods and flavorings. Most called for simmering lentils, draining them, and then tossing the still-warm lentils with a vinaigrette. More often than not, the vinaigrette contained walnut oil, wine vinegar, and other aromatics. Armed with this information, we made several batches of lentil salad. Generally, these salads were good, but there was room for improvement.

Tasters raised several issues about the vinaigrette; some felt it lacked punch, and others disliked the walnut oil. Figuring that the vinegar (everyone liked sherry vinegar best in this recipe) in the dressing lost potency when mixed with the warm lentils, we decreased the ratio of oil to vinegar. While this improved the brightness of the salad, it didn't improve it enough to meet our standards. By doubling the amount of Dijon mustard in the vinaigrette, we gave the dressing a little more bite, which in turn satisfied the problem of dull flavors. Another change we made to the vinaigrette was to omit the walnut oil, which tended to overpower the salad. Even in small amounts, its slight bitterness muted the other flavors. But keeping walnuts in mind, we moved to another issue—texture.

Many salads we made tasted fine but were rather one-dimensional. They needed crunch. Topping the salad with a sprinkling of toasted walnuts improved the salad greatly, both adding texture and accentuating the earthiness of the lentils. Introducing scallions to the mix also improved the overall texture and provided pungency. The final ingredient, roasted red peppers, sweetened the salad and rounded out the other flavors.

Lentil Salad with Walnuts and Scallions

SERVES 4 AS A SIDE DISH
TIME: 50 MINUTES (INCLUDES 15 MINUTES COOLING TIME)

This salad is a natural with grilled sausages; with the addition of lettuce leaves or other greens, it also can be served as a light vegetarian entrée. French lentils du Puy are small green lentils sold in many gourmet markets and some supermarkets. They are smaller than common brown lentils, and their color is army green. If you can't find green lentils, use common brown lentils and reduce the simmering time in step 1 by 5 to 7 minutes. See page 11 for information about jarred roasted red peppers.

1	cup lentils du Puy, picked over and rinsed
1/2	medium onion, halved
2	bay leaves
1	large sprig fresh thyme
3/4	teaspoon salt
1/2	cup coarsely chopped walnuts
2	tablespoons sherry vinegar
2	teaspoons Dijon mustard
1/8	teaspoon ground black pepper
6	tablespoons extra-virgin olive oil
2	scallions, white and green parts, sliced thin
4	ounces jarred roasted red peppers, drained and diced (about 1/2 cup)

1. Bring the lentils, onion, bay leaves, thyme, 1/2 teaspoon salt, and 4 cups water to a boil in a medium saucepan over medium-high heat. Reduce the heat and simmer until the lentils are tender but still hold their shape, 25 to 30 minutes.

2. Meanwhile, toast the walnuts in a dry skillet over medium heat, stirring frequently, until fragrant, 4 to 5 minutes; set them aside.

Whisk the vinegar, mustard, remaining ¼ teaspoon salt, pepper, and oil together in a small bowl; set the dressing aside.

3. Using a fine-mesh strainer, drain the lentils, discarding the onion, bay leaves, and thyme. Transfer the lentils to a medium bowl. Toss the warm lentils with the vinaigrette and cool to room temperature, about 15 minutes. Stir in the walnuts, scallions, and red pepper and serve immediately.

Escarole Salad with Bacon and Poached Egg

NOTHING IS AS SATISFYING AS A properly poached egg. Tender, glistening white surrounds a yolk that, when cut, oozes its rich hearty goodness. Couple a poached egg with slightly bitter greens dressed with a simple creamy vinaigrette and you'll have a combination that not only is easy to prepare but serves as a one-dish dinner salad.

Poaching eggs, however, is not always an easy task. Eggs don't respond well to water that is boiling too vigorously, nor are they appetizing when cooked too long. So we set out to develop a way to produce a perfectly poached egg without a lot of fuss. After some experimentation, we found a foolproof method.

The first thing we found was that the standard saucepan just didn't cut it. When we dropped an egg into the saucepan, it took a long time to reach the bottom of the pan. The longer the egg takes to reach the bottom of the pan, the more the egg whites are disturbed before setting. Using a skillet solved this problem. The skillet provided a floor for the eggs sooner than the saucepan did, allowing the egg whites to set without agitation.

The other variables we addressed were the temperature of the water and the cooking time. Because the white of the egg sets more quickly at higher temperatures, the ideal temperature to cook the eggs is 212 degrees (as high as you can go with boiling water). But, as you can imagine, the rapidly boiling water dispersed the whites, leaving almost nothing around the yolks—not what we were looking for. We then tried the more traditional method of poaching, with the water kept around 160 degrees. While this method worked a little better, the whites suffered without the initial blast of high temperature. This resulted in wispy egg whites, and in the end the egg was a little tough.

This led us to develop a slightly unconventional method for poaching eggs. We found that placing the eggs in boiling water and then immediately turning off the heat and covering the pan worked the best. The high temperature set the whites almost immediately and also provided enough residual heat to cook the yolks in a short amount of time. Shutting off the heat also meant we didn't have to contend with rough water, so there were no tattered whites. The result was a perfectly cooked yolk, its white still attached, with the perfect texture.

Now that we had perfected our eggs, we needed to decide what kind of salad to put them on. Because the initial inspiration for this salad was the classic French *salade Lyonnaise,* we decided to look there. Salade Lyonnaise consists of bitter greens dressed in a vinaigrette made of bacon drippings and wine vinegar and then topped with pieces of crisp bacon (lardons) and a poached egg. While this is a good salad, tasters felt it could be made better with slight modifications.

One such change was the dressing. The consensus among tasters was that while the bacon added a smoky, salty component to the salad, a vinaigrette made solely with bacon fat was heavy and greasy, overpowering the other flavors in the salad. To rectify this, we added already crisped bacon to the salad and replaced the bacon fat in the vinaigrette with olive oil. While this made a lighter vinaigrette, the dressing didn't stick well to the lettuce leaves. This problem was easily solved by adding a little sour cream to the dressing, which provided sticking power.

Tasters felt the greens also should be changed. Frisée, the classic choice, was too bitter, so we began to explore other options. While not bitter, tender leafy greens such as red and green leaf lettuce could not stand up to the richness of the egg and the bacon. Tasters felt romaine was too watery and bland. In the end, escarole was the favorite among tasters. Although it is in the same family as frisée, escarole is slightly less bitter, and it has enough texture to hold its own with the other ingredients in this salad.

Topped with cherry tomatoes for sweetness and blue cheese to balance the richness of the egg, this is a satisfying dinner salad that can be prepared in less than half an hour.

POACHING EGGS

To get four eggs into simmering water at the same time, crack each egg into a small cup with a handle. Lower the lips of the cups just into the water at the same time and tip the eggs into the pan.

Escarole Salad with Bacon and Poached Egg

SERVES 4 AS A MAIN COURSE

TIME: 25 MINUTES

See the illustration below for information about getting the eggs safely into the boiling water.

1¼	teaspoons salt
3	tablespoons white wine vinegar
4	large eggs, each cracked into a small-handled teacup
1	tablespoon juice from 1 lemon
¼	cup extra-virgin olive oil
2	tablespoons sour cream
2	teaspoons Dijon mustard
⅛	teaspoon ground black pepper
1	medium head escarole, washed, dried, and torn into pieces (about 8 cups lightly packed)
4	strips bacon, cooked until crisp, drained on paper towels, and crumbled
12	cherry tomatoes, halved
2	ounces blue cheese, crumbled (about ½ cup)

1. Fill a 10-inch nonstick skillet nearly to the rim with water, add 1 teaspoon salt and 2 tablespoons vinegar, and bring the mixture to a boil over high heat. Lowering the lips of the cups just into water at once (see the illustration at left), tip the eggs into the boiling water, cover, and remove the pan from the heat. Let sit undisturbed until the yolks are medium-firm, exactly 4 minutes. For firmer yolks (or for extra-large or jumbo eggs), increase time to 4½ minutes; for looser yolks (or for medium eggs), decrease time to 3 minutes.

2. Meanwhile, whisk together the remaining 1 tablespoon vinegar, lemon juice, oil, sour cream, mustard, pepper, and remaining ¼ teaspoon salt in a small bowl. Toss the escarole

with the vinaigrette in a large bowl and arrange the escarole on four individual plates.

3. With a slotted spoon, carefully lift and drain each egg over the skillet. Place an egg gently on top of the lettuce on each plate. Sprinkle the salads with the bacon, tomatoes, and cheese. Serve immediately.

Warm Spinach Salads

WARM SPINACH SALADS ARE VICTIMS of unfair stereotyping. Thought of as complicated and difficult to execute, they somehow are perceived as an item you can enjoy only in a restaurant. Most cooks willing to try them at home save spinach salads for the first course at fancy dinner parties. But we found the exact opposite to be true. Warm spinach salads are not only easy to make but also easily transformed into a satisfying meal without expending much effort or time. But that's not to say there aren't pitfalls you must avoid when preparing these salads.

Spinach salad at its finest is a pleasant dish of tender spinach leaves lightly wilted by a warm aromatic dressing. But after several tests in the kitchen, we found this ideal is not automatically achieved. The salads we tried ran the gamut from tough leaves covered with bland, insipid dressing to salads so overdressed they were mushy piles of greens standing in puddles of vinaigrette. To reach the goal of a satisfactory homemade spinach salad, we had to address two major factors: the type of spinach to use and how to dress it.

We tackled spinach type first. There are two categories of spinach: curly leaf and flat leaf. Curly-leaf spinach is probably the variety most people are familiar with; it is usually packaged in cellophane bags and sold at the local supermarket. This type of spinach didn't do

well in our tests. Tasters felt the leaves were too dry and chewy, and the remaining stems were fibrous. The leaves also didn't wilt with the addition of the warm vinaigrette, so we decided to reserve this type for recipes in which the spinach is cooked.

Moving on to flat-leaf spinach, our results were more encouraging. We found two types of flat-leaf spinach commonly available at the market. The larger leaf spinach, which was sold in bundles, worked well in our salad. Its tender leaves were moist and wilted well, but the bunches we bought were full of dirt and required several extended periods of soaking to rid them of all the grit. Discouraged by the amount of time it took to wash and prepare the spinach, we bought a bag of the baby spinach sold in the supermarket in the same aisle as the prepared salads-in-a-bag. Baby spinach worked perfectly. The small, tender leaves came washed and trimmed, and all we had to do was open the bag and place the spinach in a bowl. You can't get much quicker than that.

With the base of our salad tested, we could focus on how to make a flavorful dressing that didn't overpower or overwilt the greens. During testing, we found the acidic component in the warm dressing should be varied based on the accompanying salad ingredients. Tasters generally preferred wine vinegar or lemon juice, feeling they made a bright salad. We also found that if we added the acidic component of the dressing in the early stages of the cooking process, the flavors were muted. Swirling in the acid at the end, after the pan had been removed from the flame, restored some of the punch—but not quite enough. Up to this point, we had been using our standard vinaigrette ratio of 4 parts oil to 1 part vinegar. While this formula worked, the salad was a little greasy. To solve these two problems, we scaled back our ratio to 3 parts

REMOVING TENDONS FROM SCALLOPS

The small, rough-textured, crescent-shaped muscle that attaches the scallop to the shell toughens when cooked. Use your fingers to peel the tendon away from the side of each scallop before cooking.

DEVEINING SHRIMP

Some shrimp (especially very large ones) have a visible black vein that runs along the outer curved edge just under the surface. Although the veins don't affect the flavor or texture of the shrimp, many cooks remove them for aesthetic reasons. We don't bother with deveining unless the veins are quite big.

1. With a paring knife, make a shallow slit along the back of each shrimp. With the tip of the blade, lift up and loosen the vein.

2. Because the vein is quite sticky, we like to touch the knife blade to a paper towel on the counter. The vein will stick to the towel, and you can devein the next shrimp with a clean knife.

oil and 1 part vinegar. We now had a bright, fresh-tasting salad that wasn't too greasy.

Another problem with many salads we tested was overdressing. Nothing is worse than limp, soggy salad. So we tried tossing salads with various quantities of dressing and finally settled on 6 tablespoons dressing for 8 cups greens. This wilted the spinach perfectly; the leaves retained a satisfying crunch without becoming wet and slimy.

Both of the spinach salads we developed call for searing shellfish in the pan in which you eventually build the vinaigrette. While this step takes very little time and makes a satisfying one-dish meal, it can be omitted if you want to make a simple first-course salad.

Warm Spinach Salad with Seared Scallops and Roasted Pepper Vinaigrette

SERVES 4 AS A MAIN COURSE
TIME: 25 MINUTES

This recipe calls for jarred roasted red peppers. See page 11 for information about our testing of various brands of jarred peppers. See photo of this recipe on page 152.

9	ounces baby spinach (about 8 cups lightly packed)
¾	cup sliced almonds
5	tablespoons extra-virgin olive oil
I	pound medium sea scallops, tendons removed (see the illustration above) Salt
4	ounces jarred roasted red peppers, drained and cut into thin strips (about ½ cup)
2	medium shallots, sliced thin
⅛	teaspoon ground black pepper
I ½	tablespoons sherry vinegar

1. Place the spinach in a large bowl and set it aside. Toast the almonds in a 12-inch skillet

over medium heat, shaking the pan occasionally to turn the nuts, until they are fragrant and lightly browned, about 3 minutes. Transfer the almonds to the bowl with the spinach.

2. Add 2 tablespoons oil to the empty skillet, raise the heat to medium-high, and heat until the oil begins to smoke. Add the scallops, flat-side down, and cook until well browned, 2½ to 3 minutes. Using tongs, turn the scallops over, one at a time. Cook until medium-rare (the sides will have firmed up and all but the middle third of the scallop will be opaque),

about 45 seconds longer. Transfer the scallops to a plate, season with salt to taste, and set aside.

3. Lower the heat to medium and add the remaining 3 tablespoons oil to the empty skillet along with the red peppers, shallots, ¼ teaspoon salt, and pepper. Cook until the shallots soften slightly, about 2 minutes. Remove the pan from the heat and swirl in the vinegar. Pour the warm dressing over the spinach and gently toss to wilt. Divide the spinach salad among four plates and arrange the scallops on top. Serve immediately.

SEGMENTING ORANGES

For salads and other dishes where presentation matters, you want to remove segments from an orange without any white pith or membrane. The same technique can be used with grapefruits.

1. Start by slicing a small section, about ½ inch thick, from the top and bottom ends of the orange.

2. Use a very sharp paring knife to slice off the rind, including all of the bitter white pith. Slide the knife edge from the top to the bottom of the orange, following the outline of the fruit as closely as possible to minimize waste.

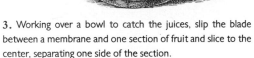

3. Working over a bowl to catch the juices, slip the blade between a membrane and one section of fruit and slice to the center, separating one side of the section.

4. Turn the blade of the knife so it faces out and lines up along the membrane on the opposite side of the section. Slide the blade from the center out along the membrane to completely free the section. Continue until all sections are removed and free of membranes.

Warm Spinach Salad with Spicy Shrimp and Orange

SERVES 4 AS A MAIN COURSE

TIME: 25 MINUTES

Some shrimp contain visible black veins, which you may want to remove before cooking. See the illustrations on page 56 for tips on deveining shrimp.

9	ounces baby spinach (about 8 cups lightly packed)
1	teaspoon fennel seeds
½	teaspoon hot red pepper flakes
½	teaspoon salt
1	pound extra-large shrimp (21 to 25 count per pound), peeled and deveined, if necessary
5	tablespoons extra-virgin olive oil
½	medium red onion, sliced thin
1	teaspoon grated zest from 1 orange
⅛	teaspoon ground black pepper
1½	tablespoons juice from 1 lemon
3	medium seedless oranges, segmented (see the illustrations on page 57)

1. Place the spinach in a large bowl and set it aside. Place the fennel seeds, red pepper flakes, and ¼ teaspoon salt in a spice grinder or coffee mill and process until finely ground but not powdery. Toss the spices with the shrimp in a medium bowl. Heat 2 tablespoons oil in a 12-inch skillet over medium-high heat until the oil begins to smoke. Add the shrimp and cook until lightly browned, about 2 minutes. Using tongs, turn the shrimp over and cook until browned on the second side, about 1½ minutes longer. Transfer the shrimp to a plate and reserve.

2. Lower the heat to medium and add the remaining 3 tablespoons oil to the empty skillet along with the onion, orange zest, remaining ¼ teaspoon salt, and pepper. Cook until the onion softens slightly, 2 to 3 minutes. Remove the pan

from the heat and swirl in the lemon juice. Pour the warm dressing over the spinach, add the orange segments, and toss gently to wilt. Divide the spinach salad among four plates and arrange the shrimp on top. Serve immediately.

SHRIMP SALAD WITH AVOCADO AND GRAPEFRUIT

THE COMBINATION OF SHRIMP SALAD and avocado is classic, a standard on luncheon menus across the country. But all too often, this salad consists of tough, tiny precooked frozen shrimp, swimming in mayonnaise and presented in a hollow avocado half—an unsightly and unappetizing mess. We wanted to develop a salad featuring properly cooked shrimp in a bright, flavorful dressing, complemented by rich avocados and bitter grapefruit.

Several of the recipes we consulted suggested using frozen precooked shrimp. While we thought this would be a big time-saver, it turned out to be a mistake in the recipe—the shrimp were chewy and rubbery. We started to explore methods of cooking shrimp.

The method of preference in most recipes was poaching. This entailed bringing a poaching liquid (we squeezed lemon juice into plain water) to temperature, adding the shrimp, and cooking for several minutes with the burner on. This method seemed to have two flaws. The first problem was that with the burner on, it was hard to regulate the temperature of the water, and this often led to overcooked and tough shrimp. Second, the shrimp was in the water so briefly it didn't pick up any flavor from the poaching liquid. Our solution was to bring the poaching medium to a boil, turn off the heat, add the shrimp, and cover the pot. With this method, the shrimp stay in the water for 8 minutes, enough time to pick up flavor, and because there is no direct heat, the danger of overcooking is eliminated.

With the method of cooking shrimp settled, we moved on to the flavors of the salad. From the start, we decided to stay away from a rich mayonnaise-based dressing. This led us to experiment with vinaigrettes and creamy dressings made with yogurt and sour cream. Tasters preferred the salad dressed with vinaigrette; they felt the creamy dressing was too heavy and weighed down the flavors of the salad. Because the salad contained grapefruit, we decided the vinaigrette should contain a citrus juice. Lime juice was favored over lemon juice for its brightness. To finish the vinaigrette, we added ginger to give it a little bite and honey to balance the acidity of the limes.

Shrimp Salad with Avocado and Grapefruit

SERVES 4 AS A LIGHT MAIN COURSE

TIME: 25 MINUTES

See page 21 for tips on handling avocados. If the shrimp have large veins, remove them according to the instructions on page 56.

1	lemon, halved
1	pound extra-large (21 to 25 count per pound) shrimp, peeled and deveined, if necessary
2	tablespoons juice from 1 lime
1/2	teaspoon honey
1	(1-inch) piece fresh ginger, minced (about 1 1/2 teaspoons)
1/2	teaspoon salt
1/4	teaspoon ground black pepper
1/3	cup canola oil
2	medium ruby grapefruits, segmented (see the illustrations on page 57)
1	tablespoon chopped fresh mint leaves
2	ounces snow peas (about 24 peas), strings removed (see the illustration on page 6) and cut crosswise into 1/8-inch strips
1	large avocado, pitted, peeled, and cut into 1/2-inch dice
16	Bibb lettuce leaves, washed and dried

1. Place 3 cups water in a medium saucepan. Squeeze the juice of both lemon halves into the water; add the squeezed halves to the water as well. Bring to a boil over high heat and boil for 2 minutes. Remove the pan from the heat and add the shrimp. Cover and let stand off the heat for 8 minutes. Meanwhile, fill a medium bowl with ice water. Drain the shrimp into a colander, discard the lemon halves, and immediately transfer the shrimp to the bowl with the ice water to stop cooking and chill them thoroughly, about 3 minutes. Drain the shrimp again into a colander and transfer them to a large bowl. Refrigerate the shrimp until needed.

2. Meanwhile, whisk together the lime juice, honey, ginger, salt, pepper, and oil in a small bowl until smooth.

3. Remove the chilled shrimp from the refrigerator and add the grapefruits, mint, snow peas, and avocado to the bowl with the shrimp. Pour the vinaigrette over the shrimp mixture and toss gently to coat. Arrange the lettuce leaves on four plates and top with the shrimp salad. Drizzle the lettuce leaves with any vinaigrette left in the bowl and serve immediately.

THAI-STYLE BEEF SALAD

THAI CUISINE IS ALL ABOUT BALANCE and contrast. The elements of sweet, sour, salt, and spice all should be in harmony. Thai salads are a perfect example of this harmony; they offer an enticing variety of tastes, textures, and colors. In Thai cuisine, salads are treated differently than in American cuisine. Instead of being served before or after a meal, Thai salads are eaten alongside main dishes, contributing to the balance of the meal as a whole. Because these salads are normally a mixture of crunchy raw vegetables with the simple addition of a single protein, they are quick to prepare and require little cooking. In addition, they are healthy to eat, as they contain little or no fat.

The most important part of a Thai salad is the dressing. This is where balance plays an important role. If any of the flavors are out of sync with the others, you end up with a dressing that is too sweet, too sour, or too salty.

Thai salads are normally dressed with *nouc cham,* a fish-based sauce mixed with ginger, garlic, chiles, sugar, and lime juice. The question we faced when creating a new recipe was whether we could achieve a balanced and traditional-tasting dressing without using so many ingredients. This required some experimentation, but we believe we've succeeded.

Even before we began, we knew we had to base the dressing on fish sauce. A salty, briny liquid made from fermented fish, fish sauce is, culinarily, the Thai equivalent of Chinese soy sauce. Lime juice would provide the sour component, and we found that an equal amount of lime juice and fish sauce struck the right balance. We tried several sweeteners, including granulated sugar, honey, and brown sugar. The granulated sugar gave the dressing a slightly artificial flavor, and even small amounts of honey were too strong, tending to inappropriately accent the dressing with a floral tinge. Brown sugar, however, provided a subtle, pleasant sweetness, complementing the sour and the salty flavors. For spiciness, we considered chiles, but we found it hard to control the heat of the chiles from one salad to another. So we settled on a small amount of hot red pepper flakes. While this approach is not authentic, we nevertheless achieved a consistent heat level—and we saved ourselves some time.

With our dressing done, we moved on to the vegetables. Because the focus of the salad is seared beef, we wanted to find a balance of flavors and textures that complemented and contrasted with the beef. We looked for vegetables that would cut the richness of the beef, which we felt would benefit the salad. Cucumber was a good choice due to its crispness and mild flavor. Thinly sliced red onion also worked well, adding pungency and crunch. Bibb lettuce lightened the salad. It wouldn't be a Thai salad without a hefty amount of fresh herbs; this job was filled by a duo of cilantro and mint, both of which added a bright, clean flavor. Topped with a little bit of chopped peanuts, our Thai-style salad was now complete.

Thai-Style Beef Salad

SERVES 4 AS A MAIN COURSE

TIME: 35 MINUTES

See the illustrations on page 190 for information about seeding the cucumber. If you prefer, omit the oil and grill the steak.

1	tablespoon vegetable oil
1¼	pounds flank steak, trimmed of excess fat and patted dry with paper towels
	Salt and ground black pepper
¼	cup fish sauce
¼	cup juice from 2 limes
4	teaspoons brown sugar
¼	teaspoon hot red pepper flakes
½	medium cucumber, peeled, seeded, and sliced thin
½	small red onion, sliced thin
1	tablespoon packed fresh cilantro leaves, torn
1	tablespoon packed fresh mint leaves, torn
1	head Bibb or Boston lettuce, washed, dried, and torn into pieces (4 cups lightly packed)

½ cup unsalted dry-roasted peanuts,
chopped coarse

1. Heat the oil in a heavy-bottomed 12-inch skillet over medium-high heat until it begins to smoke. Season the steak liberally with salt and pepper, lay it in the pan, and sauté, not moving it until well browned, 4 to 5 minutes. Turn the steak over with tongs and reduce the heat to medium. Continue to cook until the steak is browned on the second side, about 5 minutes. Transfer the steak to a plate and let rest for 10 minutes.

2. Whisk the fish sauce, lime juice, brown sugar, and red pepper flakes together in a medium bowl until the sugar is dissolved. Remove half of the dressing from the bowl and set it aside in a large bowl. Slice the steak crosswise on the bias into ⅛-inch-thick slices. Halve the longer slices into roughly 3-inch lengths. Add the steak to the smaller bowl with the dressing, toss to coat, and let marinate for 5 minutes.

3. Remove the steak from the dressing and discard the marinade. Toss the steak, cucumber, onion, cilantro, and mint with the reserved dressing in the larger bowl. Arrange the lettuce on a large serving platter or individual plates. Spoon the steak and vegetables over the lettuce. Drizzle the salad with any dressing left in the bowl and sprinkle it with peanuts. Serve immediately.

CHINESE CHICKEN SALAD

WHEN WE THINK OF CHICKEN SALAD, we imagine the traditional mix of chicken, mayonnaise, and a little bit of onion and celery for flavor. But chicken salad has gone far beyond that simple concept. Today, chicken salad is all about the addition of exotic ingredients. Inspired by the cuisines from which these new ingredients come, 21st-century chicken salads often adopt new names. Chinese chicken salad is the perfect example.

A quick search of our cookbook library yielded a handful of Chinese chicken salad recipes. Except for chicken, these recipes had little in common. The flavor of the salads varied greatly. While the ingredients used were ones we usually associate with Chinese cooking, such as bean sprouts and soy sauce, some of the recipes had upwards of 20 ingredients (one had 50!). We wanted a Chinese chicken salad that was a mix of crisp vegetables and moist chicken, all tossed with a flavorful vinaigrette—and with a minimum of ingredients.

We first set our sights on the dressing. We made several vinaigrettes from recipes we had found. Rice vinegar was the most commonly used acid, and it turned out to be the best option. The recipes calling for other vinegars, such as white wine vinegar, tended to be acidic and harsh, and these other vinegars failed to meld with other flavors. The mild acidity and slight sweetness of the rice vinegar suited the other flavors in the salad, such as scallions, red peppers, and cabbage. Minced ginger seemed a natural addition to our dressing, as did soy sauce. But the dressing still lacked depth, so we rummaged through our Asian pantry items and settled on hoisin sauce. Hoisin added both sweetness and a hint of spiciness, which contrasted well with the flavors of the soy sauce and the rice vinegar.

With the dressing developed, we moved on to the chicken. In the test kitchen, our usual procedure for cooking chicken for chicken salad calls for roasting bone-in, skin-on chicken breasts. After roasting, the meat is pulled from the bone and torn into bite-size pieces. Although this procedure produces deliciously moist and flavorful chicken, it takes 45 minutes. We opted here for broiling the chicken breasts, hoping that a quick sear would seal in moistness and save valuable time.

There was, however, a recurring problem with this method—the chicken tasted a bit bland and seemed detached from the salad. We considered marinating the chicken to increase its flavor, but this would take extra time and increase the total amount of ingredients. Next, we thought of making a little extra dressing and using that as a marinade. This, as it turned out, was the solution. Even though we let the chicken marinate for just 10 minutes, it picked up some salty seasoning from the soy sauce. Also, the sugars from the hoisin caramelized in the broiler, producing a wonderful sweet-roasted flavor.

All we had left to do was to decide which vegetables we wanted in our salad. Napa cabbage, or Chinese cabbage, was a perfect fit. Crisp and tasty, its slight mustard flavor wasn't overpowering. Bean sprouts were favored for their crunch and earthiness. Thinly sliced scallions added a slightly assertive bite, and red peppers provided sweetness, completing our Chinese chicken salad.

Chinese Chicken Salad with Hoisin Vinaigrette

SERVES 4 AS A MAIN COURSE

TIME: 30 MINUTES

Chow mein noodles, often sold in 5-ounce canisters, can be found in most supermarkets with other Asian ingredients; La Choy is the most widely available brand. These Americanized noodles add a welcome crunch to this salad.

1/3	cup rice vinegar
1/4	cup canola oil
1 1/2	tablespoons soy sauce
3	tablespoons hoisin sauce
1	tablespoon minced fresh ginger
4	boneless, skinless chicken breast halves (about 1 1/2 pounds), trimmed, with tenderloins removed and reserved for another purpose
1/2	medium head napa cabbage, sliced crosswise into 1/4-inch-thick shreds (about 4 cups)
1/2	large red bell pepper, stemmed, seeded, and sliced thin
1	cup bean sprouts
2	scallions, sliced thin on the bias
1	cup chow mein noodles (see note above)

1. Whisk the vinegar, oil, soy sauce, hoisin, and ginger together in a medium bowl. Remove 1/2 cup dressing from the bowl and set it aside. Add the chicken to the remaining dressing in the bowl, toss to coat, and let marinate 10 minutes.

2. Meanwhile, adjust an oven rack so it is 6 inches away from the broiler element and heat the broiler. Coat the broiler pan top with vegetable spray. Remove the chicken from the marinade, discard the liquid, and lay the chicken breasts on the broiler pan top. Place the broiler pan top over the broiler pan bottom and place under the broiler. Broil the chicken until lightly browned, about 4 minutes. Flip the chicken and broil until it is fully cooked, 3 1/2 to 4 minutes.

3. Place the chicken on a clean plate and cover with plastic wrap. Poke a few vent holes in the plastic wrap and refrigerate the chicken while preparing the other ingredients.

4. Shred the cooled chicken (see the illustration on page 168) and toss it with the cabbage, red pepper, sprouts, and scallions in a large serving bowl. Rewhisk the dressing, pour it over the chicken salad, and toss to combine. Sprinkle with the chow mein noodles and serve immediately.

VEGETABLES

VEGETABLE SIDE DISHES ARE ALMOST always quick, but are they interesting? Sure, you can blanch broccoli, dump it into a bowl with salt and olive oil, and put it on the table in 10 minutes. You can boil corn or grill zucchini in just about the same amount of time. While this kind of side dish is fine, it is plain, and plain fare can become boring over time.

Our goal in developing recipes for this chapter was a bit more ambitious. We wanted to make vegetable side dishes that were special—the kind you might serve to company. However, we didn't want to get complicated. An exotic vegetable recipe with two dozen ingredients may taste great, but who has the time or energy for this kind of project? The recipes that follow offer the best combination of convenience and taste, and all are easy enough to prepare on a weeknight for a family supper. See Chapter 10 for information about grilling vegetables and Chapter 11 for information about stir-frying them.

ASPARAGUS

YOU COULD, WERE YOU SO INCLINED, call asparagus the double agent of the vegetable world. It has the feel and reputation of a fancy vegetable—much more uptown than, say, broccoli or carrots. Yet—and here is the great benefit for home cooks—it is arguably quicker and easier to cook than either of those more pedestrian choices. Better yet, asparagus goes well with almost any kind of sauce. We decided to capitalize on its easygoing nature and give it the quickest, lightest sauces we could: vinaigrettes.

Broiling was our cooking method of choice because it concentrates the flavor of the asparagus and lightly caramelizes its peel, thus making the most of its delicate taste. Broiling also keeps the stovetop free for other dishes. The two primary questions related to

broiling concerned the thickness of the stalks and the distance they should be kept from the heat source during cooking.

In our tests with thick asparagus, from ¾ to 1 inch in diameter, the peels began to char before the interior of the spears became fully tender. Another disadvantage of thicker asparagus was that they often had to be peeled because their skins were generally thicker and tougher than those of more slender asparagus (with a maximum thickness of about ⅝ inch). Thinner asparagus not only let us skip the peeling step but also tended to cook more evenly, without the threat of burning.

Working now with thinner asparagus, we focused on how far to keep them from the heating element. At 3 inches, the asparagus charred a bit, just as the thicker spears had done. At 5 inches, the thinner asparagus took a little too long to cook, and they failed to caramelize adequately. The middle ground, 4 inches, proved perfect for cooking speed, control, and browning.

While the asparagus speed along in the broiler, you need only whisk together oil, an acid, such as vinegar or lemon juice, and flavorings for a bright, simple sauce that beats the clock and keeps your stovetop free and clear.

PREPARING ASPARAGUS

In our tests, we found the tough, woody part of the asparagus stem breaks off in just the right place if you hold the spear the right way. Hold the asparagus in one hand about halfway down the stalk; with the other hand, hold the cut end between the thumb and index finger about an inch or so from the bottom; bend the stalk until it snaps.

Basic Broiled Asparagus

SERVES 6 TO 8

TIME: 20 MINUTES (INCLUDES 10 MINUTES TO PREHEAT BROILER)

Plain broiled asparagus are delicious on their own; they also can be embellished slightly, as in the variations that follow. Choose spears no thicker than ⅝ inch in diameter.

2   pounds thin asparagus spears, tough ends snapped off (see the illustration on page 64)

1   tablespoon extra-virgin olive oil
    Salt and ground black pepper

1. Adjust the oven rack to the uppermost position (about 4 inches from the heating element) and heat the broiler. Toss the asparagus with the oil and salt and pepper to taste on a heavy rimmed baking sheet. Arrange the spears in a single layer on the baking sheet.

2. Broil the asparagus 4 to 5 minutes, shake the pan to turn the spears, and broil another 4 to 5 minutes until they are tender and lightly browned. Transfer the asparagus to a serving platter and serve hot or warm.

Broiled Asparagus with Lemon-Shallot Vinaigrette

SERVES 6 TO 8

TIME: 20 MINUTES

These flavors work well with fish and chicken.

⅓   cup extra-virgin olive oil

1   teaspoon grated zest and 1 tablespoon juice from 1 lemon

1   large shallot, minced (about 2 tablespoons)

1   tablespoon minced fresh thyme leaves

¼   teaspoon Dijon mustard
    Salt and ground black pepper

1   recipe Basic Broiled Asparagus

Whisk together the oil, lemon zest and juice, shallot, thyme, mustard, and salt and pepper to taste in a small bowl. Broil and arrange the asparagus on a serving platter as directed. Cool for 5 minutes, drizzle with the dressing, and serve.

Broiled Asparagus with Tomato-Basil Vinaigrette

SERVES 6 TO 8

TIME: 20 MINUTES

Serve with fish or chicken. See photo of this recipe on page 159.

1   medium ripe tomato, cored, seeded, and chopped fine (about ½ cup)

1   medium shallot, minced

1½   tablespoons juice from 1 lemon

1   tablespoon minced fresh basil leaves

3   tablespoons extra-virgin olive oil
     Salt and ground black pepper

1   recipe Basic Broiled Asparagus

Stir together the tomato, shallot, lemon juice, basil, oil, and salt and pepper to taste in a small bowl. Broil and arrange the asparagus on a serving platter as directed. Cool for 5 minutes, drizzle with the dressing, and serve.

Broiled Asparagus with Bacon, Red Onion, and Balsamic Vinaigrette

SERVES 6 TO 8

TIME: 20 MINUTES

This variation is good with meat.

6   slices bacon, cut crosswise into thin strips

¼   cup extra-virgin olive oil

2   tablespoons balsamic vinegar

2   tablespoons minced red onion

1   tablespoon minced fresh parsley leaves
     Salt and ground black pepper

1   recipe Basic Broiled Asparagus

1. Fry the bacon in a medium skillet over medium heat until brown and crisp, about 6 minutes. Using a slotted spoon, transfer the bacon to a paper towel–lined plate and set it aside.

2. Whisk together the oil, vinegar, onion, parsley, and salt and pepper to taste in a small bowl. Broil and arrange the asparagus on a serving platter as directed. Cool for 5 minutes, drizzle with the dressing, sprinkle with the bacon, and serve.

BROCCOLI

SOME PEOPLE STEAM, BOIL, OR MICROWAVE broccoli to an undesirable army-green mush. Luckily, the texture is hardly noticeable because such broccoli is often served underneath a thick, fluorescent orange cheese sauce. We wanted a quick way to produce properly cooked broccoli. We also wanted updated flavors that enhanced rather than hid the flavor of the broccoli.

Most cooks prepare the florets only, but in the test kitchen we prefer to eat the whole broccoli—both stalks and florets. We noted that the crunchy stalks, though as tasty as the florets, took longer to cook. Our first thought was to peel the stalks of their fibrous, tough outer layer, and this, in fact, made them tender and decreased cooking time. Because we didn't want to use staggered cooking times or two pots, we cut the florets into bite-size pieces, then peeled the stalks, halved them lengthwise, and cut them into ½-inch pieces. Now the florets and stalks cooked in exactly the same amount of time.

The next step was to refine the cooking process. First, we tried boiling the broccoli, but this seemed to beat it up quite a bit. Next, we steamed the broccoli in a steaming basket, then sautéed it with other ingredients. The results

were good, but working with two pans was a bother. We tried simply sautéing the florets and stalks in a frying pan with oil, but we found that the relatively dry heat took quite a while to penetrate and cook the broccoli. We were able to speed up the process, however, by adding water to the pan. When the cold water hit the hot pan, it turned into steam—which, when trapped under a lid, cooked the broccoli in merely 2 minutes. Removing the lid, we were able to evaporate the small amount of water left in the pan, resulting in perfectly steamed yet dry broccoli made using just one pan.

This technique not only is simple but also makes it easy to season the broccoli. We sautéed aromatics and other ingredients, such as garlic, ginger, and red peppers, then added the broccoli and water to the pan. This quick method ensures perfectly cooked broccoli, uses only one pan, and allows for countless flavor variations.

Steamed Broccoli with Toasted Garlic and Lemon

SERVES 4

TIME: 20 MINUTES

Watch the pan closely to make sure the garlic does not burn. It should be golden but not fully browned.

2   tablespoons extra-virgin olive oil
2   medium cloves garlic, sliced thin
     Pinch hot red pepper flakes
2   anchovies, minced (optional)
1½ pounds broccoli (about 1 medium bunch), prepared according to the illustrations on page 67
     Salt and ground black pepper
½   lemon, cut into 4 wedges

1. Heat the oil, garlic, and pepper flakes in a large nonstick skillet over medium heat until

the garlic is golden brown, about 5 minutes. Add the anchovies, if using, and cook, stirring constantly, until fragrant, about 30 seconds.

2. Increase the heat to high; add the broccoli and ½ cup water, then cover and cook until the broccoli begins to turn bright green, 1 to 2 minutes. Uncover the pan and cook, stirring frequently, until the liquid has evaporated and the broccoli is tender, 3 to 5 minutes longer. Season with salt and pepper to taste. Transfer the broccoli to a serving platter. Serve immediately with lemon wedges.

Steamed Broccoli with Red Bell Pepper and Sweet Soy Sauce

SERVES 4

TIME: 20 MINUTES

A sweetened soy sauce and rice vinegar mixture replaces plain water for steaming the broccoli in the pan. Serve with red meat.

2	tablespoons soy sauce
2	tablespoons rice vinegar
1	teaspoon sugar
2	tablespoons vegetable oil
1	medium red bell pepper, stemmed, seeded, and cut into thin strips about 1½ inches long
1	tablespoon minced fresh ginger
2	medium cloves garlic, minced or pressed through a garlic press (about 2 teaspoons)
1½	pounds broccoli (about 1 medium bunch), prepared according to the illustrations at right
	Salt and ground black pepper
2	medium scallions, sliced thin

1. Mix together the soy sauce, vinegar, sugar, and ¼ cup water in a small bowl and set the mixture aside.

2. Heat the oil in a large nonstick skillet over medium-high heat until almost smoking. Add the bell pepper and ginger and cook until the pepper is softened and slightly charred, 5 minutes. Add the garlic and cook, stirring constantly, until fragrant, about 30 seconds. Increase the heat to high; add the broccoli and the soy mixture, then cover and cook until the broccoli begins to turn bright green, 1 to 2 minutes. Uncover the pan and cook, stirring frequently, until the liquid has evaporated and the broccoli is tender, 3 to 5 minutes longer. Season with salt and pepper to taste. Transfer to a serving platter, sprinkle with the scallions, and serve immediately.

PREPARING BROCCOLI

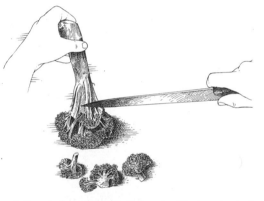

1. Place the broccoli upside down on a cutting board and cut off the florets close to their heads with a large knife.

2. Once the florets are removed, stand each stalk on the cutting board and square it with a large knife. This removes the tough outer ⅛ inch from the stalk. Cut the squared stalk in half lengthwise and then into ½-inch pieces.

Steamed Broccoli with Pine Nuts and Raisins

SERVES 4

TIME: 20 MINUTES

This variation works well with chicken or pork.

¼ cup pine nuts

2 tablespoons extra-virgin olive oil

2 medium cloves garlic, sliced thin

¼ teaspoon hot red pepper flakes

¼ cup raisins

1½ pounds broccoli (about 1 medium bunch), prepared according to the illustrations on page 67

1½ tablespoons sherry vinegar

Salt and ground black pepper

1. Toast the pine nuts in a large nonstick skillet over medium-high heat until golden and aromatic, 2 to 3 minutes. Transfer the nuts to a small bowl and reserve. Return the empty pan to medium heat; add the oil, garlic, pepper flakes, and raisins and cook until fragrant, about 30 seconds.

2. Increase the heat to high; add the broccoli and ½ cup water, then cover and cook until the broccoli begins to turn bright green, 1 to 2 minutes. Uncover the pan and cook, stirring frequently, until the liquid has evaporated and the broccoli is tender, 3 to 5 minutes longer. Remove the pan from the heat and stir in the vinegar and toasted nuts. Season with salt and pepper to taste. Transfer the broccoli to a serving platter and serve immediately.

CARROTS

THE SLICK, SACCHARINE CONFECTION often called glazed carrots belongs in a candy dish on a coffee table, not as a side dish on a dinner plate. These abused vegetables, adrift in a sea of syrup, lie limp and soggy from overcooking or retain a raw, fibrous resistance from undercooking. Most recipes for glazed carrots are hopelessly dated, residing in books from the Betty Crocker era or in more contemporary tomes by authors who feel obliged to include them. These recipes never deliver what we hope for in glazed carrots: fully tender, well-seasoned carrots with a glossy, clingy, yet modest glaze.

We began with the problem of how to prepare the carrots for cooking. Matchsticks were out from the get-go—we were looking for simplicity, not to improve our knife skills. A bag of "baby" carrots unceremoniously emptied into a pan for cooking revealed pieces of wildly different girth, with some more than twice as big around as others. Sure that these would cook unevenly, we halved the large pieces lengthwise; so much for the convenience of this product. Tasters remarked that these little carrots, cooked, were shy on both carrot flavor and good looks, so we peeled regular bagged carrots and cut them on the bias into handsome oblong shapes. Once cooked, these comely carrots earned much praise for their good flavor. Slender bunch carrots (sold with their tops on and at a higher price), also cut on the bias, were no more flavorful, and their diminutive size lacked presence. Regular bagged carrots it was.

Most recipes call for steaming, parboiling, or blanching the carrots prior to glazing, resulting in a battery of dirty utensils. Instead, we put the carrots with a bit of liquid in a skillet (nonstick, for easy cleanup), along with salt and sugar for flavor; then we covered the skillet and let the carrots simmer. Mission accomplished: The carrots were cooked through without much ado. We further found that chicken broth used for the cooking liquid lent the carrots savory backbone and a full, round flavor, whereas water left them hollow and wine turned them sour and astringent. We tried swapping more unusual sweeteners for the sugar but found brown sugar too muddy, maple syrup too assertive, and honey too floral (but good for a variation, we noted). We stood by clean, pure, easy-to-measure granulated sugar.

We moved on to the glaze. After the carrots had simmered for a few minutes and were just on the verge of tender (they would see more heat during glazing, so we simmered them shy of done), we lifted the lid from the skillet, increased the heat, and let the liquid reduce to 2 tablespoons. (If the liquid is not reduced, the glaze is thin and watery.) Finally, we added butter (cut into small pieces for quick melting) and a bit more sugar to encourage glaze formation and to increase overall sweetness. The result was a light, clingy glaze that with a few more minutes of high-heat cooking took on a pale amber hue and a light caramel flavor. A sprinkle of fresh lemon juice gave the dish sparkle, and a twist or two of freshly ground black pepper provided depth. We were surprised, as were our tasters, that glazed carrots could be this good and this easy.

SLICING CARROTS

Cut the carrots on the bias into rounds about ¼ inch thick and 2 inches long.

Glazed Carrots

SERVES 4

TIME: 20 MINUTES

Glazed carrots are a good accompaniment to any roast—beef, pork, lamb, poultry. A nonstick skillet is easiest to clean, but this recipe can be prepared in any 12-inch skillet with a cover.

I	pound carrots (about 6 medium), peeled and sliced ¼ inch thick on the bias (see the illustration at left)
½	teaspoon salt
3	tablespoons sugar
½	cup canned low-sodium chicken broth
I	tablespoon unsalted butter, cut into 4 pieces
2	teaspoons juice from I lemon
	Ground black pepper

1. Bring the carrots, salt, 1 tablespoon sugar, and broth to a boil in a 12-inch nonstick skillet, covered, over medium-high heat. Reduce the heat to medium and simmer, stirring occasionally, until the carrots are almost tender when poked with the tip of a paring knife, about 5 minutes. Uncover, increase the heat to high, and simmer rapidly, stirring occasionally, until the liquid is reduced to about 2 tablespoons, 1 to 2 minutes.

2. Add the butter and remaining 2 tablespoons sugar to the skillet. Toss the carrots to coat and cook, stirring frequently, until they are completely tender and the glaze is light gold, about 3 minutes. Off the heat, add the lemon juice and toss to coat. Transfer the carrots to a serving dish and scrape the glaze from the pan over them. Season to taste with pepper and serve immediately.

Glazed Carrots with Ginger and Rosemary

Cut a 1-inch piece of fresh ginger crosswise into ¼-inch coins. Follow the recipe for Glazed Carrots, adding the ginger to the skillet along with the carrots and adding 1 teaspoon minced fresh rosemary along with the butter. Discard the ginger pieces before serving.

Honey-Glazed Carrots with Lemon and Thyme

Follow the recipe for Glazed Carrots, substituting an equal amount honey for the sugar and adding ½ teaspoon minced fresh thyme leaves and ½ teaspoon grated lemon zest along with the butter.

Glazed Curried Carrots with Currants and Almonds

Lightly toasting the curry powder in the warm, dry skillet brings forth its full flavor.

Toast ¼ cup sliced almonds in a 12-inch nonstick skillet over medium heat until fragrant and lightly browned, about 5 minutes; transfer to a small bowl and set aside. Off the heat, sprinkle 1½ teaspoons curry powder into the skillet; stir until fragrant, about 2 seconds. Follow the recipe for Glazed Carrots, adding the carrots, salt, sugar, and broth to the skillet with the curry powder. Add ¼ cup currants along with the butter and add the toasted almonds along with the lemon juice.

CAULIFLOWER

CAULIFLOWER HAS BECOME A RARE sight on many a dinner table, but these milky-colored, earthy-sweet florets can be a welcome change of pace when cooked correctly. Yet, cauliflower is a member of the cabbage family, and it can all too easily smell and taste like its green-leafed cousin when cooked badly.

To begin, we found that cauliflower's small, dense clusters of firmly packed florets, protected by large, stiff outer leaves, demanded agile knife work to yield attractive, fork-sized pieces. We determined that ¾-inch florets with 1-inch stems were the perfect size; the bite is easy to spear but not oversized.

Cauliflower is quite porous, and it takes on moisture as it cooks. Taking advantage of these traits, we found that we could easily add flavor to the cauliflower by cooking it in a seasoned liquid. This basic technique, called *braising*, involves cooking with a small amount of liquid in a covered container.

We investigated how best to treat the cauliflower before adding the liquid. Steaming did not work, as the cauliflower soaked up so

CUTTING CAULIFLOWER INTO FLORETS

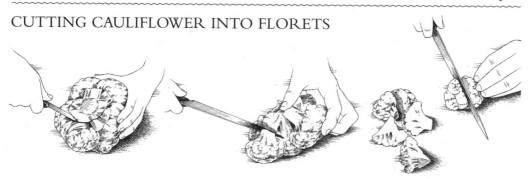

1. Trim the stem near the base of the head. Cut around and then pull out and discard the core.

2. Using a paring knife, cut the individual florets from the inner stem.

3. Cut the florets into halves or quarters to yield ¾-inch pieces.

much moisture that little room was left for it to absorb the braising liquid. Braising the cauliflower in its raw state worked well enough, but the flavor was nothing compared with florets that were first sautéed, then braised. When sautéed in a skillet with a little oil, the cauliflower became brown and toasty, and its naturally nutty-sweet flavor was enhanced. The dry heat also evaporated much of the cauliflower's own moisture, so when the flavorful braising liquid was introduced, it was soaked up readily.

Getting a good, searing brown on the cauliflower took about six minutes, after which the vegetable was nearly cooked through. In fact, we found it took only two minutes longer to braise the cauliflower until it was tender. Not wanting to load the pan with too much liquid for a two-minute braise, we found it hard to define exactly how much liquid was needed. Rather, it seemed to vary depending on the viscosity of the liquid and the moisture content of the other ingredients. For example, when adding canned, diced tomatoes, which are fairly wet even after draining, we found we needed only 2 tablespoons drained tomato juice as a braising liquid—yet we needed ½ cup thick coconut milk in another recipe that had no other moist ingredients.

Browned and Braised Cauliflower with Garlic and Tomatoes

SERVES 4 TO 6

TIME: 20 MINUTES

Serve with fish or chicken.

- 2 tablespoons extra-virgin olive oil
- 1 medium head cauliflower (about 2 pounds), prepared according to the illustrations on page 70
- 1 small red onion, quartered and sliced thin
- 3 medium cloves garlic, sliced thin
- Pinch hot red pepper flakes
- Pinch sugar
- 1 (14½-ounce) can diced tomatoes, drained, 2 tablespoons juice reserved
- 2 tablespoons minced fresh basil leaves
- Salt and ground black pepper
- ⅓ cup grated Parmesan cheese

1. Heat the oil in a large, heavy-bottomed skillet over medium-high heat until almost smoking. Add the cauliflower, onion, garlic, pepper flakes, and sugar and sauté, stirring occasionally, until the cauliflower is golden brown, 5 to 6 minutes.

2. Stir in the tomatoes and reserved tomato juice. Reduce the heat to low, cover, and continue to cook until the cauliflower is tender, about 2 minutes. Remove the pan from the heat, stir in the basil, and season with salt and pepper. Transfer to a serving platter, sprinkle with the cheese, and serve immediately.

Browned and Braised Cauliflower with Coconut Milk, Peas, and Curry

SERVES 4 TO 6

TIME: 20 MINUTES

This variation is especially nice with seafood.

- 2 tablespoons vegetable oil
- 1 medium head cauliflower (about 2 pounds), prepared according to the illustrations on page 70
- 2 medium shallots, minced
- 1 medium clove garlic, minced or pressed through a garlic press (about 1 teaspoon)
- 1 tablespoon curry powder
- ½ teaspoon brown sugar
- ½ cup frozen peas
- ½ cup unsweetened coconut milk
- 1 tablespoon minced fresh basil or cilantro leaves
- Salt and ground black pepper

1. Heat the oil in a large, heavy-bottomed skillet over medium-high heat until almost smoking. Add the cauliflower and sauté, stirring occasionally, until it is golden brown, 5 to 6 minutes. Stir in the shallots, garlic, and curry powder and cook until fragrant, about 30 seconds.

2. Stir in the brown sugar, peas, and coconut milk. Reduce the heat to low, cover, and continue to cook until the cauliflower is tender, about 2 minutes. Remove the pan from the heat, stir in the basil, and season with salt and pepper to taste. Transfer to a serving platter and serve immediately.

CORN

ALTHOUGH FROZEN VEGETABLES ARE commonly regarded as cheap and bland compared with fresh, some of them, such as corn, have just gotten a bad rap. Thanks to modern harvesting and freezing equipment, vegetables are now picked, cleaned, prepared, frozen, and bagged within hours. They can even taste fresher than those found in the produce section, which may be days, if not weeks, old.

The problem with cooking frozen vegetables, however, is that the instructions given on the bag usually indicate longer cooking times than necessary. Corn is a prime example of this; the bag directions call for bringing the corn and some water to a boil and then cooking for three to four minutes. When prepared this way, the corn turns out wet and wrinkled, with a stale, steamed flavor.

Trying other techniques, such as broiling, microwaving, and sautéing, we found that the right technique can make all the difference. Expecting the broiler to produce beautifully roasted corn, we were surprised when the broiled corn developed a strange, crisp, sticky texture. Microwaving the corn (also described

on the back of the bag) was equally unsuccessful, producing wet, mushy kernels no one liked. Sautéing over high heat, on the other hand, produced corn with a clean, fresh flavor and characteristic corn crunch. Using a large skillet and a little butter over high heat, we were able to defrost, dry, and cook the corn in only 2 minutes. Frozen corn given this fast, high-heat treatment fooled some test-kitchen tasters into thinking it was recently cut off the cob.

Cooking frozen corn in a skillet also makes it easy to incorporate other flavors, turning an otherwise bland bag into a surprisingly good side dish. By first sautéing aromatics, such as onions, garlic, and chiles, then adding the corn and fresh herbs, you'll amaze diners with how tasty this frozen convenience food can be.

Sautéed Frozen Corn with Southwestern Flavors

SERVES 4 TO 6
TIME: 20 MINUTES

If you like, omit the chile and replace the cilantro with basil for a different flavor.

4	tablespoons unsalted butter
1	medium yellow onion, minced
1	medium jalapeño chile, stemmed, seeded, and minced
2	medium cloves garlic, minced or pressed through a garlic press (about 2 teaspoons)
1	medium tomato, cored and cut into ½-inch dice
1	pound frozen corn (about 3½ cups)
¾	teaspoon salt
⅛	teaspoon ground black pepper
1	tablespoon minced fresh cilantro leaves

1. Melt the butter in a large nonstick skillet over medium-high heat until the foaming subsides. Add the onion and chile and sauté

until they are softened and beginning to brown around the edges, about 5 minutes. Add the garlic and tomato and sauté until fragrant, about 30 seconds.

2. Raise the heat to high and stir in the corn, salt, and pepper. Cook, stirring often, until the corn is warmed through but still crunchy, about 2 minutes. Stir in the cilantro and serve immediately.

➤ VARIATION

Sautéed Frozen Corn with Bacon and Scallions

Cook 6 slices bacon, cut into ½-inch pieces, in a large nonstick skillet over medium-high heat until crisp and brown, about 5 minutes. With a slotted spoon, transfer the bacon to a paper towel–lined plate and reserve. To the rendered bacon fat in the pan (you should have 2 to 3 tablespoons), add 1 to 2 tablespoons unsalted butter (for a total amount of 4 tablespoons) and heat over medium-high heat until the butter melts. Add the onion to the pan (but omit the chile) and proceed as directed in the recipe for Sautéed Frozen Corn. Add the reserved bacon and 3 scallions, sliced thin, during the final minute of cooking.

EGGPLANT

GARNERING ARDENT SUPPORTERS AND adversaries alike, eggplant is a rather tricky vegetable to cook. Most cooks have had a difficult run-in with eggplant at one point or another—the thick skin turning tough, the earthy flavor going bitter, or the porous flesh becoming spongy and wet. Most cookbooks demand the eggplant be salted, rinsed, and pressed nearly dry before cooking, but we wondered if this procedure was really necessary.

The justification given for the salting process is that it rids the eggplant of bitter-tasting liquid. However, this turns out to be invalid, especially as small to medium eggplant are rarely bitter. What the procedure does do is rid the vegetable of its incredible amount of moisture, which can easily be two-thirds of the total weight. After testing a variety of salted, salted and pressed, and unsalted eggplants side by side under various cooking conditions, we found that salting both is and is not a necessary step. Broiling and grilling sliced eggplant were far more successful when the slices were salted and pressed. However, sautéing *unsalted* slices over high heat in a nonstick skillet produced fine results. The nonstick skillet prevented the eggplant from sticking and burning, and the high heat evaporated much of the moisture from the eggplant as it cooked.

One caution about sautéing: The eggplant absorbs all of the oil as soon as it hits the pan, and we found it tempting to add more oil when the pan looked dry. However, when we did, the resulting dish was overly oily. The eggplant won't stick in a nonstick pan, and 3 tablespoons oil per 1 pound eggplant is sufficient to encourage browning.

As for the skin, we found it turned tough and sticky when cooked via the high-heat method, and tasters unanimously voted to remove it before cooking. Last, we noted that eggplant cooked by this method, which is akin to a stir-fry, was easily flavored with a simple sauce made with soy sauce, garlic, ginger, and roasted peanuts. Served with fresh lime wedges, this no-fuss eggplant not only tastes good but cooks in just 10 minutes.

Asian-Style Eggplant

SERVES 4 PEOPLE

TIME: 20 MINUTES

This assertively flavored dish works best with meat.

2 tablespoons soy sauce

1½ teaspoons Asian sesame oil

1 teaspoon sugar

2 medium scallions, sliced thin

3 tablespoons plus 1 teaspoon vegetable or peanut oil

1 pound eggplant (1 medium or 2 small), peeled and cut into ½-inch cubes

1 tablespoon minced fresh ginger

2 medium cloves garlic, minced or pressed through a garlic press (about 2 teaspoons)

2 tablespoons chopped unsalted dry-roasted peanuts

½ lime, cut into wedges

1. Mix together the soy sauce, sesame oil, sugar, and scallions in a small bowl and set aside. Heat 3 tablespoons vegetable oil in a large skillet over medium-high heat until almost smoking. Add the eggplant and cook, stirring often, until soft and well browned, about 9 minutes (do not add any extra oil to the pan).

2. Clear the center of the pan and add the ginger, garlic, and remaining 1 teaspoon oil to the clearing. Mash the aromatics with the back of a spatula and cook until fragrant, about 15 seconds. Stir the aromatics into the eggplant. Remove the pan from the heat, add the soy mixture, and toss to coat. Transfer the eggplant to a serving platter, sprinkle with the peanuts, and serve immediately with lime wedges.

Green Beans

THE TRICK TO PREPARING TASTY GREEN beans is cooking them properly. Most recipes for green beans employ one of two cooking methods: (1) cooking, then flavoring, or (2) cooking and flavoring simultaneously (braising). The first method is faster than the second, so we decided to home in on it.

By this method, the green beans are either boiled or steamed, then sautéed or simply dressed with flavorful ingredients. Sounds simple—and it is—but we still had questions. Is boiling better than steaming? Should the beans be cut before cooking? Should salt be added to the water? How long should beans cook? Should they be refreshed in cold water to stop the cooking process?

After a number of experiments with boiling and steaming, we came to prefer boiling. Steaming takes twice as long as boiling, and when steaming a pound or more of beans, we found it necessary to turn them during cooking because those at the bottom were cooking faster than those at the top of the pile. Finally, boiling cooks each bean more evenly; steamed beans are often tender on the outside but raw-tasting in the middle. Just as important, boiling permits the addition of salt during cooking. The beans need more salt after they are drained, but its presence during cooking results in more even seasoning.

As for preparation, we preferred to trim the tops and tails with our fingers but leave the beans whole otherwise. Cutting the beans into shorter lengths exposes the tender flesh to too much heat. Because the skin cooks more slowly than the exposed flesh, the inside of the beans tends to become mushy. Boiling times varied greatly in the sources we consulted. One respected Italian cookbook author recommends cooking green beans for 20 to 25 minutes. Another suggests 1½ minutes. Are they writing about the same vegetable?

We found that the freshness and thickness

of the beans greatly affect cooking time. Really fresh, thin beans, not much thicker than a strand of linguine, may be done in as little as two minutes. Most beans in the super-market, though, have traveled some distance and are considerably thicker. Due to their age and size, they need five to six minutes to become tender. Tasters didn't like mushy green beans, but beans that were too crisp or raw-tasting were likewise unappealing.

After draining, the beans can be tossed with other ingredients. Finding it best to dress them while still hot, which maximizes flavor absorption, we liked pairing beans with strong and spicy ingredients, such as garlic-chili sauce or quickly pickled onions and walnuts.

Spicy Green Beans with Sesame Seeds

SERVES 4

TIME: 15 MINUTES

Avoid buying very thick beans, as they were har-vested too late and will remain tough and chewy after cooking. Also, spend time choosing pods that are fairly uniform in size, as their thickness deter-mines the cooking time. If using haricots verts—very thin green beans—reduce the boiling time to just 2 or 3 minutes.

1	tablespoon sesame seeds
	Salt
1	pound green beans, ends snapped off
1	teaspoon Asian sesame oil
1½	teaspoons Asian garlic-chili sauce
2	tablespoons minced fresh cilantro leaves

1. Toast the sesame seeds in a small skillet over medium-high heat until golden and aro-matic, 2 to 3 minutes. Transfer the seeds to a small bowl and reserve.

2. Meanwhile, bring 2½ quarts water to a boil in a large saucepan. Add 1 teaspoon salt and the beans and cook until tender, about 5

minutes. Drain the beans and transfer them to a large serving bowl. Toss with the oil, chili sauce, cilantro, and sesame seeds. Season with salt to taste and serve immediately.

Green Beans with Pickled Red Onions and Toasted Walnuts

SERVES 4

TIME: 15 MINUTES

Although the vinegar left over from the quick pick-led onions is not used in this recipe, it is quite fla-vorful and can be stored in the refrigerator to be used in a vinaigrette or sauce.

½	cup red wine vinegar
1	tablespoon sugar
	Salt
½	medium red onion, sliced thin
½	cup walnuts
1	pound green beans, ends snapped off
2	teaspoons extra-virgin olive oil
1	tablespoon minced fresh tarragon leaves
	Ground black pepper

1. Bring the vinegar, sugar, and ¼ teaspoon salt to a boil over high heat in a small saucepan. Add the onion, return the mixture to a boil and then immediately remove the pan from the heat. Transfer the mixture to a small bowl to cool.

2. Toast the walnuts in a small skillet over medium heat until golden and fragrant, about 5 minutes. Set the nuts aside on a plate.

3. Meanwhile, bring 2½ quarts water to a boil in a large saucepan. Add 1 teaspoon salt and the beans and cook until tender, about 5 minutes. Drain the beans and transfer them to a large serving bowl. Strain the onions from the vinegar, reserving the liquid for another use. Toss the onions with the beans, toasted walnuts, oil, and tarragon. Season with salt and pepper to taste and serve immediately.

PEAS AND PEARL ONIONS

ALTHOUGH PEAS AND PEARL ONIONS are a classic duo, the disappointing truth is that they usually taste terrible. Frozen and bagged together, the peas often turn out wrinkled and overcooked, while the onions merely steam and turn mushy. Yet, when cooked properly, the flavor of the sweet, green peas alongside the mild pearl onions leaves no doubt why these two spring vegetables were originally paired.

To begin, we tossed aside the idea of using fresh peas and onions. Thanks to updated harvesting and processing equipment, frozen peas are usually picked, washed, and frozen within hours, thus tasting at least as fresh as, if not fresher than, those in the produce department, which can be several days old. We also found frozen pearl onions far more convenient than their fresh counterparts, which must be blanched, then peeled individually. Although peas and pearl onions are often frozen and packaged together, it took only a couple of tests to realize these mixtures don't work. The problem is that frozen peas and frozen pearl onions require drastically different cooking times and techniques. The peas need only a couple of minutes to shake off their frost and heat through, while the onions require much more attention.

So we bought separate bags of frozen peas and pearl onions and focused on the best way to cook each before combining them. Beginning with the onions, we found that boiling turned them mushy and bland. Yet sautéing didn't work either, as the outside layers began to fall off, while the inside remained frozen. Looking for a road between these two methods, we tried doing a little of both. First, we simmered the onions in a covered skillet with a little water to thaw them thoroughly.

INGREDIENTS: Frozen Peas

In the test kitchen, we've come to depend on frozen peas. Not only are they more convenient than their fresh comrades in the pod, but they also taste better. In test after test, we've found that frozen peas are tender and sweet, while fresh peas are starchy and bland. To understand this curious finding, which defied common sense, we did some research.

Green peas are one of the oldest vegetables known to humankind. Despite this long history, however, they are relatively delicate and have little stamina. They lose a substantial portion of their nutrients within 24 hours of being picked, which explains the starchy, bland flavor of most peas found in supermarket produce departments. These not-so-fresh peas might be several days old (or more). Frozen peas, on the other hand, are picked, cleaned, sorted, and frozen within several hours of harvest, which helps preserve their delicate sugars and flavors. When commercially frozen vegetables began to appear in the 1920s, green peas were among the first.

Finding good frozen peas is not hard. After tasting peas from the two major national frozen food purveyors, Birdseye and Green Giant, along with organically grown peas from Cascadian Farm, our panel found little difference among them. All of the peas were sweet and fresh, with a bright green color. Unless you grow your own or stop by a local farmstand for fresh-picked peas, you're best off buying frozen.

We then removed the lid, increased the heat to high, and evaporated the steaming water. This approach produced tender onions that were pleasantly browned on the outside from the high-heat finish, but they still tasted a bit bland. Adding salt seasoned the onions as they simmered, and a little butter and sugar helped caramelize the exterior during the high-heat finish. Finally, we threw the peas into the skillet toward the end; they took only two minutes to heat through as the onions finished caramelizing.

Although perfectly cooked, the peas and

onions were still a bit lackluster. We tried including bacon, but its hearty smoked flavor overpowered the rather delicate vegetables. A little pancetta (unsmoked Italian bacon), however, added just the right meaty backbone without overdoing it. When finished with a little fresh lemon juice, these fresh, tender peas and glossy caramelized pearl onions taste great and require next to no preparation.

Peas and Pearl Onions

SERVES 6

TIME: 25 MINUTES

For information about buying frozen peas, see page 76. For information about pancetta, see page 84.

2	ounces pancetta, cut into strips about 3 inches long and ¼ inch thick
8	ounces frozen pearl onions
I	tablespoon unsalted butter
I	tablespoon sugar
½	teaspoon salt
I	pound frozen peas
¼	teaspoon ground black pepper
2	teaspoons juice from I lemon

1. Cook the pancetta in a large, heavy-bottomed nonstick skillet over medium-high heat until crisp and golden brown, about 3 minutes. Using a slotted spoon, transfer the pancetta to a small plate, leaving the rendered fat in the skillet.

2. Return the skillet to medium heat and add the onions, butter, sugar, salt, and ½ cup water. Cover the pan and cook, shaking the pan occasionally to turn the onions, until the onions are tender, about 5 minutes. Uncover the pan, increase the heat to medium-high, and simmer until all the liquid has evaporated and the onions are deeply browned, 8 to 10 minutes.

3. Add the peas and continue to cook, stirring occasionally, until all the vegetables are glazed and the peas are just cooked through, about 2 minutes. Add the pepper and lemon juice. Transfer the vegetables to a serving bowl, sprinkle with the pancetta, and serve immediately.

PEAS

MUSHY PEAS ARE AN ENGLISH COMFORT food. Although the name may not be appealing, the dish itself is. Consisting of frozen peas, butter, and, sometimes, heavy cream or half-and-half, mushy peas are served alongside dishes from chicken to steak to kidney pie. Requiring negligible preparation and little cooking time, they are the epitome of a fresh and fast vegetable side dish.

Beginning with a 1-pound bag of frozen peas (frozen peas are almost always better than fresh supermarket peas; see Ingredients: Frozen Peas, page 76), we noticed immediately that small peas, often called *petite peas* or *petits pois,* didn't mush as well as their larger cousins. With a higher ratio of skin to flesh, the smaller peas mashed to a thicker, skin-heavy mixture. Switching to large peas, we then tested dairy ingredients including butter, heavy cream, and half-and-half, both alone and in combination. Tasters preferred the peas made with all butter; both heavy cream and half-and-half were too rich and dairy heavy, even in small amounts. Cooking pots of peas with increasing amounts of butter, from 2 to 8 tablespoons, side by side, tasters chose the ratio of 6 tablespoons butter to 1 pound peas as their favorite. Less butter simply tasted thin, while more was overkill. One butter trick we gleaned from our research was to reserve half of it to add at the very end; the result tastes surprisingly sweet and clean.

Up to this point, we had simply cooked the

frozen peas and butter in a covered saucepan over low heat until the peas were soft enough to mash. Some tasters, however, noted that the peas still tasted a bit bland, even after salt and pepper were added. To help bring out their fresh flavor, we found, a pinch of sugar does wonders. We also tried sautéing onions, garlic, and shallots in the butter before adding the peas; only shallots were delicate enough to add flavor without stealing the show. Finished with fresh basil or mint, these quick, buttery, mushy peas are worthy of a place in your weekday repertoire.

Mushy Peas

SERVES 4 TO 6

TIME: 15 MINUTES

You need a potato masher to turn the cooked peas into a coarse puree. See page 87 for tips on buying a potato masher.

6	tablespoons unsalted butter
1	medium shallot, minced
1	pound frozen peas
½	teaspoon salt
¼	teaspoon ground black pepper
⅛	teaspoon sugar
1	tablespoon minced fresh mint or basil leaves

1. Melt 3 tablespoons butter in a medium saucepan over medium heat until the foaming subsides. Add the shallot and sauté until softened, about 1½ minutes. Stir in the peas, salt, pepper, and sugar. Cover and cook until the peas are softened but not discolored, 8 to 10 minutes.

2. Remove the pan from the heat. Using a potato masher, mash the peas coarsely, leaving a few intact. Stir in the remaining 3 tablespoons butter until melted. Add the mint and serve immediately.

ROASTED POTATOES

WITH A CRISP, GOLDEN EXTERIOR AND a sweet, creamy interior, roasted potatoes are the ultimate crowd-pleaser. Unfortunately, most versions stray far from this ideal and are either overdone and falling apart or underdone and crunchy. Although roasted potatoes seem an easy, basic dish, success in making them can be elusive.

We began by roasting four readily available potato varieties side by side—Red Bliss, russets, Yukon Golds, and white creamers—with dramatic results. White creamers rated the lowest, with a raw potato flavor and minimal browning, while Yukon Golds were a bit dry and starchy. Russets came in second place with a golden brown skin and a soft interior, but the flavor was reminiscent of french fries. The Red Bliss came out on top with a crisp exterior, creamy interior, and a pleasingly nutty, roasted flavor.

Although some recipes call for parboiling the potatoes, we found this a time-consuming, multipot pain. Parboiled potatoes did, however, come out creamier after roasting because they maintained their interior moisture. To reproduce this effect without the hassle, we covered the potatoes tightly with foil, allowing them, in essence, to steam themselves in the oven. We further found that removing the foil partway through cooking allowed the oven-steamed potatoes to roast to a golden crisp on the outside. Testing various oven temperatures with this unique roasting technique, we discovered a 425-degree oven worked best. At higher temperatures, the potatoes cooked too fast, with too little time to develop a golden crust, while lower temperatures simply took too long.

With the cooking method nailed down, we were ready to consider various types of fats. Testing butter, vegetable oil, and olive oil, we found that the butter burned long before the potatoes were fully roasted, producing a bitter aftertaste. Both vegetable and olive oil held up well to the high roasting temperature; however, tasters preferred the pleasant fruity flavor of the olive oil. Finding that 2 pounds of potatoes easily served four people, we added 3 tablespoons olive oil, resulting in a rich mouthfeel that wasn't greasy.

Although tasty in their own right, plain roasted potatoes can be easily embellished with a few aromatics. To prevent garlic from burning and herbs from turning to sawdust in the oven, add the seasonings after the potatoes are roasted.

Roasted Potatoes with Lemon and Thyme

SERVES 4

TIME: 45 MINUTES

To roast more than 2 pounds of potatoes at once, use a second pan rather than crowding the first. If your potatoes are small, like new potatoes, cut them in half instead of wedges and turn them cut-side up during the final 10 minutes of roasting.

2	pounds Red Bliss or other red-skinned potatoes, scrubbed, halved, and cut into ³⁄₄-inch wedges
4	tablespoons extra-virgin olive oil
	Salt and ground black pepper
I	medium clove garlic, peeled
I	medium shallot, minced
¹⁄₂	teaspoon grated zest and I teaspoon juice from I lemon
I	teaspoon minced fresh thyme leaves

1. Adjust the oven rack to the middle position and heat the oven to 425 degrees. Toss the potatoes with 3 tablespoons oil in a medium bowl to coat; season generously with salt and pepper and toss again to blend. Place the potatoes, flesh-side down, in a single layer on a rimmed baking sheet. Cover tightly with aluminum foil and cook for 15 minutes. Remove the foil and continue to roast until the potatoes are cooked through and golden brown, carefully turning them with a metal spatula halfway through, about 20 minutes.

2. Meanwhile, mince the garlic with ¹⁄₈ teaspoon salt to form a smooth paste (see the illustration on page 4). Mix the garlic paste with the shallot, lemon zest and juice, thyme, and remaining 1 tablespoon oil in a large serving bowl. Toss the roasted potatoes with the shallot mixture and serve immediately.

Roasted Potatoes with Garlic, Feta, Olives, and Oregano

SERVES 4

TIME: 45 MINUTES

The Greek flavors in this dish are potent, so match it with an equally strong main course.

2	pounds Red Bliss or other red-skinned potatoes, scrubbed, halved, and cut into ³⁄₄-inch wedges
3	tablespoons extra-virgin olive oil
	Salt and ground black pepper
2	tablespoons minced fresh oregano leaves
2	medium cloves garlic, peeled
2	ounces feta cheese, crumbled (about ¹⁄₂ cup)
12	kalamata olives, pitted and coarsely chopped
I	tablespoon juice from I lemon

1. Adjust the oven rack to the middle position and heat the oven to 425 degrees. Toss the potatoes with the oil in a medium bowl to coat; season generously with salt and pepper and toss again to blend. Place the potatoes, flesh-side down, in a single layer on a rimmed baking sheet. Cover tightly with

aluminum foil and cook for 15 minutes. Remove the foil and continue to roast until the potatoes are cooked through and golden brown, carefully turning them with a metal spatula halfway through, about 20 minutes. Sprinkle the oregano over the potatoes and roast 3 minutes longer.

2. Meanwhile, mince the garlic with ⅛ teaspoon salt to form a smooth paste (see the illustration on page 4). Mix the garlic paste with the feta, olives, and lemon juice in a large serving bowl. Toss the roasted potatoes with the feta mixture and serve immediately.

HASH BROWNS

HASH BROWNS AREN'T JUST FOR breakfast. A crisp, skillet-sized potato cake is equally welcome alongside a steak or roast chicken for dinner, as is often done in Europe. Although recipes for hash browns are incredibly simple, we discovered that they differ on one main point: whether to start with raw or cooked potatoes (the split was 50-50). Other variables included the type of potato and the cooking method.

Beginning with the potatoes themselves, we tested several varieties, including all-purpose potatoes, Yukon Golds, russets, and Red Bliss. The latter, which are low in starch, did not hold together in cake form, brown well, or even taste like much. The all-purpose potatoes sold in plastic bags in the supermarket, which have a medium starch content, worked well enough to be considered an adequate choice. The Yukon Golds, another medium-starch potato, had a lovely buttery flavor and hue; however, the russets, high-starch potatoes, yielded the best results overall. They adhered well, browned beautifully, and had the most pronounced potato flavor.

With the type of potato chosen, we focused next on the big question: whether to cook the potatoes before frying them into cake form or simply to use them raw. Expecting the precooked potatoes to work better, we were pleasantly surprised when the raw potatoes won the tasting. The precooked potatoes tasted good but, when cut into chunks, did not stick together in a cohesive cake. When they were grated, we had to press them very hard to form a cake—which, unfortunately, meant they ended up with the mouthfeel of fried mashed potato. The raw grated potatoes, on the other hand, easily formed a cohesive cake. As the raw starch on the outside of the potato shreds heated, it fused the thatch of grated potatoes into a crisp, sliceable cake. The fresh starch also cooked to an attractive, deeply browned crust, while the interior of the cake remained creamy.

Having cooked many batches of hash browns by this point, we had determined that the pan itself was an important factor. A skillet with sloping sides made it considerably easier to flatten the potatoes, invert them, and slide them from the pan. All these tasks were more difficult with a straight-sided frying pan. For fast, easy cleanup and an effortless flip, we found a nonstick skillet worked best. We also found that butter, brought just to the browning point over medium-high heat before adding the potatoes, provided good color and a rich, satisfying taste. Our last test was to cover the potatoes during cooking. We found, however, that the cover trapped steam in the pan, turning the crisp crust soggy. Fortunately, as long as we began with a thin layer of potatoes in the pan, they cooked through adequately without covering.

While testing, we used only salt and freshly ground pepper for seasoning, but as soon as scallions were added, the potatoes turned a corner. Other alliums, such as onions and shallots, didn't lend themselves well to the cooking method, as they turned out tasting steamed. But the delicate flavor and color of scallions helped transform this otherwise plain hash brown into dinnerworthy fare.

~≻

Potato–Scallion Hash Browns

SERVES 4

TIME: 30 MINUTES

Hash browns are a natural partner for both meat and chicken.

1	pound russet potatoes, peeled and coarsely grated on the large holes of a box grater or with the shredding attachment of the food processor
3	medium scallions, minced
½	teaspoon salt
⅛	teaspoon ground black pepper
2½	tablespoons butter

1. Toss together the potatoes, scallions, salt, and pepper in a medium bowl. Heat 1½ tablespoons butter in a 10-inch nonstick skillet over medium-high heat until the butter just starts to brown. Scatter the potato mixture evenly over the entire pan bottom. Using a wide spatula, firmly press the potatoes to flatten. Reduce the heat to medium and cook until dark golden brown and crisp, 7 to 8 minutes.

2. Slide the hash browns onto a large plate, then invert them onto a second plate so the browned side is facing up. Add the remaining 1 tablespoon butter to the pan. Once the butter has melted, slide the hash browns back into the pan, browned side up. Continue to cook over medium heat until the second side is dark golden brown and crisp, 5 to 6 minutes longer.

3. Slide the hash browns onto a plate or cutting board, cut into wedges, and serve immediately.

SCALLOPED POTATOES

TRADITIONALLY RESERVED FOR HOLIDAYS and special events, true scalloped potatoes are unabashedly lavish. Cooked in fantastic amounts of heavy cream, butter, and cheese, their richness is hardly suitable for your average supper (or diet). Most recipes also require at least an hour in the oven. Could we lighten and speed up the classic recipe so it could join the weeknight repertoire?

To begin, we made several standard scalloped potato recipes. After rubbing a shallow dish with garlic, we laid sliced potatoes in rows among pats of butter, topped them with heavy cream and cheese, and baked them until tender. Although the ingredient lists of most recipes were similar, including garlic, cream, and sliced russets, some included half-and-half or milk, and others included flour. All of the recipes turned out incredibly rich and took up to 1½ hours to make from start to finish. Several tasted pasty from flour used as a thickener for the sauce, and almost all were dull from sheer lack of aromatics beyond garlic.

Our quest for lighter, speedier scalloped potatoes started with their main ingredient. We cooked russet, all-purpose, and Yukon Gold varieties side by side in a basic recipe. Russets, with a tender bite and earthy flavor, garnered the most compliments, while Yukon Golds and all-purpose potatoes were good but a bit waxy. Choosing to go with the traditional russets, we noted that the thickness of the potato slices made a huge difference in the final texture of the casserole. When the potatoes were cut thicker than ⅛ inch, the casserole was loose and sloppy, while thinner slices melted together into a mashed potato texture. At ⅛ inch, however, the potatoes kept their shape, yet were flexible enough to form tight layers that stuck together as they cooked. The slicing disk on the food processor is the best tool for quickly and evenly slicing potatoes.

Cooking batches of 2½ pounds of potatoes each, we tried to relieve the heaviness by augmenting and substituting for the heavy cream with less fatty liquids. First, we tried replacing it with half-and-half, but the sauce curdled in the oven. Half-and-half, it turns out, doesn't have enough fat to keep the dairy proteins from coagulating under high heat, making the sauce look curdled. Augmenting the heavy cream with milk worked great, but the dish still tasted a bit heavy and dairy-rich for an everyday meal. Last, we tried replacing half of the heavy cream with chicken broth; this successfully mitigated the cream's heaviness. Tasters also liked how the broth rounded out the flavors in the sauce. Fresh thyme and onion helped enliven the dish, too.

Up to this point, we had been using the tiresome technique of layering the raw potatoes and sauce into a shallow dish and baking it in the oven for at least an hour. To speed the process, we tried parboiling the potatoes, then combining them with a flour-thickened sauce and finishing the dish in the oven. Although this did shave nearly 45 minutes off the cooking time, the potatoes had a hollow flavor, the floury sauce tasted flat, and we spent much of the time saved washing dirty pots.

We then tried cooking the sliced potatoes in the stock and cream on top of the stove before dumping it all into a dish and finishing it in the oven. This technique gave the potatoes a head start, and they released some of their own starch (a natural thickening agent) into the sauce, which obviated the need for flour. We found it necessary to cover the pot during this brief simmer to help the potatoes cook and to prevent the sauce from reducing too quickly. When slowly simmered on top of the stove for 10 minutes, at which time the potatoes were about halfway cooked, the casserole required only 15 minutes in a 425-degree oven to finish.

Straight out of the oven, scalloped potatoes are a bubbling inferno requiring at least 10 minutes to cool. When not allowed to cool, the ripping hot potatoes and soupy sauce make for a sloppy casserole. Don't worry—they magically transform into a unified dish after the 10-minute rest.

Scalloped Potatoes

SERVES 4 TO 6

TIME: 50 MINUTES
(INCLUDES 25 MINUTES BAKING
AND COOLING TIME)

If you prefer, Parmesan can be used instead of cheddar cheese. Serve with meat or chicken.

2	tablespoons unsalted butter
1	small onion, minced
2	medium cloves garlic, minced or pressed through a garlic press (about 2 teaspoons)
1	tablespoon chopped fresh thyme leaves
1¼	teaspoons salt
¼	teaspoon ground black pepper
2½	pounds (about 5 medium) russet potatoes, peeled and cut into ⅛-inch-thick slices with the slicing disk of a food processor
1	cup canned low-sodium chicken broth
1	cup heavy cream
4	ounces cheddar cheese, shredded (1 cup)

1. Adjust an oven rack to the middle position and heat the oven to 425 degrees.

2. Melt the butter in a large Dutch oven over medium-high heat until the foaming subsides. Add the onion and cook, stirring occasionally, until soft and lightly browned, about 4 minutes. Add the garlic, thyme, salt, and pepper and cook until fragrant, about 30 seconds. Add the potatoes, broth, and cream and bring to a simmer. Cover, reduce the heat

to medium-low, and simmer until the potatoes are almost tender (a paring knife can be slipped into and out of a potato slice with some resistance), about 10 minutes.

3. Transfer the mixture to an 8-inch-square baking dish (or other 1½-quart gratin dish); sprinkle evenly with the cheese. Bake until the cream is bubbling around the edges and the top is golden brown, about 15 minutes. Cool 10 minutes before serving.

➤ VARIATION

Scalloped Potatoes with Chipotle Chile and Smoked Cheddar Cheese

Follow the recipe for Scalloped Potatoes, adding 1 large chipotle chile in adobo sauce, minced (about 1½ tablespoons), along with the garlic, and substituting smoked cheddar cheese for regular cheddar.

SPINACH

THOUGH FOR SALADS WE PREFER BAGGED baby spinach or bundled tender flat-leaf spinach, curly-leaf spinach sold in cellophane has one distinct advantage: Most of the dirt has already been removed, so it requires only a quick rinse. In contrast, flat-leaf spinach is almost always sandy and requires multiple soakings before it can be used. For this reason, curly-leaf spinach is the most appealing choice for the cook trying to prepare a quick side dish.

Wilting spinach in a covered pot is the most straightforward way to cook it; this technique yields a better texture than blanching, steaming, or microwaving. To wilt, just place the leaves, still damp from rinsing, in a pot with a small amount of hot fat over medium-high heat and cover the pot. Because spinach cooks down so much, you need to start with a lot, and that means you need a big pot; we found that a Dutch oven or stockpot works best. The water clinging to the leaves is enough to cook the spinach, which breaks down from a huge volume of raw leaves to a manageable quantity of cooked spinach in just 3 to 5 minutes. As the spinach cooks, make sure to stir it several times so the leaves wilt evenly.

To make spinach more interesting, add aromatics (onions, garlic, or shallots) to the hot fat before the spinach goes into the pot. The whole process takes less than 20 minutes.

Spinach with Garlic Chips and Pepper Flakes
SERVES 6 TO 8

TIME: 20 MINUTES

Do not heat the oil before adding the garlic; heating them together over gentle heat helps reduce the risk of burnt, bitter garlic.

3	tablespoons extra-virgin olive oil
6	medium cloves garlic, sliced thin (about ¼ cup)
¼	teaspoon hot red pepper flakes
3	bags spinach (10 ounces each), stemmed, washed, and partially dried, with water left clinging to leaves
	Salt

Heat the oil and garlic in a large Dutch oven or stockpot over medium heat. Cook, stirring occasionally, until the garlic is golden and crisp, 10 to 12 minutes. With a slotted spoon, transfer the garlic chips to a paper towel–lined plate. Add the pepper flakes to the oil and cook until fragrant, about 1 minute. Add the spinach and toss to combine. Cover the pot, increase the heat to medium-high, and cook, stirring occasionally, until the spinach is tender and wilted but still bright green, 3 to 5 minutes. Off the heat, season with salt to taste and toss with the reserved garlic chips. Serve immediately.

Spinach with Pancetta and Balsamic Vinegar

SERVES 6 TO 8

TIME: 15 MINUTES

If desired, bacon and red wine vinegar can be used in place of the pancetta and balsamic vinegar.

1   tablespoon extra-virgin olive oil

4   ounces pancetta cut into $1/4$-inch pieces

3   medium cloves garlic, minced or pressed
     through a garlic press (about
     1 tablespoon)

3   bags spinach (10 ounces each),
     stemmed, washed, and partially dried,
     with water left clinging to leaves
     Salt and ground black pepper

1   tablespoon balsamic vinegar

Heat the oil in a large Dutch oven or stock-pot over medium heat until shimmering. Add the pancetta and cook until crisp, 5 to 6 minutes. With a slotted spoon, transfer the pancetta to a paper towel–lined plate. Add the garlic to the oil and cook until fragrant, about 30 seconds. Add the spinach and toss to combine. Cover the pot, increase the heat to medium-high, and cook, stirring occasionally, until the spinach is tender and wilted but still bright green, 3 to 5 minutes. Off the heat, season with salt and pepper to taste and toss with the vinegar and pancetta. Serve immediately.

Spinach with Sautéed Shallots and Lemon

SERVES 6 TO 8

TIME: 15 MINUTES

If desired, serve with lemon wedges.

3   tablespoons extra-virgin olive oil

2   large shallots, sliced thin (about $1/2$ cup)

2   teaspoons grated zest from 1 large lemon

3   bags spinach (10 ounces each),
     stemmed, washed, and partially dried,
     with water left clinging to leaves
     Salt and ground black pepper

Heat the oil in a large Dutch oven or stock-pot over medium heat until shimmering. Add the shallots and cook until golden, 3 to 4 minutes. Add the lemon zest and spinach and toss to combine. Cover the pot, increase the heat to medium-high, and cook, stirring occasionally, until the spinach is tender and wilted but still bright green, 3 to 5 minutes. Off the heat, season with salt and pepper to taste. Serve immediately.

INGREDIENTS: Pancetta

Pancetta and American bacon come from the same part of the pig—the belly—but the curing process is different. American bacon is cured with salt, sugar, and spices (the mix varies from producer to producer) and smoked. Pancetta is not smoked, and the cure does not contain sugar—just salt, pepper, and, usually, cloves. Pancetta is cured for two weeks, rolled tightly like a jelly roll, and packed into a casing.

SWEET POTATOES

MASHED SWEET POTATOES ARE OFTEN overdressed in a Willy Wonka–style casserole topped with marshmallows and whipped cream, but when it comes to flavor, this candied concoction doesn't hold a candle to an honest sweet potato mash. With a deep, natural sweetness that requires little assistance, the humble sweet potato, we thought, would taste far better if prepared with a minimum of ingredients.

Yet even with a simple recipe, mashed sweet potatoes can pose problems. Nailing a fork-friendly puree every time is a form of cooking roulette. Mashed sweet potatoes often turn out thick and gluey or, at the other extreme, sloppy and loose. We also found that most recipes overload the dish with pumpkin pie seasonings that obscure the potato's natural flavor. We wanted a recipe that pushed that deep, earthy sweetness to the fore and that reliably produced a silky puree with enough body to hold its shape on a fork. We decided to focus first on the cooking method, test the remaining ingredients, and, finally, fiddle with the seasonings.

To determine the best cooking method, we tested a variety of techniques: baking potatoes unpeeled, boiling them whole and unpeeled, boiling them peeled and diced, steaming them peeled and diced, and microwaving them whole and unpeeled. Adding a little butter and salt to the potatoes after mashing, we found, yields a huge improvement in texture, flavor, and ease of preparation.

The baked sweet potatoes produced a mash with a deep flavor and bright color, but the potatoes took more than an hour to bake through, and handling them hot from the oven was risky. Boiling whole sweet potatoes in their skins yielded a wet puree with a mild flavor. When we used a fork to monitor the potatoes as they cooked, we made holes that apparently let the flavor seep out and excess water seep in. Steaming and boiling pieces of peeled potato produced the worst purees, with zero flavor and loose, applesauce-like textures. The microwave, although fast and easy, was also a disappointment. The rate of cooking was difficult to control, and the difference between undercooked and overdone was only about 30 seconds. Over-microwaving the potatoes, even slightly, produced a pasty mouthfeel and an odd plastic flavor. By all accounts, this first round of testing bombed. Yet it did end up pointing us in a promising direction.

We had certainly learned a few facts about cooking sweet potatoes. First, their deep, hearty flavor is surprisingly fleeting and easily washed out. Second, the tough, dense flesh reacts much like winter squash when it's cooked, turning wet and sloppy. We also found it safer to peel the sweet potatoes when raw and cold rather than cooked and hot. Taking all of this into account, we wondered if braising the sweet potatoes might work. If cut into uniform pieces and cooked over low heat in a covered pan, the sweet potatoes might release their own moisture slowly and braise themselves.

Adding a little water to the pan to get the process going, we found the sweet potatoes were tender in about 40 minutes. We then simply removed the lid and mashed them right in the pot. To our delight, they were full of flavor because they cooked, essentially, in their own liquid. We tried various pots and heat levels and found that a medium-size pot (accommodating two or three layers of potatoes) in combination with low heat worked best.

Up to this point, we had been adding only butter to the mash; we wondered what the typical additions of cream, milk, or half-and-half would do. Making four batches side by side, we tasted mashes made with only butter, with butter and milk, with butter and half-and-half, and with butter and heavy cream. Tasters found the butter-only batch tasted boring, while milk turned the mash bland and watery. The batch made with half-and-half came in second, with heartier flavor and fuller body, but the heavy cream stole the show.

As we had now made this recipe many times, a glaring oversight became obvious. Why didn't we replace the small amount of water used to cook the potatoes with the butter and heavy cream? Curious about how the recipe would react without the water, we were gratified when this streamlined technique produced the ultimate mash. The puree stood up on a fork, with a luxurious texture that was neither loose nor gluey. Further, with the water out of the picture, the sweet potato flavor was more intense than ever.

Mashed Sweet Potatoes

SERVES 4

TIME: 50 MINUTES (INCLUDES 40 MINUTES COOKING TIME)

Cutting the sweet potatoes into slices of even thickness is important in getting them to cook at the same rate. The potatoes are best served immediately, but they can be covered tightly with plastic wrap and kept relatively hot for 30 minutes. This recipe can be doubled in a Dutch oven; the cooking time must be doubled as well.

4	tablespoons unsalted butter (½ stick), cut into 4 pieces
2	tablespoons heavy cream
½	teaspoon salt
1	teaspoon sugar
2	pounds sweet potatoes (about 2 large or 3 medium-small potatoes), peeled, quartered lengthwise, and cut crosswise into ¼-inch-thick slices
	Pinch ground black pepper

1. Combine the butter, cream, salt, sugar, and sweet potatoes in a 3- to 4-quart saucepan. Cover and cook over low heat, stirring occasionally, until the potatoes fall apart when poked with a fork, 35 to 45 minutes.

2. Off the heat, mash the sweet potatoes in the saucepan with a potato masher. Stir in the pepper and serve immediately.

> VARIATIONS

Maple-Orange Mashed Sweet Potatoes

Follow the recipe for Mashed Sweet Potatoes, stirring in 2 tablespoons maple syrup and ½ teaspoon grated orange zest along with the pepper.

INGREDIENTS: Yams versus Sweet Potatoes

It's an age-old culinary question: What is the difference between a yam and a sweet potato? Answer: It depends on where you live. In U.S. markets, a "yam" is actually a mislabeled sweet potato. If you can get a glimpse of the box it's shipped in, you'll see the words *sweet potato* printed somewhere, as mandated by the U.S. Department of Agriculture. In other parts of the world, *yam* refers to a true yam, a vegetable having no relation to the sweet potato. Sold under the label "ñame" (ny-AH-may) or "igname" here in the United States, a true yam has a hairy, off-white or brown skin and white, light yellow, or pink flesh. This tuber is usually sold in log-shaped chunks that weigh several pounds each. Unlike a sweet potato, a true yam tastes bland and has an ultra-starchy texture. It cannot be used as a substitute for sweet potatoes.

SWEET POTATO   YAM

Indian-Spiced Mashed Sweet Potatoes with Raisins and Cashews

These sweet potatoes have a good balance of spice, sweetness, and crunch.

Follow the recipe for Mashed Sweet Potatoes, substituting dark brown sugar for the granulated sugar and adding ¾ teaspoon garam masala to the saucepan along with the sweet potatoes. Stir ¼ cup golden raisins and ¼ cup roasted unsalted cashews, chopped coarse, into the mashed potatoes along with the pepper.

Mashed Sweet Potatoes with African Flavors

Toast ½ teaspoon ground coriander and ⅛ teaspoon cayenne in a 3- to 4-quart saucepan over medium heat until fragrant, about 30 seconds. Follow the recipe for Mashed Sweet Potatoes, cooking the butter, cream, salt, sugar, and sweet potatoes in the saucepan with the toasted spices. Stir in 1 tablespoon chunky peanut butter and 1 tablespoon minced fresh cilantro along with the pepper.

EQUIPMENT: Potato Mashers

The two classic styles of potato masher are the wire-looped masher with a zigzag presser and the disk masher with a perforated round or oval plate. Modern mashers, as it turns out, are simply variations of these two original designs. We tested eight mashers to see which had the most comfortable grip and the most effective mashing mechanism.

When we wrapped up our mash-fest, we concluded that the wire-looped mashers were second-rate. The space between the loops made it hard to achieve a good, fast mash, and most of the potato pieces escaped between the loops unscathed. One model, the Exeter Double Masher ($9.99), is worth mentioning, however; it is spring-loaded and uses a double-tiered set of wire loops for mashing. It took some muscle to use this masher, but it was the fastest of all the mashers tested,

turning a pot of cooked potatoes into a smooth puree in just 20 strokes.

In general, the disk mashers outperformed the wire-looped models, and the Profi Plus ($15.99) was our favorite. With its small holes, this oval-based masher turned out soft and silky spuds with a reasonable 40 thrusts. Its rounded edges snuggled right into the curves of the saucepan, enhancing its efficacy, and its round handle was easy to grip. The runner-up, the Oxo Smooth Masher ($9.99), has an oval metal base and rectangular perforations. The larger perforations allowed a bit more potato through, so it took 50 mashes to get the job done; still, this squat device with its cushiony handle was easy to use. We did not like the all-plastic Oxo Good Grips Masher—it has an awkward grip and ineffective mash—so shop carefully if buying this brand.

THE BEST POTATO MASHERS

The Profi Plus Masher (left) yielded silky spuds with little effort and was testers' top choice. The Oxo Smooth Masher (middle) was comfortable but slower than the winner, making it our runner-up. The spring-loaded Exeter Double Masher (right) was the best of the wire-loop mashers. Although fast, it was a bit awkward to use.

CHERRY TOMATOES

MOST COOKS DON'T THINK ABOUT cooking cherry tomatoes. They use them for salads, but when it comes to heating tomatoes they turn to plum or round beefsteak varieties. However, cherry tomatoes can be sautéed in minutes to make a quick side dish. In addition, they generally taste pretty good, even in the dead of winter, making them even more appealing.

We did want to explore the ins and outs of this simple technique. We knew it was important to cook the tomatoes as quickly as possible so they wouldn't fall apart. We found that a large skillet (which allows the tomatoes to cook in a single layer) and medium-high heat are essential.

In our testing, we discovered that some batches of cherry tomatoes were bitter. We liked the results when we sprinkled a little sugar over the tomatoes before they went into the pan. The sugar helped with caramelization and balanced the acidity in the tomatoes. Olive oil was the tasters' favorite choice for fat, but browned butter was a close second and is used in one variation. Sautéed cherry tomatoes can be seasoned in numerous ways; fresh herbs, however, are a must.

Sautéed Cherry Tomatoes

SERVES 4

TIME: 10 MINUTES

If the cherry tomatoes are especially sweet, you may want to reduce or omit the sugar. Serve this juicy side dish with fish or chicken (especially a dish that could use extra moisture) or with beef.

1   tablespoon extra-virgin olive oil
4   cups (2 pints) cherry tomatoes, halved
    unless very small
2   teaspoons sugar
1   medium clove garlic, minced or pressed
    through a garlic press (about 1 teaspoon)
2   tablespoons thinly sliced fresh basil leaves
    Salt and ground black pepper

Heat the oil in a large skillet over medium-high heat until shimmering. Mix the tomatoes and sugar in a medium bowl and add them to the hot oil. (Do not mix the tomatoes ahead of time or you will draw out their juices.) Cook for 1 minute, tossing frequently. Stir in the garlic and cook for another 30 seconds. Remove the pan from the heat, add the basil, and season with salt and pepper to taste. Serve immediately.

➤ VARIATIONS

Sautéed Cherry Tomatoes with Curry and Mint

For a saucier dish, mix in 2 tablespoons plain yogurt just before serving. Serve with fish or chicken.

Follow the recipe for Sautéed Cherry Tomatoes, adding 1½ teaspoons curry powder along with the garlic. Substitute thinly sliced mint leaves for the basil.

Sautéed Cherry Tomatoes with Brown Butter and Herbs

This variation is especially good with mild white-fleshed fish, such as snapper and flounder.

Follow the recipe for Sautéed Cherry Tomatoes, replacing the oil with an equal amount of unsalted butter. When the butter starts to brown and the foam subsides, add the tomatoes and sugar and proceed as directed. Replace the basil with an equal amount of snipped chives or minced fresh dill or tarragon.

ZUCCHINI

ONE SURE WAY TO MAKE ZUCCHINI universally appealing is to make fritters. The crisp, fried edges are a drastic improvement over the wet, overcooked texture so common with this moisture-rich vegetable. Unfortunately, most fritters turn out soggy and bland. Our goal was to develop a recipe for highly seasoned, crisp fritters that were made as quickly as possible.

We researched several recipes and found only small differences among ingredient lists and techniques. All the recipes called for some sort of binder (usually eggs, a starch, or a combination of the two) and seasonings. According to several recipes, salting and draining the zucchini before combining them with the other fritter ingredients is vital, yet other recipes omitted this step. Also, although all the recipes cooked the fritters in a skillet, they called for different amounts of oil.

We began by testing whether or not the zucchini should be salted. After shredding zucchini on the large holes of a box grater, we tried three preparations before using the zucchini in a basic fritter recipe: (1) tossed with salt and set aside in a colander for 30 minutes, (2) spread on paper towels, sprinkled with salt, and allowed to sit for 10 minutes, and (3) left unsalted. The 30-minute salting caused the zucchini to lose a substantial amount of liquid, but the finished fritters were only marginally better than those made with zucchini that sat for just 10 minutes. In contrast, the fritters made with unsalted zucchini were soggy, not crisp. We concluded that salting for 10 minutes was essential. Placing the salted zucchini on paper towels rather than in a colander helped rid it of moisture. After 10 minutes, we simply laid fresh paper towels on top, rolled the zucchini in the towels, and gave the roll a quick squeeze. We then unrolled the towels over a large bowl, allowing the zucchini to fall into it.

Next, we tested various binders, including all-purpose flour, potato starch, and cornstarch, both with and without egg. Tasters far preferred the consistent, unified texture of the fritters made with egg. As for the starch, the differences were noticeable but minimal, so we chose flour because it is most often on hand.

Making enough fritters to serve four to six people required cooking them in two batches. We found it easy to wipe the spent oil from a large nonstick skillet after the first batch and add fresh oil to the relatively clean pan for the second. (If we skipped this step, the burnt bits from the first batch of fritters stuck to the second batch.) As for the amount of oil, we noted that using too much was simply a waste, while using too little allowed the fritters to either burn or steam. Three tablespoons oil per batch struck the perfect balance between crisp fritters and economy. Seasoned with a little garlic and scallion, these zucchini fritters taste surprisingly fresh, requiring only a squeeze of fresh lemon juice before eating.

Zucchini Fritters

SERVES 4 TO 6

TIME: 30 MINUTES

These fritters work well with meat or chicken. They can also be served as an appetizer with cocktails.

1	pound zucchini, ends trimmed
1¼	teaspoons salt
¼	teaspoon ground black pepper
1	medium clove garlic, minced or pressed through a garlic press (about 1 teaspoon)
2	medium scallions, minced
1	large egg, lightly beaten
¼	cup unbleached all-purpose flour
6	tablespoons vegetable oil
1	lemon, cut into wedges

1. Grate the zucchini on the large holes of a box grater or shred using the shredding disk of the food processor. Spread the zucchini across several layers of paper towels 4 sheets long. Sprinkle the salt evenly over the zucchini and let sit for 10 minutes. Lay several more layers of paper towels on top of the zucchini, roll up the whole stack, and squeeze gently to extract moisture. Unroll the paper towels over a large bowl, letting the zucchini fall into it and using your hands to brush loose any pieces that stick to the paper. Add the pepper, garlic, scallions, and egg to the bowl and stir to combine. Sprinkle the flour over the mixture and stir to incorporate.

2. Adjust the oven rack to the middle position and heat the oven to 200 degrees. Heat 3 tablespoons oil in a large, heavy-bottomed nonstick skillet over medium-high heat until wisps of smoke appear. Drop the batter in 2-tablespoon portions into the pan and use the back of a spoon to spread each portion into a fritter measuring about 2½ inches across. Repeat until you have 6 fritters in the pan. Fry until golden brown, about 2 minutes. Gently flip the fritters and fry on the second side until golden brown, about 2 minutes longer. Transfer the fritters to a paper towel–lined baking sheet and place the baking sheet in the warm oven. Carefully wipe the hot skillet clean with paper towels held with tongs. Return the pan to medium-high heat, add the remaining 3 tablespoons oil, and repeat with the remaining batter. Arrange the hot fritters on a platter and serve immediately with wedges of lemon.

4
GRAINS AND BEANS

MOST COOKS DO NOT ASSOCIATE grains and beans with quick cooking. Dried beans must simmer for hours, and many whole grains take quite a long time to soften. However, if you rely on quick-cooking grains (rice, polenta, quinoa, and bulgur) and grain-like pastas (couscous and orzo), grains can be ready to serve in 30 minutes or so. Likewise, if you choose canned beans rather than dried (dried lentils are the exception here because they cook so quickly), legumes can be ready to serve rather quickly.

This chapter includes simple side dishes as well as slightly more involved main courses. Many recipes rely on exotic flavorings from countries where grains and beans are culinary mainstays. However, all of these grains, legumes, and seasonings are available in any reasonably stocked supermarket.

SAFFRON COUSCOUS PILAF

IN NORTH AFRICAN COOKING, THE line between sweet and savory dishes is fuzzy. Meats and vegetables are frequently combined with dried fruits, nuts, and warm spices generally reserved for sweets in European-style cooking. So a couscous pilaf with almonds and raisins is far from extraordinary; in fact, it's a staple dish common throughout Morocco and Algeria. The pilaf's short list of ingredients and rapid cooking time are appealing.

Couscous is, technically, pasta—the tiny size is deceiving. It is made from semolina flour "rolled" with lightly salted water until the minute balls form; these are then steamed and dried for long-term storage. Traditionally, couscous is cooked in a special pot called a *couscoussier,* which is essentially a stockpot fitted with a small-holed colander. The couscous sits in the colander and plumps in the steam produced by the pot's contents—stock, soup, or stew. While an ersatz couscoussier can be rigged with a saucepan and colander, a much easier method produces entirely acceptable couscous. Hot water or stock is poured over couscous in a bowl, which is then sealed with plastic wrap. Within minutes—12, to be exact—the couscous is tender and ready to eat.

The drawback to this technique is that the couscous tends to clump into tight balls that must be separated—a labor-intensive chore that inevitably leads to burned fingertips. We found the addition of a little oil or butter to the hydrating liquid helped but didn't completely rectify the situation. Borrowing a technique from rice pilaf, we tried toasting the raw couscous in a little butter before adding the liquid. The resulting couscous was our best batch yet; the grains were discrete and the flavor nutty.

With our couscous plumped and smooth, we were ready to address the pilaf flavorings. As we had already heated a skillet to toast the couscous, it was easy to toast the almonds and sauté aromatics. We favored sliced almonds for both appearance and ease; the pale slivers rimmed with brown looked appealing against the couscous and required no preparation beyond the quick toasting. For aromatics, onions sautéed in butter lent the couscous both sweetness and a subtle sharpness.

We initially added the raisins after the onions were cooked, but they failed to fully plump and tasted too mild. We then tried adding them with the onions so they were heated for several minutes, which markedly improved their flavor and texture.

Saffron gives the couscous an alluring golden hue as well as a distinct aroma. Despite its stiff price tag, saffron can be an economical spice, as a little goes a long way. The fine threads are intensely potent, and we found just a small pinch—slightly under ¼ teaspoon—

was ideal. Any more conveyed an unappealingly medicinal flavor.

For liquid, water was the easiest choice, but it made for a bland couscous, even with the onions, raisins, and saffron. We then tried chicken broth, but it was actually too strong; the chicken flavor overpowered the mild couscous. A combination of chicken broth and water, however, worked fine, giving the couscous body and a pleasant richness. As a final touch, we chose to add a little lemon juice, which sharpened the seasonings and balanced the sweet elements in the pilaf.

Saffron Couscous Pilaf with Raisins and Almonds

SERVES 4 TO 6 AS A SIDE DISH

TIME: 35 MINUTES

If you don't have saffron or dislike its potent flavor, don't skip this dish; substitute a couple of cinnamon sticks for a pleasant flavor and aroma. Add them with the onion so they are exposed to dry heat, which intensifies their flavor. For the fluffiest texture, use a large fork to fluff the grains; a spoon or spatula can destroy the light texture. The simple flavors of the pilaf pair well with a wide variety of meat, poultry, and vegetable dishes. Specialty markets may carry couscous of varying size, but stick to the basic kind. Other sizes require different cooking methods.

4	tablespoons unsalted butter
2	cups couscous
¾	cup sliced almonds
1	small onion, chopped fine
	Pinch saffron threads, crumbled with fingertips
¾	cup raisins
	Salt
1¾	cups canned low-sodium chicken broth
1½	teaspoons juice from 1 lemon
	Ground black pepper

1. Melt 2 tablespoons butter in a large skillet over medium-high heat. When the foaming subsides, add the couscous and cook, stirring frequently with a wooden spoon, until some grains are just beginning to brown, about 3 minutes. Scrape the grains from the skillet into a large bowl and return the pan to medium heat. Add the almonds and cook, stirring frequently, until they are lightly toasted and aromatic, about 1½ minutes. Scrape them into a small bowl.

2. Add the remaining 2 tablespoons butter to the skillet. Once it melts, add the onion, saffron, raisins, and ¾ teaspoon salt and cook, stirring occasionally, until the onion has softened and is beginning to brown, about 5 minutes. Add the broth and 2 cups water, increase the heat to medium-high, and bring to a boil.

3. Add the boiling liquid to the bowl with the toasted couscous, cover tightly with plastic wrap, and allow to sit until the couscous is tender, about 12 minutes. Remove the plastic wrap, fluff the grains with a fork, and gently stir in the almonds and lemon juice. Adjust the seasonings with salt and pepper to taste and serve immediately.

TOASTED ORZO PILAF

ORZO, LIKE COUSCOUS, IS A SMALL pasta shape that is sometimes treated like a grain and used in pilaf recipes. Orzo, which is shaped like rice, can be used to produce a pilaf reminiscent in texture to risotto—but requires a quarter of the work. Cookbooks are packed with ersatz recipes for no-stir risotto that fail to deliver as promised; the secret may be in using rice-shaped pasta.

The basic concept of orzo pilaf varies little from rice pilaf—sauté aromatics, toast the orzo, and simmer in liquid until tender—but pasta, obviously, has different cooking requirements than rice. Our testing thus focused on how long and at what temperature to toast the orzo for optimum flavor and texture and how much liquid was necessary for an al dente texture. For flavor, we decided simple was best and borrowed elements from a basic risotto—butter, shallots, white wine, chicken broth, and Parmesan cheese. In homage to the Venetian *risi e bisi,* or rice and peas, we included peas.

After toasting orzo to shades varying from pale yellow to golden brown, we found that the darker the orzo, the richer the flavor (shy of burning it, of course). Well-browned orzo possessed a full, nutty flavor that tasters favored over that of more lightly toasted orzo. Temperature alone appeared to have little effect on the orzo's flavor; the key, it turned out, was timing. We opted for medium-high heat, which produced golden orzo in about 6 minutes, though it did require diligent stirring and a watchful eye to prevent scorching.

Rice, predictably, requires about 1½ times its volume in liquid to plump, but we were not sure if this ratio would work for orzo. The pilaf is not drained of excess liquid, so we needed to ascertain the minimum amount of liquid necessary. In our first test, we added 6 cups chicken broth to 1 pound orzo (2½ cups), which resulted in an extraordinarily soupy pilaf. We then tried just 3 cups broth, but the orzo was chalky and undercooked. Four cups came closer to the mark, and an additional ¼ cup proved perfect; the orzo plumped to a tender yet firm consistency, somewhere between that of pasta and rice. We replaced part of the broth with an equal amount of vermouth and tasters liked the result. (White wine also worked well.)

We tried cooking the orzo like risotto by adding the liquid a little at a time but found this time-consuming technique unnecessary, as was a low, covered simmer, like standard

pilaf. The easiest way proved the best. Once the broth came to a boil, we reduced the heat to medium-low and left the pilaf uncovered and unattended, outside of a few sporadic stirs, until done—a mere 10 minutes. To preserve the color and flavor of the peas, we added them at the last minute, once the orzo was cooked through. The peas needed only about 2 minutes of ambient heat to warm through, despite directions on the package that suggest cooking them much longer.

Toasted Orzo Pilaf with Peas and Parmesan

SERVES 4 TO 6 AS A SIDE DISH

TIME: 20 MINUTES

Because the pan gets extremely hot while the orzo is toasting, be sure to add the broth off the heat and after the pan has cooled a bit; otherwise, the ensuing steam can be dangerous. For additional flavor, a couple of bay leaves, a few sprigs of thyme, or a small pinch of saffron can be added with the garlic. Just remember to remove the herbs prior to serving. Serve this basic pilaf with almost any dish, including red meat, poultry, and fish.

2	tablespoons unsalted butter
1	medium onion, chopped fine
	Salt
2	medium cloves garlic, minced or pressed through a garlic press (about 2 teaspoons)
1	pound orzo (about 2½ cups)
¾	cup vermouth or dry white wine
3½	cups canned low-sodium chicken broth
8	ounces frozen peas
1	cup grated Parmesan cheese
	Pinch ground nutmeg
	Ground black pepper

1. Melt the butter in a large nonstick skillet over medium-high heat. Once the foaming subsides, add the onion and ¾ teaspoon salt

and cook, stirring frequently, until the onion has softened and is just beginning to brown, about 4 minutes. Add the garlic and cook until fragrant, about 30 seconds. Stir in the orzo and cook, stirring frequently with a wooden spoon, until most of the grains are lightly browned and golden, 5 to 6 minutes.

2. Slide the skillet off the heat, cool for 30 seconds, and then pour in the vermouth and broth, being careful to avoid the steam. Return the skillet to the burner and bring to a boil over medium-high heat. Reduce the heat to medium-low and simmer, stirring occasionally, until all of the liquid is absorbed and the orzo is tender, 10 to 12 minutes.

3. Stir in the peas, cheese, and nutmeg. Remove the skillet from the heat and allow to sit for 2 minutes to heat the peas through. Adjust the seasonings, adding salt and pepper to taste. Serve immediately.

BULGUR AND MUSHROOM PILAF

THROUGHOUT THE COUNTRIES RIMMING the eastern Mediterranean, including Turkey and Greece, bulgur is a staple grain. Produced from whole wheat kernels, it is highly nutritious and packed with an earthy, nutty flavor that is highly distinctive. Bulgur is used in everything from tabbouleh (most famously) to meatballs (called *kibbeh)* and—our top choice—pilaf. The relatively bland bulgur makes an ideal canvas for any number of assertive flavors. One of our favorites is a pilaf with mushrooms. Our goal was to reinvent this Mediterranean classic as a one-pan, quick-cooking pilaf—ready in minutes with a minimum of effort.

Bulgur is made of whole wheat kernels that are steamed, dried, and crushed into either coarse, medium, or fine grades, all of which require different cooking methods. Fine-grain bulgur, the variety most often seen in Middle Eastern dishes, must be rehydrated in hot liquid, not unlike couscous. Larger-grain bulgur, which we prefer for pilafs, must be simmered until tender, usually about 15 minutes.

Based on our work developing other pilaf recipes, we already had a cooking method in mind; we would use a large skillet from start to finish. The aromatics and mushrooms would be sautéed and then the bulgur and cooking liquid added and simmered until tender. Testing, then, was a matter of developing the fullest mushroom flavor and discovering how long and at what temperature to simmer the bulgur for the best texture.

For intense mushroom flavor without resorting to pricey exotics, we frequently combine standard cultivated mushrooms— white button or cremini—with dried shiitake or porcini mushrooms. Relatively inexpensive and packed with flavor, the dried mushrooms impart an intensely earthy flavor and pungent aroma to the most mild-mannered fresh mushrooms. After rehydrating in hot water, the dried mushrooms are ready to cook. The leftover soaking water can be used as a portion of the cooking liquid for the bulgur. After testing a few combinations, tasters favored the pairing of dried porcini and fresh cremini mushrooms—shiitakes tasted too Asian, and white button mushrooms lacked enough presence. To boost the mushroom flavor, we added both onion and garlic (pressed for the biggest impact) as well as soy sauce—odd in a Mediterranean dish but welcome nonetheless for its dramatic impact on mushroom flavor. Not identifiable as soy sauce per se, it deepened the mushroom flavor and color.

For the liquid, we tried both chicken broth and water. Independently, chicken broth was too strong and muddied the dish's flavors, but water made the pilaf too lean-tasting. A combination of the two, however, gave the pilaf body without calling attention to the chicken flavor. Roughly 2 parts chicken broth to 1 part water proved the ideal ratio.

As we explored the best way to cook the bulgur, we tried every approach from a full boil to a quiet simmer. Rapid simmering cooked the bulgur unevenly and gave it an unpleasant chewiness. Very low heat cooked the bulgur more evenly. While some recipes we found called for toasting the bulgur before adding liquid, we found this step unnecessary.

Herbs were necessary to enliven the monotonous palette of browns as well as for flavor. Thyme reinforced the pilaf's earthy edge but lacked visual presence. Parsley, however, brightened both flavor and color, so we chose it over thyme. We opted for a fairly generous amount: ¼ cup.

Bulgur and Mushroom Pilaf

SERVES 4 TO 6 AS A SIDE DISH

TIME: 35 MINUTES (INCLUDES 15 MINUTES SIMMERING TIME)

Don't be confused by the term cracked wheat when purchasing bulgur; while it looks like bulgur, the two are not the same. Cracked wheat is uncooked, whereas bulgur is parcooked, and the two require different cooking methods. We prefer moderately coarse bulgur, which has a texture like that of kosher salt, to finer, sandy bulgur. Cremini mushrooms, also sold as baby bellas, are juvenile portobellos.

Despite its boldness, this pilaf is at home with a wide variety of main courses, including roast chicken, pork, and firm-fleshed fish like halibut, swordfish, and sea bass. See the illustrations below for tips on rehydrating dried mushrooms.

½   ounce dried porcini mushrooms

3   tablespoons unsalted butter

REHYDRATING DRIED MUSHROOMS

We find the microwave cuts mushroom soaking time from 20 minutes at room temperature to just 5 minutes. Just place the dried porcini and water in a microwave-safe bowl, cover with plastic wrap, cut several steam vents in the plastic, and microwave on high power for 30 seconds. Remove the bowl from the microwave and let stand, covered, until the mushrooms soften, about 5 minutes. Here's how to remove the softened mushrooms from the liquid and leave the sand behind.

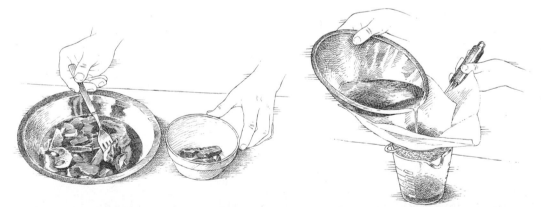

1. When dried porcini mushrooms are soaking, most of their sand and dirt falls to the bottom of the bowl. Use a fork to lift the rehydrated mushrooms from the liquid without stirring the sand. If the mushrooms still feel gritty, rinse them briefly under cool running water.

2. The soaking liquid is quite flavorful and should be reserved. To remove the grit, pour the liquid through a small strainer lined with a single layer of paper towel and placed over a measuring cup.

1   medium onion, chopped fine
      Salt
8   ounces cremini (preferably) or white
      button mushrooms, stem ends trimmed,
      quartered (or cut into 6 pieces if large)
2   medium cloves garlic, minced or pressed
      through a garlic press (about 2 teaspoons)
1 ½   cups bulgur, preferably medium-grain
1 ¾   cups canned low-sodium chicken broth
1 ½   teaspoons soy sauce
¼   cup chopped fresh parsley leaves
      Ground black pepper

1. Mix the dried porcini mushrooms with ½ cup hot tap water in a small microwave-safe bowl. Cover the bowl with plastic wrap, cut several steam vents with a paring knife, and microwave on high power for 30 seconds. Let stand until the mushrooms soften, about 5 minutes. Lift the mushrooms from the liquid with a fork and mince. Pour the liquid through a small strainer lined with a single layer of paper towel and placed over a measuring cup. Add enough water to the soaking liquid to total 1 cup and set aside.

2. Meanwhile, melt the butter in a large skillet over medium-high heat. When the foaming subsides, add the onion and ¼ teaspoon salt and cook, stirring occasionally, until the onion has softened, 3 to 4 minutes. Add the fresh mushrooms and cook until reduced in volume and beginning to brown, 3 to 4 minutes. Add the garlic and cook until fragrant, about 30 seconds. Stir in the bulgur, broth, soy sauce, and reserved mushroom soaking liquid and bring to a boil. Cover, reduce the heat to low, and simmer until the bulgur is tender, about 15 minutes. Using a fork, stir in the parsley and fluff the bulgur. Adjust the seasonings with salt and pepper to taste. Serve immediately.

QUINOA PILAF

ONE OF THE LESS FAMILIAR GRAINS IN the market, quinoa is something of a miracle food. Packed with vitamins, minerals, and protein, it puts other grains to nutritional shame. Quinoa possesses a wholesome, hearty taste that pairs well with fruits and nuts. Its texture is addictively crunchy—the individual seeds pop when chewed, not unlike caviar. Even with all these benefits, quinoa is still obscure, but we hope to change that. Quinoa is healthful, uniquely flavored—and, best of all, cooks within 15 minutes. We chose to use it in a simple pilaf with apples, pecans, and herbs—a perfect match for roast pork or chicken and, possibly, an unusual option for the Thanksgiving table.

Quinoa has been cultivated and consumed for thousands of years throughout South America. It was a staple of the Inca civilization (according to some sources, Spanish conquistadors banned it in an attempt to subjugate the Inca). Generally treated as a grain, quinoa is actually the seed of the goosefoot plant. It contains significantly more protein than most grains, and that protein is complete—that is, quinoa possesses all of the amino acids necessary for protein metabolism, unlike grains that must be consumed in conjunction with other foodstuffs, such as beans, to unlock their nutritional contribution. Other benefits include substantial amounts of calcium and vitamin E as well as traces of many other nutrients.

Given all these miraculous nutritional properties, we expected the wonders of quinoa to be balanced with some significant drawback, like intensive preparation or a finicky cooking method. We were wrong. Quinoa couldn't be easier to clean and cook. Almost every recipe we found employed the same method for cooking. Rinse the quinoa well to rid the grains of a mildly toxic protective layer (called saponin), which is unpleasantly bitter, bring it to a boil in stock or water, and simmer over low heat, covered, for 15 minutes. Despite our best efforts, we could do little to improve this method, which produced flawlessly cooked, slightly crunchy quinoa every time.

Our one surprise was the degree to which quinoa's flavor improved with dry-toasting. Although toasting grains before adding liquid is standard pilaf procedure because it ensures plumped, individual grains, this step had an unexpectedly substantial impact on quinoa, whose otherwise subtle flavor undertones were greatly intensified. About 4 minutes in a skillet over medium-high heat was enough; longer toasting was unnecessary.

We kept the pilaf flavorings simple. Besides the apples and pecans, we added sautéed onions (cooked before toasting the quinoa) and chicken broth (made with water alone, the quinoa tasted too lean and downright bland). For the apples, we favored tart, crisp Granny Smiths—our usual choice for cooking. We wanted to preserve their texture to act as a counterpoint in the pilaf, so we quickly sautéed them over high heat, just enough to lightly caramelize the surface. A teaspoon of sugar expedited browning and deepened the sweet-tart apple flavor. In our first few batches, we simmered the diced apple with the quinoa, but the small cubes turned to mush, so we opted to reserve them until the quinoa was finished and to stir in the sautéed apple with the herbs and nuts.

For herbs, tasters favored a combination of thyme and parsley. The earthiness of thyme reinforced that of the quinoa, and the parsley brought brightness and visual appeal that helped break the pilaf's monotonous color scheme.

Quinoa Pilaf with Apples and Pecans

SERVES 4 TO 6 AS A SIDE DISH

TIME: 40 MINUTES (INCLUDES 15 MINUTES SIMMERING TIME)

If your market does not carry quinoa, try the local health food store, which will certainly sell it. Quinoa must be thoroughly rinsed before cooking to remove the bitter exterior coating, called saponin. The seeds are washed before packaging, but a bit of the compound may remain; it is worth being safe, as a small amount of saponin can ruin a dish. A heatproof rubber spatula is the best tool for stirring the quinoa, although a wooden spoon works nearly as well. It's easy to tell when quinoa is done, as the brown seeds turn translucent—you don't even need to test it.

½	cup coarsely chopped pecans
3	tablespoons unsalted butter
1	large Granny Smith apple, peeled, cored, and chopped fine
1	teaspoon sugar
1	medium onion, chopped fine
	Salt
2	cups quinoa, well rinsed and drained in a fine-mesh sieve
1¾	cups canned low-sodium chicken broth
2	tablespoons coarsely chopped fresh parsley leaves
¾	teaspoon minced fresh thyme leaves
	Ground black pepper

1. Add the pecans to a large sauté pan over medium-high heat and toast, stirring frequently, until aromatic and beginning to brown, about 3 minutes. Transfer the pecans to a small bowl and set them aside.

2. Melt 1 tablespoon butter in the empty pan over medium-high heat. Once the foaming subsides, add the apple and sugar and cook, stirring occasionally, until lightly

browned, about 2 minutes. Transfer the apples to the bowl with the pecans and set them aside.

3. Reduce the heat to medium and add the remaining 2 tablespoons butter to the pan. Once the butter melts, add the onion and ¼ teaspoon salt and cook, stirring frequently, until the onion softens and is just beginning to brown, about 4 minutes. Add the quinoa and toast, stirring often, until just beginning to turn golden and aromatic, about 4 minutes. Add the broth and bring to a boil. Reduce the heat to low, cover, and simmer until the quinoa is transparent and tender but slightly crunchy, about 15 minutes.

4. Remove the cover, increase the heat to medium, and cook, stirring frequently, until the remaining liquid has evaporated, 2 to 3 minutes. Gently stir in the apple, pecans, and herbs and adjust the seasonings with salt and pepper to taste. Serve immediately.

INSTANT POLENTA
WHILE WE FAVOR THE CREAMY TEXTURE and robust corn flavor of slow-cooked polenta, time doesn't always permit such luxury. Fortunately, quick-cooking polenta, produced by several Italian companies, is pretty good—a close second to the real thing. What it lacks in flavor and texture it makes up for in convenience, requiring only a few minutes to cook. Like instant grits and boil-in-bag rice, instant polenta is fully cooked and then dried; it just needs to rehydrate before being served. Quick polenta is available in large grocery stores and virtually every Italian specialty store. To prepare it, follow the instructions on the box, as the proportions of liquid to polenta vary by brand. For the best flavor, we like to stir in a little butter once the polenta is ready.

Almost anything can grace the top of polenta to make a meal—a wedge of rich cheese, a hearty meat sauce, sautéed greens. We wanted to develop a pair of unconventional toppings made with simple ingredients. Canned tomatoes develop a whole new flavor and texture when roasted, and they make an ideal foil for creamy mozzarella cheese. Likewise, red onions cooked with brown sugar and balsamic vinegar take on a lush texture and rich flavor that tempers the sharp bite of well-aged cheddar. Best of all, both toppings require minimal preparation and no exotic ingredients.

POLENTA WITH ROASTED TOMATOES
ON THEIR OWN, CANNED TOMATOES aren't very exciting. Yes, they possess better flavor than the fresh, cardboardlike specimens populating the produce aisle most of the year, but we still don't want to eat them on their own. But while developing a tomato soup recipe for *Cook's Illustrated* a couple of years back, we found that high heat can work miracles on them. Something of a restaurant trick, roasting tomatoes intensifies their fruitiness and sweetness. The technique works equally well on fresh and canned tomatoes.

We picked canned diced tomatoes over whole tomatoes to save on preparation time—the seeds and peels were already removed and the tomatoes cut to a convenient size. The only work necessary was to extract the tomato juices; without this step, the tomatoes stew in the oven rather than roast. The best method we found was to empty the tomatoes into a colander set over a bowl or in a sink and vigorously squeeze the tomatoes with our hands.

While they can be roasted as is with a

dusting of salt and pepper, we found the tomatoes' flavor improved with a drizzle of olive oil and a spot of brown sugar, which enhanced their natural sweetness. In just under 25 minutes at 475 degrees, the tomatoes dramatically reduced in size, browned a little, and developed the intense flavor we desired. At higher heat, they cooked too quickly and burned.

The roasted tomatoes were sweet, a little tart, and chewy. To mellow their intensity, we chose to add creamy, fresh mozzarella—the good stuff from an Italian deli, not the packaged, rubbery blocks in the supermarket cheese section. Cubed, the cheese melted into the polenta and added textural contrast. Despite the tomatoes' acidity, most tasters thought the topping needed a bit more kick and suggested scallions. Thinly sliced on the bias, the scallions looked attractive and lent much-needed sharpness to the sweet polenta.

Polenta with Roasted Tomatoes and Fresh Mozzarella

SERVES 4 TO 6 AS A MAIN COURSE
TIME: 35 MINUTES (INCLUDES 25 MINUTES BAKING TIME)

If you have leftovers, you can turn the topping into a quick sandwich filling (especially good when heated) or even toss it with pasta. If you can't find fresh mozzarella or prefer a cheese with a stronger flavor, we recommend fontina. Beware of Danish fontina, as its flavor pales in comparison with the authentic Italian variety. Taleggio is another option, although it is too soft to dice; small spoonfuls will do the trick. See photo of this recipe on page 153.

3	(14 ½-ounce) cans diced tomatoes, drained well in a colander and squeezed by hand to remove remaining juices
1 ½	teaspoons light brown sugar
	Salt

1	tablespoon extra-virgin olive oil, plus more for drizzling
3	medium scallions, sliced thin on the bias
8	ounces fresh mozzarella cheese, cut into ½-inch dice
	Ground black pepper
1 ½	cups instant polenta, prepared according to package directions
2	tablespoons unsalted butter

1. Adjust an oven rack to the middle position and heat the oven to 475 degrees. Line a rimmed baking sheet with aluminum foil. Combine the tomatoes, brown sugar, ¼ teaspoon salt, and oil in a medium bowl and toss well to mix. Spread the tomato mixture in a single layer across the prepared pan. Roast until the tomatoes begin to darken and are reduced significantly in size, 22 to 25 minutes. Using a large rubber spatula, scrape the tomatoes off the pan and into a bowl. Toss with the scallions and cheese until combined. (The cheese will soften but probably won't melt.) Adjust the seasonings with salt and pepper to taste.

2. When the tomatoes are nearly done, prepare the polenta according to the package

MAKING POLENTA

Whether you are preparing instant or regular polenta, lumps can ruin its texture. To prevent them, pour the polenta into the boiling salted water in a very slow stream from a measuring cup, all the while stirring in a circular motion with a wooden spoon.

directions. Stir the butter into the finished polenta and spoon the polenta into individual shallow soup or pasta bowls. Divide the tomato mixture among the bowls of polenta and drizzle each with a little olive oil. Serve immediately.

Polenta with Sweet-and-Sour Onion Relish

SWEET-AND-SOUR ONION RELISH, OR onions *agrodolce,* as the Italians call it, is packed with an intense flavor that is an ideal accompaniment to a wide variety of dishes. When paired with polenta, the relish accents its mild corn flavor. When capped with sharp cheese and walnuts, the relish and polenta become a hearty meal with complex, satisfying flavors.

Most sweet-and-sour onion relish recipes are a fairly simple combination of onions, sugar, vinegar, and an herb or two. Tiny pearl onions (or the Italian variety called cipollini) are the most common choice, but for the sake of time and convenience, we chose standard whole onions, thinly sliced. We favored red onions over yellow for their sweetness and dark color, which made for a sharper contrast with the pale polenta. We cooked the onions until they softened, then added light brown sugar for sweetness and balsamic vinegar for acidity and its characteristic caramel flavor. Simmered for a few minutes, the onions turned jamlike and silky smooth. Thyme, cooked as whole sprigs and removed before serving, added a pleasant earthiness.

As for cheese to accompany the relish and the polenta, tasters made a surprising choice. After trying a variety of sharp imported cheeses, including pecorino, Parmesan, manchego, and Gorgonzola, everyone favored the local hero: extra-sharp cheddar. The sharpness and crumbly texture of well-aged cheddar had a natural affinity for the onions and polenta that none of the other cheeses matched—though admittedly, they weren't too far behind.

Polenta with Sweet-and-Sour Onion Relish, Cheddar, and Toasted Walnuts

SERVES 4 TO 6 AS A MAIN COURSE

TIME: 25 MINUTES

If you don't have red onions, go ahead and use whatever kind you do have; you will probably need to add a bit more sugar, however. Leftover onions work well as a sandwich spread. If you prefer, the cheese may be beaten into the polenta instead of scattered over the top.

½	cup walnuts, chopped coarse
2	tablespoons extra-virgin olive oil
2	medium red onions, sliced thin
4	sprigs fresh thyme
	Salt
1	tablespoon light brown sugar
2	tablespoons balsamic vinegar
	Ground black pepper
1½	cups instant polenta, prepared according to package directions
2	tablespoons unsalted butter
6	ounces extra-sharp cheddar cheese, shredded (about 1½ cups)

1. Add the walnuts to a large skillet over medium-high heat and toast, stirring frequently, until aromatic and beginning to brown, about 3 minutes. Transfer the walnuts to a small bowl and set them aside.

2. Return the skillet to the burner and add the oil, onions, thyme sprigs, and ½ teaspoon salt. Cook over medium-high until the

onions soften and begin to brown, 6 to 7 minutes. Reduce the heat to low and sprinkle the brown sugar, vinegar, and 2 tablespoons water across the onions. Stir to combine the mixture and simmer until the liquid has evaporated and the onions are glossy, 5 to 7 minutes. Adjust the seasonings with salt and pepper to taste. Discard the thyme.

3. While the onions are cooking, prepare the polenta according to the package directions. Stir the butter into the finished polenta and spoon the polenta into individual shallow soup or pasta bowls. Divide the onion mixture among the bowls of polenta. Sprinkle each portion with cheese and walnuts. Serve immediately.

SKILLET CHICKEN BIRYANI

GENERALLY RESERVED FOR FESTIVE meals in certain regions of India and Pakistan, biryani is, essentially, a rich rice pilaf. Heavily spiced with saffron, cardamom, cinnamon, and ginger (to name just a few commonly included spices), biryani may contain chicken or lamb as well as a long list of vegetables and herbs. Everything is combined in layers and slowly baked in the oven until the rice has plumped and the flavors have blended. The finishing touch is a spoonful of thick *raita,* the ubiquitous yogurt-based sauce served at most Indian meals. While a dish this complicated may seem out of place in this book, we were intrigued. Could we extract the fundamental flavors from the recipes we researched and develop a cooking method that circumvented unnecessary steps and streamlined the process?

Admittedly, ours was to be more of a mock biryani designed to feed a hungry crowd on a weeknight. For starters, we realized it would be easy to reconfigure the chicken and rice recipe (see page 214). After the chicken browned, we could sauté the pilaf's remaining ingredients in the hot skillet (toasting the rice, too), return the chicken to the pan to nestle in the rice, and slide the skillet into a hot oven to finish cooking—one dish for a full meal.

Cooking method in hand, we turned to the rest of the challenge: picking a variety of rice and the best vegetables and spices to flavor the biryani. Basmati rice is the most common type of rice in India, notable for its popcorn-like aroma and distinctive flavor. The name literally translates as "queen of fragrance." Unlike most rice, basmati is aged to reduce its water content. The grains cook up long and separate, especially when toasted in oil, as they are in a biryani. Most stores carry at least one brand of basmati rice, though it might be tucked away in the ethnic foods aisle. If basmati is unavailable, conventional long-grain white rice is perfectly acceptable, though it lacks the trademark aroma. As with any rice pilaf, we quickly toasted the rice grains in the hot oil, once the vegetables were cooked through, to ensure the grains cooked up fluffy and separate.

For vegetables, we chose two of the most common in the recipes we found: onions and jalapeño chiles. Onions lent the biryani sweetness and depth, and jalapeños brought a bright vegetal flavor and mild heat—too mild, in fact, when we removed the seeds and inner white ribs. Tasters preferred versions made with the seeds and ribs for a bit more kick.

Most biryani recipes we researched contained a long list of spices—way too many for our recipe. We needed to select the few that yielded the biggest impact. A pinch of saffron, for color and fragrance, and cinnamon were present in all the recipes we found, so they were kept. Ginger was common too, and we opted to add it fresh, sliced into thick coins, which required little prep work but provided plenty of flavor. To round out the spices—the biryani tasted flat to most tasters—we tried cumin, coriander, and cardamom, with the cardamom winning for its penetrating flavor and exotic aroma, which blended well with the saffron. Cardamom comes in several forms: whole, in pods, decorticated (seeds removed from the pod but still whole), and powdered. The whole pods may be black, white, or green, with the latter preferred for smoothest flavor. Cardamom possesses a high, sweet flavor, which some describe as "minty" or "eucalyptus-like." This distinctive flavor is part of many curry and Indian spice blends.

For recipes like this, we often use whole spices because they can easily be removed

---

INGREDIENTS: Yogurt

Plain yogurt may not be the world's sexiest food, but plenty of mystique surrounds this refrigerator staple, perhaps owing to that ad campaign featuring centenarian Georgians (from Russia, not the American South) who ate yogurt every day. Once consumed in the United States mainly by hippies, yogurt is now a mainstream product, available in countless flavors, including cotton candy and kiwi.

We had three questions at the outset of our research. First, does the inclusion of certain bacteria (the active cultures in yogurt) affect flavor? Second, does fat content make a difference in flavor or texture? You can buy nonfat, low-fat, and whole-milk yogurt, and we wanted to taste all three. Third, are the leading supermarket brands just fine, or is it worth seeking specialty brands, especially those found in natural foods stores?

Yogurt was probably first made by chance when milk was accidentally fermented by wild bacteria. Today, the process is controlled. Milk (whole, low-fat, or skim) is pasteurized and, usually, homogenized. (Some companies leave whole milk unhomogenized to retain a separate cream layer in their yogurt.) Active bacteria cultures are then added, and the milk is poured into cups and kept in a warm environment for several hours. The bacteria convert the milk sugar (called lactose) to lactic acid, causing the proteins in the milk to coagulate and thicken. Lactic acid also gives yogurt its characteristic tang. Finally, the yogurt is cooled and refrigerated.

We rounded up 11 leading brands of plain yogurt, including four made with whole milk, two with low-fat milk, and five with skim milk, and tasted them straight from the container. We quickly determined that the type of bacteria used to culture the milk had no discernible effect on our tasters' ratings. Fat content was more complicated. Yogurts made with low-fat milk and whole milk took the top four spots. However, two whole-milk yogurts fared poorly. Yes, our tasters appreciated the richness and flavor contributed by the extra fat, but in the end, other considerations took precedence.

In terms of flavor, a happy medium between tart and bland carried the day. Yogurts that were extremely tart landed at the bottom of the rankings.

In terms of texture, our tasters spoke loud and clear. They preferred smooth, creamy yogurts to those that were lumpy, chalky, grainy, watery, or curdlike. In fact, tasters put such a high premium on smoothness that a low-fat variety won the tasting.

THE BEST PLAIN YOGURT

Tasters gave Colombo Low-Fat Plain Yogurt (left) a big thumbs-up, praising the "clean taste" and "mild tang" of this "creamy," "silky" yogurt. "Rich and buttery" Brown Cow Organic Whole-Milk Plain Yogurt (center) finished second in the tasting, followed by "velvety but mild" Stonyfield Farm Organic Low-Fat Plain Yogurt (right).

from the finished dish. There is no messy measuring of powders, and the flavor is generally brighter than that of ground spices (which often sit on the shelf too long).

Raita is traditionally served as a garnish to mellow and brighten biryani's assertive flavors. For our version, tasters favored a simple combination of yogurt, cilantro, and a small amount of garlic.

Skillet Chicken Biryani

SERVES 4 TO 6 AS A MAIN COURSE
TIME: 55 MINUTES (INCLUDES 20
MINUTES BAKING TIME)

The cardamom pods rise to the surface by the time the dish finishes baking, so they are easy to remove. Do try to remove them all prior to serving, as biting into a pod can be unpleasant. Leftover yogurt sauce may be used as a dip or sandwich spread.

1	teaspoon vegetable oil
4	bone-in, skin-on chicken thighs (about 1¾ pounds), trimmed of excess fat and skin
	Salt and ground black pepper
1	medium onion, sliced thin
3	large jalapeño chiles, stemmed and sliced thin (with seeds for maximum flavor and heat)
8	green cardamom pods, lightly crushed with the flat side of a knife
1	(1½-inch) piece fresh ginger, cut into 4 coins
2	cinnamon sticks
1½	cups basmati or long-grain rice, well rinsed and drained
	Pinch saffron threads, crumbled with fingertips
4	medium cloves garlic, minced or pressed through a garlic press (about 4 teaspoons)
1	cup plain yogurt, preferably whole-milk
2	tablespoons minced fresh cilantro leaves

1. Adjust an oven rack to the middle position and heat the oven to 375 degrees. Heat the oil in a heavy-bottomed 12-inch oven-proof skillet over medium-high heat until almost smoking. Meanwhile, thoroughly dry the chicken with paper towels and season liberally with salt and pepper. Swirl the skillet to coat with the oil and add the chicken, skin-side down. Cook until deep golden, about 5 minutes; turn the chicken pieces over and brown until golden on the second side, about 4 minutes longer. Using tongs, transfer the chicken to a plate and cover with aluminum foil to keep warm.

2. Add the onion, jalapeños, cardamom, ginger, cinnamon, 1 teaspoon salt, and 2 tablespoons water to deglaze the pan. Cook, stirring frequently and scraping the bottom of the pan to release any browned bits, until the onion softens and begins to brown, about 4 minutes. Add the rice, saffron, and 1 tablespoon garlic and cook, continuing to stir frequently, until the grains of rice are coated with fat, about 1½ minutes.

3. Off the heat, add 2½ cups water and the browned chicken. Return the pan to the heat and bring to a boil. Cover the skillet with a lid and transfer to the oven. Bake until the chicken is cooked through, 20 to 22 minutes.

4. Meanwhile, mix together the yogurt, remaining 1 teaspoon garlic, cilantro, ½ teaspoon salt, and pepper to taste in a small bowl.

5. Remove the cardamom pods, ginger coins, and cinnamon sticks from the skillet and adjust the seasonings with salt and pepper to taste. Serve the chicken and rice immediately, passing the yogurt sauce separately at the table.

JAMBALAYA

WHO WOULD HAVE THOUGHT THAT one of the classic dishes of the Louisiana Bayou, jambalaya, could be made within an hour without stooping to prepared foods or instant rice? Loaded with chicken, shrimp, sausage, and a long list of vegetables, spices, and herbs, traditional jambalaya did not seem a strong candidate for weeknight cooking. But inspired by the challenge, we knew we could pare the dish to its essence, retain only the most important flavors and crucial cooking

INGREDIENTS: Andouille Sausage and Tasso

Andouille, a seasoned smoked sausage, is the most authentic choice for jambalaya, with tasso, also known as Cajun ham, a close second. (Tasso is a lean chunk of highly seasoned pork or, sometimes, beef that is cured and then smoked.) Because andouille and tasso can be hard to find in supermarkets, we tested the two against chorizo and linguiça (Spanish and Portuguese sausages, respectively), which are more widely available and also fit the jambalaya flavor profile.

After we made a batch of jambalaya with each sausage, tasters agreed that nothing compares with the real thing. Andouille was perfection. It had intense heat and the bold flavors of garlic and strong herbs, and it imparted a noticeable yet manageable degree of smokiness to the dish. While nicely seasoned and flavorful, tasso was too smoky and had a strange, gristly texture no one liked. Linguiça was bland and added little heat to the finished product; chorizo was slightly more piquant but still dull.

Although andouille is clearly the best choice for jambalaya, we wondered if all brands were created equal. To find out, we gathered five brands available nationally in supermarkets and by mail order and put them to the test. Here are the results of our taste test, with brands listed in order of preference:

CHEF PAUL'S REGULAR ANDOUILLE (sometimes called Mild) took the crown, one vote shy of a sweep. With its "smoky," "rich," and "earthy" flavors and "balanced heat level," it was the perfect accompaniment to the other big flavors in the jambalaya.

JACOB'S ANDOUILLE was easily the most unsightly andouille of the group. Despite its aesthetic shortcomings, this sausage was our runner-up. It had a "deeply smoky," almost sweet flavor and a substantial bite.

CHEF PAUL'S HOT ANDOUILLE was so spicy the sausage's other flavors were obscured.

POCHE'S ANDOUILLE had little flavor to offer. Its texture was equally disappointing: "chewy," "rubbery," and "tough."

NORTH COUNTRY SMOKEHOUSE ANDOUILLE received the worst marks. It was excessively spicy and had a "tinny," almost "ammonia-like" flavor.

The conclusion is clear: If you can find Chef Paul's Regular Andouille, buy it.

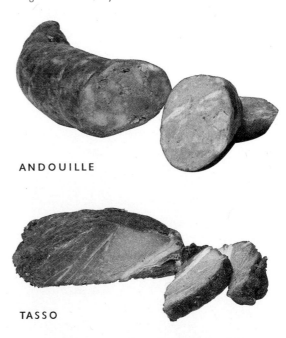

ANDOUILLE

TASSO

Tasso has great flavor, but tasters did not like its gristly texture and thought its smoke flavor was overpowering. Andouille is a better choice for jambalaya. It is spicy, bold, smoky, and perfectly textured.

steps, and bring it to the table within the hour.

Admittedly, we had something of a head start. Having already developed a simplified jambalaya recipe in the test kitchen, we had some ideas about where we could trim ingredients and streamline preparation. Much of jambalaya's unique character comes from its rich combination of chicken, shrimp, and fiery andouille sausage, but for the sake of time, we needed to exclude one of the meats or the shrimp. With jambalaya's name derived from the French *jambon,* or ham, we couldn't exclude the pork, so we had to choose between chicken and shrimp. Both tasted great, but the chicken required more preparation and longer cooking, so it was ousted.

With our limited lineup, the andouille sausage would be the star of the show. Heavily spiced and thoroughly smoked, andouille sausage was originally French and made predominantly from tripe and chitterlings. The Cajuns put their own spin on it, jazzing it up and omitting the offal. Most markets carry at least one variety, but beware—brands can vary a great deal in flavor and spice level. Our favorite? After testing several brands (see page 105), tasters preferred Chef Paul's Regular, developed by Paul Prudhomme, the man who has done more to popularize Cajun cuisine than anyone else. This sausage is available by mail order as well as in some grocery stores. The flavor is well rounded and the heat level tolerable—attributes rarely found together in the other brands we tested. If you can't get Chef Paul's, rely on your butcher for recommendations. For the fullest flavor, we browned the sausage in a Dutch oven before cooking the vegetables, then used the rendered, highly seasoned pork fat as their cooking medium.

As for the vegetables themselves, we found, through the process of elimination, that onions, red bell pepper, and garlic (lots of it) form the trinity upon which jambalaya stands.

Most Cajun cooking employs green bell peppers, but tasters did not care for their bitter, vegetal bite. To save preparation time, we tossed all the vegetables into the food processor and chopped the mixture very fine—almost to a paste. This mixture cooked quickly and broke down to flavor the dish. Jambalaya is all about the meat and rice, not the vegetables, so their obvious appearance was not missed.

Most recipes simmer the shrimp in the stew during the last few minutes of cooking. While this might work well in a fully constructed, highly seasoned jambalaya, shrimp so treated tasted too bland in this version. In a dish with so few ingredients, it was important to extract as much flavor as possible from each. We took a nontraditional approach and seared the shrimp in a skillet alongside the pot of jambalaya. The shrimp lightly caramelized in the high heat, and the flavor was markedly improved. It then occurred to us that we could cook the shrimp in the Dutch oven before the rest of the jambalaya and hold them until the end, thereby limiting production to just one pot—always a bonus.

Once everything was browned and the rice lightly toasted, we returned the sausage to the pan and added canned diced tomatoes, bottled clam juice, and water. The more traditional choice for liquid would have been a shrimp stock or chicken stock, but the former required time we didn't have, and the latter made for a muddy-tasting jambalaya. Clam juice provided just enough brininess to reinforce the shrimp's presence without being too forceful.

In 20 minutes, the rice was tender and the flavors blended. We stirred in the shrimp and a substantial amount of parsley, for color as much as for flavor, and our jambalaya was ready.

Simple Shrimp and Andouille Jambalaya

SERVES 4 TO 6 AS A MAIN COURSE

TIME: 45 MINUTES (INCLUDES 20 MINUTES SIMMERING TIME)

If andouille sausage is impossible to find in your area, kielbasa is an acceptable substitution, though you will probably need to add hot pepper sauce or cayenne pepper to make up for the missing spiciness. Be sure to spread the shrimp in an even layer in the pan; otherwise, they won't cook properly, and their flavor will suffer.

1	medium onion, chopped coarse
1	medium red bell pepper, stemmed, seeded, and chopped coarse
5	medium cloves garlic, chopped coarse
1	pound extra-large shrimp (21 to 25 per pound), shelled and deveined (if necessary)
	Salt
	Hot pepper sauce, such as Tabasco
1	tablespoon vegetable oil
¾	pound andouille sausage, halved lengthwise and cut into ¼-inch-thick half-moons
1½	cups long-grain rice
4	bay leaves
1	(14½-ounce) can diced tomatoes, briefly drained (to retain some juice)
2	(8-ounce) bottles clam juice
¼	cup chopped fresh parsley leaves

1. In a food processor, pulse the onion, red pepper, and garlic until chopped very fine, ten to twelve 1-second pulses, scraping down the sides of the bowl as necessary; set aside. Season the shrimp with salt and hot pepper sauce to taste.

2. Heat the oil in a large, heavy-bottomed Dutch oven over medium-high heat until shimmering. Add the shrimp in a single layer and cook, without stirring, for 30 seconds.

Using tongs, flip the shrimp and cook for another 30 seconds. Transfer the shrimp to a medium bowl and set aside.

3. Add the sausage to the pan and cook, stirring occasionally, until lightly browned, about 3 minutes. Using a slotted spoon, transfer the sausage to a second bowl.

4. Scrape the vegetables from the food processor into the empty pot and cook, stirring frequently, until softened, about 3 minutes. Stir in the rice and continue to stir until the grains are coated with the fat, about 1 minute. Add the bay leaves, tomatoes, clam juice, and 1 cup water and bring to a boil. Stir in the sausage, cover, and reduce the heat to low. Cook until the rice is tender, 17 to 20 minutes.

5. Off the heat, stir in the shrimp and parsley with a large fork (do not mush the rice), cover the pot, and allow to sit for 2 minutes, or until the shrimp are heated through. Discard the bay leaves and adjust the seasonings with salt and hot pepper sauce to taste. Serve immediately.

CHICKPEA AND VEGETABLE COUSCOUS

WHILE COUSCOUS IS GENERALLY served as an accompaniment to long-cooked Moroccan meat or vegetable stews called tagines, we saw no reason why we couldn't merge these two elements. Inspired by several tagine recipes we found, we sought to simplify the flavors, shorten the ingredient list, and combine the stew with couscous for a nutritious one-pot meal. Although hardly authentic, the marriage would save on preparation and cooking time as well as cleanup.

Having mastered a technique for cooking couscous—toasting the grains in butter, then steeping them in a flavorful liquid until tender—completing a new recipe was simply a matter of choosing the most suitable vegetables and seasonings and working out ideal cooking times for each. The chickpea and vegetable tagine recipes we consulted typically contained a long list of ingredients, including carrots, onions, peas, turnips, zucchini, and tomatoes. From the get-go, we chose to limit the dish to just three vegetables—carrots, onions, and peas—each of which brought a distinctive flavor and texture to the dish. Carrots and onions lent sweetness, body, and crunch, and the clean, vegetal flavor and slight snap of the fragile peas contrasted vividly with the tender grains of couscous and firm cubes of carrot. The peas further added visual appeal, the bright green standing out prominently against the light couscous.

To cook the vegetables—excluding the peas, which we reserved until later to prevent overcooking—we followed the technique from our saffron couscous recipe (page 93), sautéing the carrots along with the onions after the couscous was toasted and removed from the skillet. When the vegetables had begun to lightly caramelize (butter helped elicit their natural sweetness), we added a substantial amount of garlic, plus the spices—the ingredients that prompted the most debate.

Much of the character of North African cooking derives from an abundance of spices expertly combined. The tagine recipes we consulted included lots of spices—at least five or six per recipe—or employed a mixture called *ras el hanout*, a spice blend that can contain over 30 ingredients. For the sake of time and efficiency, we needed to limit our choices. We experimented with many combinations until tasters decided coriander and dried ginger (fresh ginger is almost never used in North African cuisine) constituted the most complementary match for the vegetables we had chosen.

The only remaining ingredients to consider were the chickpeas, broth, and frozen peas. Chickpeas are among our favorite canned beans because they pull through the canning process better than most legumes and retain their full flavor and firm texture. A quick rinse in a colander was all that was necessary to prepare them for the pot. For the liquid to hydrate the couscous, tasters favored a combination of chicken broth and water, blended in equal portions. Without the broth, the couscous tasted a little anemic (though straight water or vegetable stock would be an acceptable substitution for vegetarians). The peas went in at the last moment before the simmering mixture was added to the couscous to steep.

Despite the dish's full flavors, it screamed for an abundance of fresh herbs. We tried the usual—parsley, cilantro, and mint—and couldn't reach a consensus. Some tasters favored the clean, bright flavor of parsley, while others liked the sharpness of cilantro (cilantro and coriander are often paired, as coriander is the seed of the cilantro plant), and a few held out for the exotically aromatic mint. In the end, we decided not to decide, as they all work equally well. We leave the choice to the cook.

Moroccan Chickpea and Vegetable Couscous

SERVES 4 AS A MAIN COURSE OR
6 TO 8 AS A SIDE DISH

TIME: 45 MINUTES

Sprinkled with additional lemon juice and a tablespoon or two of extra-virgin olive oil, this dish is also good cold as a salad. Harissa, a fiery Algerian hot sauce flavored with chiles, caraway, garlic, and cumin, is an authentic accompaniment and worth looking for. Vegetable stock or water can be used instead of chicken broth, if a vegetarian version is desired. The couscous may need salt to replace that lost from the chicken broth.

4 tablespoons unsalted butter

2 cups couscous

1 medium onion, chopped fine

2 medium carrots, chopped fine

Salt

4 medium cloves garlic, minced or pressed through a garlic press (about 4 teaspoons)

1/2 teaspoon ground coriander

1/2 teaspoon ground ginger

1 (15-ounce) can chickpeas, drained and rinsed

1 3/4 cups canned low-sodium chicken broth

1 1/2 cups frozen peas

1/2 cup chopped fresh parsley, cilantro, and/or mint leaves

Ground black pepper

1 lemon, cut into wedges

1. Melt 2 tablespoons butter in a large skillet over medium-high heat. When the foaming subsides, add the couscous and cook, stirring frequently with a heatproof rubber spatula or wooden spoon, until some grains are just beginning to brown, about 3 minutes. Scrape the grains from the skillet into a large bowl and return the pan to medium heat.

2. Add the remaining 2 tablespoons butter to the empty pan. Once the butter melts, add the onion, carrots, and 1 teaspoon salt. Cook, stirring occasionally, until the onion softens and begins to brown, about 5 minutes. Stir in the garlic, coriander, and ginger and cook until fragrant, about 30 seconds. Add the chickpeas, broth, and 2 cups water, increase the heat to medium-high, and bring to a boil.

3. Stir in the peas and pour the mixture over the toasted couscous; cover tightly with plastic wrap and allow to sit for 12 minutes. Remove the plastic wrap, add the herbs, and fluff the grains with a fork. Adjust the seasonings with salt and pepper to taste. Serve immediately, accompanied by lemon wedges.

REFRIED BEANS

AUTHENTIC REFRIED BEANS ARE LEFT-over stewed beans cooked in copious quantities of lard until they soften to a smooth paste; they are served garnished with toppings like sharp, crumbly cheese, scallions, bacon, and jalapeño chiles. The texture is sinfully lush and the flavor unbeatably rich and satisfying. Delicious, yes—but healthy? We wanted to revise traditional refried beans to make them both healthier and faster—quick enough to cook a skilletful with time left in the hour to chop garnishes, assemble burritos, or fry eggs to serve with the beans for a platter of *huevos rancheros*.

The beans were the first hurdle to overcome. Canned beans are undeniably convenient, but in flavor and texture they are generally pale compared with dried beans cooked slowly with aromatics. In this case, the canned beans were to be smashed smooth, so texture wasn't an issue. But flavor, however, was paramount, as most refried bean recipes have few ingredients outside of the beans, lard, a little onion, and salt. In preliminary testing, we tried a few traditional recipes with canned beans filling in for dried, and the flavors were boring. We clearly needed to boost the dish with additional flavors. First, however, we needed to identify a cooking method that would break down the beans quickly (the traditional recipes took up to an hour) and a fat to replace the lard.

The standard procedure we came across most often involved simply mashing the beans in the pan as they cooked with a wooden spoon or potato masher. The method was labor-intensive and yielded mediocre results; the chunky mash was punctuated with bits of tough, leathery bean skin. Canned beans apparently have tougher skins than dried beans. Clearly, we needed more force than that generated by a potato masher and an arm—like a food processor or blender. The food processor did a miraculous job. We rinsed the beans, put them in the workbowl with water for lubrication, and processed the beans until smooth—about 30 seconds. The skins virtually disappeared, and the resulting puree was completely smooth. We had eliminated significant time.

With our beans pureed, it was time to fry them. Lard is a tough act to follow; we tried corn, canola, vegetable, and olive oil, and the latter won for its full flavor and rich mouthfeel—mild compared with lard but infinitely healthier. We tried every quantity from a scant tablespoon (unnoticeable) to ½ cup (overkill) for three cans of beans and settled on 5 tablespoons, which is generous but not hedonistic.

The last job was to choose seasonings that would deepen the flavor of the otherwise plain-tasting beans. Onions, which are traditional, added depth and body as well as sweetness. Jalapeño chiles brought a hint of heat and a vegetal edge that tasters liked. Garlic and cumin rounded out the seasonings. We cooked the flavorings in the olive oil, added the bean puree, and within 10 minutes the beans were rich-tasting and smooth.

❧ Refried Kidney Beans

SERVES 4 TO 6 AS A SIDE DISH

TIME: 25 MINUTES

If you have a spice grinder, you can enjoy freshly ground whole cumin seeds. The flavor is markedly better than that of store-bought ground cumin. Simply toast the seeds in a skillet for a couple of minutes or until fragrant, then grind them until finely processed. If you like your beans on the spicy side, don't bother to seed the chiles. Refried beans can be served with a variety of garnishes, including tortilla chips, salsa (see the quick recipe on page 16), pickled jalapeño chiles (sold in cans in most supermarkets), sliced scallions, shredded Monterey Jack or cheddar cheese, sour cream, and pickled red onions (see page 48). Refried beans can be served with almost any dish but are especially good with beef, pork, or eggs.

3 (15-ounce) cans red kidney beans, drained and rinsed
5 tablespoons olive oil
1 medium onion, chopped fine
1 large jalapeño chile, stemmed, seeded, and minced
   Salt
2 medium cloves garlic, minced or pressed through a garlic press (about 2 teaspoons)
1 teaspoon ground cumin
½ cup coarsely chopped fresh cilantro leaves (optional)
   Hot pepper sauce, such as Tabasco

1. Process the beans and 1 cup water in a food processor until smooth, scraping down the sides of the workbowl with a rubber spatula as necessary, about 30 seconds; set aside.

2. Put the oil, onion, chile, and ½ teaspoon salt in a large nonstick skillet over medium-high heat. Cook, stirring occasionally, until the onion softens and just begins to brown, about 5 minutes. Add the garlic and cumin and cook, stirring frequently, until aromatic, about 30 seconds. Stir in the bean mixture until thoroughly combined and reduce the heat to medium. Cook, stirring occasionally, until the beans have thickened and the flavors have blended, about 10 minutes. Stir in the cilantro, if using, and adjust the seasonings with salt and hot pepper sauce to taste. Serve immediately.

REFRIED BLACK BEANS WITH BACON

FOR THOSE CRAVING THE RICHNESS and meaty flavor of more traditional refried beans cooked in pork fat, we decided a bacon-based refried bean recipe was necessary. For this variation, we opted for black beans over kidney beans because of their natural affinity with bacon. Their strong, assertive flavor stands up well to the sweet smokiness of the cured pork. We found the method needed little change. Instead of completely browning the bacon and removing the crispy bits, we left them in to enrich the beans. We discovered it was unnecessary to fully render the bacon before adding the aromatics; the bits of meat browned and the remaining fat rendered as the onion and chile cooked. We experimented with different amounts of bacon and decided that anything more than 4 ounces (about four slices), was too rich.

Refried Black Beans with Bacon

SERVES 4 TO 6 AS A SIDE DISH

TIME: 25 MINUTES

See the note to Refried Kidney Beans for garnishes. These hearty beans are great with meat or eggs.

- 3   (15-ounce) cans black beans, drained and rinsed
- 4   ounces bacon, diced (about 4 slices)
- 1   medium onion, chopped fine
- 1   large jalapeño chile, stemmed, seeded, and minced
      Salt
- 2   medium cloves garlic, minced or pressed through a garlic press (about 2 teaspoons)
- 1   teaspoon ground cumin
- ½   cup coarsely chopped fresh cilantro leaves (optional)
      Hot pepper sauce, such as Tabasco

1. Process the beans and 1 cup water in a food processor until smooth, scraping down the sides of the workbowl with a rubber spatula as necessary, about 30 seconds; set aside.

2. Cook the bacon in a large nonstick skillet over medium-high heat until it just begins to brown and most of the fat has rendered, about 4 minutes. Add the onion, chile, and ¼ teaspoon salt and cook, stirring occasionally, until the onion softens and just begins to brown, 3 to 4 minutes. Add the garlic and cumin and cook, stirring frequently, until aromatic, about 30 seconds. Stir in the bean mixture until thoroughly combined and reduce the heat to medium. Cook, stirring occasionally, until the beans have thickened and the flavors have blended, about 10 minutes. Stir in the cilantro, if using, and adjust the seasonings with salt and hot pepper sauce to taste. Serve immediately.

REFRIED BEAN TOSTADAS

TOSTADAS ARE CRISP CORN TORTILLAS crowned with beans, meat, or poultry and finished with cheese, salsa, and any number of garnishes. With our quick refried bean recipe in hand, we set out to develop a tostada recipe with authentic flavor—but ready in minutes using grocery store staples. We would keep the dish simple, pared to the minimum—corn tortillas, refried beans, salsa, and cheese—for clean flavor and quick preparation.

Small corn tortillas—6 inches or so in diameter—are the best bet because they possess enough structural integrity to support the toppings. Larger tortillas snap easily, and soft flour tortillas are best reserved for burritos, soft tacos, and quesadillas. Frying is a must for the fullest corn flavor and crisp texture, but the small size of the tortilla means little oil is necessary. We found the best method was to fry the tortillas one at a time in an 8-inch skillet. In less than two minutes, the tortilla was crisp and lightly browned. Figuring on two tostadas per serving, this meant frying took 15 minutes, though this time may be split between monitoring the tortillas and preparing the other ingredients.

Freshly made salsa has an unbeatable brightness and clarity that puts even the best jarred salsas to shame. Our quick salsa (page 16) uses a food processor and canned tomatoes to cut down on labor. It is not quite as attractive as hand-chopped salsa, but the flavor is great, and it is ready in moments.

With tortillas fried, beans made, and salsa assembled, we needed to pick a type of cheese to finish off our tostadas. Traditionally, tostadas are sprinkled with one of several Mexican cheeses in textures from fresh and stringy to dry and crumbly—but most of these can be hard to find outside Latino markets. Monterey Jack is probably the closest to one of the fresh cheeses (asadero or Oaxacan string cheese, if you're searching for authenticity), though a mild cheddar works well too. Both Monterey Jack and cheddar are readily available and melt smoothly. It is important to remember that tostadas are not pizzas, and a little cheese goes a long way. We found just ¼ cup melted across the top of each tostada lent richness and flavor without overshadowing the beans.

In a very hot oven, the cheese melted in less than five minutes. We found it important to melt the cheese as quickly as possible because moisture from the beans can turn the tortillas soggy if they spend too much time baking.

Refried Bean Tostadas

SERVES 4 AS A MAIN COURSE

TIME: 40 MINUTES

If time is short, use a good-quality store-bought salsa. Although we don't like commercial salsa with chips, it's fine in this recipe. Look for cans of pickled jalapeños with the other Mexican ingredients in the supermarket. To save time, prepare the salsa first, then the refried beans. While the beans are cooking, heat the oven and fry the tortillas.

¾	cup corn or vegetable oil
8	(6-inch) corn tortillas (white or yellow)
2	cups refried beans (either of the preceding recipes works well)
8	ounces Monterey Jack or mild cheddar cheese, shredded (about 2 cups)
I	cup Five-Minute Salsa (page 16)
½	cup sliced pickled jalapeños (optional)
I	lime, cut into thin wedges (optional)
	Hot pepper sauce, such as Tabasco (optional)

1. Adjust an oven rack to the middle position and heat the oven to 475 degrees.

2. Heat the oil in an 8-inch heavy-bottomed skillet over medium heat to 350 degrees, about 5 minutes (the oil should bubble when a small piece of tortilla is dropped in; the tortilla piece should rise to the surface in 2 seconds). Meanwhile, line a rimmed baking sheet with a double thickness of paper towels. Using tongs, slide 1 tortilla into the hot oil. Fry until the tortilla has stiffened and is just beginning to brown, about 45 seconds. Using tongs, flip the tortilla and cook the other side until it is lightly browned, about 45 seconds. Transfer the crisp tortilla to the paper towels to drain and repeat the process with the remaining tortillas.

3. To assemble the tostadas, smear each tortilla with ¼ cup refried beans and sprinkle evenly with ¼ cup cheese. Lay the tostadas in

a single layer on a rimmed baking sheet and bake until the cheese is just melted, about 5 minutes. Spread 1 to 2 tablespoons salsa over each tostada. Serve immediately, accompanied by pickled jalapeños, lime wedges, and hot pepper sauce, if desired.

RED LENTILS WITH COCONUT MILK

BEAN STEWS, CALLED DALS, ARE A staple dish at almost every Indian meal. Red lentils, also sold under the Indian name *masoor dal,* are one of the more common legumes of India. They are mild-tasting and slightly nutty, fading to a light mustard hue once cooked. They come both whole and split. The split variety cooks significantly faster and breaks down to a smooth puree within about 20 minutes without soaking— a time that's hard to beat for dried legumes.

To deepen the flavor of the otherwise bland lentils, we briefly sautéed onion, garlic, and ginger before adding the lentils and liquid. Many Indian recipes we researched called for adding the aromatics raw or skipping them altogether, relying for flavor entirely on spices and garnishes like chutney, but our method boosted flavor more easily. Traditionally, the spices are toasted in a separate pan (sometimes in oil but more often in *ghee,* or clarified butter). The spices and fat are then stirred into the lentils. This method would have meant employing a second pan and fat beyond the butter we were already using to sauté the aromatics. For the sake of efficiency, we chose the Western approach and added the spices to the aromatics.

For complex flavors without a lot of work, we chose garam masala, a spice mixture that contains a blend of coriander, cloves, cardamom, cumin, cinnamon, black

BUILDING BLOCK RECIPE
Fluffy White Rice
SERVES 4 AS A SIDE DISH
TIME: 35 MINUTES

This recipe yields American-style rice with fluffy, separate grains.

1	tablespoon unsalted butter or oil (vegetable or olive)
1½	cups long-grain white rice (not converted)
2¼	cups water
¾	teaspoon salt

1. Heat the butter or oil in a medium saucepan over medium heat. Add the rice and cook, stirring constantly, for 1 to 3 minutes, depending on desired amount of nutty flavor. Add the water and salt. Bring to a boil, swirling the pot to blend ingredients.

2. Reduce the heat to low, cover tightly, and cook until the liquid is absorbed, about 15 minutes.

3. Turn off the heat; let the rice stand on the burner, still covered, to finish cooking, about 15 minutes longer. Fluff with a fork and serve.

pepper, and nutmeg. Slightly sweet and not very spicy, garam masala is best when toasted in dry heat, so we incorporated the blend into the onion mixture before adding the lentils and liquid.

Despite the aromatics, the lentils tasted too lean, so we decided to add coconut milk, which is the source of the lush, creamy texture and full mouthfeel of many South Asian dishes. For garnishes, we added cilantro for its refreshing bite and diced raw tomato for both sweetness and acidity.

Red Lentils with Coconut Milk

SERVES 4 TO 6 AS A MAIN COURSE

TIME: 40 MINUTES (INCLUDES 20 MINUTES SIMMERING TIME)

Because the kick of garam masala is quite mild, add a pinch of ground cayenne pepper if you like spicy foods. Make sure to purchase coconut milk, not cream of coconut—they are very different products. The lentils may be made up to 3 days ahead of time and stored in an airtight container, but the cilantro should be withheld until just before serving, as its flavor quickly fades. Serve with Basmati Rice, Pilaf-Style (right), which can be prepared as the lentils simmer.

2	tablespoons vegetable oil
I	small onion, chopped fine
	Salt
4	medium cloves garlic, minced or pressed through a garlic press (about 4 teaspoons)
I	tablespoon minced fresh ginger
I	teaspoon garam masala
I ¼	cups split red lentils
I	cup unsweetened coconut milk
½	cup coarsely chopped fresh cilantro leaves
	Ground black pepper
3	medium plum tomatoes, cored, seeded, and diced medium

1. Combine the oil, onion, and 1 teaspoon salt in a large saucepan. Cook over medium-high heat, stirring occasionally, until the onion softens and just begins to brown around the edges, 4 to 5 minutes. Add the garlic, ginger, and garam masala and cook until fragrant, about 45 seconds. Add the lentils, coconut milk, and 3 cups water and bring to a boil.

2. Reduce the heat to low, partially cover, and simmer until the lentils break down and form a thick puree, 20 to 30 minutes. Stir in the cilantro, adjust the seasonings with salt and pepper to taste, and serve immediately, garnished with tomatoes and accompanied by basmati rice.

BUILDING BLOCK RECIPE
Basmati Rice, Pilaf-Style

SERVES 4 AS A SIDE DISH

TIME: 30 MINUTES

While plain long-grain rice is perfectly suitable, basmati is the traditional accompaniment to lentil dishes. It has an exotic aroma and distinctive flavor some liken to popcorn. The addition of cardamom pods is common and adds a new flavor dimension. For efficiency, begin cooking the rice once the lentils are simmering; they will be ready at about the same time.

4	teaspoons vegetable oil
4	whole green cardamom pods, lightly smashed with the flat side of a chef's knife
½	cup thinly sliced onion
I ½	cups basmati rice, well rinsed and drained
¾	teaspoon salt

1. Heat the oil in a medium saucepan over high heat until almost smoking. Add the cardamom pods and onion and cook, stirring occasionally, until the onion is translucent, 2 to 3 minutes. Stir in the rice and cook until fragrant, 1 to 2 minutes.

2. Add 2¼ cups water and the salt and bring to a boil. Reduce the heat to low, cover tightly, and simmer until all the water is absorbed, about 17 minutes. Fluff with a fork, discard the cardamom pods, and serve immediately.

Spanish-Style Braised Lentils with Sausage

THE PAIRING OF BEANS WITH CURED meat is common in many cuisines. Think Cuban black beans, split pea soup, even Boston baked beans—all have rich ham, bacon, or sausage as a prime ingredient. The beans absorb the robust flavor and stretch the meat so a small amount can feed more people. For quick one-pot meals, the pairing makes perfect sense. Fast-cooking legumes, like lentils, cook within the hour and are a perfect foil to hearty sausage. Because of the meat's assertive flavor, the dish requires few additional ingredients, which limits both preparation and shopping time. Inspired by a classic Spanish dish of green lentils flavored with paprika and *morcilla,* or blood sausage, we wanted to develop a recipe that would cook as quickly as possible and taste authentic. Morcilla is rarely available in the United States, so a less exotic sausage would have to do.

Our first step was to evaluate the traditional recipes we found and uncover where time might be trimmed in cooking and preparation. Recipes required slow simmering—that is, braising—in the oven with aromatics and sausage, a method that took hours. We didn't have this kind of time, so we opted to give the lentils a head start on the stovetop while we assembled the remaining ingredients. Then, once the lentils were almost tender, we combined all of the dish's components and finished it in the oven. This final step reduced the cooking liquid to a glossy glaze and browned the sausage, lending flavor that stovetop cooking alone could not accomplish.

Glossy green lentils du Puy were our bean choice for this dish. Their firm texture—they retain their shape better than other lentils—

and hearty flavor are ideal with sausage. For the fullest flavor, we simmered them in diluted chicken broth flavored with a bundle of fresh thyme leaves; the whole herbs imparted a great deal of flavor with no preparation required. In 20 to 25 minutes, the lentils were just shy of tender—the perfect state for finishing in the oven.

We knew the lentils needed flavor help from aromatics like onion and garlic. The traditional recipes included these as well as tomato and, after tasting, we saw no reason to alter the ingredient list. The onions and garlic gave the lentils sweetness and depth, while the tomato provided fruitiness and acidity. Our only change was to toast the garlic in olive oil to a light golden color for the roundest flavor. Once the aromatics were sautéed, we added the lentils to the skillet (its greater surface area relative to the saucepan in which the lentils were simmered made for faster cooking in the oven), and the dish was ready for the oven—with the addition of sausage, of course.

As for spices, paprika—smoked paprika, in particular—gave the dish all the punch it needed. Produced only in the Vera region of Spain, smoked paprika is made from pimiento peppers that are slowly smoked over oak prior to crushing. The flavor is intensely smoky and comes in three grades: sweet, hot, and bittersweet. Despite its localized Spanish production, smoked paprika is widely available in specialty stores and large markets. For this dish, we favored bittersweet paprika, as sweet was too mild and hot numbed the palate. For the best flavor, we found it important to toast the smoked paprika briefly in the skillet before adding liquid—the heat activates the volatile oils.

Replacing morcilla sausage was a tall order. We opted for convenience rather than authenticity and tried a wide range of readily available sausages, including chorizo, linguiça, hot and sweet Italian sausage, and kielbasa. The latter won out for its smoky, sweet flavor and compact texture. In addition, kielbasa is sold ready to eat, which meant it just needed to heat through and brown a little for flavor.

As the sausage was already cooked, the dish's stay in the oven could be fast and furious. High heat quickly reduced the cooking liquid and browned the sausage—just what we wanted. Temperatures ranging from 400 to 500 degrees all worked fine, but 475 degrees produced the most consistent results. In 10 to 15 minutes, the lentils were glossy, the cooking liquid had evaporated, and the sausage was lightly browned but still juicy.

Our final touch, though nontraditional, was to scatter thinly sliced scallions across the lentils. Tasters enjoyed the piquant scallion punch and the added visual appeal.

Spanish-Style Braised Lentils with Sausage
SERVES 4 AS A MAIN COURSE
TIME: 45 MINUTES

Search the lentils carefully for small pebbles and other detritus; lentils often have hidden grit. A white plate or bowl makes foreign objects easy to see. Smoked paprika is available from many specialty stores. Be sure to choose the bittersweet variety unless you have a penchant for very spicy food; hot smoked paprika is exactly that. You can use regular paprika if you can't find smoked; the difference is, of course, that regular paprika lacks smokiness. If you like your lentils on the mushy side, leave them in the oven for an additional 5 minutes. The dish reheats well and may even be eaten at room temperature with a drizzle of lemon juice or sherry vinegar.

I	cup lentils du Puy, picked over and rinsed
5	sprigs fresh thyme, tied into a bundle with kitchen twine
I ¾	cups canned low-sodium chicken broth
2	tablespoons extra-virgin olive oil
4	medium cloves garlic, slivered
I	medium onion, diced
	Salt
I ¼	teaspoons smoked bittersweet paprika or regular sweet paprika
I	(14½-ounce) can diced tomatoes, drained
8	ounces kielbasa, split lengthwise, then halved crosswise to yield 4 pieces
	Ground black pepper
2	medium scallions, sliced thin on the bias

1. Bring the lentils, thyme sprigs, broth, and 1½ cups water to a boil in a medium saucepan over medium-high heat. Reduce the heat to medium-low and simmer until the lentils are almost tender but still a little crunchy, 20 to 25 minutes.

2. Meanwhile, adjust an oven rack to the middle position and heat the oven to 475 degrees. Heat the olive oil and garlic in an ovenproof 12-inch skillet over medium-high heat. As the oil begins to sizzle, shake the pan gently back and forth to prevent the garlic from clumping (stirring with a spoon will cause the garlic slivers to stick together). Once the garlic turns very light golden brown, after 2 to 3 minutes, add the onion and ½ teaspoon salt and cook, stirring occasionally, until the onion softens, about 4 minutes. Add the paprika and cook until aromatic, about 1 minute. Stir in the tomatoes. (If the lentils are not ready, set the skillet aside.)

3. When the lentils are ready, add them and any liquid left in the saucepan to the skillet with the other ingredients and arrange the kielbasa, cut-side up, across the top of the pan. Set the skillet in the oven and cook until the liquid has evaporated and the lentils are soft, 10 to 12 minutes. Cool for at least 5 minutes. Discard the thyme, adjust the seasonings with salt and pepper to taste, and garnish with the scallions. Serve immediately.

CANNELLINI BEANS WITH ROASTED PEPPERS AND KALE

SOME OF THE MOST INSPIRED Mediterranean bean dishes come from Tuscany, in northern Italy. Dubbed *mangiafagiole,* or "bean eaters," by Italians from other regions, Tuscans have historically consumed tremendous amounts of legumes in numerous and ingenious combinations. One of our favorite dishes is beans and greens. Full-flavored and healthful to a fault, this one-pot meal can, with the aid of canned beans, be ready in minutes. For our version, we chose to pair cannellini beans and kale, plus jarred roasted red peppers for flavor and color.

What canned beans lack in flavor and texture they make up for in convenience. When combined with assertive flavors, as they are in this dish, they taste fine. All they need is a quick rinse to rid them of the viscous liquid that coats them, a task best accomplished by emptying the cans into a colander set in the sink and passing the beans under gently running water.

Traditionally, for a dish like this, the beans and kale would be stewed together and flavored with a slow-cooked *soffrito,* a mixture of olive oil, onions, and garlic. We knew we didn't have the time for a full-fledged soffrito, but we could sauté garlic and onions to deepen the dish. We could then add the remaining ingredients, in effect treating the dish as a sauté. Once assembled, the dish could simmer until the flavors married. We quickly identified our vessel of choice as a large skillet. A Dutch oven or saucepan would have been more conventional, but the large surface area of the skillet meant ingredients cooked quickly, liquid evaporated efficiently, and the dish was easy to monitor.

Onions and olive oil (a fairly substantial amount enriches this otherwise lean combination) were the first ingredients into the pan. We began testing with yellow onions but quickly switched to red, as their more intense sweetness better complemented the beans. Garlic was the next ingredient we tested, though it quickly replaced the onion as the first into the pan. While northern Italian dishes classically demonstrate a restrained hand with garlic, most tasters felt that, in this instance, a healthy dose was necessary to give body to the mild-tasting cannellini beans. Tasters preferred the nutty flavor of toasted garlic, which necessitated cooking it before the onion. The golden slivers also looked appealingly rustic in the final dish. Along with the garlic, we added a few hot red pepper flakes; their spiciness cut the sweetness of the beans and roasted peppers.

After the onions, we added jarred roasted red peppers (see page 11 for more information on our testing of leading brands). Like canned beans, jarred peppers are extremely convenient, and they work well in this kind of recipe. Kale, sliced into thin ribbons, was next. Kale's sturdy texture and sweet, full flavor are perfectly suited to pair with beans. Unlike more delicate greens, such as spinach, kale holds up well and retains its distinctive texture. All told, the kale simmered for about 10 minutes without any compromise in flavor, texture, or appearance.

The beans were last into the pan, in order to preserve their delicate structure. We also added white wine and water to moisten the mixture. Chicken broth muddied the flavors, but wine brought a desirable acidity that accented the sweetness of the beans and complemented the kale. The dish now became a balancing act between flavor and texture. The longer it simmered, the better the flavors but the softer the beans. After taste-testing on a minute-by-minute basis, we decided 10 minutes was enough to blend the flavors without damage to the beans.

As with most bean dishes, this mixture benefited from a hint of acidity added at the end. In this case, we chose a spritz of lemon juice, though balsamic vinegar or (nontraditional) sherry vinegar would also work well. Some tasters liked the nuttiness and extra richness provided by a dusting of Parmesan cheese, but others preferred the beans without, so we left it as an option.

Cannellini Beans with Roasted Peppers and Kale

SERVES 4 AS A MAIN COURSE,
6 TO 8 AS A SIDE DISH

TIME: 30 MINUTES

While substantial enough to serve as a main course, with a crusty loaf of bread and a salad, this recipe also works as a side dish with roasted pork, chicken, and firm fish like sea bass and cod; be sure to omit the cheese if you serve this dish with fish. If kale is unavailable, try chard. The chard stems may be included in the recipe—cut them into ¼-inch pieces and sauté the stems with the onions. Leftover beans served on bruschetta make an excellent appetizer. Most tasters liked this dish with a somewhat brothy consistency—the broth may be soaked up with bread. If you prefer a drier texture, exclude the added water. For a nonvegetarian version, add 2 ounces finely diced pancetta with the onion.

¼ cup extra-virgin olive oil, plus more for drizzling

4 medium cloves garlic, sliced thin

¼ teaspoon hot red pepper flakes

1 small red onion, sliced thin
   Salt

10 ounces jarred roasted red peppers, drained and sliced thin (about 1¼ cups)

1 pound kale, stemmed and sliced thin (about 4 heaping cups)

2 (15-ounce) cans cannellini beans, drained and rinsed

½ cup dry white wine or dry vermouth
   Ground black pepper

½ cup grated Parmesan cheese (optional)

1 lemon, cut into wedges

1. Combine the oil, garlic, and red pepper flakes in a large skillet over medium-high heat. As the oil begins to sizzle, shake the pan gently back and forth to prevent the garlic from clumping (stirring with a spoon causes the garlic slices to stick together). Once the garlic turns very light golden brown, after 2 to 3 minutes, add the onion and ¾ teaspoon salt and cook, stirring frequently, until the onion softens and begins to brown around the edges, 2 to 3 minutes. Add the peppers and cook until softened and glossy, about 3 minutes.

2. Using tongs, stir in the kale. When it wilts, add the beans, wine, and ½ cup water. Reduce the heat to medium-low, cover, and simmer until the flavors have blended, about 10 minutes. Adjust the seasonings with salt and pepper to taste. Serve in warmed bowls garnished with cheese and a drizzle of olive oil and with lemon wedges on the side.

5

PASTA AND NOODLES

FEW FOODS RIVAL PASTA IN TERMS OF either speed or convenience. Pasta is almost always on hand, it cooks in minutes, and it can serve as the basis for literally hundreds of one-dish meals. That said, many cooks (even experienced ones) have questions about preparing pasta. How much water do you need to cook a pound of pasta? Is salt necessary in the cooking water? How about oil? How thoroughly do you drain the pasta? What happens if you rinse the pasta after draining?

Many cooks tend to skimp on water for the obvious reason that the less you use, the faster it comes to a boil. To test this variable, we cooked 1 pound pasta in 2 quarts water and discovered two major problems straight off. First, the water tends to foam and boil over the pan edges. Second, the pieces of pasta are more inclined to stick together than when more water is used.

When we talked to Dr. Patricia Berglund, director of the Northern Crops Institute in Fargo, North Dakota, she explained that pasta consists primarily of starch but also contains about 10 percent protein. For dried pasta to make the change from its brittle state to a tender, toothsome noodle, the starch granules must absorb enough hot water to make them burst, thereby giving pasta its tenderness, while the small amount of protein sets up to provide the noodle with its characteristic bite. We noticed that between absorption and evaporation, 1 quart or more of water can be lost in the process of cooking 1 pound pasta. During cooking, a lot of starch also leaches into the cooking water. Without enough water to dilute the leached starch, Berglund said, the pieces of pasta are likely to stick together and the water to foam, which is precisely what we observed. Thus, we recommend you not skimp on the water—use at least 4 quarts per pound of pasta.

While ample water proved key to preventing

BUILDING BLOCK RECIPE
How to Cook Pasta
SERVES 4
TIME: 20 MINUTES

This recipe summarizes our findings about cooking dried semolina pasta. For information about cooking Asian noodles, see specific recipes later in this chapter. Refer here when cooking pasta to go with your favorite sauces. It's best to combine pasta and sauce when both are hot and fresh, so if your sauce requires long cooking, have it nearly complete when you start cooking the pasta. Many simple sauces can be cooked simultaneously with the pasta.

4	quarts water
1	tablespoon salt
1	pound dried pasta

Bring the water to a rolling boil in a 6-quart (or larger) stockpot or Dutch oven. Add the salt and pasta; stir to separate the noodles. Cover the pot and return to a boil. Remove the cover and boil the pasta, stirring frequently to keep the noodles separate. Taste for doneness 3 minutes short of the cooking time indicated on the box. If the noodles are not done, taste every 30 seconds until the pasta is just shy of al dente—that is, the noodles are tender but resist slightly more than desired (an opaque white core should be faintly visible in the noodle you bit into). If necessary for the sauce, reserve ½ cup pasta cooking water (as suggested in many recipes in this chapter); drain the pasta in a large colander for 30 seconds without shaking. Transfer the pasta to the now-empty cooking pot or to a warm serving bowl; toss with the sauce and serve immediately.

pasta from sticking, we also found (no great surprise) that frequent stirring makes a difference. It is particularly important to stir the moment the pasta goes into the water. Otherwise, pasta can get remarkably comfortable stuck to the pan bottom or nestled up against its kind. In most cases, any spoon or even a pair of tongs will do for stirring. For long noodles, like spaghetti, we found the tines of a pasta fork most effective in separating the strands. We prefer plastic or stainless-steel pasta forks; wood forks can split with use.

Of course, what many people do to prevent sticking is add oil to the boiling water. We tried this repeatedly and determined that oil definitely did not minimize pasta's sticking potential while cooking. Americans tend to fill a bowl with pasta and glop the sauce on top. Italians toss the just-cooked pasta and the sauce together. The Italian method

evenly distributes the sauce and, in effect, prevents sticking. Cooking in a large quantity of water prevents the pasta from sticking together.

As with oil, opinions vary widely about whether or not salt should be added to the cooking water. Other than contributing to flavor, salt had no discernible effect on the pasta or the cooking process itself; in fact, the small amounts of salt we added to the water never increased the boiling point (a plus suggested by several sources). As for flavor, every participating taster found the addition of 2 tablespoons salt excessive once the pasta was tossed with an already seasoned sauce. While a couple of tasters preferred 1½ teaspoons salt in the water, the overall opinion was that 1 tablespoon salt to 4 quarts water worked best to round out the pasta flavor.

Most important to the cooking process is determining when the pasta is done, or al

MATCHING PASTA SHAPES AND SAUCES

SHORT PASTAS

Short tubular or molded pasta shapes do an excellent job of trapping chunky sauces. Sauces with large chunks are best with rigatoni or other large tubes. Sauces with small chunks work best with fusilli or penne. Clockwise from top right, the shapes shown are penne, shells, farfalle, orecchiette, rigatoni, and fusilli.

STRAND PASTAS

Long strands are best with smooth sauces or sauces with very small chunks. In general, wide noodles, such as pappardelle and fettuccine, can support slightly chunkier sauces (such as pasta primavera) than can very thin noodles. Clockwise from top right, the shapes shown are fettuccine, linguine, spaghetti, capellini, and pappardelle.

INGREDIENTS: Dried Pasta

In the not-so-distant past, American pasta had a poor reputation, and rightly so. It cooked up gummy and starchy, and experts usually touted the superiority of Italian brands. We wondered if this were still the case.

To find out, we tasted eight leading brands of spaghetti—four American and four Italian. American brands took two of the three top spots, while two Italian brands landed at the bottom of the rankings. It seems American companies have mastered the art of making pasta.

American-made Ronzoni was the top finisher, with tasters praising its "nutty, buttery" flavor and superb texture. Mueller's, another American brand, took third place. Tasters liked its "clean," "wheaty" flavor.

DeCecco was the highest-scoring Italian brand, finishing second in the tasting. It cooked up "very al dente" (with a good bite) and was almost chewy. Other Italian brands did not fare quite so well. Martelli, an artisanal pasta that costs nearly $5 a pound, finished in next-to-last place, with comments like "gritty" and "mushy" predominating on tasters' score sheets. Another Italian brand, Delverde, sank to the bottom of the ratings.

Our conclusion: Save your money and don't bother with most imported pasta. American pastas are just fine. If you must serve Italian pasta in your home, stick with DeCecco.

THE BEST PASTA

Ronzoni won tasters over with its firm texture and nutty, buttery flavor.

dente. We cooked up a number of pasta types made by a variety of manufacturers and found that, overall, the cooking time given in the box instructions is too long. We also found that the old, curious trick of tossing a noodle against the wall (which applies to spaghetti or fettuccine noodles only) isn't accurate. The surefire test is simply biting into the pasta about three minutes before the package directions indicate doneness. Undercooked pasta has a clearly visible white core and is crunchy in the center. When pasta is cooked al dente, which translates as "to the tooth," it should have some bite but still be tender throughout. The white core may be just faintly visible.

While there is no exact science to determining doneness and each person has a different doneness preference, taste-testing the pasta once or twice every minute during the last few minutes of cooking helps the cook gain a better sense of when pasta is just right. The pasta will continue to soften a bit as you drain and sauce it, so pull it off the flame about 30 seconds before you think it will be perfectly cooked.

The only time you might want to rinse drained pasta is if you plan to make pasta salad. (Also, some Asian noodles are best rinsed to remove excess starch.) Rinsing flushes starch from the surface of the noodles, which causes two problems. First, starch helps the sauce adhere to the pasta; without it, the sauce can drain off and pool at the bottom of the bowl. Second, rinsing cools the noodles, which are best served hot.

Finally, some pasta aficionados warn against shaking the strainer after draining the pasta. As with the recommendation against rinsing, there is some cause for this. Shaking drains off some of the starchy moisture that helps the sauce cling to the pasta. But don't worry if by impulse you shake the strainer; it is no grave offense. We found that you lose only about 2 tablespoons liquid. (Many of our recipes suggest reserving some pasta cooking water to moisten the pasta as it is tossed with the sauce.)

We find it is important to match the sauce with the right pasta shape. A chunky sauce is better with shells or rigatoni than spaghetti because the short shapes can trap and hold pieces of the sauce, while large chunks of vegetables, for instance, just sit on top of long, thin noodles. The idea is to eat sauce and pasta in the same mouthful. The illustrations on page 121 give additional specific examples.

Once the pasta is sauced, it must be served immediately. You may want to warm the serving bowls, either with the hot cooking water or by placing them in a very low oven.

The first two-thirds of this chapter deals with Italian-style pasta, and the recipes call for dried semolina pasta. (For our tasting of major brands, see page 122.) The chapter concludes with several Asian noodle recipes. These noodles require slightly different cooking methods. Information about each type is given with the appropriate recipe.

PASTA WITH RAW TOMATO SAUCES

ONE OF THE CORNERSTONES OF Italian cooking is the ability to take a few fresh, flavorful ingredients, prepare them with minimal effort, and create simple but exceptional dishes. Raw tomato sauces typify this kind of Italian cooking. These sauces can be made in the time it takes to boil water and cook pasta. A word of wisdom, however: Making these sauces in mid-January with supermarket tomatoes will be disappointing. Only the freshest summer-ripe tomatoes are good enough for these sauces.

The most perplexing question we faced when developing recipes for raw tomato sauces was how to prepare the tomatoes. After consulting many leading Italian cookbooks, we found that opinions truly varied. Some chefs preferred to use peeled and seeded tomatoes, others called for seeded but unpeeled tomatoes, and several simply used the whole tomato—peel, seeds, and all.

With tomatoes in hand, we set out to try all possible methods. Our first test was to peel and seed the tomatoes before making the sauce. The process of peeling and seeding was time-consuming, and the results were mediocre. Some of the tomatoes we bought at the farmers' market had thin skins, and trying to peel them resulted in maiming them. Also, once peeled and added to the pasta, the tomatoes did not hold up well, providing the sauce little body.

Our next test was to seed but not peel the tomatoes, and the results were promising. With the skin left on, the tomatoes held their shape and provided the sauce with a rich presence; the tomato flavor stayed in the foreground rather than disappearing into the pasta as it did with the sauces made with peeled tomatoes. Also, scooping out the seeds was much easier than peeling and seeding.

We also tried to make our sauce with tomatoes that were neither peeled nor seeded. The sauce made in this way was clearly not what we wanted. Once the sauce sat for several minutes, it became watery, and when mixed with pasta, the high amount of liquid diluted the flavors of the pasta, making the dish bland. In the end, we opted to make our sauces with unpeeled, seeded tomatoes.

Once we had determined how to prepare the tomatoes, we focused on other flavors for our sauces. We thought olive oil should be the other main ingredient. The oil not only provides moisture but also helps coat the pasta and join the pasta and sauce together. Because these sauces are raw, extra-virgin olive oil is a vital ingredient. In addition to olive oil, we found dozens of ingredients (including herbs, cheese, hot red pepper flakes, olives, and capers) to add to these sauces for variations. As long as the ingredients are fresh and flavorful and don't require cooking, the possibilities are nearly endless.

Fusilli with Tomatoes and Fresh Mozzarella

SERVES 4

TIME: 20 MINUTES

We found the texture of the cheese in this dish is more pleasing if it softens rather than melts. Therefore, add the cheese after the tomatoes have been added and the pasta has cooled slightly. Make sure to use high-quality fresh mozzarella, not shrink-wrapped cheese, in this recipe. See the illustrations on page 125 for tips on seeding tomatoes.

	Salt
I	pound fusilli
I ½	pounds ripe tomatoes, halved, seeded, and cut into ½-inch dice
3	medium scallions, sliced thin
¼	cup extra-virgin olive oil
	Ground black pepper
7	ounces fresh mozzarella cheese, cut into ½-inch cubes

1. Bring 4 quarts water to a rolling boil in a large pot. Add 1 tablespoon salt and the pasta, stir to separate, and cook until al dente. Drain the pasta and return it to the cooking pot.

2. Meanwhile, mix the tomatoes, scallions, oil, ¼ teaspoon pepper, and ½ teaspoon salt in a medium bowl. Add the tomato mixture to the pot with the pasta and mix to combine. Add the mozzarella and toss to combine. Adjust the seasonings with salt and pepper to taste. Serve immediately.

Farfalle with Tomatoes, Feta, and Mint

SERVES 4

TIME: 20 MINUTES

Adding the feta at the same time as the tomatoes will cause it to melt slightly, so, as with the mozzarella, we found it best to add the cheese after the tomatoes—that is, once the pasta has cooled slightly.

	Salt
I	pound farfalle
I ½	pounds ripe tomatoes, halved, seeded, and cut into ½-inch dice
I	tablespoon chopped fresh mint leaves
¼	cup extra-virgin olive oil
½	cup kalamata olives, pitted and roughly chopped
	Ground black pepper
6	ounces feta cheese, crumbled

CORING FENNEL

Fennel bulbs contain a hard core that should be removed when using the fennel raw in a pasta sauce. Cut the trimmed bulb in half through the base; then, use a paring knife to cut out the pyramid-shaped piece of the core in each half. The fennel can now be sliced thin.

MAKING PARMESAN SHAVINGS

Run a sharp vegetable peeler along the length of a piece of Parmesan cheese to remove paper-thin curls.

1. Bring 4 quarts water to a rolling boil in a large pot. Add 1 tablespoon salt and the pasta, stir to separate, and cook until al dente. Drain the pasta and return it to the cooking pot.

2. Meanwhile, mix the tomatoes, mint, oil, olives, ¼ teaspoon pepper, and ½ teaspoon salt in a medium bowl. Add the tomato mixture to the pot with the pasta and mix to combine. Add the feta and toss to combine. Adjust the seasonings with salt and pepper to taste. Serve immediately.

Orecchiette with Tomatoes, Fennel, and Parmesan

SERVES 4

TIME: 20 MINUTES

If you don't have ear-shaped orecchiette on hand, shells are a good substitute. See the illustration on page 124 for tips on coring the fennel.

> Salt
> 1   pound orecchiette

1 ½   pounds ripe tomatoes, halved, seeded, and cut into ½-inch dice

1   small bulb fennel, fronds and stems removed, bulb halved, cored, and sliced thin (about 1 ½ cups)

¼   cup extra-virgin olive oil

¼   cup chopped fresh basil leaves
    Ground black pepper

2   ounces Parmesan cheese, cut into thin shavings (see the illustration on page 124)

1. Bring 4 quarts water to a rolling boil in a large pot. Add 1 tablespoon salt and the pasta, stir to separate, and cook until al dente. Drain the pasta and return it to the cooking pot.

2. Meanwhile, mix the tomatoes, fennel, oil, basil, ¼ teaspoon pepper, and ½ teaspoon salt in a medium bowl. Add the tomato mixture to the pot with the pasta and mix to combine. Adjust the seasonings with salt and pepper to taste. Serve immediately, garnishing each bowl with shaved Parmesan.

SEEDING TOMATOES

Because of their different shapes, round and plum (also called Roma) tomatoes are seeded differently.

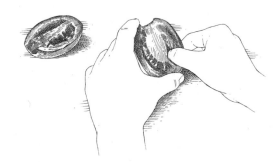

ROUND TOMATOES

Halve the cored tomato along its equator. Gently squeeze each half and shake out the seeds and gelatinous material. Use your finger to scoop out any seeds that remain.

PLUM TOMATOES

Halve the cored tomato lengthwise, cutting through the core end. Scoop out the seeds and gelatinous material with your finger.

PASTA WITH SAUTÉED CHERRY TOMATOES AND SUMMER SQUASH

THE COMBINATION OF SUMMER SQUASH and tomatoes epitomizes summer. The mild flavor and firm texture of the squash mixed with the sweet-acidic tomatoes is appealing. Added to pasta, this duo makes a fresh and easy dinner. Unless it is properly prepared, however, this dish may be nothing more than a watery, flavorless mess.

Wondering what types of recipes we would find combining these two summery ingredients, we did a little bit of research. The majority of the recipes called for simply sautéing summer squash and tomatoes, then tossing the two with pasta. Sounds easy enough, and it was, but the results were not good. Most of the recipes were bland and textureless.

First, we focused on the squash. This vegetable is almost entirely water, so its tendency to release this moisture when cooked is not surprising. Even when sautéed, squash inevitably ends up steaming in its own moisture. We had the idea to salt the squash before we sautéed it. We figured that by salting the squash, we could rid it of some of its moisture. We also decided to increase the temperature at which we cooked the squash in hopes of evaporating the liquid in the pan rapidly. These two techniques worked well. We no longer had the problem of limp, bland squash. In fact, we were able to brown the squash and develop a slight charred flavor similar to grilled squash.

The tomatoes in the recipes we tested suffered a similar fate. When sautéed, they too diluted the pasta. We considered adding the tomatoes raw to the dish, but tasters felt the slightly cooked tomatoes had a more intense flavor. We also tried peeling and seeding the tomatoes to reduce the water problem, but this work was to no avail. Our next thought was to try different tomatoes. We gathered several varieties, including plum tomatoes and cherry tomatoes. The plum tomatoes, which tend to have less moisture than globe tomatoes, certainly worked better, but still they were too watery. The cherry tomatoes, however, were a success. Added at the end of the cooking process and quickly sautéed over a hot flame, they added a burst of flavor without releasing too much moisture. We finished this simple sauce with an abundant amount of basil and grated Parmesan.

Farfalle with Sautéed Cherry Tomatoes and Summer Squash

SERVES 4

TIME: 30 MINUTES

Although this recipe can be prepared any time of year, it is best in the summer months. To save time, heat the pasta water and salt the zucchini before beginning to prepare the other ingredients. Orecchiette can be substituted for the farfalle.

1	medium zucchini or summer squash, halved lengthwise and cut crosswise into ¼-inch-thick half-circles
	Salt
2	tablespoons extra-virgin olive oil
1	small onion, minced
1	pint cherry tomatoes, halved
2	medium cloves garlic, minced or pressed through a press
¼	cup minced fresh basil leaves
	Ground black pepper
1	pound farfalle
¼	cup grated Parmesan cheese

1. Bring 4 quarts water to a rolling boil in a large pot for cooking the pasta.

2. Spread the zucchini on several layers of paper towels, sprinkle with 1 teaspoon salt, and allow to stand for 10 minutes.

3. Heat 1 tablespoon oil in a large nonstick skillet over medium-high heat until just smoking. Add the zucchini and cook until golden brown and slightly charred, 5 to 7 minutes. Transfer the zucchini to a clean bowl.

4. Return the pan to medium heat and add the remaining 1 tablespoon oil. Add the onion and cook until lightly browned and softened, about 5 minutes. Increase the heat to high, stir in the tomatoes and garlic, and cook briefly to heat through, about 1 minute. Remove the pan from the heat and add the basil and pepper to taste.

5. Soon after you start to cook the zucchini, add 1 tablespoon salt and the pasta to the boiling water. Stir to separate, then cook until al dente. Drain the pasta and return it to the cooking pot. Add the tomato mixture, zucchini, and cheese and toss to combine. Adjust the seasonings with salt and pepper to taste. Serve immediately.

PASTA WITH RICOTTA

CREAMY, SLIGHTLY SWEET RICOTTA makes a wonderful background for many flavors. We wanted to develop a pasta recipe that highlighted these desirable traits. Ricotta, peas, and prosciutto are a familiar combination in Italian cooking, and we liked the ease of this appealing trio. When we tried several recipes, tasters liked the overall flavors but complained the dish wasn't creamy and rich enough.

We tackled the issue of the pasta sauce first. Most recipes simply added ricotta in small bits to the bowl of hot drained pasta. This method did not work well. Although the cheese melted slightly, it failed to coat the entire quantity of pasta in a consistent or pleasing fashion. In fact, the graininess of the ricotta stood out, making for a strange overall texture. A few recipes suggested whisking the ricotta with a small amount of reserved pasta cooking water before mixing it with the pasta. This technique was a success. The hot water smoothed out the graininess of the ricotta and made a lovely uniform coating for our pasta. However, the water tended to make the ricotta bland, so we searched for a flavor booster. We decided to add Parmesan to the mixture; thus, we regained some flavor and added a pleasant nuttiness.

We next turned to the prosciutto. While we liked the flavor of the prosciutto in the dish generally, some tasters felt its texture was bothersome. Raw prosciutto is silky, but warm prosciutto can be slightly rubbery and chewy. We tried cutting it into smaller pieces, but we felt it didn't impart enough flavor that way. We then considered using the prosciutto in a manner more along the lines of bacon or pancetta. We hoped we could cook the prosciutto in a little oil, crisping its texture and rendering some of its fat. We would then sauté onion and garlic in the remaining oil. This technique turned out to be the best option. By sautéing the aromatics in the rendered fat from the prosciutto, we retained the salty meatiness we liked in previous tests but avoided the texture problems. Topping the completed dish with crispy bits of prosciutto provided welcome textural contrast.

We hoped to cook the peas in the same water as the pasta. To that end, we added frozen peas shortly before the pasta was al dente. This worked perfectly. We tested fresh peas as well, but their timing was more variable, and tasters preferred the consistently sweet flavor of the frozen peas.

127

Shells with Ricotta, Peas, and Prosciutto

SERVES 4

TIME: 25 MINUTES

It pays to use a high-quality ricotta rather than a watery supermarket brand. Look for fresh, creamy (not curdy) ricotta at an Italian grocer, gourmet market, or specialty cheese shop. This dish calls for a lot of black pepper, but the heat works well with the mild, creamy cheese. You can use penne in place of the shells.

1	cup whole-milk ricotta
1/2	cup grated Parmesan cheese
2	tablespoons unsalted butter, cut into 8 pieces
	Salt and ground black pepper
1	tablespoon extra-virgin olive oil
1/4	pound thinly sliced prosciutto, cut into 1/4-inch strips
1	medium onion, chopped fine
2	medium cloves garlic, minced or pressed through a garlic press (about 2 teaspoons)
1	pound small shells
2	cups frozen peas
1	tablespoon juice from 1 lemon

1. Bring 4 quarts water to a rolling boil in a large pot for cooking the pasta.

2. Place the ricotta, Parmesan, butter, 1/4 teaspoon salt, and 1/2 teaspoon pepper in a bowl large enough to hold the cooked pasta and set it aside.

3. Heat the oil and prosciutto in a medium nonstick skillet over medium-high heat, stirring occasionally, until the prosciutto is well browned and crisp, 4 to 5 minutes. Using a slotted spoon, transfer the prosciutto to a paper towel–lined plate. Add the onion to the empty pan, reduce the heat to medium, and cook until lightly golden, about 3 minutes. Add the garlic and continue to cook until fragrant, about 1 minute. Transfer the onion mixture to the bowl with the ricotta mixture.

4. Meanwhile, add 1 tablespoon salt and the pasta to the boiling water and stir to separate. When the pasta is about 1 minute shy of al dente, add the peas and continue to cook until the peas are warmed through and the pasta is al dente. Reserving 1 cup cooking water, drain the pasta and peas. Add 1/2 cup reserved cooking water and the lemon juice to the ricotta mixture and whisk until smooth. Add the pasta and peas to the bowl and toss to coat, adding more reserved cooking water as necessary to moisten the pasta. Adjust the seasonings with salt and pepper to taste. Serve immediately, garnishing each portion with crisp prosciutto.

PASTA WITH BUTTERNUT SQUASH AND THYME

THE SWEET, SMOOTH FLESH OF WINTER squash pairs well with the toothsome bite of pasta. Considering that winter squashes require a longer cooking time than their summer cousins do, we wondered if it was possible to include them in our quick-cooking repertoire.

Our major concern as we developed this recipe was how to cook the squash. In past recipes, we've preferred to peel and dice squash, then roast it. While roasting brings out the squash's natural sweetness, we felt preheating the oven and roasting was too time-consuming, and the flavor benefits were questionable in a pasta sauce.

We tried simmering the squash in a separate pot. This did not produce a favorable result; the squash was bland and soggy, and when added to the pasta it disintegrated. Our next thought was to steam the squash in the pan and build the other flavors of the sauce around it. We started by softening onions in a sauté pan, after which we added the squash, chicken broth, and thyme. We covered the pan and allowed the squash to steam for several minutes. This method resulted in a good sauce with full flavor. The high heat of the steam cooked the squash in no time at all, and the chicken broth added a little richness to the dish. This method also allowed all the flavors to blend so we didn't end up with a watered-down sauce.

We next turned to brightening the flavors and adding contrasting texture. Tasters repeatedly observed that the combination of the squash and pasta lacked textural contrast; in other words, the dish needed crunch. Nuts seemed a logical solution to this problem. Slivered almonds beat out hazelnuts, with their mild flavor complementing the sweet squash. Almonds could also be toasted in the sauté pan for several minutes before we made the sauce.

RESERVING PASTA COOKING WATER

Many recipes suggest reserving some of the pasta cooking water to help spread the sauce evenly over the noodles. However, in that last flurry of activity before saucing the pasta, it's easy to forget to save a bit of the pasta cooking water. To make sure you always have pasta cooking water when you need it, set up the colander in the sink and place a measuring cup inside the colander. The cup will nudge your memory to scoop out some cooking water before draining the pasta.

We were nearly done, but a few tasters felt the sauce still lacked depth. Because its flavors were slightly rich and sweet, we figured that additional acidity would brighten them. A small amount of lemon juice intensified the other flavors in the dish.

Gemelli with Butternut Squash and Thyme
SERVES 4
TIME: 25 MINUTES

We like the twisted corkscrew shape of gemelli, but penne works as well in this recipe. You will need about half a butternut squash. Even the best chef's knife can struggle with the thick skin and odd shape of this squash. See the illustrations on page 130 for a tip on using a cleaver and mallet to halve winter squash. A heavy-duty vegetable peeler is the best tool for removing its thick skin.

½	cup slivered almonds
1	tablespoon extra-virgin olive oil
½	medium onion, chopped fine
1½	pounds butternut squash, peeled, seeded, and cut into ½-inch dice
1	tablespoon chopped fresh thyme leaves
¾	cup canned low-sodium chicken broth
	Salt
1	pound gemelli
2	tablespoons chopped fresh parsley leaves
½	cup grated Parmesan cheese, plus more for the table
1	tablespoon juice from 1 lemon
	Ground black pepper

1. Bring 4 quarts water to a rolling boil in a large pot for cooking the pasta.

2. Place the almonds in a large skillet and set over medium-high heat. Toast, stirring often, until the almonds are fragrant and lightly browned, about 3 minutes. Transfer the toasted nuts to a small plate.

3. Return the pan to medium-high heat, add the oil, and heat until the oil is shimmering but not smoking. Add the onion and cook until just softened, about 3 minutes. Add the squash, thyme, and broth; reduce the heat to medium and cover. Cook until the squash is tender but retains its shape, 4 to 5 minutes.

4. Meanwhile, add 1 tablespoon salt and the pasta to the boiling water, stir to separate, then cook until al dente. Reserving 1 cup cooking water, drain the pasta and return it to

HALVING A BUTTERNUT SQUASH

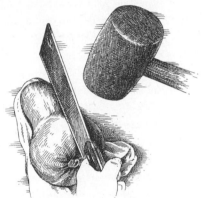

1. Set the squash on a damp kitchen towel to hold it in place. Position the cleaver on the skin of the squash.

2. Strike the back of the cleaver with a mallet to drive the blade deep into the squash. Continue to hit the cleaver with the mallet until the cleaver cuts through the squash and opens it up.

the cooking pot. Add the squash mixture, parsley, Parmesan, lemon juice, and ½ cup reserved cooking water. Mix until combined, adding more cooking water as necessary to moisten the pasta. Adjust the seasonings with salt and pepper to taste. Serve immediately, passing more cheese separately.

PASTA WITH BROCCOLI RABE AND SAUSAGE

SOUTHERN ITALY IS BEST KNOWN FOR its pasta dishes. One of these renowned dishes is the combination of broccoli rabe and orecchiette, which loosely translates as "little ears." With the addition of sausage, this pasta dish from Puglia, in the heel of the Italy boot, quickly makes a satisfying meal.

A search of Italian cookbooks turned up a number of recipes for orecchiette and broccoli rabe. After several tests, we identified a number of problems with these recipes. The first was that they used three pans to cook a dish with just a handful of ingredients. The second was that the sauces were bland and the pasta dry. We wanted to rectify these problems and streamline the cooking process without sacrificing flavor.

The first issue we tackled was the cooking procedure. Most recipes call for blanching the broccoli rabe in one pot, sautéing the sausage in another pan, and finally cooking the pasta in a third pot. Thinking we could eliminate the pot in which the rabe was blanched, we tried several cooking methods. Our first thought was to add the rabe directly to the pot with the pasta. While this worked, we found it hard to judge the proper time to put the rabe into the pot so that both it and the pasta would be done at the same time. The other method we tried was to cook the rabe in the pan in which we cooked the sausage. We first tried to sauté the rabe in the hot pan along with the sausage, but this did not work. Some of the rabe was fully cooked while other pieces were still underdone. It was obvious that the rabe required moist-heat cooking, like steaming, rather than dry heat, like sautéing. So we tried adding a small amount of liquid to the hot pan after we browned the sausage. Because the pan was quite hot, it created a fair amount of steam. By covering the pan, we captured this steam to cook the rabe. This method of pan-steaming turned out to be the solution. We eliminated the extra pot and still had consistently cooked pasta and rabe.

Now that we had mastered a cooking method for the rabe, we focused on the blandness problem. The blanching of the rabe in previous tests resulted in loss of flavor, and our new cooking method seemed to alleviate this problem, but not fully. We therefore decided to steam the rabe in chicken broth rather than water. This did the trick. As the broth reduced, it added richness and depth to the dish. In addition, it moistened the pasta and eliminated the last problem we had encountered.

Orecchiette with Broccoli Rabe and Sausage

SERVES 4

TIME: 20 MINUTES

If you prefer to use broccoli instead of broccoli rabe in this recipe, use 2 pounds broccoli cut into 1-inch florets and increase the cooking time by several minutes. If you prefer a less spicy dish, use sweet Italian sausage.

> Salt
>
> 1 pound orecchiette
>
> 8 ounces hot Italian sausage, casings removed
>
> 6 medium cloves garlic, minced or pressed through a garlic press (2 tablespoons)
>
> ½ teaspoon hot red pepper flakes
>
> 1 bunch broccoli rabe (about 1 pound), trimmed and cut into 1½-inch lengths (see the illustrations below)
>
> ½ cup canned low-sodium chicken broth
>
> 1 tablespoon extra-virgin olive oil
>
> ½ cup grated Parmesan cheese

1. Bring 4 quarts water to a rolling boil in a large pot. Add 1 tablespoon salt and the

PREPARING BROCCOLI RABE

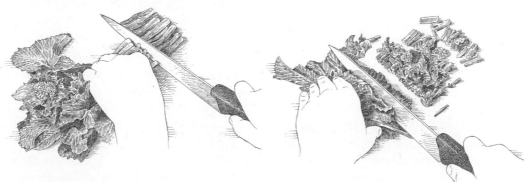

1. The thick stalk ends of broccoli rabe should be trimmed and discarded. Use a sharp knife to cut off the thickest part (usually the bottom 2 inches) of each stalk.

2. Cut the remaining stalks and florets into bite-size pieces about 1½ inches long.

pasta, stir to separate, and cook until al dente. Drain and return the pasta to the pot.

2. While the pasta is cooking, cook the sausage until browned in a large nonstick skillet over medium-high heat, breaking it into ½-inch pieces with a wooden spoon, about 3 minutes. Stir in the garlic, red pepper flakes, and ½ teaspoon salt. Cook, stirring constantly, until the garlic is fragrant and slightly toasted, about 1½ minutes. Add the broccoli rabe and broth, cover, and cook until the broccoli rabe turns bright green, 2 minutes. Uncover and cook, stirring frequently, until most of the broth has evaporated and the broccoli rabe is tender, 2 to 3 minutes.

3. Add the sausage-rabe mixture, oil, and cheese to the pot with the pasta and toss to combine. Serve immediately.

PASTA WITH LENTILS

THE COMBINATION OF LENTILS AND pasta may seem strange to many Americans, but it is commonplace in Italy. The earthy, smoky undertones of the lentils are a perfect foil for mild pasta. Enhanced with vegetables, this dish makes a satisfying, quick vegetarian meal. Arriving at an intensely flavored sauce with pleasing texture, however, proved harder than we expected.

Our initial focus was on the lentils. What type should we use, and how should we cook it? Looking back on past experiences, we favored the small green French lentils, commonly called lentils du Puy, for both their flavor and texture. We cooked several batches of green lentils and mixed them with pasta. We found the lentils were so small in relation to the pasta that they got lost, contributing little flavor to the dish. Tasters also felt the overall dish was dry and lacked texture.

The reason why we've liked green lentils in

the past is that they hold their shape when cooked. In this case, however, we thought we might prefer to have the lentils cooked down a little and thicken the sauce. We tried the more common brown lentils, and the results were more in line with what we were looking for. By the time the lentils were fully cooked and tender, some had started to lose their seed coat, causing them to disintegrate slightly. In breaking down, they gave the pasta sauce body and flavor. But the overall dish still lacked intense flavor.

Until this point, we had been cooking lentils with lightly sautéed vegetables and water and simmering them until tender. Then we drained any excess liquid from the lentils and tossed them with cooked pasta. We assumed that if we used chicken broth instead of water in this process, we would have a much more flavorful result. While flavor did increase slightly, however, the broth didn't make a large difference. Also, the broth changed a previously vegetarian dish into a nonvegetarian one. Next, we tried using both red wine and water to cook the lentils. We knew something was amiss when after 25 minutes the lentils were still tough and chalky. It turned out the acidity of the wine prevented the lentils from absorbing water and thereby cooking through. The one good result of this test was that tasters liked the flavor of the wine, feeling it accented the earthiness of the lentils and added depth to the dish. We therefore added several tablespoons of wine to the fully cooked lentils, achieving the same flavor without affecting their cooking time.

It occurred to us that by cooking the lentils in a large amount of water and dumping the cooking water, we might be pouring flavor down the drain. Experimenting with the ratio of water to lentils, we learned that 2 cups water and ½ cup lentils yielded fully cooked lentils and enough remaining moisture to coat the pasta. We also found this increased flavor, but we wanted more. Knowing we could extract more flavor from the vegetables, we sautéed them in butter instead of oil, and we also lightly browned the vegetables. This slight alteration had a significant impact on the flavor. The browned vegetables added sweetness, and the butter added richness. Our final ingredient was a piece of Parmesan rind. This might seem a strange addition, but the degree of flavor it imparts is surprising. Simmered with the rind, the lentils pick up the salty, tangy richness of the Parmesan.

Campanelle with Lentils

SERVES 4

TIME: 50 MINUTES

Campanelle, also called gigli, are small pieces of pasta shaped like trumpets with ruffled edges. If you cannot find this type of pasta, any small pasta, such as orecchiette, cavatelli, or shells, will work in this recipe. To ensure the lentils don't become chalky and tough, cook them fully before adding the red wine.

2	tablespoons unsalted butter
1	medium onion, cut into ¼-inch dice (about 1 cup)
2	medium carrots, peeled and cut into ¼-inch dice (about 1 cup)
1	stalk celery, cut into ¼-inch dice (about ½ cup)
½	cup brown lentils, picked over and rinsed
1	small piece Parmesan rind (about 2 by 2 inches)
	Salt
3	tablespoons red wine
1	pound campanelle or other small pasta shape
¼	cup chopped fresh parsley leaves
	Ground black pepper
	Grated Parmesan cheese

1. Heat the butter in a medium saucepan over medium-high heat. When the foaming subsides, add the onion, carrots, and celery and cook, stirring occasionally, until the vegetables are lightly browned, about 4 minutes. Add the lentils, 2 cups water, Parmesan rind, and 1 teaspoon salt. Cover and simmer until the lentils are fully cooked and tender, 20 to 25 minutes. Add the wine and simmer for an additional minute. Set the lentil mixture aside.

2. Meanwhile, bring 4 quarts water to a rolling boil in a large pot. Add 1 tablespoon salt and the pasta, stir to separate, and cook until al dente. Reserving ¼ cup cooking water, drain the pasta and return it to the cooking pot. Toss the pasta with the lentils, the reserved cooking water, and the parsley. Season with salt and pepper to taste. Serve immediately, passing the grated cheese separately.

PASTA WITH WHITE BEANS AND GREENS

THE IDEA OF PASTA AND BEANS MIGHT lead you to expect an overly starchy dish, but as it happens, the combination of creamy beans and al dente pasta is wonderful. When you add just a bit of fresh greens, the dish turns into an Italian classic.

While you would normally start preparing this dish by cooking dried white beans, this approach doesn't make sense in a quick recipe. Our goal was to develop a recipe using canned beans that nevertheless had as much flavor as possible. A number of recipes we gathered called for rendering bacon or pancetta before adding the beans and aromatics to the pasta, so we tried both to see what would happen. Both bacon and pancetta added a tremendous amount of flavor to the finished dish, and their salty meatiness complemented the white beans. However, we found the smokiness of the American bacon overpowered the other ingredients, so we opted for the milder pancetta for this recipe.

Simply sautéing the beans in the fat from the rendered pancetta, however, didn't provide enough flavor. When we mixed the beans with the pasta, the overall dish was dry and the pasta bland. Even adding reserved pasta water didn't help. Wanting to build a more flavorful sauce, we added chicken broth to the beans while they were cooking. In addition, as the beans cooked, we pressed some of the beans against the side of the pan, thickening the sauce. This technique proved successful, yielding a creamy sauce that coated the pasta and evenly distributed the flavor of the beans. A squeeze of lemon juice helped cut some of the richness of the beans and pancetta.

Many types of greens held promise for rounding out this dish. The recipes we consulted called for kale, spinach, escarole, and arugula. Because we wanted to keep preparation simple, we wanted to add the greens to the pasta at the end of the cooking process to avoid another cooking step. As it turned out, this technique cooked the greens with the residual heat of the dish, wilting them slightly while retaining a slight crunch. This efficient approach quickly ruled out greens that required prolonged cooking, such as kale and escarole. We tried spinach and arugula, and arugula was, hands down, the preferred choice. Favored for its peppery bite, the arugula added more flavor to the dish than spinach.

Penne with White Beans, Pancetta, and Arugula

SERVES 4

TIME: 20 MINUTES

Any short, stubby pasta like penne will work well in this dish. Remove any thick stems from the arugula. *The residual heat of the pasta and the sauce will wilt tender arugula leaves, but thick stems will remain too crunchy.*

Salt and ground black pepper
1 pound penne
1 tablespoon extra-virgin olive oil
3 ounces pancetta, chopped fine
1 medium onion, chopped fine
3 medium cloves garlic, minced or pressed through a garlic press (about 1 tablespoon)
1 (19-ounce) can cannellini beans, drained and rinsed
3/4 cup canned low-sodium chicken broth
1 large bunch arugula, washed and dried (about 5 cups)
1 tablespoon juice from 1 lemon
Grated Parmesan cheese

1. Bring 4 quarts water to a rolling boil in a large pot. Add 1 tablespoon salt and the pasta, stir to separate, and cook until al dente. Reserving 1/2 cup cooking water, drain the pasta and return it to the cooking pot.

2. Meanwhile, heat the oil and pancetta in a large skillet over medium-high heat. Cook, stirring occasionally, until the pancetta renders its fat and browns, 3 to 4 minutes. Reduce the heat to medium, add the onion, and cook until softened, about 4 minutes. Add the garlic and cook until fragrant, 30 seconds. Add the beans, broth, and 1/2 teaspoon salt. Simmer until the beans are heated through, about 3 minutes. As the beans are simmering, press some against the sides of the pan with the back of a spoon until the sauce thickens.

3. Add the bean mixture, arugula, lemon juice, and reserved cooking water to the pasta. Stir until the arugula wilts and the ingredients are well mixed. Adjust the seasonings with salt and pepper. Serve immediately, passing the grated cheese separately.

PASTA WITH MUSSELS

AFTER SALMON, MUSSELS ARE PROBABLY aquaculture's most successful crop. Despite this success, Americans have been slow to warm to mussels, perhaps fearing they will be gritty. But this is not the case. Aquafarmers have learned to grow these bivalves suspended from ropes so many of their unpleasant traits are things of the past. Go to any supermarket or fishmonger and you'll find mesh bags of clean, grit-free mussels.

For the purposes of quick cooking, mussels are a particularly attractive ingredient. They take very little time to cook—about 6 minutes—and their briny mildness melds well with other flavors. The question was what ingredients would best pair with our mussels. Thinking the combination of mussels and pasta seemed Mediterranean, we decided to try fennel as an aromatic addition.

A main goal was to restrict the cooking of the mussels to one pot. Because the liquid the mussels shed as they cook would be invaluable to the flavor of the dish, we did not want to lose any of it. The first question, then, was in what liquid do we steam the mussels? We tried wine, water, and clam juice. White wine was the clear winner. Tasters felt its crispness and acidity complemented the mussels perfectly, while the water and clam juice tasted flat. Next in the procedure, we softened fennel in oil, added the mussels and wine, covered the pan, and allowed the mussels to steam open. We added the pasta to finish. Unfortunately, the result was disappointing. The flavors seemed a little flat, and because the sauce was watery, the mussels and pasta seemed disconnected.

To avoid the watery sauce problem, we tried steaming the mussels beforehand, removing them from the pan, and reducing the liquid to concentrate flavors and limit the amount of liquid we added to the pasta. This worked better, but it didn't solve the problem completely. Believing that if we added body to the sauce we could avoid the issue altogether, we decided to add a can of tomatoes to the pan before we steamed the mussels. This did the trick. By making the sauce more substantial from the outset, the sauce and pasta were more easily combined.

Unfortunately, adding the tomatoes to the dish masked the fennel's flavor to the point where the only reminder of its presence was its crunch. Trying to increase the fennel's potency, we doubled the amount. The increase in flavor, however, was marginal. Our next option was to use an anise-flavored liquor, like ouzo or Pernod. Although both brought out the anise flavor, tasters disliked the hint of sweetness they added to the sauce. When we considered that most people don't have either liquor on hand, keeping them on our ingredient list did not seem appropriate. Our last thought was to add a healthy dose of chopped tarragon right before serving. The result was

DEBEARDING MUSSELS

A weedy beard often protrudes from the crack between the mussel shells. It's fairly small and can be difficult to tug out. To remove it easily, trap the beard between the side of a small knife and your thumb and pull. The flat surface of a paring knife gives you leverage to remove the beard.

exactly what we wanted. The tarragon added a vibrant anise flavor that brought out the fennel and gave the dish a burst of freshness. A pinch of hot red pepper flakes also enlivened the flavor and finished this recipe.

Linguine with Mussels and Fennel

SERVES 4

TIME: 30 MINUTES

Look closely at the package before you buy mussels. We found that farmed mussels grown on ropes suspended in the water are the best bet for this recipe. They have little or no grit compared with wild mussels and mussels cultivated along the ground, so you don't have to worry about straining the sauce. When cleaning the mussels, throw out any that won't close or have broken shells. Start cooking the pasta right before the mussels go into the sauce.

3	tablespoons extra-virgin olive oil
½	medium onion, chopped fine
l	medium fennel bulb, chopped fine (about l cup)
½	cup white wine
l	(28-ounce) can diced tomatoes in juice
½	teaspoon hot red pepper flakes
2	pounds mussels, scrubbed and debearded (see the illustration on page 135)
	Salt
l	pound linguine
2	tablespoons chopped fresh tarragon leaves

1. Bring 4 quarts water to a rolling boil in a large pot for cooking the pasta.

2. Heat 2 tablespoons oil in a large Dutch oven over medium heat until shimmering but not smoking. Add the onion and fennel and cook until slightly softened, 5 minutes. Add the wine and tomatoes, including their juice, and the red pepper flakes. Simmer until the sauce reduces slightly, about 10 minutes. Add the mussels, cover, and steam until they are fully open, 6 to 7 minutes. With a slotted spoon, transfer the mussels to a bowl and cover to keep them warm.

3. Just before the mussels go into the sauce, add 1 tablespoon salt and the pasta to the boiling water. Stir to separate the pasta and cook until al dente. Reserving ¼ cup cooking water, drain the pasta and transfer it to the pot with the sauce. Toss with the remaining 1 tablespoon oil and tarragon, moistening the pasta as needed with the reserved cooking water. Adjust the seasonings with salt to taste. Divide the pasta among individual bowls and top with the mussels. Serve immediately.

GNOCCHI WITH SWISS CHARD

POTATO GNOCCHI ARE ITALIAN COMFORT food. Simple and satisfying gnocchi are something to look forward to on a cold winter night—but could they be included in a collection of quick recipes? Until recently, we thought not.

Gnocchi in some form have been around for centuries, tracing their lineage back to the Renaissance, when they were nothing more than wheat flour dumplings served in broth. Over the years, the broth disappeared and the base of the gnocchi changed from flour (or semolina) to potato. Today, gnocchi are flavored with a range of ingredients, including spinach, tomatoes, squash, and porcini mushrooms. Regardless of their flavorings, gnocchi shouldn't be the chewy, leaden plugs that, unfortunately, are often served in bad Italian-American restaurants. They should be light and airy, with the rich flavor of potato.

Recently we noticed several new types of gnocchi available at supermarkets. We wondered if it was possible to use one of them and avoid the hours it takes to make gnocchi by hand. Although we found that none of these convenience products can rival freshly prepared gnocchi, several were surprisingly good, especially considering that they require no more effort to cook than dried pasta.

We tested three types of gnocchi sold in supermarkets: frozen, fresh in the refrigerated section, and dry in vacuum-sealed packages in the pasta aisle. We prepared several batches of each with a simple sauce to find out which one was preferable. The frozen gnocchi did not fare well. They were heavy, dense, flavorless balls; moreover, some of them developed a slimy coating, a characteristic tasters universally loathed. The fresh gnocchi from the refrigerator case weren't much better. They had a strange springy quality and never seemed to become properly tender. They also did not have much potato flavor. Given these poor results, we were pleasantly surprised by the vacuum-packed gnocchi sold with the dried pasta. These gnocchi were much lighter than the other choices and had a decidedly more intense potato flavor. They also didn't have the artificial texture of the frozen and fresh varieties.

Now that we had found an alternative to freshly made gnocchi, we concerned ourselves with the sauce. Although tomato sauce and dairy-based sauce with butter or cream are options, we wanted something lighter that would complement the delicate potato flavor of the gnocchi without overwhelming it.

In a previous test, tasters had responded positively to spinach, stating that the earthiness of the greens complemented the gnocchi. Making several sauces using spinach, we ran into problems. Simply adding sautéed spinach to the gnocchi proved uninteresting, and the water content of the spinach made the dish bland. Adding a little stock to the sauce also

didn't work because the spinach overcooked and became slightly slimy. We thus turned to other leafy greens that might be good substitutes for spinach.

We immediately thought of Swiss chard, which we hoped would respond better to cooking and provide more flavor than the spinach. Our hunch was right. Because chard is more substantial than spinach, it didn't cook down as much and thus gave the final dish substantially more body and flavor. Another advantage of chard was that we were able to use the stems as well as the leaves. In addition to deepening the flavors of the dish, the stems provided a pleasing crunch that contrasted well with the tender gnocchi.

Considering our ongoing problems with watery sauces, we decided to sauté the chard in a hot pan before building the sauce instead of adding the raw greens in at the end. Once the chard was tender, we transferred it to a colander and squeezed out the excess moisture. We then built the sauce in the empty pan and returned the dried chard to it at the last minute.

SEPARATING CHARD STEMS AND LEAVES

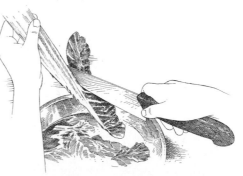

Hold each leaf at the base of the stem over a bowl filled with water. Use a sharp knife to slash the leafy portion from either side of the thick stem. The cutting motion here is the same you would use with a machete. This technique also works well with kale and mustard greens.

Gnocchi with Swiss Chard

SERVES 4

TIME: 20 MINUTES

We tried several brands of vacuum-packed gnocchi and found that Delverde tasted most like home-made. See the illustration on page 137 for tips on handling chard.

3	tablespoons extra-virgin olive oil
2	medium cloves garlic, minced or pressed through a garlic press (about 2 teaspoons)
1	pound Swiss chard, stems removed, washed, and cut into ¼-inch pieces; leaves washed, dried, and torn into large pieces (keep stems and leaves separate)
	Salt
1	large shallot, minced
1	cup canned low-sodium chicken broth
3	tablespoons unsalted butter
1	pound dried gnocchi
⅓	cup grated Pecorino Romano cheese
	Ground black pepper

1. Bring 4 quarts water to a rolling boil in a large pot for cooking the gnocchi.

2. Meanwhile, heat 2 tablespoons oil and the garlic in a 12-inch skillet over medium-high heat. Cook until the garlic becomes fragrant and slightly brown, about 2 minutes. Add the Swiss chard leaves by handfuls, tossing with tongs to coat them with oil. Once all the chard is added, sprinkle with ¼ teaspoon salt. Cook until the leaves are just wilted, about 1½ minutes. Transfer the chard to a colander set in a sink and use the tongs to squeeze out excess water. Leave the colander in a sink.

3. Return the pan to medium-high heat, add the remaining 1 tablespoon oil, and heat until it is shimmering. Add the shallot and cook, stirring frequently, until it softens, about 1 minute. Add the chard stems and sauté for

another 2 minutes. Add the broth, reduce the heat to medium, and simmer until the sauce is reduced slightly and the stems are crisp-tender, about 2½ minutes. Add the butter and stir until it melts and the sauce thickens slightly.

4. When the sauce is nearly done, add 1 tablespoon salt and the gnocchi to the boiling water. Cook until the gnocchi start to float to the top, 1½ to 2 minutes. Drain thoroughly.

5. Add the gnocchi, chard leaves, and cheese to the pan with the sauce. Toss to combine and adjust the seasonings with salt and pepper to taste. Serve immediately.

FOUR-CHEESE PASTA

PASTA AI QUATTRO FORMAGGI, THE classic Italian pasta dish with four cheeses and heavy cream, is a great idea—in theory. In reality, however, it often turns into a virtually inedible mess: tasteless, stringy, heavy, and greasy. We wanted to discover what made this dish great in the first place, delivering a pasta dinner that was silky smooth and rich but not heavy—a grown-up, sophisticated version of macaroni and cheese with Italian flavors.

Of course, the cheese was the first issue with respect to both flavor and texture. We committed to Italian cheeses, but this barely diminished our choices; research turned up varying combinations and amounts (1 cup to 6½ cups cheese per 1 pound pasta) of asiago, fontina, Taleggio, Pecorino Romano, mascarpone, mozzarella, Gorgonzola, Parmesan, and ricotta. Initial testing reduced the scope quickly. Mascarpone and ricotta added neither flavor nor texture, and asiago was bland. Pasta tossed with mozzarella was gooey and greasy, whereas Taleggio not only was difficult to obtain but also made the pasta too rich and gluey. After testing numerous combinations of the remaining cheeses, tasters favored a

2½-cup combination of Italian fontina (which is creamier and better-tasting than versions of this cheese made elsewhere), Gorgonzola, Pecorino Romano, and Parmesan.

Both heating the cheeses and cream together and adding the cheeses separately to the hot pasta produced nasty messes. Each attempt caused the cheeses to curdle, separate, or turn greasy. Some recipes solved this problem by beginning with a *besciamella* (known in French as a *béchamel*). This basic white sauce is made by cooking butter and flour together, then adding milk or cream. The cheeses can then be added to the white sauce, which doesn't separate because of the flour. As we soon found out, the white sauce kept the pasta sauce from breaking, but it also had an unintended side effect: The flavor of the cheeses was now diminished. The solution was to radically reduce the amount of flour and butter to 2 teaspoons each instead of the usual 3 or 4 tablespoons each. Now the sauce was silky and smooth and allowed the flavor of the cheeses to stand out.

After making this recipe a half-dozen more times, we were bothered by the notion of heating the cheeses ahead of time with the béchamel. We wanted to cook the cheeses as little as possible for the best flavor, so we put the shredded/crumbled/grated cheeses in a large bowl and added the hot pasta and hot béchamel. A quick toss melted the cheeses without actually cooking them. We had now both simplified the recipe and produced a cleaner-tasting, more flavorful dish.

Tubular pasta shapes (penne is ideal) allow the sauce to coat the pasta inside and out and are the best choice. Many recipes suggest cooking the pasta fully, then baking it for 20 or 30 minutes. This is a recipe for mushiness. Two moves keep the pasta from overcooking: draining it several minutes before it is al dente, then minimizing the baking time. Just seven minutes in a 500-degree oven (the pasta heats more quickly in a shallow baking dish) is enough to turn the pasta and sauce into a casserole.

Many recipes add a bread crumb topping that browns and crisps in the oven. We tried this casserole with and without the crumb topping; tasters unanimously voted for the topping, which contrasts nicely with the creamy pasta and helps balance the richness of the sauce.

Creamy Baked Four-Cheese Pasta

SERVES 4 TO 6

TIME: 35 MINUTES

For maximum efficiency, shred, crumble, and grate the cheeses while the pasta water comes to a boil. This dish is quite rich and can also be served as a side dish.

BREAD CRUMB TOPPING

3–4	slices white sandwich bread with crusts, torn into quarters
¼	cup (½ ounce) grated Parmesan cheese
¼	teaspoon salt
⅛	teaspoon ground black pepper

PASTA AND CHEESE

4	ounces Italian fontina cheese, shredded (about 1 cup)
3	ounces Gorgonzola cheese, crumbled (about ¾ cup)
½	cup (1 ounce) grated Pecorino Romano cheese
¼	cup (½ ounce) grated Parmesan cheese
	Salt
1	pound penne
2	teaspoons unsalted butter
2	teaspoons unbleached all-purpose flour
1½	cups heavy cream
¼	teaspoon ground black pepper

139

1. FOR THE TOPPING: Pulse the bread in a food processor until it resembles coarse crumbs, about ten 1-second pulses (you should have about 1½ cups). Transfer the crumbs to a small bowl; stir in the Parmesan, salt, and pepper. Set the mixture aside.

2. FOR THE PASTA: Adjust an oven rack to the middle position and heat the oven to 500 degrees.

3. Bring 4 quarts water to a rolling boil in a large pot. Combine the cheeses in a large bowl; set the bowl aside. Add 1 tablespoon salt and the pasta to the boiling water and stir to separate. While the pasta is cooking, melt the butter in a small saucepan over medium-low heat. Whisk the flour into the butter until no lumps remain, about 30 seconds. Gradually whisk in the cream, increase the heat to medium, and bring to a boil, stirring occasionally. Reduce the heat to medium-low and simmer 1 minute to ensure the flour cooks. Stir in the remaining ¼ teaspoon salt and the pepper. Cover the cream mixture to keep it hot.

4. When the pasta is al dente (when bitten into, the pasta should be opaque and slightly underdone at the center), drain about 5 seconds, leaving the pasta slightly wet. Add the pasta to the bowl with the cheeses. Immediately pour the cream mixture over the pasta, cover the bowl with foil or a large plate, and let stand 3 minutes. Uncover the bowl and stir with a rubber spatula, scraping the bottom of the bowl, until the cheeses are melted and the mixture is thoroughly combined.

5. Transfer the pasta to a 13 by 9-inch baking dish and sprinkle evenly with the reserved bread crumbs, pressing down lightly. Bake until the topping is golden brown, about 7 minutes. Serve immediately.

➤ VARIATIONS

Baked Four-Cheese Pasta with Tomatoes and Basil

Follow the recipe for Creamy Baked Four-Cheese Pasta, adding 1 (14½-ounce) can diced tomatoes, drained, to the pasta along with the cream mixture and stirring in ¼ cup coarsely chopped basil leaves just before transferring the pasta to the baking dish.

Baked Four-Cheese Pasta with Prosciutto and Peas

Follow the recipe for Creamy Baked Four-Cheese Pasta, omitting the salt from the cream mixture and adding 4 ounces prosciutto, chopped, and 1 cup frozen peas to the pasta along with the cream mixture.

SOPA SECA

THE NAME OF THIS MEXICAN DISH, literally translated, is "dry soup." Don't let the name fool you, however; sopa seca is neither dry nor a soup. Although it starts off looking like a soup, when completed it is a distinctive pasta dish with robust flavors.

We started by doing a little research in order to learn more about sopa seca. Of the dozen recipes we found, the one aspect they all shared was the use of fideos as a base. Fideos are coils of vermicelli that have been toasted until golden brown. The wonderful nuttiness they bring to this dish underscores all the other flavors. The fideos are placed in a baking dish, topped with an ample amount of liquid (the soup part), and baked until all the liquid is absorbed and the pasta is tender (the dry part). The similarities among the sopa seca recipes stopped there. The liquid and garnish ingredient choices made the search for the perfect sopa seca recipe an adventure.

The use of tomatoes among the recipes varied greatly. Some recipes called for fresh tomatoes, others canned, and still others listed jarred salsa as the tomato ingredient. We tried all three variations and found that canned tomatoes worked the best and yielded the most consistent results. The fresh tomatoes, while preferred slightly over canned for their flavor, led to inconsistent results due to the varied moisture content in fresh tomatoes. Jarred salsa was considered the worst option because it gave the finished dish an artificial flavor. In addition to the tomato base, sopa seca recipes usually include a liquid component, normally chicken broth or water. In our tests, chicken broth was favored slightly over water because of its greater richness.

The use of chiles also varied from recipe to recipe. We tried four options. Our first test used no chiles at all. It was soon obvious, however, that if we wanted multiple dimensions to our sopa seca, chiles were a must. Next up were fresh jalapeños. Although they definitely added a spark, some tasters felt they gave the dish too much raw chile flavor. The third trial used dried ancho chiles. Many testers liked the smokiness of these chiles, but they required a lengthy soaking period that complicated the cooking process and added time. Our final alternative was to use canned chipotle chiles. These turned out to be the best option. They provided a smoky background, like the anchos, without the long preparation time, and they added spiciness, like the jalapeños, without the raw taste.

In addition to the chiles, we liked onions, garlic, and ground cumin for extra flavor. To finish the dish, we topped it with chopped cilantro for freshness and a dollop of sour cream to temper the chile heat.

Sopa Seca

SERVES 4

TIME: 45 MINUTES (INCLUDES 20 MINUTES BAKING TIME)

We used straight vermicelli as opposed to the ones in coils because they are more readily available. If you prefer to use the vermicelli in coils, decrease the amount of chicken broth by ¼ cup. If you want a less spicy dish, use only one chipotle chile.

2	tablespoons vegetable oil
½	pound vermicelli, broken in half
1	medium onion, diced
2	medium cloves garlic, minced or pressed through a garlic press (about 2 teaspoons)
½	teaspoon ground cumin
1	(14½-ounce) can diced tomatoes in juice
1–2	canned chipotle chiles in adobo sauce, chopped fine
1½	cups canned low-sodium chicken broth
½	teaspoon salt
½	cup grated Monterey Jack cheese
¼	cup chopped fresh cilantro leaves
½	cup sour cream

1. Adjust an oven rack to the middle position and heat the oven to 350 degrees.

2. Heat 1 tablespoon oil and the vermicelli in a 12-inch skillet over medium-high heat. Cook, stirring constantly, until the noodles are golden brown, 4 to 5 minutes. Transfer the noodles to a 13 by 9-inch baking dish.

3. Add the remaining 1 tablespoon oil and the onion to the empty pan. Cook, stirring frequently, until the onion softens and browns slightly, about 2½ minutes. Add the garlic and cumin and toast until fragrant, 30 seconds. Add the tomatoes and their juice along with the chiles, broth, and salt. Bring the mixture to a boil, then pour it over the pasta.

4. Place the baking dish in the oven and bake

until all the liquid is absorbed and the pasta is tender, about 15 minutes. Remove the baking dish from the oven, stir to combine the ingredients, and then sprinkle evenly with the cheese. Return the baking dish to the oven and bake until the cheese melts, 2 to 3 minutes. Spoon portions onto individual plates and garnish with cilantro and sour cream. Serve immediately.

➤ VARIATIONS

Sopa Seca with Chorizo

Adding chorizo to this recipe makes it a more substantial meal. If the chorizo is very spicy, omit the chipotle chiles.

Follow the recipe for Sopa Seca, adding ½ pound diced chorizo sausage with the tomatoes, chiles, and broth.

Sopa Seca with Black Beans

Adding black beans and replacing the chicken broth with water makes this recipe a robust one-dish vegetarian meal.

Follow the recipe for Sopa Seca, adding one (19-ounce) can black beans, drained and rinsed, with the tomatoes and chiles. Replace the broth with water.

VEGETABLE LO MEIN

LO MEIN IS A SIMPLE DISH—BASICALLY a stir fry with boiled noodles. So why is lo mein so often poorly executed? The lo mein served in many Chinese restaurants is frequently oily and uninteresting; the noodles are often a tasteless mass. We wanted something different—flavorful strands of noodles coated in a light tangy sauce.

Most lo mein recipes call for fresh Chinese egg noodles, which are somewhat different from their Italian counterparts. Most fresh Chinese noodles are more tender and chewier and absorb flavors more readily than fresh Italian pasta. After testing both kinds of fresh noodles, we preferred the authentic Chinese-style noodles, which were significantly more substantial. However, these larger noodles often congealed in a huge mass as they cooled. Up to this point, we had been cooking the noodles until al dente, draining them, and holding them before adding them to the stir fry. We obviously needed to change this procedure.

We started by cooking our noodles less, a move that showed promise. By draining the

BREAKING LONG-STRAND PASTA IN HALF

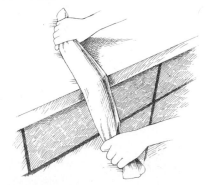

1. Though we don't normally recommend breaking pasta strands in half, this step makes it easier to toast vermicelli when making sopa seca. To keep the pasta from flying every which way in the kitchen, roll up the bundle of vermicelli in a kitchen towel that overlaps the pasta by 3 or 4 inches at both ends.

2. Holding both ends firmly, center the rolled bundle over the edge of a table or counter. Push down with both hands to break the pasta in the middle of the bundle.

noodles about a minute before they were al dente, we found we could avoid the sticky-mass problem, and the noodles stayed toothsome rather than overcooked in the finished dish. In addition to undercooking the noodles slightly, we rinsed the drained noodles with cold water and tossed them with a little bit of sesame oil. Sure enough, rinsing the noodles rid them of excess starch. Tossing them with oil further prevented the noodles from sticking together, and the sesame oil enhanced the flavor of the completed dish.

Now that we had solved the noodle problems, we moved on to the sauce. Our thought here was to generate the greatest flavor with the fewest ingredients. We also wanted to keep the sauce light and therefore an improvement on the goopy Chinese takeout sauces.

INGREDIENTS: Oyster Sauce

Oyster sauce, also called *oyster-flavored sauce*, is a rich, concentrated mixture of oyster extracts, soy sauce, brine, and assorted seasonings. It is brown, thick, salty, and strong.

A trip to our local grocery store and Asian markets turned up five brands of bottled oyster sauce. Lee Kum Kee dominated the shelves with three varieties: Choy Sun, Panda Brand, and Premium. Coin Tree and Sa Cheng rounded out the list. We tested each brand in a simple stir-fry sauce with sherry, soy sauce, sesame oil, sugar, and pepper.

The most authentic of the group was the Lee Kum Kee's Premium Oyster-Flavored Sauce. Admittedly intense and fishy, it was the only sauce with true depth of flavor; its saltiness was balanced by sweet caramel undertones, and the oyster flavor was strong. This sauce is not for the faint of heart; one taster proclaimed, "My American taste buds can't take it." Tasters, especially those with less experienced palates, liked Sa Cheng Oyster-Flavored Sauce, which was mild and "gravylike." The other three sauces were fine but indistinguishable.

Switching from fresh shiitake mushrooms (the common choice in many recipes) to dried shiitake allowed us to use the rehydrating liquid as a base for the sauce. This was perfect; it deepened the flavors and kept the sauce from being too thick. (In the beef lo mein variation, chicken broth had the same results.) Soy sauce was another essential component; we found that a light-bodied soy did the job. The darker, sweeter soy sauces were too cloying and sweet and not well suited for our purposes. To finish the dish, we chose oyster sauce. While not exactly a household staple, oyster sauce was listed in most of the recipes we consulted. We found, and tasters agreed, that the oyster sauce gave lo mein an interesting brininess and an appealing gloss.

Vegetable Lo Mein
SERVES 4
TIME: 35 MINUTES

Look for fresh Chinese egg noodles in the produce section of your supermarket. If you cannot find fresh noodles, you can substitute dry, either Asian or Italian. If you do so, choose a noodle the thickness of spaghetti. See left for information about buying oyster sauce.

8	dried shiitake mushrooms (about 2 ounces)
I	tablespoon salt
12	ounces fresh Chinese egg noodles
I	tablespoon Asian sesame oil
2	tablespoons oyster sauce
2	tablespoons soy sauce
I½	tablespoons vegetable oil
½	small head napa cabbage, sliced crosswise into ⅛-inch strips (about 3 cups)
4	medium scallions, greens only, cut into 1-inch pieces
I	tablespoon minced fresh ginger
I	cup bean sprouts

1. Cover the mushrooms with ½ cup hot tap water in a small microwave-safe bowl. Cover with plastic wrap, cut several steam vents with a paring knife, and microwave on high power for 30 seconds. Let stand until the mushrooms soften, about 5 minutes. Carefully lift the mushrooms from the liquid with a fork; pour ¼ cup soaking liquid through a small strainer lined with a single layer of paper towel and placed over a measuring cup and set aside. Trim and discard the mushroom stems and slice the caps in ¼-inch strips.

2. Bring 4 quarts water to a rolling boil in a large pot. Add the salt and noodles, stir to separate, and cook until the noodles are slightly underdone, about 2 minutes. Drain thoroughly, rinse the noodles under cold running water, and drain again. Toss with the sesame oil in a large bowl and set aside.

3. Mix the reserved mushroom broth, oyster sauce, and soy sauce in a small bowl and set the mixture aside.

4. Heat a 12-inch nonstick skillet over high heat for 3 minutes. Add 1 tablespoon oil and swirl so it evenly coats the bottom of the pan. Add the mushrooms and stir-fry until seared and three-quarters cooked, about 2 minutes. Add the cabbage and stir-fry until just wilted, about 1 minute. Clear the center of the pan and add the scallions, ginger, and remaining ½ tablespoon oil. Cook until fragrant, about 10 seconds, then stir the aromatics into the vegetables.

5. Add the noodles, sprouts, and mushroom broth mixture to the pan. Stir-fry and toss to combine all ingredients until the noodles are heated through, about 1 minute. Serve immediately.

Beef and Pepper Lo Mein

SERVES 4

TIME: 35 MINUTES

For information about preparing flank steak for a stir fry, see page 326. See page 143 for information about buying oyster sauce.

1	tablespoon salt
12	ounces fresh Chinese egg noodles
1	tablespoon Asian sesame oil
¼	cup canned low-sodium chicken broth
2	tablespoons oyster sauce
1	tablespoon soy sauce
2½	tablespoons vegetable oil
8	ounces flank steak, trimmed and sliced thin across the grain on the bias
½	small head napa cabbage, sliced crosswise into ⅛-inch strips (about 3 cups)
1	medium red bell pepper, stemmed, seeded, and sliced thin
4	medium scallions, greens only, cut into 1-inch pieces
1	tablespoon minced fresh ginger
1	cup bean sprouts

1. Bring 4 quarts water to a rolling boil in a large pot. Add the salt and noodles, stir to separate, and cook until the noodles are slightly underdone, about 2 minutes. Drain thoroughly, rinse the noodles under cold running water, and drain again. Toss with the sesame oil in a large bowl and set aside.

2. Mix the broth, oyster sauce, and soy sauce in a small bowl and set the mixture aside.

3. Heat a 12-inch nonstick skillet over high heat for 3 minutes. Add 1 tablespoon oil and swirl so it evenly coats the bottom of the pan. Add the flank steak and stir-fry until seared and three-quarters cooked, about 2 minutes. Transfer the steak to a bowl. Heat 1 tablespoon oil in the empty pan until shimmering.

Add the cabbage and bell pepper and stir-fry until softened slightly, about 1 minute. Clear the center of the pan and add the scallions, ginger, and remaining ½ tablespoon oil. Cook until fragrant, about 10 seconds, and then stir the aromatics into the vegetables.

4. Add the noodles, beef (and any accumulated juices), sprouts, and broth mixture to the pan. Stir-fry and toss to combine all ingredients until the noodles are heated through, about 1 minute. Serve immediately.

CRISPY NOODLE CAKE WITH STIR-FRIED CHICKEN

STIR-FRIES ARE THE QUINTESSENTIAL weeknight dinner because they are both quick and complex. The problem is that they are usually served on a lackluster mound of boiled rice. On several excursions to Chinatown, however, we've had stir-fries served on top of pan-fried noodle cakes, a superior marriage of protein and starch. These cakes, which have a crisp, crunchy exterior and a tender, chewy middle, appeared to be the solution to our rice doldrums.

Finding a noodle that would achieve this textural balance, however, was difficult. A stroll down the local supermarket international aisle turned up an overwhelming number of dried Asian noodles of all sizes and flavors. After we boiled up batches of noodles and pan-fried numerous cakes, the results, for the most part, were disastrous. We found that thin noodles lacked the body to achieve the balance of crisp and tender, and that the finished cake was overly dry—not unlike raw pasta. Wide noodles were not much better. The noodles wouldn't hold together to form a cake and therefore did not develop the contrasting textures we were looking for.

We finally hit upon a solution when we tried fresh Chinese egg noodles. These noodles, which are a little thicker than spaghetti, tend to be starchy. As a result, they yielded a cohesive cake with a crunchy exterior and a chewy interior. Also, the slightly doughy consistency of the noodles allowed them to retain more moisture. When pan-fried, these noodles are crisp without seeming raw. Given our success with fresh Chinese noodles, we wondered if fresh Italian pasta would work. Although not as starchy as its Chinese counterparts, fresh Italian spaghetti from the supermarket refrigerator case performed well in kitchen tests, better than any dried Asian noodles. It is the best substitute for fresh Chinese egg noodles.

Now that we had determined the type of noodle we wanted to use, we needed to perfect a technique that would yield consistent noodle cakes. Using a nonstick skillet turned out to be crucial (to avoid both sticking and excess oil), and 1 tablespoon oil per side proved just the right amount to achieve a crisp exterior, neither greasy nor burnt. Trying to flip this unwieldy disk, however, was a challenge. In the end, we found that sliding the cake onto a plate, inverting it onto another, and sliding it back into the skillet, browned-side up, was the best (and safest) method.

With the noodle cake perfected, we turned our attention to the stir fry itself. Considering that making the noodle cake requires a little more effort than steaming rice, we felt the stir fry should be kept simple. The duo of chicken and bok choy is hard to beat, and this classic combination coupled with the noodle cake makes a complete dinner. As for the sauce, we were able to build complex flavor with just four ingredients—soy sauce and sherry (which doubled as a quick marinade for the chicken), hoisin sauce for sweetness, and a healthy dose of chili garlic sauce for heat.

Crispy Noodle Cake with Spicy Stir-Fried Chicken and Bok Choy

SERVES 4

TIME: 40 MINUTES

Fresh Chinese egg noodles are often kept in the produce section of the grocery store. If you can't find fresh egg noodles, substitute the same amount of fresh Italian spaghetti. See the illustrations on page 148 for tips on handling bok choy. See the illustrations on page 331 for tips on slicing chicken breasts for a stir fry.

2½	tablespoons soy sauce
2½	tablespoons dry sherry
4	boneless, skinless chicken breasts (about 1¼ pounds), trimmed of excess fat, tenderloins removed and halved lengthwise, breasts cut crosswise into ½-inch strips
¼	cup hoisin sauce
1	tablespoon Asian chili garlic sauce
1	teaspoon salt
12	ounces fresh Chinese egg noodles
4	medium scallions, white and light green parts, sliced thin; dark green parts sliced thin on the bias, for garnish
4	tablespoons vegetable oil
1	small head bok choy (about 1 pound), stalks and greens separated, stalks cut crosswise into ¼-inch slices and greens cut crosswise into ½-inch strips
1	tablespoon minced fresh ginger

1. Bring 3 quarts water to a rolling boil in a large pot for cooking the noodles.

2. Meanwhile, combine 1 tablespoon soy sauce, 1 tablespoon sherry, and the chicken in a small bowl; set aside to marinate. Mix together the hoisin, chili garlic sauce, and remaining 1½ tablespoons each soy sauce and sherry in a small bowl; set aside.

3. Add the salt and noodles to the boiling water, stir to separate, and cook until just tender, 2 to 3 minutes. Drain thoroughly, then toss with the white and light green scallions in a bowl.

4. Heat 1 tablespoon oil in a 12-inch non-stick skillet over medium-high heat until shimmering but not smoking. Spread the noodles evenly across the bottom of the skillet; press with a spatula to flatten and cook until crisp and golden brown, about 4 minutes. Slide the noodle cake onto a large plate. Add 1 tablespoon oil to the skillet and swirl to coat. Invert the noodle cake onto a second plate and slide it, browned-side up, back into the skillet. Cook until crisp and golden brown on the second side, about 4 minutes. Slide the noodle cake onto a cutting board; set it aside.

5. Add 1 tablespoon oil to the skillet and heat until just beginning to smoke. Pour off the excess marinade from the chicken and discard. Add the chicken to the skillet. Stir-fry until just cooked, about 2 minutes. Transfer the chicken to a small clean bowl and set it aside.

6. Add the remaining 1 tablespoon oil to the skillet and heat until just beginning to smoke. Add the bok choy stalks and stir-fry for 1 minute. Clear the center of the pan, add the ginger, and cook until fragrant, about 10 seconds. Stir the ginger into the stalks and continue to stir-fry until the stalks are tender-crisp, about 20 seconds longer. Stir in the bok choy greens, chicken, and hoisin mixture and cook until the greens are wilted and the ingredients are coated with sauce, about 30 seconds. Set the skillet aside off the heat.

7. Using a chef's knife, cut the noodle cake into 8 wedges. Place 2 wedges on each of 4 individual plates. Spoon a portion of the stir fry and sauce over the noodle cake, sprinkle with the scallion greens, and serve immediately.

ASIAN NOODLES WITH WINTER GREENS

THE SHARP, PEPPERY FLAVOR OF WINTER greens is a perfect match for the mild, wheaty flavor and silken texture of Asian noodles. We wanted to find a way to combine greens and noodles with simple sauces to create quick meals.

Blanching turned out to be the optimal method for cooking the greens; this technique maintained their vibrant color but tamed their bitterness. When we started testing, we had three pots going—one for greens, one for noodles, and one for the sauce. After a few experiments, we found that it worked fine to cook the greens with the noodles. This approach cut one pot and two steps from the recipe. We didn't have to worry about removing the greens from the boiling water or about running them under cold water to stop them from cooking because once the noodles and greens are done, they are simply drained together and added to the sauce.

We found that fresh noodles should go into the pot after the greens but that dried noodles will need a head start on the greens. See the recipe headnotes for more detailed cooking instructions.

Mustard Greens and Udon Noodles with Shiitake-Ginger Sauce

SERVES 4

TIME: 20 MINUTES

You can find fresh Japanese udon noodles in the produce section of many supermarkets. If they are not available, use dried udon and add them to the pot in step 3 first. Cook the noodles for 3 minutes, then add the greens and continue cooking until both the noodles and greens are tender, another 2 or 3 minutes.

1½	cups canned low-sodium chicken broth
2	tablespoons rice vinegar
¼	cup mirin (sweet Japanese rice wine)
½	pound shiitake mushrooms, sliced thin
1	(2-inch) piece fresh ginger, peeled and cut into ¼-inch coins
½	teaspoon Asian chili garlic sauce
2	tablespoons soy sauce
1	Asian sesame oil
	Salt and ground black pepper
1½	pounds mustard greens (1 large bunch), leaves trimmed from stalks; stalks discarded and leaves cut into 2-inch pieces
14	ounces fresh udon noodles

1. Bring 5 quarts water to a boil in a large pot for cooking the greens and noodles.

2. Bring the broth, vinegar, mirin, mushrooms, ginger, chili garlic sauce, soy sauce, and sesame oil to a boil in a medium saucepan over high heat. Simmer briskly until the liquid thickens and reduces by half, 8 to 10 minutes. Off the heat, remove the ginger, season with salt and pepper to taste, and cover to keep warm.

3. Meanwhile, add 1 tablespoon salt and the greens to the boiling water. Cook until the greens are almost tender, 2 to 4 minutes. Add the noodles, stir to separate them, and cook until both greens and noodles are tender, about 2 minutes longer. Reserving ¼ cup noodle cooking water, drain the noodles and greens and return them to the pot. Add the sauce and reserved water and cook over medium-low heat, stirring to meld flavors, about 1 minute. Adjust the seasonings with salt and pepper to taste. Serve immediately.

Bok Choy and Chinese Egg Noodles with Spicy Beef Sauce

SERVES 4

TIME: 20 MINUTES

Dried linguine can be substituted for fresh egg noodles, but you will need to cook the pasta first in step 3. Cook until almost al dente (about 7 minutes), add the bok choy, and cook until both the pasta and greens are tender, another 3 to 4 minutes. See photo of this recipe on page 154.

1	tablespoon vegetable oil
1	(3-inch) cinnamon stick, broken in half
3	star anise pods
4	medium cloves garlic, sliced thin
1	tablespoon minced fresh ginger
1	cup canned low-sodium chicken broth
1	tablespoon Asian chili garlic sauce
	Salt and ground black pepper
¾	pound beef sirloin or rib-eye steak, halved crosswise, each half sliced thin across the grain
1½	pounds bok choy, bottom inch of base discarded, washed well, and cut crosswise into ¾-inch pieces
12	ounces fresh Chinese egg noodles

1. Bring 5 quarts water to a boil in a large pot for cooking the greens and noodles.

2. Heat the oil in a medium saucepan over medium-high heat until shimmering. Add the cinnamon and star anise and cook, stirring often, until the cinnamon begins to unfurl, about 1 minute. Add the garlic and ginger and cook until they soften, about 2 minutes. Add the broth and chili garlic sauce, reduce the heat to medium-low, and simmer until the liquid reduces by half, about 5 minutes. Remove and discard the cinnamon stick and star anise and season with salt and pepper to taste. Add the beef and simmer until the meat is gray around the edges and still slightly pink in the center, 1 minute.

3. Meanwhile, add 1 tablespoon salt and the bok choy to the boiling water. Cook until the bok choy is almost tender, 2 to 3 minutes. Add the noodles, stir to separate them, and cook until both the bok choy and noodles are tender, about 2 minutes longer. Reserving ⅓ cup cooking water, drain the noodles and bok choy and return them to the pot. Add the sauce and reserved water and cook over medium-low heat, stirring to meld the flavors, about 1 minute. Adjust the seasonings with salt and pepper to taste. Serve immediately.

PREPARING BOK CHOY

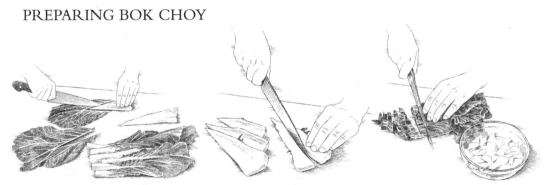

1. Cut the leafy green portions away from either side of the fleshy white stalks.

2. Cut the stalks in half lengthwise and then crosswise into thin strips.

3. Stack the leafy greens and then slice them crosswise into thin strips. Keep the stalks and leaves separate.

SINGAPORE NOODLES

BEING CLOSE TO CHINA, JAPAN, AND India, Singapore is a unique blend of these diverse cultures. Singapore noodles (or *curry noodles,* as they are called in some American restaurants) exemplify this culinary diversity. The Singapore noodles we've had in American restaurants have been greasy tangles of rice noodles with so much curry you couldn't taste anything else. We did a little research to see if we could make something closer to the real thing.

After sifting through our library, we turned up a half-dozen recipes for Singapore noodles. All were quite different, except for the use of curry powder and rice noodles, and drew on the influence of many nations. To best determine what style we wanted to follow, we cooked several batches of noodles, each with distinct influences.

The sauce seemed to have three major components: a salty component, a sweet component, and a base that provided moisture and flavor. The most common salty ingredient was soy sauce, but we also tried fish sauce and oyster sauce. Almost all tasters preferred soy over the other two, commenting that the soy sauce was the only one that didn't leave a fishy aftertaste. As for the sweet element, most recipes called for granulated sugar, while a minority of others used brown sugar or mirin (sweetened Japanese rice wine). While both the granulated and brown sugars performed the job of sweetening the dish, some testers felt the sweetness tasted slightly artificial. The mirin, however, provided a subtler sweetness that emphasized the other flavors of the dish rather than overpowering them.

We also needed to address the base of our sauce. Most recipes called for chicken broth. After a couple of trials with other ingredients, such as coconut milk and water, we concurred that chicken broth was the best base. It gave the dish moisture without heaviness.

With our sauce completed, we now could address the other ingredients in our Singapore noodles. We thought adding a protein would round out our one-dish meal. All but one of the recipes we found called for both shrimp and pork. We quickly cut this down to shrimp for several reasons. First, the Chinese-style pork cited in most recipes is impossible to find outside of well-stocked Chinese grocery stores. Second, without authentic Chinese-style pork, the only other option would be to marinate pork loin and then stir-fry it—which is time-consuming. Thankfully, we thought the dish was just fine with the shrimp alone. By quickly sautéing shrimp before proceeding with the rest of the recipe, we found we had made a light, satisfying dish with a minimal expense of time. Shallots for a mellow onion flavor, a red pepper for sweetness, and a handful of beans sprouts for crunch and a peppery bite finished our ingredient list.

The important choice of noodles was our last task. At the supermarket, we found many brands of rice noodles. We read the ingredient lists on the packages and found that most of the packaged noodles were the same; the only evident variation was in thickness. So we proceeded by making our recipe with two types of noodles: a thick noodle about the thickness of linguine and a thin version more like vermicelli. While both noodles worked equally well with respect to flavor, we found the thinner noodles mixed better with the other ingredients. This made for a more even distribution of the sauce and other ingredients and put the pasta and sauce on equal footing. We did have one recurring problem with our noodles: how to prepare them before stir-frying.

Most of the packages of rice noodles we purchased called for soaking the noodles in water before stir-frying. This softens the noodles and enables them to be fully cooked, even

149

with a very brief cooking time. The soaking method varied by brand. Some recommended soaking in warm water for at least 20 minutes. We tried this, with horrible results: The noodles were dry and chewy. Increasing the soaking time helped somewhat, but the idea of a quick recipe soon disappeared. We next tried another method suggested by the package directions, which was to soak the noodles in very hot tap water or boiling water. The results were more encouraging, but the noodles still had a semiraw texture.

Most Asian experts frown on the idea of preboiling rice noodles, feeling it causes the noodles to adhere into a large mass upon draining. However, we felt in this case that our noodles needed to be 100 percent cooked before adding them to the pan, so we boiled them for just 1 minute. While the noodles did stick to themselves slightly, they soon separated when we put them in the pan with our sauce. We also avoided the problem of partially cooked noodles.

Singapore Noodles

SERVES 4

TIME: 25 MINUTES

This recipe was developed using Muchi curry powder, a spicy version from the southern part of India. Madras curry powder is similar. Most other curry powders are milder, so if you prefer spicy noodles, you can add a pinch of cayenne pepper.

½	pound medium shrimp (41 to 50 count), peeled
2½	teaspoons curry powder
2	medium cloves garlic, minced or pressed through a garlic press (about 2 teaspoons)
¾	cup canned low-sodium chicken broth
¼	cup soy sauce
2	tablespoons mirin (sweet Japanese rice wine)
	Salt
6	ounces rice vermicelli (also called rice sticks)
4	teaspoons vegetable oil
3	medium shallots, sliced thin (about ¼ cup)
1	medium red bell pepper, stemmed, seeded, and cut into 1½ by ¼-inch strips
1	cup bean sprouts

1. Bring 3 quarts water to a boil in a large saucepan for cooking the noodles.

2. Mix the shrimp and ½ teaspoon curry powder in a small bowl and set it aside. Mix the garlic and remaining 2 teaspoons curry powder together in another bowl and set it aside. Mix the broth, soy sauce, and mirin together in a third bowl and set it aside.

3. Add 1 teaspoon salt and the noodles to the boiling water, stir to separate, and boil until tender, about 1 minute. Drain thoroughly and set the noodles aside.

4. Meanwhile, heat 2 teaspoons oil in a 12-inch nonstick skillet over medium-high heat until shimmering but not smoking. Add the shrimp and cook until slightly browned, about 45 seconds. Turn the shrimp with tongs and continue to cook for another 45 seconds. Remove the shrimp from the pan and set them aside in bowl.

5. Reduce the heat to medium and add the remaining 2 teaspoons oil. Add the garlic and curry powder mixture and cook until fragrant, about 30 seconds. Add the shallots and stir-fry until they begin to soften, about 30 seconds. Add the bell pepper and stir-fry until crisp-tender, about 1½ minutes. Add the softened noodles, shrimp, broth mixture, and bean sprouts and toss until the ingredients are combined and the noodles heated through, about 1 minute. Serve immediately.

SPICY THAI-STYLE SHRIMP SOUP **PAGE 192**

151

WARM SPINACH SALAD WITH SEARED SCALLOPS AND ROASTED PEPPER VINAIGRETTE **PAGE 56**

POLENTA WITH ROASTED TOMATOES AND FRESH MOZZARELLA **PAGE 100**

153

BOK CHOY AND CHINESE EGG NOODLES WITH SPICY BEEF SAUCE **PAGE 148**

154

STIR-FRIED SHRIMP AND SNOW PEAS IN COCONUT CURRY SAUCE **PAGE 334**

SKILLET FAJITAS **PAGE 226**

156

GRILLED SCALLOPS WITH CHILI-LIME GLAZE AND CORN SALAD **PAGE 322**

157

CHICKEN AND RICE WITH LEMON, PEAS, AND SCALLIONS **PAGE 214**

BROILED ASPARAGUS WITH TOMATO-BASIL VINAIGRETTE **PAGE 65**

OVEN-FRIED CHICKEN AND ROASTED SWEET POTATO SALAD **PAGE 209**

CORNMEAL BISCUITS WITH CORN KERNELS **PAGE 369**

160

PAN-SEARED SALMON WITH BRAISED LENTILS AND CHARD **PAGE 263**

TUSCAN-STYLE STEAK WITH ARUGULA AND PARMESAN **PAGE 233**

30-MINUTE TARTE TATIN **PAGE 414**

163

JELLY ROLL CAKE WITH RASPBERRY JAM   **PAGE 386**

BLUEBERRY COBBLER **PAGE 418**

165

30-MINUTE CHOCOLATE MOUSSE **PAGE 435**

SOUPS

THE TERM QUICK SOUP SEEMS OXYMORONIC. You would think "quick soup" means "canned soup." However, because homemade soups can be hearty enough to serve as one-dish meals (all the recipes in this chapter fit this description), they appeal to the cook who doesn't have time to assemble several dishes per meal. So how do you make good soup in less than an hour? Clearly, homemade stock is never an option. We found that commercial broths make good soup, as long as you make sure to pump up the flavor. Simmering herbs, garlic, chiles, and other flavorful ingredients in the broth helps in this respect. The recipes in this chapter prove that good homemade soup doesn't have to take all day.

QUICK CHICKEN NOODLE SOUP

WHEN YOU ARE LAID UP SICK OR chilled to the bone, nothing is as restorative as a steaming bowl of chicken noodle soup. Simple, rich, and hearty, it is just what the doctor ordered. Unfortunately, good chicken noodle soup takes a long time to make because its flavor depends on a slow-cooked chicken broth. This means you are out of luck if the need for a bowlful hits and you don't have homemade stock squirreled away in the freezer. Inspired by the idea of a quick-cooking chicken noodle soup, we hoped to create a recipe using canned chicken broth that could be ready within an hour.

Homemade chicken stock derives its rich flavor from bones and dark meat. Long, slow simmering transfers flavors from the chicken to the water. Our goal was to enrich canned broth in a similar manner, with chicken parts. Boneless, skinless chicken breasts seemed the most convenient, but we found they gave the canned broth almost no additional flavor.

(They also were expensive.) Further, the breast meat dried out and lost flavor—a big problem, as we hoped to use the poached meat in the soup. Clearly, bones were necessary. We tried in rapid succession bone-in legs, breasts, and thighs (skin and excess fat removed to prevent the broth from becoming too greasy) and found that thighs were the best choice. After 40 minutes of simmering, the thighs had imparted richness to the canned broth, and the chicken meat was moist and tender.

Diced chicken wouldn't do for such a rustic soup, so we shredded the meat. While it's easiest to shred the chicken with your fingers after it has cooled, we contrived a method that worked almost as well with the hot chicken fresh from the pot. Using two forks facing each other, anchor the thigh with one fork and use the other to pull off shreds (see the illustration below). It took just a couple of minutes to shred all the meat into thin threads.

Almost universally, chicken noodle soup is flavored with onions, carrots, and celery. The onions and carrots lend sweetness and body, and the celery imparts a clean vegetal flavor

SHREDDING CHICKEN

Hold one fork in each hand, with the prongs down and facing each other. Insert the prongs into the chicken meat and gently pull the forks away from each other, breaking the meat apart into long, thin strands.

that balances the broth. Many recipes we consulted added the vegetables raw to the stock to simmer until softened. While the method worked adequately, it failed to concentrate the flavors of the vegetables, and they tasted bland and waterlogged. We chose to sauté the vegetables prior to adding broth; the resulting flavors were more intense, which in turn improved the overall flavor of the soup. Because the soup cooked so quickly, the vegetables retained their firm texture.

The sky is the limit when it comes to noodles, from thick and eggy to dried and fresh Italian-style. To keep the soup as traditional as possible, we limited our selection to egg noodles. Tasters preferred the hearty texture of thick "extra-broad" egg noodles to delicate "fine" noodles. The larger style took a little bit longer to cook, but the noodles possessed a more substantial presence and homespun charm. For the best flavor, we found it important to cook the noodles in the broth. When cooked in boiling salted water, the noodles tasted flat and underseasoned.

As for herbs, we chose the simple pairing of bay leaves and thyme. Bay leaves imparted their trademark note to the broth, and the thyme brightened both the soup's flavor and its visual appeal. Dried thyme failed to do much as the soup cooked so briefly, so we went with fresh leaves added at the last minute for the strongest flavor.

Quick Chicken Noodle Soup

SERVES 4 TO 6

TIME: 60 MINUTES

If you plan on having leftovers, reserve a portion of the soup before adding the noodles in step 3. Otherwise, the noodles will swell in the liquid and fall apart. You will need 3 (14-ounce) cans chicken broth for this recipe.

2	tablespoons vegetable oil
1	medium onion, diced
2	small carrots, peeled and cut into ¼-inch rounds
2	small celery ribs, cut on the bias into ¼-inch slices
	Salt
5¼	cups canned low-sodium chicken broth
1½	pounds bone-in chicken thighs, skin removed and trimmed of excess fat
4	bay leaves
2	cups extra-broad egg noodles (about 3 ounces)
1	teaspoon finely minced fresh thyme leaves
	Ground black pepper

1. Heat the oil in a large Dutch oven over medium-high heat until shimmering. Add the onion, carrots, celery, and ½ teaspoon salt and cook, stirring occasionally, until the vegetables soften and begin to brown, 5 to 6 minutes. Add the broth, chicken thighs, bay leaves, and 2 cups water and bring to a boil. Reduce the heat and simmer until the chicken is cooked through, about 40 minutes.

2. Remove and discard the bay leaves. Remove the chicken from the broth and use two forks to remove the meat from the bones and shred it into thin strands (see the illustration on page 168). Return the shredded chicken to the broth and increase the heat to medium-high to return the soup to a simmer.

3. Add the noodles and cook, stirring occasionally, until they are tender, about 8 minutes. Stir in the thyme and adjust the seasonings with salt and pepper to taste. Serve immediately.

QUICK TORTILLA SOUP

DESPITE WHAT THE NAME SUGGESTS, tortilla soup is not nachos in a bowl—though it does share many of the same ingredients. It is a chicken-based soup thickened with tortilla chips and garnished with a wide variety of condiments, including avocado, cilantro, tomatoes, and lime, to name just a few. Essentially, the broth is a blank canvas for diners to personalize. Spicy hot with diced jalapeño chiles, or creamy and rich with avocado, the details of the soup are entirely up to their discretion—outside of tortillas, of course. Like Mongolian hot pot and Japanese *shabu-shabu,* tortilla soup is a meal where diners craft their own portions, which makes it ideal for a large group of uncertain tastes. Let's face it: There is always somebody who doesn't like spicy food or cilantro. More importantly for this collection of recipes, tortilla soup cooks quickly and looks great. As we found, however, some effort is required to make a good soup. In many versions we tested, the liquid is little more than canned chicken broth that the garnishes cannot resuscitate, or it's so overly seasoned that the garnishes are superfluous.

Our first step was to build a full-flavored broth. With time of the essence, we knew canned chicken broth would be our starting point. The challenge would be to deepen its chicken flavor and add Mexican seasonings. Chicken stock develops flavor through the slow simmering of chicken parts and meat. While we couldn't simmer a whole bird in the broth within our allotted time, we could add chicken pieces and then use the cooked chicken as a garnish for the soup. As we discovered when developing our recipe for Quick Chicken Noodle Soup (page 169), bone-in thighs add the most flavor to the broth. Thigh meat also tastes better than the other options, staying moist, tender, and flavorful.

With a rich chicken base at the ready, it was time for seasonings. For a smoky chile touch, we first tried chili powder, but it lacked depth, and its additional flavors—cumin, garlic powder, and dried oregano—muddied the broth. We wanted a cleaner, smokier chile flavor. We then gave one of our favorite dried chiles, chipotle, a whirl, but it was too strong and brashly hot. Then, when we reduced the amount of chipotle enough to make the heat level tolerable, the chile flavor wasn't strong enough. We switched to the less hot but still smoky New Mexico chile and found a flavor tasters loved. It lent a rich smokiness and mild heat level to the broth, but it did not overpower the chicken flavor. We toasted the chiles in the dry pan for a couple of minutes for maximum flavor.

For a sweet, vegetal flavor, we knew garlic was essential. Whole cloves smashed, skins and all, added the desired flavor, but a Mexican technique brought another dimension to the broth. We toasted the garlic in the pan with the chiles until they were aromatic and a little brown. The dry heat intensified the sweetness of the garlic, and the browning complemented the smokiness of the chiles.

The final touch to the broth was fresh herbs to lighten the deep flavors. Oregano and cilantro are two of the most common herbs used in Mexican cooking, and both seemed like a good choice for the broth. Dried herbs proved a poor substitute for fresh—especially dried cilantro, which offered little to no flavor. To keep preparation simple, we bundled together oregano sprigs and cilantro stems for easy retrieval; mincing the herbs would have been a waste of time. From experience, we knew cilantro stems are more strongly flavored than the leaves, which we saved for garnish.

Many of the recipes we researched listed a seemingly endless list of garnishes, but we chose to edit the selection to tasters' favorites to save preparation time. After trying a dozen toppings, tasters identified five that were essential. Red onion added sharpness that balanced the broth's sweetness. The aroma of chopped cilantro leaves was intoxicating. Avocado was favored over sour cream and cheddar cheese for richness. Surprisingly, tomatoes received mixed reviews, although we decided the fruitiness and color were important to the broth. Finally, a squirt of lime juice brightened the other flavors.

Quick Tortilla Soup

SERVES 4 TO 6

TIME: 55 MINUTES

The broth may be prepared ahead of time—even frozen—and heated at the last minute. Err on the side of underseasoning the broth, as the tortilla chips add a fair amount of salt. You will need 4 (14-ounce) cans chicken broth for this recipe. See the illustrations on page 125 for tips on seeding tomatoes. Dried New Mexico red chiles have a smooth, shiny, brick-red skin and a crisp, slightly acidic, earthy flavor. California chiles, which are similar to New Mexicos in appearance but have a slightly milder flavor, can be used in this recipe, too.

5	sprigs fresh oregano
5	cilantro stems, plus ½ cup roughly chopped fresh cilantro leaves
4	medium cloves garlic, lightly crushed with skins on
2	dried New Mexico red chiles, brushed clean, stemmed, and cracked open to remove seeds
7	cups canned low-sodium chicken broth
1½	pounds bone-in chicken thighs, skin removed and trimmed of excess fat
	Salt
	Hot pepper sauce, such as Tabasco
1	(8-ounce) bag tortilla chips
1	small red onion, diced fine
2	medium avocados, pitted, peeled, and cut into ½-inch dice (see the illustrations on pages 20 and 21)
2	very ripe medium tomatoes, cored, seeded, and chopped coarse
1	lime, cut into wedges

1. With a short length of kitchen twine, tie together the oregano sprigs and cilantro stems. Place the garlic cloves and dried chiles in a large Dutch oven over medium-high heat. Cook, stirring frequently, until the garlic begins to darken and is aromatic, 2 to 2½ minutes. Remove the pan from the heat for 30 seconds to cool it down. Return the pan to medium-high heat and add the bundled herbs, broth, and chicken thighs and bring to a boil. Reduce the heat and simmer until the chicken is cooked through, about 40 minutes.

2. Remove the chicken from the broth and use two forks to remove the meat from the bones and shred it into thin strands (see the illustration on page 168). Strain the broth through a fine-mesh strainer into a large bowl; return the broth to the pan over low heat to keep warm. Add the shredded chicken and season with salt and hot pepper sauce to taste.

3. To serve, gently crumble a small handful of chips into individual bowls and divide the broth evenly among them. Serve the chopped cilantro leaves, onion, avocados, tomatoes, and lime wedges at the table.

QUICK CORN CHOWDER

SWEET CORN CHOWDER IS A SUMMER time classic, especially in New England. Kernels of sweet tender corn float in a creamy, rich broth. Corn chowder is not a quick dish; the corn must be shucked and the kernels cut free of the cob, the cobs simmered for flavor, and the aromatics slowly sweated for sweetness. Most recipes we found (including our favorite version, developed in the test kitchen several years ago) required at least two hours of preparation and cooking. So is there really such a thing as quick corn chowder?

We are proud to say, emphatically, yes— with the aid of ultraconvenient frozen corn. After extensive testing, we found that frozen corn was a great substitute for fresh in chowder and, with a few interesting techniques, we found that chowder could be finished in just shy of an hour. Unlike fresh corn chowder, the quick version is under no seasonal constraints; chowder made with frozen corn tastes just as good in the dead of the winter as it does in high summer.

Chowder, by definition, is a dairy-based soup (despite the anomalous tomato-based Manhattan clam chowder) flavored with bacon or salt pork and thickened with potatoes. Generally a simple affair with few ancillary ingredients, the soup highlights its main ingredient, usually corn, clams, or fish. Most corn chowder recipes we found used both the corn kernels and the cobs to flavor the broth, simmering the cobs in stock or water to extract a surprising amount of flavor. In our favorite slow-cooked recipe, we circumvented the cob-simmering by grating a portion of the corn off the cob with a box grater, which released both flavorful juices and valuable starch from the kernels and cob; the starch thickens the broth. After developing this recipe, we knew that for the best flavor, the corn must be added both grated and as whole kernels; the grated corn breaks down to enrich the broth, and the whole kernels punctuate the soup with both clean corn flavor and crisp texture.

Clearly, we could not grate frozen corn on a box grater, but we could grind it in a food processor to similar effect—or so we thought.

Partially defrosted corn quickly turned to mush when processed and lent a rich corn flavor to the soup, but the broth was marred by tough bits of skin that failed to soften despite long cooking. Frozen corn, or at least the brands we tried, appeared tougher than fresh. Still liking the basic idea, we switched from the food processor to a blender, added milk (already designated as the liquid in the soup), and met with success. After just one minute in the blender, the corn and milk mixture was relatively smooth, surprisingly creamy from the starches released by the corn, and decidedly corn-flavored. It was everything we had hoped for in a quick chowder broth.

To flavor the broth, we now needed to choose aromatics and seasonings. For a cooking medium, bacon fat or rendered salt pork is the classic choice. While tasters thought the bacon was delicious, they agreed that its smokiness overshadowed the subtle flavor of the corn. Salt pork proved a better choice, as its milder flavor did not compete with the corn. Salt pork, however, took at least eight to ten minutes to render enough fat in which to sauté the aromatics—too long for our quick-cooking parameters. We discovered, though, that the salt pork did not have to be completely rendered to season the chowder. It could be cooked in butter in conjunction with the aromatics; not all of the fat was rendered from the meat, but by the end of simmering, when the salt pork was removed, the chowder definitely tasted porky. And we had saved at least eight minutes of cooking.

For aromatics, onions and garlic were essential for depth. Tasters liked a mellow garlic flavor, so we started cooking the garlic with the onion, roughly chopping it so it would not scorch and turn the soup bitter. For additional sweetness and color, we included diced red bell pepper. Herbs were kept to a minimum, with fresh thyme and bay leaf winning out. Neither required prep work, as they could be added whole (the thyme sprigs bundled together for convenience) and removed with the cubed salt pork once the soup finished cooking,

With the basic flavors out of the way, we looked at minor points like the best type of potatoes to use and if heavy cream was necessary. Red Bliss potatoes won out for their waxy texture, colorful jackets, and clean flavor. Starchy russets broke down too easily and tasted mealy; they are not recommended for this soup. We tested cream and half-and-half, but both proved superfluous. The starch from the corn thickened the soup just fine, lending a lush, rich mouthfeel to the milky broth.

For once, time was on our side, as long cooking did little to benefit the chowder's flavor. All the soup needed was just enough simmering to cook the potatoes through and marry the flavors. We reduced the temperature to low after the soup came to a simmer to prevent it from developing a cooked milk flavor.

The final hurdle was how to add the remaining whole corn kernels. After exhaustive testing, we finally accepted that the less you cook it, the better frozen corn tastes. We sautéed, blanched, microwaved, and roasted corn in the quest for flavor, but nothing helped. Further, the texture of the corn suffered, turning tougher and more fibrous with every moment of cooking. Simply adding the frozen corn to the chowder for the final few minutes of simmering made for the most tender, flavorful corn.

Quick Corn Chowder

SERVES 4 TO 6

TIME: 50 MINUTES

As the soup simmers, it must be routinely stirred to prevent scorching; the pureed corn tends to stick to the pan bottom and burn if left unattended.

Gentle heat is important, too. If your burners run hot, use a Flame Tamer (see page 174 for details).

2	pounds frozen corn, I pound defrosted in a microwave for I minute
4	cups whole milk
2	tablespoons unsalted butter
6	ounces salt pork, rind removed, cut into 4 pieces
4	medium cloves garlic, chopped coarse
I	medium onion, diced fine
I	small red bell pepper, stemmed, seeded, and diced fine
4	bay leaves
6	fresh thyme sprigs, tied into a bundle with kitchen twine
	Salt
½	pound Red Bliss potatoes (about 2 medium), scrubbed and cut into ¾-inch dice
	Ground black pepper

1. Combine the defrosted corn and milk in the jar of a blender and process on high speed until creamy and smooth, about 1 minute. Set aside.

2. Heat the butter and salt pork in a large Dutch oven over medium-high heat. When the butter has melted and the foaming subsides (2 to 2½ minutes), add the garlic, onion, bell pepper, bay leaves, thyme, and ¾ teaspoon salt and cook, stirring frequently, until the onion softens and is just beginning to turn golden about the edges, about 4 minutes. Add the milk–corn mixture and the potatoes and bring to a simmer. Immediately reduce the heat to low and cook, stirring occasionally, until the potatoes are very tender, 20 to 25 minutes. Discard the bay leaves and thyme.

3. Add the remaining frozen corn and cook until the corn is heated through, about 4 minutes. Adjust the seasonings with salt and pepper to taste. Serve immediately.

ROASTED RED PEPPER SOUP

VIBRANTLY COLORED ROASTED RED pepper soup looks as rich as it tastes. Although traditional recipes call for roasting, steaming, peeling, and seeding red bell peppers, we felt confident that a fully respectable version could be whipped up at home in minutes with the aid of reliable jarred roasted peppers.

At its simplest, roasted red pepper soup is little more than aromatics like onion and garlic, roasted peppers, and broth simmered together to blend the flavors, then pureed to a velvety consistency. We decided the best strategy would be to develop a basic recipe and fine-tune the flavors afterward.

While we normally reach for standard yellow onions for soup, we favored red onions in this instance for their intense sweetness and red color, which intensified the soup's hue once pureed. For richness, butter won out over olive oil and vegetable oil as the cooking medium. Butter also browned the onions faster than either oil.

Garlic and broth were the next ingredients to try. We wanted a definite garlic bite to the soup to accent the sweetness of the peppers, but we did not want the garlic to overpower them. Roasted garlic proved too sweet, as did garlic cloves simmered in the broth. Quickly sautéed minced garlic—the fastest and easiest method—delivered the best flavor. For broth, chicken broth was favored over both beef and vegetable broth. Its mild, rich flavor took a back seat to the peppers but provided much-needed body. Beef broth tasted too tinny, and vegetable broth lacked presence.

With the basics settled, we moved on to the star of the soup: the peppers. While freshly roasted red peppers are the usual choice, we employed jarred roasted peppers. After testing a variety of brands (see page 11 for details), we definitely have our favorite. Divina roasted peppers possess a rich, sweet flavor superior to that of the competition, although no brand we tried was truly unacceptable. For use in the soup, we found it important to rinse jarred peppers well to rid them of the tart brine they come packed in. Unwashed peppers made the soup unpalatably sour. Coarsely chopped peppers quickly softened and blended into the soup, and the total cooking time, once everything was assembled, was just 20 minutes.

Once pureed, the soup tasted full-bodied and sweet—everything we wanted from red pepper soup. The final addition was a dose of

EQUIPMENT: Flame Tamer

A Flame Tamer or heat diffuser is a metal disk that can be fitted over an electric or a gas burner to reduce the heat output. This device is especially useful when trying to keep a pot at the barest simmer. If you don't own a Flame Tamer (it costs less than $10 and is stocked at most kitchenware stores), you can fashion one from aluminum foil. Take a long sheet of heavy-duty foil and shape it into a 1-inch-thick ring that fits on your burner. Make sure the ring is an even thickness so a pot will rest flat on it. A foil ring elevates the pot slightly above the flame or electric coil, allowing you to keep a pot of chowder at the merest simmer.

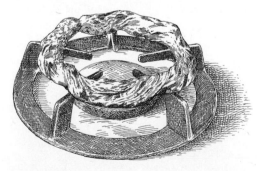

HOMEMADE FLAME TAMER
A homemade Flame Tamer made with aluminum foil keeps soups and sauces from simmering too briskly, even on a stovetop that runs fairly hot.

heavy cream, which made the texture especially lush.

With a basic recipe mastered, we were ready to tackle additional seasonings. We wanted to keep them simple and nonintrusive—just zippy enough to highlight the peppers. Spanish cooking has a classic sauce called romesco that employs roasted peppers to great effect. The peppers are ground with almonds, garlic, thyme, and paprika. The flavors work so well in a sauce that we hoped they would work equally well in soup.

While we had already included sautéed garlic in the basic soup, we felt toasted garlic would have a nuttier, sweeter flavor. Minced and pressed garlic tended to burn quickly, so we opted to sliver the cloves, which allowed for slower, more easily controlled cooking. The toasting brought out the garlic's sweet, nutty edge as we had hoped—reminiscent of the nuts and garlic combination in romesco sauce. A serendipitous side effect of toasting the garlic was that the butter browned as well, which further deepened the nutty flavor in the soup.

For the fullest thyme flavor, we found it necessary to add whole sprigs to the soup as it cooked and to use some minced as a garnish. Fresh thyme sprigs bundled together and simmered in the broth were both convenient and flavorful (thyme leaves are so small they can take a long time to pick, clean, and mince, so we try to use whole sprigs whenever possible). The garnish provided aroma and visual appeal.

Surprisingly, paprika didn't give us the slightly sweet and smoky flavor we hoped for. We opted for chipotle chiles, which possess a deep smokiness and potent heat level. These smoked jalapeños come dried and in cans rehydrated in a tomato-based adobo sauce. We prefer the convenience of the canned chiles. Because chipotles are so intense, we found

little was needed to flavor the soup. Any more than half a chile overwhelmed the mild flavor of the bell peppers and made the soup too spicy.

We garnished the soup with simple toasted croutons. We tried flavoring the croutons with sautéed garlic and adobo sauce reserved from the chipotle chile, but tasters preferred the simplicity of plain buttered croutons.

Roasted Red Pepper Soup
SERVES 4 TO 6
TIME: 40 MINUTES

Be vigilant when toasting the garlic and keep the color to a light golden brown; overbrowned garlic tastes bitter and will ruin the soup. See page 11 for information about buying jarred roasted red peppers. You will need about 1½ (13-ounce) jars for this recipe. For chicken broth, you will need 2 (14-ounce) cans. This soup makes a light meal, especially when paired with a leafy salad.

5	tablespoons unsalted butter, 3 tablespoons melted
4	medium cloves garlic, slivered
I	medium red onion, diced fine
	Salt
¼	cup unbleached all-purpose flour
24	ounces jarred roasted red peppers, drained and coarsely chopped (about 3 cups)
½	small chipotle chile in adobo, chopped (about 1½ teaspoons)
5	sprigs fresh thyme, tied into a bundle with kitchen twine, plus ½ teaspoon minced leaves
3½	cups canned low-sodium chicken broth
6	slices white sandwich bread, crusts removed, slices cut into ½-inch cubes (about 3 cups)
	Ground black pepper
¾	cup heavy cream

175

1. Heat 2 tablespoons butter in a large Dutch oven over medium-high heat until just melted. Add the garlic and cook, stirring frequently, until lightly browned, 1 to 1½ minutes (the butter will brown a little as well). Add the onion and ½ teaspoon salt and cook, stirring frequently, until the onion softens and begins to brown, 4 to 5 minutes. Add the flour and stir constantly until the flour is lightly toasted, about 45 seconds. Add the red peppers, chipotle, thyme sprigs, broth, and 1 cup water and bring to a boil. Reduce the heat, partially cover, and simmer until the peppers are soft, about 20 minutes.

2. Meanwhile, adjust an oven rack to the upper-middle position and heat the oven to 400 degrees. Combine the bread cubes with salt and pepper to taste in a medium bowl and drizzle with the melted butter; toss well with a rubber spatula to combine. Spread the croutons in a single layer on a rimmed baking sheet. Bake the croutons, turning at the halfway mark, until golden brown and crisp, 8 to 10 minutes. Set aside.

3. Remove the thyme sprigs from the soup and, working in batches, puree the soup in a

PUREEING SOUP SAFELY

Many vegetable soups are best pureed in a blender to create a smooth texture. Blending hot soup can be dangerous, though. To prevent mishaps, don't fill the blender jar more than halfway and hold the lid in the place with a folded kitchen towel.

blender until smooth and creamy. Stir in the cream and adjust the seasonings with salt and pepper to taste. Serve immediately, garnishing the individual bowls of soup with croutons and minced thyme leaves.

SWEET POTATO AND PEANUT SOUP

SWEET POTATOES ARE A DELICIOUS and nutritious vegetable unjustly relegated to side dish status in most American meals. In other parts of the world, however, sweet potatoes are used more widely, and they are the star of the meal in many regions of Africa. One common preparation is a thick soup flavored with protein-rich peanuts and a variety of seasonings. When well prepared, this soup is smooth, creamy, and fragrant with pungent spices. Because sweet potatoes cook faster than their starchier namesakes (yams), we thought an African-style sweet potato soup could be finished within our quick-cooking parameters.

During our initial research, we found dozens of recipes for sweet potato and peanut soup, many including a long list of spices and flavorings. After cooking and tasting a few, the test kitchen decided the simplest recipes did the best job of highlighting the mild flavor of the sweet potato—a definite bonus for quick turnaround. Our task, then, was to combine sweet potatoes and peanuts with just a few complementary flavors.

The first step was choosing the proper sweet potatoes. The most common variety of sweet potato sold in American markets is the Beauregard. These possess the familiar dusty orange hue and mild flavor, and they performed well in our kitchen tests in soup. Two other varieties of sweet potato—Jewel and Red Garnet—which are often sold erroneously as yams (see page 86 for more information on the difference between yams and sweet potatoes)—also work well in the soup. Both have more intense color than the Beauregard and a slightly different flavor.

With pounds and pounds of Beauregards at the ready, we began recipe development. Onions and garlic were a given, as they provided depth and richness. We finely diced the onion so it would cook quickly, browning in just five minutes. Tasters favored the pungency and body conveyed by a healthy dose of minced garlic. After testing both butter and vegetable oil as cooking mediums, we favored butter because the aromatics appeared to brown faster and have a sweeter, nuttier flavor.

Chicken broth seemed the best option for liquid, as it provided just enough richness without dominating the other flavors. We did find, however, that the best-flavored soup came from slightly diluting the chicken broth with water; the flavor of straight chicken broth competed with the sweet potatoes and peanuts.

Peanuts may sound eccentric in soup, but they paired surprisingly well with the sweet potatoes. While many recipes we found used whole peanuts, we liked the lushness imparted by peanut butter. Both creamy and chunky varieties worked fine; the soup is pureed in the end.

For spices, recipes offered dozens of choices. Many of them, like cinnamon, cloves, and cumin, muddied the sweet potato flavor. Coriander was almost a standard in our research recipes—and, as we found, for good reason. Its slightly floral flavor and aroma perfectly complemented the sweet potato. Little used in most American cooking, coriander is the seed of the coriander plant, which, when used as a leafy herb, is called cilantro. A little coriander goes a long way. We started off the soup with upward of a teaspoon and, through subsequent tests, scaled the amount back to a scant half-teaspoon. We also added a little cayenne pepper to the soup. Some tasters enjoyed the soup downright spicy, while others felt too much heat ruined it; we leave the heat level to your discretion.

With the basic flavors chosen, we looked at saving valuable cooking time in the recipe. The biggest savings was obtained by cutting the potatoes so they would cook swiftly and evenly. Our early attempts with thick chunks failed to cook in the allotted time. However, thin slivers—pieces roughly ¼-inch thick— worked well, as they cooked through in about 25 minutes. Because the soup is pureed, precision cutting was largely unnecessary. We roughly quartered the potatoes, then sliced them into slivers.

Fresh cilantro was the ideal final touch. Its fresh bite reinforced the coriander, and the flecks of green in the orange puree were visually appealing.

Sweet Potato–Peanut Soup

SERVES 4 TO 6

TIME: 50 MINUTES

Although the recipe was developed with standard sweet potatoes (called Beauregards), Jewel and Red Garnet sweet potatoes also work well. Do stick to the orange-fleshed varieties; white-fleshed sweet potatoes, in conjunction with the peanut butter, would blend to an unappetizing color. Ground coriander seemingly loses its flavor even faster than most ground spices, so give yours a taste prior to making this recipe; you may want to pick up a fresh supply. If you have a spice grinder, grind whole coriander seeds for the best flavor. Both smooth and crunchy peanut butter work fine here, as the soup is pureed. You will need 2 (14-ounce) cans chicken broth for this recipe. This soup can be prepared in advance (it will hold for 2 days in the refrigerator), but don't add the cilantro until just before serving.

2   tablespoons unsalted butter

1   medium onion, diced fine

     Salt

1   teaspoon light brown sugar

3   medium cloves garlic, minced or pressed through a garlic press (about 1 tablespoon)

$1/2$ teaspoon ground coriander

$1/8$–$1/4$ teaspoon cayenne pepper

$3^1/2$ cups canned low-sodium chicken broth

2   pounds sweet potatoes (about 3 medium), peeled, quartered lengthwise, and sliced thin

3   tablespoons peanut butter

     Ground black pepper

1   tablespoon minced fresh cilantro leaves

1. Melt the butter in a large Dutch oven over medium-high heat. Once the foaming subsides, add the onion, 1 teaspoon salt, and brown sugar and cook, stirring frequently, until the onion softens and begins to brown, about 5 minutes. Add the garlic, coriander, and cayenne and cook until aromatic, about 30 seconds. Add the broth, sweet potatoes, peanut butter, and 2 cups water. Cover, increase the heat to high, and bring to a boil. Once boiling, reduce the heat to low and partially uncover the pan. Cook until the sweet potatoes begin to crumble and are easily pierced with a knife, 25 to 30 minutes.

2. Working in batches, puree the soup in a blender until smooth. Adjust the seasonings with salt and pepper to taste and stir in the cilantro. Serve.

MULLIGATAWNY SOUP

MULLIGATAWNY MAY BE A MOUTHFUL for English speakers, but Tamil-speaking people who inhabit southern India and Sri Lanka hear "pepper water," an apt name for this spicy yet refined soup. Dating back to the mid-nineteenth-century British colonization of India, mulligatawny soup was created by local cooks to suit the timid palates of the British. Originally nothing but a lightly seasoned vegetable soup enriched with coconut milk, mulligatawny has developed into an often fiery broth loaded with everything from chicken and lamb to a cupboard's-worth of spices. Despite its generally long list of ingredients, we knew mulligatawny soup was a strong contender for quick cooking because, behind its complex seasoning and exotic flavors, it actually takes little time and effort to make. We had previously developed a recipe that came pretty close to our quick-cooking criteria, though it needed editing. Our task was to trim it to fit the rigors of quick cooking without significant impact to its flavor.

Luckily for us, our original version of mulligatawny soup was done quickly; actual cooking was little more than half an hour—just long enough for the vegetables to soften and the spices to mellow. The problem was the ingredient list. Even though it was relatively simple compared with many recipes we found, our version still possessed a substantial list of ingredients that all took time to prepare. Our first step was to make our recipe and determine which ingredients were essential. Tasters agreed that the core flavors were carrot, curry powder, garlic, ginger, coconut, and a subtle yet important hint of banana. The other ingredients melted into the background—undoubtedly important, but to what extent?

Our testing, then, was a matter of excluding ingredients one by one from the recipe and tasting the results. The first victim was celery. While its crisp vegetal flavor was appreciated, it was fairly insignificant in the big picture. Tomato paste was the next to go, though we did miss its sweetness. We were able to compensate by sautéing the onions and carrots longer than in the original recipe to bring out more of their natural sweetness. We hoped to cut back on the amount of carrots and onion to save preparation time, but to no avail; the soup tasted anemic with less.

The next omissions were spices. Curry powder packed such a punch that we hoped to be able to cut other seasonings. Most commercially prepared curry powders contain, at the least, cumin, coriander, fenugreek, turmeric, mustard seeds, and black pepper. In the original recipe, we had included cumin and cayenne in addition to a healthy amount of prepared curry powder. While tasters preferred the soup with the extra spices, they agreed it was fine without. The heat was milder and the fenugreek more pronounced, but the taste was still good.

Coarsely chopped cilantro and yogurt were the garnishes in the original recipe, and tasters would part with neither. The cilantro added brightness to the soup, and the yogurt effectively unified the flavors and tempered the curry's bite. Our stripped-down mulligatawny still tasted full-bodied and complex—and was prepared within an hour.

Mulligatawny Soup

SERVES 6 TO 8

TIME: 40 MINUTES

If you use a banana that is less than very ripe, you might need to adjust the soup's sweetness with a pinch of sugar. If you can find sweetened shredded coconut only, soak it in water for 5 minutes to remove some sugar; otherwise, the soup will taste too sweet. You will need 4 (14-ounce) cans chicken broth for this recipe.

3	tablespoons unsalted butter
2	medium onions, chopped fine
2	medium carrots, chopped coarse
½	cup shredded unsweetened coconut
1	(1½ inch) piece fresh ginger, peeled and grated (about 1½ tablespoons)
4	medium cloves garlic, 2 minced or pressed through a garlic press (about 2 teaspoons), 2 peeled and left whole
1½	tablespoons curry powder, preferably Madras
¼	cup unbleached all-purpose flour
7	cups canned low-sodium chicken broth
1	medium-to-large very ripe banana, peeled and cut into 1-inch lengths
	Salt and ground black pepper
2	tablespoons minced fresh cilantro leaves
¾	cup plain yogurt

1. Melt the butter in a large Dutch oven over medium-high heat until the foaming subsides. Add the onions and carrots and cook, stirring frequently, until softened and just beginning to lightly brown, 5 to 6 minutes. Add the coconut, 1 tablespoon ginger, and minced garlic and cook until fragrant, about 1 minute. Add the curry powder and flour and stir until evenly combined and the curry is fragrant, about 1 minute. Whisking constantly, stir in the broth. Add the banana, cover, and bring to a boil. Reduce the heat to low and simmer, stirring occasionally, until the vegetables are fully softened, about 15 minutes.

2. Puree the remaining 2 garlic cloves and 1½ teaspoons ginger with ¼ cup water in a blender until smooth, about 30 seconds. Working in batches, puree the soup in the blender with the garlic mixture until smooth. Adjust the seasonings with salt and pepper to taste. (The soup can be refrigerated in an airtight container for a day or two.) Serve, garnishing individual bowls with cilantro and a dollop of yogurt.

INGREDIENTS: Commercial Chicken Broth

Few of the dozens of commercial broths in our tasting came close to the full-bodied consistency of a successful homemade stock. Many lacked even a hint of chicken flavor. Interestingly, the four broths we rated best were all products of the Campbell Soup Company, of which Swanson is a subsidiary. In order, they were Swanson Chicken Broth, Campbell's Chicken Broth, Swanson Natural Goodness Chicken Broth (with 33 percent less sodium than regular Swanson chicken broth), and Campbell's Healthy Request Chicken Broth (with 30 percent less sodium than regular Campbell's chicken broth). The remaining broths were decidedly inferior and hard to recommend.

We tried to find out why Campbell's broths are superior to so many others, but the giant soup company declined to respond to questions, explaining that its recipes and cooking techniques are considered proprietary information. Many of the answers, however, could be found on the products' ingredient labels. As it turned out, the top two broths contain the highest levels of sodium. Salt has been used for years in the food industry to make foods with limited flavor tastier. The top two products also contained the controversial monosodium glutamate (MSG), an effective flavor enhancer.

Sadly, most of the products that had lower levels of salt and lacked the benefit of flavor enhancers simply tasted like dishwater. Their labels did indicate that ingredients included "chicken broth" or "chicken stock," sometimes both. But calls to the U.S. Food and Drug Administration and the U.S. Department of Agriculture revealed that no standards define chicken broth or stock, so an ingredient list that includes chicken broth or chicken stock may mean anything as long as some chicken is used.

Ingredients aside, we found one more important explanation for why most commercial broths simply cannot replicate the full flavor and body of homemade stock. Most broths are sold canned, which entails an extended heating process carried out to ensure a sterilized product. The immediate disadvantage of this processing is that heat breaks down naturally present flavor enhancers found in chicken protein. Further, as it destroys other volatile flavors, the prolonged heating concentrates flavor components that are not volatile, such as salt.

A few national brands of chicken broth have begun to offer their products in aseptic packaging (special cartons). Compared with traditional canning, in which products are heated in the can for up to nearly an hour to ensure sterilization, the process of aseptic packaging entails a flash heating and cooling process that is said to help products better retain both their nutritional value and their flavor.

We decided to hold another tasting to see if we could detect more flavor in the products sold in aseptic packaging. Of the recommended broths in the tasting, only Swanson broths are available in aseptic packaging, and even these are not yet available nationwide. We tasted Swanson's traditional and Natural Goodness chicken broths sold in cans and in aseptic packages. The results fell clearly in favor of the aseptically packaged broths; both tasted cleaner and more chickeny than their canned counterparts. Our conclusion: For the best of the best in commercial broths, choose one of the two Swanson broths sold in aseptic packaging. An opened aseptic package is said to keep in the refrigerator for up to 2 weeks (broth from a can is said to keep, refrigerated, for only a few days).

THE BEST CHICKEN BROTHS

Swanson Chicken Broth (left) and its reduced-sodium counterpart, Swanson Natural Goodness Chicken Broth (center), are our top choices in the test kitchen. In testing, we've found that broth packaged in aseptic cartons (right) tastes better than canned broth.

Cuban-Style Black Bean Soup

IT IS HARD TO THINK OF CUBAN food without envisioning a steaming bowl of black bean soup, redolent with sweet garlic and pungent spices and thick with savory beans and shreds of smoked pork. Unfortunately, such gustatory pleasure comes at a stiff price. Black bean soup takes hours of slow simmering to build its robust flavor. When we have all day to cook, we follow traditional methods and make it with dried beans, smoked ham hocks, and a variety of aromatics and seasonings. But on a weekday night, time does not allow for such patience. Could we possibly make black bean soup in an hour? With the aid of canned beans and a food processor, yes.

To abbreviate the recipe, we tackled the three major components of Cuban-style black bean soup independently—the *sofrito,* meat, and beans—to identify where we could save time. Generally composed of onions, garlic, and bell pepper, sofrito is nothing more than the Spanish name for the sautéed vegetables on which the soup is built. Unfortunately, a classic sofrito takes a long time to cook; the vegetables are slowly cooked down in lard or oil until they are mere shadows of their former selves—mellow, sweet, and concentrated. We tried making soup with a quickly sautéed sofrito, but it tasted thin and boring. We then tried a different angle. Instead of dicing all the vegetables, we tried finely mincing them in a food processor—almost to a pulp. The processed vegetables cooked through in about half the time of diced vegetables but possessed most of the flavor. So we saved time on both prep work and cooking.

As the soup is cooked so briefly, we knew the classic ham hock would do us little good. It takes hours before the meat is fully softened and its flavors blended with the beans. But its rich flavor is essential, so we looked at other pork products with similar intensity. After we tested salt pork, a variety of sausages, and bacon, the latter won out. Salt pork lent lushness but little depth, and the sausage seasonings overwhelmed the soup. Bacon rendered enough fat to sauté the vegetables, and the crisp bits were an ideal garnish for the finished soup, adding both flavor and a pleasing crunch.

All that was left was to fine-tune the supporting flavors and the soup's texture. Tasters all enjoyed the spice mixture of cumin, cayenne, and dried oregano, especially when lightly toasted in the pan before the liquid was added. The dry heat intensified their flavors by drawing out the volatile oils of the spices. For liquid, beef broth tasted tinny, and all chicken broth detracted from the bean flavor. Part chicken broth and part water proved the best bet, lending richness without being intrusive.

With respect to texture, opinions varied; some tasters preferred an utterly smooth soup, while others chose a slightly thickened version. A blender aerated the beans, and tasters deemed the texture "weird." A food processor (still set up from pureeing the vegetables) yielded a smooth, thick puree punctuated with bits of beans that most tasters enjoyed, although some wanted a chunkier texture. Deciding that pureeing a portion of the soup was the best method, we succeeded in pleasing everyone.

Classic garnishes run the gamut from diced red onion to sieved hard-cooked eggs and even a splash of rum. We preferred to keep them simple and top bowls of soup with a sprinkle of cilantro, the reserved bacon bits, and a spritz of lime juice.

Cuban-Style Black Bean Soup

SERVES 4 TO 6

TIME: 45 MINUTES

For a strictly vegetarian version, replace the bacon with 3 tablespoons olive oil and use all water or vegetable broth instead of chicken broth. Grated cheese or sour cream can replace the bacon bits as a garnish. This soup can be prepared in advance and refrigerated for several days, although you should fry fresh bacon for the garnish just before serving. You will need 2 (14-ounce) cans chicken broth for this recipe.

6	ounces bacon, diced
1	medium onion, chopped coarse
1	medium red bell pepper, stemmed, seeded, and chopped coarse
6	medium cloves garlic, chopped coarse
1	teaspoon dried oregano
½	teaspoon ground cumin
¼	teaspoon cayenne pepper
4	(15-ounce) cans black beans, drained and rinsed
3½	cups canned low-sodium chicken broth
	Salt
	Hot pepper sauce, such as Tabasco
½	cup coarsely chopped fresh cilantro leaves
2	limes, quartered

1. Cook the bacon in a large Dutch oven over medium-high heat, stirring frequently, until the fat is rendered, about 5 minutes.

2. Meanwhile, combine the onion, bell pepper, and garlic in the workbowl of a food processor and process until finely minced, about twenty-five 1-second pulses, scraping down the sides of the workbowl with a rubber spatula as necessary. With a slotted spoon, transfer the browned bacon bits to a paper towel to drain. Add the minced vegetables to the Dutch oven (do not wash the food processor workbowl) and cook, stirring frequently, until dramatically reduced in volume and just beginning to brown, about 6 minutes. Add the oregano, cumin, and cayenne pepper and toast until fragrant, about 30 seconds. Add the beans, broth, and 3 cups water and bring to a boil. Reduce the heat to medium-low, partially cover, and simmer until the flavors are fully blended, about 20 minutes.

3. Transfer 2½ cups soup (both beans and broth) to the workbowl of the food processor and process until smooth, about 30 seconds. Return the pureed soup to the pot, stir to combine, and adjust the seasonings with salt and hot pepper sauce to taste. Serve immediately, garnishing individual bowls with the reserved bacon and cilantro and offering lime wedges at the table.

ITALIAN LENTIL SOUP

ITALIAN CUISINE BOASTS A WIDE variety of hearty peasant-style soups that are nutritious, quick, and economical. A few vegetables, a bit of meat, beans, and even stale bread find their way into the pot to become deeply flavored, irresistible soups. The downside to these recipes is that they tend to take a long time to cook. Low, steady heat is responsible for the rich flavor. We were curious about whether we could make soup with such flavor in a fraction of the normal cooking time. We decided to focus on a Tuscan lentil soup flavored with Parmesan and rosemary.

Our first step was to figure out the fastest method to cook both the lentils and the vegetables. Italian soups and stews are classically built on a mixture of sautéed aromatic vegetables called a soffritto, which literally translates as "underfried." While the exact combination of vegetables differs regionally, most soffrittos are essentially the same: vegetables slowly sweated in copious amounts of olive oil, butter, or lard. The slow cooking teases out the sweetness of the vegetables, and the mixture takes on a depth of flavor that cannot easily be replicated with quick cooking. Clearly, we could not cook the vegetables for long enough before starting the lentils; we would never be done in an hour. But could we cook the lentils in a separate pot and add the vegetables once they finished? Would the dish taste as good as that made by the traditional method?

We started with the lentils. Lentils come in a rainbow of colors, from pale yellow to pink, brown, gray, and green. Brown lentils are the most commonly used in Italy and what we chose for the soup, though dark green lentils du Puy from France worked well too. They are less readily available than brown but have a richer flavor and more compact texture. Brown and green both cooked in 30 to 40 minutes—perfect for a quick soup.

Because the lentil cooking liquid would become the soup broth, it needed to be moderately flavored. At the outset, we chose canned chicken broth, but it overpowered the delicate lentil flavor. Cutting the chicken broth by half with water solved this problem. The finished soup possessed the richness of the broth but did not taste particularly chickeny—something we wanted to avoid.

To pep up the broth, we included several bay leaves (the standard single bay leaf failed to do anything in such a brief period), which imparted a mildly earthy, herbal flavor that paired perfectly with the beans. Garlic was next, and we used a neat trick sent in by a reader of *Cook's Illustrated*. We sliced off the top of a whole garlic head (loose skins removed) and added it to the broth. The cloves inside softened by the time the beans were tender and could be squeezed out like roasted garlic and returned to the broth to impart a sweet, rich garlic flavor.

Many Italian soups rely on the rind of a wedge of Parmesan cheese for flavor. Even in the relatively short time the lentils simmered,

TWO WAYS TO FLAVOR SOUPS QUICKLY

Garlic and herbs are often used to flavor soup. Instead of being minced, they can be added whole to the soup as follows.

A. Add a whole head of garlic (with the top and papery outer skins removed) to the pot and let it simmer until the soup is done. Use tongs to remove the garlic and either discard it or squeeze out the softened cloves with the tongs and return the garlic to the soup.

B. Instead of stripping leaves off branches of rosemary or thyme and then mincing them, we often throw a fresh sprig of either herb right into the pot as the soup cooks. Remove the spent sprig much as you would remove a bay leaf before serving the soup. Rosemary can be very strong, so don't let it simmer for more than 20 minutes or so.

183

we found that a good-sized Parmesan rind gave the broth depth and complexity.

With the beans simmering away, we turned our attention to the soffritto. An authentic soffritto generally includes onion, celery, carrot, and garlic, but we hoped to pare it down. The garlic was already taken care of—it simmered in the broth—and onions were essential, so it came down to a choice between carrot and celery. After a few batches, tasters unanimously preferred the sweet taste and bright color of the carrot, so celery was out. We slowly sweated the diced vegetables in an abundance of olive oil until they were very soft and reduced in volume—but not browned, as Italian recipes so adamantly warned against. By using a 12-inch skillet, we were able to reduce the cooking time to about 20 minutes. The mixture then went into the beans and simmered until the flavors married—about 20 minutes longer.

The soup tasted surprisingly full-bodied and rich despite our unconventional method. The soffritto blended easily into the beans, and the substantial amount of garlic added sweetness and an irresistible aroma. To garnish the soup, tasters favored a splash of olive oil for a lush mouthfeel and a drizzle of balsamic vinegar to accent the mild lentil flavor.

Italian Lentil Soup

SERVES 4 TO 6

TIME: 55 MINUTES

While brown lentils taste just fine, pricier French lentils du Puy offer a slightly richer flavor and maintain their shape better. If a meatier flavor is desired, ¼ cup diced pancetta may be added to the vegetables. If you don't have a supply of Parmesan rinds, you can purchase them cheaply at Italian markets. Stored in the freezer, the rinds keep indefinitely. You will need 2 (14-ounce) cans chicken broth for this recipe.

1½	cups lentils (about ¾ pound), rinsed and picked over
1	large Parmesan rind (about 3 by 4 inches)
4	bay leaves
1	medium head garlic, top third cut off and discarded, loose outer skins removed and discarded
3½	cups canned low-sodium chicken broth
¼	cup extra-virgin olive oil, plus more for drizzling
2	medium carrots, peeled and diced
1	large red onion, diced
	Salt
1	sprig fresh rosemary
	Ground black pepper
	Balsamic vinegar for drizzling

1. Bring the lentils, Parmesan rind, bay leaves, garlic, broth, and 3 cups water to a boil in a large saucepan over medium-high heat. Reduce the heat to low, partially cover the pan, and simmer for 20 minutes, until the lentils are tender.

2. Meanwhile, combine the ¼ cup oil, carrots, onion, and ½ teaspoon salt in a large skillet over medium heat. Cook, stirring occasionally, until the vegetables are soft and have shrunk considerably in size but are not browned, about 20 minutes. Using a rubber spatula, scrape the vegetables into the saucepan with the lentils. Add the rosemary sprig and cook until the flavors fully blend and the lentils are tender, about 20 minutes longer.

3. Remove and discard the rosemary sprig, bay leaves, and rind. Using tongs, remove the garlic head from the soup and squeeze the head to remove the cloves. Coarsely chop the cloves and return them to the pan. Adjust the seasonings with salt and pepper to taste. (This soup can be refrigerated in an airtight container for several days.) Serve, drizzling bowls with oil and vinegar to taste.

MOROCCAN CHICKPEA SOUP

MOROCCAN COOKING IS A HEADY amalgam of Asian, African, and European cuisines rich with exotic tastes and flavors. Many dishes are characterized by complex combinations of spices and a keen balance of sweet and savory elements. *Harira* is one of Morocco's most important dishes. Traditionally served as the main meal of the day during the monthlong Muslim holiday Ramadan (which involves fasting until sunset, hence the need for a nutritious meal), harira is a hearty stew composed of chickpeas and/or lentils and cubed lamb in a spicy tomato broth. Laced with herbs and spices, it is an ideal one-pot meal. Despite its traditionally long list of ingredients and even longer cooking time, we sensed that, with judicious trimming and a few shortcuts, a delicious version could be made within the hour.

There are literally thousands of recipes for harira, as it is customized to suit the cook's taste and budget. Some versions we researched included several varieties of meat and many vegetables, while others were abbreviated to just a few ingredients. The few standard elements include chickpeas, tomatoes, and a starch of some sort—pasta, bread dough, or potatoes. The basic seasonings were saffron, cumin, ginger, garlic, and lemon juice. In a taste test, the most spare versions we tried lacked the rounded flavor we desired, and the most complicated versions were simply out of our league for both exotic ingredients and extensive time necessary for preparation. Our aim was to find a midpoint between the extremes and develop a recipe that communicated harira's richness and unique flavor with just an hour of effort.

As with most soups, onions were the place to start. Without them, the soup tasted hollow and bland. While we normally would have sautéed the onions in olive oil to best blend with the other flavors, a little research suggested that butter was the more authentic choice, and to good effect. (Moroccans typically use a clarified salted butter called *smen,* similar to India's *ghee.*) The butter both browned the onions faster than oil and added a sweet nuttiness that, in the finished soup, boosted the spices. A little sugar and salt mixed with the onions further expedited the browning process, as the salt drew out the onion's moisture and the sugar caramelized in the pan's relatively high heat.

A substantial amount of garlic was the next addition, followed by the spices, which must be dry-toasted in the pan for the best flavor. After experimenting with a variety of spices (the amounts included in authentic recipes were often staggeringly large), we chose saffron (for its rich color as much as its pungent aroma and distinct flavor), hot paprika, ginger, and cumin. Coincidentally, these spices—along with cinnamon and cardamom—form the base for Morocco's ubiquitous spice mixture, *ras el hanout.*

Chickpeas and tomatoes were the next additions, as was choosing the broth that best matched the flavors. Dried chickpeas rehydrated through a long, slow simmer would be the traditional choice, but this approach was far too time-consuming for us. We have long thought canned chickpeas are an excellent shortcut, and their use in this recipe was no exception; they possessed all the flavor and firm texture of dried beans and took virtually none of the effort.

For most of the year, high-quality canned tomatoes are superior to fresh tomatoes in the produce aisle. They are consistently sweet and fruity, unlike their flavorless siblings grown for aesthetics above flavor. And canned tomatoes are convenient—no prep work necessary beyond opening the can. While we often discard the juices the tomatoes are packed in, they tasted fine in this instance, boosting the flavor of the chicken broth, which tasters preferred to vegetable broth or water.

Tasters preferred potatoes to pasta for flavor and superior thickening properties. With a little gentle persuasion and a wooden spoon, the potatoes broke down a bit and lent a pleasant viscosity to the thin broth. Small red potatoes added the best flavor and could be used without peeling, saving prep time and adding color to the soup.

It would have been unthinkable not to finish the soup with fresh herbs and lemon juice. Mint, parsley, and cilantro, either independently or in combination, are classic choices. Tasters favored parsley, with mint a close second. Cilantro, on the other hand, faced mixed reviews, as some tasters felt the combination of cilantro and saffron was odd. In any case, the herbs in conjunction with the lemon pleasantly brightened the soup.

RELEASING STARCH FROM POTATOES

Once the potatoes are tender, use the back of a wooden spoon to press some of them against the side of the pot. This releases more starch and helps thicken the soup.

Moroccan-Style Chickpea Soup

SERVES 4 TO 6

TIME: 50 MINUTES

Feel free to enliven this dish with your favorite hot sauce. In Morocco, it would be jazzed up with harissa, a fiery chili paste seasoned with caraway or cumin seeds, garlic, and coriander. Fresh mint, in addition to the parsley, makes a soothing, traditional accompaniment. Although tasters preferred chicken broth, vegetable broth makes an acceptable vegetarian substitution. You will need 2 (14-ounce) cans chicken broth for this recipe.

3	tablespoons unsalted butter
I	medium onion, diced fine
I	teaspoon sugar
	Salt
4	medium cloves garlic, minced or pressed through a garlic press (about 4 teaspoons)
¼	teaspoon saffron threads, crumbled
½	teaspoon hot paprika
¼	teaspoon ground ginger
¼	teaspoon ground cumin
I	(14 ½-ounce) can diced tomatoes, including juices
2	(15-ounce) cans chickpeas, drained and rinsed
I	medium zucchini (about 8 ounces), cut into ½-inch dice
I	pound small red potatoes, scrubbed and cut into ½-inch dice
3 ½	cups canned low-sodium chicken broth
¼	cup chopped fresh parsley and/or mint leaves
I	medium lemon, cut into wedges

1. Melt the butter in a large Dutch oven over medium-high heat. Once the foaming subsides, add the onion, sugar, and ½ teaspoon salt and cook, stirring frequently, until the onion softens and begins to brown, about 5

minutes. Add the garlic, saffron, paprika, ginger, and cumin and cook, stirring frequently, until aromatic, about 30 seconds.

2. Add the tomatoes, chickpeas, zucchini, potatoes, and broth; increase the heat to high and bring to a boil. Reduce the heat to medium-low and simmer, stirring occasionally, until the potatoes are tender, 20 to 25 minutes.

3. With a wooden spoon, mash a small amount of the potatoes against the side of the pot (see the illustration on page 186) and stir to thicken the broth. Remove the pan from the heat, stir in the herbs, and adjust the seasonings with salt to taste. (This soup can be refrigerated in an airtight container for several days; add the herbs just before serving.) Serve with the lemon wedges.

RAMEN NOODLE SOUP

EVERYONE, AT SOME POINT, HAS BEEN desperate enough to eat ramen noodles—those tightly compressed noodle bricks with the mysterious seasoning packet. Just add boiling water for a meal in minutes. Although filling, ramen are generally not very appetizing.

However, ramen noodles are more than just a bargain convenience food; they have a culinary pedigree. Ramen is the Japanese translation of *lo mein,* the Chinese term for "boiled noodles," which have been consumed for thousands of years. In China and Japan, noodle shops are as prolific as pizza joints in the United States, open at all hours and serving noodle dishes of innumerable varieties. Cellophane-packed ramen noodles, then, are not the problem; it's the MSG-heavy seasoning packet, which provides weak flavor and a heavy dose of sodium. We wondered if we could put the noodles to better use in a

heartier, healthier broth that, in the spirit of things, could still be both inexpensive and ready in minutes.

Our challenge was to pick just a handful of assertive ingredients that packed enough flavor to make a rich broth quickly—ideally, within half an hour. We chose chicken broth as our base for its rich yet neutral flavor and diluted it a little so the chicken flavor was not overwhelming. For aromatics, garlic and ginger were natural choices. We simply smashed the garlic cloves and ginger coins (¼-inch-thick slices), skins and all, with the flat side or butt end of a chef's knife. We found that bruising the aromatics helps release their volatile oils faster. Leaving the skins on meant the broth had to be strained, but that was easier than peeling and mincing the garlic and ginger.

For a rich, meaty flavor, we chose dried shiitake mushrooms, a common flavoring in Asian soups and readily available in supermarkets. Dried shiitakes possess a potent meaty flavor and a musty, earthy aroma—much more vigorous than their fresh counterparts, which

INGREDIENTS: Ramen Noodles

Ramen are sold in cellophane packages in most American supermarkets. They have a distinctive wavy appearance and chewy texture. Ramen are called instant noodles because they cook so quickly, in just two to three minutes. They almost always come with a separate flavor packet, which we simply throw out. We prefer to make our own broth and add meat, seafood, tofu, and vegetables.

In Japan, ramen noodles are available fresh and with egg in the dough. We are hard pressed to find fresh ramen in the United States and have to settle for the instant variety. Unlike fresh ramen, instant ramen never contain egg. Be wary of noodles with an unnaturally bright yellow color, which often comes from a list of chemicals and dyes. Read labels and avoid noodles with ingredients other than flour, water, and salt.

we also tried. We quickly found a little shiitake goes a long way. Just four mushrooms were needed to lend a deep but not overpowering flavor to the broth. We added the mushrooms whole—dried and shriveled (but rinsed)—and by the time the flavors had blended, the mushrooms were tender enough to thinly slice, adding texture to the soup.

For saltiness and color, soy sauce was essential. Its strong flavor gave body to the soup and colored it a rich caramel hue. After trying several varieties, including light, black, and tamari, we favored standard soy sauce. Light versions lacked depth, and black soy and tamari both made the broth too sweet (they contain sugar). Along with the soy sauce, we added a small amount of mirin, or sweetened rice wine, for a hint of sharpness and extra sweetness.

The final touch, for a distinctly Asian flavor and aroma, was star anise. A key component in five-spice powder, star anise has a rich, sweet black licorice flavor—much more robust than anise and fennel seeds. The flavor boosted the mushroom flavor and added a mysterious note that tasters enjoyed. Just two pods were enough—any more and the broth tasted of nothing but licorice.

With the broth ready, it took just minutes to finish the soup. Ramen noodles are available everywhere, so finding them was no problem. When we added the bricks whole, the noodles were so long they were difficult to eat. The noodles are about 16 inches long—fine for those who like to slurp their soup, but none of our tasters fell into that category. For easier consumption, we chose to break the raw noodles into smaller bits that easily fit onto a soupspoon. The ramen cooked in just three minutes in the pot.

Tofu is a common addition to Japanese noodle soups, and we thought this protein-rich ingredient could help turn the soup into a complete meal. When we added the tofu to the pot, it tended to break up and cloud the broth. As it didn't need to cook—it just heats through in the broth—we added it instead to the individual bowls and ladled the soup over top. Tasters chose firm tofu for its mild resistance. Soft and silken tofu fell apart too easily, and extra firm was disconcertingly chewy in the soup. A garnish of scallions finished the soup.

~

Ramen Noodle Soup with Shiitake Mushrooms and Tofu

SERVES 4 TO 6

TIME: 40 MINUTES

The broth may be prepared a couple of days ahead of time and stored in an airtight container. If you are leery of tofu, you can replace it with an equal amount of diced roast chicken or pork or exclude the protein altogether. You will need 3 (14-ounce) cans chicken broth for this recipe.

5¼	cups canned low-sodium chicken broth
2	tablespoons soy sauce
¼	cup mirin or dry sherry
1	(1-inch) piece fresh ginger, cut into 4 coins and smashed (see the illustration on page 189)
4	medium cloves garlic, lightly crushed with skins on
2	whole star anise pods
4	dried shiitake mushrooms, rinsed
2	(3-ounce) packages ramen noodles, flavor packets discarded, noodles broken into ½-inch pieces
12	ounces firm tofu, cut into small cubes
4	medium scallions, sliced thin on the bias

1. Bring the broth, soy sauce, mirin, ginger, garlic, star anise, mushrooms, and 2 cups water to a boil over medium-high heat in a large

saucepan. Reduce the heat to low and simmer for 20 minutes. Remove the mushrooms with a slotted spoon and thinly slice them. Strain the broth through a fine-mesh strainer into a large bowl and return the strained broth to the saucepan; discard the solids.

2. Bring the broth to a simmer over medium-high heat and add the noodles and sliced mushrooms. Cook, stirring frequently, until the noodles soften, about 3 minutes. Divide the tofu equally among individual bowls, then ladle the soup over the tofu. Serve immediately, garnishing the soup with scallions.

CUCUMBER AND SHRIMP SOUP

TORRID SUMMER DAYS CALL FOR light meals to temper the heat. Gazpacho is the first soup that comes to mind, but all that chopping of vegetables takes time. For a change of pace, we make buttermilk-based cucumber soup. Light and refreshing, this soup is the perfect antidote to the wilting sun. Little but cucumber, buttermilk, and a flavoring or two, this soup comes together in minutes with little preparation; the blender does all the work. Best of all, no cooking is necessary. The trick is overcoming the inherent blandness of cucumbers and making them substantial enough for a light meal. For this version, we chose to pair cucumber and buttermilk with dill and shrimp.

The first recipe we tried underwhelmed most tasters. It was little more than dill- and mustard-flavored buttermilk with diced cucumber and shrimp stirred in. It tasted thin and lacked presence, though tasters enjoyed the overall flavor combination. We wanted to stick with the basic flavors while thickening the texture and pumping up the flavors—the soup needed more complexity to make it worthwhile.

Our first step was to puree cucumbers into the buttermilk. The subtly sweet flavor of the cucumber blended well with the tangy buttermilk and thickened it as well. We played with the ratio of cucumber and buttermilk until they were balanced—sweet and tart, with a fruity edge. We also decided to reserve some cucumber to add as garnish for a clean burst of cucumber flavor.

To add depth to the soup, we knew it needed fat. A shot of heavy cream did not do much, and plain yogurt was too harsh, although most tasters felt a less acidic ingredient might do the trick. Sour cream, then, seemed the next logical step, and it did, in fact, add the brightness and lush texture we wanted. The creaminess tied the flavors together and made the soup more substantial.

With the basics down, we worked on the seasonings. Mustard and dill were givens, but in what form? After trying several types of mustard, tasters preferred the refined bite

SMASHING GINGER

To release flavorful oils from fresh ginger, thinly slice an unpeeled knob and then use the end of a chef's knife to smash each piece. This technique works best when you want to infuse the flavor of ginger into a liquid. Best of all, the ginger does not need to be peeled or chopped; fish the coins out of the liquid when they are spent.

of Dijon, the acidity of which balanced the sweetness in the soup. A little went a long way, though. We ended up scaling back the amount to a mere teaspoon—an amount where it was more noticeable by its absence than presence. For a hint of heat, we added a small amount of hot pepper sauce—just enough to remind tasters how soothing the soup really was. Despite these seasonings, the soup was still a little flat and needed a kick. Onions, shallots, and scallions all helped, but tasters favored garlic most of all. Again, we decided on just enough to be noticed yet not interfere: one small clove.

Finally, we focused on the garnishes. We wanted to use precooked shrimp to save on preparation and cooking but found little consensus about size; different stores carried different-size precooked shrimp. To alleviate confusion, we decided to dice the shrimp (size really didn't matter, then) and make a relish of sorts that included some reserved diced cucumber. The combination looked a little plain on its own, but more dill perked it up. The final touch was a little more sour cream to bind the relish together. With a fat dollop of the relish in the middle of each bowl, the soup was austerely elegant—as pretty as any restaurant meal.

SEEDING CUCUMBERS

Halve the cucumber (already peeled, if necessary) lengthwise. Run a small spoon inside each cucumber half to scoop out the seeds and surrounding pulp.

Cucumber and Shrimp Soup

SERVES 4 TO 6

TIME: 45 MINUTES (INCLUDES 30 MINUTES IN THE REFRIGERATOR)

If precooked shrimp are unavailable, poach raw peeled shrimp in seasoned (2 teaspoons salt to 2 quarts water) boiling water just until pink (about 2 minutes) and shock under cold water to stop the cooking. Any size shrimp works because they are diced. See the illustration at left for tips on seeding cucumbers.

½	pound cooked peeled shrimp, diced medium
3	medium cucumbers, peeled and seeded, ½ cucumber cut into medium dice, remaining cucumbers chopped coarse
I	tablespoon plus ⅓ cup sour cream
3	tablespoons minced fresh dill leaves
	Salt
I	small clove garlic, peeled
3	cups buttermilk
I	teaspoon Dijon mustard
⅛	teaspoon hot pepper sauce, such as Tabasco
I ¼	teaspoons sugar
	Ground black pepper

1. With a rubber spatula, combine the shrimp, diced cucumber, 1 tablespoon sour cream, and 1 tablespoon dill in a medium bowl. Add salt to taste and refrigerate until needed.

2. Combine the remaining ingredients, including 1 teaspoon salt and black pepper to taste, in a blender and blend until smooth, about 1 minute. Adjust the seasonings with salt and pepper to taste and refrigerate until chilled, about 30 minutes.

3. Ladle the soup into chilled shallow bowls. Spoon a large dollop of the shrimp mixture in the center of each bowl. Serve immediately.

Spicy Thai-Style Shrimp Soup

QUICK THAI SOUPS LACK THE RICH body of long-cooked European-style soups, but they possess a unique freshness. One of the best-known Thai soups is called tom yum. It is a spicy, slightly sour chicken broth–based soup flavored with shrimp, mushrooms, tomato, lemon grass, and kaffir lime leaves. While this combination may sound odd, the flavors blend surprisingly well. Despite its exotic roots, we felt confident that a Thai-style shrimp soup could be replicated by the home cook with a minimum of effort and without a run to the specialty market. For once, preparation wasn't a race against the clock; the soup could easily be ready within the hour. The problem was ingredients. How could we best imitate the soup's exotic flavors without authentic ingredients like lemon grass and kaffir lime leaves?

Making the soup involves two steps. First, the broth is mixed, simmered, and strained; then shrimp, mushrooms, and tomato are added and simmered until just cooked through—a matter of moments. Canned chicken broth was our starting point, but we had our work cut out for us building the broth from grocery store staples and creating its uniquely Thai flavor palette, with hot, salty, sweet, and sour elements.

Heat, or spiciness, traditionally comes from innocuous-looking little red chiles called Thai or bird chiles. Despite their benign appearance, these chiles pack an incendiary punch. We made the decision to pick a more accessible option, such as dried red pepper flakes or cayenne pepper. Hot red pepper flakes, however, lacked the bright, clean spiciness of fresh chiles—an important component in the broth. We went back to fresh chiles but chose milder jalapeños, which provided the brightness and green vegetal flavor we wanted at a

more tolerable heat level.

Saltiness comes from the fish sauce. "Pungent" may be a polite description for fish sauce's odd charm, but it lends a trademark body to Thai foods that cannot be obtained from any other source. Luckily, fish sauce is readily available in most markets. A little goes a long way with fish sauce. We tried amounts from $\frac{1}{2}$ cup to a scant tablespoon and found that 2 tablespoons imparted a pleasantly fishy edge to the broth that tasters found ideal.

While it may seem odd to add sugar as a seasoning to savory dishes, it is routine in Southeast Asian cooking to balance spiciness and sourness. Raw palm sugar—light brown in color and slightly earthy-tasting—is the traditional choice, but it is rarely available outside of specialty markets. Luckily, we found plain white sugar worked just as well. Just a scant teaspoon was needed in the broth.

The sourness authentically comes from a combination of lemon grass, kaffir lime leaves, and lime juice. Though lemon grass and kaffir lime share names with common citrus fruits, the similarities end there. Kaffir lime leaves are intensely aromatic, almost floral, and can impart a mild bitterness. Lemon grass is a narrow, fibrous grass with a rich aroma and sweet lemon flavor tasters described as "fresh-tasting." Both ingredients were irreplaceable, though we realized their role was as much about citrus smell as flavor. Instead of trying to find perfect substitutions for them, we focused on coaxing the most aroma and flavor out of lime juice. Adding lots of juice tipped the delicate balance of the broth. We discovered that adding the lime juice off the heat just before serving the soup maximized its impact. The pleasant pungency of the lime juice hit diners directly. With this method, even the most die-hard Thai food lover in the test kitchen was pleased despite the absence of lemon grass and kaffir lime leaves.

To round out the broth's flavors, we included garlic, ginger, and cilantro. Because we planned to strain the broth, we pounded the garlic and ginger with the end of a chef's knife to release their volatile oils and added skins and all to the broth—a standard Asian cooking technique. We also followed tradition and used cilantro stems in the broth, reserving the leaves for a garnish. We were impressed by the significantly more potent flavor the stems had than the leaves. When we cooked leaves in the broth, their flavor was mild and fleeting at best.

Within 20 minutes, the broth was richly flavored and ready to be strained. The rest of the ingredients—shrimp, mushrooms, and tomato—were then simmered in the broth until just cooked. While oyster mushrooms are the authentic choice, tasters also enjoyed meaty cremini mushrooms and even conventional white button mushrooms. Because of their dense texture, we gave the mushrooms a head start over the shrimp, which took just a minute to cook. Tasters favored medium-size, one-bite shrimp, though larger shrimp take a little less time to peel and can be cut down to size. Because the soup is rustic, we coarsely chopped the tomatoes, seeds and all, and added them at the last minute. For a burst of fresh heat, we added more sliced jalapeño. In the end, this soup offers exotic flavors with pedestrian ingredients—everything we hoped for.

Spicy Thai-Style Shrimp Soup

SERVES 4 TO 6

TIME: 40 MINUTES

The broth (through step 1) can be prepared up to 2 days in advance. Just remember to withhold the lime juice until the last moment; otherwise, its flavor and aroma will dissipate. If you can locate lemon grass at the market, feel free to add a stalk to the broth, trimmed of its fibrous top and bruised with the flat side of a knife. For maximum heat, do not seed the chiles. See photo of this recipe on page 151.

5¼	cups canned low-sodium chicken broth
1	(½-inch) piece fresh ginger, cut in half and smashed (see the illustration on page 189)
2	large cloves garlic, lightly crushed with skins on
2	tablespoons fish sauce
4–6	cilantro stems, including roots, plus ¼ cup roughly chopped fresh cilantro leaves
1	teaspoon sugar
2	medium jalapeño chiles, stemmed and sliced crosswise into ¼-inch rings
2	medium tomatoes, cored and chopped coarse
½	pound cremini, oyster, or button mushrooms, wiped clean and quartered (or cut into sixths if large)
½	pound medium shrimp (about 41 to 50 per pound), peeled
3	tablespoons juice from 2 limes

1. Bring the broth, ginger, garlic, fish sauce, cilantro stems, sugar, half of the sliced chiles, and one-quarter of the chopped tomatoes to a boil in a large saucepan over medium-high heat. Reduce the heat to low and simmer for 20 minutes. Strain the broth through a fine-mesh strainer into a large bowl, pushing on the solids to extract as much liquid as possible.

2. Return the broth to the pan and bring it to a simmer over medium-high heat. Add the mushrooms and the remaining chiles and cook for 2 minutes. Add the shrimp and cook for 1 minute longer. Remove the soup from the heat and add the lime juice. Evenly portion the remaining chopped tomato and the chopped cilantro among individual bowls and ladle the soup over top. Serve immediately.

BOURRIDE

ALTHOUGH BOUILLABAISSE IS THE most famous fish stew of Marseilles, the Provençal port city, bourride deserves to share the limelight. Simpler than its more celebrated sibling, bourride is a tomato- and wine-based broth studded with chunks of tender monkfish and enriched by a pungent *aïoli* (garlic- and lemon-flavored mayonnaise). The soup's flavors are clean and bright, and it needs just a handful of ingredients and little preparation.

Classically, bourride has three major components: broth, fish, and aïoli. The broth is simmered until its ingredients are blended; then the fish is poached in the broth. The broth and fish are served with a fat dollop of aïoli and thick slices of toasted baguette. In most recipes we found, the broth is little more than tomato, onion, garlic, wine, fish stock, and a strip or two of orange zest—a trademark flourish. Everything was easy to find and quick to prepare, but fish stock posed a problem. There was no way we could make it quickly, and we have yet to find an adequate commercially produced fish stock. Bottled clam juice can work well in some cases, but it failed us in this instance; tasters felt it muddied the pure flavor of the sweet monkfish. Evidently, we had to tweak the classic recipe to make up for the absence of fish stock.

We developed more flavor by sautéing the aromatics (onions and garlic), although the broth still tasted thin without fish stock. We then revisited a technique used to great effect in our recipe for black bean soup (page 182). We processed the onion and garlic in the food processor until almost a paste and then sautéed the mixture. The broth's flavor was deeper still, and the minuscule bits of onion and garlic virtually melted into the broth. As another bonus, we saved on preparation time; the onions just had to be coarsely chopped before processing. Tasters agreed that the fruity, sharp

broth needed a green note and recommended parsley. We reserved parsley leaves for a garnish and threw the stems into the pot to simmer, along with several bay leaves. The sweet, almost vanilla flavor of bay was a perfect match for the monkfish.

Monkfish has a firm texture and sweet flavor reminiscent of lobster. All of the monkfish meat is within the tail, which is divided into two fillets. These vary in size with the size of the fish, and some authorities suggest the larger fillets taste better, though we did not find that to be true. The fillets may be covered in a dark, viscous membrane that must be removed before cooking. This is easy to do with a sharp paring knife, but the fishmonger should do it if asked. We tried cutting the fish into chunks of various sizes, and tasters preferred 1-inch pieces; smaller pieces cooked too quickly and dried out. Within 8 to 10 minutes, the fish poached in the broth.

The aïoli is more than a garnish; it flavors both the broth and the fish. Heady with garlic and olive oil, it brightens and enriches the lean broth. Aïoli is nothing but mayonnaise with garlic and lemon juice, so we thought we could get away with doctoring commercial mayonnaise. We were proved wrong, as this faux aïoli proved to be loose, flabby, and flavorless, and it had none of the charms of the freshly prepared sauce. The good news was that real aïoli couldn't be easier to make. We already had the food processor out for chopping the onions and garlic, so we were halfway there; the workbowl didn't even have to be cleaned because the residual juices only added flavor. Into the bowl went garlic, egg yolks (with the whites, the aïoli came out too loose), lemon juice, and salt. Once these ingredients were combined, we added a thin, steady stream of olive oil. Within two minutes, we achieved a thick, creamy traditional aïoli.

After trying a few versions of aïoli, we

made some alterations to our original approach. We preferred regular olive oil to extra-virgin, which turned the aïoli bitter. We also switched to orange juice from lemon juice. The broth included orange peel, and the fresh juice reinforced the flavor.

Bourride

SERVES 6

TIME: 50 MINUTES

Some canned tomatoes are more acidic than others. If the broth tastes too acidic, feel free to add a pinch of sugar for balance. A dry white wine such as Sauvignon Blanc works well in this recipe. If monkfish is unavailable, substitute another firm-fleshed white fish—cod, grouper, or striped bass. Thick slices of toasted baguette are ideal for soaking up the broth. Either serve them on the side or place a slice in each bowl before adding the soup. Be sure to ask your fishmonger to trim the membrane from the monkfish fillets. The broth (through step 1) can be prepared up to 2 days in advance, but the fish should be cooked just before serving, and the aïoli is best made at the last minute. To streamline your work, toast the baguette slices and make the aïoli as the broth cooks.

2 medium onions, chopped coarse

6 medium cloves garlic

2 tablespoons plus ¾ cup olive oil

2 (3-inch-long) pieces rind plus 2 table-spoons juice from 1 small orange
Salt

2 cups dry white wine

1 (28-ounce) can diced tomatoes with juices

4 bay leaves

8 parsley stems tied together with kitchen twine, plus ¼ cup chopped fresh parsley leaves

1 baguette, cut into ½-inch-thick slices and toasted

2 large egg yolks
Ground black pepper

2 pounds monkfish fillets, trimmed of membrane and cut into 1-inch pieces

1. Process the onions and 4 garlic cloves in the workbowl of a food processor until finely minced, about twenty-five 1-second pulses, scraping down the sides of the workbowl with a rubber spatula as necessary. Transfer the mixture to a Dutch oven; do not wash the food processor. Add 2 tablespoons oil, the orange rind pieces, and ½ teaspoon salt to the Dutch oven and cook over medium-high heat, stirring occasionally, until the onions soften, about 8 minutes. Add the wine, tomatoes, bay leaves, parsley stems, and 2½ cups water and bring to a boil. Reduce the heat to low and simmer until the flavors are fully combined, about 20 minutes.

2. Meanwhile, adjust an oven rack to the middle position and heat the oven to 400 degrees. Arrange the bread in a single layer on a baking sheet. Bake, turning the bread slices once, until dry and crisp, about 10 minutes.

3. Combine the remaining 2 garlic cloves, orange juice, egg yolks, and ¼ teaspoon salt in the food processor workbowl and process until the garlic is finely pureed, about 30 seconds. With the machine running, pour the remaining ¾ cup oil in a thin steady stream through the feed tube until fully incorporated, about 1 minute. Adjust the seasonings with salt and pepper to taste.

4. Remove the orange rind, bay leaves, and parsley stems from the broth and discard; stir in the monkfish. Simmer until the fish is cooked through, 8 to 10 minutes. Stir in the chopped parsley and adjust the seasonings with salt and pepper to taste. Ladle the soup into shallow bowls and dollop each with a large spoonful of aïoli. Serve immediately with the toasted baguette on the side.

POULTRY

OUR GOAL IN THIS CHAPTER WAS TO create complete meals with chicken (or turkey) as a jumping-off point. Most of the following recipes use boneless breasts (either chicken or turkey) or chicken parts (split breasts or thighs), although we did figure out a way to cook a whole chicken in less than an hour (see the recipe on page 217). The grilling and stir-frying chapters include several chicken recipes as well.

SAUTÉED CHICKEN BREASTS

SAUTÉING IS THE ULTIMATE FAST-cooking technique. Beyond speed, the real benefit of sautéing is the golden bits left behind in the pan. These glistening brown gems make it easy to make a pan sauce in minutes, turning a boneless, skinless piece of chicken into a special dish.

The real trick to sautéing is to use the right pan and get it really hot. Although you would naturally think sauté pans are best for this task, we found their straight, high sides make them less than ideal for this recipe. The low, sloped sides of a skillet, on the other hand, work perfectly. This seemingly minor variance makes all the difference in how moisture evaporates from the pan. The low, outward-sloping sides of the skillet encourage moisture to evaporate from the cooking chicken and, later, the reducing sauce. On the other hand, the taller, straight sides of the sauté pan prevent moisture evaporation by getting in the way. Using a sauté pan instead of a skillet results in paler chicken and less flavorful drippings. The sauce then not only does not taste as good but also takes longer to cook. We found it necessary to use a heavy-bottomed 12-inch skillet to cook four boneless, skinless chicken breasts (sometimes referred to as *chicken cutlets*). Using a

smaller pan crowded the chicken as it cooked and trapped moisture in the pan.

We found that preheating the pan for several minutes is absolutely necessary. The best way to tell when the pan is hot enough is to heat it with some oil. When the oil shimmers and begins to smoke slightly, the pan is ready to go. Again, using a cold pan makes for improperly browned chicken.

Dusting the chicken in flour before cooking also helps it achieve a golden crust and aids in the making of golden drippings. With such high heat, boneless breasts require only about 3 minutes per side. Transfer the chicken to a plate in a warm oven and return the "dirty" pan to the stove to make the sauce.

A basic pan sauce consists of three components: aromatics, liquid, and butter. Quickly soften garlic, shallots, and tough herbs (such as rosemary) in the pan over low heat and then add liquid just in time to prevent the browned bits from burning. The liquid, usually a combination of wine and stock, helps remove the browned bits from the bottom of the pan and incorporates them into the sauce; this process is known as *deglazing*. The liquid is then brought to a simmer over high heat, which both intensifies its flavor and thickens its consistency. Finally, the mixture is finished with butter, elevating the reduced liquid to sauce status by enriching its flavor and body.

By mixing green beans into the equation, you can easily produce the better part of a dinner in about the same amount of time. Making a generous amount of sauce means you can drizzle some over the beans as well. We undercooked the beans in boiling, lightly salted water (we found they continued to cook even after being drained) and then tossed them with a little butter and then some pan sauce. When timed correctly, the beans have the perfect crunch at the moment the sauce is finished.

Sautéed Chicken and Green Beans with Lemon and Thyme

SERVES 4

TIME: 35 MINUTES

See the illustration below for information on safely sautéing chicken breasts. Serve with roasted potatoes (page 79), hash browns (page 81), plain rice, or toasted orzo pilaf (page 94).

½	cup unbleached all-purpose flour
4	boneless, skinless chicken breasts (5 to 6 ounces each), trimmed (see the illustrations on page 199) Salt and ground black pepper
3	tablespoons vegetable oil
¾	pound green beans, ends snapped off
4	tablespoons unsalted butter, cut into 4 pieces
2	medium shallots, minced
I	cup canned low-sodium chicken broth
½	cup vermouth or dry white wine
I	tablespoon juice from I lemon
2	teaspoons minced fresh thyme leaves

1. Bring 2½ quarts water to a boil in a large pot. Adjust an oven rack to the lower-middle position, set a large heatproof plate on it, and heat the oven to 200 degrees. Place the flour in a shallow dish. Season both sides of the chicken with salt and pepper. One at a time, coat both sides of each chicken piece with flour. Lift each breast by the tapered end and shake to remove excess flour; set aside.

2. Heat the oil in a heavy-bottomed 12-inch skillet over medium-high heat until just smoking. Place the floured chicken in a single layer in the skillet and cook until golden brown, about 3 minutes. Using tongs, flip the chicken; cook until the second side is golden brown and the meat feels firm when pressed with a finger, about 3 minutes. The meat should no longer be pink in the center. Transfer the chicken to the heated plate and return the plate to the oven.

3. Add 1 tablespoon salt and the beans to the boiling water and cook until crisp-tender, about 5 minutes. Drain the beans and transfer them to a large serving bowl. Toss with 1 tablespoon butter and salt and pepper to taste.

4. Meanwhile, return the skillet to low heat; add the shallots and cook, stirring occasionally, until soft, about 1 minute. Add the broth and vermouth, increase the heat to high, and simmer vigorously, scraping the browned bits from the pan bottom, until the sauce is slightly syrupy and measures ½ cup, 6 to 8 minutes. Reduce the heat to low and stir in the lemon juice, thyme, and any accumulated juices from the chicken. Whisk in the remaining butter, 1 tablespoon at a time, and season with salt and pepper to taste.

5. Arrange a portion of green beans on individual plates and place a chicken breast on top. Pour the sauce over the chicken and beans and serve immediately.

SAUTÉING CHICKEN BREASTS SAFELY

To avoid being splashed with hot fat, lay the breasts in the pan thick side first, hanging on to the tapered end until the rest of the breast is in the pan. Position the tapered end of the breast at the edge of the pan, where the heat is less intense.

➤ VARIATIONS

Sautéed Chicken and Green Beans with Sherry, Green Olives, and Almonds

Toast the almonds in the skillet before you cook the chicken, about 3 to 5 minutes over medium-high heat. Transfer the toasted almonds to a separate bowl and reserve. Wipe the skillet clean of any almond crumbs with a wad of paper towels. Add the oil and cook the chicken as directed.

Follow the recipe for Sautéed Chicken and Green Beans with Lemon and Thyme, replacing the vermouth with ½ cup sherry and replacing the lemon juice and thyme with ⅓ cup green olives, pitted and slivered. Just before serving, sprinkle the plated chicken and beans with ¼ cup toasted almonds.

Sautéed Chicken and Green Beans with Dried Porcini and Rosemary

See page 96 for information about rehydrating dried mushrooms. The soaking liquid is not used in this recipe.

Follow the recipe for Sautéed Chicken and Green Beans with Lemon and Thyme, replacing the shallot with 2 minced garlic cloves, 1 teaspoon minced rosemary, and ½ ounce dried porcini mushrooms, rehydrated and chopped. Omit the lemon juice and thyme.

BUILDING BLOCK RECIPE

Sautéed Chicken Breasts

SERVES 4

TIME: 20 MINUTES

Once the breasts are cooked and in the oven, you will want to make a pan sauce. Start by cooking several tablespoons of aromatics (shallots, leeks, onion, or garlic) in the drippings over low heat. Once the aromatics soften, deglaze the pan with about 1½ cups liquid (stock, wine, and/or juice) and simmer until the liquid reduces to about ½ cup. At this point, flavorful ingredients (herbs, lemon juice, lime juice, olives, capers, or dried fruit) can be added. Finish the sauce by whisking in several tablespoons of butter. Taste for seasonings, adding salt and pepper as needed, and spoon the pan sauce over the breasts.

½ cup unbleached all-purpose flour
4 boneless, skinless chicken breasts (5 to 6 ounces each), trimmed (see the illustrations on page 199)
  Salt and ground black pepper
3 tablespoons vegetable oil

1. Adjust an oven rack to the lower-middle position, set a large heatproof plate on the rack, and heat the oven to 200 degrees. Place the flour in a shallow dish. Season both sides of the chicken with salt and pepper. One at a time, coat both sides of each chicken piece with flour. Lift each breast from the tapered end and shake to remove excess flour; set aside.

2. Heat the oil in a heavy-bottomed 12-inch skillet over medium-high heat until just smoking. Place the floured chicken in a single layer in the skillet and cook until golden brown, about 3 minutes. Using tongs, flip the chicken; cook until the second side is golden brown and the meat feels firm when pressed with a finger, about 3 minutes longer. The meat should no longer be pink in the middle. Transfer the chicken to the heated plate and return the plate to the oven. Make a pan sauce in the empty skillet and spoon it over the breasts.

BREADED CHICKEN FINGERS

FEW KIDS (BOTH YOUNG AND OLD) don't like the crunchy simplicity of chicken fingers—tender, boneless lengths of chicken pan-fried with a cloak of mildly flavored crumbs. They are easily served with a variety of dipping sauces or turned into sandwiches. Yet, as with most things so simple, they are best made well or not at all. Wanting to avoid rubbery chicken and a bland coating that falls off the chicken, we set out to find the best, yet simplest, way to make chicken fingers.

Cutting boneless, skinless chicken breasts into finger-length pieces was incredibly simple and required little skill. We did note, however, that chicken breasts can range in size drastically. We found it easiest to cut uniformly sized fingers from breasts weighing 5 to 6 ounces each. Cutting the chicken diagonally into ¾-inch-wide strips, we found it unnecessary to pound them. Also, the chicken tenderloins attached to the back of each breast make perfect fingers after the white tendon is removed.

What really makes or breaks a good chicken finger is the coating. Ideally, it should taste mild and comforting and have a solid crunch. It should not be dull or greasy. To get the coating to adhere to the chicken, we found it necessary to use a bound breading, or *panade*, whereby the chicken is dipped into flour, dragged through a lightly whisked egg, and then, finally, coated with bread crumbs. We found the type of bread crumbs can make a big difference. Making our own out of sliced bread tasted great but required too much time and effort for a midweek meal. Packaged bread crumbs from the store were disappointing, offering only a stale, mass-market flavor that pleased no one. Japanese *panko* crumbs (commonly found in the ethnic aisle of the supermarket) offered a mild wheaty flavor and shatteringly crisp texture that not only won the test kitchen over but also required no work beyond the opening of a bag.

We tried to omit the flouring step noted above but found that without it, the coating

TRIMMING CHICKEN BREASTS

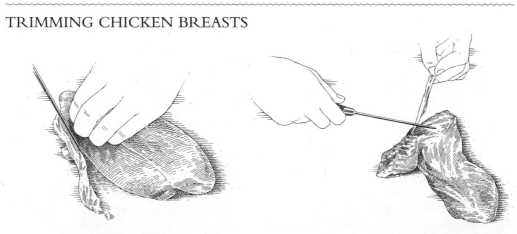

1. Lay each breast tenderloin-side down and smooth the top with your fingers. Any fat will slide to the periphery, where it can be trimmed with a knife.

2. To remove the tough, white tendon, turn the breasts tenderloin-side up and peel back the thick half of the tenderloin so it lies top-down on the work surface. Use the point of a paring knife to cut around the top of the tenderloin to expose the tendon, then scrape the tendon free with the knife.

merely peeled off. The flour ensured that the surface of the chicken was absolutely dry before being dipped into the egg, which guaranteed a coating with staying power. We also learned that mixing a little oil into the egg wash helped keep the breading from getting too heavy and produced a deeper, golden brown color during frying. Last, we noted the importance of pressing the crumbs into the chicken for an absolutely even distribution. As for seasoning, we found it easiest to add salt and pepper to the egg wash.

Using a heavy-bottomed 12-inch skillet, we were able to fry all the fingers in only two batches. Although this makes for a fairly crowded pan, usually a no-no when frying, we found that the small chicken fingers did not suffer a bit. Rather, they cooked through quickly and browned evenly. Pitting vegetable oil against olive oil, we preferred the light, unobtrusive flavor of the vegetable oil to the potent and slightly bitter flavor of olive oil. We found it unnecessary to use fresh oil for the second round of frying. After cooking the first batch over medium-high heat, we simply reduced the heat to medium for the second batch to prevent burning.

Breaded Chicken Fingers

SERVES 4

TIME: 30 MINUTES

Chicken breasts can range drastically in size from 4 to 10 ounces. For this recipe, we used what we consider the average size: 5 to 6 ounces. Look for panko (extra-crunchy Japanese bread crumbs) in the ethnic food aisle at your supermarket. These fingers are classically served with any number of condiments, including ketchup, barbecue sauce, honey-mustard sauce (our favorite), hot sauce, relish, mayonnaise, or a simple wedge of lemon. The fingers can be held for up to 15 minutes in a 200-degree oven before serving. Chicken fingers can

easily be turned into Chicken Parmesan Hoagies (see page 201). Serve with a basic leafy salad or green vegetable.

4	boneless, skinless chicken breasts (5 to 6 ounces each), tenderloins removed whole, breasts sliced on the diagonal into ¾-inch-wide strips
1	cup unbleached all-purpose flour
3	cups panko (Japanese-style bread crumbs)
2	large eggs
1	tablespoon plus 1 cup vegetable oil
	Salt and ground black pepper
1	lemon, cut into wedges, or Honey-Mustard Dipping Sauce (recipe follows)

1. Adjust the oven rack to the middle position and heat the oven to 200 degrees. Thoroughly dry the breasts with paper towels. Spread the flour and panko in two separate shallow dishes. Lightly beat the eggs, 1 tablespoon oil, 1 teaspoon salt, and ½ teaspoon pepper in a third shallow dish. Working with several pieces of chicken at a time, drop the chicken into the flour and shake the pan to coat them. Shake the excess flour from each piece; then, using tongs, dip the chicken into the egg mixture, turning to coat well and allowing the excess to drip off. Drop the chicken into the panko and press the crumbs lightly onto the chicken. Shake off excess crumbs and place the breaded chicken on a wire rack set over a rimmed baking sheet. Repeat with the remaining chicken.

2. Heat the remaining 1 cup oil in a heavy-bottomed 12-inch skillet over medium-high heat until it reaches 350 degrees—the oil will shimmer but should not smoke—3 to 4 minutes. Lay half of the chicken gently in the skillet and cook until golden brown and crisp on the first side, about 2 minutes. Using tongs, flip the chicken; continue to cook until the second

side is deep golden brown and crisp, and the chicken is no longer pink in the center, about 2 minutes longer. Transfer the chicken to a clean rimmed baking sheet lined with paper towels and place it in the warm oven. Return the skillet to medium heat and repeat with the remaining chicken. Serve immediately with the lemon wedges or honey-mustard sauce.

Honey-Mustard Dipping Sauce

MAKES A SCANT $^1/_2$ CUP, ENOUGH FOR
1 RECIPE OF CHICKEN FINGERS

TIME: 2 MINUTES

This sauce is both sweet and spicy and is a grown-up choice to go with Breaded Chicken Fingers.

3 tablespoons honey
4 tablespoons Dijon mustard

Mix the honey and mustard in a small bowl until smooth.

KEEPING SANDWICHES UPRIGHT

After slicing the rolls partially open, place them on a foil-lined rimmed baking sheet. Balancing the rolls slit-side up, crimp the foil around them to help them stay upright so they can be filled and finished in the oven.

Chicken Parmesan Hoagies

MAKES 4 LARGE SANDWICHES,
SERVING 6 TO 8 PEOPLE

TIME: 1 HOUR (INCLUDES MAKING
THE CHICKEN FINGERS)

We found it easiest to make the tomato sauce first and then prepare and fry the chicken and, finally, assemble the sandwiches.

2 (14½-ounce) cans diced tomatoes
2 tablespoons extra-virgin olive oil
4 large cloves garlic, minced or pressed through a garlic press (about 4 tablespoons)
1 teaspoon dried oregano
⅛ teaspoon hot red pepper flakes
 Salt and ground black pepper
4 (12-inch) hoagie rolls, slit partially open
12 ounces sliced deli mozzarella cheese (about 12 slices)
1 recipe Breaded Chicken Fingers (page 200), omitting lemon wedges and Honey-Mustard Dipping Sauce

1. Process the tomatoes in the workbowl of a food processor fitted with a steel blade until smooth, about five 1-second pulses. Heat the oil, garlic, oregano, and pepper flakes in a medium saucepan over medium heat until the garlic sizzles, about 40 seconds. Stir in the tomatoes, bring to a simmer, and cook, uncovered, until the sauce thickens, about 15 minutes. Remove the pan from the heat and season with salt and pepper to taste; set aside.

2. Meanwhile, adjust an oven rack to the middle position and heat the oven to 450 degrees. Place the rolls side by side, cut-side up, on a foil-lined rimmed baking sheet. Crimp the outer edges of the foil around the rolls to prevent them from flopping on their sides (see the illustration at left). Lay 3 ounces sliced mozzarella (about 3 slices) inside each roll. Lay

201

4 or 5 chicken fingers on the mozzarella and top with ½ cup tomato sauce. Bake until the cheese is melted and the rolls are lightly toasted, about 10 minutes. Serve immediately.

NUT-CRUSTED CHICKEN BREASTS

BY REPLACING BREAD CRUMBS WITH nuts, a simple breaded chicken breast can be quickly transformed. Yet, for the transformation to be a success, we had to uncover a few key tricks.

Using boneless, skinless chicken breasts, we began by adapting our standard breading technique: dredging the chicken in flour and then an egg wash, and, finally, bread crumbs. We first tried replacing the bread crumbs with sliced almonds, but the thin almond slices refused to stick to the chicken. We had more success when the almonds were processed into fine crumbs in the food processor, but even then the crust tasted dense, oily, and sodden after it was cooked. In an effort to lighten the crust, we mixed the nuts with bread crumbs. Testing various ratios of nuts to bread crumbs, we landed on a ratio of 2 parts freshly ground nuts to 1 part crumbs. We found that light Japanese-style bread crumbs, called panko, worked especially well.

Given the density of the nut–bread crumb mixture, we wondered if the initial step of flouring the chicken was necessary. Cooking two nut-crusted pieces of chicken, one floured and one not, side by side, we found the differences minor; in the spirit of streamlining, we decided to omit the flouring step.

Cooking the chicken turned out to be fairly straightforward. The important factors were to use a skillet large enough to comfortably cook four pieces of chicken and to use plenty of oil. Much like regular breaded chicken, the breasts have to be pan-fried rather than sautéed. As for flavor, we were surprised to find the nut crust tasted relatively mild. To spruce it up, flavoring the egg wash with ingredients such as Dijon mustard, citrus zest, or both was easy and effective.

Noticing how well the nut-crusted chicken tasted with fruit, we made the short jump to pairing it with a wilted spinach salad and a fruit-based dressing. Holding the chicken warm in a 200-degree oven, we simply wiped the oil out of the pan and returned it to the stove to make a warm dressing. This method lightly wilted baby spinach without turning it wet or slimy. Cooked from start to finish in 45 minutes, this exotic-tasting meal is far from your average chicken and salad supper.

~+~

Almond-Crusted Chicken Breasts with Wilted Spinach-Orange Salad

SERVES 4

TIME: 45 MINUTES

It should take about 10 seconds to process the almonds into fine crumbs; don't overprocess them or the nuts will become oily. If you want to add a starch, try a couscous or quinoa pilaf (see Chapter 4) made without nuts.

2	large eggs
1	teaspoon Dijon mustard
1¼	teaspoons grated zest and 4 wedges from 1 orange
	Salt and ground black pepper
1	cup sliced almonds, processed into fine crumbs in the food processor
½	cup panko (Japanese-style bread crumbs)
4	boneless, skinless chicken breasts (5 to 6 ounces each), trimmed (see the illustrations on page 199) and dried thoroughly with paper towels
8	tablespoons vegetable oil

5   ounces baby spinach (about 6 cups)
2   medium oranges, peel and pith removed
     (see the illustration on page 57)
     and then quartered through the ends
     and sliced across the segments into
     ¼-inch-thick pieces
1   small shallot, minced (about
     2 tablespoons)

1. Lightly beat the eggs, mustard, 1 teaspoon orange zest, ½ teaspoon salt, and ¼ teaspoon pepper in a shallow dish. Mix the almonds and panko in a separate shallow dish. Working with one piece of chicken at a time, use tongs to dip it into the egg mixture; turn to coat well and allow excess to drip off. Drop the chicken into the nut mixture and press the nuts into it with your fingers. Transfer the breaded chicken to a wire rack set over a baking sheet and repeat with the remaining chicken. Adjust an oven rack to the middle position and heat the oven to 200 degrees.

2. Heat 6 tablespoons oil in a heavy-bottomed 12-inch nonstick skillet over medium-high heat until just smoking. Lay the chicken gently in the skillet and cook until golden brown and crisp on the first side, about 2½ minutes. Using tongs, flip the chicken; reduce the heat to medium and continue to cook until the meat feels firm when pressed gently, the second side is deep golden brown and crisp, and the chicken is no longer pink in the center, 2 minutes longer. Transfer the chicken to a paper towel–lined plate and place the plate in the oven. Discard the oil in the skillet and, using tongs and paper towels, wipe the skillet clean.

3. Place the spinach in a large bowl. Heat 1 tablespoon oil in the cleaned skillet over high heat until just smoking. Add the orange slices and cook until lightly browned around the edges, 1½ to 2 minutes. Remove the pan from the heat, add the remaining 1 tablespoon oil, shallot, remaining ¼ teaspoon zest, ¼ teaspoon salt, and ⅛ teaspoon pepper and allow residual heat to soften the shallot, 30 seconds. Pour the warm dressing with the oranges over the spinach and toss gently to wilt. Remove the chicken from the oven and serve it immediately with the salad and orange wedges.

➤ VARIATION

Macadamia Nut–Crusted Chicken Breasts with Wilted Spinach-Pineapple Salad
Buy peeled and cored fresh pineapple at the supermarket to save time. The exotic flavors in this dish are best paired with plain white rice.

Follow the recipe for Almond-Crusted Chicken Breasts with Wilted Spinach-Orange Salad, omitting the mustard. Substitute lime zest and lime wedges for the orange zest and orange wedges and macadamia nuts for the almonds. Substitute 2 cups fresh pineapple cut into ¾-inch dice for the orange slices in step 3, sautéing the pineapple for 2 minutes.

STUFFED CHICKEN BREASTS

AN OBVIOUS WAY TO DOCTOR UP A simple chicken breast is to stuff it with interesting ingredients. The problem, however, is that most stuffed chicken breast recipes take forever, requiring that the chicken first be butterflied and pounded and then stuffed, rolled, chilled, breaded, and—finally—fried. We wanted to simplify this process.

Using boneless, skinless chicken breasts, we began by testing various ways to make a pocket for a simple filling. At first, our goal was to create a large pocket inside the chicken breast without making a large incision that would allow the filling to leak out. This, however, was difficult, as most boneless, skinless chicken pieces are fairly thin and leave little room for error. We realized we needed to switch gears and look for a simpler method. Clearly, we needed to butterfly the cutlets. But was pounding really necessary? We found that as long as we used medium-size cutlets, we could skip pounding.

We simply placed the filling over half of the butterflied breast and folded the chicken over it, back into its original shape. Using a wooden skewer, we then "sewed" the incision closed and trimmed off excess skewer. We worried that the filling might leak out with only the skewer holding it in and so were pleasantly surprised when the chicken fried up without incident. No rolling or chilling to firm the filling was necessary.

We found it best to use a bound breading, whereby we dragged the chicken through flour and then an egg wash and, finally, through crisp Japanese bread crumbs called panko. It was easy to get a golden, crisp crust, but we encountered trouble cooking the chicken through without burning the crust. We tried frying it for a longer period over lower heat, but this simply turned the coating greasy. In the end, we discovered that finishing the browned chicken in the oven

for 10 minutes ensured it was cooked through and the filling was hot.

We chose rich, full-flavored ingredients to use as fillings. Ham and Swiss cheese; roasted red peppers and basil; and chutney and cheddar were all well received by tasters. A lemon wedge cuts the richness of these stuffed breasts.

Chicken Breasts Stuffed with Ham and Cheese
SERVES 4

TIME: 40 MINUTES

Serve with one of the vegetable side dishes in Chapter 3 made with broccoli, cauliflower, carrots, green beans, or peas. Freeze the tenderloins for later use in a stir-fry.

4   boneless, skinless chicken breasts (5 to 6 ounces each), tenderloins removed and reserved for another use
     Salt and ground black pepper
4   teaspoons Dijon mustard
4   ounces sliced Black Forest deli ham (about 4 slices), cut into 1 ½-inch-wide lengths

STUFFING CHICKEN BREASTS

1. Holding the knife parallel to the cutting board, slice the chicken breast in half but not quite all the way through.

2. Open the chicken breast like a book and arrange the filling over one half.

3. Fold the chicken back into its original shape. Use a wooden skewer to sew the open edges of the chicken together. Trim off any skewer excess with scissors.

2 ounces sliced deli Swiss or Gruyère cheese (about 2 slices), cut into 1½-inch-wide lengths

½ cup unbleached all-purpose flour

2 cups panko (Japanese-style bread crumbs)

2 large eggs

1 tablespoon plus 1 cup vegetable oil

1 lemon, cut into wedges

1. Following the illustrations on page 204, butterfly the chicken breasts and season them with salt and pepper to taste. Brush the inside of each breast with 1 teaspoon mustard and lay 1 ounce ham and ½ ounce cheese over half of each breast. Fold the chicken back into its original shape and secure the seam with a wooden skewer, cutting off any excess skewer with scissors.

2. Spread the flour and panko in two separate shallow dishes. Lightly beat the eggs, 1 tablespoon oil, 1 teaspoon salt, and ½ teaspoon pepper in a third shallow dish. Working with one piece of stuffed chicken at a time, drop it into the flour, shake the pan to coat, and shake off the excess flour. Using tongs, dip the chicken into the egg mixture; turn to coat well and allow excess to drip off. Drop the chicken into the panko and press the crumbs lightly onto it with your fingers. Shake off excess crumbs and place the chicken on a wire rack over a rimmed baking sheet. Repeat with the remaining chicken. Adjust an oven rack to the middle position and heat the oven to 350 degrees.

3. Heat the remaining 1 cup oil in a heavy-bottomed 12-inch nonstick skillet over medium-high heat until it reaches 350 degrees—the oil will shimmer but should not smoke—3 to 4 minutes. Lay the chicken gently in the skillet and cook until golden brown and crisp on the first side, 2 to 3 minutes. Using tongs, flip the breasts; continue to cook until the second side is deep golden brown and crisp, about 2 minutes longer. Transfer the chicken to a clean wire rack set over a baking sheet and bake until the chicken is cooked through, 8 to 10 minutes. The meat should no longer be pink in the center. Serve immediately with lemon wedges.

➤ VARIATIONS

Chicken Breasts Stuffed with Roasted Red Peppers, Provolone, and Basil

This recipe is especially good with Steamed Broccoli with Toasted Garlic and Lemon (page 66).

Follow the recipe for Chicken Breasts Stuffed with Ham and Cheese, substituting 4 teaspoons chopped fresh basil leaves for the mustard, 4 ounces jarred roasted red peppers, rinsed, dried, and cut into ½-inch-wide strips for the ham, and 2 ounces sliced deli provolone cheese (about 2 slices), cut into 1½-inch-wide lengths, for the Swiss cheese. Fill each breast with 1 teaspoon basil, 1 ounce peppers, and ½ ounce cheese.

Chicken Breasts Stuffed with Mango and Cheddar

Serve with Glazed Curried Carrots with Currants and Almonds (page 70) or Browned and Braised Cauliflower with Coconut Milk, Peas, and Curry (page 71). Major Grey mango chutney works well in this recipe.

Follow the recipe for Chicken Breasts Stuffed with Ham and Cheese, substituting 4 teaspoons minced fresh cilantro leaves for the mustard, ¼ cup jarred mango chutney for the ham, and 4 ounces sliced deli cheddar cheese (about 4 slices), cut into 1½-inch-wide lengths, for the Swiss cheese. Fill each breast with 1 teaspoon cilantro, 1 tablespoon chutney, and 1 ounce cheese.

Broiled Chicken and Asparagus

FAR FROM GLAMOROUS, BROILED chicken is nevertheless the kind of weeknight staple you can depend on. The high heat of the broiler makes the skin crisp, and the chicken itself cooks quickly. The problem is that broiled chicken often tastes about as good as it sounds: boring. We wanted not only a fail-safe way to produce good broiled chicken but also a way to make it taste worthwhile.

We determined it would be easiest to use just one cut of chicken. This would not only ensure that the chicken cooked evenly but also simplify both shopping and prepping. We tried using split breasts but found their teardrop shape made them difficult to cook. By the time the thicker part of the breast was cooked through, the tapered end was over-done and dry. Turning our attention to bone-in thighs, we found their symmetrical shape broiled well. The ample skin and dark meat also helped keep the chicken from drying out as it cooked, producing a juicier, more flavor-ful dish.

Cooking the chicken at a fixed distance from the broiler element was disastrous. When too close, the skin burned by the time the chicken was cooked through. When cooked too far from the element, the skin remained pale and flabby. By cooking the chicken first at a distance, then directly under the element, we achieved both perfectly cooked meat and crisp, golden skin. We found it necessary to start the chicken skin-side down and then flip it to crisp the skin. To get the skin really crisp, we discovered it was best to slash it several times with a paring knife. This created extra surface area and allowed more of the fat underneath the skin to render during broil-ing. Just make sure you don't cut into the meat or juices will be lost as the chicken cooks.

Tossing aside the time-consuming idea of marinating, we turned our attention instead to flavorful herb rubs and pastes. Rubbing the chicken with an herb-garlic paste before broiling did not work; it burned by the time the chicken was cooked through. Brushing the paste onto the crisp skin at the last minute, however, worked well. Although this last-minute rub gave the skin a good hit of flavor, we still wanted to find a way to flavor the meat. We did this by placing a slice of lemon on each piece of chicken as it cooked. We started with the lemon on top of the chicken so its juices basted the meat for the first half of the cooking time. When we flipped the chicken for the second half of the cooking time, we simply flipped the lemon underneath the chicken so the skin had unobstructed exposure to the broiler element. The broiled lemon wedges can be served with the chicken for even more flavor.

With the broiler hot and the broiler pan already dirty, the opportunity to cook an accompanying vegetable was too good to pass up. While the chicken rested on the counter (uncovered so the skin wouldn't turn soggy), we poured off most of the fat from the broiler pan bottom, laid some asparagus in the pan, and cooked it directly under the broiler until tender. To give it some flavor, we tossed the cooked asparagus with reserved herb-garlic paste in the hot broiler pan.

Full of flavor and taking only 45 minutes to prepare, this classic combination of broiled chicken and asparagus will surprise you.

Broiled Chicken Thighs and Asparagus with Lemon and Garlic

SERVES 4

TIME: 1 HOUR

This recipe will work only in broilers with adjustable racks, not fixed-height broilers in drawers under the oven. An orzo, couscous, or bulgur pilaf (see Chapter 4) would nicely round out the meal.

- 4 medium cloves garlic, peeled
  Salt and ground black pepper
- ¼ cup extra-virgin olive oil
- 1 teaspoon minced fresh thyme leaves
- 8 bone-in, skin-on chicken thighs (about 3 pounds), trimmed of excess fat
  Nonstick cooking spray
- 2 lemons, 1 trimmed and cut into 8 (¼-inch-thick) rounds, 1 cut into wedges
- 2 pounds thin asparagus spears, tough ends snapped off (see the illustration on page 64)

1. Mince the garlic with ¾ teaspoon salt to form a smooth paste (see the illustration on page 4). Mix the garlic paste, ¼ teaspoon pepper, oil, and thyme in a small bowl. Measure 1½ tablespoons garlic-thyme mixture into a separate bowl and reserve it for the asparagus. With a sharp knife, make 3 diagonal slashes in the skin of each chicken piece (do not cut into the meat). Season both sides of the chicken pieces with salt and pepper to taste.

2. Adjust one oven rack to the lowest position and the other to the upper-middle position (the top rack should be about 5 inches from the heating element; the bottom rack should be 13 inches away) and heat the broiler. Place a slotted broiler pan top over a broiler pan bottom and coat lightly with nonstick cooking spray. Place the chicken on the broiler pan top, skin-side down. Lay a slice of lemon on each piece of chicken.

3. Broil the chicken on the bottom rack until just beginning to brown, 12 to 16 minutes. Using tongs, flip the chicken so it rests on the lemon slice. Continue to broil on the bottom rack until the skin is slightly crisp and the thickest part of the meat registers 160 degrees on an instant-read thermometer, about 15 minutes. Brush the chicken with the garlic-thyme mixture and move the pan to the upper rack. Broil until the chicken is crisp and dark brown in spots, about 1 minute.

4. Transfer the chicken and lemon slices to a serving platter. Remove the broiler pan top from the broiler pan bottom (use caution, as it will still be hot) and pour off all but 1 teaspoon of the fat accumulated in the broiler pan bottom. Add the asparagus and broil, shaking the pan halfway through to turn the spears, until tender and lightly browned, 7 to 10 minutes. Remove the asparagus from the oven and, still in the hot pan, toss with the reserved garlic-thyme mixture. Serve the chicken, broiled lemon slices, and asparagus immediately with the lemon wedges.

➤ VARIATION

Broiled Chicken Thighs and Asparagus with Lime and Jalapeño

Mince 2 medium garlic cloves with ¼ teaspoon salt to form a smooth paste (see the illustration on page 4). Mix the garlic paste, ¼ teaspoon pepper, 1½ tablespoons minced fresh ginger, 1 minced jalapeño chile, 2 tablespoons brown sugar, 1 tablespoon minced fresh cilantro leaves, and 2 tablespoons lime juice. Reserve 1½ tablespoons of this mixture for tossing with the broiled asparagus. Proceed as directed, using the rest of this mixture in place of the garlic-thyme paste and replacing the lemons with 2 limes.

OVEN-FRIED CHICKEN AND SWEET POTATOES

OVEN-FRIED CHICKEN HAS BECOME A popular low-fat, no-mess alternative to regular fried chicken. Regrettably, it usually tastes terrible, with a rubbery, greasy, or dry coating and a flavor that is either artificial or bland. Was it possible to make oven-fried chicken that had real crunch and good flavor?

Right off the bat, we noted that the coating makes the difference between good and bad oven-fried chicken. Looking at a number of recipes, we came up with a huge list of coating possibilities, from bread crumbs to crackers to cornflakes. Trying nearly 20 coating options from already published recipes, we found no clear winner. Both fresh and dried bread crumbs offered a lackluster texture, while a variety of crackers from Ritz to saltines turned soft and did not toast in the oven. Cornflakes was just one of the losing candidates from the cereal aisle; its flavor was too sweet and its texture too tough. Stuffing mixes tasted, well, too much like stuffing, and good old Shake 'n Bake made tasters gag with its overwhelmingly artificial flavor.

These tests did, however, help us to narrow the scope of our search. We wanted a crunchy coating that didn't damage our gums and an honest, recognizable flavor that didn't taste commercial. Also, it was necessary that the crumbs toast to a copper-colored brown as the chicken cooked in the oven.

Moving further into the cracker aisle, we found a selection of hearty possibilities such as bagel chips, lavash, Swedish crisps, pita chips, bread sticks, and Melba toast. All of these crackers were far more successful than any of our previous tests, but one cracker was particularly well liked. Melba toast was crunchy, had great

flavor, and toasted to a beautiful golden hue.

Throughout our testing of crumb coatings, we also played with the breading technique. Most recipes begin by rolling the chicken in a flavorful liquid such as butter, egg, or milk before dipping it into the crumbs. The liquid not only adds flavor but creates a wet surface for the crumbs to stick to. We tested a host of ingredients, including water, eggs, milk, buttermilk, butter, yogurt, mayonnaise, sour cream, and even ranch dressing. The fattier options—butter, ranch dressing, and mayonnaise—did not work well, as the surface they created was too slick for the crumbs to stick to. The other dairy possibilities—sour cream, yogurt, milk, and buttermilk—were too wet, which prevented the crumbs from getting crisp. Lightly whisked egg, on the other hand, worked great. The egg made the surface of the chicken tacky and therefore easy for the Melba toast crumbs to stick to. By whisking in a little Dijon and dried thyme with the eggs, we were able to subtly flavor the chicken without compromising the effectiveness of the eggs.

Last, we noted that the crumbs benefited not only from a bit of salt and pepper but oil as well. When containing vegetable oil, the crust turned an even, dark brown, much like real fried chicken right out of the oil. Baking the chicken at 400 degrees, we found, yielded both cooked chicken and a beautifully browned crust. To ensure a perfectly golden crust all around the chicken, we baked it on a wire rack set over a rimmed baking sheet, which helped the oven heat get underneath the chicken.

With an eye bent toward cooking time economy, we couldn't overlook the possibility of baking a side dish in the oven alongside the chicken. Sweet potatoes fit the bill in terms of cooking time and flavor; however, it took us a few tries to get them just right. We tried making steak fries but found that the high moisture content of the sweet potatoes made this nearly impossible to do in the oven. We cut the sweet potatoes into smaller pieces and tried roasting them on a preheated baking sheet with a fair amount of oil. The potatoes made an impressive sizzle when they hit the hot pan, but the resulting crisp edges were only a minor victory, as the potatoes still turned a bit sodden.

Up to now, we had been simply roasting the potatoes on a rack underneath the chicken in the oven. Wary of ruining the chicken's gorgeous brown crust, we wondered if this technique was preventing the oven heat from getting to the potatoes. On a hunch, we tried switching the chicken and potatoes around in the oven halfway through the cooking time. Without compromising the chicken in the least, this switch made all the difference to the potatoes, which emerged golden and crisp. The sweet potatoes tasted far more interesting when tossed with scallions, roasted red peppers, and Dijon mustard for a quick salad.

Oven-Fried Chicken and Roasted Sweet Potato Salad

SERVES 4

TIME: 1 HOUR

Round out the meal with Sautéed Frozen Corn with Southwestern Flavors (page 72) or Cornmeal Biscuits (page 369) and salad. See photo of this recipe on page 160.

2   large sweet potatoes (about 2 pounds), scrubbed, quartered lengthwise, then sliced crosswise into ¹/₂-inch-thick pieces

¹/₃ cup plus ¹/₄ cup vegetable oil
    Salt and ground black pepper

1   box (5 ounces) plain Melba toast, ground to a sand-and-pebble texture in a food processor

¹/₂ teaspoon garlic powder

2   large eggs

2   teaspoons Dijon mustard

1   teaspoon dried thyme

4   split chicken breasts, bone-in, skin-on, 8 to 10 ounces each, skin removed

2   medium scallions, white and green parts, sliced thin

5   ounces jarred roasted red peppers, drained, dried, and cut into ¹/₄-inch pieces (about ¹/₂ cup)

1. Adjust the oven racks to the upper-middle and the lowest positions, place a rimmed baking sheet on the lower rack, and heat the oven to 400 degrees.

2. In a large bowl, toss the potatoes with ¹/₃ cup oil, ¹/₂ teaspoon salt, and ¹/₄ teaspoon pepper; set aside.

3. Toss the Melba crumbs with the remaining ¹/₄ cup oil, ³/₄ teaspoon salt, ¹/₂ teaspoon pepper, and garlic powder in a shallow dish. Whisk the eggs with 1 teaspoon Dijon mustard and the thyme in another shallow dish. Using tongs, dip a chicken piece into the egg mixture, turning to coat well and allowing excess to drip off. Drop the chicken into the Melba crumb mixture and press the crumbs into it with your fingers. Transfer the chicken to a wire rack set over a second rimmed baking sheet. Repeat with the remaining chicken.

4. Spread the potatoes on the preheated baking sheet on the lowest rack in the oven and place the chicken on the upper rack. Bake for 20 minutes, shaking the pan of potatoes occasionally. Switch the potatoes to the top rack and the chicken to the bottom rack; continue to cook until the chicken is a deep, nutty brown and registers 160 degrees on an instant-read thermometer, about 20 minutes longer. Remove the chicken and potatoes from the oven. Transfer the potatoes to a large bowl and toss with the remaining 1 teaspoon mustard, scallions, and roasted red peppers. Season the potatoes with salt and pepper to taste. Serve the chicken and potato salad immediately.

209

CHICKEN MAQUE CHOUX

UNLESS YOU'RE FROM LOUISIANA, chances are you've never heard of maque choux (pronounced "mach shu"). Although lots of ingredients can be included, the only essential ingredient in this braise is corn. With the addition of chicken and kielbasa sausage, we transformed a classic maque choux from a simple side dish to a one-pot supper.

The method of cooking maque choux is fairly standard. Onions are sautéed, then corn is added along with spices. The pot is covered, and the mixture simmers until the corn is tender and the sauce is flavorful. Because the corn is simmered for so long, we found that frozen corn simply didn't work. It withered into wrinkly bits that offered little flavor to the sauce. Fresh corn kernels are a must for this recipe.

To incorporate the chicken and sausage, we found it necessary to do a little shuffling of ingredients in and out of the pot. Wanting both the sausage and the chicken to get a good sear before being simmered with the corn, we decided to brown them separately. By searing them in the same pot, we were able to create layers of tasty drippings, giving the sauce a remarkably deep flavor.

We tried using boneless, skinless chicken breasts but found they overcooked and dried out too easily while simmering. Split breasts posed the same problem. Bone-in thighs worked much better. The dark meat remained tender and juicy, and their ample layer of skin browned well, leaving wonderful drippings behind. The only issue was that the skin turned flabby after simmering. To avoid this unsightly result, we simply removed the browned skin before adding the chicken back to the pot to simmer. Once all the ingredients were in the pot, we noted that it took about 25 minutes to cook the chicken through, by which time the corn was tender and the sauce tasted amazingly good.

The addition of cayenne, red peppers, and herbs made it even better. The only complaint now was that the essential ingredient—the corn—was hard to taste. Increasing the amount of corn seemed the obvious response, but it didn't produce the desired effect. We then tried scraping the corn pulp out of the cobs and found the potent, sweet, fragrant corn flavor we were looking for.

Last, we found it beneficial to add ¼ cup water to the pot before simmering to avoid all risk of sticking and burning. Although the corn and chicken release a lot of moisture as they begin to heat through, the pot stays dangerously dry in the first few minutes of cooking. We also found it best to simmer the stew uncovered for the last 5 minutes to adjust the sauce to the right consistency.

Chicken Maque Choux

SERVES 6

TIME: 1 HOUR

Serve with hot sauce and a crusty, rustic loaf to help sop up the sauce. Plain steamed rice (page 113) is another good option, as are Cornmeal Biscuits (page 369). If you like, add a leafy salad, such as Bitter Salad with Creamy Garlic Vinaigrette (page 30).

6   ears corn, husked and silked

6   bone-in, skin-on chicken thighs (about 2 pounds), trimmed of excess fat
     Salt and ground black pepper

2   teaspoons vegetable oil

1   pound kielbasa, sliced crosswise into ¼-inch rounds

2   medium onions, minced

½   teaspoon cayenne pepper

2   medium red bell peppers, stemmed, seeded, and cut into ½-inch dice

3   medium cloves garlic, minced or pressed through a garlic press (about 1 tablespoon)

1   teaspoon minced fresh thyme leaves

2   tablespoons minced fresh parsley leaves

1. Stand an ear of corn on end inside a large bowl. Using a chef's knife, cut the kernels off the cob. Using the back of the knife, scrape any remaining pulp off the cob and into the bowl. Repeat with the remaining ears of corn. Set the corn kernels and pulp aside; discard the cobs.

2. Season the chicken liberally with salt and pepper. Heat the oil in a Dutch oven until just smoking. Add the chicken, skin-side down, and cook until golden, about 6 minutes. Flip the chicken and continue to cook until the second side is golden, about 3 minutes longer. Transfer the chicken to a plate. Using paper towels, pull the skin off the chicken and discard it.

3. Return the pot to medium heat, add the kielbasa, and cook until it is lightly browned around the edges, 1 to 2 minutes. Transfer the kielbasa to a plate.

4. Pour all but 1 tablespoon fat from the pan and return it to medium heat. Add the onions, cayenne, and 1 teaspoon salt and cook until the onions are translucent and soft, 3 to 4 minutes. Stir in the bell peppers, garlic, thyme, corn kernels and pulp, kielbasa, chicken, and ¼ cup water. Cover, reduce the heat to medium-low, and cook until the chicken registers 155 degrees on an instant-read thermometer, about 25 minutes.

5. Remove the lid and simmer to reduce the sauce and finish cooking the chicken to 160 degrees, about 5 minutes. Remove the pot from the heat, stir in the parsley, and adjust the seasonings with salt and pepper to taste. Serve immediately.

BRAISED CHICKEN

IN THEORY, A FAST CHICKEN BRAISE can be as soothing as a long-simmered stew. Unlike stew meat, which requires hours of simmering to become tender, chicken requires just enough simmering time to cook through (it's already tender).

The term *braise* is actually the name of the cooking technique, which involves simmering something partially submerged in liquid underneath a lid. Many braises are started on the stove and then transferred to the oven, where they can simmer on their own for hours. Because chicken cooks so quickly, it can be easily braised on the stove.

We began with the classic braising technique. First, the meat is seared in the pot, then removed. The aromatics are then sautéed in the drippings left behind. The meat is then returned to the pot along with liquid, covered, and simmered until done. Testing this method on a variety of chicken parts, we noted that breast meat cooked unevenly, with the meat at the tapered end overcooked by the time the thicker end was cooked through. Bone-in thighs, in contrast, cooked evenly and remained moist and flavorful, thanks to their uniform shape and dark meat. Tasters did not like the rubbery skin of the thighs after they had been braised, yet we noticed a loss of flavor when the thighs were seared without their skin. To solve the problem, we removed the browned skin after the thighs were seared but before they were returned to the pot to simmer. The thighs cooked in only 35 minutes.

As for the braising liquid, we found that a mixture of wine and water worked well. When the braise is flavored with hearty ingredients such as olives and pancetta, we found that chicken broth (which is called for in many recipes) is unnecessary. Last, we found it necessary to add flour to the braise, helping the liquid thicken to a sauce.

Chicken Provençal

SERVES 4

TIME: 1 HOUR

The garlic toasts makes this braise a complete main course. You might round out the meal with a leafy salad.

8	bone-in, skin-on chicken thighs (about 3 pounds), trimmed of excess fat
	Salt and ground black pepper
4	ounces pancetta, cut into ¼-inch pieces
1	large onion, chopped fine
5	medium cloves garlic, minced or pressed through a garlic press (about 5 teaspoons), plus 1 large clove garlic, peeled
1	tablespoon unbleached all-purpose flour
½	cup vermouth or dry white wine
1	(14½-ounce) can diced tomatoes, drained
8	slices high-quality rustic or Italian bread, each about ½ inch thick
½	cup small black olives, such as niçoise, pitted
¼	cup minced fresh basil leaves

1. Season the chicken with salt and pepper to taste. Cook the pancetta in a Dutch oven over medium-high heat until crisp, 5 to 6 minutes. Using a slotted spoon, transfer the pancetta to a small bowl, leaving the rendered fat in the pot. Return the pot to high heat and add the chicken, skin-side down. Cook until golden brown and crisp, about 6 minutes. Using tongs, flip the chicken; continue to cook until the second side is golden, about 3 minutes. Remove the pot from the heat and transfer the chicken to a large plate.

2. Drain off all but 2 tablespoons fat from the pot. Add the onion and ½ teaspoon salt. Return the pot to medium heat and cook, scraping the browned bits off the bottom of the pan, until the onion is soft and translucent,

4 to 5 minutes. Meanwhile, remove and discard the skin from the browned chicken. Stir the minced garlic and flour into the onion and cook until fragrant, about 1 minute. Stir in the vermouth, tomatoes, and ½ cup water, scraping the browned bits off the bottom of the pan. Return the chicken and pancetta to the pan and bring to a simmer. Cover, reduce the heat to medium-low, and cook until the chicken is tender and nearly cooked through, about 30 minutes, turning the chicken over with tongs halfway through.

3. Meanwhile, adjust an oven rack to the middle position and heat the oven to 400 degrees. Arrange the bread slices in a single layer on a baking sheet and bake until dry and crisp, about 10 minutes, turning them over halfway through baking. While the bread is still hot, rub each slice with the whole garlic clove and set aside.

4. Stir the olives into the pot and continue to cook, uncovered, until they are heated through and the braising liquid is thickened slightly, about 5 minutes longer. Transfer the chicken to a serving platter or individual plates. Stir the basil into the sauce and adjust the seasonings with salt and pepper to taste. Pour the sauce over the chicken and serve immediately with the garlic toasts.

Moroccan Chicken, Chickpea, and Apricot Stew with Couscous

SERVES 4 TO 6

TIME: 1 HOUR

This Moroccan-style braise incorporates the perfume of cardamom and cinnamon along with dried apricots (some of which are cut in half to further flavor the sauce). Classically, this type of stew is cooked in a special pot with a shallow, perforated insert for the couscous, which steams over the fragrant, simmering chicken. Without this special pot, we found it necessary to cook plain couscous on the side and make the stew a bit more potent so that the flavors of the two elements are balanced. This braise is a bit soupier than the previous recipe so that the couscous can soak up the extra liquid.

8	bone-in, skin-on chicken thighs (about 3 pounds), trimmed of excess fat
	Salt and ground black pepper
2	tablespoons extra-virgin olive oil
2	medium onions, chopped fine
5	medium cloves garlic, minced or pressed through a garlic press (about 5 teaspoons)
2	cinnamon sticks
½	teaspoon ground cardamom
I	teaspoon hot paprika
8	ounces dried apricots (about I cup), 4 ounces cut in half, the rest left whole
2	cups couscous
I	(15-ounce) can chickpeas, drained and rinsed
¼	cup minced fresh cilantro leaves

1. Season the chicken with salt and pepper. Heat 1 tablespoon oil in a Dutch oven over medium-high heat until just smoking. Add the chicken, skin-side down, and cook until golden, about 6 minutes. Using tongs, flip the chicken; continue to cook until the second side is golden, about 3 minutes. Remove the pot from the heat and transfer the chicken to a large plate.

2. Drain off all but 1 tablespoon fat from the pot. Add the onions and ½ teaspoon salt, return the pot to medium heat, and cook, scraping the browned bits off the bottom of the pot, until the onions are soft and translucent, about 4 minutes. Meanwhile, remove and discard the skin from the browned chicken. Stir the garlic, cinnamon, cardamom, paprika, and apricots into the onions and cook until fragrant, about 30 seconds. Add 2 cups water and scrape up any browned bits from the pot.

Add the chicken to the pot and bring to a simmer. Cover, reduce the heat to medium-low, and cook until the chicken is tender and nearly cooked through, about 30 minutes, using tongs to turn over the chicken at the halfway point.

3. Meanwhile, heat the remaining 1 tablespoon oil in a medium saucepan over medium-high heat until shimmering. Add the couscous and toast, stirring often, until it just begins to turn golden, about 5 minutes. Transfer the toasted couscous to a large bowl and toss with ½ teaspoon salt and ⅛ teaspoon pepper. Pour 3¾ cups boiling water over the couscous and cover with a tight-fitting lid or sheet of plastic wrap. Allow to sit for 12 minutes. Remove the lid and fluff the grains with a fork.

4. Stir the chickpeas into the Dutch oven and continue to cook, uncovered, until the chickpeas are warmed through and the sauce is slightly reduced, about 5 minutes. Remove the Dutch oven from the heat, discard the cinnamon sticks, stir in the cilantro, and adjust the seasonings with salt and pepper to taste. To serve, portion the couscous into individual shallow bowls, top with a piece or two of chicken, and then ladle the chickpea and apricot sauce over the top.

CHICKEN AND RICE

CHICKEN AND RICE IS A CLASSIC weeknight supper around the world. Usually cooked in the same pot under a lid, the chicken rests on the rice, basting it with flavor as the rice steams underneath. Yet this one-pot meal has its fair share of problems. Keeping the chicken from drying out and the rice from turning sticky or cooking unevenly can be tricky.

We decided to keep the shopping simple and stick to one cut of chicken. Starting with boneless, skinless chicken breasts, we found the meat turned out both flavorless and far overdone by the time the rice had cooked through. Moving on to split breasts, we found the cooking time between chicken and rice was closer, but the chicken still emerged from the pot tasting dry and with an ugly, flabby skin. To boot, we noted that the rice cooked unevenly under the weight of the chicken; some of the grains were overdone while others remained crunchy. Giving the rice a stir partway through the cooking helped it cook more evenly; however, the chicken still emerged subpar.

Up to now, we had been using the classic chicken and rice method. First, we browned the chicken in a Dutch oven, then removed it and sautéed onions with the browned bits the chicken left behind in the pot. To the sautéed onions we added rice and toasted it for a few minutes to intensify its flavor. We then added water, placed the chicken on the rice, covered the pot, and let it all cook. Finding no way to alter this method to produce crisp chicken and perfect rice, we decided to abandon this approach altogether. After browning the chicken in the pot to crisp the skin, we transferred it to the oven and let it roast on its own. This chicken emerged from the oven juicy and tender, with a beautiful golden crust. As the chicken roasted, we returned the pot to the stove and cooked the rice pilaf-style, incorporating the flavorful drippings left from browning the chicken. Happily, the chicken roasted in exactly the same amount of time it took to cook the rice.

Because the chicken was no longer being cooked in the pot with the rice, the pilaf tasted bland and lacked its original chicken flavor. To rectify this, we simply replaced some of the pilaf's water with canned chicken broth. Using all broth was overpowering, so we cut the broth with water.

The last trick we discovered to making perfectly cooked rice was to let it finish off the heat with a towel draped under the lid. This way, we prevented the rice from sticking and burning on the bottom of the pot. Draping a towel underneath the lid as it rested prevented condensing drips from hitting the rice and turning it soggy.

Our updated cooking technique is just as simple as the classic one-pot method, yet far more reliable.

Chicken and Rice with Lemon, Peas, and Scallions

SERVES 4

TIME: 1 HOUR

This recipe is hearty enough to stand on its own, although you could add glazed carrots (page 69) or green beans (page 75). See photo of this recipe on page 158.

4	split chicken breasts, bone-in, skin-on, 10 to 12 ounces each
	Salt and ground black pepper
2	teaspoons vegetable oil
1	large onion, chopped fine
1½	cups long-grain or basmati rice
⅛	teaspoon hot red pepper flakes
3	medium cloves garlic, minced or pressed through a garlic press (about 1 tablespoon)
1½	teaspoons grated zest and 2 tablespoons juice from 1 lemon, plus 1 lemon, cut into wedges
1¾	cups canned low-sodium chicken broth
1	cup frozen peas
5	medium scallions, green and white parts, sliced thin

1. Adjust the oven rack to the middle position and heat the oven to 350 degrees. Season the chicken liberally with salt and pepper. Heat the oil in a Dutch oven over medium-high heat until just smoking. Add the chicken, skin-side down, and cook until golden brown,

about 6 minutes. Transfer the chicken, skin-side up, to a casserole dish and bake until it reaches 160 degrees on an instant-read thermometer, 30 to 35 minutes.

2. Meanwhile, remove all but 2 tablespoons fat from the pot and return it to medium heat. Add the onion and 1 teaspoon salt and cook, scraping the browned bits off the bottom of the pot, until soft and translucent, 3 to 4 minutes. Add the rice and red pepper flakes and cook, stirring often, until the rice begins to turn translucent, about 3 minutes. Add the garlic and lemon zest and cook until fragrant, about 30 seconds. Add the broth and 1 cup water, scraping any browned bits off the bottom of the pot. Turn the heat to low, cover, and cook until all the liquid is absorbed, 16 to 18 minutes. Remove the pot from the heat. Sprinkle the peas over the rice, place a towel across the top of the pot, and replace the lid (see the illustration below). Allow the rice to stand for 10 minutes.

3. When ready to serve, gently fold the lemon juice and scallions into the rice with a fork and season with salt and pepper to taste. Serve the rice and chicken with lemon wedges.

STEAMING RICE

After the rice is cooked, cover the pan with a clean dish towel and then the lid; allow the rice to sit for 10 minutes. The towel absorbs moisture and helps produce dry, fluffy rice.

Chicken and Rice with Coconut Milk and Pistachios

SERVES 4

TIME: 1 HOUR

By replacing the chicken broth with coconut milk, we were able to change the flavor of the dish drastically. Because the coconut milk has a thicker viscosity than broth, the rice emerges with a slightly heavier texture.

4	split chicken breasts, bone-in, skin-on, 10 to 12 ounces each
	Salt and ground black pepper
2	teaspoons vegetable oil
1	medium onion, chopped fine
1½	cups long-grain or basmati rice
3	medium cloves garlic, minced or pressed through a garlic press (about 1 tablespoon)
1½	grated teaspoons zest and 2 tablespoons juice from 1 large lime, plus 1 lime, cut into wedges
½	teaspoon ground cardamom
1	(14-ounce) can unsweetened coconut milk
¼	cup minced fresh cilantro leaves
½	cup shelled pistachios, chopped coarse

1. Adjust the oven rack to the middle position and heat the oven to 350 degrees. Season the chicken liberally with salt and pepper. Heat the oil in a Dutch oven over medium-high heat until just smoking. Add the chicken, skin-side down, and cook until golden brown, about 6 minutes. Transfer the chicken to a casserole dish and bake until it reaches 160 degrees on an instant-read thermometer, 30 to 35 minutes.

2. Meanwhile, remove all but 2 tablespoons fat from the pot and return it to medium heat. Add the onion and 1 teaspoon salt and cook, scraping the browned bits off the bottom of

the pot, until soft and translucent, 3 to 4 minutes. Add the rice and cook, stirring often, until it begins to turn translucent, about 3 minutes. Add the garlic, lime zest, and cardamom and cook until fragrant, about 30 seconds. Add the coconut milk and 1 cup water, scraping the browned bits off the bottom of the pot. Turn the heat to low, cover, and cook until all the liquid is absorbed, 16 to 18 minutes. Remove the pot from the heat, place a towel across the top, and replace the lid (see the illustration on page 215). Allow the rice to stand for 10 minutes.

3. When ready to serve, gently fold the lime juice, cilantro, and pistachios into the rice with a fork and season with salt and pepper to taste. Serve the rice and chicken with lime wedges.

Chicken Under a Brick with Herb-Roasted Potatoes

COOKING A BUTTERFLIED CHICKEN under a brick in a skillet not only looks cool but shaves half an hour off the cooking time of a regular roast chicken *and* produces an amazingly crisp skin. The brick helps keep the chicken flat as it cooks, forcing all of the skin to make contact with the pan. Yet, after trying a few recipes, we noted two big problems. First, the beautiful, crisp skin often turned soggy or greasy as the chicken finished cooking. Second, the chicken is often marinated, but we found the marinade scorches in the hot pan.

We also noted a few problems that could be immediately rectified. Not only did we find that the weight of two bricks set on a rimmed baking sheet or cast-iron skillet offered a better distribution of weight but that few people actually have loose bricks hanging about in the kitchen. Also, we found that chickens much larger than 3 pounds were difficult to fit into a 12-inch skillet.

To start, we set the idea of a marinade aside for the moment and focused on the cooking method. With two unmarinated butterflied chickens, we tested the difference between pounding the chicken to an even thickness with a mallet and simply pressing it flat by hand. When pounded, the superflat chicken cooked evenly, and more of the skin made contact with the pan, thus turning crisp. By

BUTTERFLYING A CHICKEN

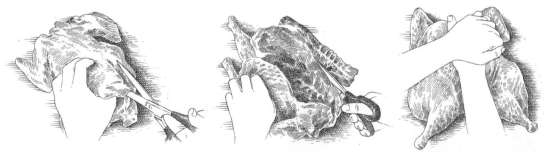

1. With the breast-side down and the tail of the chicken facing you, use poultry shears to cut along the length of one side of the backbone.

2. With the breast-side still down, turn the neck end to face you, cut along the other side of the backbone, and remove it.

3. Turn the chicken breast-side up. Open the chicken on the work surface. Use the palm of your hand to flatten the chicken, then pound it with the flat side of a mallet to a fairly even thickness.

comparison, only the portions of skin on the thicker sections of the chicken flattened by hand were nicely browned.

We cooked these chickens according to the method cited in most of the recipes we researched—skin-side down first with bricks on top, then flipped to cook the underside, replacing the bricks to help keep the chicken flat. This, however, didn't work. After the chickens were flipped and the weight placed back on top, the skin, which was now crisp and delicate, was torn to pieces and steamed itself flaccid. We then tried not replacing the bricks after the chicken was flipped, but the skin still turned rubbery from the steam and splattering oil. Next, we tried cooking the underside of the chicken first, finishing breast-side down, but this didn't work either. By flipping time, the pan was so loaded with grease and burned bits that the skin had no chance of looking pretty. It was greasy, spotty, and slightly bitter.

We then decided to try a different approach altogether. We cooked the chicken, skin-side down, underneath the bricks until it had a beautiful color. We then removed the bricks, flipped the chicken over, and finished it—still in the skillet—in a 450-degree oven. The hot, dry air of the oven ensured that the skin remained crisp and intact as the meat finished cooking. As for the bricks, we found that heavy cans and a cast-iron pot worked just as well (see the recipe headnote for more ideas).

Based on our oven-finish method, we quickly figured out an easy way to include a flavorful marinade as well as accompanying potatoes. Brushing the marinade onto the crisp chicken before finishing it in the oven was the obvious answer to our initial scorching problem. The heat of the oven fused the marinade to the skin without ruining its crisp texture, and the brief cooking time made it easy to retain the fresh, potent flavors in the

marinade. Tasters preferred a simple oil-based marinade made with garlic, lemon, thyme, and a kick of red pepper flakes.

We found an easy method for roasting potatoes. We simply threw them into the pan underneath the chicken before it went into the oven. Emerging fragrant and gorgeous, the chicken must rest for 10 minutes, during which time the potatoes are returned to the oven to finish cooking and pick up some color.

Chicken Under a Brick with Herb-Roasted Potatoes

SERVES 4
TIME: 1 HOUR

Instead of two bricks and a rimmed baking sheet, use a heavy cast-iron skillet loaded with several cans or a large stockpot partially filled with water. Be careful when removing the pan from the oven, as the handle will be hot. Serve with Peas and Pearl Onions (page 77) or a leafy salad.

1	small whole chicken (about 3 pounds)
	Salt and ground black pepper
1	teaspoon plus 2 tablespoons vegetable oil
3	medium cloves garlic, minced or pressed through a garlic press (about 1 tablespoon)
3	teaspoons minced fresh thyme
1/8	teaspoon hot red pepper flakes
2	tablespoons juice from 1 lemon, plus 1 lemon, cut into wedges
1 1/2	pounds small Red Bliss potatoes, scrubbed, dried, and cut into 3/4-inch wedges
1	tablespoon minced fresh parsley leaves

1. Following the illustrations on page 216, remove the backbone from the chicken and pound flat with a rubber mallet. Season the chicken with salt and pepper to taste.

2. Adjust the oven rack to the lowest position and heat the oven to 450 degrees. Heat 1 teaspoon oil in a heavy-bottomed 12-inch ovenproof nonstick skillet over medium-high heat until it begins to smoke. Swirl the skillet to coat evenly with oil. Place the chicken, skin-side down, in the hot pan and reduce the heat to medium. Place the weight (see headnote) on the chicken and cook, checking every 5 minutes or so, until evenly browned, about 25 minutes. (After 20 minutes, the chicken should be fairly crisp and golden; if not, turn the heat up to medium-high and continue to cook until well browned.)

3. Meanwhile, mix the remaining 2 tablespoons oil, garlic, 1½ teaspoons thyme, pepper flakes, lemon juice, ½ teaspoon salt, and ¼ teaspoon black pepper in a small bowl and set aside.

4. Using tongs, carefully transfer the chicken, skin-side up, to a clean plate. Pour off any accumulated fat in the pan and add the potatoes, sprinkling them with ¼ teaspoon salt, ⅛ teaspoon black pepper, and the remaining 1½ teaspoons thyme. Place the chicken, skin-side up, on the potatoes and brush the skin with the reserved thyme–lemon juice mixture.

5. Transfer the pan to the oven and roast until the thickest part of the breast registers 160 degrees on an instant-read thermometer, about 10 minutes longer. Transfer the chicken to a cutting board and let rest 10 minutes.

6. Return the skillet with the potatoes to the oven and roast until browned and cooked through, about 10 minutes. Using a slotted spoon, transfer the potatoes to a large bowl, leaving the fat behind. Toss the potatoes with the parsley. Cut the chicken into pieces. Serve the chicken and potatoes immediately with the lemon wedges.

THAI-STYLE GROUND CHICKEN IN LETTUCE CUPS

CONSIDERED COMMON STREET FOOD (or fast food) in Thailand, *laab gai* is as simple as dinner can get. Sort of like a stir-fry, this exotic-tasting dish consists of spicy, quickly cooked ground chicken that is eaten not with a fork but with the aid of a lettuce leaf. The ground filling is spooned into a lettuce leaf, which is folded shut and then eaten with your fingers, much like you eat a taco.

To start, we noted that ground chicken is sold in a variety of textures, from finely ground to coarsely processed. The finely ground chicken was easy to break into small, bite-size pieces as it cooked. Coarsely ground chicken cooked up to an unappetizing worm-like texture. Because it can be hard to tell how finely ground your chicken is, we found it best to give the raw chicken a once-over with the chef's knife to ensure it is finely textured.

Most recipes we researched called for similar flavorings, including fish sauce, lime juice, scallions, and chiles. Lime zest gave the laab gai a good punch that was nicely tempered with brown sugar and fragrant basil. Many recipes also included a surprising ingredient: toasted rice powder. We tried making laab gai without it but found its sweet flavor made the dish taste absolutely authentic. The rice powder also thickened the mixture slightly and kept it from becoming too sloppy and wet. We simply toasted several tablespoons of white rice in the skillet before cooking the chicken and then ground them to a powder in a spice mill.

Although any type of lettuce leaves could be used to eat the laab gai, we found the small leaf size and pronounced curvature of Boston and Bibb lettuce to work best.

Thai-Style Ground Chicken in Lettuce Cups

SERVES 4

TIME: 30 MINUTES

When serving, we found it easiest to put the laab gai in a shallow serving bowl on a large plate. If you arrange the leaves of lettuce around the edge of the plate and equip everyone with a soupspoon, the platter can be placed in the center of the table and people can serve themselves. Serve with Spicy Green Beans with Sesame Seeds (page 75).

2	tablespoons long-grain white rice
2	tablespoons fish sauce
2	tablespoons juice and 1 teaspoon grated zest from 1 large lime
1	tablespoon brown sugar
1	pound ground chicken
1 1/2	tablespoons vegetable oil
1	medium Thai red or jalapeño chile, stemmed, seeded, and minced
3	tablespoons minced fresh basil leaves
2	medium scallions, green and white parts, sliced thin
1	head Boston lettuce, leaves separated from root end, washed, dried, and left whole

1. Toast the rice in a 10-inch nonstick skillet over medium-high heat until golden and aromatic, about 3 minutes. Transfer the hot rice to a spice grinder and grind to a powder; reserve. Mix the fish sauce, lime juice, and sugar in a small bowl and set aside. Using a chef's knife, chop the ground chicken further to a finely ground texture.

2. With paper towels, wipe any remaining rice dust from the skillet. Add the oil and heat over medium-high heat until the oil is just about to smoke. Add the chicken, chile, and lime zest, reduce the heat to medium, and cook, using a wooden spoon to break the chicken into small pieces, until the meat is no longer pink, about 5 minutes. Remove the skillet from the heat and stir in the toasted rice powder, fish sauce mixture, basil, and scallions. Transfer the chicken to a bowl and serve alongside the lettuce leaves (see headnote). Spoon some of the mixture into a lettuce leaf, fold the leaf edges up to form a taco shape, and eat with your hands.

SAUTÉED TURKEY CUTLETS

TURKEY IS NOW RIDING THE WAVE OF poultry popularity and can be bought in many forms, including quick-cooking cutlets. We discovered a few tricks to buying and cooking turkey cutlets that ensure they turn out tender and flavorful rather than tough and rubbery.

A cutlet is a thin slice of meat, often no thicker than 3/8 inch, usually cut from the breast. The ideal cutlet has an even thickness from end to end. It is cut across the grain of the breast so its edges won't curl when it cooks. Also, it is usually cut on the diagonal to increase its surface area.

We tried all the brands of cutlets we could get our hands on and found them inconsistent in terms of size, shape, and thickness. One regional brand, Shady Brook, was pretty good, while one national brand, Perdue Fit 'n Easy, was quite disappointing. Short of cutting your own cutlets, which takes practice and seriously curtails the speed and ease of preparing this dish, the best you can do is to inspect the packages carefully before you buy and sample the brands in your area to find the most uniform product. Buy cutlets with neat (not ragged) edges and make sure all the cutlets are roughly the same size.

Many recipes call for flouring the meat

before cooking to prevent it from turning dry and to help develop a golden crust. After making a few batches of cutlets, both floured and unfloured, we determined that flouring wasn't necessary; we were able to get a golden crust without flour. Also, when it was necessary to cook the cutlets in batches, the residual flour left in the pan after the first batch tended to burn.

Sometimes the cutlets are sliced in such a way that six of them (serving four people) fit easily into a 12-inch pan. Other times, their size and shape make it necessary to cook them in batches. If you must batch-cook, do so. Because the cutlets are so thin, it is nearly impossible to get a golden color on both sides without overcooking them, resulting in a dry and rubbery texture. Instead, we focused the cooking time on one side of the cutlet to achieve a golden color, cooking the second side only long enough to cook the cutlet through. The cutlets are then served golden-side up. Last, we found it is important for the cutlets to be dried thoroughly before cooking—not just blotted, but dried thoroughly on both sides. Damp cutlets form poor crusts.

Cooked in just 3 minutes and complemented by an unusual pan sauce, these turkey cutlets are a welcome change from the same old boneless chicken breasts.

Sautéed Turkey Cutlets with Dried Cherry Sauce

SERVES 4

TIME: 20 MINUTES

One cutlet per person makes a skimpy serving, so we call for a total of six to serve four people. If you cannot fit all the cutlets in the pan without overlapping, cook them in two batches, using 1½ tablespoons oil for each. This dish is especially nice with couscous pilaf (page 93) and a green vegetable.

6	turkey cutlets (about 1½ pounds), rinsed and thoroughly dried
	Salt and ground black pepper
2½–4	tablespoons vegetable oil
2	medium shallots, minced
½	cup dried cherries
1	teaspoon minced fresh thyme leaves
½	cup ruby port
½	cup orange juice
2	tablespoons unsalted butter, cut into 2 pieces

1. Adjust the oven rack to the middle position, set a large heatproof plate on it, and heat the oven to 200 degrees. Sprinkle both sides of the cutlets with salt and pepper.

2. Heat 1½ tablespoons oil in a heavy-bottomed 12-inch skillet over medium-high heat until just smoking. Lay the cutlets in the pan, not overlapping, and cook without moving until light golden brown, about 2 minutes. Using tongs, turn the cutlets; cook until the meat feels firm when pressed, 30 to 60 seconds longer. Transfer the cutlets to the warm plate in the oven. If necessary, repeat with the remaining cutlets and more oil.

3. Add 1 tablespoon oil to the empty skillet and return the pan to medium heat. Add the shallots, cherries, and thyme and cook, scraping the browned bits off the bottom of the pan, until the shallots soften, about 1 minute. Add the port and orange juice, scraping the browned bits off the bottom of the pan. Turn the heat to high and simmer until the liquid is well reduced and syrupy, 3 to 4 minutes. Whisk in the butter, 1 tablespoon at a time, along with any accumulated juices from the cutlets. Remove the pan from the heat and season the sauce with salt and pepper to taste. To serve, arrange the cutlets on a platter or individual plates and pour the sauce over them.

BUILDING BLOCK RECIPE
Sautéed Turkey Cutlets
SERVES 4
TIME: 20 MINUTES

Once the cutlets are in the oven, make a pan sauce in the empty skillet. Start by cooking several tablespoons of aromatics (shallots, leeks, onion, or garlic) in 1 tablespoon oil in the empty skillet over low heat. Once the aromatics soften, deglaze the pan with about 1 cup liquid (stock, wine, and/or juice) and simmer until the liquid reduces to about ½ cup. At this point, flavorful ingredients (herbs, lemon juice, lime juice, olives, capers, or dried fruit) can be added. Finish the sauce by whisking in several tablespoons of butter. Taste for seasonings, adding salt and pepper as needed, and spoon the pan sauce over the cutlets.

6	turkey cutlets (about 1½ pounds), rinsed and thoroughly dried
	Salt and ground black pepper
1½–3	tablespoons vegetable oil

1. Adjust the oven rack to the middle position, set a large heatproof plate on it, and heat the oven to 200 degrees. Sprinkle both sides of the cutlets with salt and pepper.

2. Heat 1½ tablespoons oil in a heavy-bottomed 12-inch skillet over medium-high heat until just smoking. Lay the cutlets in the pan, not overlapping, and cook without moving until light golden brown, about 2 minutes. Using tongs, turn the cutlets; cook until the meat feels firm when pressed, 30 to 60 seconds longer. Transfer the cutlets to the warm plate in the oven. If necessary, repeat with the remaining cutlets and more oil. Make a pan sauce in the empty skillet and spoon it over the cutlets.

Sautéed Turkey Cutlets with Hard Cider and Thyme Sauce
SERVES 4
TIME: 20 MINUTES

One cutlet per person makes a skimpy serving, so we call for a total of six to serve four people. If you cannot fit all the cutlets in the pan without overlapping, cook them in two batches, using 1½ tablespoons oil for each batch. Serve with plain steamed rice or couscous pilaf (page 93) and a green vegetable.

6	turkey cutlets (about 1½ pounds), rinsed and thoroughly dried
	Salt and ground black pepper
2½–4	tablespoons vegetable oil
½	small red onion, minced
	Pinch sugar
1	teaspoon minced fresh thyme leaves
1	cup hard cider
2	tablespoons sour cream

1. Adjust the oven rack to the middle position, set a large heatproof plate on it, and heat the oven to 200 degrees. Sprinkle both sides of the cutlets with salt and pepper.

2. Heat 1½ tablespoons oil in a heavy-bottomed 12-inch skillet over medium-high heat until just smoking. Lay the cutlets in the pan, not overlapping, and cook without moving until light golden brown, about 2 minutes. Using tongs, turn the cutlets; cook until the meat feels firm when pressed, 30 to 60 seconds longer. Transfer the cutlets to the warm plate in the oven. If necessary, repeat with the remaining cutlets and more oil.

3. Add 1 tablespoon oil to the empty skillet and return the pan to medium heat. Add the onion, sugar, and a pinch of salt and cook, scraping the browned bits from the bottom of the pan, until the onion softens and is lightly browned, about 5 minutes. Add the thyme and

cider, scraping the browned bits off the bottom of the pan. Turn the heat to high and simmer until the liquid is syrupy, 3 to 4 minutes. Remove the pan from the heat and whisk in the sour cream, 1 tablespoon at a time, along with any accumulated juices from the cutlets. Season with salt and pepper to taste. To serve, arrange the cutlets on a platter or individual plates and pour the sauce over them.

Turkey Saltimbocca

SERVES 4

TIME: 45 MINUTES

Because of the prosciutto, this dish requires little salt. Serve with Toasted Orzo Pilaf with Peas and Parmesan (page 94).

6	thin slices prosciutto (about 3 ounces)
6	turkey cutlets (about 1 ½ pounds), rinsed and thoroughly dried
6	large fresh sage leaves
	Ground black pepper
2 ½–4	tablespoons extra-virgin olive oil
½	small onion, minced
1	cup sweet Marsala
2	tablespoons unsalted butter, cut into 2 pieces
1	tablespoon juice from 1 lemon
1	tablespoon minced fresh parsley leaves
	Salt

1. Adjust the oven rack to the middle position, set a large heatproof plate on it, and heat the oven to 200 degrees. Place 1 slice prosciutto on each turkey cutlet and lay 1 sage leaf in the center, pressing them into the turkey with the palm of your hand. Following the illustration at right, secure all 3 layers with a toothpick. Sprinkle both sides of the cutlets with pepper.

2. Heat 1½ tablespoons oil in a heavy-bottomed 12-inch skillet over medium-high heat until just smoking. Lay the cutlets in the pan, prosciutto-side down, not overlapping, and cook without moving until light golden brown, about 2 minutes. Using tongs, turn the cutlets; cook until the meat feels firm when pressed, 30 to 60 seconds longer. Transfer the cutlets to the warm plate in the oven. If necessary, repeat with the remaining cutlets and more oil.

3. Add 1 tablespoon oil to the empty skillet and return the pan to medium heat. Add the onion and cook, scraping the browned bits off the bottom of the pan, until the onion softens and is lightly browned, about 5 minutes. Add the Marsala, scraping the browned bits off the bottom of the pan. Turn the heat to high and simmer until the liquid is well reduced and syrupy, 3 to 4 minutes. Whisk in the butter, 1 tablespoon at a time, along with any accumulated juices from the cutlets, the lemon juice, and the parsley. Remove the pan from the heat and season the sauce with salt and pepper to taste. To serve, arrange the cutlets on a platter or individual plates and pour the sauce over them.

MAKING SALTIMBOCCA

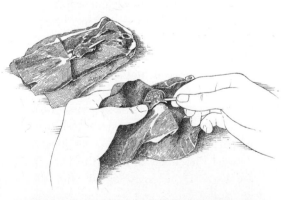

Using a toothpick as if it were a stickpin, secure the sage and prosciutto to the turkey cutlet by poking the toothpick down through the layers, then back out again. The toothpick should be parallel to the cutlet and as flat as possible.

MEAT

WE RELY ON SEVERAL BASIC TECHNIQUES to cook steaks, chops, and roasts quickly. (For information on stir-frying small bits of sliced meat, see Chapter 11). Grilling is always an option for cooking steaks, chops, and roasts (see Chapter 10). Indoors, we tend to rely on three methods: We pan-sear steaks and chops, we pan-fry boneless cutlets, and we pan-roast small roasts that are too large to cook through by pan-searing alone. Some notes on each of these indoor methods follow.

Pan-searing is best for chops and steaks of moderate thickness. (A 2-inch-thick T-bone steak should be grilled.) The meat is cooked in a bare film of oil in a blazing hot pan until both sides are well browned and a flavorful crust forms. At this point, the interior is done and the meat need only rest for 5 to 10 minutes before being sliced or served.

The caramelized browned bits left in the pan, called *fond*, can be turned into a quick sauce while the meat rests. Aromatics such as minced shallots can be sautéed; then, in a process called *deglazing*, liquid (usually wine, stock or broth, or both) is poured in and the fond is scraped up with a wooden spoon. The liquid is simmered and reduced to concentrate flavors and thicken the texture; in a final and sometimes optional step, the reduction is enriched and slightly thickened by whisking in butter. (For more on pan sauces, see page 232.)

Tempting though it may be to use a nonstick skillet for searing or sautéing, if you intend to make a pan sauce, opt for a traditional (not nonstick) skillet. Nonstick skillets will not develop the fond that a traditional one will, and because fond supplies a pan sauce with richness and depth, a nonstick skillet will make a less flavorful sauce. Also important is the size of the skillet, which should comfortably hold the food being cooked. If it is overcrowded, the food will steam and fail to create much fond.

If unenameled cast iron is your cookware of choice, be sure the pan is well seasoned and free of rusty spots; when tested in our kitchen, a sauce made in a well-seasoned cast-iron pan tasted fine. Poorly maintained cast iron, however, will make a metallic-tasting sauce. If you are just pan-searing but not making a sauce, cast iron is an excellent option.

Pan-frying is a second indoor method that cooks meat quickly. It is ideal for boneless breaded cutlets. Here, a nonstick skillet is best because no sauce will be made in the pan. Add enough oil to come halfway up the sides of the food. Typically, this is less oil than you might think—usually about ½ cup. Breaded meat should be fried just until the exterior is crisp—a process that takes just minutes. (For more information about breading and pan-frying, see page 236.)

Pan-roasting is the third indoor method we use to cook meat quickly. This technique is suited to cuts that are too thick to pan-sear. (With a small roast, for example, the exterior would burn long before the inside was cooked through by pan-searing.) We like to cook tenderloins and small pork loins by this method. The roast is coated generously with salt and pepper and then browned on all sides in a hot ovenproof skillet. Once the exterior is browned, the roast (still in the pan) goes into a preheated oven to finish cooking. By using a high oven temperature (and keeping the meat in the hot skillet), the roasting time for a 1-pound tenderloin or a 2-pound pork loin is 15 to 30 minutes.

Once the meat is nearly up to temperature, it should be transferred to a cutting board, covered with foil, and allowed to rest for 10 minutes. During this time, the juices will redistribute themselves evenly through the roast, and the internal temperature will continue to climb as residual heat cooks the meat a bit further. After the meat rests, it should be sliced thin and served immediately.

The recipes that follow demonstrate these basic techniques as well as a few more unusual ways to cook meat quickly.

SKILLET FAJITAS

IT SEEMS LIKE EVERY TEX-MEX JOINT, from the tiniest hole in the wall to the strip mall chains, offers some hackneyed version of fajitas well distanced from the authentic recipe—which is a combination of grilled meat and peppers tucked into a flour tortilla. Nevertheless, fajitas are probably the Southwest's greatest culinary export. This dish is simple at heart and quick cooking by design. We wanted to develop a fajita recipe that could be made without lugging out the grill.

Traditionalists swear by skirt steak as the cut of choice for fajitas, though flank steak has long surpassed it because of its readier availability and lower cost, with only a slightly milder flavor. Skirt steak, however, is well worth searching out for its full flavor (see page 226 for details). Prior to cooking, the meat conventionally is marinated overnight in a mixture of lime juice and seasonings. Despite tradition, we knew from experience that marinating doesn't significantly affect the meat's flavor (although, depending on the marinade's acidity, it can adversely affect the texture). Most tasters found that a quick drizzle of lime juice added just before cooking contributed as much flavor as a 12-hour marinade.

One point everyone agrees on is that flank steak is at its best when cooked fast and furious over high heat. Extended cooking robs the meat of its juices, rendering it tough and fibrous. In addition, flank steak should be cooked to rare to medium-rare; when cooked further, the meat becomes dry, tough, and livery. Grilling is the first choice for fajitas, but we wanted to stay

BUILDING BLOCK RECIPE
Pan-Seared Flank Steak
SERVES 4
TIME: 20 MINUTES

When it is just too cold to grill, pan-searing is the best way to cook most steaks. A dry steak will brown best, so be sure to pat the meat with paper towels right before it goes into the pan. Sliced flank steak can be used in sandwiches and salads or served on its own with a potato and a vegetable side dish.

2	tablespoons vegetable oil
1½	pounds flank steak, trimmed of excess fat and patted dry with paper towels
	Salt and ground black pepper

Heat the oil in a heavy-bottomed 12-inch skillet over medium-high heat until smoking. Meanwhile, season the steak liberally with salt and pepper. Lay the steak in the pan and cook, without moving, until well browned, 4 to 5 minutes. Using tongs, flip the steak. Reduce the heat to medium. Continue to cook until the second side is browned, 4 to 5 minutes. Transfer the steak to a plate, tent loosely with aluminum foil, and let rest for 10 minutes. Slice the steak very thinly against the grain and serve.

indoors and chose to pan-sear the meat. We followed our standard method for steaks: We heated vegetable oil in the skillet until it smoked and seared each side of the steak until it was well browned. As with smaller steaks, it was important to move the steak as little as possible as it cooked to preserve the rich brown crust. The thin steak cooked quickly, requiring less than 10 minutes to reach rare. When it was fresh from the skillet, we drizzled more lime juice over the

INGREDIENTS: Three Flat Steaks

Like flank steak, the two other cuts most similar to it—skirt steak and hanger steak—have recently undergone a transformation to fashionable. These now-popular steaks all come from the chest and side of the cow. Hanger and flank both come from the rear side, while skirt comes from the area between the abdomen and the chest cavity. In addition to location, these steaks share certain other basic qualities: all are long, relatively thin, quite tough, and grainy, but with rich, deep, beefy flavor.

Of course, these flavorful steaks also have differences. When a cow is butchered, the hanger, a thick muscle attached to the diaphragm, hangs into the center of the carcass—hence the name. Because this cut is used in a classic French bistro dish, it is highly prized in restaurants and therefore difficult to find in butcher shops. We don't think this is a great loss because the hangers we sampled had the toughest texture and least rich flavor of these three cuts.

Fortunately, flank steak is easy to find in any supermarket. It has great beef flavor and is quite tender if cooked rare or medium-rare and sliced thin against the grain. Because of the popularity of fajitas, flank steak has become somewhat expensive, often retailing for $7 a pound.

Skirt steak, the cut originally used for fajitas, can be hard to locate in supermarkets and even butcher shops. This is a real pity because this cut has more fat than the flank steak, which makes it juicier and richer-tasting. At the same time, it has a deep, beefy flavor that outdoes both hanger and flank steak. If you see skirt steak, buy it and cook it like flank.

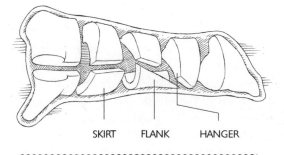

SKIRT   FLANK   HANGER

steak so that the bright citrus flavor would penetrate into the hot meat.

As the steak rested, we cooked the peppers and onions in the same pan, taking advantage of the flavorful fond left by the meat. As the peppers and onions sautéed, the fond was effectively deglazed and lent the vegetables a full flavor that needed little enhancement. (A little water added to the pan helped this process along.) We did, however, experiment with a variety of spices and settled on cumin seeds, which added a characteristically Southwestern touch to the mix. Left whole, the seeds also added a little crunch that contrasted with the soft texture of the peppers.

The fajitas were now all but ready for the table. We tried topping them with the common garnishes, from salsa and guacamole to cheese and sour cream. Tasters enjoyed them all except for the cheese, which seemed out of place. Seeking to save time, we found we could reduce the guacamole to its fundamental ingredient, diced avocado.

Skillet Fajitas

SERVES 4 TO 6
TIME: 40 MINUTES

If you like spicy food, add sliced jalapeño peppers with the red bell peppers, or a finely chopped chipotle chile once the peppers finish cooking. If you have only ground cumin, reduce the amount to ¼ teaspoon and add it for the last 30 seconds of cooking; otherwise, it could burn and turn the peppers bitter. Leftover fajitas reheat well and can be turned into a sandwich or the filling for an omelet— Southwestern-style steak and eggs. See pages 20 and 21 for tips on handling avocado. If you can find skirt steak, by all means use it in this recipe. See photo of this recipe on page 156.

1 ½   pounds flank steak, trimmed of excess fat
       and patted dry with paper towels

Salt and ground black pepper

4 tablespoons juice from 2 to 3 limes

2 tablespoons vegetable oil

2 medium red bell peppers, stemmed, seeded, and sliced thin

1 large red onion, halved and sliced thin

½ teaspoon cumin seeds

8–12 large flour tortillas

1 cup Five-Minute Tomato Salsa (page 16) or prepared salsa

½ cup sour cream

1 medium avocado, pitted, peeled, and diced medium

1. Sprinkle each side of the steak with a liberal coating of salt and pepper followed by 1 tablespoon lime juice (2 tablespoons in total). Heat the oil in a heavy-bottomed 12-inch skillet over medium-high heat until smoking. Lay the steak in the pan and cook, without moving, until well browned, 4 to 5 minutes. Using tongs, flip the steak. Reduce the heat to medium. Continue to cook until the second side is browned, 4 to 5 minutes. Transfer the steak to a plate, drizzle with the remaining 2 tablespoons lime juice, tent loosely with aluminum foil, and let rest for 10 minutes.

2. Meanwhile, return the skillet to medium-high heat and add the bell peppers, onion, cumin seeds, ½ teaspoon salt, and 2 tablespoons water. Cook, stirring occasionally and scraping the bottom of the skillet to release any browned bits, until the onion is very soft and browned, 5 to 6 minutes. Transfer the vegetables to a serving bowl and adjust the seasonings with salt and pepper to taste.

3. Heat a large nonstick skillet over medium heat for 2 minutes and lightly toast each tortilla in the pan for 10 to 15 seconds per side. Stack the toasted tortillas in a clean towel and wrap to keep warm.

4. To serve: Slice the steak very thinly against the grain and place the meat in a serving bowl.

Pour any released juices over the vegetables. Serve the vegetables, meat, and tortillas along with bowls of salsa, sour cream, and avocado so diners can assemble their own fajitas.

BEEF TERIYAKI

WHAT IN THE WORLD IS TERIYAKI? Most every Asian restaurant has some version of it, generally a sickly sweet, shellac-thick sauce varnished on tough mystery meat. But teriyaki can be a well-balanced sauce napping tender pieces of flavorful beef, chicken, or fish. Despite its simplicity, however, teriyaki is prone to problems. We set out to rectify them, as it is ideal for a quick meal.

Teriyaki is a Japanese term that refers to a particular sauce and cooking style. *Teri* translates as "luster," and *yaki* is a cooking method in which food is broiled. Traditionally, the teriyaki sauce is applied toward the end of cooking. Beef teriyaki generally appears as strips of beef—on skewers or not—flash-cooked so they are pink on the inside and glossy mahogany on the outside.

When we assessed the recipes we gathered, we found little consensus about the cut of beef to use for teriyaki. Sirloin and top round appeared, but so did flank steak and even rib eye. All the choices proved acceptable, but in the end, we favored a more unorthodox choice: blade steak. Richly flavored and inexpensive, blade steak is an underutilized cut of beef. Most people dismiss it because of a minor flaw: a thick ribbon of gristle running through the middle. However, the gristle serves here as a guide for slicing the meat; keeping the knife parallel to the gristle ensures you are cutting against the grain—a job, we have found, that can be confusing for home cooks. We kept the strips thin—about ¼ inch thick—to facilitate fast cooking.

Traditional teriyaki recipes dictate that the meat be marinated in a mixture of soy and sherry for several hours. Clearly, we didn't have several hours, but we found that as little as 10 minutes in the marinade improved the meat's flavor, especially when the marinade was punched up with ginger and garlic. In addition, the seasonings cooked along with the meat, which eliminated the task of cooking them separately.

While grilling the meat is the most traditional approach, we wanted to stay indoors and use just one pan. Pan-searing was the natural choice, and a 12-inch skillet provided all the surface area necessary to spread the meat in a single layer in a single batch. (In smaller skillets, the meat overlapped and stewed when cooked in a single batch—and, for the sake of time, we wanted to avoid two batches.)

Teriyaki sauce itself is a simple combination of three to four ingredients finely balanced between sweet and salty. Soy sauce and sugar are the primary flavoring agents along with sherry or mirin, a sweetened rice wine used specifically for cooking in Japan. As the sauce is reduced to a thick glaze, attaining the proper balance of flavors was a matter of trial and error; too much soy and the sauce was inedible, but too little and the sauce was bland and one-dimensional. After several attempts came out too thin, we tried adding a small amount of cornstarch. Tasters appreciated both the thicker texture and glossier sheen a scant amount provided. We walked a fine line, however; as little as an extra ¼ teaspoon cornstarch made the sauce too viscous.

Finishing the dish was a simple matter of turning the meat in the hot sauce for a couple of minutes until each of the slices was glossy. The reduced sauce was finely balanced and lustrous, not too sweet or sticky, and the meat was tender—a perfect medium-rare.

Beef Teriyaki

SERVES 4 TO 6

TIME: 30 MINUTES

See the column at left for more information about buying and cutting blade steak. The meat and sauce may be prepared ahead of time, although the garlic and ginger are best prepared when needed. As for accompaniments, rice is a must and steamed broccoli is traditional, although nearly any blend of vegetables would be acceptable. If you have leftovers, you can make the sliced meat into a sandwich with mayonnaise and spicy greens like arugula or watercress; several test cooks swear by the combination.

2	pounds top blade steaks, 1 inch thick, sliced against the grain into ¼-inch-thick strips, gristle discarded
1	(1-inch) piece fresh ginger, peeled and grated fine
2	medium cloves garlic, minced or pressed through a press
¼	cup plus 1 tablespoon soy sauce
½	cup mirin (Japanese rice wine)

TOP BLADE STEAKS

Top blade steaks, also called blade or flatiron steaks, are cut from the shoulder (or chuck) area of the cow. These small steaks are especially flavorful and tender. They are easy to spot in markets, as each has a line of gristle running down the center. When slicing these steaks, cut parallel to the gristle to ensure you are working against the grain. When you reach the gristle, turn the steak around and cut from the other side. Once all the meat is sliced away, discard the gristle.

2 tablespoons sugar
½ teaspoon cornstarch
2 teaspoons peanut or vegetable oil
  Sticky White Rice (page 328)
2 teaspoons sesame seeds
2 medium scallions, sliced thin on the bias

1. Toss the meat slices with the ginger, garlic, and 1 tablespoon soy sauce in a medium bowl and marinate for at least 10 minutes. Whisk together the remaining ¼ cup soy sauce, mirin, sugar, cornstarch, and ½ cup water in a small bowl.

2. Heat the oil in a 12-inch nonstick skillet over medium-high heat until smoking. Using tongs, place the meat in a single layer in the pan (using the sloping sides, if necessary); cook without moving until browned, 2 to 2½ minutes. Starting with the first strips placed in the pan, flip the meat and cook until the second side is browned, about 2 minutes. Use tongs to transfer the meat to a clean bowl.

3. Add the sauce mixture to the skillet, scraping with a wooden spoon to release any browned bits. Cook until the sauce reduces by half, about 2 minutes. Reduce the heat to medium and return the meat to the pan. Cook, stirring continuously, until the sauce reduces to a syrupy glaze and the meat is well coated, about 2 minutes.

STRIP STEAKS

Strip steaks, also known as top loin or shell steaks, are long, narrow, and triangular in shape. The strip meat is a bit chewy, with a tight, noticeable grain. It is a bit less fatty than other premium steaks and is a good choice for pan-searing.

4. Divide the rice among individual plates. Place the meat and sauce over the rice and garnish with sesame seeds and scallions. Serve immediately.

PAN-SEARED STRIP STEAKS WITH SAUTÉED MUSHROOMS

STEAK AND MUSHROOMS ARE A CLASSIC combination, appearing on menus from down-home diners to uptown steakhouses. Too often, however, the dish is marred by improperly seared, insipid beef and waterlogged, bland mushrooms. Simple combinations require flawless techniques to coax the best flavors from each component. Developing the best steak and mushrooms recipe was a task we relished, and in the spirit of quick-cooked, one-pot meals, we opted to update the dish with the addition of spicy greens and pungent blue cheese—ideal, irresistible complements.

Strip steaks were our choice for this dish. They pack a rich flavor, and the tight-grained texture seemed ideal, as the steak was to be paired with a variety of other textures, from the dense, resilient bite of sautéed mushrooms to crisp leafy greens and creamy cheese. These steaks are also convenient, requiring little preparation beyond some negligible trimming of extraneous fat (if the butcher was inattentive) and the thin line of gristle delineating the steak's longer side. Further, the steaks come ideally portioned—about 8 to 10 ounces each and neatly fitting in a large skillet without touching one another. We dusted the steaks with salt and pepper and then seared them on each side until a thick crust developed.

An important byproduct of pan-searing is

BUILDING BLOCK RECIPE

Pan-Seared Strip Steaks

SERVES 4

TIME: 20 MINUTES

Boneless strip steaks are our favorite premium cut for pan-searing. The steaks will leave browned bits, called fond, in the pan. The fond should be used as the basis for a quick pan sauce (see page 232).

1   teaspoon vegetable oil
4   boneless strip steaks, 1 to 1¼ inches thick (8 to 10 ounces each), trimmed of exterior gristle and patted dry with paper towels
     Salt and ground black pepper

Heat the oil in a large, heavy-bottomed skillet over medium-high heat until smoking. Meanwhile, season the steaks liberally with salt and pepper. Lay the steaks in the pan and cook, without moving, until a well-browned crust forms, 5 to 6 minutes. Using tongs, flip the steaks. Reduce the heat to medium. Cook 3 to 4 minutes more for rare (120 degrees on an instant-read thermometer) or 5 to 6 minutes for medium-rare (125 degrees). Transfer the steaks to a cutting board, tent with aluminum foil, and let rest for 5 minutes. Serve immediately.

the crusty bits that stick to the skillet's bottom. Known formally as fond, the bits are packed with flavor and by all means should be used. Generally speaking, the fond becomes the basis for a quick pan sauce, but in this instance, we used it to flavor the mushroom sauté that would top the steaks. The liquid shed by the mushrooms—encouraged with a little salt, which draws out moisture—effectively washed the fond free from the pan, and the

fond in turn suffused the mushrooms with its full, meaty flavor.

Because small mushrooms can take a long time to clean and prepare, we opted for a shortcut: large portobello mushroom caps. With a quick sweep of a pastry brush or paper towels, the caps were wiped clean and ready to chop. Just five to six caps totaled ¾ pound, more than enough for the topping. Portobello mushrooms are best if the dark gills are removed, as they may stain the sauté an inky brown, but with the aid of a sharp paring knife, this task takes moments.

Like the steaks, the mushrooms developed the best flavor over fairly high heat. The exterior browned and the interior remained juicy but far from waterlogged. To add depth and sweetness to the mushrooms, we included a few additional flavors. Onion—red onion in particular—lent sweetness and body. We assumed garlic would be a given and were surprised when tasters found its flavor superfluous because of the other assertive flavors in the dish. For herbs, we added thyme, which accented the woodsy flavor of the mushrooms. A splash of red wine, added off the heat, was enough liquid to loosen the fond and brighten the otherwise deep flavors.

While a more conventional presentation would involve positioning the salad beside the steak, we found the brash spiciness of the watercress benefited from both the mild warmth and juices yielded by the meat. A member of the mustard family, watercress packs some heat and is a traditional accompaniment to rich meat. The greens needed no dressing; the combination of steak juices and blue cheese provided enough flavor.

The mineral tang of good beef has a natural affinity for the funky ripeness of blue cheese, and their textural contrast—creamy cheese and toothy meat—heightens the experience. After trying several varieties of blue cheese, tasters preferred the big, tangy flavor of Gorgonzola—one of Italy's finest cheeses. With a heady cheese like Gorgonzola, a little goes a long way. Tasters preferred a light garnish of crumbled cheese (no more than 1 ounce per serving) sprinkled over the steak and mushrooms just before they went to the table.

Pan-Seared Strip Steaks with Sautéed Mushrooms, Gorgonzola, and Watercress

SERVES 4

TIME: 35 MINUTES

See page 229 for more information about buying strip steak. We find that the black gills on the underside of the portobellos can make the sauce inky brown, so we scrape them off with a paring knife before slicing the mushrooms. In this recipe, tasters preferred a potent aged Gorgonzola to a milder dolce Gorgonzola. If you prefer, replace the Gorgonzola with Stilton or any other strong blue cheese.

I	teaspoon vegetable oil
4	boneless strip steaks, I to I ¼ inches thick (8 to 10 ounces each), trimmed of exterior gristle and patted dry with paper towels
	Salt and ground black pepper
2	tablespoons unsalted butter
I	small red onion, halved and sliced thin
12	ounces portobello mushroom caps (5 or 6 medium), gills removed, caps cut in half and then into ½-inch-wide slices
4	sprigs fresh thyme, tied into a bundle with kitchen twine
2	tablespoons red wine
8	cups watercress, coarse stems removed
4	ounces Gorgonzola, crumbled (about ¾ cup)

1. Heat the oil in a large, heavy-bottomed skillet over medium-high heat until smoking. Meanwhile, season the steaks liberally with salt and pepper. Lay the steaks in the pan and cook, without moving, until a well-browned crust forms, 5 to 6 minutes. Using tongs, flip the steaks. Reduce the heat to medium. Cook 3 to 4 minutes more for rare (120 degrees on an instant-read thermometer) or 5 to 6 minutes for medium-rare (125 degrees). Transfer the steaks to a cutting board and tent with aluminum foil to keep warm.

2. Add the butter to the empty pan and increase the heat to medium-high. When the foam subsides, add the onion, mushrooms, thyme bundle, and ½ teaspoon salt. Cook, stirring occasionally, until the onion is soft and the mushrooms are well browned, 6 to 7 minutes. Remove the skillet from the heat and stir in the wine, scraping the pan bottom to remove any browned bits. Discard the thyme bundle and adjust the seasonings with salt and pepper to taste.

3. Divide the watercress evenly among 4 individual plates. Slice each steak crosswise into thin strips. Lay the steak over the greens, followed by the mushroom mixture. Drizzle any juices that collected from the meat over the greens and then sprinkle a little cheese over the top. Serve immediately.

TUSCAN-STYLE STEAK WITH ARUGULA AND PARMESAN

MUCH HAS BEEN MADE OF THE FOOD of northern Italy, from the superiority of its ingredients to the ethos of simplicity that guides its cooking. Simple cooking is harder than it looks. Ingredients and methods must be at their very best; there's nothing to cover up mistakes or imperfect flavors. Tuscan-style steak is a case in point. Simply grilled and anointed with an olive oil–based vinaigrette, the flavor rests solely on the quality of the meat and olive oil. We were inspired to develop a recipe in the spirit of Tuscan steak, extended to a full meal with the addition of greens and Parmesan.

An authentic Tuscan-style steak is a T-bone or porterhouse, over 2 inches thick, charred on the grill. For ease and efficiency, we opted to pan-sear the steak, so our choices were limited to steaks that were small enough to fit in a skillet and skinny enough to finish on the stovetop. We didn't want to finish them in the oven, which excluded the classic 2-inch-thick behemoth. From experience, we knew strip steaks fit the bill; perfectly sized and richly marbled, they beat out

sirloins, rib eyes, and filets. In a smoking-hot pan, 1-inch-thick steaks took about 8 to 9 minutes to reach rare; we pulled them at 120 degrees to take into consideration the five or so degrees that internal temperature increases as the steaks rest.

Steaks seared, we tackled the vinaigrette. The finest extra-virgin olive oil is the classic base for the dressing, and we could find little reason to argue with this. For acidity, we tried red and white wine vinegars, balsamic vinegar, and lemon juice; tasters favored the clean, bright taste of lemon juice. Garlic added punch to the vinaigrette, and tasters wanted enough for an assertive kick. Two cloves, pressed through a garlic press for the

---

BUILDING BLOCK RECIPE

Red Wine Pan Sauce for Strip Steaks

MAKES ABOUT ⅔ CUP, ENOUGH

FOR 4 STEAKS

TIME: 10 MINUTES

Once the meat is seared and transferred to a cutting board to rest, a pan sauce can be quickly made in the empty skillet. The choices of aromatics, liquids, and seasonings are endless. Here's a favorite combination for beef.

1	large shallot, minced (about 4 tablespoons)
1	tablespoon balsamic vinegar
½	cup red wine
¾	cup canned low-sodium chicken broth
1	teaspoon minced fresh rosemary leaves
3	tablespoons unsalted butter, cold, cut into 3 pieces
	Salt and ground black pepper

Once the steaks are removed from the pan, pour off all but 2 teaspoons fat. Add the shallot and cook over medium heat, stirring frequently, until it softens, about 1½ minutes. Add the vinegar, wine, and broth and deglaze the pan by scraping up the browned bits with a wooden spoon. Simmer until the sauce reduces to ½ cup, about 5 minutes. Add any meat juices that have accumulated and simmer for 1 minute longer. Whisk in the rosemary and butter and season with salt and pepper to taste. Serve immediately over steaks.

➤ VARIATION

Cognac and Mustard Sauce

Follow the recipe for Red Wine Pan Sauce for Strip Steaks, omitting the vinegar, replacing the wine with ⅓ cup cognac or brandy, and increasing the broth to 1 cup. Replace the rosemary with thyme, reduce the butter to 2 tablespoons, and add 1 tablespoon Dijon mustard with the butter.

most flavor, proved just right. A healthy dose of herbs was the last addition, though the most contentious; tasters couldn't agree on an ideal pairing. Some favored the piney bite of rosemary, while others preferred the milder flavor of parsley. After trying several permutations, we agreed on a combination of parsley and oregano, which was fresh-tasting and complementary to the steak and greens but neither too mild nor too rough.

While any assertive, full-flavored green would have stood up to the rich meat, arugula was the crowd-pleaser, as its peppery bite best cut the meat's richness. Positioned beneath the steak, the greens caught the meat juices and softened from their residual heat. Larger pieces wilted more slowly, so we left the leaves whole.

The finishing touch was a garnish of nutty Parmesan cheese, a perfect foil to the sharp greens and rich meat. While we normally finely grate Parmesan for pasta, the powdery dusting looked odd on the steak and greens. Tasters much preferred finely shaved slivers scattered over the dish. The cheese didn't melt as quickly as when grated, so it packed a stronger flavor.

Tuscan-Style Steak with Arugula and Parmesan

SERVES 4

TIME: 30 MINUTES

For the best results, use high-quality extra-virgin olive oil and genuine Parmesan cheese. The greens may be washed and dried up to a day ahead of time, but the vinaigrette should be made the same day for the best flavor. If the arugula is very mature, tear the leaves into 2 or 3 pieces. Serve a crusty loaf of bread alongside to soak up any remaining vinaigrette and juices from the steak. See page 229 for more information about buying strip steaks. See photo of this recipe on page 162.

5   tablespoons extra-virgin olive oil
1   tablespoon juice from 1 lemon
2   medium cloves garlic, minced or pressed through a garlic press (about 2 teaspoons)
1   tablespoon chopped fresh parsley leaves
1   tablespoon chopped fresh oregano leaves
    Salt and coarsely ground black pepper
1   teaspoon vegetable oil
4   boneless strip steaks, 1 to 1 1/4 inches thick (8 to 10 ounces each), trimmed of exterior gristle and patted dried with paper towels
8   cups loosely packed arugula
3   ounces Parmesan cheese, cut into thin shavings (see the illustration on page 124)

1. Whisk together the olive oil, lemon juice, garlic, parsley, oregano, and a pinch each of salt and pepper in a small bowl until smooth.

2. Heat the vegetable oil in a large, heavy-bottomed skillet over medium-high heat until smoking. Meanwhile, season the steaks liberally with salt and pepper. Lay the steaks in the pan and cook, without moving, until a well-browned crust forms, about 5 to 6 minutes. Using tongs, flip the steaks. Reduce the heat to medium. Cook 3 to 4 minutes more for rare (120 degrees on an instant-read thermometer) or 5 to 6 minutes for medium-rare (125 degrees). Transfer the steaks to a cutting board, tent with aluminum foil, and let rest for 5 minutes.

3. Divide the arugula evenly among 4 individual plates. Cut each steak crosswise into thin strips and arrange the steak over the arugula. Drizzle any juices that collected from the meat over the greens. Rewhisk the dressing and drizzle it over the steak and greens. Sprinkle with the Parmesan and serve immediately.

Pan-Seared Veal Chops

SOMETIMES THE SIMPLEST CUT OF meat, plainly presented, can make the biggest impact. Veal chops are a case in point. With their crisp, thick brown crust yielding to a juicy, creamy pink interior, they are as austere as a piece of meat can be. Veal chops can stand alone, needing the barest accompaniment to add flavor. In this case, we chose to match pan-seared veal chops with lemon-flavored wilted spinach (a classic Italian preparation) and a sprinkling of gremolata, a traditional, bracing blend of parsley, lemon, and garlic.

For the cooking method, we planned to sear the chops on the stovetop and then, while they rested, to wilt spinach in the same pan. The juices exuded from the spinach would release the *fond* (browned bits) stuck to the skillet, which in turn would flavor the greens.

When it comes to choosing veal chops, we have found rib chops to possess the fullest flavor and juiciest, most tender meat. Admittedly, they are expensive—around $15 a pound—but they are well worth it, especially when presented as simply as they are in this dish. Loin chops, which look like little T-bone steaks, are a close second if your market doesn't carry rib chops.

We knew the secrets to successful pan-searing were simple: The skillet must be smoking hot and the cook patient. The best indication of a pan ready to sear meat is smoking vegetable oil. A thin slick of oil across the skillet bottom is all that's necessary; once smoke is wafting from the surface, the pan is ready. On most ranges, this takes about 4 minutes. If the chops are added too early, the meat will take too long to form a crust and is liable to overcook—not worth risking with meat this expensive.

Once the chops are in the pan, patience comes to play again. It is crucial to not move the chops for at least 2½ minutes; otherwise, the meat may stick to the pan and its surface be marred. After about 3 minutes, we found, the perfect crust is formed and the chop is ready to be flipped to the uncooked side. We found it important to reduce the pan temperature to medium for the second side; when we did not, the exterior of the chop burned before the interior reached the desired doneness.

Having chosen the cut of meat and the cooking method, we just had to pick the ideal thickness of the chop. If the meat was too thin, it dried out and overcooked long before the desired crust formed. If the meat was too thick, the center was still rosy pink by the time the exterior approached overcooked. Extra-thick chops must be finished in a high-heat oven—a step we preferred to avoid. After

RIB VERSUS LOIN VEAL CHOPS

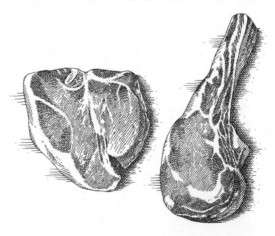

The best veal chops come from the rib area and the loin. (We find that shoulder chops can be tough and are best braised or cut off the bone and used in stews.) A loin chop (left) looks like a T-bone steak, with the bone running down the center and meat on either side. A rib chop (right) has the bone running along one side of the meat. We find that rib chops are juicier and more flavorful than loin chops, but both are quite good cuts.

plowing through pounds of chops, tasters agreed that 1 to 1¼ inches yielded the best results. Both sides had a thick, golden brown crust, and the center was a juicy medium-rare—ideal for veal of this cut.

Once the chops were finished and removed from the pan to a cutting board for their requisite rest, we jacked the heat back up and added the spinach. As the spinach exuded water, the fond released to season the spinach. The spinach wilted to surprisingly little, and we found it necessary to increase the amount of raw spinach several times before we arrived at the proper yield. It seemed like a huge amount of spinach—more than one test cook wondered how it would all fit into the skillet—but it wilted to a shadow of itself almost instantaneously. Tongs were the best tool for stirring the spinach, providing much more dexterity than a wooden spoon or spatula. A spritz of lemon juice, added once the spinach wilted, was all that was needed to sharpen its flavor.

As for the garnish, we made quick work of mincing the parsley, lemon zest, and garlic for the gremolata. Classically, gremolata is made from equal parts of these three ingredients, but most tasters preferred a mellower mix that was heavy on the parsley; too much garlic overwhelmed the veal's delicate flavor. One caveat: Gremolata is best when prepared as close as possible to consumption, as the flavors quickly lose their freshness and the garlic turns unpleasantly bitter.

To finish the dish, we tried drizzling the chops with extra-virgin olive oil, as Italians would do, but tasters preferred the flavor of the oil when it was combined with the gremolata and spooned over the chops. The oil enriched the flavors in the garnish and made plating even easier.

Pan-Seared Veal Chops with Wilted Spinach and Gremolata

SERVES 4

TIME: 25 MINUTES

If your market doesn't carry rib chops, use loin chops, which are nearly as good. The spinach may be washed ahead of time, but the rest of the preparation should be done just before cooking. Be particularly careful when zesting the lemon to avoid the pith, as it will turn the gremolata bitter. You will need about three bunches of flat-leaf spinach, each weighing about 10 ounces, for this recipe.

- 3 tablespoons extra-virgin olive oil
- 1 teaspoon finely minced zest and 2 teaspoons juice from 1 medium lemon
- 1 medium clove garlic, minced or pressed through a garlic press (about 1 teaspoon)
- 2 tablespoons minced fresh parsley leaves
- 2 teaspoons vegetable oil
- 4 bone-in rib veal chops, 1 to 1¼ inches thick, trimmed of excess fat and patted dry with paper towels
  Salt and ground black pepper
- 3 bunches flat-leaf spinach (about 10 ounces each), tough stems removed and leaves washed and spun dry (about 4 quarts loosely packed)

1. Combine 2 tablespoons olive oil and the lemon zest, garlic, and parsley in a small bowl.

2. Heat the vegetable oil in a large skillet over medium-high heat until smoking. Meanwhile, liberally season the chops with salt and pepper. Lay the chops in the pan and cook without moving until well browned, about 3 minutes. Using tongs, flip the chops. Reduce the heat to medium. Cook 5 to 6 minutes more for medium (130 degrees on an instant-read thermometer). Transfer the chops to a large plate and tent with foil to keep warm.

3. Increase the temperature to medium-high and add the remaining 1 tablespoon olive oil to the empty pan. Add the spinach by handfuls and ¼ teaspoon salt; use tongs to stir and coat the leaves with oil. Continue stirring with the tongs until the spinach is uniformly wilted and glossy green, 1½ to 2 minutes. Sprinkle the lemon juice over the top and adjust the seasonings with salt and pepper to taste.

4. Divide the spinach evenly among 4 individual plates. Place a veal chop on top of the spinach on each plate, spooning any released meat juices over the top. Drizzle the gremolata mixture over each chop and serve immediately.

PORK CUTLETS

THERE'S SOMETHING FEW PEOPLE CAN resist about a properly fried pork cutlet. Spartanly seasoned with a spritz of lemon juice or gussied up with fixings and nestled in a sandwich, the juicy, tender meat is perfectly accented by the sweet, crisp crunch of the breading. A pork cutlet is all about technique; proper breading and frying are crucial to the best results. Luckily, good technique need not take long. We found perfect fried cutlets were entirely possible even when time is tight.

The natural place to commence testing was the pork itself. In the recipes we researched, boneless pork chops and tenderloin were the most common cuts, and after the first test, tasters overwhelmingly preferred the sweeter, moister tenderloin. The tenderloin cutlets we purchased, however, were uneven and raggedly cut, broadly ranging in thickness; evidently, we would have to prepare our own cutlets. This gave us complete control over portion size and thickness, which proved the secret to success. A 1- to 1¼-pound tenderloin yielded six portions—two cutlets per person for a typical entrée or one cutlet per sandwich.

The trick was finding a thickness at which the pork would cook through by the time the crumbs browned—which, as we found, was easier said than done. Pounded very thin, under ¼ quarter inch, the pork was tough and chewy by the time the coating cooked. When lightly pounded to about 1 inch thick, the pork was blushing pink at the center when the coating was just shy of burnt. Aiming for a happy medium, we pounded the cutlets to a thickness of ½ inch and met with success. Both the coating and the meat were cooked to near perfection; the meat was juicy and tender and the crust crisp and golden.

While the cutlet thickness was essential to success, a few minor points helped too. When breading the cutlets, we found it was crucial to remove as much excess flour as possible prior to dipping the cutlet into the egg. For the crumbs, it was important to make sure each cutlet was thoroughly coated but not to pack it on, which can make for a dense exterior. We normally prefer freshly ground crumbs made from white sandwich bread, but for the sake of time in this case, we chose Japanese *panko* crumbs. These are crisp and a much better choice than other commercial bread crumbs. The final step prior to frying was a quick rest, during which the breading firmly adhered to the meat; without this rest, the breading is liable to slough off during frying.

For pan-frying, we prefer the clean flavor of vegetable oil. It also has a fairly high smoke point when compared with olive oil, so it's much safer to fry in and little risk that it will turn and develop an acrid flavor. Pan-frying takes much less oil than most people imagine. After frying cutlets in oil of varying depths, we found the oil needed to reach just halfway up the sides of the cutlets. In this case, a 12-inch skillet with three cutlets in the pan required ½ cup oil per batch.

Pan-Fried Pork Cutlets

SERVES 3

TIME: 30 MINUTES

Look for panko bread crumbs in the Asian foods section at the supermarket. For an Asian touch, replace the lemon wedges with tonkatsu sauce, a ketchup-based sweet brown sauce that can be prepared in just minutes with pantry items (see the variation below). Serve the cutlets with rice (either the sticky Asian-style rice on page 328 or the fluffy American-style rice on page 113) and a simple green vegetable, such as Steamed Broccoli with Toasted Garlic and Lemon (page 66) or Spicy Green Beans with Sesame Seeds (page 75).

½ cup unbleached all-purpose flour

2 large eggs

1 tablespoon plus 1 cup vegetable oil

2 cups panko (Japanese-style bread crumbs)

1 pork tenderloin (1 to 1¼ pounds), trimmed of silver skin, cut crosswise into 6 pieces, and pounded to a thickness of ½ inch (see the illustrations on page 238)

   Salt and ground black pepper

1 lemon, cut into wedges

1. Adjust an oven rack to the lower-middle position, set a large heatproof plate on it, and heat the oven to 200 degrees. Spread the flour in a pie plate, beat the eggs with 1 tablespoon oil in a second pie plate, and put the panko in a third pie plate. Position the three pie plates in a row on the work surface.

2. Blot the cutlets dry with paper towels and sprinkle thoroughly with salt and pepper. Working with one at a time, dredge each cutlet thoroughly in the flour, shaking off excess. Using tongs, dip both sides of the cutlet into the egg mixture, allowing the excess to drip back into the pie plate to ensure a thin coating. Dip both sides of the cutlet in the panko

bread crumbs, pressing the crumbs with your fingers to form an even, cohesive coat. Place the breaded cutlets in a single layer on a wire rack set over a baking sheet and allow the coating to dry for 5 minutes.

3. Meanwhile, heat ½ cup oil in a heavy-bottomed 12-inch nonstick skillet over medium-high heat until shimmering but not smoking. Lay 3 cutlets in the skillet. Fry until deep golden brown and crisp on the first side, gently pressing down on the cutlets with a wide metal spatula to help ensure even browning; check browning partway through, at about 2½ minutes (smaller cutlets from the tail end of the tenderloin may cook quickly). Using tongs, flip the cutlets; reduce the heat to medium and continue to cook until the meat feels firm when pressed gently and the second side is deep golden brown, again checking browning partway through, about 2½ minutes longer. Line the warmed plate with a double layer of paper towels and set the cutlets on top; return the plate to the oven. Discard the oil in the skillet and wipe it clean using tongs and a large wad of paper towels.

4. Repeat step 3, using the remaining ½ cup oil and the now-clean skillet and preheating the oil for just 2 minutes to cook the remaining cutlets. Serve immediately with lemon wedges or use the cutlets in one of the recipes on the following pages.

➤ VARIATION

Pork Cutlets with Tonkatsu Sauce

While the breaded cutlets are resting, mix ½ teaspoon dry mustard powder with 1 teaspoon water in a small bowl until smooth. Stir in ½ cup ketchup, 2 tablespoons Worcestershire sauce, and 2 teaspoons soy sauce. Cut the fried cutlets into ¾-inch-wide strips and drizzle with the sauce.

Pan-Fried Pork Cutlets with Pepper and Onion Sauté

WE KNEW IT WOULD BE EASY TO MAKE a quick sauce in the skillet when it was still hot from frying the cutlets. The trick was to develop a sauce that could be cooked in a short enough time that the cutlets could rest in a warm oven but retain their crisp crust. The sauce had to meet certain criteria, however. It needed to be fairly dry so as to not compromise the crust (the whole point of pan-frying the cutlets). Our thoughts gravitated toward a mixture of peppers and onions—something like Spain's *piperade*. The peppers and onions were easy to prepare, and their sweetness would complement the pork. Most important, the mixture was dry enough to not make the cutlets soggy.

In essence, the sauce was nothing but a quick vegetable sauté. For a cooking medium, we turned to flavorful extra-virgin olive oil. We started the garlic first so it would lightly brown and develop a mild nuttiness, ideally suited to the pork's sweet flavor. In next went the onion and peppers to soften and brown. Red bell peppers were the tasters' favorite,

CUTTING A PORK TENDERLOIN INTO SIX CUTLETS

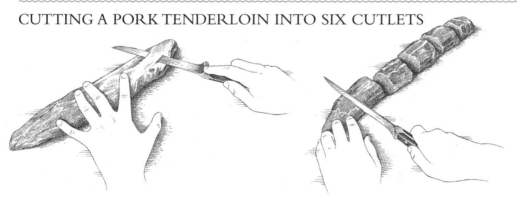

1. Slip a knife under the silver skin, angle it slightly upward, and use a gentle back-and-forth motion to remove it.

2. Cut the tenderloin crosswise into six equal pieces, including the tapered tail end.

3. Standing it on its cut side, sandwich one piece of tenderloin between two sheets of plastic wrap or parchment. Pound gently with a mallet or meat pounder to an even thickness of ½ inch.

4. The thin tail piece of the tenderloin requires extra care to produce a cutlet. Fold the tip of the tail under the cut side before pounding between the sheets of parchment or plastic wrap.

though yellow or a combination of the two worked fine as well.

For flavoring the vegetables, tasters were divided between the piney flavor and aroma of rosemary and the simple freshness of parsley. Both had their own charms, so we left the choice to the cook. The rosemary was left whole on the sprig so it could be removed when the flavor was potent enough. From experience, we knew that rosemary could overpower a dish all too quickly.

We wanted the sauce to remain on the dry side, but liquid was needed to release the flavorful bits that adhered to the skillet as the vegetables browned. Stock accomplished little and water even less, but white wine added a pleasant acidity that sharpened the flavors. A scant ½ cup quickly reduced in the hot skillet, leaving just enough liquid to moisten the vegetables.

Pan-Fried Pork Cutlets with Pepper and Onion Sauté

SERVES 3

TIME: 45 MINUTES

If you would like to add some heat, add a pinch of hot red pepper flakes with the garlic; the chile flavor will be intensified by the toasting. A sprig of marjoram or oregano would be a suitable replacement for the rosemary.

I	recipe Pan-Fried Pork Cutlets (page 237)
2	tablespoons extra-virgin olive oil
3	medium cloves garlic, slivered
2	small red bell peppers, stemmed, seeded, and sliced thin
I	small onion, halved and sliced thin
I	small sprig fresh rosemary or 2 tablespoons chopped fresh parsley leaves
	Salt
½	cup dry white wine
	Ground black pepper

Prepare the cutlets as directed. Thoroughly wipe the skillet clean using tongs and a wad of paper towels. Add the olive oil and garlic to the skillet and heat over medium-high heat, sliding the pan back and forth over the burner to cook the garlic evenly. Cook until the garlic just begins to turn golden brown, 1 to 1½ minutes. Add the peppers, onion, rosemary sprig (if using), and ¼ teaspoon salt. Cook, stirring frequently, until the onion and peppers soften and begin to brown, about 7 minutes. Remove the skillet from the heat and add the white wine, scraping the pan with a wooden spoon to release any browned bits. (If using parsley, stir it in now. Discard the rosemary sprig.) Adjust the seasonings with salt and pepper and serve alongside (or on top of) the pork cutlets.

PAN-FRIED PORK CUTLETS, PO' BOY–STYLE

CAJUN AND CREOLE COOKING REPRESENT some of this country's finest indigenous cooking, from humble street snacks to fine dining feasts. Even the lowly sandwich is given royal treatment. The po' boy, probably the most famous New Orleans sandwich, is simple at heart but worthy of kings, despite its origins as a humble, filling snack. Po' boys (a contraction of "poor boys") come in all stripes, from grilled steak and fried oysters to a seemingly oddball combination of french fries and roasted pork.

A pork cutlet sandwich takes little work beyond frying the cutlets. Essentially, the po' boy is little more than what in other regions is called a hoagie, torpedo, grinder, or submarine; it's a Dagwood sandwich constructed on a long roll or baguette. We favor our po' boys "dressed," which, in New Orleans patois, means the sandwich is laden with lettuce, tomato, mayonnaise, and pickles.

As one might expect, little technique is involved with making a po' boy; the sandwich is all about the ingredients. For bread, a fresh, crusty baguette is essential. The crisp exterior holds in the exuded juices and provides textural contrast to the softer filling. The soft, chewy crumb acts as a blotter for the juices. Staying true to tradition, we scooped out a portion of the crumb to make room for the filling—of which there is plenty to pack in.

First things first; a layer of mayonnaise is thickly slathered on the bread. Next comes the pickle so its juices can mingle with the mayonnaise and lubricate the otherwise dry sandwich. With the pork cutlet, tasters preferred the sweet-and-sour bite of bread-and butter pickles; dill was a close second. Pickle chips work fine, but the planks make assembly even easier. The lettuce goes on top of the pickle. Sweet, hearty romaine worked well; green leaf lettuce was a close second. We preferred the lettuce sliced into ribbons.

The cutlet itself and thin slices of tomato complete the po' boy. To fit a whole cutlet into the sandwich, we found it best to cut it into three pieces and squeeze them into place by laying them diagonally across the width of the baguette. The tomato, wedged into place, added a mild sweetness and a bit more juice to lubricate the roll. With a stack of napkins and a bottle of cold beer, dinner (or lunch) was served.

BUILDING BLOCK RECIPE

Pan-Roasted Pork Tenderloins

SERVES 4 TO 6

TIME: 35 MINUTES

While the tenderloins rest, build a quick sauce in the empty pan. Start by sautéing aromatics (garlic, shallots, or onions) until softened and then deglaze the pan with a liquid (stock, wine, or juice) and simmer until the sauce thickens. Finish with herbs and seasonings (anything from capers or olives to mustard, honey, or maple syrup). Serve sliced pork tenderloin with noodles, rice, or potatoes and add a salad or vegetable to round out the meal.

2	pork tenderloins (about 1 pound each), trimmed of silver skin (see illustration 1 on page 238) and patted dry with paper towels
1	teaspoon salt
3/4	teaspoon ground black pepper
2	teaspoons vegetable oil

1. Adjust an oven rack to the middle position and heat the oven to 425 degrees. Thoroughly rub the tenderloins with the salt and pepper. Heat the oil in a large ovenproof skillet over medium-high heat until smoking. Add the tenderloins to the skillet and cook until browned on the bottom, 1 to 1½ minutes. Using tongs, rotate the tenderloin a quarter-turn; cook until well browned, 1 to 1½ minutes. Repeat two more times until the roast is well browned on all sides.

2. Transfer the skillet to the oven and cook until an instant-read thermometer registers 135 to 140 degrees, 15 to 18 minutes. Remove the skillet from the oven, transfer the meat to a cutting board, tent the tenderloins with aluminum foil, and let rest until the internal temperature registers 145 to 150 degrees, about 10 minutes. Cut the tenderloins crosswise into thin slices and serve immediately.

Pan-Fried Pork Cutlet Po' Boys

SERVES 6

TIME: 35 MINUTES

Pickled red onions (page 48) are another good addition to this sandwich.

2	baguettes, cut into 3 equal pieces each (crusty end pieces removed), each piece split open
¾	cup mayonnaise
12	bread-and-butter pickle planks or 20 to 25 pickle slices
4	cups lightly packed thinly sliced romaine or green leaf lettuce leaves
1	recipe Pan-Fried Pork Cutlets (page 237), each cutlet sliced lengthwise into 3 pieces
2	medium tomatoes, cored and sliced thin Salt and hot pepper sauce, such as Tabasco

Using your fingers, evenly pull out a 1-inch-wide channel of interior crumb from the top and bottom of each piece of baguette. Spread 1 tablespoon mayonnaise over the insides of each piece of baguette. Into each bottom half layer the pickles, lettuce, pork, and tomatoes. Adjust the seasonings with salt and hot pepper sauce to taste. Add the baguette tops and serve immediately.

ROAST PORK TENDERLOINS, CHINESE-STYLE

QUICK-COOKING, LEAN, AND MODERATELY priced, pork tenderloin is among our favorite cuts of pork. It is easily turned into a variety of dishes, from roasts to cutlets, all simple to prepare and ready in minutes. One of our favorite pork preparations is a Chinese dish called *char siu,* or roasted pork marinated in a variety of seasonings. While we accepted that traditional char siu was out of our league for both time and ingredient considerations, we thought we could make a version with similar flavors that was accessible to the home cook, calling for few exotic ingredients and prepared within a tight time budget.

Most Americans have had char siu at one point or another, whether they've recognized it or not. This roasted pork is used in many Chinese restaurant dishes, such as fried rice, pork stir-fries, and dim sum variations. The meat's exterior is characteristically a vibrant red or pinkish hue from a combination of caramelized sugar and red food color. The flavor is both sweet and salty, with a deep hoisin flavor and backnotes of five-spice power, ginger, and garlic. Generally, it is purchased from Asian specialty markets, where it is roasted in large cuts in intensely hot ovens designed for the purpose. Char siu is typically incorporated into dishes, not used on its own, and is therefore potently flavored. Our goal, then, was to tone down the seasoning and make the dish into a main-course dish, suitable on its own but good in other dishes too, if there happened to be leftovers.

From the start, we had a game plan for our ersatz char siu. In hopes of keeping preparation easy, we wanted to sear the tenderloins on the stovetop for flavor and color and then finish them in a very hot oven. Then, once the meat was cooked through, we would coat it with a thick sauce featuring all the flavors normally present in the marinade. We borrowed the technique from our Beef Teriyaki (page 228). Tenderloins couldn't be easier to prepare, as they require minimal trimming. For this dish, we found it important to remove the silver skin (the tough connective tissue striating the tenderloin's exterior) so it didn't roll up

241

onto itself; the silver skin tightens more than the meat, causing it to arc. We left the untrimmed fat alone. Tenderloins are so lean that they need all the help they can get, and most of the fat renders off as the meat cooks.

After consulting a tall stack of recipes, we reckoned the base flavors of char siu marinade—and therefore our sauce—were five-spice powder, ginger, garlic, hoisin sauce, soy sauce, and a sweetener. Our testing, then, centered on the proper proportion of ingredients and how to best flavor the pork with the seasonings. We learned quickly how important it was to expose the five-spice powder to direct, dry heat. When we added it to the other sauce components, its potent flavor dominated the mix, even when scaled back significantly. The cinnamon in the five-spice powder likewise was too potent, tasting like a cheap cookie. But after toasting, the five-spice powder—especially the cinnamon—took a back seat and lent attractive mystery to the sauce's sweet edge without a distinct presence. To save on cooking steps, we found we could use the five-spice powder (combined with salt) as a spice rub on the tenderloin, thereby toasting the spices as the meat seared.

The rest of the sauce ingredients proved easier to nail, though balancing the sweet and salty tastes took some work. What tasted balanced raw didn't always work once reduced. After starting off with plain white sugar for a sweetener, we found honey a better choice, as its floral tones emphasized the flavor of the hoisin sauce and its thickness added visual luster.

Building the sauce in the skillet, post roast, also allowed us to use the *fond* (caramelized browned bits in the pan)—an easy and effective way to bolster flavor. Because the pork was so lean, we had to use additional oil to sauté the garlic and ginger; then we added the rest of the sauce components to reduce and blend. Once the sauce was syrupy, we returned the tenderloins to the skillet and turned them to coat. The result was stunning; the meat was thickly glossed with a mahogany color. Yes, it lacked the trademark scarlet red hue (nobody in the test kitchen complained), but the flavor was just as good.

Roast Pork Tenderloins, Chinese-Style

SERVES 4 TO 6

TIME: 40 MINUTES

Serve the pork with Sticky White Rice (page 328) and Steamed Broccoli with Toasted Garlic and Lemon (page 66) or Spinach with Sautéed Shallots and Lemon (page 84). Leftover pork may be used to flavor a stir-fry, make fried rice, or prepare a sandwich with spicy greens like watercress.

- 1½ teaspoons five-spice powder
  Salt
- 2 pork tenderloins (about 1 pound each), trimmed of silver skin (see illustration 1 on page 238) and patted dry with paper towels
- 4 teaspoons vegetable oil
- 1 tablespoon honey
- 1 tablespoon soy sauce
- ¼ cup hoisin sauce
- 2 medium cloves garlic, minced or pressed through a garlic press (about 2 teaspoons)
- 1 tablespoon minced fresh ginger

1. Adjust an oven rack to the middle position and heat the oven to 425 degrees. Combine the five-spice powder and 1 teaspoon salt in a small bowl. Thoroughly rub the tenderloins with the spice mixture. Heat 2 teaspoons oil in a large ovenproof skillet over medium-high heat until smoking. Add the tenderloins to the skillet and cook until browned on the bottom, 1 to 1½ minutes. Using tongs, rotate the tenderloins a

quarter-turn; cook until well browned, 1 to 1½ minutes. Repeat two more times until the meat is well browned on all sides. Transfer the skillet to the oven and cook until an instant-read thermometer registers 135 to 140 degrees, 15 to 18 minutes. Remove the skillet from the oven, transfer the meat to a cutting board, and tent the tenderloins with aluminum foil to keep warm.

2. While the tenderloins are in the oven, mix the honey, soy sauce, hoisin sauce, and ½ cup water in a small bowl and set aside.

3. Return the empty skillet to medium-high heat, add the remaining 2 teaspoons oil, and swirl to coat the pan. Add the garlic and ginger and cook, stirring frequently, until aromatic, about 30 seconds. Add the sauce mixture and cook, stirring frequently and scraping the bottom of the pan with a wooden spoon to remove any browned bits, until syrupy, 3 to 4 minutes. Return the pork to the pan and, using tongs, roll the tenderloins several times to coat thoroughly with the sauce. Transfer the meat to a cutting board and cut the tenderloins crosswise into thin slices. Arrange the meat on a platter and pour the remaining sauce over top. Serve immediately.

ROAST PORK TENDERLOINS WITH FIGS AND BALSAMIC SAUCE

PORK AND FIGS MAY SEEM AN ODD couple at first thought, but they are natural together, playing off each other's flavor to intensify the meat's sweet and nutty flavors. The dish we conceived, inspired by a French bistro recipe, has a complex flavor but is ready within the hour using just one pan. Pair it with an assertive salad and it's the perfect meal for entertaining on a weeknight.

Having mastered a technique for roasting pork tenderloins while developing Roast Pork Tenderloins, Chinese-Style (page 242), we knew we wanted to sear the tenderloins for flavor and color and then roast them in a 425-degree oven to finish. To replace the five-spice powder employed as a rub in that recipe, we favored a combination of salt, black pepper, and fennel seed. Once the pork was seared and in the oven, it was a matter of waiting; the rest of the recipe would be finished while the cooked pork rested.

With a skillet hot from the oven, it was quick work to sauté the figs to elicit the most flavor from them. For the strongest visual appeal, we browned them on their cut side only so they retained a brightly colored skin to contrast with the browned surface. Within just 2 minutes, the cut surface was richly caramelized, but the figs retained much of their firm texture. We discovered that sprinkling the cut side of the figs with salt just before setting them in the pan helped draw out moisture from the fruit and promoted better caramelization. Once browned, the figs joined the pork under the aluminum foil on the cutting board to keep warm—browned-side up to preserve the crust.

As the pork and figs rested, we prepared the pan sauce. To temper the sweet figs, we chose a sauce based on the assertive flavor of reduced balsamic vinegar, which has been something of a restaurant favorite for years. Squiggled around a plate's perimeter or slicked on a steak, it lends a finishing touch to any dish needing a jolt of sweet, sharp, intense flavor. Luckily, there's nothing to it, as restaurants use the same grade of balsamic vinegar you find in the market. The trick, we found, was to keep the reduction slow and steady. During testing, rapid reduction (boiling) inevitably led to a harsh-tasting sauce. One poorly attended pot boiled over, leaving a charred, sticky mess on the range. The wide surface area of the skillet allowed for quick reduction at a slow temperature. A bare simmer reduced the vinegar in less than 10 minutes.

To round out the vinegar's sweet but one-dimensional flavor, we added bay leaves and fresh thyme sprigs, herbs that are complementary to both pork and figs. Once the vinegar reduced by half to a syrupy consistency, we whisked in butter to both thicken the sauce and enrich an otherwise lean dish.

Roast Pork Tenderloins with Figs and Balsamic Sauce

SERVES 4 TO 6

TIME: 50 MINUTES

Most markets sell ground fennel seed, but it is easy to grind whole seeds at home if you have a spice grinder; toast the whole seeds briefly in a dry skillet, cool briefly, and then grind. Choose fairly firm figs, as they will be hard to move if they are too soft. Don't try to substitute dried figs for fresh; they won't work in this recipe.

Different brands of balsamic vinegar may require different amounts of sugar to balance the acidity. For both flavor and visual contrast, pair the pork with a simple salad of spicy greens, like watercress or arugula, and a crusty loaf of bread to soak up the sauce. Leftover pork and figs make an excellent, if unconventional, sandwich, combined with a baguette and arugula or baby spinach.

1	teaspoon ground fennel seed
	Salt and ground black pepper
2	pork tenderloins (about 1 pound each), trimmed of silver skin (see illustration 1 on page 238) and patted dry with paper towels
2	teaspoons vegetable oil
3	tablespoons unsalted butter
1	pint fresh green or black figs (about 12), halved lengthwise
¾	cup balsamic vinegar
¼	teaspoon sugar, plus more if necessary
6	sprigs fresh thyme, tied into a bundle with kitchen twine, plus 1 teaspoon minced leaves
2	bay leaves

1. Adjust an oven rack to the middle position and heat the oven to 425 degrees. Combine the fennel seed with 1 teaspoon salt and ¾ teaspoon pepper in a small bowl. Thoroughly rub the tenderloins with the spice mixture. Heat the oil in a large oven-proof skillet over medium-high heat until smoking. Add the tenderloins to the skillet and cook until browned on the bottom, 1 to 1½ minutes. Using tongs, rotate the tenderloins a quarter-turn; cook until well browned, 1 to 1½ minutes. Repeat two more times until the meat is well browned on all sides. Transfer the skillet to the oven and cook until an instant-read thermometer registers 135 to 140 degrees, 15 to 18 minutes. Remove the skillet from the oven, transfer the meat to a cutting board, and tent the tenderloins with aluminum foil to keep warm.

2. Return the empty skillet to medium-high heat and add 1 tablespoon butter; when melted, swirl to coat the pan. Sprinkle the figs lightly with salt and place them, cut-side down, in the pan. Cook without moving until lightly browned, about 2 minutes. Very carefully use a thin spatula to transfer the figs, cut-side up, to the cutting board and tent with aluminum foil. Reduce the heat to medium-low and add the balsamic vinegar, sugar, thyme sprigs, and bay leaves. Using a wooden spoon, scrape the bottom of the pan to release any browned bits and simmer, stirring occasionally, until the vinegar is just barely covering the bottom of the pan, 7 to 8 minutes.

Remove the skillet from the heat, discard the herbs, and slowly whisk in the remaining 2 tablespoons butter. Adjust the seasonings with salt and pepper to taste (and additional sugar, if necessary).

3. Cut the tenderloins crosswise into thin slices. Serve slices of pork accompanied by figs, lightly drizzled with the balsamic sauce, and garnished with the minced thyme leaves. Pass additional sauce at the table, if desired.

PORK TINGA

WHILE THE NAME SOUNDS LIKE A Tuesday-night special at Trader Vic's, pork tinga is actually a stewlike pork dish from Mexico. Fiercely spiced with chorizo sausage, chipotle chiles, and garlic, it is heady stuff.

Authentic pork tinga comprises shredded stewed or braised pork shoulder simmered with chorizo in a tomato-based sauce. The texture is fairly dry, more like a saucy stir-fry than a stew. The braised pork, of course, would not be possible with our time constraints, but thinly sliced and sautéed pork could fill its role—not quite authentic but, by our reckoning, the sauce was the star of the show anyhow.

We experimented with several cuts of pork, and tenderloin proved the easiest to prepare as well as the most flavorful. To cook the meat as quickly as possible, we prepared the meat as we would for a stir-fry, thinly slicing it from the whole tenderloin into cutlets and then shredding it into thin strips. A brief spell in the freezer firmed the pork, making it easier to cut. The meat browned within a couple of minutes in a large smoking-hot skillet, which improved its overall flavor and deepened the final dish.

While the pork was easy to figure out, the sauce took some effort. The best versions of pork tinga we tasted were finely balanced between hot and sweet, suffused with smoky heat from chorizo and chiles, and lightened with fresh oregano. Onions, tomatoes, and garlic rounded out the flavors and provided depth.

The first step, then, was to sauté the chorizo, which would provide the fat necessary to soften the onions and garlic. Chorizo is integral to both Mexican and Spanish cooking and is available in most markets. We found it sold in medium-size links as well as thicker links. We cut the skinnier links into small wedges; thicker sausages must have their casings removed and the meat diced. The sausage browned quickly and rendered plenty of fat in which to cook the onions and garlic. We sautéed the onions until soft and then added a large amount of garlic at the last minute so it retained its sharp bite. Canned diced tomatoes were agreeable, especially as they needed no prep work outside of a quick drain.

Chipotle chiles, the last addition to the sauce, were the star of the show—searingly hot and smoky-tasting. Chipotle chiles, also known as *smoked jalapeños,* are available dried as well as rehydrated and packed in an adobo sauce, which contains tomato, onion, oil, and herbs. Whereas dried chiles must be toasted and rehydrated, the canned chilies were ready to go, saving valuable preparation time. Chipotle chiles are hot; discretion is important. After trying multiple batches, tasters favored 1½ chiles—any more and it was hard to taste anything beneath the spiciness.

For the most balanced flavor, we simmered the sauce for about 10 minutes, just long enough to blend the flavors, break down the tomatoes, and reduce the liquid. We found it necessary to add more liquid for a smoother flavor and texture; canned chicken broth filled the bill. We reserved the pork until the final moments to prevent it from overcooking—always a risk when simmering thin pieces of meat.

Pork Tinga

SERVES 4 TO 6

TIME: 45 MINUTES

This recipe is best made with thin chorizo, about an inch thick. If you can find plump links only, remove the casings and crumble the meat before cooking the chorizo. If you can't find chorizo sausage, substitute kielbasa, though the flavor won't be quite as intense. Pork tinga can be served over rice, with tortillas, or even tucked into French bread or a roll as a sandwich. If you choose a sandwich, melt a soft cheese, like Monterey Jack or colby, over the meat. The meat (strained of excess sauce) may replace the bean mixture (or be included with it) in the tostada recipe on page 112.

1	pork tenderloin (1 to 1¼ pounds), cut into thin strips (see the illustrations on page 328)
	Salt and ground black pepper
4	teaspoons vegetable oil
8	ounces chorizo, quartered lengthwise and then cut crosswise into ¼-inch-thick pieces
1	medium onion, chopped fine
4	medium cloves garlic, minced or pressed through a garlic press (about 4 teaspoons)
1½	chipotle chiles in adobo sauce, minced
1	(14½-ounce) can diced tomatoes, drained
1¾	cups canned low-sodium chicken broth
1	tablespoon brown sugar
1½	teaspoons coarsely chopped fresh oregano leaves

1. Toss the pork with salt and pepper to taste in a medium bowl. Heat 2 teaspoons oil in a large skillet over medium-high heat until smoking. Add the pork in a single layer and cook without stirring until browned, 1½ to 2 minutes. Using tongs, flip the pork strips; brown the second side, another 1½ to 2 minutes. Transfer the pork to a clean bowl and cover with aluminum foil to keep warm.

2. Add the remaining 2 teaspoons oil and the chorizo to the empty skillet. Cook, stirring infrequently, until lightly browned, about 2 minutes. Add the onion, ¼ teaspoon salt, and 2 tablespoons water to loosen the browned bits. Cook, stirring often, until the onion softens, 2 to 3 minutes. Stir in the garlic and chipotles and cook until fragrant, about 30 seconds. Add the tomatoes, broth, and brown sugar and bring to a boil. Reduce the heat to medium-low and simmer until the liquid is reduced by half, about 10 minutes. Stir in the pork and oregano and cook until heated through, 2 to 3 minutes. Serve immediately.

HONEY-GLAZED PORK LOIN WITH VEGETABLES

CRISP AND GLISTENING WITH RENDERED fat, it's hard to beat the visual appeal and flavor of a well-browned pork roast. It's the center of any festive spread, though preparation time is well beyond the limit of weeknight dinners. We wondered, however, if it were possible to cook a small roast—enough for four—at high heat so it would be ready in under an hour. After a long game of trial and error, we found that yes, it is possible—and, as a bonus, we roasted vegetables alongside the meat for a complete meal made in one pan.

Blade-end pork loin is among the most flavorful and tender cuts of pork, and it has the added benefit of a blanket of fat that helps protect the meat from drying out—something we found especially important with high-heat roasting. Blade-end roasts are available in a variety of sizes, but we chose to use the smallest we could find, which meant 1½ pounds to just over 2 pounds.

Small roasts can take intense heat because of their small diameter; the exterior does not overcook before the interior is finished. A large roast needs a moderate roasting temperature so the heat slowly and evenly penetrates the meat's inner core. After we cooked small roasts at temperatures ranging from 375 to 500 degrees, we found 475 degrees was ideal (after a stovetop sear to add both flavor and color to the roast). We were certainly surprised by the results, having guessed that the pork would be charred at such an extreme temperature. The pork finished in 30 to 35 minutes, gorgeously browned and moist to a fault. Total cooking time—including preparation, stovetop sear, and a rest once cooked (for the roast's juices to redistribute themselves)—was less than an hour.

Cooking technique mastered, our testing shifted gears to accent flavors for the pork roast and the vegetables we would roast alongside it. We knew a dry rub could add flavor with minimal effort, so we experimented with combinations—variations on classic pork seasonings. Tasters favored a simple blend of ground fennel seed, black pepper, and salt. To intensify the sweetness of the fennel seed, we tried a honey glaze to finish the roast, which worked well; tasters loved it for both the sweet taste and the enticing aroma it gave the pork. Minutes before the loin was finished, we thickly slicked it with honey, which then concentrated to a shiny veneer in the high oven heat.

For our roasted vegetable accompaniment, any number of root vegetables would have tasted fine, but we looked for the one that would require the least preparation. A quick survey of the produce department made our decision easy: bagged baby carrots. Peeled and trimmed, they were oven ready straight from the store. After the first couple of batches, most tasters found the flavor of the carrots to be lacking, even with fresh thyme sprigs thrown into the pan. Because we were using fennel seeds in the spice rub, fennel bulb was a natural addition. Thickly sliced into long fingers approximately the size of the carrots, the fennel browned and attained a meltingly soft texture.

Normally, when we roast meats, we try to make either a pan sauce or a gravy from the drippings, but in this case, we had little need. Between the honey and the liquid released by the vegetables, flavorful juices were already in the bottom of the skillet—not enough for a true sauce but plenty to toss with the vegetables to give them a glossy, glazed appearance.

Honey-Glazed Pork Loin with Roast Carrots and Fennel

SERVES 4 TO 6

TIME: 60 MINUTES

Despite its small size, the roast needs tying to promote even cooking. Make sure to use all-cotton or linen kitchen twine, as synthetic string may burn or impart an off flavor to the roast at such a high temperature. Most markets sell ground fennel seed, but it is easy to grind whole fennel seeds at home if you have a spice grinder; toast the whole seeds briefly in a dry skillet, cool briefly, and then grind. Simple mashed potatoes would be the ideal accompaniment. See page 37 for tips on coring fennel.

I	pound baby carrots
I	medium fennel bulb (about ¾ pound), halved, cored, and cut into ½-inch-thick strips
8	sprigs fresh thyme, tied into a bundle with kitchen twine
I	tablespoon plus 2 teaspoons vegetable oil
	Salt and ground black pepper
I	teaspoon ground fennel seed
I	boneless blade-end pork loin roast (1½ to 2 pounds), tied at even intervals along its length with 3 pieces butcher's twine
2	tablespoons honey

1. Adjust the oven rack to the middle position and heat the oven to 475 degrees.

2. Toss the carrots, fennel, thyme sprigs, 1 tablespoon oil, ½ teaspoon salt, and pepper to taste in a medium bowl; set aside. Combine the fennel seed with ¾ teaspoon salt and ¾ teaspoon pepper in a small bowl; thoroughly rub the roast with the spice mixture.

3. Heat the remaining 2 teaspoons oil in a large ovenproof skillet over medium-high heat until just beginning to smoke. Place the roast, fat-side down, in the skillet and cook until well browned on the bottom, 2 to 2½ minutes. Using tongs, rotate the roast one-quarter turn; cook until well browned, about 2 minutes. Repeat two more times until the roast is well browned on all sides (about 8

minutes total). Remove the roast from the skillet and add the vegetables, stirring until the browned bits on the bottom of the pan are partially released, 20 to 30 seconds. Clear the center of the pan and return the roast to the skillet; slide the skillet into the oven.

4. Roast for 15 minutes. Using tongs, flip the roast and stir the vegetables; return the skillet to the oven and roast for 10 minutes more. Using a pastry brush, coat the roast with the honey; return the pan to the oven. Cook until the center of the roast registers 140 degrees on an instant-read thermometer, 5 to 10 minutes longer. Remove the roast from the pan and put it on a plate or cutting board, tented with aluminum foil. Let the roast rest until the internal temperature reaches 145 to

BUILDING BLOCK RECIPE

Pan-Roasted Pork Loin

SERVES 4

TIME: 55 MINUTES

By starting the roast on the stovetop, it's possible to cook, rest, and slice a 2-pound roast in under an hour. Jazz up the roast by applying a spice rub before it goes into the skillet or brush a sticky, sweet glaze onto the meat during the last 5 or 10 minutes of roasting.

- 1   boneless blade-end pork loin roast (1½ to 2 pounds), tied at even intervals along its length with 3 pieces butcher's twine
- 1   teaspoon salt
- ¾   teaspoon ground black pepper
- 2   teaspoons vegetable oil

1. Adjust an oven rack to the middle position and heat the oven to 475 degrees. Thoroughly rub the roast with the salt and pepper. Heat the oil in a large ovenproof

skillet over medium-high heat until just beginning to smoke. Place the roast, fat-side down, in the skillet and cook until well browned on the bottom, 2 to 2½ minutes. Using tongs, rotate the roast one-quarter turn; cook until well browned, about 2 minutes. Repeat two more times until the roast is well browned on all sides (about 8 minutes total).

2. Transfer the skillet to the oven and roast for 15 minutes. Using tongs, flip the roast. Continue cooking until the center of the roast registers 140 degrees on an instant-read thermometer, 15 to 20 minutes longer. Remove the roast from the skillet and put it on a cutting board, tented with aluminum foil. Let the roast rest until the internal temperature reaches 145 to 150 degrees, about 10 minutes. Cut the pork crosswise into thin slices and serve immediately.

150 degrees, about 10 minutes.

5. Discard the thyme sprigs and stir the vegetables in the pan to coat with any juices. Transfer the vegetables to a serving bowl and keep warm. Cut the pork crosswise into thin slices and serve immediately, accompanied by the vegetables.

ROAST PORK LOIN WITH MOJO SAUCE AND ORANGES

OUR SUCCESS WITH THE ROASTED pork loin with carrots and fennel (page 247) encouraged us to try our hand at another classic pork dish, roast pork with mojo sauce. No, it has nothing to do with Austin Powers, as the name might suggest. It's a Cuban dish assertively flavored with garlic, cumin, and tart citrus.

Next to cigars, mojo sauce is probably Cuba's most notable sensory export. It appears in many guises but always contains, at the very least, garlic, cumin, olive oil, and sour orange juice. Sour oranges (also known as *Seville oranges*) are hard to find in all but the best-stocked supermarkets and Latino specialty stores. They are gnarled and rough looking, a far cry from the unblemished Valencias they are related to. The flavor is tart; we approximated it with a mixture of 1 part lime juice to 2 parts orange juice.

We aimed for the simplest mojo with the biggest impact. A healthy dose of minced garlic—quickly cooked for intense flavor—and cumin provided most of the flavor, and extra-virgin olive oil provided the body. While herbs like cilantro, oregano, and parsley are common, we excluded them for the sake of time.

To jazz up the pork, we made a simple spice rub. After testing a variety of rubs that included cayenne and paprika, we decided to keep it simple and went with a mixture of cumin, black pepper, and salt. While tasters liked the bright heat the cayenne lent the pork, the fumes produced as the roast seared on the stovetop were noxious; everyone in the test kitchen was coughing. Hot paprika lacked the cayenne's toxicity, but it sloughed off the roast as it cooked and left an intractable crust in the pan.

We wanted to roast a vegetable alongside the pork in the oven. Red onions proved a natural. When cut through the root end so the layers would stay together, the onions browned attractively and took on a jammy texture and intense flavor that accented the sweet pork and muted the mojo's tang.

The combination of pork and onions left a rich *fond* (browned bits) in the skillet that we wanted to use. We already had a sauce, so a pan sauce would have been redundant. A test cook came up with the perfect solution: Why not quickly sear oranges in the pan to deglaze the fond and accompany the onions as a garnish? The orange slices would intensify the citrus notes in the mojo sauce. Peeled of rind and pith and sliced into rounds, the oranges caramelized beautifully in the pan, effectively deglazing it and absorbing the flavor of the fond.

Roast Pork Loin with Mojo Sauce and Oranges

SERVES 4

TIME: 60 MINUTES

If you like spicy food, feel free to add a large pinch of cayenne pepper to the mojo sauce. For the ground cumin, we recommend grinding freshly toasted cumin seed, as the spice's flavor is central to this dish. When cooking the oranges, be careful handling the pan; it's easy to forget the skillet's handle is hot. We have a little trick in the test kitchen for pans hot from the oven: We stick a hot pad or kitchen mitten over the handle so everyone knows it is too hot to touch. To streamline this recipe, make the mojo sauce while the pork is in the oven.

Salt and ground black pepper

1¼ teaspoons ground cumin

1 boneless blade-end pork loin roast (1½ to 2 pounds), tied at even intervals along its length with 3 pieces butcher's twine

4 teaspoons vegetable oil

1 large red onion, halved through the root end and cut into 8 equal wedges with root attached (or use 2 medium onions, each quartered)

¼ cup extra-virgin olive oil

6 medium cloves garlic, minced or pressed through a garlic press (about 2 tablespoons)

¼ cup juice from 1 large orange

2 tablespoons juice from 1 lime

3 navel oranges, peel and pith removed (see illustrations 1 and 2 on page 57) and then each cut horizontally into 4 rounds

1. Adjust an oven rack to the middle position and heat the oven to 475 degrees.

2. Combine 1 teaspoon salt, 1 teaspoon pepper, and 1 teaspoon cumin in a small bowl; thoroughly rub the roast with this spice mixture. Heat 2 teaspoons vegetable oil in a large ovenproof skillet over medium-high heat until just beginning to smoke. Place the roast, fat-side down, in the skillet and cook until well browned on the bottom, 2 to 2½ minutes. Using tongs, rotate the roast one-quarter turn; cook until well browned, about 2 minutes. Repeat two more times until the roast is well browned on all sides (about 8 minutes total). While the roast sears, toss the onion with the remaining 2 teaspoons vegetable oil in a small bowl. Once the roast is completely browned, add the onions to the skillet and set it in the oven.

3. Roast for 15 minutes. Using tongs, flip the roast and turn the onions; return the skillet to the oven. Cook until the center of the roast registers 140 degrees on an instant-read thermometer, 15 to 20 minutes longer. Remove the roast from the skillet and put it on a cutting board, tented with aluminum foil. Transfer the onions to a plate and keep warm. Let the roast rest until the internal temperature reaches 145 to 150 degrees, about 10 minutes.

4. While the pork is cooking, heat the olive oil in a small saucepan over medium heat until shimmering. Add the garlic and remaining ¼ teaspoon cumin and cook until fragrant but not browned, 30 to 45 seconds. Remove the pan from the heat and add the orange juice, lime juice, and salt and pepper to taste. Return the pan to the heat and bring to a simmer; cook for another minute. Remove the pan from the heat and cool the sauce.

5. Set the empty skillet in which the pork was cooked over medium-high heat. When the oil remaining in the pan sizzles, add the orange slices in a single layer. Cook without moving until lightly browned on the bottom, 1½ to 2 minutes. Flip and cook until the second side browns, 1½ minutes.

6. Cut the pork crosswise into thin slices and arrange the pork on a platter with the onions and oranges. Drizzle the pork, onions, and oranges with mojo sauce and serve immediately, passing the remaining sauce at the table.

FRIED HAM STEAK WITH CIDER GRAVY

WITH CRISP BROWN EDGES AND sweet, nutty-tasting meat, pan-fried ham steaks are a Southern treat. Luckily, when the craving hits, they cook in minutes. For this version, we chose to gussy up the ham steaks a bit with a cider-based gravy—not too fancy, just a little something to moisten the meat and dunk biscuits into.

Ham steaks are sold in two sizes: small, individual portions and large slices obviously crosscut from a whole ham. Initially, we were attracted to the individual portions, but we quickly found that their flavor paled in comparison to the larger steaks. Also, the texture was significantly tougher. On close inspection, they appeared to be cut from pressed or canned hams (bits of ham trimmings packed together) rather than whole large hams. Clearly, large steaks were the way to go—portioning would be done after cooking. Most large ham steaks weigh between 1 and 1½ pounds. Some companies do produce extra-thick steaks closer to 2 pounds, but we found that these are best reserved for other purposes, like baking or grilling, as they take too long to heat through in the skillet. Premium ham steaks (which we recommend) are cut from the center of the ham, the leanest section, though it can be hard to tell unless specifically marked on the package.

Admittedly, frying ham steaks is not rocket science. The meat is already cooked; it is just a matter of heating it through and creating a well-browned crust. We tried temperatures from low to high and found medium-high yielded the best results and well-browned, crisp edges. Butter proved a better bet than oil as a frying medium because it made for a richer crust.

With the ham fried and resting in a warm oven, we tackled the gravy. The recipes we found included everything from cider thickened with flour to a complicated sauce worthy of a three-star restaurant. We aimed for the middle ground—a full-flavored gravy that did not require inordinate effort; we are talking a simple ham steak, after all.

The steak left a thick *fond* (browned coating) that started the gravy off on the right foot. We deglazed the skillet with cider, vigorously scraping it with a spoon to free the brown bits firmly affixed to the bottom. We had to decide how much cider to start with and how much it should be reduced. When it boiled down too far, the resulting gravy was sickly sweet to most tasters—more like the base for a dessert sauce. Too little boiling, however, and the gravy was bland. After several tests, we found reducing 2 cups cider to 1 cup yielded a slightly viscous liquid with a strong apple flavor that was not too sweet—just what we wanted. In fact, we had to add a pinch of brown sugar to appease some tasters.

Despite the cider's syrupy texture, most tasters desired a slightly thicker gravy, so we had to add a thickener. Flour made the gravy pasty, but cornstarch was flavorless and added an appealing luster. A scant ¾ teaspoon packed all the thickening power necessary for a glossy gravy just stiff enough to nap the ham.

To add a little more character to the gravy, we looked for a seasoning or two that would complement the ham's sweet flavor. After sampling a few, tasters agreed on thyme for earthiness and mustard for an assertive punch.

Fried Ham Steak with Cider Gravy

SERVES 3 TO 4

TIME: 20 MINUTES

The size of the ham steak ultimately determines the serving size. We were able to feed four from a single large steak (with a couple of side dishes), but feel free to fry two steaks; you will need to reduce the skillet's temperature to medium for the second steak. You may want to taste a small bite of the cooked ham steak before adjusting the gravy's seasoning to prevent oversalting; some brands of ham steak are saltier than others. Ideal accompaniments would be sweet potato biscuits (page 370) or cornmeal biscuits (page 369) and a simple leafy green salad such as *Mellow Salad with Red Wine Vinaigrette* (page 29) or sautéed kale or collard greens.

¾ teaspoon cornstarch
½ teaspoon brown sugar
1 teaspoon Dijon mustard
1 tablespoon plus 2 cups cider
1 tablespoon unsalted butter
1 large ham steak (about 1½ pounds), patted dry with paper towels
2 sprigs fresh thyme, tied into a bundle with kitchen twine
Salt and ground black pepper

1. Adjust an oven rack to the middle position and heat the oven to 200 degrees.

2. Whisk together the cornstarch, brown sugar, mustard, and 1 tablespoon cider in a small bowl.

3. Heat the butter in a 12-inch skillet over medium-high heat until the foaming subsides. Add the ham steak and cook without moving until browned, 3½ to 4 minutes. Using tongs and a large spatula, flip the steak; cook the second side until browned, about 3 minutes. Transfer the ham steak to an ovenproof plate or baking sheet and place it in the oven.

4. Return the skillet to medium-high heat and add the remaining 2 cups cider and thyme sprigs, scraping the bottom of the pan with a wooden spoon to release any browned bits. Cook until the cider is reduced by half, about 6 minutes. Whisk in the cornstarch mixture and cook, stirring frequently, until the sauce thickens, about 2 minutes. Remove and discard the thyme sprigs and adjust the seasonings with salt and pepper to taste.

5. Cut the ham steak into 3 or 4 pieces and place them on individual plates. Spoon the gravy over the ham steaks and serve immediately.

ONE-SKILLET BRATWURST AND SAUERKRAUT

SOME MIGHT CALL THE DISTINCT FLAVOR of sauerkraut an acquired taste, but it is a healthy and traditional foundation for several classic German and Alsatian meals, of which bratwurst and sauerkraut may be the best known. Well-browned, flavorful sausage nestled in meltingly soft sauerkraut—what's not to love? Unfortunately, the dish traditionally relies on a long list of ingredients and a slow simmer in the oven for its full flavor. Despite these challenges, however, we sensed the dish was ripe for a quick-cooking makeover.

We were not out to reinvent the dish, just to find a way to cook it quickly without compromising its essential flavors. This meant employing our deductive skills and examining the classic technique and flavors to find shortcuts and identify the core ingredients. Our first realization was that surface area was crucial to quickly cooking the sauerkraut, so we ditched the conventional Dutch oven in favor of a 12-inch heavy-bottomed skillet with a lid; this offered plenty of surface area for the sauerkraut to cook. The *fond* (browned bits) that developed when the sausage was browned would, in turn, flavor the sauerkraut.

Browning the sausages was the first step, just a minute or two per side to intensify flavor and develop fond to flavor the sauerkraut. Bratwurst is the classic choice, though knackwurst follows closely; feel free to combine them if you like. Authentic bratwurst are made from a combination of pork and veal seasoned with a variety of spices, including ginger, nutmeg, and caraway. Knackwurst is a combination of beef and pork flavored with cumin and garlic. Both are fresh sausages and must be thoroughly cooked; browning starts the process and steaming in the sauerkraut finishes it. While we recommend a trip to your local German butcher for the best-quality sausages, your local supermarket should carry them—often in the deli department, and sometimes next to bags of sauerkraut.

With recipes dating to the early Middle Ages, sauerkraut has a long lineage. At its simplest, sauerkraut is nothing but thinly sliced cabbage tightly packed with salt and slowly fermented. Depending on the temperature at which the cabbage is stored, fermentation may last a year before the sauerkraut is ready. Rarely does it go this long; 1 or 2 months is more conventional. Clearly, our aim was not to make our own; store-bought would have to do. Luckily, all the brands we tested were perfectly acceptable, especially when well rinsed to expel the potent brine.

To boost the flavor of the sauerkraut, we stuck to conventional flavorings like onion, carrot, and apple. Apple and carrot (grated coarsely on a box grater) cooked the fastest, breaking down to enrich the sauerkraut. We tried grating the onions but found they did not brown as well as when sliced, and the sauerkraut suffered, lacking depth. Despite the sweetness provided by the onion, carrot, and apple, tasters agreed that the sauerkraut needed more. White sugar worked adequately, but brown sugar lent a new dimension to the dish. A scant tablespoon did the job.

For liquid, everything from cider and beer to chicken broth and water appeared in our researched recipes. Cider made the cabbage taste too sweet and fruity for most tasters, even when diluted with water. Beer added a malty note that some tasters enjoyed but the majority felt clashed with the sauerkraut's tang, so we skipped it. Water lent little, so chicken broth was chosen; it added richness and depth without altering the dish's balanced flavors.

In the recipes we consulted, traditional seasonings included sage, caraway seeds, garlic, cloves, bay leaves, and juniper berries. We tried most of them—solo and in tandem—but tasters most enjoyed the woodsy, almost camphorlike flavor of the juniper, as it added complexity without competing with the assertive spiciness of the sausage.

One final though crucial lesson we learned was the importance of pricking the sausages prior to cooking. Without a liberal pricking, the sausages were prone to explode—an unsightly mess, to say the least.

One-Skillet Bratwurst and Sauerkraut

SERVES 4

TIME: 50 MINUTES (INCLUDES 30 MINUTES SIMMERING TIME)

Don't be alarmed when the grated apple rapidly oxidizes; the brown color won't affect the finished dish. The dish may be prepared ahead of time and reheated, but add water or chicken broth to keep the cabbage moist. An ideal accompaniment would be potatoes, either mashed or boiled. Juniper berries can be found in the spice section of the supermarket.

1	tablespoon unsalted butter
4	bratwurst or knackwurst, punctured liberally with a small skewer
1	small onion, halved and sliced thin
10	whole juniper berries
1	medium carrot, peeled and grated on the large holes of a box grater
	Salt
2	pounds packaged sauerkraut, well rinsed and drained
1	medium Granny Smith apple, peeled and grated on the large holes of a box grater
1	tablespoon brown sugar
1¾	cups canned low-sodium chicken broth
	Ground black pepper

1. Heat the butter in a 12-inch skillet over medium-high heat. Once the foaming subsides,

add the sausages and reduce the heat to medium. Cook until well browned, 1 to 1½ minutes. Using tongs, rotate the sausages one-quarter turn; brown the next side, about 1 minute. Repeat two more times until browned on all sides (about 4 minutes total). Transfer the sausages to a plate.

2. Add the onion, juniper berries, carrot, and ¼ teaspoon salt to the empty skillet. Cook, stirring frequently, until the onion softens, about 3 minutes. Stir in the sauerkraut, apple, brown sugar, and broth, increase the heat to medium-high, and bring to a simmer. Nestle the sausages into the sauerkraut, evenly spaced around the skillet, cover, and reduce the heat to low. Simmer until the liquid is almost evaporated, about 30 minutes. Adjust the seasonings with salt and pepper to taste and serve immediately, with the sausages resting on top of the sauerkraut on a platter.

Pan-Seared Lamb Chops with Quick Apricot Chutney

LAMB IS, UNFORTUNATELY, OFTEN given short shrift in the modern American kitchen. Our guess is that most people have lingering memories of gamy, overcooked meat slathered with a mentholated sauce or mysterious brown gravy. But, by our reckoning, lamb deserves better. Pan-seared lamb chops are quick, easy, and flavorful—perfect for a meal in a hurry. When paired with a highly seasoned, exotic-tasting chutney—a classic British combination—lamb chops are hard to beat. Our goal, then, was to concoct a homemade chutney in half an hour to top lamb chops that were ready in minutes.

From experience, we knew the three chop options: loin, rib, and shoulder. Shoulder

chops are the least expensive of the three (usually a third or half the price) and the chewiest, though not tough by any means. They also remained juicier than the more expensive cuts when cooked beyond medium-rare. The price of loin and rib chops can be prohibitively high, but tasters appreciated the fine texture and sweet flavor of the meat, especially when cooked rare. (The meat becomes dry and tough if cooked past medium-rare.) We decided to develop our recipe with shoulder chops, as they are more forgiving if cooked past medium-rare. That said, you can use loin or rib chops if you don't mind paying two or three times as much for them. These chops tend to be smaller than shoulder chops, and you may want two per person.

Whatever chop you choose, lamb chops respond well to pan-searing. Liberally coated with salt and ground black pepper and set into a smoking-hot pan, the chops develop a thick mahogany crust in minutes. For the most even cooking, we found it important to reduce the temperature to medium once the first side is cooked; otherwise, the second side burned before the center was cooked.

With our meat testing under our belt, we focused on the chutney. Chutneys appear in many forms in Indian cooking, from simple, fresh concoctions similar to salsas to long-cooked, fruit-based blends close to jam. Slow-cooked chutneys, according to most sources, were developed during the 19th-century colonial period in India; the British could not stomach the high acidity and spiciness of the fresh versions. Mango chutney is probably the most widely sold slow-cooked version (Major Grey is a popular brand), though a long list of fruits—from apples and tomatoes to cherries and peaches—can be used in chutney. For our quick chutney, we chose to use dried apricots. A pantry staple for many, dried apricots pack a bright, sharp flavor ideally suited to lamb's robustness. The other ingredients we had to choose through testing were aromatics, vinegar, sweetener, and spices.

Making chutney requires little technique. Generally, the ingredients are combined and simmered until the flavors meld and a jammy consistency is reached. The issue was time. Most chutneys require at least an hour or two of simmering. Our initial attempts at chutney using coarsely chopped apricots proved we had to alter the traditional method. After a half hour of cooking, the chutney tasted raw and unbalanced. We figured we could reduce total cooking time by chopping everything finely in a food processor. The chopping reduced the cooking to about 15 minutes—well within our time frame.

Technique in hand, we needed to balance the sweet and sour tastes in the chutney and to choose a few key flavors to complement the apricots. Shallots were common to many recipes we consulted, so we included a large one, processed in the food processor before the apricots to ensure it was chopped finely. Along with the shallot, we processed a jalapeño chile for its bright, hot, fresh taste. Just one medium chile provided all the heat most tasters desired.

Sweet and sour came from a fine balance of cider vinegar and brown sugar. Too much vinegar was overwhelmingly tangy, while too little made the chutney one-dimensional. Brown sugar was favored over white by tasters for its fuller, earthier flavor. For spices, we opted for a combination of ginger and cloves, as their bright flavor complemented the lamb and sharpened the chutney's sweetness. Two whole cloves and some fresh ginger coins provided all the spice necessary.

With the chutney finished, it took just minutes to cook the chops. The result: a simple, classic combination streamlined from hours to minutes.

Pan-Seared Lamb Chops with Quick Apricot Chutney

SERVES 4

TIME: 30 MINUTES

Leftover chutney is likely, but it keeps well and may be put to a variety of uses, including as a sandwich condiment or an accompaniment to rich cheese. A simple basmati rice pilaf (page 114)

INGREDIENTS: Lamb Shoulder Chops

Lamb shoulder is sliced into two cuts: blade and round-bone chops. Blade chops are roughly rectangular in shape, and some are thickly striated with fat. Each blade chop includes a piece of the chine bone (the backbone of the animal) and a thin piece of the blade bone (the shoulder blade of the animal).

Round-bone chops, also called arm chops, are more oval in shape and, as a rule, are substantially leaner than blade chops. Each contains a round cross section of the arm bone; the chop looks a bit like a small ham steak. In addition to the arm bone, a tiny line of riblets is on the side of each chop.

We didn't find any difference in taste or texture between the two types except that the blade chops generally have more fat.

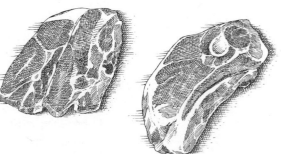

BLADE CHOP   ROUND-BONE CHOP

would be an ideal side dish, as would a simple leafy salad, such as Mellow Salad with Red Wine Vinaigrette (page 29).

1	large shallot, peeled and chopped coarse
1	medium jalapeño chile, stemmed and chopped coarse
8	ounces dried apricots (about 1¼ cups)
2	whole cloves
1	(1-inch) piece fresh ginger, cut crosswise into 4 coins
⅓	cup cider vinegar
¼	cup packed light or dark brown sugar Salt and ground black pepper
2	teaspoons vegetable oil
4	lamb shoulder chops (¾ to 1 inch thick), patted dry with paper towels

1. Process the shallot and jalapeño in the bowl of a food processor fitted with a steel blade until finely chopped, about ten 1-second pulses. Add the apricots and process until finely chopped, about twenty-five 1-second pulses, scraping down the sides of the workbowl with a rubber spatula as necessary. Transfer the mixture to a small saucepan and add the cloves, ginger, vinegar, brown sugar, ¼ teaspoon salt, and ½ cup water. Bring to a simmer over medium-high heat, reduce the heat to low, and cook, stirring occasionally, until the mixture is stiff and the liquid is evaporated, about 15 minutes. Remove and discard the cloves and ginger; adjust the seasoning with salt and pepper to taste.

2. While the chutney simmers, heat the oil in a large, heavy-bottomed skillet over medium-high heat until smoking. Meanwhile, season the chops liberally with salt and pepper. Lay the chops in the pan and cook, without moving, until a well-browned crust forms, 3 to 4 minutes. Using tongs, flip the chops. Reduce the heat to medium. Cook 4 to 5 minutes more for rare (120 degrees on an

instant-read thermometer), 5 to 6 minutes for medium-rare (125 degrees), or 6 to 7 minutes for medium (130 degrees). Transfer the chops to a cutting board, tent with aluminum foil, and let rest for 5 minutes.

3. Serve the chops garnished with a large dollop of chutney. Pass the remaining chutney at the table.

MIDDLE EASTERN–STYLE LAMB PITA SANDWICHES

WHETHER YOU CALL THEM KEFTA, *kibbe, kofta,* or simply *ground meat patties,* lamb-based patties appear all over the Middle East. Generally sold by street vendors, the patties are stuffed into sandwiches with any number of toppings, from incendiary sauces and exotic pickles to a simple tahini- or yogurt-based sauce and lettuce. We think these sandwiches are an ideal recipe for an exotic weeknight dinner. A Middle Eastern spice palette and subtly exotic lamb can turn an otherwise prosaic meatball sandwich into something special.

The sandwich comprises three parts: the meat, the garnishes, and the bread. The patty recipes we researched ran the gamut with respect to flavor and technique. Some included a long list of ingredients that necessitated a great deal of effort, while others kept the flavors simple and preparation brief. A quick taste test of extremes suggested we seek a comfortable medium. The simplest versions tasted bland, while the fancy versions buried the meat under a mass of spices and took entirely too long to assemble.

After looking at numerous ingredient lists, we broke down the patty into three components: the meat, the binding, and the seasoning. Unlike ground beef, ground lamb is normally available only in one unspecified fat content. You could ask your butcher to grind fresh meat for you, but we found it unnecessary, as additional fat renders out. Much of lamb's somewhat gamy flavor is located in the fat, so we found leaner meat tasted milder, if this is a concern.

In contrast to European-style meat patties, most Middle Eastern recipes do not contain much binding, relying instead on tight packing of the patty or an occasional handful of bulgur or bread crumbs. Most tasters found the authentic texture on the dense side and suggested bread crumbs and dairy to help tenderize the meat and prevent the patties from drying out while frying. Just one slice of bread yielded all the crumbs necessary. For dairy, a little milk worked fine, but keeping in the spirit, yogurt proved the best choice; its sharp tang and rich flavor worked well with the robust lamb flavor.

Many recipes we researched contained lots of spices. Patties from Morocco employed the spice blend *ras-el-hanout,* which includes up to 20 spices; recipes from Lebanon and Syria were more restrained, including cinnamon, allspice, cumin, cayenne pepper, coriander, and turmeric. To reduce complexity, we opted to use cumin for a deep musky flavor and cayenne for bright heat. To round out the flavorings, a handful of chopped cilantro brought a pleasant sharpness. The resulting patties tasted distinctly Middle Eastern and were full-flavored, all with a minimum of ingredients and labor.

Borrowing a technique we learned while developing a meatball recipe, we briefly chilled the patties prior to frying. The cold firms them and helps them retain definition.

Traditionally, the patties are grilled on skewers, but for the sake of convenience, we opted for pan-frying. Broiling would have been the logical indoor replacement for grilling, but we found pan-frying offered more control, and the patties developed a crisper crust—a definite bonus, according to most tasters. All of the patties could fit into a large skillet at one time and were cooked through in less than 10 minutes. After a quick blot on paper towels, they were ready to eat.

To finish the sandwich, we needed the sauce, lettuce, and the bread. Yogurt-based sauces appear throughout the Middle East and were a perfect accompaniment, as the yogurt's sharpness cuts the lamb's richness. To keep the ingredient list brief, we chose to reuse some of the ingredients in the patties, including cilantro for brightness and cayenne pepper for spiciness. To add pungency and round out the yogurt's tang, we included minced garlic—just one clove, as to not overwhelm the other flavors.

Any mild, sweet lettuce will do, but tasters most enjoyed romaine for its sturdy leaves and crisp bite. For bread, your favorite pita is perfect—just pick up the largest size you can find and cut off the top arc to facilitate filling.

Middle Eastern–Style Lamb Pita Sandwiches with Yogurt Sauce

SERVES 4

TIME: 30 MINUTES

If you would like to include more garnishes, tomato, pickled red onions (page 48), cucumber slices, and even sliced pickled pepperoncini would be appropriate. If you do not like cilantro, feel free to substitute fresh mint. If you don't have sandwich bread, ¼ large pita will do as a binder for the patties. Simply crumble it roughly and pulse it in a food processor until reduced to coarse crumbs. You will need large pita—at least 8 inches in diameter—to hold all the filling.

1 pound ground lamb

Salt

1 teaspoon ground cumin

¼ teaspoon cayenne pepper, plus more to taste

3 tablespoons chopped fresh cilantro leaves

3 tablespoons plus 1 cup plain yogurt

1 slice white bread, crumbled into rough crumbs

1 small clove garlic, minced or pressed through a garlic press (about 1 teaspoon)

3 tablespoons vegetable oil

4 large pita breads, top ½ inch sliced off each

4 cups coarsely chopped romaine lettuce

1. With your hands, mix the lamb, 1 teaspoon salt, cumin, cayenne, 2 tablespoons cilantro, 3 tablespoons yogurt, and white bread crumbs in a medium bowl. Divide the mixture into 12 equal pieces and roll them into balls. Gently flatten the balls into round disks, 1½ to 2 inches thick. Place the shaped patties on a large plate or baking sheet and set in the freezer for 5 minutes.

2. While the patties are chilling, combine the remaining 1 cup yogurt, remaining 1 tablespoon cilantro, garlic, and salt and cayenne pepper to taste in a small bowl. Set the sauce aside.

3. Heat the oil in a large nonstick skillet over medium-high heat until shimmering. Using a spatula, place the patties in the skillet in a single layer; cook until well browned, about 2 minutes. Flip the patties, reduce the heat to medium, and cook until well browned on the second side, about 6 minutes. Transfer the patties to a paper towel–lined plate.

4. Divide the patties evenly among the pita rounds and fill each with 1 cup lettuce and a spoonful of the yogurt sauce. Serve immediately, passing the remaining yogurt sauce at the table.

FISH AND SHELLFISH

FISH AND SHELLFISH COOK IN MINUTES, quite literally, and are a natural starting point for quick dinners. Our goal in creating recipes for this chapter was to use widely available fish and shellfish in recipes that make complete (or nearly complete) meals. The first half of the chapter covers favorite fish, including salmon, halibut, monkfish, sole, trout, and cod. The second half deals with shellfish: shrimp, scallops, squid, clams, and mussels. In addition to the recipes in this chapter, several grilling and stir-frying recipes in Chapters 10 and 11 rely on fish and shellfish.

MAPLE-SOY GLAZED SALMON

SOMETIMES RECIPES JUST MATERIALIZE, sprung half-formed from the collective conscious of the test kitchen. This recipe for maple-soy glazed salmon is a case in point; a test cook had picked it up from a friend, who had learned it from another cook, and on and on. Whatever its origin, this unusual dish is packed with deep, rich flavors, and it couldn't be any easier to make. We knew it was ideal for inclusion in this collection.

The title says it all: salmon fillets coated with a maple syrup and soy sauce glaze. Clearly a riff on teriyaki sauce (by some adventurous Vermonter, perhaps), the glaze is simply maple syrup and soy sauce reduced to a thick, salty-sweet liquid that is then shellacked onto salmon fillets. As the fish cooks, the glaze further concentrates to a thick mahogany varnish, and the results are stunningly attractive and delicious. Our testing focused on the proper proportions of sauce ingredients, the best cooking method for the salmon, and the most opportune moment to apply the glaze.

Although the glaze has just two ingredients, it took some work to master, as proper proportions and thickness were essential to success. Regarding the latter, the sauce had to be thin enough to brush onto the fish but syrupy enough to stick. First things first, however, so we began by tackling the proportions. Equal parts maple syrup to soy sauce produced a wickedly salty glaze that ruined the fish; clearly, the ratio had to lean in favor of the maple syrup. After several more tests, we found that twice as much maple syrup as soy sauce produced the most balanced flavor. As for thickness, reducing the liquid by one-third made it syrupy but still pourable. Reducing it further made the sugars in the maple syrup begin to stiffen to a caramel consistency.

The two options for cooking the fish were broiling and roasting. Broiling is one of the best methods for cooking fish, as the extreme heat preserves the fish's delicate flavor and texture, but with its sugary glaze, the salmon tended to burn quickly. Roasting, however, proved faultless. The salmon cooked perfectly, and the glaze tightened to a thick veneer without any signs of burning. We experimented with roasting temperatures and discovered that 500 degrees yielded the juiciest fish and best flavor. Answering the last question—when to apply the glaze—took just a few trials. We soon found that glazing the fish before it went into the oven was too soon; the glaze just slid off the fillets. On the other hand, adding it in the last couple of minutes was too late for the glaze to concentrate. About halfway through—once the fillets were opaque and firm—yielded the best texture and most lustrous sheen.

With the salmon wrapped up, we sought ways to turn this dish into a more complete meal—with a minimum of effort, of course. As the dish was both sweet and rich, we knew we wanted a side dish that was light and crisp to serve as a foil. Because the salmon's flavors were Asian-inspired, bok choy seemed ideal. While bok choy is generally braised, steamed, or stir-fried, we wanted to confine cooking to the oven and took a leap of faith (as we often do, as test cooks) and attempted to roast it. We prepared for the worst and were surprised with the tender, well-cooked results. The bok choy stems possessed enough moisture that, in effect, it steamed itself.

For additional flavor, we tossed the bok choy in vegetable oil—which also prevented the leaves from sticking to the baking sheet— and grated ginger, which cut the richness of the fish. For a bit of crunch, we garnished the finished bok choy with sesame seeds.

Maple-Soy Glazed Salmon with Gingered Bok Choy

SERVES 4

TIME: 25 MINUTES

An ideal accompaniment to this dish is plain steamed rice, white or brown. If you happen to have extra glaze, drizzle it over the bok choy or pass it at the table. The glaze may be prepared several days ahead and reheated, though you may need to add a splash of water to loosen it. Leftover

salmon can be used cold in a sandwich with spicy greens, such as watercress or arugula.

½	cup maple syrup
¼	cup soy sauce
1	tablespoon grated fresh ginger
1	tablespoon plus 1 teaspoon vegetable oil
1	large head bok choy (about 2 pounds), root end removed, cut crosswise into 1-inch-wide pieces
	Salt and ground black pepper
4	center-cut salmon fillets (each about 6 ounces and 1¼ inches thick), pin bones removed (see the illustrations below) and patted dry with paper towels
2	teaspoons sesame seeds

1. Adjust one oven rack to the lowest position and a second rack to the upper-middle position. Heat the oven to 500 degrees. Bring the maple syrup and soy sauce to a simmer in a small saucepan over medium-high heat. Cook, stirring occasionally, until syrupy and reduced to ½ cup, 8 to 9 minutes.

2. Meanwhile, combine the grated ginger and 1 tablespoon oil in a large bowl. Add the bok choy, ¼ teaspoon salt, and pepper to taste

REMOVING PIN BONES FROM SALMON

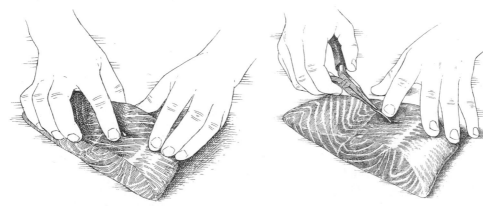

1. Using the tips of your fingers, gently rub the surface of the salmon to locate any pin bones.

2. If you feel any bones, use a pair of needle-nose pliers or tweezers to pull them out.

and toss to coat. Spread the bok choy on a rimmed baking sheet in a single layer. Grease a second rimmed baking sheet with the remaining 1 teaspoon oil and position the salmon fillets, skin-side down, on the sheet, with at least 1 inch between them. Sprinkle the salmon with salt and pepper to taste.

3. Place the bok choy on the bottom rack and the salmon on the upper rack. Cook for 5 minutes; then pull the salmon from the oven and, using a pastry brush, spread a thick layer of the glaze over each fillet (tops and sides). Return the salmon to the oven. Continue to cook until the bok choy leaves are wilted, the stems are tender, and the fish is just firm to the touch, about 3 minutes longer. Transfer the bok choy to a serving platter and sprinkle with the sesame seeds. Brush the fillets with another layer of glaze and transfer them to individual plates. Serve the fish immediately, accompanied by the bok choy.

PAN-SEARED SALMON WITH BRAISED LENTILS AND CHARD

THE ASSERTIVE FLAVOR AND FLAKY texture of oily fish pairs well with the starchy mildness of beans. Salmon and lentils are a case in point; the bright pink, meaty fish is ideally complemented by the mild earthiness and olive-green hue of small lentils du Puy. For good reason, the match has become something of a restaurant darling in recent years, appearing on hundreds of menus in one variation or another. One of our favorites includes leafy green chard.

Restaurant cooking has little to do with home cooking, as it is generally labor-intensive (batteries of line cooks chop those perfect dice) and, more odious, dish-intensive. No line cook gives a second thought to the number of dishes he or she generates—that's left to the dishwasher to worry about. For example, this particular dish, as it has three components, would warrant three skillets for just one serving. In the home kitchen, the cook is the dishwasher, and the last thing he or she wants to worry about after a long day is a deep sink full of pots and pans. Our idea was to limit our version of salmon and lentils to the core flavors and a single pan by cutting extraneous ingredients. With a large (12-inch) nonstick skillet in mind, our plan proved practical. Aromatics were sautéed to flavor the lentils, the lentils were braised, the greens were wilted (once the lentils were removed), and, finally, the salmon fillets were seared, all in the same skillet.

For the braised lentils, we experimented with a variety of aromatics, including garlic, shallots, scallions, and onions, and settled on the latter for their sweetness and body. The other options proved too forthright. Much of the flavor in the lentils, however, was to come from an unexpected ingredient: chard stems. Chard is an unusual green in that the stems are

WIPING A SKILLET CLEAN

A quick wipe of the skillet with paper towels allows you to prepare the chard and then the salmon in a single pan. After the chard is removed from the pan, crumple a wad of paper towels, grab it with the tongs, and use it to swab the extra oil from the pan before cooking the fish.

as desirable as the leaves. Chard stems possess an earthy, beetlike flavor that betrays the fact that chard is, in fact, a relative of beets, bred for its leaves instead of its roots. Chard stems are at their best sautéed in butter, so that is how we prepared them, cooking them with the onions. Fresh thyme sprigs complemented the other flavors in the braised lentils. Tasters favored the rich yet neutral taste of chicken broth over other cooking liquids. Within 30 minutes, the lentils were tender; a quick burst of high heat evaporated any remaining broth.

Once the lentils were cooked, it took just minutes to finish the dish. The chard greens, roughly chopped, were the next ingredient to go into the skillet. We normally favor the addition of garlic and lemon to sautéed greens, but in this case we let them stand alone, simply seasoned with salt and the butter in which they were cooked.

A quick wipe of the skillet with paper towels prevented burning and adverse effects on the salmon's crisp crust. As with searing any meat, it was important to dry the salmon fillets well with paper towels before cooking and to apply salt and ground black pepper liberally. The salt both flavors the fish and aids in proper crust development. We found that the scantest amount of oil—just 2 teaspoons—was enough to deeply brown the fish and crisp the skin. A sprinkling of lemon juice adds a finishing touch.

With all the components cooked independently and ready to go, it was time to assemble the meal. This is certainly a time for restaurant-style plating, so get inspired—the diners will be impressed that such a meal can be whipped up so quickly and without a sink full of dishes.

Pan-Seared Salmon with Braised Lentils and Chard

SERVES 4

TIME: 50 MINUTES

Some tasters loved the salmon skin crisped in the hot skillet, and others were strongly opposed. If you don't like salmon skin, you can easily remove it before serving. Lentils du Puy are widely available in most markets, but if you have trouble finding them, check the gourmet aisle of your local market. Your local health food store is another good bet; the lentils may be in the bulk bins. The lentils can be cooked ahead of time and reheated, but the fish and greens should be cooked at the last minute for the best flavor. See photo of this recipe on page 161.

3	tablespoons unsalted butter
1	small onion, chopped fine
1	bunch chard (10 to 12 ounces), stems and leaves separated (see the illustration on page 137), stems chopped medium, leaves sliced thin
4	sprigs fresh thyme, tied into a bundle with kitchen twine
	Salt
1	cup lentils du Puy, picked over and rinsed
1¾	cups canned low-sodium chicken broth
	Ground black pepper
2	teaspoons vegetable oil
4	center-cut salmon fillets (each about 4 ounces and 1¼ inches thick), pin bones removed (see the illustrations on page 261) and patted dry with paper towels
1	lemon, cut into wedges

1. Heat 2 tablespoons butter in a large non-stick skillet over medium-high heat until the foaming subsides. Add the onion, chard stems, thyme bundle, and ¼ teaspoon salt and cook, stirring frequently, until the vegetables soften and begin to brown, 3 to 4 minutes. Add the lentils and broth and bring to a boil. Reduce

Pan-Seared Salmon

SERVES 4

TIME: 15 MINUTES

Although you can serve the salmon with just lemon or lime wedges, it is even better with a salsa, chutney, or relish.

2   teaspoons vegetable oil
4   center-cut salmon fillets (each about 6 ounces and 1¼ inches thick), pin bones removed (see the illustrations on page 261) and patted dry with paper towels
     Salt and ground black pepper
1   lemon or lime, cut into wedges

Heat the oil in a large nonstick skillet over medium-high heat until smoking. Meanwhile, season the fillets with salt and pepper to taste. Place the fillets in the skillet, flesh-side down, and cook without moving until well browned, 2½ to 3 minutes. Using tongs and a spatula, flip the fish and cook until the fish is opaque and just firm, 2½ to 3 minutes longer. Serve immediately with the lemon or lime wedges.

the heat to low, cover the skillet, and cook until the lentils are tender, 25 to 30 minutes. Increase the heat to medium-high and cook, uncovered and stirring frequently, until excess liquid is evaporated, 1 to 2 minutes. Remove and discard the thyme, season with salt and pepper to taste, transfer the lentils to a bowl, and cover with aluminum foil to keep warm.

2. Return the skillet to medium-high heat and melt the remaining 1 tablespoon butter. Once the foaming subsides, add the chard greens and salt and pepper to taste. Using tongs, stir the chard until it is completely wilted and glossy green, 1½ to 2 minutes. Transfer the chard leaves to a small bowl and cover with aluminum foil to keep warm.

3. Using tongs and paper towels, wipe the skillet clean. Return the skillet to medium-high heat and heat the oil until smoking. Meanwhile, season the fillets with salt and pepper to taste. Place the fillets in the skillet, flesh-side down, and cook without moving until well browned, 2½ to 3 minutes. Using tongs and a spatula, flip the fish and cook until the fish is opaque and just firm, 2½ to 3 minutes longer.

4. Spoon a small pile of lentils in the center of four plates and then rest a salmon fillet on top. Divide the chard equally among the plates, placing it in a circle around the lentils. Serve immediately with the lemon wedges.

Pan-Seared Halibut and Potatoes

FISH AND POTATOES ARE A CLASSIC combination. From fish and chips to brandade, starchy white potatoes are the perfect foil for flaky white fish. Instead of trying to rework some classic dish, we opted to take a slightly different route. We decided to create a simple recipe—tipping our hat to French country cooking—that could be confined to one pan but would highlight the flavor and texture of both the fish and potatoes.

For the fish, we gravitated toward the clean flavor and pristine appearance of halibut. Depending on the region of the country, halibut can be one of the more expensive offerings of the fish counter, but for this dish, it is well worth it. Halibut is sold in either steak or fillet form; in this case, we favored fillets because they brown better and require less preparation. Because the potatoes were going to be roasted, we opted for Red Bliss potatoes, which possess a creamy interior and sweet flavor. Also, they don't need to be peeled—a bonus when time is tight.

We thought the simplest method would be to roast the potatoes and, when they were almost ready, add the fish to the pan, but we quickly realized that this approach had some drawbacks. Neither the fish nor the potatoes browned as effectively as we had hoped, despite manipulating oven temperatures and cooking pans. We achieved the best results by cooking both elements of the dish independently on the stovetop. We browned the potatoes first, then cleaned the pan and seared the fish. Any additional effort required for stovetop cooking was limited to an occasional stir.

To flavor our potatoes, we leaned toward a simple combination of onions, garlic, and herbs. We decided to cook an onion with the potatoes for added flavor. The garlic, however, tended to burn regardless of how it was prepared. Then we tried a slightly unconventional approach. We left the cloves in their skins and removed the peels once the potatoes were tender. The cloves slipped their skins easily and cooked to a soft, creamy state that easily blended with the potatoes and suffused them with the full, sweet flavor of roasted garlic.

For herbs, a wide variety worked, but tasters liked the woodsy note of fresh thyme best. We took the lazy route and added whole sprigs to the potatoes. Once the potatoes were done, the sprigs were easily removed, along with the bay leaves we had also included. For a shot of freshness, we threw in minced parsley just before serving.

Once the potatoes were tender and the onions caramelized, we gave the skillet a quick cleaning and proceeded to sear the fish. As it is with meat, a smoking-hot skillet is the key to

attaining the best crust on fish. The crust is flavorful and visually appealing—both important to this simple dish. Halibut is sturdy enough to brown well without flaking apart. To be on the safe side, however, we were careful to flip the fish gingerly.

Pan-Seared Halibut and Potatoes

SERVES 4

TIME: 50 MINUTES

This rustic-looking dish is best served family-style on a large platter. If you prefer to plate the meal individually, cut the fillet into 4 portions before cooking; the cooking times will remain the same. A simple green salad would be an ideal accompaniment.

3	tablespoons unsalted butter
1	medium red onion, halved and cut into ½-inch-thick slices
1½	pounds Red Bliss potatoes, scrubbed and cut into ¾-inch wedges
8	medium cloves garlic, unpeeled
8	sprigs fresh thyme
4	bay leaves
	Salt
1	tablespoon chopped fresh parsley leaves
	Ground black pepper
2	teaspoons vegetable oil
1½	pounds halibut fillet (in a single piece)
1	lemon, cut into wedges

1. Adjust an oven rack to the middle position and heat the oven to 200 degrees. Heat the butter in a large nonstick skillet over medium-high heat. When the foaming subsides, add the onion, potatoes, garlic, thyme, bay leaves, and 1 teaspoon salt. Cook, stirring occasionally, until the potatoes begin to brown, about 10 minutes. Reduce the heat to medium and cook, stirring occasionally, until the potatoes are well browned and easily

pierced with a knife, about 20 minutes. Remove the thyme sprigs, bay leaves, and garlic cloves; discard the thyme and bay leaves. Using tongs, squeeze the garlic cloves from their skins and roughly chop. Toss the garlic and parsley with the potatoes and adjust the seasonings with salt and pepper. Transfer the potatoes to an ovensafe bowl and place the bowl in the oven to keep warm.

2. Using tongs and paper towels, wipe the skillet clean. Add the oil and heat over medium-high heat until smoking. Meanwhile, liberally season the fish with salt and pepper. Place the fillet, skin-side down, in the pan and cook until well browned, about 5 minutes. Using a large spatula, gently flip the fish and cook until the fish is cooked through and opaque, 4 to 5 minutes. Place the potatoes on a serving platter and set the fish over them. Garnish with the lemon wedges and serve immediately.

Pan-Seared Monkfish with Quick Succotash

MONKFISH HAS ONLY RECENTLY BECOME popular in America, but it has long been revered in Europe for its flavor and texture. Granted, the fish's appearance—all teeth and fleshy maw—is hideous, but the flesh is meaty and sweet—not unlike that of lobster, to which it is often compared. In fact, monkfish is sometimes called "poor man's lobster," as its price is less than half that of lobster.

We wanted to make monkfish the center of a quick-cooked meal, so we needed to find an appropriate accompaniment. Surprisingly, succotash—the classic American vegetable blend—came to mind and proved the perfect match. With the aid of frozen vegetables, this became an upscale dish with bargain-priced ingredients ready for the table within half an hour.

The word *succotash* is derived from the Narragansett tribe's word for "boiled kernels of corn"; it is most commonly a blend of corn, lima beans, and red or green peppers. The sweet flavor and blend of textures—crisp, starchy, and soft—are ideal complements to fish. From previous recipe development, we knew that good succotash could be made, in part, with frozen corn and frozen lima beans. To lend depth to this version, we employed bacon fat as the cooking medium and then used the browned bacon bits as a garnish that gave the dish additional flavor and texture.

For freshness, we briefly sautéed red bell pepper—green peppers tasted unpleasantly bitter—and red onion, which caramelized and took on sweetness and depth. The lima beans also benefited from a bit of browning, which intensified their mild flavor. We added them still frozen to the pan. Frozen corn, on the other hand, was at its best when just warmed through. If cooked too long, we found, it lost flavor and turned tough and fibrous. For herbs, tasters favored a light amount of tarragon, as the mild anise flavor improved both the succotash and the fish's flavor.

Once the succotash was finished, we transferred it to a bowl to keep warm and proceeded to cook the fish, having wiped the pan to remove any detritus that might burn. Monkfish is sold in fillets, which are actually the tail (the head comprises most of the fish and is generally removed at sea—yes, it's that ugly). The fillets are slightly round, tapering to a small tail, so they cannot be browned like a conventional fillet. Often, monkfish fillets are roasted whole, but for this recipe, we wanted to keep all the cooking on the stovetop. Cutting cross sections of the fillets—essentially, cutting them into small steaks—proved the best method, as the pieces cooked efficiently and browned attractively.

After experimenting with thicknesses, we settled on 1-inch-thick pieces, as the meat browned and cooked through quickly without drying out. We simply cut these pieces ourselves. Like halibut, monkfish is best when thoroughly cooked; otherwise, it can be rubbery. For additional color, we tossed the fish pieces with sweet paprika before cooking. The peppery sweetness of the paprika helped tie the fish to the succotash.

Pan-Seared Monkfish with Quick Succotash

SERVES 4

TIME: 30 MINUTES

Monkfish fillets are generally sold with a membranous gray coating still attached that, if you ask, will be removed by the fishmonger. Otherwise, use a sharp paring knife to trim it off. Try to purchase large fillets (about 2½ inches in diameter) and then cut them into 1-inch-thick medallions. If monkfish is unavailable, swordfish or halibut is a good substitute, although these fish should be cooked as individual steaks or fillets. A simple green salad and crusty loaf of bread are both ideal accompaniments.

1 ½	pounds monkfish fillets, trimmed of membrane and cut crosswise into 1-inch-thick pieces
¾	teaspoon paprika
1	tablespoon plus 2 teaspoons olive oil Salt and ground black pepper
4	ounces bacon (about 4 slices), diced
1	small red onion, diced fine
1	small red bell pepper, stemmed, seeded, and diced fine
1	pound frozen lima beans
8	ounces frozen corn
1	tablespoon chopped fresh tarragon leaves
1	lemon, cut into wedges

1. Toss the monkfish with the paprika, 1 tablespoon oil, ¼ teaspoon salt, and pepper to taste in a medium bowl.

2. Heat the bacon in a large nonstick skillet over medium-high heat, stirring occasionally, until the fat is rendered and the bacon browned, 4 to 5 minutes. Using a slotted spoon, remove the browned bits to a paper towel–lined plate and set aside.

3. Add the onion, bell pepper, and ½ teaspoon salt to the bacon fat in the empty pan and cook, stirring frequently, until softened and just beginning to brown, 2 to 3 minutes. Add the lima beans and cook, stirring occasionally, until softened and lightly browned, 6 to 7 minutes. Stir in the corn and cook until heated through, 1 to 2 minutes. Stir in the tarragon and adjust the seasonings with salt and pepper to taste. Transfer the succotash to a bowl and cover with foil to keep warm.

4. Using tongs and paper towels, wipe the skillet clean. Add the remaining 2 teaspoons oil and heat over medium-high heat until smoking. Add the monkfish in a single layer and cook until browned, about 2 minutes. Using tongs, flip the monkfish and cook until browned on the second side, about 2 minutes. Reduce the heat to medium and cook, stirring occasionally, until the fish is just firm and cooked through, 4 to 5 minutes longer.

5. To serve, place the succotash on a large platter or individual plates. Top the succotash with the monkfish. Garnish with the bacon bits and serve immediately, accompanied by lemon wedges.

SOLE MEUNIÈRE

MEUNIÈRE, WHICH TRANSLATES AS "miller's wife," is a classic French preparation. The technique involves dredging food in flour—hence the miller association—and then quickly sautéing it in butter. This simple dish typifies humble French country cooking. It is particularly attractive because it can be prepared in a short time.

Probably the most famous meunière preparation is sole. While the butter and flour create a beautifully golden brown exterior, the inside of the fish remains moist and flavorful. However, it is important to choose fillets with the right thickness to achieve this balance. If the fillets are too thick, the outside overcooks before the inside is done; if the fillets are too thin, the fish overcooks before the exterior browns. We tried fillets of varying thickness to find the size best suited to the meunière preparation.

Our first test involved fillets about ⅛ inch thick. As we expected, these fillets cooked in less than 2 minutes, but the flour coating hadn't had time to cook, leaving it pasty and raw. A ¼-inch-thick fillet performed a little bit better, but it still was not what we were looking for. Moving on to a ⅜-inch-thick fillet, we finally achieved the perfect results. Cooking for about 3 minutes per side allowed the fish to achieve both a flavorful, nutty-tasting exterior and a moist, creamy interior. Another benefit to using these ⅜-inch-thick fillets was that we could easily fit all of them into a 12-inch pan, eliminating the need for either two pans or two batches.

With the thickness of the fillets determined, we explored the temperature of the pan to see how it would affect our sole meunière. We started by cooking the sole over low heat, but the result was not good; the fish just poached in the butter, and as it did not brown, the taste was bland and lackluster. Cooked over medium heat, the fish was much better, but the exterior browning still fell short. High heat turned out to be excessive; by the time the interior was cooked, the butter in the pan had burned and left the fish tasting bitter and unappealing. We settled on cooking the sole over medium-high heat.

The other component of this dish is the sauce. Traditionally, the sauce served with meunière is *beurre noisette*, or brown butter sauce. Made by browning the milk solids in butter, this sauce adds a wonderful nuttiness to the fish. However, when improperly prepared, it is no more than a pool of melted butter with little flavor. We found several recipes in French cookbooks. Most utilized the same procedure: Heat the butter in a hot pan until foaming, add a little bit of lemon juice (to cool the butter and to prevent it from coloring further), and then pour the lemon-flavored butter over the fish. We tried these recipes and found them too light and lacking in the full nuttiness we desired. We did, however, like the flavor of the lemon juice. Feeling that the butter had to brown more, we let it cook past the point where the foaming subsided and then added our lemon juice. This method yielded what we wanted: a deep golden color and an intensely nutty flavor.

Many traditional recipes also include capers and shallots in the butter. These additions did wonders for our sauce. The capers added brininess, the shallot added a pungent bite, and both elements contrasted nicely with the mild, slightly sweet flavor of the sole.

To round out the meal, we blanched green beans, tossed them with butter, and set them aside while we finished the sauce. (It's best to cook the beans at the same time as the fish.) At serving time, we piled beans on each plate, set a fillet on top of the beans, and then drizzled the brown butter sauce over both the fish and the beans.

Sole Meunière

SERVES 4

TIME: 25 MINUTES

We strongly recommend using ⅜-inch-thick sole fillets for this recipe. If you can't find this size, use slightly thicker fillets rather than thinner ones. Timing is the key to the recipe. While the fish is cooking, add the beans to the boiling water. Once the fish goes into the oven, drain and butter the beans and then quickly make the butter sauce. Add rice, mashed potatoes, or crusty bread to finish the meal.

½	cup unbleached all-purpose flour
4	sole fillets, each 5 to 6 ounces and ⅜ inch thick
	Salt and ground black pepper
8	tablespoons unsalted butter, cut into 8 pieces
¾	pound green beans, ends snapped off
2	tablespoons drained capers
I	small shallot, minced (about 2 tablespoons)
I	tablespoon juice from I lemon
I	tablespoon chopped fresh parsley leaves

1. Bring 2½ quarts water to a boil in a large saucepan. Adjust an oven rack to the lower-middle position, set a large heatproof plate on the rack, and heat the oven to 200 degrees. Place the flour in a shallow dish. Season both sides of the sole fillets with salt and pepper to taste. Coat both sides of 1 fillet with flour. Shake excess flour from the fillet and set it aside on a plate. Repeat with the remaining fillets.

2. Heat 1 tablespoon butter in a 12-inch nonstick skillet over medium-high heat. Once the foaming subsides, place the floured fillets in a single layer in the skillet and cook until golden brown, about 3 minutes. Using a spatula, gently flip the fish and cook on the second side until the flesh feels firm when

pressed with a finger, 2 to 3 minutes longer. Transfer the fillets to the heated plate and return the plate to the oven.

3. Meanwhile, add 1 tablespoon salt and the beans to the boiling water and cook until tender, about 5 minutes. Drain the beans and transfer them to a large serving bowl and toss with 1 tablespoon butter, ⅛ teaspoon salt, and ⅛ teaspoon pepper.

4. Return the skillet to medium heat and add the remaining 6 tablespoons butter. Cook until the butter is golden and smells nutty and fragrant, 1 to 2 minutes. Remove the pan from the heat and add the capers, shallot, lemon juice, and parsley. Season the sauce with salt and pepper to taste.

5. Arrange portions of green beans on individual plates and place a piece of sole on each. Pour the sauce over both the fish and the beans and serve immediately.

HADDOCK AND VEGETABLES EN PAPILLOTE

COOKING FISH EN PAPILLOTE IS A classic French method that involves baking fish in a tightly sealed parchment paper pouch. In effect, the fish steams in its own juices, developing a flaky, delicate texture and an intense, clean flavor. With the addition of vegetables and seasonings, the fish becomes a complete main course with a side of showmanship, as each diner receives his or her own pouch to open. Best of all, this dish takes little work outside of assembly; there's no stovetop cooking and little mess.

Traditional French methods for cooking en papillote are somewhat arcane. Pieces of thick parchment must be trimmed to an exact size, and folding patterns reminiscent of

269

origami are employed to ensure a tight seal. Admittedly, the results make for a dramatic presentation. The paper balloons and browns in the oven and is slit open at the table by the diner. Because many home kitchens do not have parchment paper squirreled away, however, we opted to use aluminum foil as a more convenient, modern upgrade. While it lacks the drama of the parchment, aluminum foil works just as effectively and doesn't require labor-intensive folding. The seams can simply be crimped together.

We kept certain limitations in mind as we designed this recipe. All the components must cook at roughly the same rate, driven by the cooking time necessary for the fish. That meant dense vegetables like carrots or potatoes were excluded and that the vegetables we did choose must be thinly cut.

After trying a variety of fish fillets, we favored flaky, mild fish over more assertive, oilier fish like salmon or tuna, which can hold their own with more aggressive cooking methods. Haddock became our first choice for flavor and texture, although red snapper was a close second. Fillets about 1 inch thick proved ideal, becoming flaky without drying.

Clearly, ascertaining the fish's degree of doneness involved guesswork; it was hard to nick and peek when the fish was sealed tight in foil. The old rule of thumb—10 minutes cooking time per inch of fish—failed in this case, as the fish was barely opaque within that period. After experimenting with oven temperatures, we found that the fish cooked best at 450 degrees for 20 minutes. While it seemed like an excessive length of time at such a high heat, the fish was well insulated within the sealed pouch. Cooking the pouches on the lowest rack of the oven helped concentrate the exuded liquid so neither the fish nor the vegetables were waterlogged.

With the technique mastered and the fish selected, we set to work choosing vegetables and flavorings. Light, clean-tasting zucchini and summer squash were crowd-pleasers, and it took little work to thinly slice them into rounds. For sweetness and body, we added sliced tomatoes. For flavorings, we turned to garlic for an assertive kick and anchovies to intensify the mild haddock. A splash of dry white wine brought acidity to the dish, and basil complemented both the fish and the squash.

ASSEMBLING THE PAPILLOTE

1. Shingle the vegetables in three 5-inch-long rows in the center of each piece of foil. (Make one row of zucchini, one row of tomato, and one more row of zucchini.) Season the vegetables with salt and pepper to taste and sprinkle each grouping with 1 tablespoon basil.

2. Place the fish on the vegetables. With an icing spatula, spread the butter on the fish. Sprinkle each piece of fish with 1 tablespoon basil and drizzle with 1 tablespoon wine.

3. Place the remaining pieces of aluminum foil over each fillet. Tightly crimp the bottom and top edges of the foil together to form a tight circle.

While tasters liked the dish, they felt that it tasted too lean—it needed fat. Olive oil lent a light and summery flavor to the fish, but tasters wanted more depth—the kind of depth provided only by butter. Simply putting a pat on the fish before sealing the pouch helped, but we took a different approach and made a compound butter by adding the garlic and anchovies to the butter. The potent flavors better suffused the dish and made a delicious broth to be sopped up with bread.

Haddock and Vegetables en Papillote

SERVES 4

TIME: 40 MINUTES

Ask your fishmonger to remove the skin from the fillets. The pouches may be assembled several hours ahead of time and refrigerated, but they should be baked just before serving. Because the fish is sealed tightly in the pouch, it will continue to cook out of the oven. To prevent overcooking, open each pouch promptly after baking. As the broth is quite flavorful, we recommend passing a hearty loaf of bread at the table.

4	tablespoons unsalted butter, softened
4	anchovy fillets, chopped fine
3	medium cloves garlic, minced or pressed through a garlic press (about 1 tablespoon)
2	medium zucchini and/or summer squash (about 1 pound), cut crosswise into ¼-inch-thick rounds
3	medium ripe round tomatoes (about 1 pound), cored and sliced thin
	Salt and ground black pepper
½	cup coarsely chopped fresh basil leaves
4	haddock or red snapper fillets (each about 6 ounces)
¼	cup dry white wine
1	lemon, cut into wedges

1. Adjust an oven rack to the lowest position and heat the oven to 450 degrees. With a fork, combine the butter, anchovies, and garlic in a small bowl.

2. Cut eight 12-inch squares of heavy-duty aluminum foil. Lay 4 pieces of foil on a work surface. Layer the squash, tomatoes, salt and pepper to taste, basil, fish, anchovy-garlic butter, and wine on the foil pouches according to illustrations 1 and 2 on page 270. Seal the pouches with the remaining foil squares according to illustration 3 on page 270. Set the pouches on a rimmed baking sheet and place the baking sheet in the oven. Cook until the fish is just cooked through, about 20 minutes. Immediately serve each packet on a plate, allowing each diner to slice it open at the table. Pass the lemon wedges at the table.

ROASTED STUFFED TROUT

RAINBOW TROUT, WHOLE OR IN FILLETS, are an underappreciated staple available at most fish counters. Sweet and mild, they appeal to even the most finicky eater. Their mildness makes them attractive for any number of dishes; one of our favorites is trout stuffed with a simple filling and roasted. Each fish is a meal unto itself (at roughly 7 to 10 ounces, cleaned, each trout is the perfect serving size), requiring only a simple salad or grain dish to round out the meal.

When developing fillings, we chose to step off the beaten path of standard bread-based stuffing and create vegetable stuffings with flavors borrowed from classic fish dishes. Fennel, red onion, and orange came out of bouillabaisse, the famous Provençal fish stew, and the combination of spinach, bacon, and red pepper has its roots in American cooking.

But before we could tackle the fillings, we

needed to figure out the best method for roasting the trout, which involved choosing the proper pan and testing various oven temperatures and oven rack positions. Small Pyrex baking dishes and roasting pans both caused the fish to exude liquid and steam, which was detrimental to both flavor and texture. The fish needed more room for the oven's hot air to circulate. Spreading the trout on a large rimmed baking sheet allowed for the best circulation, and as a result, the baked fish had a significantly better texture than when prepared in the smaller pan. The trout also cooked faster on a rimmed baking sheet.

We experimented with temperatures ranging from 400 to 500 degrees and found little difference in flavor or texture; the advantage boiled down to a difference in cooking time—so 500 degrees it was. In 10 to 12 minutes, the fish were perfectly flaky yet still moist. As for rack placement, we stuck with the middle position, as the fish seemed to cook most evenly there.

With our fish cooked, it was time to focus on the fillings. The flavors of orange and fennel are essential to bouillabaisse. To add body and sweetness to the fennel, we favored red onion. As in bouillabaisse, which gets a shot of Pernod for an anise kick, the filling needed more anise than the fennel bulb alone could provide. We felt Pernod was too oddball an ingredient for most home cooks, but we found fennel seed provided ample flavor. Left whole and sautéed along with the fennel and onion, the seeds softened and lent a bit of texture to the otherwise soft filling.

Orange juice gave much-needed acidity to the vegetables and helped deglaze the browned bits adhering to the bottom of the pan. Juice alone, however, failed to provide enough orange flavor. A scant ½ teaspoon zest was enough to convey flavor without developing bitterness. After several soggy fish, we learned

it's important to make the filling as dry as possible. When it's too wet, the moisture steams the fish, which makes for an unpleasant texture.

Bacon and trout are a classic pairing, most likely a serendipitous match first made by a camping fisherman cooking brookside. For our second filling, we paired the bacon with sweet bell peppers, onions, and spinach.

Our cooking method varied little from the previous filling although, for the fullest flavor, we sautéed the peppers and onions in the fat rendered from the bacon. The browned bacon bits were reserved until after the trout was roasted and used as a garnish, as they turned unappetizingly chewy when cooked in the filling. Preparing the spinach was simply a matter of wilting it in the skillet, which took just moments. We tried several styles of spinach, including sturdy crinkle-leaf, mature flat-leaf, and baby. The flavor differences were slight, but preparation was not. The baby spinach won, as it is purchased already cleaned. The leaves wilted in less than 2 minutes.

As the fennel stuffing did, the spinach mixture needed a shot of acidity to brighten the flavors. In this case, citrus tasted too sharp, so we turned to vinegar. Cider vinegar was the tasters' favorite.

—✦—

Roasted Stuffed Trout
SERVES 4
TIME: 30 MINUTES (INCLUDES TIME TO MAKE STUFFING)

The filling may be made up to 2 days ahead of time, but the fish should be stuffed and roasted at the last minute. With either filling, the trout pairs well with the bulgur and quinoa pilafs in Chapter 4. The fennel filling also pairs nicely with saffron couscous (page 93). Use olive oil to grease the baking sheet if using the fennel stuffing; vegetable oil works better with the bacon stuffing. Ask your fishmonger to gut and clean the fish.

2 tablespoons extra-virgin olive oil or
   vegetable oil
4 whole rainbow trout, gutted, cleaned (7
   to 10 ounces each), and patted dry inside
   and out with paper towels
   Salt and ground black pepper
1 recipe Fennel and Red Onion Stuffing or
   Bacon, Red Pepper, and Spinach Stuffing
   (recipes follow)
1 lemon, cut into wedges

1. Adjust an oven rack to the middle position and heat the oven to 500 degrees. Grease a rimmed baking sheet with the appropriate oil and place the trout on the sheet, spaced at least 2 inches apart. Season the cavity of each fish with salt and pepper. Using a spoon, divide the filling equally among the cavities of the fish.

2. Place the baking sheet in the oven and cook until the fish is opaque and the meat flakes upon touch, 10 to 12 minutes. Serve immediately, 1 trout per diner, garnished with a lemon wedge.

Fennel and Red Onion Stuffing

MAKES ENOUGH FOR 4 TROUT

Some markets sell fennel bulbs with the stalks and fronds already removed, so the fennel fronds are optional; use parsley if the fronds are not available. See the illustration on page 37 for information about coring the fennel bulb.

2 tablespoons extra-virgin olive oil
1 large fennel bulb (about 1 pound),
   fronds reserved and stems discarded,
   bulb halved, cored, and sliced thin
1 medium red onion, halved and sliced thin
1 teaspoon fennel seeds
   Salt
½ teaspoon grated zest and ¼ cup juice
   from 1 large orange

1 tablespoon chopped fennel fronds or
   fresh parsley
   Ground black pepper

Heat the oil in a 12-inch nonstick skillet over medium-high heat until shimmering. Add the sliced fennel bulb, onion, fennel seeds, and ¾ teaspoon salt and cook, stirring frequently, until the vegetables soften and brown, about 12 minutes. Stir in the orange zest and juice and cook until the liquid is evaporated, about 30 seconds. Remove the pan from the heat, stir in the fennel fronds, and adjust the seasonings with salt and pepper to taste.

Bacon, Red Pepper, and Spinach Stuffing

MAKES ENOUGH FOR 4 TROUT

The bacon bits become too chewy if cooked inside the fish. Once the trout emerges from the oven, use a spatula to gently open each fish and sprinkle the bacon bits into the cavity over the stuffing.

4 ounces bacon (about 4 slices),
   diced fine
1 medium onion, halved and sliced thin
1 medium red bell pepper, stemmed,
   seeded, and sliced thin
   Salt
9 ounces baby spinach (about 12 cups)
2 teaspoons cider vinegar
   Ground black pepper

Cook the bacon in a 12-inch nonstick skillet over medium-high heat, stirring frequently, until the fat is rendered and the bits are browned, about 5 minutes. Using a slotted spoon, transfer the bacon to a paper towel–lined plate (see the headnote about adding the bacon after the stuffed fish is cooked). Add the onion, bell pepper, and ½ teaspoon salt to the fat in the empty skillet and cook, stirring frequently, until the onion softens and begins to brown, about 5 minutes. Add the spinach by the handful and, using tongs, stir it in until wilted and any moisture is evaporated, about 2 minutes. Off the heat, stir in the vinegar and adjust the seasonings with salt and pepper to taste.

FISH TACOS

BORN IN THE BAJA REGION OF Mexico, fish tacos have become a staple street snack throughout much of that country and Southern California. While they appear in many guises, the standard version—made famous by a chain called Rubio's based in San Diego—is composed of battered white fish tucked into a corn tortilla with shredded lettuce and a tangy white sauce. It sounded like an odd pairing to many of us in the test kitchen, but those of us who had tasted fish tacos knew better. With few components and little preparation needed, we knew we could pull a quick recipe together without compromising flavor.

The fish itself was the natural starting point. In Southern California, the favored fish is a sturdy white fish, like cod, halibut, or haddock. We experimented with the three and found them all acceptable, although tasters preferred the flavor and texture of the halibut. We cut skinned fillets into 1-inch-thick pieces about 4 to 5 inches long, or just about the diameter of a small tortilla.

Rubio's uses beer batter with their fish, and we could find little reason to change. Beer batters are just flour, beer, and seasoning; the beer's carbonation keeps the batter loose and light—part of the fish's charm. We discovered that a thin, pourable batter (similar to a crêpe batter) yielded fried fish that was light and

crisp. Thicker batters produced fish that was leaden and gummy. All-purpose flour worked fine, and a light lager (like Budweiser or Corona) added a complementary sweetness that didn't overpower the fish the way heartier beers did. To spice the batter, we added cumin and cayenne pepper—simple seasonings that perked up the mild flavor of the fish.

Rubio's sauce is nothing more than mayonnaise and yogurt spiked with lime juice. While it was deemed acceptable by tasters (and thousands of Californians), we wanted a sauce with a bit more character. Not wedded to the Rubio's recipe, we opted to exclude the yogurt and add minced chipotle chiles for both heat and flavor. The addition of the chipotle intensified the mayonnaise enough that additional condiments were superfluous.

Corn tortillas are the only option for fish tacos, with white preferable to yellow corn. They may be heated in a variety of ways, but our favorite method is in a hot skillet on the stovetop; they essentially toast, which intensifies the sweet corn flavor. Once pliant and speckled with brown—20 to 30 seconds per side in a medium-hot skillet—the tortillas are ready. Thinly sliced lettuce finished off these tacos.

Fish Tacos

SERVES 4 TO 6

TIME: 40 MINUTES

The dry ingredients of the batter may be combined ahead of time, but the beer should be whisked in just before frying. The chipotle mayonnaise may be made up to a day ahead. If you prefer a spicier mayonnaise, add an extra chile or a small spoonful of the adobo sauce the chiles are packed in. If you want additional garnishes, try tomato salsa (page 16), pickled red onions (page 48), guacamole, or diced avocado. Use a light-flavored lager, such as Budweiser or Corona, in the batter. Serve the tacos with the beer.

1	cup mayonnaise
1 ½	teaspoons juice from 1 lime, plus 1 lime cut into wedges
1	chipotle chile packed in adobo sauce, minced to a paste
	Salt
4	cups vegetable oil
1	cup unbleached all-purpose flour
½	teaspoon ground cumin
¼	teaspoon cayenne pepper
1	cup beer
1 ½	pounds sturdy white fish fillets (cod, halibut, or haddock), cut into 4 by 1-inch pieces
12	small corn tortillas, preferably white
½	head iceberg lettuce, cored and shredded fine
	Hot pepper sauce, such as Tabasco

1. Adjust an oven rack to the middle position and heat the oven to 200 degrees. Mix the mayonnaise, lime juice, chile, and salt to taste in a small bowl; set aside.

2. Meanwhile, heat the oil in a large Dutch oven or heavy-bottomed saucepan over medium heat until the oil registers 350 degrees on a thermometer. Whisk together the flour, cumin, cayenne, and 1 teaspoon salt in a large bowl. Whisk in the beer until the batter is completely smooth. Add half of the fish to the batter and stir to coat. Cover a wire cooling rack with several layers of paper towels and set it over a rimmed baking sheet.

3. Using tongs, transfer the fish to the oil and fry until golden brown (making sure the pieces don't touch), 4 to 5 minutes. Transfer the fish to the paper towel–lined rack and set the baking sheet in the oven to keep the fish warm. Repeat the process with the remaining fish. While the fish cooks, toast the tortillas, 1 at a time, in a skillet over medium-high heat until softened and speckled with brown, 20 to 30 seconds per side. Wrap the tortillas in a slightly moistened kitchen towel to keep warm.

4. For assembly, smear each tortilla with mayonnaise and top with shredded lettuce. Add 1 piece of fish to each tortilla and serve immediately, folded in half, passing hot pepper sauce and lime wedges at the table.

COD BRANDADE

THE HISTORY OF BRANDADE SEEMS TO begin in the French town of Nîmes in Provence, even though it is made with salt-preserved cod—which is not a local fish. The theory is that Icelandic cod made its way to Nîmes via trade, shortly after which brandade was born. Classically, the dried pieces of salt cod are soaked and rinsed for several days to rehydrate and rid them of excess salt. The bones and, sometimes, the skin are removed, and the fish is then ground with olive oil and a bit of milk. Over the years, garlic and potatoes have become standard additions to this basic formula. Because good salt cod can be hard to find and fresh cod can be found nearly everywhere, we wondered if brandade could be made using fresh cod.

We discovered a few published recipes for fresh cod brandade and noted that they fell into two categories: mashed with milk and pureed with oil. The first method simmers the cod and the potatoes in milk; they are then drained and mashed together, adding back as much of the flavorful milk as necessary to achieve the correct consistency. The other method marinates and cooks the cod in olive oil, then purees it with already-cooked potatoes, adding more olive oil as needed to achieve the correct consistency. After giving both of these techniques a try, tasters were decidedly in favor of the milk-simmered approach. Although the olive oil style comes closer to authentic salt-cod brandade, we found its flavor overpowering and its texture a bit greasy when used with fresh cod. The milk-simmered brandade, on the other hand, had a mild, approachable flavor and a creamy texture. We did, however, find it tasted a bit lean and bland, and we were disappointed that much of the milk used for cooking was simply discarded.

Most of these initial recipes called for 1 pound cod and 1 pound potatoes, which seemed to work well in terms of balance and served four people easily. (We liked the buttery flavor and golden color of Yukon Gold potatoes, but russets also worked well in this recipe.) Wanting a richer mouthfeel, we tried replacing the milk with half-and-half, but we found that it separated, or broke, as it simmered. Next, we tried enriching the milk with heavy cream, which worked much better. We found a ratio of 1 part milk to 1 part cream added just the right amount of heft, and the cream did not separate as it simmered.

Up to now, we had been simmering the cod (which had been cut into small pieces that would cook quickly) in the milk-cream mixture, then straining it out and returning the liquid to the pot. Then we simmered and strained the potatoes and mashed them with the cod, adding cooking liquid as needed. Finding this technique fussy and wasteful, we figured out an easy way to streamline it. Cutting the cod into 5-inch lengths, we found we could simply remove them from the pot with a slotted spoon, thus avoiding the mess and fuss of straining. We then added the potatoes, cut into small pieces, to the pot and simmered them until tender. Rather than straining them, however, we simply mashed them right in the pot with the simmering liquid, folding the cooked cod in at the end so it retained some if its flaky texture.

To boost the flavor, we found it necessary to season the milk-cream mixture with garlic, salt, and herbs. Yet, we were still missing the intense cod flavor that is the hallmark of brandade. Looking through the pantry, we found an ingredient that returned the flavor of our fresh cod brandade to its roots: anchovies. By mincing no fewer than three anchovies, we were able to round out and deepen the flavor of brandade significantly without turning it overly fishy or salty. We finished our brandade with a handful of minced chives.

We also found a way to incorporate the classic flavor of olive oil: We served our brandade with toasted bread slices brushed with garlic and olive oil. Taking minutes rather than days to make, this brandade may be labeled heretical in Nîmes, but it rivals its authentic cousin in flavor.

Fresh Cod Brandade
SERVES 4
TIME: 40 MINUTES

Serve this potato and cod puree with Garlic Toasts (recipe follows) and a leafy salad.

I	cup heavy cream
I	cup milk
4	medium cloves garlic, minced or pressed through a garlic press (about 4 teaspoons)
2	bay leaves
4	sprigs fresh thyme
3	anchovy fillets, minced fine
	Salt and ground black pepper
I	pound cod, skinned and cut into 5 by 2-inch pieces
I	pound Yukon Gold potatoes, peeled and cut into ½-inch dice
4	tablespoons minced fresh chives

1. Stir the cream, milk, garlic, bay leaves, thyme, anchovies, 1¼ teaspoons salt, and ¼ teaspoon pepper in a large, heavy-bottomed saucepan until the salt dissolves. Add the cod and bring to a simmer over medium-high heat. Reduce the heat to medium and continue to simmer until the fish flakes apart easily, about 3 minutes. Using a slotted spoon, transfer the fish to a bowl and reserve.

2. Add the potatoes to the cream mixture and bring the liquid to a simmer over medium-high heat. Reduce the heat to low, cover, and cook, stirring often, until the potatoes are tender, 10 to 15 minutes. Remove the pot from the heat and discard the bay leaves and thyme. Using a potato masher, mash the potatoes and the cream mixture until smooth.

3. Gently fold 3 tablespoons chives and the reserved cod into the potatoes, trying to keep the flakes of cod intact. Adjust the seasonings with salt and pepper to taste. Transfer the mixture to a serving bowl and sprinkle with the remaining 1 tablespoon chives. Serve immediately with the garlic toasts.

Garlic Toasts

MAKES 8 TOASTS, SERVING 4

These garlicky toasts work well with a wide variety of soupy and saucy seafood dishes. You may want to make extras—they are that good.

8	slices rustic bread, each about ½-inch thick
1	medium clove garlic, peeled
2	tablespoons extra-virgin olive oil

Adjust an oven rack to the middle position and heat the oven to 400 degrees. Arrange the bread in a single layer on a baking sheet and bake until dry and crisp, about 10 minutes, turning the slices over halfway through baking.

While still hot, rub each slice of bread with the raw garlic clove and drizzle with the olive oil. Serve hot or warm.

SHRIMP IN SPICY CHIPOTLE SAUCE

WE HAVE HAD SHRIMP PREPARED IN more ways than we can remember, and we were somewhat bored with them when it came time to develop shrimp recipes for this book. Then we came across a Mexican dish in a local restaurant called *camarones enchipolatas* (also called shrimp in chipotle sauce) that jolted our jaded palate. This dish is fiery yet sweet and full of depth. Research proved that the dish's deep flavor came from a surprisingly short ingredient list. By our reckoning, shrimp in chipotle sauce could easily be prepared in under an hour, and we enthusiastically began recipe development.

According to the recipes we gathered, the chipotle sauce is prepared first and then the shrimp are simmered in it. Naturally, then, the sauce was the place to begin. The manner of making traditional Mexican sauces is distinctly different from the European approach. The ingredients—onions, garlic, chiles, tomatoes, and so on—are roasted until browned and even slightly blackened, and then they are pureed together with a liquid of some sort. The sauce is then fried or cooked over very high heat to blend and intensify the flavors. These sauces are easy to make, as they require little preparation; everything is left whole or roughly chopped to roast, and the blender does all the work.

The base for this particular sauce is a blend of tomatoes, onions, and garlic—all roasted. At first, we roasted each ingredient independently on a large rimmed baking sheet, tossing each with olive oil and salt, but we quickly realized they all cooked at similar rates and could therefore be roasted together. We employed well-drained diced canned tomatoes (to save on preparation) and roughly chopped onions and garlic; appearance counted for little, as it was all destined for the blender. With respect to oven temperature and rack placement, we started off with the hottest possible combination by placing the vegetables on the bottom rack in a 500-degree oven. Within 20 minutes, the vegetables were browned and the flavors intensified. Lower temperatures and higher rack settings failed to produce better results, so we stuck with our first method.

To effectively puree the vegetables, we had to add liquid. Water contributed no flavor, of course, but the reserved liquid from the drained tomatoes added a bright fruitiness without increasing the short ingredient list. For spices, chipotle chiles and cloves are the classic duo. While the dish is supposed to be fiery, we scaled back the traditional volume of chipotles to appease the more sensitive tasters. As for cloves, any more than a pinch was jarring.

The final steps were frying the sauce and cooking the shrimp. Frying the sauce could not have been easier. Once added to a hot pan, it bubbled ferociously and reduced in volume. The flavors intensified and the hue darkened slightly, all in a couple of minutes.

Traditional recipes for this dish simply simmer the shrimp in the sauce, but we found the result tasted bland; the shrimp lost definition in the assertive sauce. We found the shrimp had a better flavor when they were seared before being added to the sauce. The speckled brown surface emphasized the natural sweetness of the shrimp and gave depth to the smoky sauce.

Shrimp in Spicy Chipotle Sauce

SERVES 4 TO 6
TIME: 40 MINUTES

Serve with corn tortillas or steamed white rice. A leafy salad is a good addition, too. If the shrimp have particularly large veins, you may want to remove them. See the illustrations on page 56 for tips on deveining shrimp.

2	(14½-ounce) cans diced tomatoes, drained well, ¾ cup tomato liquid reserved
1	medium onion, chopped coarse
4	medium cloves garlic, peeled
4	tablespoons olive oil
	Salt and ground black pepper
1½	canned chipotle chiles in adobo sauce
	Small pinch ground cloves
1	teaspoon vegetable oil
1½	pounds extra-large shrimp (21 to 25 count per pound), peeled and deveined, if desired
¼	cup coarsely chopped fresh cilantro leaves

1. Adjust an oven rack to the lowest position and heat the oven to 500 degrees. Combine the drained tomatoes, onion, garlic, 3 tablespoons olive oil, ¼ teaspoon salt, and pepper to taste in a large bowl. Spread the mixture on a foil-lined rimmed baking sheet and place the baking sheet in the oven. Cook until reduced in volume and speckled with brown, about 20 minutes (a little blackening is okay). Transfer the mixture to the jar of a blender, add the chipotles, ground cloves, and reserved tomato liquid; puree until smooth. Adjust the seasonings with salt and pepper.

2. Heat the vegetable oil in a large skillet over medium-high heat until smoking. Meanwhile, toss the shrimp in a bowl with the

remaining 1 tablespoon olive oil, ½ teaspoon salt, and pepper to taste. Add half the shrimp to the hot pan in a single layer and cook until speckled brown, 30 to 45 seconds. Using tongs, flip the shrimp and cook until speckled brown on the second side, 30 to 45 seconds longer. Transfer the shrimp to a bowl. Repeat the process with the remaining shrimp.

3. Off the heat, carefully pour the sauce into the skillet. Return to the heat and cook, stirring frequently, until thickened, about 2 minutes. Stir in the shrimp and cook until they are heated through, about 1 minute. Sprinkle with the cilantro. Serve immediately.

SKILLET SHRIMP PAELLA

IN THE PANTHEON OF RICE DISHES, paella is near the top. Packed with meats and seafood—from chicken and snails to rabbit and shrimp—myriad vegetables, and plump yet discrete grains of rice, this dish is rightly famous around the world. As is true of many classic dishes, however, it can take hours of preparation and arduous stoveside attendance (or grillside, for truly authentic paella). But when deconstructed, paella is a one-pan main dish that, with some adjustments to technique and ingredients, can easily be made within the hour. To keep our version simple, we decided to employ shrimp as our prime flavor, leaving the snails and rabbit for another day.

Paella is traditionally cooked on a stovetop or the dying embers of a wood fire. The flavorings are sautéed and then the rice and liquid are added and simmered, uncovered, until the rice grains are tender and the liquid has evaporated. The authentic cooking vessel is called a *paellera,* and it is a large, shallow round pan made from thin steel. We found that a large skillet is an acceptable substitute, as the

sides gently slope and the pan itself is shallow, which allows for quick evaporation of the cooking liquid.

The heart of paella is the rice. Paella rice must be medium grain and starchy. The traditional choices are Valencian and Calasparra rice, which can be tricky to find. We found that Arborio rice (typically used in risotto) is a suitable substitute, as it possesses the same ability to absorb a lot of liquid.

Sautéed aromatics form the foundation on which paella is built. For our simplified version, we favored a simple combination of onion and garlic sautéed in olive oil. For seasonings, we included thyme sprigs, left whole to save preparation time, and sweet paprika. Saffron is another common ingredient, but tasters felt that, in this case, it added little. Once the paprika had toasted in the dry skillet (which intensified its flavor), we added well-drained canned diced tomatoes for sweetness and color.

Water as the cooking liquid made the dish taste bland, and chicken broth tasted out of place. As shrimp was to be the primary flavor in the dish, clam juice proved the best choice.

Cooking paella takes a leap of faith, as the method is different from most rice cookery. Once the liquid is added, the pan is left uncovered and the rice simmers rapidly (and unstirred) until tender. We had the best luck with medium-low heat; the grains were uniformly tender and discrete in 18 to 20 minutes. At lower temperatures, the rice turned starchy, and at higher heat, it cooked unevenly.

Tasters unanimously favored extra-large shrimp for their full flavor, tenderness, and visual appeal. To cook the shrimp, we first followed conventional recipes and added them to the rice during the final minutes of cooking. While the result was acceptable, the shrimp tasted bland, so we searched for another method. Seared shrimp packed the most flavor, so we cooked them alongside the paella in a second skillet and added them at the last minute. In a moment of clarity, we realized we could sear the shrimp in the skillet beforehand and incorporate the *fond* (browned bits) from the shrimp into the paella, thereby improving the overall flavor. Before cooking them, we tossed the shrimp with olive oil, salt, and paprika to improve their flavor and color; the paprika darkened and intensified their red hue. The seared shrimp held well in a bowl, and a brief warming before serving brought them back to temperature. Finishing touches included a scattering of scallions over the top and a spritz of lemon.

To serve paella, it is customary to bring the pan to the table and allow diners to serve themselves. Even though our version was less than authentic, it looked the part, and we saw no reason to break with this serving tradition.

One-Skillet Shrimp Paella

SERVES 4 TO 6

TIME: 45 MINUTES

If you want a little heat, add a pinch of cayenne pepper with the paprika or mix sweet and hot paprika. If the shrimp have particularly large veins, you may want to remove them. See the illustrations on page 56 for tips on deveining shrimp.

1	teaspoon vegetable oil
1½	pounds extra-large shrimp (21 to 25 count per pound), peeled and deveined, if desired
3	tablespoons extra-virgin olive oil
3	teaspoons paprika
	Salt
1	medium onion, diced fine
6	medium cloves garlic, slivered thin
6	sprigs fresh thyme
1	(14½-ounce) can diced tomatoes, drained well
1½	cups Arborio rice
2	(8-ounce) bottles clam juice
	Ground black pepper
3	medium scallions, sliced thin on the bias
1	lemon, cut into wedges

1. Heat the vegetable oil in a large skillet over medium-high heat until smoking. Meanwhile, toss the shrimp with 1 tablespoon olive oil, 1 teaspoon paprika, and ½ teaspoon salt in a large bowl. Add half of the shrimp in a single layer and cook until speckled brown, 30 to 45 seconds. Using tongs, flip the shrimp and cook until speckled brown on the second side, about 30 seconds longer. Transfer the shrimp to a bowl. Repeat the process with the remaining shrimp. Cover the bowl with aluminum foil to keep the shrimp warm.

2. Reduce the heat to medium and add the remaining 2 tablespoons olive oil, onion, garlic, thyme sprigs, and ½ teaspoon salt to the empty skillet. Cook, stirring frequently, until softened and beginning to brown, 3 to 4 minutes. Stir in the remaining 2 teaspoons paprika and cook until fragrant, about 30 seconds. Stir in the tomatoes, rice, clam juice, and 2 cups water. Once the liquid comes to a boil, reduce the heat to medium-low and cook, without covering or stirring, until the rice is tender and the liquid is absorbed, about 18 minutes. Spread the shrimp over the rice and cover until the shrimp are heated through, about 2 minutes. Remove and discard the thyme springs. Adjust the seasonings with salt and pepper to taste, sprinkle the scallions over the top, and serve immediately, bringing the skillet to the table along with the lemon wedges.

SEAFOOD SCAMPI

SCAMPI IS NOT AUTHENTIC ITALIAN cuisine; however, it is one of the most popular dishes found on Italian restaurant menus. Most often, though, restaurant scampi is disappointing, with a heavy sauce that drowns overcooked shrimp. Although making scampi at home is far more successful, most recipes call for cooking the shrimp for far too long, turning them rubbery and dry. We find scampi tastes much more interesting when made with a combination of shrimp and scallops, lightly dressed in a potent garlic-lemon-butter sauce that pools a bit on the plate, just waiting for a piece of bread.

Noting that 2 pounds shrimp and scallops easily serves four to six people, we found it necessary to use a large skillet and to cook the seafood in batches. Not only do the scallops and shrimp require different cooking times but also, when they are piled into the skillet all at once, the heat of the skillet is instantly quelled. We found the sea scallops cooked through in just over a minute, while the shrimp took just over 2 minutes.

Because these cooking times are so short, it is important to have the pan as hot as possible. The scallops and shrimp will get a little brown around the edges, which intensifies their flavor. In contrast, a lukewarm pan steams rather than sautés the seafood, making it taste bland and look pale. Knowing when the skillet is hot enough can be difficult, but we found the cooking oil to offer the best clue. Heating the oil in the otherwise empty pan, you can watch its consistency become more fluid and begin to shimmer. As soon as you see wisps of smoke, the pan is ready.

Many recipes build a sauce in the pan alongside the seafood, but obviously this doesn't work. Not only does the sauce prevent the shrimp and scallops from cooking properly but also, by the time the sauce is done, the seafood is far overcooked. Placing the cooked shrimp and scallops off to the side in a bowl, we returned the empty, slightly dirty pan to the stove to make the sauce. Many recipes make the sauce with olive oil, but we far preferred the flavor and body of sauce made with butter. After melting butter in the pan, we quickly sautéed garlic before adding the lemon juice. Six garlic cloves and ¼ cup lemon juice made for a potent sauce. Some recipes also call for white wine or vermouth, and we found that they too deepened the flavor of the sauce significantly. (We liked the herbal flavor of the vermouth better, but white wine works well, too.) Once the sauce is finished with a pinch of cayenne and parsley, the shellfish need only be tossed with the sauce briefly before serving.

Seafood Scampi

SERVES 4 TO 6

TIME: 30 MINUTES

If the shrimp have particularly large veins, you may want to remove them. See the illustrations on page 56 for tips on deveining shrimp. Serve this juicy scampi with Garlic Toasts (page 277) or crusty bread.

2	tablespoons olive oil
1	pound extra-large shrimp (21 to 25 count per pound), peeled and deveined, if desired
1	pound medium sea scallops, tendons removed (see the illustration on page 56)
4	tablespoons unsalted butter
6	medium cloves garlic, minced or pressed through a garlic press (about 2 tablespoons)
¼	cup juice from 1 large lemon
3	tablespoons dry vermouth or white wine
2	tablespoons minced fresh parsley leaves
⅛	teaspoon cayenne pepper
	Salt and ground black pepper

1. Heat 1 tablespoon oil in a 12-inch skillet over high heat until almost smoking. Add the shrimp and cook, stirring occasionally, until just opaque, 2 to 2½ minutes. Transfer the shrimp to a medium bowl. Return the pan to medium-high heat, add the remaining 1 tablespoon oil, and heat until almost smoking, about 5 seconds. Add the scallops and cook, stirring occasionally, until just opaque, 1 to 1½ minutes. Transfer the scallops to the bowl with the shrimp.

2. Return the empty skillet to medium-low heat and melt 1 tablespoon butter in the pan. Add the garlic and cook, stirring occasionally, until fragrant, about 30 seconds. Off the heat, add the lemon juice and vermouth. Return the pan to medium heat and simmer until the sauce thickens slightly, about 1 minute. Whisk in the remaining 3 tablespoons butter. Add the parsley and cayenne and season with salt and black pepper to taste.

3. Remove the pan from the heat and return to it the shrimp and scallops, along with any accumulated juices. Toss to combine and serve immediately.

SEARED SQUID WITH PEPPERS AND SPICY ASIAN SAUCE

ONE OF OUR FAVORITE SQUID DISHES is a sauté of squid, red bell peppers, and peanuts, tossed with spinach and a spicy Asian-style sauce. Not quite a salad or a stir-fry, it can serve equally well as a first course or a main course, if accompanied by steamed rice. Other than the sauce, the dish has only four components: squid, red bell pepper, peanuts, and spinach. Each contributes a distinctive flavor and texture—there's nothing superfluous. The spicy sweet and sour sauce ties the ingredients together.

As we do in preparing a stir-fry, we broke the dish into batches of ingredients that cook at similar rates. The red peppers and peanuts went into the pan first, trailed by the squid. Even novice cooks know how time-sensitive cooking fish can be. Seconds can make or break the quality of many a seafood dish, squid being among the most sensitive. The rule of thumb—which we won't argue with—is that squid must be cooked in under 2 minutes or over an hour. Clearly, in this case, we were taking the short route.

A smoking-hot skillet proved a close approximation of the intense heat a wok provides, and we achieved perfectly cooked squid every time, once we broke the volume of squid into two batches so as to not drop the heat of the skillet precipitously low. Within seconds, the edges of the squid began to brown and char. Within 1½ minutes, the squid was cooked; the pieces showed color around the edges and were tender to a fault.

The sauce we envisioned was a riff on the classic Vietnamese dipping sauce *nuoc cham*, which is a balanced blend of fish sauce, lime juice, chiles, and sugar. Nuoc cham is traditionally served raw at the table as a dipping sauce for numerous dishes. We experimented with several recipes and settled on what we considered an ideal balance of sweet, sour, salty, and hot—the primary flavors of Southeast Asian cooking. We did make a couple of changes to the classic recipe, including the substitution of brown sugar for white, for deeper flavor, and of Asian chili paste for fresh, incendiary bird's-eye chiles, which can be hard to find outside of specialty markets.

While the sauce tasted fine on its own, the heat of the squid brought out the assertive flavor and heady bouquet of fish sauce, which some tasters found objectionable. We first tried reducing the amount of fish sauce, but this left the final sauce bland tasting and the sauté one-dimensional. Adjusting the other components of the sauce also failed to improve it. A quick turn in the hot skillet, however, allowed us to keep the original amount of fish sauce but temper its pungency to a more tolerable level. We seized this opportunity to deglaze the browned bits left by the seared squid, further increasing the sauce's flavor.

The idea is for the spinach to retain much of its raw shape and texture; the dish is not a wilted spinach salad. Clearly, cooking the spinach in the skillet would expose it to too much heat. Adding the hot sauce, with the warm ingredients, to the spinach in a bowl proved the best approach. The leaves retained much of their raw flavor and crisp texture, making them a perfect foil to the chewy squid and crunchy nuts.

Seared Squid with Bell Peppers, Peanuts, Spinach, and Spicy Asian Sauce

SERVES 4

TIME: 15 MINUTES

This dish must be served over steamed white rice (page 113). Good-quality roasted peanut oil is a nice addition, but vegetable oil is fine. Make sure to ask the fishmonger to clean the squid. (Most squid sold in supermarkets is already clean.)

¼	cup juice from 2 limes
3	tablespoons fish sauce
2	teaspoons Asian chili paste
5	teaspoons brown sugar
1	pound cleaned squid, tentacles left whole and bodies sliced into ½-inch-thick rings
2	tablespoons peanut or vegetable oil
	Salt and ground black pepper
8	ounces baby spinach (about 10 cups)
1	large red bell pepper, stemmed, seeded, and sliced into thin strips about 1½ inches long
¾	cup unsalted dry-roasted whole peanuts

1. Whisk the lime juice, fish sauce, chili paste, and brown sugar together in a small bowl. Toss the squid with 2 teaspoons of the oil, ½ teaspoon salt, and pepper to taste in a medium bowl. Place the spinach in a large bowl.

2. Heat 1 tablespoon oil in a large nonstick skillet over medium-high heat until smoking. Add the bell pepper and peanuts and cook, stirring frequently, until the pepper softens and the peanuts are lightly browned, about 2 minutes. Using a spatula, transfer the pepper and peanuts to the bowl with the spinach.

3. Add the remaining 1 teaspoon oil to the empty pan and heat until smoking. Add half of the squid in a single layer and cook, without stirring, until the edges begin to brown, 30 to 45 seconds. Using tongs, turn the squid over to brown on the second side, about 30 seconds, and then stir continuously until the squid is opaque, about 30 seconds longer. Transfer the squid to the bowl with the spinach and repeat the process with the remaining squid (adding the squid to the pan without more oil).

4. Off the heat, pour the sauce mixture into the skillet (be careful to avoid the steam) and return the skillet to the burner. Cook until slightly thickened, 30 to 45 seconds. Pour the sauce over the squid and spinach and, using tongs, toss the mixture to disperse the ingredients. Serve immediately.

CLAMS AND CHORIZO

THE SOMEWHAT ODD-SOUNDING COM-bination of clams and chorizo hails from the coast of Portugal. It is a robust mix of spicy pork sausage and plump clams steamed in tomato broth. Sometimes called *cataplana*, which refers to the vessel it's traditionally cooked in, this dish is similar to paella, but it is less elaborate and can

~~~~~~

easily be made in less than 30 minutes.

Just because something is simple doesn't mean it is always prepared well. This was obvious after we tested a handful of recipes. Many recipes called for too many ingredients that masked the flavor of the clams. What we wanted was to highlight the plump, briny clams and keep the other flavors in the background.

We steamed three batches of clams: littlenecks, tiny Manila clams, and soft-shell clams (better known as *steamers*). We quickly ruled out the steamers, agreeing they were too brittle and gritty for this application. The littlenecks were nice and plump, although some testers felt that they were slightly bland. The Manila clams proved the most flavorful of the three, but in the end we chose the littlenecks, feeling they were more widely available and consistently flavored.

The next ingredient to test was the pork. Most recipes called for a dried sausage, like chorizo or linguiça, although some called for small pieces of fresh pork to be added to the dish. We found we preferred the meatiness the sausages added to the dish to the bland, chewy pieces of pork. We found that ½ pound sausage added abundant flavor to the dish but

didn't overpower the other flavors. We also preferred our sausage cut into larger pieces than most recipes suggested, agreeing they added more textural contrast than a small dice.

Our next step was to address the broth. Onions and garlic were the unanimous choice for its aromatic base; the onions added a mild sweetness, and a healthy dose of garlic heightened the spiciness of the dish. Some of the recipes we consulted included additional vegetables, such as red bell peppers and mushrooms, but we felt these ingredients just muddied the broth and didn't add much. Tomatoes were also a big part of the broth, and canned diced tomatoes worked well. To finish the broth, we added white wine for acidity; ¾ cup was enough to brighten the flavors of the dish without leaving an alcohol aftertaste.

~~≻≺~~

Clams and Chorizo

SERVES 4

TIME: 30 MINUTES

Tasters preferred chorizo to the more traditional linguiça sausage in this recipe, but linguiça can be used depending on your preference or local availability. Serve with Garlic Toasts (page 277) or crusty bread to sop up the heady broth.

I	tablespoon extra-virgin olive oil
½	pound chorizo sausage, cut in half lengthwise and then cut crosswise into ⅛-inch-wide half-moons
I	medium onion, diced small
3	medium cloves garlic, minced or pressed through a garlic press (about I tablespoon)
¾	cup white wine
I	(14½-ounce) can diced tomatoes in juice
4	pounds littleneck clams, well scrubbed (see the illustration at left)
2	tablespoons chopped fresh parsley leaves

SCRUBBING CLAMS

Use a soft brush, sometimes sold in kitchen shops as a vegetable brush, to scrub away any bits of sand trapped in the shell.

1. Heat the oil in a heavy-bottomed Dutch oven over medium heat until shimmering. Add the chorizo and cook, stirring occasionally, until the sausage browns and renders some of its fat, about 4 minutes. With a slotted spoon, transfer the chorizo to a paper towel–lined plate.

2. Add the onion to the fat in the empty pot and cook until it softens, about 2 minutes. Add the garlic and continue to cook until fragrant, about 30 seconds. Add the wine and tomatoes (including their juices) and let simmer until thickened slightly, about 3 minutes. Increase the heat to high and add the clams and chorizo to the pot. Cover and cook, stirring once, until all the clams open, 4 to 8 minutes. Discard any unopened clams.

3. Use a slotted spoon to transfer the clams to a large serving bowl or individual bowls. Stir the parsley into the liquid in the pot. Pour the broth over the clams and serve immediately.

STEAMED MUSSELS WITH RICE

AN OVERFLOWING BOWL OF STEAMED mussels has irresistible charm. Meaty mussels, with a hearty aromatic broth as a chaser, are a one-pot meal, especially with bread or rice to bulk it up. We knew we wanted to include a steamed mussel recipe in this chapter, as mussels cook so quickly and require so little effort, but finding the ideal recipe was a challenge. Most of the recipes we found—generally French or Italian—left us uninspired. A Thai-style recipe, however, caught our attention. With rich coconut milk and fiery chiles, this dish is nothing like boring.

Mussels possess such intense flavor that the dish did not need gussying up with too many other ingredients. The cooking method was simple. The aromatics were sautéed, coconut milk and the mussels added, and then the pot covered to steam the shellfish open. In minutes, the dish was ready to shower with fresh herbs and serve.

In the recipes we researched, shallots, garlic, and chiles usually formed the base of the sauce, but they were often hidden, ground into a curry paste. We took liberties with the classic approach and sliced the shallots and chiles into skinny rings—which, serendipitously, wrapped themselves around the cooked mussels, lending texture and flavor. We put the garlic through a press to save preparation time so its flavor suffused the sauce.

Virtually every recipe we found included lemon grass—either left in long lengths or ground into paste—yet few markets stock it. For the sake of authenticity, we tried it side by side with a batch flavored with lime juice for a citrus note; tasters felt both versions tasted equally delicious, and we concluded that lemon grass was not essential.

The mussels were the last ingredient into the pot. Most mussels sold in markets are farm-raised and therefore impeccably clean, requiring little but a rinse and debearding. It is, however, crucial to make sure your mussels are alive. It's easy to tell: If a mussel fails to close, it's a good bet that it's dead and should be discarded immediately. (Note that sometimes mussels can take their time closing, especially if fresh from refrigeration.)

Like most seafood, mussels can be easily overcooked, and we found close attention was essential to success with this dish. Mussels are cooked the moment the shells open—any longer and they turn rubbery. If they have fallen from their shells, they are certainly overcooked. At medium heat, the mussels cooked in the broth in just 4 to 6 minutes. To ensure even cooking, we found it helpful to stir the mussels after 2 minutes.

We tossed the cooked mussels with an ample amount of coarsely chopped cilantro. Although the taste was good, tasters desired a bit more color—with just the mussels, broth, and herbs, the dish looked a little drab. A sprinkling of diced tomatoes proved ideal, and the fruity flavor added yet another dimension to the dish. We left the lime juice up to the diner, passing wedges at the table.

Southeast Asian–Style Steamed Mussels with Rice

SERVES 4

TIME: 25 MINUTES

As when making a stir-fry, it is imperative to have the ingredients ready and nearby. All can be prepared well ahead of time, however, and the dish finished at the last minute.

1½	cups jasmine rice, well rinsed and drained
	Salt
1	tablespoon vegetable oil
2	large shallots, sliced thin
2	medium jalapeño chiles, stemmed, seeded (if desired to reduce heat), and sliced thin
3	medium cloves garlic, minced or pressed through a garlic press (about 1 tablespoon)
1	cup unsweetened coconut milk
½	teaspoon brown sugar
2	pounds mussels, well rinsed and debearded (see the illustration on page 135)
3	medium plum tomatoes, cored, seeded, and diced medium
½	cup coarsely chopped fresh cilantro leaves
1	lime, cut into wedges

1. Bring the rice, 2¼ cups water, and ¼ teaspoon salt to a boil in a medium saucepan over high heat. Reduce the heat to low, cover, and cook until the liquid evaporates, about 17 minutes. Remove the pan from the heat, fluff the rice with a fork, and sandwich a clean kitchen towel between the lid and the pan to absorb excess moisture (see the illustration on page 215).

2. While the rice is cooking, heat the oil in a large Dutch oven over medium-high heat until shimmering. Add the shallots, chiles, and ½ teaspoon salt and cook, stirring frequently, until the shallots soften and are just beginning to brown, 2 to 3 minutes. Add the garlic and cook until aromatic, about 30 seconds. Reduce the heat to medium and stir in the coconut milk and brown sugar (add the coconut milk slowly and stand back to protect yourself from the steam). Add the mussels and cover. Cook for 2 minutes. Using a wooden spoon, stir the mussels. Cover and cook until all the mussels are just open, 2 to 4 minutes longer.

3. Stir in the tomatoes and cilantro. Transfer the mussels to a serving bowl, pour the sauce over them, and serve immediately with the rice, passing the lime wedges at the table.

10

GRILLING

GRILLING IS THE QUICK COOKING OR searing of foods over an open fire. Relatively thin cuts, such as steaks, chops, and fish fillets, as well as seafood and vegetables take well to grilling. Once the food is seared on both sides, it's probably done. Grilling is hot and fast.

Our preference is to use charcoal for grilling, as it burns a bit hotter than gas and puts a nicer crust on steaks and chops. To put a good crust on foods, especially grilled meats, you must use enough charcoal. Because heat is so important, we prefer irregularly shaped chunks of lump hardwood charcoal to pillow-shaped briquettes when grilling. Hardwood charcoal burns a bit hotter than briquettes and is well suited to this kind of outdoor cooking. That said, briquettes will work fine for our recipes. However, do not use Match Light charcoal or other brands that contain lighter fluids. We find they can give delicate foods an off flavor. In any case, if you use a chimney starter (see the illustration on page 289), charcoal will light reliably with just one piece of newspaper and a single match.

Although charcoal is our preference, we know that gas is convenient to use. All the

THREE TYPES OF CHARCOAL FIRES

BUILDING A SINGLE-LEVEL FIRE

Once the lit charcoal is in the grill, the coals can be arranged in an even layer to create a single-level fire. This kind of fire delivers even heat and is best for quick searing at a moderate temperature.

BUILDING A TWO-LEVEL FIRE

Another option is to build a two-level fire, which permits searing over very hot coals and slower cooking over cooler coals to cook through thicker cuts. To build a two-level fire, spread some of the lit coals in a single layer over half of the grill. Leave the remaining coals in a pile that rises to within 2 or 2½ inches of the cooking grate. If necessary, add unlit charcoal on the hot side of the grill. Wait 10 minutes or so for these coals to heat.

BUILDING A MODIFIED TWO-LEVEL FIRE

When we build a two-level fire, we generally follow the method outlined in the drawing to the left. With foods that are susceptible to burning but require a long cooking time (such as chicken breasts), we sometimes build a modified two-level fire. We pile all the lit coals in half the grill to create a hot place for searing, leaving the remaining portion of the grill empty. Some heat from the coals will still cook foods placed over the empty part of the grill, but the heat is gentle, and little browning will occur here. We often cover foods on the cool part of the grill with a disposable aluminum pan to trap heat and create an ovenlike cooking environment (see page 294). We also build a modified two-level fire when we want to grill a small piece of meat (such as a flank steak) over an intense fire. By piling the coals in just half the grill, we use relatively little charcoal but still get a very hot fire.

recipes in this book are written for a charcoal grill but have also been tested on a gas grill. You may need to add a minute or two to the cooking times if using gas.

Grilling over gas requires slightly different (but similar) procedures. We find that gas grills work best with the lid down in all instances. Gas flames put out less heat than a charcoal fire, and foods won't brown properly if the lid is left open. Because gas burns cleanly, soot does not build up on the inside of the lid, so foods cooked in a covered gas grill are not in danger of picking up an off flavor.

However, when grilling with charcoal, we always leave the cover off because, over time and unlike with gas grills, soot and resinous compounds can build up on the inside of a kettle grill lid, which can then impart an off flavor, reminiscent of stale smoke, to the food. This effect is most noticeable in fish and poultry. When we want to trap heat on an open charcoal grill to make sure the food cooks

LIGHTING A CHARCOAL FIRE

Our favorite way to start a charcoal fire is with a chimney starter, also known as a flue starter. To use this simple device, fill the bottom section with crumpled newspaper, set the starter on the grill grate, and fill the top with charcoal. (Most starters can hold about 6 quarts of charcoal.) When you light the newspaper, flames shoot up through the charcoal, igniting it. When the coals are burning and covered with a layer of gray ash, dump them onto the grate and arrange according to one of the illustrations on page 288.

through, we prefer to cover it with a disposable aluminum roasting pan or pie plate.

Whether cooking on charcoal or gas, using the right level of heat is imperative. To make our recipes easy to follow, we have devised a system that quantifies the heat level by measuring the amount of time you can comfortably hold your hand above the cooking grate (see page 291 for details). If you use this system, the cooking times in our recipes will be excellent guidelines. However, we always recommend that you test foods often on the grill.

Grilling over a live fire is not like cooking in a precisely calibrated oven. Be prepared to adjust the timing, especially if grilling in cool or windy weather. An instant-read thermometer is the best way to gauge the progress of most foods on the grill. The other option is to remove a test piece and peek into the food with the tip of a knife.

GRILLED CHICKEN BREASTS

IN TODAY'S INCREASINGLY HEALTH-conscious world, people are eating chicken more often without the skin. In addition to being low in fat, boneless and skinless chicken breasts are convenient (they require no preparation) and quick cooking. For these reasons, the popularity of grilled chicken breasts has rocketed in the past few years. All too often, however, the chicken comes off the grill dry and overcooked because it lacks the protective layer of skin to moisten it. We wanted moist, juicy chicken with a good hit of smoke from the grill.

Our preferred method when dealing with chicken breasts is to brine them in a salt solution to keep them from drying out while cooking. However, brining adds at least 45 minutes to the preparation time, so we sought an alternate (and faster) method for keeping the chicken moist.

Our initial thought was to coat the breasts liberally with oil, hoping it would act like skin and keep the outer surface of the meat from drying out. The method seemed to work, but dousing the breasts with oil seemed to negate the health benefits of removing the skin in the first place. Next, we considered using some sort of glaze as a protective coating. After experimentation, we found that glazes did prevent the chicken from drying out. Normally we recommend adding the glaze to grilled foods at the end of the cooking process, but we found that because the breasts took so little time to cook, we could glaze them before they went on the grill. This not only protected the chicken throughout the cooking process but also added significant flavor. We glazed the chicken again as it cooked.

As for the glaze itself, many tasters liked a variation made with orange juice concentrate and grated ginger. It had, however, one drawback. Some felt the orange juice concentrate (which we had chosen for its viscosity) tasted slightly artificial. We tried replacing the concentrate with fresh juice. While the glaze tasted much better, the juice was too thin and failed to achieve a thick, glossy glaze. By simmering the orange juice on a burner while the grill was heating, we managed to keep the fresh orange flavor without diluting the glaze. In addition to the orange juice and ginger, we added ground coriander and cayenne to boost

---

BUILDING BLOCK RECIPE

Grilled Chicken Breasts

SERVES 4

TIME: 40 MINUTES

To keep the breasts from drying out, brush them with a sticky, moist glaze, such as barbecue sauce. The tenderloins cause the meat to cook unevenly and are best removed before grilling. Freeze the tenderloins for later use in a stir-fry.

4   boneless, skinless chicken breasts
    (5 to 6 ounces each), tenderloins
    removed and reserved for
    another use
½   cup barbecue sauce or other
    sticky glaze
    Salt and ground black pepper

1. Light a large chimney starter filled with charcoal and allow it to burn until all the charcoal is covered with a layer of fine gray ash. Build a modified two-level fire by spreading all the coals evenly over half of the grill (see the illustration on page 288).

Set the cooking rack in place, cover the grill with the lid, and let the rack heat, about 5 minutes. Use a wire brush to scrape clean the cooking grate. The grill is ready when the coals are hot (see page 291 for information about taking the temperature of a grill fire).

2. Brush the chicken with half the sauce or glaze and season with salt and pepper to taste. Place the chicken breasts, smooth-side down, directly over the hot coals. Grill, uncovered, until the chicken is opaque about two-thirds up the sides and rich grill marks appear, 4 to 5 minutes. Brush with the remaining sauce or glaze and turn. Continue to cook until the chicken is fully cooked, 4 to 6 minutes. To test for doneness, peek into the thickest part of the chicken with the tip of a small knife (it should be opaque at the center) or check the internal temperature with an instant-read thermometer, which should register 160 degrees. Serve.

the flavor. Brown sugar finished our glaze and helped create a thick, sticky consistency.

To turn the chicken into a meal, we tested a variety of vegetables. Tasters preferred asparagus because it worked well with the orange glaze. Because asparagus grills in just minutes and holds well, we found it best to cook the spears before the chicken.

Grilled Chicken Breasts and Asparagus with Orange Glaze

SERVES 4

TIME: 50 MINUTES

The tenderloins cause the breasts to cook unevenly and are best removed before grilling. Freeze the tenderloins for later use in a stir-fry. If you like, add rice or the saffron couscous pilaf (page 93) to round out this meal.

1 ½	cups orange juice
1	tablespoon grated fresh ginger
½	teaspoon ground coriander
⅛	teaspoon cayenne pepper
2	tablespoons light brown sugar
1 ½	pounds asparagus, tough ends snapped off
1	tablespoon vegetable oil

Salt and ground black pepper

4   boneless, skinless chicken breasts (5 to 6 ounces each), tenderloins removed and reserved for another use

1. Light a large chimney starter filled with charcoal and allow it to burn until all the charcoal is covered with a layer of fine gray ash. Build a modified two-level fire by spreading all the coals evenly over half of the grill (see the illustration on page 288). Set the cooking rack in place, cover the grill with the lid, and let the rack heat, about 5 minutes. Use a wire brush to scrape clean the cooking grate. The grill is ready when the coals are hot (see below for information about taking the temperature of a grill fire).

2. Meanwhile, bring the orange juice, ginger, coriander, and cayenne to a boil in a medium saucepan over high heat. Reduce the heat to medium-high and simmer until the juice mixture is syrupy and reduced to ½ cup, 6 to 8 minutes. Transfer the juice mixture to a small bowl and stir in the brown sugar.

3. Toss the asparagus with the oil in a medium bowl or on a rimmed baking sheet and season with salt and pepper to taste. Grill directly over the hot coals, turning once, until

TAKING THE TEMPERATURE OF THE FIRE

Use the chart below to determine the intensity of the fire. The terms hot, medium-hot, medium, and medium-low are used throughout this chapter. When using a gas grill, ignore dial readings such as medium or medium-low in favor of actual measurements of the temperature, as described here.

INTENSITY OF FIRE	TIME YOU CAN HOLD YOUR HAND 5 INCHES ABOVE GRATE
Hot	2 seconds
Medium-hot	3 to 4 seconds
Medium	5 to 6 seconds
Medium-low	7 seconds

Once the coals are spread in the bottom of the grill, put the cooking grate in place and put the cover on for 5 minutes to heat the grate. (On gas grills, preheat with the lid down and all burners on high for 15 minutes.) Scrape the cooking grate clean and then take the temperature of the fire by holding your hand 5 inches above the cooking grate and counting how long you can comfortably leave it in place. If the fire is not hot enough, add more coals and wait 10 minutes for them to heat. If the fire is too hot, wait for the coals to cool slightly.

tender and streaked with grill marks, 4 to 5 minutes. Transfer to a serving platter and cover loosely with foil.

4. Brush the chicken with half the glaze and season with salt to taste. Place the chicken breasts, smooth-side down, directly over the hot coals. Grill, uncovered, until the chicken is opaque about two-thirds up the sides and rich grill marks appear, 4 to 5 minutes. Brush with the remaining glaze and turn. Continue to cook until the chicken is fully cooked, 4 to 6 minutes. To test for doneness, peek into the thickest part of the chicken with the tip of a small knife (it should be opaque at the center) or check the internal temperature with an instant-read thermometer, which should register 160 degrees. Transfer the chicken to the platter with the asparagus and serve immediately.

GRILLED TANDOORI-STYLE CHICKEN

TO MOST PEOPLE, TANDOORI CONJURES pieces of unnaturally red dyed chicken from local Indian restaurants. What they often don't realize is that *tandoori* is not a dish per se but a cooking device. A tandoor oven is a beehive-shaped structure that cooks both meats and breads at a very high temperature in a very short time. While not exactly a tandoor oven, the grill works on the same principles: high temperatures and short cooking times. Our goal was to replicate the flavors of tandoori chicken on our grill.

We were hoping to avoid the dry and flavorless chicken that arrives when you order tandoori chicken in many restaurants. We also wanted to flavor the chicken in the time that it took for the grill to heat, and we didn't want to use any exotic spices. During our research, we ran across many recipes that called for marinating the chicken in spiced yogurt from 6 to 24 hours. Marinating was not within the quick-cooking guidelines, however, so we choose to forgo it in favor of a dry spice rub.

Consulting the recipes we had gathered, we compiled a list of spices to try in our rub. The three flavors that topped the list were ginger, coriander, and cumin. Our initial attempt was to combine equal amounts of all three, but we found that the cumin was too aggressive and masked the other flavors. Reducing the cumin by half took care of this problem. After these three spices, the combinations were endless. After much testing, we chose turmeric for color and pungency, a small amount of cinnamon for sweetness, and a pinch of cayenne pepper for heat.

Once we had determined the makeup of the spice rub, we had to decide what type of chicken we wanted to use. A half-chicken was out of the question because of its long cooking time. Chicken legs and thighs worked well, but tasters felt that while the chicken meat was moist, it did not absorb enough flavor from the rub. Our next test was with boneless, skinless breasts. The result was the exact opposite of the legs: The breasts were well flavored but dry. Seeking the middle ground, we tried bone-in, skin-on chicken breasts, which turned out to be the answer. The skin protected the meat from drying out, and direct contact between the meat and rub was enough to give the chicken good flavor.

Tasters noticed that the tanginess normally associated with tandoori chicken was missing in our version. This was because we didn't marinate our chicken in yogurt. We decided instead to introduce the yogurt in the form of *raita*. A common Indian condiment, raita is a yogurt-based sauce served with a variety of foods. Mixing yogurt with garlic and cilantro provided a fresh and flavorful sauce that complemented the flavors in the spice rub.

Grilled Tandoori-Style Chicken Breasts with Raita

SERVES 4

TIME: 60 MINUTES

A simple cucumber salad rounds out the meal; basmati rice (see the pilaf recipe on page 114) is another option. We found the raita tastes much better with whole-milk yogurt, although low-fat yogurt can be used. Do not use nonfat yogurt; the sauce will be hollow-tasting and bland.

1	cup whole-milk yogurt
2	tablespoons chopped fresh cilantro leaves
1	medium clove garlic, minced or pressed through a garlic press (about 1 teaspoon)
	Salt and cayenne pepper
1	tablespoon grated fresh ginger

1	tablespoon ground coriander
1 ½	teaspoons ground cumin
1	teaspoon turmeric
½	teaspoon ground cinnamon
4	split chicken breasts, bone-in, skin-on, 10 to 12 ounces each

1. Light a large chimney starter filled with charcoal and allow it to burn until all the charcoal is covered with a layer of fine gray ash. Build a modified two-level fire by spreading the coals over half of the grill (see the illustration on page 288). Set the cooking rack in place, cover the grill with the lid, and let the rack heat, about 5 minutes. Use a wire brush to scrape clean the cooking grate. The grill is ready when the coals are hot (see page 291 for information about

---

BUILDING BLOCK RECIPE

Grilled Bone-In Chicken Breasts

SERVES 4

TIME: 50 MINUTES

This recipe is quite plain. Either coat the chicken with a spice rub before grilling or brush it with barbecue sauce or a sticky glaze during the last 2 minutes of grilling time.

4	split chicken breasts, bone-in, skin-on, 10 to 12 ounces each
	Salt and ground black pepper

1. Light a large chimney starter filled with charcoal and allow it to burn until all the charcoal is covered with a layer of fine gray ash. Build a modified two-level fire by spreading the coals over half of the grill (see the illustration on page 288). Set the cooking rack in place, cover the grill with the lid, and let the rack heat, about 5 minutes.

Use a wire brush to scrape clean the cooking grate. The grill is ready when the coals are hot (see page 291 for information about taking the temperature of a grill fire).

2. Generously sprinkle both sides of the chicken breasts with salt and pepper to taste. Cook the chicken, uncovered, over the hotter part of the grill until well browned, 2 to 3 minutes per side. Move the chicken to the cooler side of the grill and cover with a disposable aluminum roasting pan (see the illustration on page 294); continue to cook, skin-side up, for 10 minutes. Turn and cook for 5 minutes more or until done. To test for doneness, either peek into the thickest part of the chicken with the tip of a small knife (you should see no redness near the bone) or check the internal temperature at the thickest part with an instant-read thermometer, which should register 160 degrees. Serve.

taking the temperature of a grill fire).

2. Meanwhile, mix the yogurt, cilantro, and garlic together in a medium bowl. Season with salt and cayenne pepper to taste and refrigerate until needed. Mix the ginger, coriander, cumin, turmeric, cinnamon, ½ teaspoon salt, and ¼ teaspoon cayenne together in a small bowl.

3. Coat both sides of the chicken breasts with the spice mixture. Cook the chicken, uncovered, over the hotter part of the grill until well browned, 2 to 3 minutes per side. Move the chicken to the cooler side of the grill and cover with a disposable aluminum roasting pan (see the illustration below); continue to cook, skin-side up, for 10 minutes. Turn and cook for 5 minutes more or until done. To test for doneness, either peek into the thickest part of the chicken with the tip of a small knife (you should see no redness near the bone) or check the internal temperature at the thickest part with an instant-read thermometer, which should register 160 degrees. Transfer to a serving platter. Serve immediately with the yogurt mixture.

GRILLING BONE-IN CHICKEN BREASTS

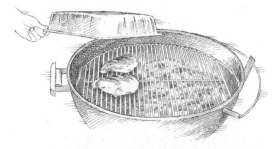

Covering chicken breasts with a disposable aluminum roasting pan while they cook on a charcoal grill creates an oven-like effect that speeds grilling but still allows air to circulate. Do not use the grill cover; built-up soot on the inside of the cover can give the chicken an off flavor.

HOISIN-GLAZED CHICKEN LEGS WITH ASIAN SLAW

GO TO ANY COMPANY PICNIC OR backyard barbecue and you are almost guaranteed to see two foods: chicken and coleslaw. Smoky grilled chicken covered with a spicy-sweet glaze and paired with crispy-crunchy slaw is a great combination. We wanted to put an Asian spin on the tomato-based barbecue sauces and sweet slaw dressings that are the norm.

The challenge in making barbecue sauce is finding a balance of flavors without a long list of ingredients. For the base of our sauce, we choose hoisin sauce. Because it already contains soy sauce, chiles, garlic, and other spices, hoisin sauce offers variety and depth of flavor. We added rice vinegar for acidity and brightness and minced ginger and Asian chili paste for pungency and heat. For spices, we chose five-spice powder. Chinese five-spice powder is a blend of cinnamon, fennel, peppercorns, star anise, and cloves; like the hoisin, it allowed us to gain depth of flavor from a single ingredient.

For the slaw, we wanted the crispiness of a traditional slaw, but a lighter, less sweet dressing than the typical mayonnaise-based dressing. Our initial thought was to take a little bit of the sauce for the chicken and perhaps thin it with water or oil. The result was disastrous, however. The dressing was too heavy, and the raw spices gave it a chalky mouthfeel. Not wanting to complicate the recipe with any more ingredients, we instead made a separate dressing based on a few of the sauce ingredients. Combining rice vinegar, ginger, and soy sauce with oil, we made a quick, simple dressing without expanding our ingredient list. We chose napa cabbage over regular green cabbage because it was lighter in texture and blended better with the Asian ingredients.

Hoisin-Glazed Grilled Chicken Legs with Napa Cabbage Slaw

SERVES 4

TIME: 60 MINUTES

Although this dish makes a fairly complete meal, you could add rice. If you prefer, replace the 4 whole legs with either 8 drumsticks or 8 bone-in, skin-on thighs and reduce the cooking time by several minutes.

½	small head napa cabbage (about ¾ pound), halved through the core end, tough core removed, and cut crosswise into ⅛-inch strips (about 4 cups)
1	medium red bell pepper, stemmed, seeded, and cut into thin strips
4	tablespoons rice vinegar
2	tablespoons soy sauce
3	teaspoons minced fresh ginger
¼	cup vegetable oil
⅓	cup hoisin sauce
1	tablespoon Asian chili paste
¼	teaspoon five-spice powder
4	whole chicken legs, trimmed of overhanging fat and skin

1. Light a large chimney starter filled with charcoal and allow it to burn until all the charcoal is covered with a layer of fine gray ash. Build a two-level fire by stacking most of

---

BUILDING BLOCK RECIPE

Grilled Chicken Legs

SERVES 4

TIME: 50 MINUTES

This recipe is quite plain. Either coat the chicken with a spice rub before grilling or brush it with barbecue sauce or a sticky glaze during the last 2 minutes of grilling time. To prevent flare-ups, make sure to trim excess fat or skin before the chicken goes onto the grill.

4	whole chicken legs, trimmed of overhanging fat and skin
	Salt and ground black pepper

1. Light a large chimney starter filled with charcoal and allow it to burn until all the charcoal is covered with a layer of fine gray ash. Build a two-level fire by stacking most of the coals on one side of the grill and arranging the remaining coals in a single layer on the other side of the grill (see the illustration on page 288). Set the cooking rack in place, cover the grill with the lid, and let the rack heat, about 5 minutes. Use a wire brush to scrape clean the cooking grate. The grill is ready when the temperature of the stacked coals is medium-hot and that of the remaining coals is medium-low (see page 291 for information about taking the temperature of a grill fire).

2. Generously sprinkle the chicken with salt and pepper to taste. Cook the chicken, uncovered, over the hotter part of the grill until seared, about 2 to 3 minutes on each side. Move the chicken to the cooler part of the grill; continue to grill, uncovered, turning occasionally, until dark and fully cooked, 12 to 16 minutes. To test for doneness, either peek into the thickest part of the chicken with the tip of a small knife (you should see no redness near the bone) or check the internal temperature at the thickest part with an instant-read thermometer, which should register 165 degrees. Serve.

the coals on one side of the grill and arranging the remaining coals in a single layer on the other side of the grill (see the illustration on page 288). Set the cooking rack in place, cover the grill with the lid, and let the rack heat, about 5 minutes. Use a wire brush to scrape clean the cooking grate. The grill is ready when the temperature of the stacked coals is medium-hot and that of the remaining coals is medium-low (see page 291 for information about taking the temperature of a grill fire).

2. Meanwhile, toss the cabbage and bell pepper in a large bowl and set aside. For the dressing, whisk together 2 tablespoons vinegar, 1½ tablespoons soy sauce, 1½ teaspoons ginger, and the oil in a medium bowl until smooth. For the hoisin glaze, mix the remaining 2 tablespoons vinegar, remaining ½ tablespoon soy sauce, and remaining 1½ teaspoons ginger in a small bowl with the hoisin sauce, chili paste, and five-spice powder.

3. Cook the chicken, uncovered, over the hotter part of the grill until seared, about 2 to 3 minutes on each side. Move the chicken to the cooler part of the grill; continue to grill, uncovered, turning occasionally, until dark and fully cooked, 12 to 16 minutes. To test for doneness, either peek into the thickest part of the chicken with the tip of a small knife (you should see no redness near the bone) or check the internal temperature at the thickest part with an instant-read thermometer, which should register 165 degrees.

4. During the last 2 minutes of cooking, brush the chicken with the hoisin glaze. Cook about 1 minute, turn the chicken over, brush it again, and cook 1 minute more. Transfer the chicken to a serving platter. Rewhisk the dressing and toss with the cabbage. Serve the chicken immediately, with the slaw passed separately at the table.

GRILLED FLANK STEAK WITH CHIMICHURRI SAUCE

THE ONLY NATION THAT RIVALS THE Unites States in consumption and production of beef is Argentina. The pampas of that country, vast fertile plains similar to the Great Plains in the United States, provide a plentiful area in which to raise livestock and are virtually devoid of humans other than the gauchos who tend the cattle. One of the favorite local dishes is *churrasco,* which is beef roasted on a spit over coals and served with various condiments. *Chimichurri* is a sauce that often accompanies grilled beef. Similar to a pesto but looser in consistency and based on parsley rather than basil, chimichurri is a flavorful addition to grilled steak, and it can be made in the time that it takes to heat the grill.

We did a bit of research to get a better understanding of chimichurri and how it should be served, and we rounded up almost a dozen recipes. Although the basic technique used in most of the recipes was the same (make a paste with garlic and fresh herbs and then add an acidic component and oil), the choice of ingredients varied greatly.

Because this sauce is based on fresh herbs, we felt the choice of herbs was the best place to start our testing. A majority of recipes called for parsley, while others called for cilantro, oregano, or some combination of the three. We quickly found that the sauces made with just oregano or cilantro did not work. Both herbs were too strong and overpowered the other ingredients in the dish. Parsley was the clear winner in our testing. Its freshness and grassy notes worked perfectly with the other ingredients without being overbearing. We also tried combinations of the herbs and found that for cilantro and oregano not to overpower the dish, they had to be used in such small amounts that it was not worth the bother.

The acid was the next ingredient we addressed. Most recipes called for vinegar, although several called for lemon juice. The recipes made with white distilled or cider vinegar were jaw-numbingly tart, and we quickly dismissed them. Lemon juice fared a little better, but some tasters felt its bright flavor clashed with the parsley. The recipes with red or white wine vinegar performed the best. The sharp, clean flavors of the wine vinegars heightened the freshness of the sauce. In the end, we favored red wine vinegar over white because of its greater complexity.

The options for the other flavorings in the sauce were wide open. Garlic was by far the most common ingredient in the recipes we researched. The amount, however, ran the gamut of one to eight cloves. After several trials, we found that five medium cloves gave a healthy garlic bite. A lot of recipes also called for fresh or dried chiles. Trying both, we found that, in conjunction with the raw garlic, the fresh chiles were incendiary. Dried chiles worked better by adding subtle heat, but in large quantities they were too spicy. In the end, we settled on just ¼ teaspoon hot pepper flakes to round out the dish.

To finish the meal, we grilled red onions; their sweetness was a good balance to the sharp sauce and rich meat.

Grilled Flank Steak and Red Onions with Chimichurri Sauce

SERVES 4

TIME: 55 MINUTES

This dish can be served with bread, rice, or potatoes. It can also be served with other grilled vegetables, including zucchini or eggplant.

1	cup packed fresh parsley leaves
5	medium cloves garlic, peeled
½	cup plus 1 tablespoon extra-virgin olive oil
¼	cup red wine vinegar
¼	teaspoon hot red pepper flakes
	Salt and ground black pepper
1	large red onion (about 12 ounces), cut into ½-inch-thick rounds
1	flank steak (2 to 2½ pounds)

1. Light a large chimney starter filled with charcoal and allow it to burn until all the charcoal is covered with a layer of fine gray ash. Build a modified two-level fire by spreading the coals over half of the grill (see the

PREPARING ONIONS FOR THE GRILL

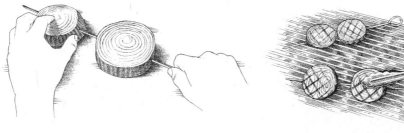

1. Cut thick slices from large onions and then skewer them all the way through with a slender bamboo skewer, about the same thickness as a toothpick, or a thin metal skewer.

2. The skewered onion slices remain intact as they are grilled. Even better, they can be flipped easily with tongs.

297

illustration on page 288). Set the cooking rack in place, cover the grill with the lid, and let the rack heat, about 5 minutes. Use a wire brush to scrape clean the cooking grate. The grill is ready when the coals are hot (see page 291 for information about taking the temperature of a grill fire).

2. Meanwhile, process the parsley and garlic in the workbowl of a food processor fitted with the steel blade, stopping as necessary to scrape down the sides of the bowl with a rubber spatula, until the ingredients are chopped fine; transfer the mixture to a medium bowl. Whisk in ½ cup oil, the vinegar, red pepper flakes, 1 teaspoon salt, and 2 tablespoons water until thoroughly blended.

3. Place the onion on a baking sheet; brush both sides lightly with the remaining 1 tablespoon oil and season with salt and pepper to taste. Thread the onion onto skewers (see the illustration on page 297).

4. Generously sprinkle both sides of the steak with salt and pepper to taste. Place the onion and steak directly over the hot coals. Grill the onion, turning once, until streaked with dark grill marks, 10 to 12 minutes. Grill the steak until well seared and dark brown on one side, 5 to 7 minutes. Using tongs, flip the steak; continue grilling on the other side until the interior of the meat is slightly less done than you want it to be when you eat it, 2 to 5 minutes more for rare or medium-rare (depending on the thickness of the steak and the heat of the fire).

5. Transfer the meat to a cutting board, cover loosely with foil, and let it rest for 5 minutes. Slice the steak very thinly on the bias against the grain; adjust the seasonings with salt and pepper to taste. Remove the onion from the skewers and separate the rings. Place the onion rings on a large platter and then arrange the meat over the onions. Serve immediately, passing the sauce at the table.

BUILDING BLOCK RECIPE
Grilled Flank Steak
SERVES 4

TIME: 50 MINUTES

Make sure to let the steak rest after grilling so the juices can redistribute themselves evenly throughout the meat. The meat will continue to cook a bit as it rests, so take the steak off the grill just before it's cooked to your liking.

I   flank steak (2 to 2½ pounds)
     Salt and ground black pepper

1. Light a large chimney starter filled with charcoal and allow it to burn until all the charcoal is covered with a layer of fine gray ash. Build a modified two-level fire by spreading the coals over half of the grill (see the illustration on page 288). Set the cooking rack in place, cover the grill with the lid, and let the rack heat, about 5 minutes. Use a wire brush to scrape clean the cooking grate. The grill is ready when the coals are hot (see page 291 for information about taking the temperature of a grill fire).

2. Generously sprinkle both sides of the steak with salt and pepper to taste. Place the steak directly over the hot coals. Grill the steak until well seared and dark brown on one side, 5 to 7 minutes. Using tongs, flip the steak; continue grilling on the other side until the interior of the meat is slightly less done than you want it to be when you eat it, 2 to 5 minutes more for rare or medium-rare (depending on the thickness of the steak and the heat of the fire).

3. Transfer the meat to a cutting board, cover loosely with foil, and let it rest for 5 minutes. Slice the steak very thinly on the bias against the grain; adjust the seasonings with salt and pepper to taste. Serve.

GRILLED STEAK AND POTATOES

NOTHING IS MORE COMFORTING THAN a perfectly grilled steak accompanied by potatoes. Normally, when steaks are grilled, the potatoes are baked or made into mayonnaise-based salad. What we wanted was meat and potatoes that could be cooked on the grill side by side. This seemingly easy task was more difficult than we expected.

We tackled first what would be the easiest part of this recipe: the steak. We found that strip steak had just the right ratio of fat to meat to make it flavorful and tender without drying out from the intense heat of the grill. After trying several thicknesses, we found that steaks in the range of 1¼ to 1½ inches thick were the best. We were able to get a deeply browned crust and a perfectly cooked center in a reasonably short period.

Grilling the potatoes, however, proved a little more difficult. Our initial thought was that we would simply slice potatoes, oil them lightly, and put them alongside the steaks on the grill. This did not work. No matter how thinly sliced they were or how long they remained on the grill, the potatoes always tasted slightly raw and had an unpleasant mealy texture. We realized that using partially cooked potatoes would avoid these problems.

Considering that we wanted this recipe to be quick and easy, our first thought was to buy potatoes in the freezer section of the grocery store. Most of these products are parcooked (normally in oil), so we figured they would grill up perfectly and we wouldn't have to spend time parboiling raw potatoes. Again, we were wrong. To keep the potatoes from falling through the cooking grid, we had to buy fairly large wedges. These wedges, even though they were partially cooked, still had a disagreeable oily taste and raw texture. We were going to have to blanch our own potatoes in water before we grilled them.

Slicing the potatoes into slabs, we covered them with water and gently simmered them until they just started to become tender, whereupon we drained them, tossed them with a little oil, and grilled them. This process yielded tasty potatoes that were better than any others we had tried. They actually tasted like potatoes and were fully cooked and creamy. We still had to tackle a bit of dryness and starchiness. Additionally, the large slabs tended to break apart when we coated them with oil, and some stuck to the grill.

Up to this point, we had been using russet potatoes because they can be cut into large slabs that are easy to grill. Wondering if a different variety of potato would change our results, we tried large Red Bliss potatoes. Because the Red Bliss potatoes had less starch and more moisture than the russets, they were creamier and less dry when fully cooked. They also could be cut slightly thicker without increasing their cooking time, which made grilling them more manageable. As for the slices sticking to the grill, we found that by laying the potato slices on an oiled baking sheet, we could evenly coat them with the necessary lubrication without risking broken slices that might result if we tossed the potatoes to coat them.

We opted for a compound butter to finish off our meat and potatoes. A flavored butter increased the richness of the meat and, as it melted, provided moisture and flavor. In this case, we chose to add blue cheese to the butter, feeling that its creamy bite would provide a nice contrast to the rich beefy steak. We didn't bother to roll and chill the compound butter, as is customary. Because the butter melts anyway, we did not want to take the time; instead, we spooned the softened butter mixture onto the cooked steaks.

Grilled Strip Steaks and Potatoes with Blue Cheese Butter

SERVES 4

TIME: 55 MINUTES

Watch the potatoes closely as they are blanching; it is important to take them out of the water before they are fully tender. Trying to grill potatoes that are already fully cooked is nearly impossible. See page 229 for more information about strip steaks.

2   pounds medium Red Bliss potatoes, scrubbed and cut crosswise into ½-inch-thick rounds
    Salt
2   tablespoons vegetable oil
    Ground black pepper
4   tablespoons unsalted butter, softened
3   tablespoons crumbled blue cheese
1   small shallot, minced (about 2 tablespoons)
1   small clove garlic, minced or pressed through a garlic press (about ½ teaspoon)
1   teaspoon chopped fresh parsley leaves
4   strip steaks, 1¼ to 1½ inches thick (12 to 16 ounces each)

1. Place the potatoes in a large pot. Cover with 1½ quarts cold water. Add 1 teaspoon salt and bring to a boil over high heat. Reduce the heat to medium and simmer until the potatoes are barely tender, about 6 minutes. Drain the potatoes in a colander, being careful not to break them. Transfer the potatoes to a baking sheet coated with 1 tablespoon oil. Drizzle the remaining 1 tablespoon oil over the potatoes and season with salt and pepper to taste.

2. While the potatoes are cooking, light a large chimney starter filled with charcoal and allow it to burn until all the charcoal is covered with a layer of fine gray ash. Build a two-level fire by stacking most of the coals on one side of the grill and arranging the remaining coals in a single layer on the other side of the grill (see the illustration on page 288). Set the cooking rack in place, cover the grill with the lid, and let the rack heat, about 5 minutes. Use a wire brush to scrape clean the cooking rack. The grill is ready when the temperature of the stacked coals is medium-hot and that of the remaining coals is medium-low (see page 291 for information about taking the temperature of a grill fire).

3. Meanwhile, beat the butter with a large fork in a medium bowl until light and fluffy. Add the cheese, shallot, garlic, parsley, ¼ teaspoon salt, and ⅛ teaspoon pepper.

4. Generously sprinkle both sides of the steaks with salt and pepper to taste. Cook them, uncovered, over the hotter part of the grill until well browned on one side, about 3 minutes. Turn the steaks; grill until well browned on the other side, 3 minutes. Once browned, move the steaks to the cooler part of the grill. Continue grilling, uncovered, to the desired doneness, 7 to 8 minutes more for rare (120 degrees on an instant-read thermometer), 9 to 10 minutes for medium-rare on the rare side (125 degrees), 11 to 12 minutes for medium-rare on the medium side (130 degrees), or 12 to 13 minutes for medium (135 to 140 degrees). Remove the steaks from the grill and let rest for 5 minutes.

5. Once the steaks are moved to the cooler part of the grill, place the potatoes on the hotter part. Cook, turning once, until grill marks appear and the potato slices are cooked through, 6 to 8 minutes.

6. To serve, place one steak and some of the potatoes on each plate. Top each steak with 2 tablespoons butter mixture and serve immediately.

Free-Form Beef Wellington

BEEF WELLINGTON IS ONE OF THOSE dishes we always envision being served on a silver platter by a waiter in a tuxedo and white gloves. This decadent beef tenderloin is topped with foie gras and mushrooms and then wrapped in pastry and baked. As such, beef Wellington isn't a dish that anyone would consider quick and simple—but, as the combination of flavors and texture is so appealing, we sought to update this classic and create our own version of beef Wellington on the grill.

Having made beef Wellington in the past, we wanted to avoid what we knew to be a common pitfall: cooking both the pastry and the beef properly. If the beef was well cooked, the pastry was soggy; if the pastry was light and flaky, the beef was overcooked. We found that by grilling the ingredients separately and assembling them afterward, we could avoid the problematic discrepancy in cooking times.

Traditionally, Wellington is made with filet mignon, a cut of beef that has little intramuscular fat, meaning it lacks the intense beefy flavor of a strip or rib-eye steak. We preferred it for a Wellington, however, because the milder steak allowed the other ingredients to show off. Filet mignon was the right choice

---

BUILDING BLOCK RECIPE

Grilled Strip Steaks

SERVES 4

TIME: 55 MINUTES

See page 229 for more information about strip steaks. Make sure to let the steaks rest after grilling so the juices can redistribute evenly throughout the meat. The meat will continue to cook a bit as it rests, so take the steaks off the grill just before they are cooked to your liking.

4   strip steaks, 1 1/4 to 1 1/2 inches thick
       (12 to 16 ounces each)
       Salt and ground black pepper

1. Light a large chimney starter filled with charcoal and allow it to burn until all the charcoal is covered with a layer of fine gray ash. Build a two-level fire by stacking most of the coals on one side of the grill and arranging the remaining coals in a single layer on the other side of the grill (see the illustration on page 288). Set the cooking rack in place, cover the grill with the lid, and let the rack heat, about 5 minutes. Use a wire brush to scrape clean the cooking rack. The grill is ready when the temperature of the stacked coals is medium-hot and that of the remaining coals is medium-low (see page 291 for information about taking the temperature of a grill fire).

2. Generously sprinkle both sides of the steaks with salt and pepper to taste. Cook the steaks, uncovered, over the hotter part of the grill until well browned on one side, about 3 minutes. Turn the steaks; grill until well browned on the other side, 3 minutes. Move the browned steaks to the cooler part of the grill. Continue grilling, uncovered, to the desired doneness, 7 to 8 minutes more for rare (120 degrees on an instant-read thermometer), 9 to 10 minutes for medium-rare on the rare side (125 degrees), 11 to 12 minutes for medium-rare on the medium side (130 degrees), or 12 to 13 minutes for medium (135 to 140 degrees). Remove the steaks from the grill and let rest for 5 minutes. Serve immediately.

after all. Grilling over a two-level fire was the best way to cook the steaks. This way, we were able to sear them over high heat for a flavorful crust and then move them to the cooler part of the grill to finish cooking. This arrangement was also perfect for the next part of our Wellington, the mushrooms.

Normally, Wellington contains mushroom *duxelles,* which are finely chopped mushrooms that have been slowly cooked in butter until they devolve into a paste. This method seemed impractical for our purposes, so we opted to grill portobello mushrooms instead. With the hot part of the fire free, we could grill the mushrooms quickly. We found that the portobellos were much tastier cooked over a hot fire than a cooler fire, where they tend to steam and won't brown.

The next step was preparing the foie gras—which we quickly decided not to do, mainly because it is so expensive but also because we were unsure how to grill it. Instead, we looked for alternative ingredients. We tried duck and chicken livers, but we found they were not meant for the grill due to their small size. Next, we tried several store-bought pâtés. Our innovative solution was to use duck liver pâté, which has a flavor similar to that of foie gras but is a lot less expensive and doesn't require cooking.

Spreading the pâté lightly on grilled bread (rather than pastry, which can't be grilled) and then topping it with slices of the portobello and steak completed our free-form Wellington. When assembled, however, it seemed a little dry. Without the time to make a proper reduction sauce, which usually accompanies beef Wellington, we decided to abbreviate the process. By reducing red wine and port with shallots and thyme until they reached a syrupy consistency, we made a sauce that enhanced the flavors of our Wellington as well as provided welcome moisture.

Free-Form Beef Wellington with Port Syrup

SERVES 4

TIME: 60 MINUTES

This recipe calls for three steaks but feeds four people. We found that four 8-ounce steaks, when served with the pâté and mushrooms, was simply too rich.

1 ½	cups ruby port
1 ½	cups red wine
1	teaspoon whole fresh thyme leaves
1	small shallot, minced (about 2 tablespoons)
3	filet mignon steaks, about 2 inches thick (8 ounces each), patted dry
2	tablespoons olive oil
	Salt and ground black pepper
4	large portobello mushroom caps (each 4 inches in diameter)
4	slices country bread (each 5 inches across and ½ inch thick)
4	ounces smooth duck liver pâté

1. Light a large chimney starter filled with charcoal and allow it to burn until all the charcoal is covered with a layer of fine gray ash. Build a two-level fire by stacking most of the coals on one side of the grill and arranging the remaining coals in a single layer on the other side of the grill (see the illustration on page 288). Set the cooking rack in place, cover the grill with the lid, and let the rack heat, about 5 minutes. Use a wire brush to scrape clean the cooking grate. The grill is ready when the temperature of the stacked coals is medium-hot and that of the remaining coals is medium-low (see page 291 for information about taking the temperature of a grill fire).

2. Meanwhile, bring the port, red wine, thyme, and shallot to a boil in a medium saucepan over high heat. Reduce the heat to medium and simmer until the mixture thickens

and is reduced to ½ cup, about 15 minutes.

3. Lightly rub the steaks with 1 tablespoon oil and sprinkle with salt and pepper to taste. Brush the portobellos with the remaining 1 tablespoon oil and season with salt and pepper to taste.

4. Cook the steaks, uncovered, over the hotter part of the fire until well browned on one side, 2 to 3 minutes. Turn the steaks; grill until well browned on the other side, 2 to 3 minutes. Move the browned steaks to the cooler part of the grill. Continue grilling, uncovered, to the desired doneness, 7 to 8 minutes for rare (120 degrees on an instant-read thermometer), 8 to 9 minutes for medium-rare on the rare side (125 degrees), 10 to 11 minutes for medium-rare on the medium side (130 degrees), or 11 to 12 minutes for medium (135 to 140 degrees). Allow the steaks to rest for 5 minutes.

5. Once the steaks are moved, set the mushrooms over the hotter coals. Grill, turning once, until tender and lightly browned, 8 to 10 minutes. Transfer the mushrooms to a platter and cover with foil. After both the steaks and the mushrooms are removed from the grill, set the bread over the cooler part of the grill and toast until golden brown on both sides, 1 to 1½ minutes.

6. To assemble: Spread 1 ounce pâté over each piece of grilled bread. Slice the mushrooms into wide strips and arrange them uniformly over the bread. Cut the beef into ¼-inch-thick strips and place some on top of the mushrooms. Drizzle with the port syrup and serve immediately.

GRILLED PORK CHOPS

INEVITABLY, GRILLED PORK CHOPS seem dry. This is, in part, because pork is bred to have so little fat that no matter how it is cooked, it tends to be dry. Because of this, we would normally brine the pork in a salt solution before cooking, but brining and quick cooking are incompatible. We wanted to figure out how to get moist chops without spending extra time brining.

The thickness of the chop played a big role in our testing. We tried pork chops of varying thickness. The thin chops (under ¾ inch) turned out overcooked and desert-dry by the time they developed an attractive and well-seared exterior. With thicker chops (over 1½ inches), we found that by the time the pork was cooked medium-rare on the inside, it was burned on the outside. The chops of medium thickness (1 inch) proved best. We were able to prepare them with a well-caramelized exterior and a moist interior.

Choosing the right chop (see left for details) also made a big difference. With their extra fat, rib loin chops easily won our test kitchen tasting.

As for accompaniments, we knew that the sweetness of fruit complements pork nicely. The fruit would also add moisture to the

RIB VERSUS CENTER-CUT PORK CHOPS

We tested four kinds of chops on the grill; tasters preferred the rib loin chop. Don't confuse this cut with a center-cut chop, which also comes from the loin. In some markets, both of these are simply labeled "loin chop." To keep them straight, remember that a bone runs through the center-cut chop (left), while the bone runs along the side of the rib chop (right).

CENTER-CUT CHOP   RIB CHOP

chops. Apples were our first choice, but because most grilling is enjoyed during the summer, apples did not seem to be the right fruit for this recipe. Our second choice was peaches. At the peak of ripeness in the summer, peaches were excellent grilled alongside the pork. Loaded with natural sugar, peaches became nicely browned and caramelized on the grill.

Even with the peaches as an accompaniment, the recipe needed something more. We considered coating the pork with a spice rub before grilling, but many of the rubs didn't pair well with the peaches. We had the same problem with marinades. Then we considered vegetables that would pair well with both the pork and the peaches. The sweetness of peppers and onions was too similar to the pork and the peaches. Something more bitter would be better for contrast. While normally used in its raw state, radicchio is excellent on the grill, with a mildly bitter and smoky flavor. The leaves become slightly crisp and they are, indeed, a perfect contrast to the pork and peaches in both taste and texture. A bit of balsamic vinaigrette drizzled over the dish added extra moisture and flavor contrast.

PREPARING RADICCHIO

Remove any brown outer leaves. Cut the radicchio in half through the core. Cut each half again through the core to make four wedges.

Grilled Pork Chops with Peaches, Radicchio, and Balsamic Vinaigrette

SERVES 4

TIME: 55 MINUTES

Use ripe but not mushy peaches in this recipe. Don't bother grilling hard peaches; they will be mealy and unappetizing. Nectarines may be substituted for the peaches. See page 303 for more information about buying pork chops.

I	tablespoon balsamic vinegar
7	tablespoons extra-virgin olive oil
I	small shallot, minced (about 2 tablespoons)
	Salt and ground black pepper
4	bone-in rib loin pork chops, each I inch thick (about 8 ounces each)
2	small peaches, halved and pitted
2	small heads radicchio, cut into quarters with core intact (see the illustration at left)

1. Light a large chimney starter filled with charcoal and allow it to burn until all the charcoal is covered with a layer of fine gray ash. Build a two-level fire by stacking most of the coals on one side of the grill and arranging the remaining coals in a single layer on the other side of the grill (see the illustration on page 288). Set the cooking rack in place, cover the grill with the lid, and let the rack heat, about 5 minutes. Use a wire brush to scrape clean the cooking grate. The grill is ready when the temperature of the stacked coals is medium-hot and that of the remaining coals is medium-low (see page 291 for information about taking the temperature of a grill fire).

2. Meanwhile, whisk together the vinegar, 4 tablespoons oil, shallot, ¼ teaspoon salt, and a pinch of pepper in a small bowl until smooth. Lightly rub the chops with 1 tablespoon oil

and season with salt and pepper to taste. Brush the peaches with 2 teaspoons oil and season with salt and pepper to taste. Brush the radicchio with the remaining 4 teaspoons oil and season with salt and pepper to taste.

3. Cook the chops, uncovered, over the hotter part of the grill until browned, about 3 minutes on each side. Move the chops to the cooler side of the grill and cover with a disposable aluminum roasting pan. Continue grilling, turning once, until an instant-read thermometer inserted through the side of the chop and away from the bone registers 130 degrees, 4 to 6 minutes longer. Transfer the chops to a platter, cover with the foil pan, and let rest about 5 minutes.

4. Once the chops are moved, place the peach halves, skin-side up, on the hotter part of the grill. Cook until well caramelized, 3 to 4 minutes. Turn and continue to cook until slightly softened, about 3 minutes more. Transfer the peaches to the platter with the chops.

5. Place the radicchio on the hotter part of the grill. Cook, turning every 1½ minutes, until the edges are browned and wilted but the center remains slightly firm, about 4½ minutes total. Transfer the radicchio to the platter with the pork and peaches.

6. Rewhisk the balsamic vinaigrette and drizzle it over the pork, peaches, and radicchio. Serve immediately.

BUILDING BLOCK RECIPE

Grilled Pork Chops

SERVES 4

TIME: 55 MINUTES

We find that rib loin chops (see the illustration on page 303) are the best choice for grilling. As with chicken breasts, we find that pork chops are best seared over the hot coals and then moved to a cooler part of the grill and covered with a disposable roasting pan to finish cooking (see the illustration on page 294).

4   bone-in rib loin pork chops, each 1
    inch thick (about 8 ounces each)
1   tablespoon extra-virgin olive oil
    Salt and ground black pepper

1. Light a large chimney starter filled with charcoal and allow it to burn until all the charcoal is covered with a layer of fine gray ash. Build a two-level fire by stacking most of the coals on one side of the grill and arranging the remaining coals in a single layer on the other side of the grill (see the illustration on page 288). Set the cooking rack in place, cover the grill with the lid, and let the rack heat, about 5 minutes. Use a wire brush to scrape clean the cooking grate. The grill is ready when the temperature of the stacked coals is medium-hot and that of the remaining coals is medium-low (see page 291 for information about taking the temperature of a grill fire).

2. Lightly rub the chops with the oil and season with salt and pepper to taste. Cook the chops, uncovered, over the hotter part of the grill until browned, about 3 minutes on each side. Move the chops to the cooler side and cover with a disposable aluminum roasting pan. Continue grilling, turning once, until an instant-read thermometer inserted through the side of the chop and away from the bone registers 130 degrees, 4 to 6 minutes longer. Transfer the chops to a platter, cover with the foil pan, and let rest about 5 minutes. Serve immediately.

CARIBBEAN–STYLE GRILLED PORK TENDERLOIN

JAMAICAN JERK HAS BECOME POPULAR in all kinds of restaurants. This highly spiced seasoning mix is the perfect rub to use on meat destined for the grill. However, matters have recently taken a turn for the worse. On many menus, what passes as "Jamaican jerk" is nothing more than a powdery spice mix lacking depth or character. We did a bit of research in an effort to develop a true jerk spice rub for pork tenderloin. Our research turned up the surprising fact that the best kind of jerk seasonings were wet rubs—not the more common dry variety, with its unpleasant chalky aftertaste.

Chiles, usually Scotch bonnets, were common to most of the seasoning mixes we uncovered in our research. While extremely hot, these chiles added floral undertones to the pork, and tasters favored them over milder jalapeños. Dry thyme was also an ingredient found in most traditional recipes. We favored fresh thyme, however, and appreciated the citrusy flavor it added to the rub. As for aromatics, a lot of the recipes called for onions and garlic. Tasters liked the bite of garlic but felt that onion, even in small amounts, was too strong. We went with scallion for milder allium flavor.

The spices used in the various Jamaican jerk recipes include cinnamon, nutmeg, cloves, and allspice. After several tests, we found that allspice was neither too sweet nor too strong. To our best rub we also added lime juice for brightness and brown sugar to help the flavors adhere to the pork and to create a well-browned crust.

We thought a sauce or relish to accompany the Jamaican jerk would make the dish a little more interesting. During our research, we discovered that several of the recipes were served with a fruit salsa or relish. Most of these accompaniments garnished the meat, and their sweet tropical flavors toned down the heat of the chiles. We tried several types of fruit salsas featuring bananas, mango, and papaya. Most tasters liked the sweet-tart flavor and firm texture of papaya better than mango, which has a somewhat stringy texture, and bananas, which are mushy. We mixed a little bit of lime juice and scallions into the papaya and created a simple, flavorful relish with hardly any extra time, energy, or ingredients.

Caribbean-Style Grilled Pork Tenderloin with Papaya Salsa

SERVES 4

TIME: 55 MINUTES

Serve this Caribbean-inspired dish with rice or, better yet, plantains. If you cannot find a papaya, two ripe mangoes are a suitable alternative.

1	medium Scotch bonnet or habanero chile, stemmed, seeded, and minced (about 1 teaspoon)
4	medium scallions, white and green parts, minced
1½	teaspoons chopped fresh thyme leaves
2	large cloves garlic, minced or pressed through a garlic press (about 2 teaspoons)
1	tablespoon grated zest plus 1 tablespoon juice from 1 lime
1	tablespoon light brown sugar
2	tablespoons olive oil
	Pinch ground allspice
2	pork tenderloins (about 1 pound each), trimmed of silver skin (see illustration 1 on page 238)
	Salt
1	ripe papaya, peeled, halved, seeded, and cut into ¼-inch dice

1. Light a large chimney starter filled with charcoal and allow it to burn until all the charcoal is covered with a layer of fine gray ash. Build a modified two-level fire by spreading all of the coals on half of the grill (see the illustration on page 288). Set the cooking rack in place, cover the grill with the lid, and let the rack heat, about 5 minutes. Use a wire brush to scrape clean the cooking grate. The grill is ready when the coals are hot (see page 291 for information about taking the temperature of a grill fire).

2. Meanwhile, mix half the chile and half the scallions with the thyme, garlic, lime zest, sugar, oil, and allspice in a medium bowl. Rub the tenderloins with the spice mixture and season with salt to taste. Mix the papaya, remain-ing chile and scallions, lime juice, and ¼ tea-spoon salt in a small bowl. Set the salsa aside.

3. Cook the tenderloins, uncovered, directly over the hot coals until browned on all four sides, about 2½ minutes on each side. Move the tenderloins to the cooler side and cover with a disposable aluminum roasting pan. Grill, turning once, until an instant-read thermometer inserted in the thickest part of the tenderloin registers 145 degrees, or until the meat is slightly pink at the center when cut with a paring knife, 2 to 3 minutes. Transfer the tenderloins to a cutting board, cover with the disposable aluminum pan, and let rest about 5 minutes. Slice crosswise into 1-inch-thick pieces and serve imme-diately with the papaya salsa.

BUILDING BLOCK RECIPE

Grilled Pork Tenderloin

SERVES 4

TIME: 55 MINUTES

Grilled pork tenderloin is best coated with a spice rub before grilling and then served with a juicy salsa.

2 pork tenderloins (about 1 pound each), trimmed of silver skin (see illustration 1 on page 238)
   Salt and ground black pepper

1. Light a large chimney starter filled with charcoal and allow it to burn until all the charcoal is covered with a layer of fine gray ash. Build a modified two-level fire by spreading all of the coals on half of the grill (see the illustration on page 288). Set the cooking rack in place, cover the grill with the lid, and let the rack heat, about 5 minutes. Use a wire brush to scrape clean the cooking grate. The grill is ready when the coals are hot (see page 291 for infor-mation about taking the temperature of a grill fire).

2. Season the tenderloins with salt and pepper to taste. Cook the tenderloins, uncovered, directly over the hot coals until browned on all four sides, about 2½ min-utes on each side. Move the tenderloins to the cooler side and cover with a disposable aluminum roasting pan. Grill, turning once, until an instant-read thermometer inserted in the thickest part of the tender-loin registers 145 degrees, or until the meat is slightly pink at the center when cut with a paring knife, 2 to 3 minutes. Transfer the tenderloins to a cutting board, cover with the disposable aluminum pan, and let rest about 5 minutes. Slice cross-wise into 1-inch-thick pieces and serve immediately.

Grilled Lamb Chops with Mint

IN OUR EXPERIENCE, LAMB DOES VERY well on the grill. The hot fire renders the fat, and this flavorful fat helps keep the meat moist and tender. And what is better served with lamb than the classic mint sauce?

Our first decision was whether or not to introduce the mint flavor to the lamb before we started to cook it (in order to develop the most intense mint flavor)—and, if so, to identify the best way of doing this. In our first test, we made a quick marinade with olive oil, mint, and spices and grilled the lamb over a hot fire. This test nearly burned down the neighborhood. The oil in conjunction with

the lamb fat was too much. The constant flare-ups gave the lamb a resinous flavor completely devoid of mint. Our next attempt was to make a mint-flavored paste to rub into the chops before they went on the grill. We processed mint with a small amount of oil, which yielded a pestolike rub. While this technique yielded some mint flavor, it wasn't intense. It seemed that as the fat rendered from the chops drained away, so too did the rub and its mint flavor. It was obvious that we would be better off grilling the lamb plain and serving it with a separate mint sauce.

After several attempts at making a sauce, we found it better to have a small amount of a concentrated sauce rather than a thin, less intense but voluminous sauce. Seeking a

---

BUILDING BLOCK RECIPE

Grilled Lamb Chops

SERVES 4

TIME: 60 MINUTES

See page 310 for more information about loin and rib lamb chops. Lamb chops are prone to flare-ups, so keep a squirt bottle of water near the grill to extinguish any flames.

8   loin or rib lamb chops,
     1¼ to 1½ inches thick
1   tablespoon extra-virgin olive oil
     Salt and ground black pepper

1. Light a large chimney starter filled with charcoal and allow it to burn until all the charcoal is covered with a layer of fine gray ash. Build a two-level fire by stacking most of the coals on one side of the grill and arranging the remaining coals in a single layer on the other side of the grill (see the illustration on page 288). Set the cooking rack in place, cover the grill with the lid,

and let the rack heat, about 5 minutes. Use a wire brush to scrape clean the cooking rack. The grill is ready when the temperature of the stacked coals is medium-hot and that of the remaining coals is medium-low (see page 291 for information about taking the temperature of a grill fire).

2. Lightly rub the chops with the oil and season with salt and pepper to taste. Cook the chops, uncovered, over the hotter side of the grill, turning once, until well browned, about 4 minutes. (If the chops start to flame, drag them to the cooler side for a moment and/or extinguish the flames with a squirt bottle.) Move the chops to the cooler side and continue cooking, turning once, to the desired doneness, about 6 minutes for rare (120 degrees on an instant-read thermometer) or about 8 minutes for medium (130 degrees). Remove the chops from the grill and let rest for 5 minutes. Serve immediately.

consistency along the lines of a pesto, we processed mint leaves with olive oil and red wine vinegar. Although this worked fine, we felt several things could be improved upon. Some tasters commented that the red wine vinegar tasted too harsh. Replacing the vinegar with lemon juice rectified this problem, and the mint flavor was intensified. Some of us also felt that the sauce lacked depth, so we tempered the mint with chives and shallots, giving the sauce more complexity.

To make this a meal, tasters agreed, zucchini was the best choice. Its mild flavor let the lamb and mint take center stage. Eggplant was a close second in our testing and can be used if you prefer.

Grilled Lamb Chops and Zucchini with Mint Sauce

SERVES 4

TIME: 60 MINUTES

If you prefer, replace the zucchini with 3 small eggplants sliced the same way. See page 310 for more information about loin and rib lamb chops.

½   cup minced fresh mint leaves

2   tablespoons minced fresh chives

1   small shallot, minced (about 2 tablespoons)

2   tablespoons juice from 1 lemon

½   cup plus 3 tablespoons extra-virgin olive oil

     Salt and ground black pepper

8   loin or rib lamb chops, 1¼ to 1½ inches thick

3   medium zucchini (1¼ to 1½ pounds), trimmed and sliced lengthwise (see the illustrations below)

1. Light a large chimney starter filled with charcoal and allow it to burn until all the charcoal is covered with a layer of fine gray ash. Build a two-level fire by stacking most of the coals on one side of the grill and arranging the remaining coals in a single layer on the other side of the grill (see the illustration on page 288). Set the cooking rack in place, cover the grill with the lid, and let the rack heat, about 5 minutes. Use a wire brush to scrape clean the cooking rack. The grill is ready when

SLICING ZUCCHINI FOR THE GRILL

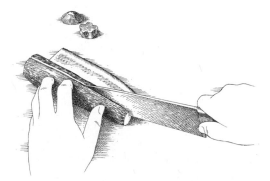

1. Cut a thin slice from each end of the zucchini. Slice the trimmed zucchini lengthwise into ½-inch-thick strips.

2. For aesthetic reasons, you may want to trim the peel from the outer slices so they match the others. (You can do the same thing with outer eggplant slices.) Besides developing more attractive grill marks, the flesh cooks better when directly exposed to the heat.

the temperature of the stacked coals is medium-hot and that of the remaining coals is medium-low (see page 291 for information about taking the temperature of a grill fire).

2. Meanwhile, stir together the mint, chives, shallot, lemon juice, ½ cup oil, and salt and pepper to taste in a medium bowl. Lightly rub the chops with 1 tablespoon oil and season with salt and pepper to taste. Lay the zucchini on a baking sheet and brush both sides of each slice with the remaining 2 tablespoons oil and season with salt and pepper to taste.

3. Cook the chops, uncovered, over the hotter side of the grill, turning once, until well browned, about 4 minutes. (If the chops start to flame, drag them to the cooler side for a moment and/or extinguish the flames with a squirt bottle.) Move the chops to the cooler side and continue cooking, turning once, to the desired doneness, about 6 minutes for rare (120 degrees on an instant-read thermometer)

or about 8 minutes for medium (130 degrees). Remove the chops from the grill and let rest for 5 minutes on a platter.

4. Once the chops are moved, place the zucchini over the hot coals. Grill, turning once, until streaked with dark grill marks, 8 to 10 minutes. Transfer the zucchini to the platter with the lamb. Spoon the mint sauce over the lamb and zucchini and serve immediately.

SHISH KEBAB

SHISH KEBAB IS THE ORIGINAL ONE-dish grill meal. Regrettably, most of the time little thought is given to the items on the skewers, and the result is a combination of raw meat and overcooked vegetables. Knowing we had to avoid this problem, we sought to develop a kebab with intense and interesting flavors, crisp-tender grilled vegetables, and tender meat.

Our first question was to identify the cut of lamb best suited for kebabs. Using meat from loin or rib chops was a waste of money, and it seemed foolish to turn these tender cuts into the small pieces required for the kebabs. Cuts from the shoulder were more economical and flavorful, but they often required cutting the meat from the bone before trimming and cubing, which is a time-consuming task. We finally settled on using the meat from the leg of the lamb. The cut was flavorful and inexpensive and required minimal trimming.

We tried two ways of introducing flavor to the meat. The first option was a dry spice rub. While this created flavorful meat, the lamb wasn't on the grill long enough for the juice to mix with the spices, so the exterior of the lamb was chalky. Our other option was a wet marinade, which seemed to do the trick. The marinade provided a layer of moisture that prevented the meat from drying out, and it also allowed the flavors to penetrate the meat more. We also learned

RIB AND LOIN LAMB CHOPS

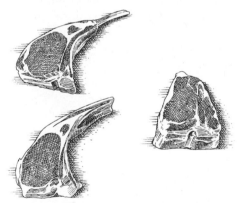

A rib chop (bottom left) often contains a lot of fat on the bone. Have your butcher french the chop (top left) by scraping away this fat. Like a T-bone steak, a loin chop (right) has meat on both sides of the bone. The small piece on the right side of the bone on this chop is very tender and fine-grained. The larger piece of meat on the other side of the bone is chewier. The rib chop has a slightly milder, more tender texture than a loin chop, which is a bit firmer (but not chewy). We found that both rib and loin chops do well on the grill.

that the marinade had to be intensely flavored because the actual marination time is so brief.

Because shish kebabs originated in the Middle East, many of the flavors in traditional shish kebab marinades reflect the cuisine of the region. Often, these marinades are herb pastes highly seasoned with aromatic spices and other flavorful ingredients, like ginger and garlic. We tried several marinades made with cilantro and parsley. The pastes with cilantro were too strong and tended to overpower the other flavors. Parsley, on the other hand, provided a great deal of freshness while allowing the other flavors to come through. Garlic was a logical choice, adding pungency and a mellow bite. Olive oil added moisture, while lemon juice contributed much-needed acidity.

Next, we added a small amount of raisins to the marinade. While this may seem odd, we found that the use of dried fruits in marinades sweetens the lamb and helps form a pleasant crust on the exterior of the meat. Choosing the spices for the marinade was difficult. In the end, we found that the Indian spice mixture garam masala was the best bet. This approach allowed us to enjoy a wide range of flavors, from sweet to spicy, without fussing with a long list of ingredients.

We finished the recipe by adding fresh figs to the skewers. Tasters wanted extra sweetness, and the figs softened beautifully over the fire.

Lamb and Fig Kebabs with Garlic-Parsley Marinade
SERVES 4 TO 6
TIME: 50 MINUTES

This recipe uses just half of the large red onion mentioned in the ingredient list. Don't try to use a whole small onion instead; it's easier to cut the large onion into pieces that skewer properly. Look for garam masala in the ethnic aisle of the supermarket or at an Indian market.

½	cup packed fresh parsley leaves
3	medium cloves garlic, peeled
¼	cup dark raisins
½	teaspoon garam masala
1 ½	tablespoons juice from 1 lemon
½	cup olive oil
	Salt and ground black pepper
1 ½	pounds boned meat from a leg of lamb, trimmed of fat and cut into 1-inch cubes
9	figs (about 1 pint), cut in half lengthwise
1	large red onion, prepared according to the illustrations below

PREPARING AN ONION FOR KEBABS

1. Trim away the stem and root end and cut the onion into quarters. Reserve two quarters for another use. Peel the three outer layers of the onion away from the inner core on the remaining two quarters. Discard the inner layers.

2. Working with the outer layers only, cut each quarter from pole to pole into 3 equal strips.

3. Cut each of the 6 strips crosswise into 3 pieces. You should have eighteen 3-layer stacks of separate pieces of onion.

311

1. Process the parsley, garlic, raisins, garam masala, lemon juice, oil, 1 teaspoon salt, and ⅛ teaspoon pepper in the workbowl of a food processor fitted with a steel blade until smooth, about 1 minute, stopping to scrape down the sides of the workbowl as needed. Toss the marinade with the lamb cubes in a large bowl and refrigerate.

2. Light a large chimney starter filled with charcoal and allow it to burn until all the charcoal is covered with a layer of fine gray ash. Build a single-level fire but spread the coals over just three-quarters of the grill (see the illustration on page 288). Set the cooking rack in place, cover the grill with the lid, and let the rack heat, about 5 minutes. Use a wire brush to scrape clean the cooking grate. The grill is ready when the coals are hot (see page 291 for information about taking the temperature of a grill fire).

3. After the lamb has marinated for at least 20 minutes, skewer the lamb on six 12-inch metal skewers. Thread each skewer with a cube of meat, followed by a piece of onion (three-layer stack) and a fig half. Repeat this order twice and end with a cube of lamb (each skewer should have 4 pieces of lamb, 3 pieces of onion, 3 fig halves). Brush any remaining marinade over the skewers.

4. Grill the kebabs directly over the coals, uncovered, turning each kebab one-quarter turn every 1¾ minutes, until the meat is well browned, grill-marked, and cooked to medium-rare, about 7 minutes. Transfer the kebabs to a platter and serve immediately.

GRILLED SALMON

SALMON IS PROBABLY THE EASIEST fish to grill. Its firm flesh is easy to handle and turn on the grill without falling apart. Salmon also contains a fair amount of natural oil, which makes it particularly attractive for grilling. This fattiness keeps the salmon from drying out while cooking, and it also reduces the chances of the fish sticking to the grill, which other fish tend to do. That same high fat content can also cause flare-ups, which can result in a resinous flavor and overly charred exterior. Our task was to intensify and complement the positive characteristics of the fish and find a suitable ingredient to grill alongside it, all the while keeping flare-ups under control.

As is true of many meats, salmon's high fat content makes it a great candidate for dry spice rubs. The oils that render from the fish combine with the spices to form a crisp crust; they add a great deal of flavor to the fish. We were fairly sure that salmon's richness would benefit from a spice rub that contrasted with its oiliness. This theory led us to search for slightly sweet spices. However, spices such as cinnamon, nutmeg, and cloves were quickly

OILING THE GRILL RACK

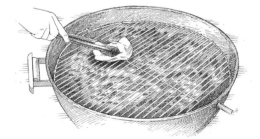

We find it helpful to oil the grill grate just before cooking fish, which is prone to stick. Dip a small wad of paper towels into vegetable oil, hold the wad with tongs, and wipe the grill rack thoroughly to lubricate it. Wiping the grill rack also cleans off any residue your wire brush may have missed. An impeccably clean grill is especially important when cooking fish, which can easily pick up off flavors.

excluded because in any significant amount they left the salmon with a powdery aftertaste. While using coriander and cumin seed allowed us to bulk up the spice rub, many of us felt that these flavors tasted too floral and didn't go well with the fish. Fennel seeds were our next attempt, and they turned out to be the right choice. The slight sweetness of the fennel complemented the salmon's oiliness without being candylike. Using whole fennel seeds allowed us to control both the texture and the intensity of the spice rub. Grated orange zest added both sweetness and bitterness to the rub, and hot red pepper flakes added heat. The final addition to the spice rub was sugar, which helped the rub stick to the fish and promoted caramelization. For this

purpose, tasters favored brown sugar over granulated sugar.

Our next task was to pick the right side dish for our salmon. We immediately thought of grilling fennel bulbs to mirror the flavors of the spice rub. When grilled, fennel becomes attractively browned, and its sweetness intensifies. Its crunchy texture also nicely complements the texture of the salmon. But grilling fennel proved tricky. It was a challenge to maximize the surface area of the fennel exposed to the grill while preventing the pieces from falling through the grill grate. In our initial attempt, we cut the fennel into wedges. While this kept the fennel from falling into the fire, the outside of the bulb became charred before the center was properly

---

BUILDING BLOCK RECIPE

Grilled Salmon Fillets

SERVES 4

TIME: 50 MINUTES

If the fillets are thicker than 1½ inches, extend the cooking time another minute or two when the salmon is flesh-side down. Make sure to keep a close eye on the salmon while grilling. If it is charring too much, move it to a cooler place on the grill.

4   center-cut salmon fillets, each 6 to 7 ounces and 1½ inches thick, pin bones removed (see the illustrations on page 261)
Salt and ground black pepper
Vegetable oil for the grill rack

1. Light a large chimney starter filled with charcoal and allow it to burn until all the charcoal is covered with a layer of fine gray ash. Build a single-level fire by spreading the coals evenly over the bottom of the

grill (see the illustration on page 288). Set the cooking rack in place, cover the grill with the lid, and let the rack heat, about 5 minutes. Use a wire brush to scrape clean the cooking grate. The grill is ready when the coals are medium-hot (see page 291 for information about taking the temperature of a grill fire).

2. Generously sprinkle the flesh of the salmon with salt and pepper to taste. Lightly dip a small wad of paper towels into vegetable oil. Holding the wad with tongs, wipe the grill rack (see the illustration on page 312). Place the fillets, skin-side down, on the grill. Grill, uncovered, until the skin shrinks, separates from the flesh, and blackens, 2 to 3 minutes. Gently flip the fillets with a metal spatula. Grill, uncovered, until the fillets are opaque almost throughout and translucent only at the very center, 3 to 4 minutes. Serve immediately.

cooked. We also tried to slice the cored fennel into rings, but by the time the rings were properly cooked, most of them had fallen into the fire. Our most successful attempt involved slicing the fennel vertically into slices without removing the core. The large surface area allowed us to pick up a lot of grill flavor, and the slices were fully cooked before becoming too dark. Leaving the core in the slices helped them hold together, so they didn't fall into the flames below.

As a finishing touch and in an effort to invigorate the dish with a quick sauce, we pulled the orange from our ingredient list and put it to work. Already providing the zest for the rub, the orange could contribute juice to form the basis of a sauce as well. By squeezing some of its juice and adding a bit of oil, shallot, and garlic, we made a simple citrus vinaigrette that moistened the salmon and the fennel and tied the flavors together.

Grilled Salmon and Fennel with Orange Vinaigrette

SERVES 4
TIME: 55 MINUTES

If the fillets are thicker than 1½ inches, extend the cooking time another minute or two when the salmon is flesh-side down. Make sure to keep a close eye on the salmon while grilling. If it is charring too much, move it to a cooler place on the grill. You will need a spice grinder (a coffee grinder is fine) for this recipe.

2   teaspoons fennel seeds
1   teaspoon hot red pepper flakes
2   teaspoons light brown sugar
     Salt
1   tablespoon grated zest and ¼ cup juice from 1 orange
1   tablespoon juice from 1 lemon
1   small shallot, minced (about 2 tablespoons)

1   medium clove garlic, minced or pressed through a garlic press (about 1 teaspoon)
6   tablespoons extra-virgin olive oil
     Ground black pepper
4   center-cut salmon fillets, each 6 to 7 ounces and 1½ inches thick, pin bones removed (see the illustrations on page 261)
2   medium fennel bulbs (about 2 pounds), prepared according to the illustrations on page 315
     Vegetable oil for the grill rack

1. Light a large chimney starter filled with charcoal and allow it to burn until all the charcoal is covered with a layer of fine gray ash. Build a single-level fire by spreading the coals evenly over the bottom of the grill (see the illustration on page 288). Set the cooking rack in place, cover the grill with the lid, and let the rack heat, about 5 minutes. Use a wire brush to scrape clean the cooking grate. The grill is ready when the coals are medium-hot (see page 291 for information about taking the temperature of a grill fire).

2. Meanwhile, place the fennel seeds and pepper flakes in a spice grinder and process until finely ground but not powdery. Transfer the spices to a small bowl and combine with the brown sugar, ¼ teaspoon salt, and orange zest; set the spice mixture aside. Whisk together the orange juice, lemon juice, shallot, garlic, 4 tablespoons olive oil, and salt and pepper to taste in another small bowl; set the vinaigrette aside.

3. Generously sprinkle the flesh of the salmon with the spice mixture. Toss the fennel with the remaining 2 tablespoons olive oil in a large bowl and season with salt and pepper to taste.

4. Lightly dip a small wad of paper towels into vegetable oil; holding the wad with tongs, wipe the grill rack (see the illustration on page 312). Place the fillets, skin-side down, on the grill. Grill, uncovered, until the skin

shrinks, separates from the flesh, and blackens, 2 to 3 minutes. Gently flip the fillets with a metal spatula. Grill, uncovered, until the fillets are opaque almost throughout and translucent only at the very center, 3 to 4 minutes. Transfer the salmon to 4 individual plates.

5. Place the fennel on the grill at the same time as the salmon and grill, turning once, until tender and streaked with dark grill marks, 8 to 10 minutes. Divide the fennel among the plates. Rewhisk the vinaigrette and drizzle a little over each piece of salmon and the fennel. Serve immediately.

GRILLED SWORDFISH WITH CHERMOULA

SWORDFISH IS A FAVORITE ON THE grill. Its smooth, firm flesh makes it easy to grill, and it is flavorful enough to stand up to assertive sauces—such as *chermoula,* a Moroccan condiment made with copious amounts of cilantro, lemon, and garlic. It is a perfect accompaniment to the smoky meatiness of grilled swordfish.

Wondering about the best way to make chermoula, we read through our library and turned up several recipes. According to these recipes, the base of chermoula is herbs—either cilantro or a mixture of cilantro and mint—which are processed with olive oil, lemon juice, and garlic and then flavored with various other spices.

We made several batches of the sauce, one using straight cilantro and the other using a combination of cilantro and mint. The majority of tasters preferred the sauce with just cilantro, feeling that in the other, the cilantro and mint were fighting for prominence. As with a basic vinaigrette, we determined that a ratio of 4 parts oil to 1 part acid (lemon juice) was the best balance for chermoula when tasted on its own. On swordfish, however, chermoula made this way tasted a bit greasy, so we increased the lemon juice slightly to balance the oiliness of the swordfish. Also, searching for a more pestolike consistency to our sauce, we upped the amount of cilantro from ½ cup (the amount called for in most recipes) to ¾ cup. The amount of garlic in the recipes we found varied from 1 clove up to a whopping 6 cloves; we settled on 4 cloves, feeling that the garlic should be assertive but not

PREPARING FENNEL FOR THE GRILL

1. Cut off the stems and feathery fronds.

2. Trim a very thin slice from the base and remove any tough or blemished outer layers from the bulb.

3. Slice the bulb vertically through the base into ¼-inch-thick pieces that resemble fans.

315

overpowering. For the spices, we chose cumin for its characteristic muskiness, paprika for smokiness, and cayenne for heat.

In addition to the chermoula and swordfish, we grilled skewered cherry tomatoes to serve on the side. Cherry tomatoes grill in a matter of minutes and impart a sweetness that made a welcome contrast to the chermoula and the swordfish.

Grilled Swordfish and Cherry Tomatoes with Chermoula

SERVES 4

TIME: 50 MINUTES

Serve with couscous to make a North African–inspired dinner.

¾	cup packed fresh cilantro leaves
4	medium cloves garlic, peeled
I	teaspoon ground cumin
I	teaspoon paprika
¼	teaspoon cayenne pepper
	Salt
3	tablespoons juice from I large lemon
½	cup plus 2 tablespoons extra-virgin olive oil
4	swordfish steaks, each about 8 ounces and I to I¼ inches thick
	Ground black pepper
I	pint cherry tomatoes
	Vegetable oil for the grill rack

1. Light a large chimney starter filled with charcoal and allow it to burn until all the charcoal is covered with a layer of fine

---

BUILDING BLOCK RECIPE

Grilled Swordfish

SERVES 4

TIME: 50 MINUTES

We found that, unlike salmon and tuna, swordfish is best cooked to medium.

4	swordfish steaks, each about 8 ounces and I to I¼ inches thick
2	tablespoons extra-virgin olive oil
	Salt and ground black pepper
	Vegetable oil for the grill rack

1. Light a large chimney starter filled with charcoal and allow it to burn until all the charcoal is covered with a layer of fine gray ash. Build a two-level fire by stacking most of the coals on one side of the grill and arranging the remaining coals in a single layer on the other side of the grill (see the illustration on page 288). Set the cooking rack in place, cover the grill with the lid, and let the rack heat, about 5 minutes. Use a wire brush to scrape clean the cooking grate. The grill is ready when the heat level of the stacked coals is medium-hot and that of the remaining coals is medium-low (see page 291 for information about taking the temperature of a grill fire).

2. Brush the swordfish with the olive oil and generously sprinkle with salt and pepper to taste. Lightly dip a small wad of paper towels into vegetable oil; holding the wad with tongs, wipe the grill rack (see the illustration on page 312). Cook the swordfish, uncovered and turning once, over the hotter side of the grill until the steaks are covered with dark grill marks, 6 to 7 minutes. Move the fish to the cooler side and cook, uncovered and turning once, until the center is longer translucent, 3 to 5 minutes. Serve immediately.

316

gray ash. Build a two-level fire by stacking most of the coals on one side of the grill and arranging the remaining coals in a single layer on the other side of the grill (see the illustration on page 288). Set the cooking rack in place, cover the grill with the lid, and let the rack heat, about 5 minutes. Use a wire brush to scrape clean the cooking grate. The grill is ready when the heat level of the stacked coals is medium-hot and that of the remaining coals is medium-low (see page 291 for information about taking the temperature of a grill fire).

2. Meanwhile, place the cilantro, garlic, cumin, paprika, cayenne, ¼ teaspoon salt, lemon juice, and ½ cup olive oil in the workbowl of a food processor. Process, scraping down the sides several times, until smooth, 10 to 15 seconds. Set the chermoula aside.

3. Brush the swordfish with 4 teaspoons olive oil and generously sprinkle with salt and pepper to taste. Thread the tomatoes onto skewers through the stem ends, brush with the remaining 2 teaspoons olive oil, and season with salt and pepper to taste.

4. Lightly dip a small wad of paper towels into vegetable oil; holding the wad with tongs, wipe the grill rack (see the illustration on page 312). Cook the swordfish, uncovered and turning once, over the hotter side of the grill until the steaks are covered with dark grill marks, 6 to 7 minutes. Move the fish to the cooler side and cook, uncovered and turning once, until the center is no longer translucent, 3 to 5 minutes.

5. Once the swordfish is moved, place the tomatoes over the hotter coals. Grill the tomatoes, turning once or twice, until dark grill marks appear and the skins begin to blister, about 3 minutes. Divide the swordfish and tomatoes among individual plates and spoon the chermoula over the top. Serve immediately.

GRILLED TUNA WITH SOY AND GINGER

TUNA'S DENSE, MEATY FLESH IS FLAVORFUL but not fishy, and it easily pairs with many sauces and side dishes. But the best thing about tuna is that it is easy to grill. Unlike flakier fish, tuna's firm, oily flesh is less apt to stick to the grill. However, we found that grilling tuna is not always foolproof. Too often, the fish comes off the grill dry in texture and tasting too much like canned tuna.

Our idea of a perfect tuna steak was to have it well seared on the outside and moist and pink on the inside, but this goal was harder to attain than we expected. Although the flesh of tuna is oily, this fish, unlike salmon, contains little fat. For this reason, we found that by the time the tuna was well seared on the outside, the inside was tough and dry. Thinking that perhaps the grill temperature should be hotter, we added more fuel and tried again. The results were better; we got a sear in a shorter time, but we still found the tuna too well done and a little strong in taste. We tried using a two-level fire and cooking the tuna with indirect heat. With this procedure, the results were worse than before. We now had pale, overcooked tuna. Obviously, we had to focus our efforts on something other than the fire.

We thought perhaps if we were to grill thicker tuna steaks, we might be able to avoid the problems we were encountering. Indeed, by increasing the thickness of the steaks to 1½ inches, we found we could sear the exterior of the tuna and still maintain a moist, rare steak. In addition, we learned that a wet marinade or a glaze helped prevent the tuna from drying out.

In our first test, we quickly marinated the fish in a mixture of soy and ginger while the grill came up to temperature. Although the resulting fish was moister than the tuna without the marinade, which also helped achieve a nice, dark crust, the flavor it provided the tuna was too subtle. The answer was to use a glaze.

Keeping soy and ginger as the base of the glaze, we tried various ingredients, seeking to form a thin, highly flavored coating for the fish. We definitely had to add a sweet ingredient both to temper the saltiness of the soy and to promote caramelization. Our first choice was mirin, a sweetened rice wine. Mirin helped make a good glaze, but the amount we had to use left an unpleasant alcohol aftertaste. Replacing a portion of the mirin with brown sugar did the trick; this combination yielded a thick glaze without any alcohol aftertaste. We finished the glaze with rice vinegar for added brightness.

With the Asian flavors in the glaze, baby bok choy (the size of your hand) seemed a natural vegetable choice to complete the meal. This vegetable can be halved and grilled in a matter of minutes. A final sprinkling of sliced scallions made an attractive and tasty garnish for the dish.

Grilled Tuna and Bok Choy with Soy-Ginger Glaze

SERVES 4

TIME: 45 MINUTES

When grilling the bok choy, mist the leaves lightly with water to prevent them from drying out and becoming too crisp. For those who prefer tuna cooked medium to well-done, we recommend buying thinner steaks. A 1-inch-thick steak will cook to the proper doneness without the glaze becoming too dark. Serve this dish with steamed white rice.

- 2 tablespoons rice vinegar
- 2 tablespoons mirin

BUILDING BLOCK RECIPE

Grilled Tuna

SERVES 4

TIME: 45 MINUTES

For those who prefer tuna cooked medium to well-done, we recommend buying thinner steaks. The exterior of thicker steaks will burn by the time the interior cooks to a higher internal temperature.

- 4 tuna steaks, each about 8 ounces and at least 1½ inches thick
- 2 tablespoons extra-virgin olive oil
  Salt and ground black pepper
  Vegetable oil for the grill rack

1. Light a large chimney starter filled with charcoal and allow it to burn until all the charcoal is covered with a layer of fine gray ash. Build a single-level fire by spreading the coals evenly over the bottom of the grill (see the illustration on page 288). Set the cooking rack in place, cover the grill with the lid, and let the rack heat, about 5 minutes. Use a wire brush to scrape clean the cooking grate. The grill is ready when the coals are medium-hot (see page 291 for information about taking the temperature of a grill fire).

2. Brush the tuna with the olive oil and season with salt and pepper to taste. Lightly dip a small wad of paper towels into vegetable oil; holding the wad with tongs, wipe the grill rack (see the illustration on page 312). Grill the tuna, uncovered and turning once, to the desired doneness, about 6 minutes for rare or 7 to 8 minutes for medium-rare. Serve immediately.

¼ cup packed (1 ¾ ounces) light
brown sugar

2 tablespoons minced fresh ginger

6 tablespoons soy sauce

4 heads baby bok choy (about
1 ¼ pounds), cut in half through the
stem and rinsed but not dried

1 tablespoon vegetable oil, plus more for
the grill rack
Salt and ground black pepper

4 tuna steaks, each about 8 ounces and at
least 1 ½ inches thick

2 medium scallions, sliced thin on the bias

1. Light a large chimney starter filled with charcoal and allow it to burn until all the charcoal is covered with a layer of fine gray ash. Build a single-level fire by spreading the coals evenly over the bottom of the grill (see the illustration on page 288). Set the cooking rack in place, cover the grill with the lid, and let the rack heat, about 5 minutes. Use a wire brush to scrape clean the cooking grate. The grill is ready when the coals are medium-hot (see page 291 for information about taking the temperature of a grill fire).

2. Meanwhile, mix the vinegar, mirin, brown sugar, ginger, and soy sauce in a small bowl; set aside ¼ cup glaze to dress the finished dish. Brush the bok choy with 1 tablespoon oil and season with salt and pepper to taste.

3. Lightly dip a small wad of paper towels into vegetable oil; holding the wad with tongs, wipe the grill rack (see the illustration on page 312). Brush one side of the tuna liberally with glaze and put the tuna, glaze-side down, on the grill. Grill, uncovered, for 3 minutes, brush with more glaze, and turn with a spatula. Grill for 2 minutes, brush with more glaze, turn the fish, and cook for 1 minute more for rare or 2 to 3 minutes more for medium-rare.

4. While the tuna is grilling, place the bok choy around the outside edge of the grill. Grill, turning once, until crisp-tender, 6 to 7 minutes. Serve the tuna steaks and the bok choy immediately, topped with the reserved glaze and sprinkled with scallions.

GRILLED SHRIMP

THE RICH, SWEET, BRINY FLAVORS OF shellfish are well complemented by the smokiness of the grill. Even better, most shellfish require just a few minutes of cooking time. However, when grilled over intense heat, shellfish, unfortunately, tend to dry out and become tough. Shrimp are often the first to suffer this fate. We wanted to find a technique that would keep grilled shrimp moist and plump.

Part of the problem with shrimp is their thinness; by the time they are nicely colored on the outside, they are overcooked on the inside. In trying various techniques to prevent the shrimp from drying out, we had the most success when we skewered them in such a way as to reduce their surface area touched by the heat of the grill. We initially did this by interlocking them, which sheltered the inside arc of the shrimp from the flames. We got even better results when we skewered each shrimp around

SKEWERING SHRIMP WITH PINEAPPLE

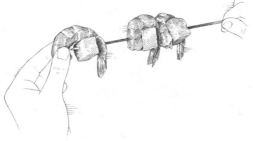

Thread the tail of a shrimp, then a chunk of pineapple, and finally the head of the shrimp onto a skewer, so the shrimp forms a half-circle around the pineapple.

juicy chunks of pineapple. This method had several advantages: The pineapple decreased the surface area of the shrimp exposed to the grill, as we had hoped, and the pineapple juices basted the shrimp and kept it from drying out.

It made sense to serve the shrimp and pineapple with a dipping sauce that would add moisture after the shrimp were cooked. Wanting a light yet flavorful sauce, we chose a Thai-style sauce, feeling that the balanced flavors would enhance the contrast between the sweet pineapple and the rich shrimp. We started with equal amounts of salty fish sauce and tart lime juice. To this we added chopped basil for freshness and a healthy dose of fresh chiles for heat. Although this sauce tasted good by itself, when it was eaten with the sweet shrimp and pineapple, the flavors became skewed. Adding more lime juice made the sauce too harsh. In the end, we chose to add rice vinegar, the mellow acidity of which pulled the sauce back into balance. A little water also helped mellow the intense flavors in the dipping sauce without disrupting their balance.

Grilled Thai-Style Shrimp with Pineapple

SERVES 4

TIME: 45 MINUTES

Serve with Basmati Rice, Pilaf Style (page 114), and/or Spinach with Sautéed Shallots and Lemon

(page 84). Although a red Thai chile is authentic, any small, hot fresh chile can be used in this recipe. To save time, buy peeled and cored pineapple at the supermarket. If you prepare the pineapple yourself, reserve half a large pineapple for this recipe.

2	tablespoons fish sauce
2	tablespoons juice from 1 lime, plus 1 lime cut into wedges
1	tablespoon sugar
1	tablespoon rice vinegar
1	red Thai chile, stemmed, seeded, and minced (about 1/2 teaspoon)
2	tablespoons chopped fresh basil leaves
2	pounds large shrimp (21 to 25 count per pound), peeled and deveined, if desired
2	cups fresh pineapple cut into 1-inch pieces

1. Light a large chimney starter filled with charcoal and allow it to burn until all the charcoal is covered with a layer of fine gray ash. Build a single-level fire by spreading the coals evenly over the bottom of the grill (see the illustration on page 288). Set the cooking rack in place, cover the grill with the lid, and let the rack heat, about 5 minutes. Use a wire brush to scrape clean the cooking grate. The grill is ready when the coals are medium-hot (see page 291 for information about taking the temperature of a grill fire).

2. Mix the fish sauce, lime juice, sugar,

PREPARING CORN FOR THE GRILL

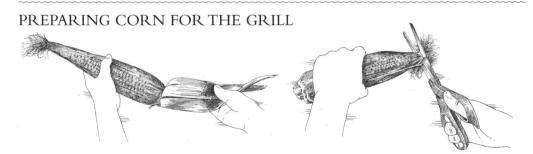

1. Remove all but the innermost layer of the husk. The kernels should be covered by (but visible through) the last husk layer.

2. Use scissors to snip off the tassel, or long silk ends, from the tip of the ear.

vinegar, chile, basil, and 3 tablespoons water in a small bowl. Following the illustration on page 319, thread the shrimp and pineapple onto six 12-inch metal skewers. Each skewer should hold 7 to 8 shrimp.

3. Grill, uncovered and turning the skewers once, until the shrimp and pineapple are charred and the shrimp is bright pink, 5 to 6 minutes. Serve the shrimp and pineapple immediately, passing the dipping sauce and lime wedges.

GRILLED SCALLOPS WITH CORN SALAD

CORN IS TRANSFORMED ON THE GRILL. The sweet kernels become wonderfully toasted and caramelized and pick up a hint of smokiness. By cutting the kernels off the ear after grilling, you can make a quick and tasty salad to accompany other grilled foods.

For our corn salad, we wanted ingredients that contrasted with the sweetness of the corn itself. We tried tossing the grilled corn with dressings made with white wine vinegar, lemon juice, and lime juice, all mixed with olive oil. Most tasters preferred the lime juice, feeling it paired best with the sweet corn. Besides the acidity in the dressing, we wanted a spicy dimension, so we added minced jalapeños to one salad and minced chipotle peppers to another. The chipotles, which are smoked jalapeños, were the clear winner; they gave the salad a smokiness that accentuated the grilled corn and provided a subtle lingering heat, whereas the jalapeños' heat was more assertive and vegetal. The addition of several tablespoons of chopped cilantro gave the salad freshness.

While corn salad goes well with almost anything grilled, we chose scallops for this particular recipe. The sweet, chewy flesh of the scallop is the perfect complement to the crunchy corn salad. However, our initial test of plain grilled scallops left much to be desired. The scallops tasted bland, and, as they spent so little time on the grill, they weren't able to develop the deep grill marks we wanted. We went searching for a way to help the scallops achieve the color and intense flavor we wanted.

Our first attempt was to make a dry spice rub, using flavors we thought would complement the corn salad. We gave the scallops a liberal dusting of cumin and chili powder and then proceeded to grill them. While we succeeded in adding a lot of flavor, the scallops didn't contain enough moisture to blend with the raw spices and therefore failed to develop a nice crust. The resulting scallops were chalky, not crisp and flavorful.

The next option was to use a marinade. Liking the flavors of the cumin and chili powder from our previous test, we began there and added lime juice and olive oil. The results from this test were better—but not good enough. The scallops achieved a more caramelized exterior but still lacked sufficient flavor. Our next option, which turned out to be the best, was a glaze. Building from the rub and the marinade, we removed the oil and

SKEWERING SCALLOPS

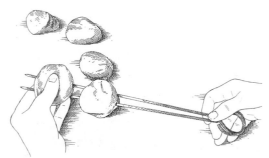

Thread the scallops onto doubled skewers so that the flat sides of each scallop will directly touch the cooking grate. This promotes better browning on each scallop. To turn the skewers, gently hold one scallop with a pair of tongs and flip.

added brown sugar. This became the key to our success, forming a thick paste that helped the spices adhere to the scallops. The result was the intense flavor we were looking for *plus* a beautifully browned exterior.

~

Grilled Scallops with Chili-Lime Glaze and Corn Salad

SERVES 4

TIME: 55 MINUTES

When buying scallops, be sure to ask the fishmonger for dry scallops. These scallops have not been chemically treated and are much sweeter and less watery than scallops that have been treated. If the scallops are swimming in milky white liquid, you can assume they have been treated. See photo of this recipe on page 157.

½	cup juice from 4 limes, plus 1 lime cut into wedges
3	tablespoons light brown sugar
2	teaspoons chili powder
½	teaspoon ground cumin
1	medium red bell pepper, stemmed, seeded, and cut into ¼-inch dice
1	small shallot, minced (about 2 tablespoons)
2	tablespoons chopped fresh cilantro leaves
1	canned chipotle chile in adobo sauce, minced to a paste
¼	cup olive oil
	Salt
1½	pounds large sea scallops, tendons removed (see the illustration on page 56)
4	ears corn, all but innermost layer of husk and silk removed (see the illustrations on page 320)
	Vegetable oil for the grill rack

1. Light a large chimney starter filled with charcoal and allow it to burn until all the charcoal is covered with a layer of fine gray ash. Build a single-level fire by spreading the coals evenly over the bottom of the grill (see the illustration on page 288). Set the cooking rack in place, cover the grill with the lid, and let the rack heat, about 5 minutes. Use a wire brush to scrape clean the cooking grate. The grill is ready when the coals are medium-hot (see page 291 for information about taking the temperature of a grill fire).

2. Meanwhile, combine ¼ cup lime juice and the brown sugar, chili powder, and cumin in a small bowl for the glaze. For the salad, toss the bell pepper, shallot, cilantro, chipotle chile, remaining ¼ cup lime juice, olive oil, and ¼ teaspoon salt in a medium bowl. Thread the scallops onto doubled skewers (see the illustration on page 321) so that the flat side of the scallops will directly touch the cooking grate.

3. Grill the corn, turning the ears every 1½ to 2 minutes, until the kernels leave dark outlines in the husk and the husk is charred and beginning to peel away from the tip to expose some kernels, 8 to 10 minutes. Remove the corn from the grill and cool slightly. Peel the husks from the corn and cut the kernels from the ears. Add the corn to the bell pepper mixture, mix well to combine the ingredients, and adjust the seasoning with salt to taste.

4. Lightly dip a small wad of paper towels into the vegetable oil; holding the wad with tongs, wipe the grill rack (see the illustration on page 312). Brush the scallops with glaze and grill on one side until caramelized, about 3 minutes. Brush the scallops with more glaze and turn with tongs. Continue to grill until the sides of the scallops are firm and all but the middle third of each scallop is opaque, 2 to 3 minutes. Brush the scallops with the remaining glaze before removing them from the grill. Serve the scallops immediately with the corn salad and lime wedges.

11

STIR-FRYING

BY DEFINITION, STIR-FRYING IS QUICK. Most recipes require no more than 5 or 10 minutes of actual cooking time. In most cases, the time and effort is expended in preparing the ingredients. Although good stir-fries require a fair number of ingredients (three ingredients do not a stir-fry make), there's no need to get carried away. Recipes in this chapter were developed to keep prep time to a minimum.

To stir-fry properly, you need plenty of intense heat. The pan must be hot enough to caramelize sugars, deepen flavors, and evaporate unnecessary juices. All this must happen in minutes. The problem for most American cooks is that the Chinese wok and the American stovetop are a lousy match that generates moderate heat at best.

Woks are conical because in China they traditionally rest in cylindrical pits that contain the fire. Food is cut into small pieces to shorten cooking time, thus conserving fuel. Only one vessel is required for many cooking methods, including sautéing (stir-frying), steaming, boiling, and deep-frying.

Unfortunately, what is practical in China makes no sense in the United States. A wok was not designed for stovetop cooking, where heat comes from the bottom only. On an American stove, the bottom of the wok gets hot, but the sides are only warm. A horizontal heat source requires a horizontal pan. Therefore, for stir-frying at home, we recommend a large skillet, 12 to 14 inches in diameter, with a nonstick coating. If you insist on using a wok for stir-frying, choose a flat-bottomed model. It won't have as much flat surface area as a skillet, but it will work better on an American stove than a conventional round-bottomed wok. (An electric wok is another option; see page 337 for more information.)

American stoves necessitate other adjustments. In Chinese cooking, intense flames lick the bottom and sides of a wok, heating the whole surface to extremely high temperatures. Conventional stoves simply don't generate enough British thermal units (BTUs) to heat any pan—wok or skillet—sufficiently. American cooks must accommodate the lower horsepower of their stoves. Throw everything into the pan at one time and the ingredients will steam and stew, not stir-fry.

One solution is to boil the vegetables first so they are merely heated through in the pan with the other stir-fry ingredients. We find this approach burdensome. Who wants to clean more pots? We prefer to cut the vegetables quite small and add them to the pan in batches. By adding just a small volume of food at a time, the heat in the pan does not dissipate. Slow-cooking vegetables such as carrots and onions go into the pan first, followed by quicker-cooking items such as zucchini and bell peppers. Leafy greens and herbs go in last.

For vegetables that won't soften even after several minutes of stir-frying, we add a bit of water to the pan and cover it to trap some steam. This method works especially well with broccoli and green beans. Once the vegetables are crisp-tender, the cover comes off so the excess water can evaporate.

We found that cooking times are affected by how the vegetables are prepared. For instance, sliced mushrooms cook more quickly than whole mushrooms. In some cases, we've found it necessary to remove cooked vegetables from the pan before adding the next batch. This is especially important if you are cooking a large volume of vegetables.

Most stir-fries start with some sort of protein—beef, chicken, pork, shrimp, scallops, squid, or tofu. All protein must be cut into bite-size pieces. We find it best to freeze beef, pork, and chicken for an hour or so to make slicing easier. We marinate all protein, once sliced, in a mixture of soy sauce and dry sherry to improve flavor. Don't add more than 4 teaspoons marinade per ¾ pound protein or the excess liquid will inhibit browning.

Many stir-fry recipes call for adding the aromatics (scallions, garlic, and ginger) too early, causing them to burn. In our testing, we found it best to cook the aromatics after the vegetables. When the vegetables are done, we push them to the sides of the pan, add a little oil and the aromatics to the center, and cook until the aromatics are fragrant but not colored, about 45 seconds. To keep them from burning and becoming harsh-tasting, we then stir them into the vegetables. At this point, the seared meat, chicken, seafood, or tofu is

---

Basic Stir-Fry

SERVES 4

TIME: 30 TO 45 MINUTES (DEPENDING ON HOW LONG IT TAKES TO PREPARE THE VEGETABLES AND SAUCE)

This is more a formula than a recipe, with a ratio of 1 part protein to 2 parts vegetables. Plug in your favorite vegetables and a sauce from the end of this chapter. Use oil as needed to cook the vegetables and make sure the harder, longer-cooking vegetables go into the pan before the softer, quicker-cooking vegetables. Increase the garlic or ginger to taste. These are just some possibilities to explore once you master this basic formula.

¾	pound protein (meat, chicken, seafood, or tofu), cut into small, even pieces
2	teaspoons soy sauce
2	teaspoons dry sherry
1	tablespoon minced garlic
1	tablespoon minced fresh ginger
2	tablespoons minced scallion, white parts only
2–3	tablespoons peanut or vegetable oil
1½	pounds prepared vegetables, cut into small pieces and divided into batches based on cooking times
½	cup sauce (see pages 340–342)

1. Toss the protein with the soy sauce and sherry in a medium bowl. Combine the garlic, ginger, scallion, and 1½ teaspoons oil in a small bowl.

2. Heat 2 teaspoons oil in a 12-inch nonstick skillet over high heat until smoking. Add the protein and cook, stirring occasionally and breaking up clumps, until well browned, 1 to 3½ minutes. Transfer the protein to a clean bowl.

3. Add 1½ teaspoons to 1 tablespoon oil to the now-empty skillet and heat until shimmering. Add the first batch of longer-cooking vegetables and cook, stirring occasionally, until crisp-tender, 1 to 5 minutes. Leaving the vegetables in the pan (or removing them if the pan will cool too much), heat another 1½ teaspoons to 1 tablespoon oil and add the faster-cooking vegetables. Cook until the vegetables are crisp-tender, 1 to 2 minutes.

4. Clear the center of the pan and add the garlic mixture. Cook, mashing the garlic mixture with the back of a spatula, until fragrant, about 45 seconds. Stir the garlic mixture into the vegetables. Add the protein and toss to combine. Whisk the sauce to recombine and add it to the skillet. Remove the pan from the heat and toss until all ingredients are well coated with sauce and sizzling hot. Serve immediately.

returned to the pan along with the sauce.

A good stir-fry for four people generally calls for only ¾ pound protein to 1½ pounds prepared vegetables. This ratio keeps the stir-fry from becoming too heavy and is also more authentic, as protein is a luxury used sparingly in China. The recipes in this chapter are designed to serve four as a main course. Serve the following recipes with plenty of rice (see the recipes on pages 113 and 328).

MEAT AND POULTRY STIR-FRIES

BEEF STIR-FRIES ARE BEST MADE WITH flank steak, which slices thin and stays tender when cooked over high heat. We tried other cuts, such as top round, and found that they toughen when stir-fried. Flank steak is easier to slice thin when slightly frozen than when at room temperature. The same is true of chicken and pork. Ten or 15 minutes in the freezer firms the texture nicely. Another option is to defrost meat in the refrigerator

and slice it before defrosting is complete.

Although some stir-fry recipes call for ground pork, we find that strips of lean meat from the tenderloin are the best option. (We tested boneless chops, but the meat was not as tender and flavorful.)

The chicken recipes in this chapter call for boneless, skinless breasts cut into ½-inch-wide strips. If you can find boneless, skinless thighs, go ahead and use this tasty dark meat. Thighs should be cut into 1-inch pieces because smaller chunks will fall apart. In the world of stir-frying, both breast and thigh meat require a fairly long time to cook through and brown slightly—at least 2 or 3 minutes.

Stir-Fried Beef and Eggplant in Oyster Sauce

SERVES 4

TIME: 45 MINUTES

If you like, add 1 teaspoon minced fresh chile to the garlic mixture in step 1. Let the beef marinate as you make the sauce and prepare the vegetables and aromatics.

SLICING FLANK STEAK FOR STIR-FRIES

1. Slice partially frozen flank steak lengthwise into 2-inch-wide pieces.

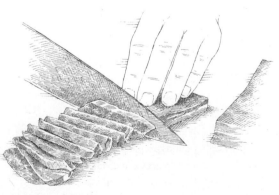

2. Cut each piece of flank steak against the grain into very thin slices.

3/4   pound flank steak, sliced thin (see the
      illustrations on page 326)
2   teaspoons soy sauce
2   teaspoons dry sherry
2   tablespoons minced garlic
1   tablespoon minced fresh ginger
3   medium scallions, green parts cut into
      1/4-inch lengths and white parts minced
8   teaspoons peanut or vegetable oil
1   small eggplant (about 3/4 pound), cut into
      1/2-inch cubes
1   small red bell pepper, stemmed, seeded,
      and cut into 1/2-inch-wide strips
1   recipe Oyster Sauce (page 341)

1. Toss the beef with the soy sauce and
sherry in a medium bowl. Combine the garlic, ginger, scallion whites, and 1½ teaspoons
oil in a small bowl.

2. Heat 2 teaspoons oil in a 12-inch nonstick skillet over high heat until smoking. Add
the beef and cook, stirring occasionally and
breaking up clumps, until well browned, 2 to
3 minutes. Transfer the beef to a clean bowl.

3. Add 1 tablespoon oil to the now-empty
skillet and heat until shimmering. Add the
eggplant and cook, stirring occasionally, until
browned and no longer spongy, about 5 minutes; transfer the eggplant to the bowl with
the beef. Add 1½ teaspoons oil to the now-
empty skillet and heat until shimmering. Add
the bell pepper and cook, stirring occasionally,
until crisp-tender, 1 to 2 minutes.

4. Clear the center of the pan and add the
garlic mixture. Cook, mashing the garlic mixture with the back of a spatula, until fragrant,
about 45 seconds. Stir the garlic mixture into
the vegetables. Add the scallion greens, beef,
and eggplant and toss to combine. Whisk the
sauce to recombine and add it to the skillet.
Remove the pan from the heat and toss until
all ingredients are well coated with sauce and
sizzling hot. Serve immediately.

Stir-Fried Beef and Broccoli with Walnuts in Garlic Sauce

SERVES 4

TIME: 30 MINUTES

*Walnuts add richness to this simple stir-fry. See the
illustrations on page 67 for tips on peeling broccoli
stalks. Let the beef marinate as you make the sauce
and prepare the vegetables and aromatics.*

3/4   pound flank steak, sliced thin (see the
      illustrations on page 326)
2   teaspoons soy sauce
2   teaspoons dry sherry
1   tablespoon minced garlic
1   tablespoon minced fresh ginger
2   tablespoons minced scallions, white parts
      only
5   teaspoons peanut or vegetable oil
1/4   cup walnuts, chopped coarse
1½   pounds broccoli, florets broken into bite-
      size pieces; stalks peeled and cut cross-
      wise into 1/4-inch-thick pieces
1   recipe Garlic Sauce (page 340)

1. Toss the beef with the soy sauce and
sherry in a medium bowl. Combine the garlic, ginger, scallions, and 1½ teaspoons oil in a
small bowl.

2. Toast the walnuts in a 12-inch nonstick
skillet over medium-high heat until golden
and aromatic, 2 to 3 minutes. Transfer the nuts
to a bowl and set aside. Wipe any remaining
walnut dust out of the pan with paper towels.

3. Add 2 teaspoons oil to the now-empty
skillet and heat until smoking. Add the beef
and cook, stirring occasionally and breaking
up clumps, until well browned, 2 to 3 minutes. Transfer the beef to a clean bowl.

4. Add 1½ teaspoons oil to the now-empty
skillet and heat until shimmering. Add the
broccoli and ½ cup water, cover, and cook

BUILDING BLOCK RECIPE
Sticky White Rice
SERVES 4 AS A SIDE DISH

TIME: 30 MINUTES (INCLUDES
25 MINUTES SIMMERING TIME)

This traditional Chinese cooking method yields sticky rice that works well as an accompaniment to a stir-fry, especially if you're eating with chopsticks. The rice is first boiled hard to release starches and then covered and steamed over very low heat until tender.

2   cups long-grain rice
3   cups water
1/2   teaspoon salt

1. Bring the rice, water, and salt to a boil in a medium saucepan over medium-high heat. Cook, uncovered, until the water level drops below the top surface of the rice and small holes appear in the surface of the rice, about 10 minutes.

2. Reduce the heat to very low, cover, and cook until the rice is tender, about 15 minutes longer.

until the broccoli begins to turn bright green, 1 to 2 minutes. Uncover and cook, stirring frequently, until the liquid evaporates and the broccoli is crisp-tender, 2 to 4 minutes longer.

5. Clear the center of the pan and add the garlic mixture. Cook, mashing the garlic mixture with the back of a spatula, until fragrant, about 45 seconds. Stir the garlic mixture into the broccoli. Add the beef and toss to combine. Whisk the sauce to recombine and add it to the skillet. Remove the pan from the heat and toss until all ingredients are well coated with sauce and sizzling hot. Sprinkle the toasted walnuts over the top and serve immediately.

Stir-Fried Pork and Napa Cabbage in Hot-and-Sour Sauce
SERVES 4

TIME: 45 MINUTES

See the illustrations on page 329 for more information about shredding cabbage. Let the pork marinate as you make the sauce and prepare the vegetables and aromatics. Due to the high moisture content of the cabbage, this stir-fry is a bit saucier than most of the other recipes in this chapter.

SLICING PORK FOR STIR-FRIES

1. Cut the partially frozen tenderloin crosswise into 1/4-inch-thick medallions.

2. Slice each medallion into 1/4-inch-wide strips.

¾ pound pork tenderloin, cut into thin strips (see the illustrations on page 328)

2 teaspoons soy sauce

2 teaspoons dry sherry

1 tablespoon minced garlic

1 tablespoon minced fresh ginger

2 tablespoons minced scallions, white parts only

8 teaspoons peanut or vegetable oil

1 medium red bell pepper, stemmed, seeded, and cut into ¼-inch-wide strips

½ medium napa cabbage (about 1 pound), shredded (about 8 cups)

1 recipe Hot-and-Sour Sauce (page 340)

1. Toss the pork with the soy sauce and sherry in a medium bowl. Combine the garlic, ginger, scallions, and 1½ teaspoons oil in a small bowl.

2. Heat 2 teaspoons oil in a 12-inch nonstick skillet over high heat until smoking. Add the pork and cook, stirring occasionally and breaking up clumps, until no longer pink, about 2 minutes. Transfer the pork to a clean bowl.

3. Add 1½ teaspoons oil to the now-empty skillet and heat until shimmering. Add the bell pepper and cook, stirring occasionally, until crisp-tender, about 1 minute.

Add 1½ teaspoons oil and half of the cabbage and stir-fry until crisp-tender, about 1 minute. Transfer the peppers and cabbage to a bowl. Heat the remaining 1½ teaspoons oil in the pan, add the remaining cabbage, and stir-fry until crisp-tender, about 1 minute. Return the first batch of cabbage and the bell peppers to the pan and toss to combine.

4. Clear the center of the pan and add the garlic mixture. Cook, mashing the garlic mixture with the back of a spatula, until fragrant, about 45 seconds. Stir the garlic mixture into the vegetables. Add the pork and toss to combine. Whisk the sauce to recombine and add it to the skillet. Remove the pan from the heat and toss until all ingredients are well coated with sauce and sizzling hot. Serve immediately.

Stir-Fried Chicken, Pineapple, and Red Onion in Sweet-and-Sour Sauce

SERVES 4

TIME: 45 MINUTES

Let the chicken marinate as you make the sauce and prepare the vegetables and aromatics. Most markets sell fresh pineapple chunks that can be used in this recipe.

SHREDDING CABBAGE

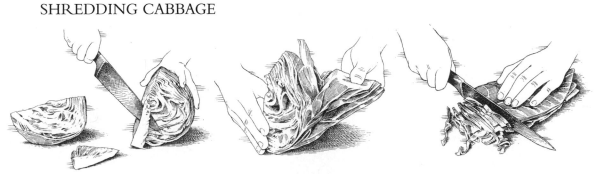

1. Cut a whole head of cabbage into quarters. Cut away the hard piece of the core attached to each quarter.

2. Separate the cored cabbage quarters into stacks of leaves that flatten when pressed.

3. Use a chef's knife to cut each stack of cabbage leaves into thin strips.

³/₄   pound boneless, skinless chicken breast, cut into uniform pieces (see the illustrations on page 331)

2   teaspoons soy sauce

2   teaspoons dry sherry

1   tablespoon minced garlic

1   tablespoon minced fresh ginger

3   medium scallions, white parts minced and green parts cut into ¼-inch lengths

5   teaspoons peanut or vegetable oil

2   small red onions, halved and cut into ½-inch-thick wedges

2   cups fresh pineapple cut into 1-inch pieces

1   recipe Sweet-and-Sour Sauce (page 341)

1. Toss the chicken with the soy sauce and sherry in a medium bowl. Combine the garlic, ginger, scallion whites, and 1½ teaspoons oil in a small bowl.

2. Heat 2 teaspoons oil in a 12-inch non-stick skillet over high heat until smoking. Add the chicken and cook, stirring occasionally and breaking up clumps, until cooked through, 2 to 3 minutes. Transfer the chicken to a clean bowl.

3. Add the remaining 1½ teaspoons oil to the now-empty skillet and heat until shimmering. Add the onions and cook, stirring occasionally, until lightly browned, about 2 minutes. Add the pineapple and cook until heated through, about 1 minute.

4. Clear the center of the pan and add the garlic mixture. Cook, mashing the garlic mixture with the back of a spatula, until fragrant, about 45 seconds. Stir the garlic mixture into the vegetables. Add the scallion greens and chicken and toss to combine. Whisk the sauce to recombine and add it to the skillet. Remove the pan from the heat and toss until all ingredients are well coated with sauce and sizzling hot. Serve immediately.

Stir-Fried Chicken, Celery, and Peanuts in Sichuan Chile Sauce

SERVES 4

TIME: 30 MINUTES

Salted or plain roasted peanuts can be used in this recipe. Let the chicken marinate as you make the sauce and prepare the vegetables and aromatics.

³/₄   pound boneless, skinless chicken breast, cut into uniform pieces (see the illustrations on page 331)

2   teaspoons soy sauce

2   teaspoons dry sherry

1   tablespoon minced garlic

1   tablespoon minced fresh ginger

2   tablespoons minced scallions, white parts only

6½   teaspoons peanut or vegetable oil

8   celery ribs, sliced thin on the bias

½   cup dry-roasted peanuts

1   recipe Sichuan Chile Sauce (page 342)

1. Toss the chicken with the soy sauce and sherry in a medium bowl. Combine the garlic, ginger, scallions, and 1½ teaspoons oil in a small bowl.

2. Heat 2 teaspoons oil in a 12-inch non-stick skillet over high heat until smoking. Add the chicken and cook, stirring occasionally and breaking up clumps, until cooked through, 2 to 3 minutes. Transfer the chicken to a clean bowl.

3. Add 1½ teaspoons oil to the now-empty skillet and heat until shimmering. Add half of the celery and cook, stirring occasionally, until crisp-tender, 1½ to 2 minutes. Transfer the celery to a small bowl. Heat the remaining 1½ teaspoons oil in the pan, add the remaining celery, and cook, stirring occasionally, until crisp-tender, 1½ to 2 minutes. Return the first batch of celery to the pan.

4. Clear the center of the pan and add the garlic mixture. Cook, mashing the garlic mixture with the back of a spatula, until fragrant, about 45 seconds. Stir the garlic mixture into the celery. Add the chicken and peanuts and toss to combine. Whisk the sauce to recombine and add it to the skillet. Remove the pan from the heat and toss until all ingredients are well coated with sauce and sizzling hot. Serve immediately.

Stir-Fried Chicken with Green Beans in Spicy Orange Sauce

SERVES 4

TIME: 30 MINUTES

Let the chicken marinate as you make the sauce and prepare the vegetables and aromatics.

¾   **pound boneless, skinless chicken breast, cut into uniform pieces (see the illustrations below)**

2   **teaspoons soy sauce**

2   **teaspoons dry sherry**

I   **tablespoon minced garlic**

I   **tablespoon minced fresh ginger**

2   **tablespoons minced scallions, white parts only**

5   **teaspoons peanut or vegetable oil**

I   **tablespoon sesame seeds**

I   **pound green beans, cut on the bias into 1 ½-inch lengths**

I   **recipe Spicy Orange Sauce (page 342)**

1. Toss the chicken with the soy sauce and sherry in a medium bowl. Combine the garlic, ginger, scallions, and 1½ teaspoons oil in a small bowl.

2. Toast the sesame seeds in a 12-inch non-stick skillet over medium heat until golden, 2 to 3 minutes. Transfer the seeds to a small bowl and set aside.

3. Heat 2 teaspoons oil in the now-empty skillet over high heat until smoking. Add the chicken and cook, stirring occasionally and breaking up clumps, until cooked through, 2 to 3 minutes. Transfer the chicken to a clean bowl.

4. Add the remaining 1½ teaspoons oil to the now-empty skillet and heat until shimmering. Add the green beans and ½ cup water, cover, and cook until the beans begin to turn bright green, 1 to 2 minutes. Uncover and cook, stirring frequently, until the liquid evaporates and the beans

SLICING CHICKEN FOR STIR-FRIES

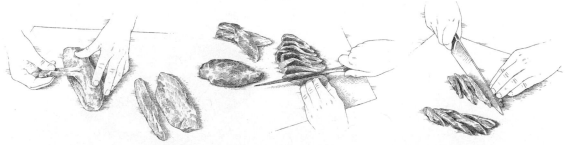

1. To produce uniform pieces of chicken, separate the tenderloins from the partially frozen skinless, boneless breasts.

2. Slice the breasts across the grain into ½-inch-wide strips that are 1½ to 2 inches long. Center pieces need to be cut in half so they are approximately the same length as the end pieces.

3. Cut the tenderloins on the diagonal to produce pieces about the same size as the strips of breast meat.

331

EQUIPMENT: Inexpensive Nonstick Skillets

We prefer a 12- or 14-inch nonstick skillet for stir-frying. This pan requires a minimum of oil and prevents foods from burning onto the surface as they stir-fry. You can use a regular skillet, but without the nonstick coating, you will need to use more oil. Do not use a smaller skillet; the ingredients will steam and stew rather than stir-fry.

Most cooks would rather purchase a relatively inexpensive pan for stir-frying. (It makes more sense to spend the big bucks on a conventional skillet for searing steaks and browning chicken breasts.) We assembled eight inexpensive skillets (all priced under $50) to see if we could find one we liked.

The material used for nonstick coatings—polytetrafluoroethylene, or PTFE—was developed by chemists at DuPont in the late 1930s. Trademarked originally as Teflon, the formula has evolved over the years, and now several companies in addition to DuPont sell PTFE to cookware manufacturers. Our understanding, however, is that the majority of today's nonstick coatings are made from the same basic substance.

Every pan in our group received a good score in release ability and cleaning tests, the raisons d'être for nonstick. We tested both traits in a purposefully abusive manner by burning oatmeal into the pans over high heat for 45 minutes. That kind of treatment would trash a traditional pan, but the scorched cereal slid out of our nonstick pans without fuss, and the pans wiped clean.

Most manufacturers recommend using plastic, rubber, coated, or wooden utensils to avoid scratching the nonstick coating. Makers of only three of our pans, the Farberware, Innova, and Bialetti, sanction the use of metal utensils.

In their new, off-the-shelf condition, all of our pans turned in a reasonable to good performance cooking the foods best suited to nonstick cooking: eggs and fish. In fact, every pan but the Revere produced evenly cooked omelets and released them with ease. The omelet made in the Farberware pan was especially impressive. The Farberware also did a particularly nice job searing salmon fillets to an even, crusty medium brown. Overall, however, our tests indicate that any of these pans can easily handle such light-duty tasks as cooking eggs. Low cost does not mean a big trade-off in this instance.

Sauté speed is also an important measure of a pan's performance. We tested this by sautéing 1½ cups chopped onions over medium heat for 10 minutes in the hope of ending up with pale gold onions that bore no trace of burning. And you know what? For the most part, we did. The Wearever, T-Fal, Innova, and Revere pans, which were all on the light side in terms of weight, turned out the darkest onions, but they were still well within an acceptable color range. Onions sautéed in the Farberware, Meyer, Calphalon, and Bialetti pans were a shade lighter, indicating a slightly slower sauté speed. The Farberware onions, however, took top honors based on how evenly all the pieces colored.

Of course, construction quality is a concern with any piece of cookware but especially with inexpensive models. Will the thing hold up, or will you have to replace it in 6 months? Based on our experience, you may well sacrifice a measure of construction quality with a budget pan. Pans with handles that were welded or riveted to the pan body, including the Farberware, Innova, Meyer, and Calphalon, all felt solid and permanent. But the heat-resistant plastic (called *phenolic*) handles on the T-Fal, Revere, Bialetti, and Wearever pans were not riveted in place, and all three came loose during testing. That does not bode well for their future.

THE BEST INEXPENSIVE NONSTICK SKILLET

Of the pans we tested, the $30 Farberware Millennium offered the best combination of good nonstick performance (in suitable applications), pleasing heft at almost 3½ pounds, and solid construction.

are crisp-tender, 2 to 4 minutes longer.

5. Clear the center of the pan and add the garlic mixture. Cook, mashing the garlic mixture with the back of a spatula, until fragrant, about 45 seconds. Stir the garlic mixture into the green beans. Add the chicken and toss to combine. Whisk the sauce to recombine and add it to the skillet. Remove the pan from the heat and toss until all ingredients are well coated with sauce and sizzling hot. Sprinkle with the toasted sesame seeds and serve immediately.

SEAFOOD STIR-FRIES

FRESH SEAFOOD WORKS WELL WITH A variety of flavors and is well suited to stir-fries. Shrimp, scallops, and squid are all good choices because they cook quickly. Shrimp may be stir-fried in the shell, but they are easier to eat when shelled (and deveined, if the veins are particularly large) before cooking. Buy large shrimp, which can be peeled more quickly than smaller shrimp. We bought 1 pound shrimp in order to have ¾ pound shelled shrimp ready to stir-fry. Shrimp should be stir-fried until bright pink, about 1½ minutes.

If you can find good-quality bay scallops, which are small, use them whole in stir-fries, but avoid inexpensive calicos that are about the same size or smaller. Otherwise, select sea scallops and cut them into 1-inch pieces. With either variety, remove the tendon attached to the side of each scallop, as it becomes unpleasantly tough when cooked. Scallops cook in just 1 minute. For optimum browning on the outside, turn scallops only once when stir-frying them.

Whole squid, either fresh or frozen, should be purchased cleaned at a fish market or supermarket. The tentacles may be stir-fried as is, while the bodies should be cut crosswise into ½-inch rings. Do not cook squid for more than 1 minute (it should turn opaque) or you risk toughening it.

Stir-Fried Shrimp, Scallions, and Peppers in Garlic Sauce
SERVES 4

TIME: 45 MINUTES

Sliced scallion whites and greens are used as a vegetable in this recipe. You will need four or five bunches of scallions (about ¾ pound). If you want to devein the shrimp, see the illustrations on page 56. Let the shrimp marinate as you make the sauce and prepare the vegetables and aromatics.

1	pound large shrimp (21 to 25 count per pound), peeled and deveined, if desired
2	teaspoons soy sauce
2	teaspoons dry sherry
1	tablespoon minced garlic
1	tablespoon minced fresh ginger
6½	teaspoons peanut or vegetable oil
1	cup scallion whites, sliced on the bias into 1-inch pieces
2	medium red bell peppers, stemmed, seeded, and cut into ¾-inch squares
1½	cups scallion greens, sliced on the bias into ½-inch pieces
1	recipe Garlic Sauce (page 340)

1. Toss the shrimp with the soy sauce and sherry in a medium bowl. Combine the garlic, ginger, and 1½ teaspoons oil in a small bowl.

2. Heat 2 teaspoons oil in a 12-inch non-stick skillet over high heat until smoking. Add the shrimp and cook, stirring occasionally, until curled and lightly browned, about 1½ minutes. Transfer the shrimp to a clean bowl.

3. Add 1½ teaspoons oil to the now-empty skillet and heat until shimmering. Add the scallion whites and cook, stirring occasionally, until tender, about 1 minute. Add the remaining 1½ teaspoons oil and the bell peppers and

cook, stirring occasionally, until crisp-tender, 1 to 2 minutes.

4. Clear the center of the pan and add the garlic mixture. Cook, mashing the garlic mixture with the back of a spatula, until fragrant, about 45 seconds. Stir the garlic mixture into the vegetables. Add the scallion greens and shrimp and toss to combine. Whisk the sauce to recombine and add it to the skillet. Remove the pan from the heat and toss until all ingredients are well coated with sauce and sizzling hot. Serve immediately.

Stir-Fried Shrimp and Snow Peas in Coconut Curry Sauce

SERVES 4

TIME: 45 MINUTES

If you want to devein the shrimp, see the illustrations on page 56. Let the shrimp marinate as you make the sauce and prepare the vegetables and aromatics. See photo of this recipe on page 155.

1	pound large shrimp (21 to 25 count per pound), peeled and deveined, if desired
2	teaspoons soy sauce
2	teaspoons dry sherry
1	tablespoon minced garlic
1	tablespoon minced fresh ginger
3	medium scallions, white parts minced and green parts cut into ¼-inch lengths
6½	teaspoons peanut or vegetable oil
1	medium red bell pepper, stemmed, seeded, and cut into ¼-inch-wide strips
¾	pound snow peas, strings removed (see the illustration on page 6)
¼	cup minced fresh basil leaves
1	recipe Coconut Curry Sauce (page 342)

1. Toss the shrimp with the soy sauce and sherry in a medium bowl. Combine the garlic, ginger, scallion whites, and 1½ teaspoons oil in a small bowl.

2. Heat 2 teaspoons oil in a 12-inch non-stick skillet over high heat until smoking. Add the shrimp and cook, stirring occasionally, until curled and lightly browned, about 1½ minutes. Transfer the shrimp to a clean bowl.

3. Add 1½ teaspoons oil to the now-empty skillet and heat until shimmering. Add the bell pepper and cook, stirring occasionally, until crisp-tender, 1 to 2 minutes. Transfer the bell

JULIENNING VEGETABLES

1. Long vegetables such as carrots, zucchini, and summer squash can be cut into thin julienned strips (also called *matchsticks*) that cook quickly. Start by slicing the vegetables on the bias into rounds.

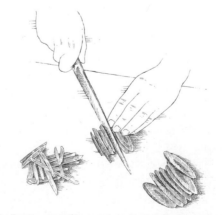

2. Fan the vegetable rounds and cut them into strips that measure about 2 inches long and ¼ inch thick.

pepper to a small bowl. Add the remaining 1½ teaspoons oil and the snow peas to the skillet and cook, stirring occasionally, until crisp-tender, about 1 minute. Return the bell peppers to the skillet and toss to combine.

4. Clear the center of the pan and add the garlic mixture. Cook, mashing the garlic mixture with the back of a spatula, until fragrant, about 45 seconds. Stir the garlic mixture into the vegetables. Add the scallion greens, basil, and shrimp and toss to combine. Whisk the sauce to recombine and add it to the skillet. Remove the pan from the heat and toss until all ingredients are well coated with sauce and sizzling hot. Serve immediately.

Stir-Fried Scallops and Asparagus in Lemon Sauce

SERVES 4

TIME: 45 MINUTES

Use whole bay scallops or sea scallops cut into 1-inch pieces for this dish. Let the scallops marinate as you make the sauce and prepare the vegetables and aromatics. This dish is fairly subtle and benefits from the addition of salt and pepper just before serving.

¾	pound scallops, tendons removed (see the illustration on page 56) and scallops cut, if necessary
2	teaspoons soy sauce
2	teaspoons dry sherry
1	tablespoon minced garlic
1	tablespoon minced fresh ginger
3	medium scallions, white parts minced and green parts cut into ¼-inch lengths
6½	teaspoons peanut or vegetable oil
1	pound asparagus, tough ends snapped off, sliced on the bias into 2-inch lengths
2	medium carrots, peeled and julienned (see the illustrations on page 334)
1	recipe Lemon Sauce (page 342) Salt and ground black pepper

1. Toss the scallops with the soy sauce and sherry in a medium bowl. Combine the garlic, ginger, scallion whites, and 1½ teaspoons oil in a small bowl.

2. Heat 2 teaspoons oil in a 12-inch non-stick skillet over high heat until smoking. Add the scallops and cook, turning once, until opaque, about 1 minute. Transfer the scallops to a clean bowl.

3. Add 1½ teaspoons oil to the now-empty skillet and heat until shimmering. Add the asparagus and cook, stirring occasionally, until crisp-tender, 2 to 3 minutes. Transfer the asparagus to a small bowl. Add the remaining 1½ teaspoons oil and the carrots to the skillet and cook, stirring occasionally, until crisp-tender, about 2 minutes. Return the asparagus to the pan and toss to combine.

4. Clear the center of the pan and add the garlic mixture. Cook, mashing the garlic mixture with the back of a spatula, until fragrant, about 45 seconds. Stir the garlic mixture into the vegetables. Add the scallion greens and scallops and toss to combine. Whisk the sauce to recombine and add it to the skillet. Remove the pan from the heat and toss until all ingredients are well coated with sauce and sizzling hot. Adjust seasonings with salt and pepper to taste. Serve immediately.

Stir-Fried Squid and Vegetables in Black Bean Sauce

SERVES 4

TIME: 45 MINUTES

Cleaned squid costs just a bit more than uncleaned squid and is much quicker to prepare—simply slice and cook. Let the squid marinate as you make the sauce and prepare the vegetables and aromatics. Squid can overcook quite easily and become very tough, so follow the cooking time in the recipe.

¾ pound cleaned squid, bodies cut crosswise into ½-inch rings, tentacles left
   whole

2 teaspoons soy sauce

2 teaspoons dry sherry

1 tablespoon minced garlic

1 tablespoon minced fresh ginger

2 tablespoons minced scallions, white parts
   only

8 teaspoons peanut or vegetable oil

½ pound small shiitake mushrooms, stems
   discarded and caps cut into ½-inch-wide
   strips

1 medium red bell pepper, stemmed,
   seeded, and cut into ¼-inch-wide strips

½ pound sugar snap peas, strings removed
   (see the illustration on page 6)

1 recipe Black Bean Sauce (page 341)

1. Toss the squid with the soy sauce and sherry in a medium bowl. Combine the garlic, ginger, scallions, and 1½ teaspoons oil in a small bowl.

PROTECTING NONSTICK SURFACES

If you stack your cookware (as we do), you run the risk of scratching the nonstick surface. Some cooks slip each pan into a large zipper-lock bag before stacking it, while others place plastic lids (from sour cream, coffee, or yogurt containers) between pans to keep them from scratching each other. Our favorite way to protect nonstick cookware is to slide a doubled piece of paper towel between the pans.

2. Heat 2 teaspoons oil in a 12-inch non-stick skillet over high heat until smoking. Add the squid and cook, stirring occasionally, until opaque, about 1 minute. Transfer the squid to a clean bowl.

3. Add 1½ teaspoons oil to the now-empty pan and heat until shimmering. Add the mushrooms and cook, stirring occasionally, until tender, about 1 minute. Add 1½ teaspoons oil and the bell pepper and cook, stirring occasionally, until crisp-tender, about 1 minute. Add the remaining 1½ teaspoons oil and the peas and cook, stirring occasionally, until softened, about 1 minute.

4. Clear the center of the pan and add the garlic mixture. Cook, mashing the garlic mixture with the back of a spatula, until fragrant, about 45 seconds. Stir the garlic mixture into the vegetables. Add the squid and toss to combine. Whisk the sauce to recombine and add it to the skillet. Remove the pan from the heat and toss until all ingredients are well coated with sauce and sizzling hot. Serve immediately.

STIR-FRIED TOFU

TOFU WORKS WELL IN STIR-FRIES FOR several reasons. It absorbs the flavors of the sauce well, and in the process of browning acquires a pleasantly crisp exterior. It also adds a protein element. Firm or extra-firm tofu (rather than soft or silken varieties) holds its shape best and is the best choice for stir-fries.

Like dairy products, tofu is perishable and should be kept well chilled to maximize its shelf life. We prefer to use it within a few days of opening. If you want to keep an open package of tofu fresh for several days, cover the tofu with fresh water and store in the refrigerator in an airtight container. Change the water daily to keep the tofu fresh. Any hint of sourness and the tofu is past its prime.

When you're ready to stir-fry, drain the tofu and pat it dry with paper towels. Cutting the tofu into 1-inch cubes speeds cooking. Exterior caramelization is promoted by turning the tofu as little as possible, no more than two or three times, as it sears. Because it is hard to overcook, you can let it brown for 3 or 3½ minutes.

Because tofu is quite bland, it works best in stir-fries when paired with highly flavorful sauces, such as those made with fermented black beans or chiles and vinegar.

EQUIPMENT: Electric Woks

We don't like regular woks. The relatively small base of a wok means only modest burner contact, which translates to less than maximum heat. Quite simply, the design of the wok is not meant for cooking on a Western stovetop, where a large, open skillet is much more successful at achieving optimum sizzle and sear.

We wondered, however, if electric woks offered advantages over stovetop woks. Are their heating elements capable of really cranking up the heat and producing first-rate stir-fries? We collected six electric woks ranging in price from $30 to $100 and set up shop in a corner of the test kitchen. We stir-fried and deep-fried in each wok and looked for differences in heating ability and design. Quite frankly, we were surprised to find one wok—and a modestly priced one, at that—that excelled in all areas and another that did quite well.

The runaway winner was the Maxim Nonstick Electric Wok with Dome Cover ($60). It stir-fried on par with a skillet, and it managed the oil for deep-frying like a pro. The temperature dial stayed cool during cooking and was relatively accurate and easy to read. Its size was generous (14 inches in diameter, 6½ quarts in capacity), and the long-handled design made it possible to simultaneously empty and scrape ingredients out of the wok when cooking in batches.

The runner-up was the Toastmaster High-Performance Electric Wok ($30). This wok had the heat output of the winner, but it was not nearly as commodious (just 12¾ inches in diameter and 4½ quarts in capacity). With use, its temperature dial became hot to the touch, and its two short handles were less than ideal for cooking in batches because it was impossible to scrape out food while turning to empty the wok.

The remaining four woks tested—Rival Stainless-Steel Electric Wok ($90), West Bend Electric Wok ($48), Martin Yan Professional Wok ($90), and Circulon Hard Anodized Electric Wok ($100)—weren't worth the space they occupied on the countertop. Problems included flimsy construction, odd design, and hot spots. Moreover, none of these woks had good heat output; in fact, three couldn't get the oil for deep-frying above 350 degrees, though their thermostats were set for 375 and indicated that the temperature had been reached (in one, the oil stayed at only 312 degrees). In comparison, our favorite woks maintained temperatures of 365 to 375 degrees, ideal for deep-frying.

Should you purchase an electric wok? Probably, if you're a frequent fryer or like to use a bamboo steamer (which requires a wok of some sort, electric or not). However, if stir-frying is your limit, stick with a large, heavy, totally utilitarian nonstick skillet.

THE BEST ELECTRIC WOKS

This Maxim wok (left) was easily the best of the six models we tested. The Toastmaster wok (right) heats well and costs less than the Maxim wok, but this model is smaller and not quite as well designed as our top choice.

Stir-Fried Tofu and Asparagus in Black Bean Sauce

SERVES 4

TIME: 45 MINUTES

A red or orange bell pepper can be used in this recipe, but don't use a green pepper—it's bitter and offers no contrast in color with the asparagus. Let the tofu marinate as you make the sauce and prepare the vegetables and aromatics.

¾	pound firm or extra-firm tofu, drained and cut into 1-inch cubes
2	teaspoons soy sauce
2	teaspoons dry sherry
1	tablespoon minced garlic
1	tablespoon minced fresh ginger
3	medium scallions, white parts minced and green parts cut into ¼-inch lengths
6½	teaspoons peanut or vegetable oil
1	pound asparagus, tough ends snapped off, sliced on the bias into 2-inch lengths
1	medium yellow bell pepper, stemmed, seeded, and cut into ¼-inch-wide strips
1	recipe Black Bean Sauce (page 341)

1. Toss the tofu with the soy sauce and sherry in a medium bowl. Combine the garlic, ginger, scallion whites, and 1½ teaspoons oil in a small bowl.

2. Heat 2 teaspoons oil in a 12-inch nonstick skillet over high heat until smoking. Add the tofu and cook, turning several times, until lightly browned on several sides, 3 to 3½ minutes. Transfer the tofu to a clean bowl.

3. Add 1½ teaspoons oil to the now-empty skillet and heat until shimmering. Add the asparagus and cook, stirring occasionally, until crisp-tender, 3 to 4 minutes. Transfer the asparagus to a small bowl. Add the remaining 1½ teaspoons oil and the bell pepper and cook, stirring occasionally, until crisp-tender,

1 to 2 minutes. Return the asparagus to the pan and toss to combine.

4. Clear the center of the pan and add the garlic mixture. Cook, mashing the garlic mixture with the back of a spatula, until fragrant, about 45 seconds. Stir the garlic mixture into the vegetables. Add the scallion greens and tofu and toss to combine. Whisk the sauce to

INGREDIENTS: Soy Sauce

Few condiments are as misunderstood as soy sauce, the pungent, fragrant, fermented flavor mainstay of Asian cooking. Its simple, straightforward composition—equal parts soybeans and a roasted grain, usually wheat, plus water and salt—belies the subtle, sophisticated contribution it makes as an all-purpose seasoning, flavor enhancer, tabletop condiment, and dipping sauce.

The three products consumers are likely to encounter are regular soy sauce, light soy sauce (made with a higher percentage of water and hence lower sodium), and tamari (made with fermented soybeans, water, and salt—no wheat). Tamari generally has a stronger flavor and thicker consistency than soy sauce. It is traditionally used in Japanese cooking.

In a tasting of leading soy sauces, we found that products aged according to ancient customs were superior to synthetic sauces, such as La Choy, which are made in a day and almost always contain hydrolyzed vegetable protein. Our favorite soy sauce, Eden Selected Shoyu Soy Sauce (*shoyu* is the Japanese word for soy sauce), is aged for 3 years. Tasters also liked products made by San-J and Kikkoman.

THE BEST SOY SAUCE

Eden Selected Shoyu Soy Sauce was described by tasters as "toasty, caramely, and complex." The saltiness was tangible but not overwhelming. Among the 12 brands tested, it was the clear favorite.

recombine and add it to the skillet. Remove the pan from the heat and toss until all ingredients are well coated with sauce and sizzling hot. Serve immediately.

Stir-Fried Tofu, Red Onion, and Sugar Snap Peas in Hot-and-Sour Sauce

SERVES 4

TIME: 45 MINUTES

Crunchy sugar snap peas are a good foil for tender tofu, and caramelized onions add a sweet note. See the illustration on page 6 for tips on stringing the peas. Let the tofu marinate as you make the sauce and prepare the vegetables and aromatics.

¾	pound firm or extra-firm tofu, drained and cut into 1-inch cubes
2	teaspoons soy sauce
2	teaspoons dry sherry
1	tablespoon minced garlic
1	tablespoon minced fresh ginger
2	tablespoons minced scallions, white parts only
8	teaspoons peanut or vegetable oil
2	medium carrots, peeled and julienned (see the illustrations on page 334)
1	medium red onion, halved and cut into ½-inch-thick wedges
½	pound sugar snap peas, strings removed (see the illustration on page 6)
1	recipe Hot-and-Sour Sauce (page 340)

1. Toss the tofu with the soy sauce and sherry in a medium bowl. Combine the garlic, ginger, scallions, and 1½ teaspoons oil in a small bowl.

2. Heat 2 teaspoons oil in a 12-inch nonstick skillet over high heat until smoking. Add the tofu and cook, turning several times, until lightly browned on several sides, 3 to 3½ minutes. Transfer the tofu to a clean bowl.

3. Add 1½ teaspoons oil to the now-empty skillet and heat until shimmering. Add the carrots and cook, stirring occasionally, until crisp-tender, about 2 minutes. Transfer the carrots to a small bowl. Add 1½ teaspoons oil to the now-empty skillet and heat until shimmering. Add the onion and cook, stirring occasionally, until lightly browned, about 2 minutes. Add the remaining 1½ teaspoons oil and the peas and cook, stirring occasionally, until crisp-tender, about 2 minutes. Return the carrots to the pan and toss to combine.

4. Clear the center of the pan and add the garlic mixture. Cook, mashing the garlic mixture with the back of a spatula, until fragrant, about 45 seconds. Stir the garlic mixture into the vegetables. Add the tofu and toss to combine. Whisk the sauce to recombine and add it to the skillet. Remove the pan from the heat and toss until all ingredients are well coated with sauce and sizzling hot. Serve immediately.

STIR-FRY SAUCES

STRONGLY FLAVORED SAUCES ARE THE key to vibrant stir-fries. In our testing, we found that too much cornstarch (many recipes call for 1 tablespoon or more) makes sauces thick and gloppy. We prefer the cleaner flavor and texture of sauces made with a minimum of cornstarch—no more than 1 teaspoon for a typical stir-fry. With so little cornstarch, it is necessary to limit the amount of liquid ingredients in the sauce—about ½ cup in the recipes that follow. A half-cup of sauce will nicely coat the ingredients in our standard stir-fry without being too liquid. We have made a specific sauce suggestion for each stir-fry, but feel free to create your own combinations of sauce, vegetables, and protein.

A caution about the use of sugar: Even sweet sauces, such as sweet-and-sour, should contain only a minimum of sugar. Too much Chinese food prepared in the United States is overly sweet. A little sugar is authentic (and delicious) in many recipes; a lot of sugar is not.

Hot-and-Sour Sauce

MAKES ENOUGH FOR
1 STIR-FRY RECIPE

TIME: 5 MINUTES

For a spicier sauce, increase the chili paste to 2 tablespoons.

3	tablespoons rice vinegar
2	tablespoons canned low-sodium chicken broth
2	tablespoons dry sherry
1	tablespoon soy sauce
4	teaspoons Asian chili paste
1	teaspoon Asian sesame oil
1	teaspoon sugar
1	teaspoon cornstarch

Combine all the ingredients in a small bowl and set aside.

INGREDIENTS: Asian Sesame Oil

Also known as dark or toasted sesame oil, this aromatic brown oil is used as a seasoning in sauces. Because of its low smoke point, it is not used for cooking. Do not substitute regular sesame oil, which is pressed from untoasted seeds and meant for salad dressings and cooking. Japanese brands of sesame oil are commonly sold in American supermarkets and are generally quite good. Sesame oil tends to go rancid quickly, so store it in a cool cabinet or refrigerate an opened bottle if you will not use it up within a couple of months.

INGREDIENTS: Sichuan Peppercorns

Sichuan peppercorns have a mildly peppery, herbal flavor and aroma. If possible, smell peppercorns before buying them to gauge freshness and intensity. Twigs and tiny leaves will be mixed in with the peppercorns (just pick them out of the amount you are using), but there should be a minimum of black seeds. To bring out their flavor, toast peppercorns in a dry skillet until fragrant and then grind them in a coffee mill set aside for spices.

Garlic Sauce

MAKES ENOUGH FOR
1 STIR-FRY RECIPE

TIME: 5 MINUTES

This sauce adds a rich garlic flavor to beef and seafood but does not overpower other ingredients. Adjust the heat as desired by adding more hot red pepper flakes to the stir-fry.

3	tablespoons dry sherry
3	tablespoons canned low-sodium chicken broth
2	tablespoons soy sauce
1/2	teaspoon Asian sesame oil
1 1/2	teaspoons minced garlic
1	teaspoon cornstarch
1/2	teaspoon sugar
1/8	teaspoon hot red pepper flakes

1. Combine all the ingredients except the pepper flakes in a small bowl and set aside.

2. Add the pepper flakes to the garlic mixture in step 1 of the stir-fry recipe.

INGREDIENTS: Chili Paste

Sometimes labeled *chili sauce*, chili paste is a spicy seasoning made with crushed chile peppers, vinegar, and, usually, garlic. The texture is thick and smooth, and the color is bright red. Brands vary from mild to incendiary, so taste before using and adjust the amount as needed. Opened jars can be refrigerated for many months.

Sweet-and-Sour Sauce

MAKES ENOUGH FOR
1 STIR-FRY RECIPE

TIME: 5 MINUTES

Pineapple juice can be used in this recipe instead of orange juice, if desired. This is especially appropriate when pineapple is in the stir-fry. The flavors in this sauce are good with chicken, pork, and seafood. Due to the thick consistency of the ketchup, less cornstarch than usual is needed in this sauce.

3	tablespoons red wine vinegar
3	tablespoons orange juice
3	tablespoons sugar
1 1/2	tablespoons ketchup
1/2	teaspoon cornstarch
1/4	teaspoon salt

Combine all the ingredients in a small bowl and set aside.

Black Bean Sauce

MAKES ENOUGH FOR
1 STIR-FRY RECIPE

TIME: 5 MINUTES

Chinese fermented black beans are available in Asian food shops. They should be moist and soft to the touch. Don't buy beans that are dried out or shriveled. High-quality fermented beans should not be overly salty.

3	tablespoons dry sherry
3	tablespoons canned low-sodium chicken broth
2	tablespoons soy sauce
1	tablespoon Asian sesame oil
1	teaspoon cornstarch
1/2	teaspoon sugar
1/8	teaspoon ground black pepper
1	tablespoon Chinese fermented black beans, chopped

1. Combine all the ingredients except the beans in a small bowl and set aside.

2. Add the black beans to the garlic mixture in step 1 of the stir-fry recipe.

Oyster Sauce

MAKES ENOUGH FOR
1 STIR-FRY RECIPE

TIME: 5 MINUTES

As the name suggests, jarred oyster sauce is made from fermented oysters, along with salt and spices (see page 143 for more information and our tasting of leading brands). The flavor is not overly fishy, but it is quite salty, so a little goes a long way. This sauce works well with beef and seafood. Due to the thick consistency of the oyster sauce, less cornstarch than usual is needed in this sauce.

3	tablespoons dry sherry
3	tablespoons jarred oyster sauce
1	tablespoon Asian sesame oil
1	tablespoon soy sauce
1/2	teaspoon sugar
1/2	teaspoon cornstarch
1/8	teaspoon ground black pepper

Combine all the ingredients in a small bowl and set aside.

Coconut Curry Sauce

MAKES ENOUGH FOR
I STIR-FRY RECIPE

TIME: 5 MINUTES

Use canned unsweetened coconut milk in this recipe, not sweetened coconut cream. This velvety sauce coats food especially well and doesn't require any cornstarch.

- 1/3   cup unsweetened coconut milk
- 3   tablespoons canned low-sodium chicken broth
- 1 1/2   teaspoons yellow curry powder
- 1/4   teaspoon sugar
- 1/4   teaspoon salt
- 1/8   teaspoon hot red pepper flakes

1. Combine all the ingredients except the pepper flakes in a small bowl and set aside.

2. Add the pepper flakes to the garlic mixture in step 1 of the stir-fry recipe.

Lemon Sauce

MAKES ENOUGH FOR
I STIR-FRY RECIPE

TIME: 5 MINUTES

The flavors in this sauce are mild and work especially well with seafood.

- 1/2   teaspoon minced zest and 3 tablespoons juice from I large lemon
- 2   tablespoons canned low-sodium chicken broth
- 2   tablespoons dry sherry
- 1   tablespoon soy sauce
- 2   teaspoons sugar
- 1   teaspoon cornstarch
- 1/8   teaspoon ground black pepper

Combine all the ingredients in a small bowl and set aside.

Sichuan Chile Sauce

MAKES ENOUGH FOR
I STIR-FRY RECIPE

TIME: 5 MINUTES

This sauce gets its heat from chili paste, and Sichuan peppercorns give it an herbal, floral quality.

- 3   tablespoons dry sherry
- 2   tablespoons canned low-sodium chicken broth
- 1 1/2   tablespoons soy sauce
- 1   tablespoon Asian sesame oil
- 1   tablespoon Asian chili paste
- 1   teaspoon cornstarch
- 1/4   teaspoon toasted and ground Sichuan peppercorns
- 1/4   teaspoon sugar

Combine all the ingredients in a small bowl and set aside.

Spicy Orange Sauce

MAKES ENOUGH FOR
I STIR-FRY RECIPE

TIME: 5 MINUTES

The citrus flavors in this sauce are especially good with chicken and seafood.

- 1/2   teaspoon minced zest and 1/4 cup juice from I large orange
- 2   tablespoons dry sherry
- 1   tablespoon Asian sesame oil
- 1   tablespoon soy sauce
- 2   teaspoons Asian chili paste
- 1   teaspoon sugar
- 1   teaspoon cornstarch

Combine all the ingredients in a small bowl and set aside.

BECAUSE EGGS COOK IN MINUTES, they are a natural choice for quick meals. In this chapter, we focus on egg dishes that are substantial enough to serve as a light dinner, especially when you add potatoes, a vegetable side dish, or a leafy salad.

From experience, we found that eggs suffer more from the vagaries of improper storage than age. Despite the built-in egg cups, the refrigerator door is far from ideal storage for two reasons: temperature and protection. The American Egg Board recommends storing eggs at 40 degrees, but we found the average door temperature in our six test kitchen refrigerators closer to 45 degrees. The top shelf is a better bet; ours registered between 38 and 40 degrees. When removed from the protective cardboard carton, the eggs may absorb off flavors; we've made oniony cakes and cookies with improperly stored eggs. The carton also helps maintain humidity—ideally, 75 to 85 percent.

We were curious how eggs from different sources might stack up when tasted side by side. We recently put four varieties—farm-fresh eggs (less than a week old); Egg Innovations organic eggs ("free roaming"); Eggland's Best brand eggs from hens raised on a vegetarian feed (the label says these eggs are guaranteed to possess "25% less saturated fat than regular eggs" and "100 mg of omega-3 fatty acids"); and standard supermarket eggs—to the test by cooking each sunny-side up. The farm-fresh eggs were standouts. The large yolks were shockingly orange and sat high above the comparatively small white. Their flavor was exceptionally rich and complex. The organic eggs followed in second place, with eggs from hens raised on a vegetarian diet in third place and the standard supermarket eggs last.

Our conclusion? If you have access to eggs fresh from the farm, they are worth it for the rich flavor. Otherwise, organic eggs are worth the premium (about a dollar more than standard supermarket eggs), especially if you frequently eat them on their own.

SCRAMBLED EGGS

WHAT CAN BE DIFFICULT ABOUT cooking scrambled eggs? They contain only a few ingredients, and the whole process—from walking into the kitchen to sitting down at the table—takes but a few minutes. But the simplest things are not always the easiest. Ideally, scrambled eggs have large, fluffy curds of egg that remain moist and tender after cooking. All too often, however, you end up with the opposite: dry, flat, tough curds.

The majority of recipes we found called for a liquid, normally water or milk, to be added to the eggs prior to scrambling. Milk was overwhelmingly favored by tasters because the eggs with milk developed larger curds with more flavor. We decided not to add spices or dried herbs, other than salt and pepper, because the eggs became dry and powdery when we did. As for other ingredients, we found it was best to add warm, fully cooked items (raw ingredients were not done when the eggs were, and cold ingredients cooled the eggs, prolonged the cooking time, and resulted in tougher eggs).

Next, we investigated the type of pan in which to cook our eggs. A nonstick pan was the obvious choice, so size became the next question. We started with eight eggs and a 12-inch pan but soon found the surface area was too great and the eggs tended to overcook. Our next attempt was with a 10-inch pan. The eggs cooked quickly and evenly without becoming dry. An 8-inch pan was too small; it didn't allow the eggs to cook quickly enough, making them tough and rubbery.

12

EGGS

BUILDING BLOCK RECIPE
Scrambled Eggs
SERVES 4
TIME: 5 MINUTES

8	large eggs
½	teaspoon salt
⅛	teaspoon ground black pepper
½	cup milk
1	tablespoon unsalted butter

1. Crack the eggs into a medium bowl. Add the salt, pepper, and milk. Whip with a fork until the streaks are gone and the color is pure yellow; stop beating while the bubbles are still large.

2. Heat the butter in a 10-inch nonstick skillet over medium-high heat. When the butter foams, swirl it around and up the sides of the pan. Before the foam completely subsides, pour the beaten eggs into the pan. With a wooden or heatproof rubber spatula, push the eggs from one side of the pan to the other, slowly and deliberately lifting and folding them as they form into curds, until they are nicely clumped into a single mound but remain shiny and wet, 1½ to 2 minutes. Serve immediately.

The last variable we tested was the temperature of the burner. Our first test was the slow and low method. The results—scrambled eggs with small, dry curds—were bad. Medium heat wasn't much better; the eggs spent too much time in the pan, and while the curds were bigger, they were still tough and chewy. High heat proved the best option; the eggs coagulated almost instantly and were fully cooked, yet moist.

The utensil used to stir the eggs while cooking unexpectedly turned out to be a factor in the quality of the finished dish. We found that mixing slowly and deliberately with a wide spatula yielded curds much bigger and moister than those that formed when we beat the mixture with a fork, as suggested in most recipes.

With the addition of cooked sausage, ham, vegetables, and/or cheese, these scrambled egg recipes are perfect for a hearty breakfast or a quick weeknight dinner.

Scrambled Eggs with Linguiça Sausage and Red Peppers
SERVES 4
TIME: 15 MINUTES

Linguiça is a mildly spicy Portuguese sausage. Other spicy sausages, including chorizo and hot Italian links, can be used in this recipe. If the sausage is particularly fatty, you may need to remove some of the rendered fat from the pan; there should be no more than 1 tablespoon.

8	large eggs
½	teaspoon salt
⅛	teaspoon ground black pepper
½	cup milk
2	teaspoons vegetable oil
6	ounces linguiça sausage, cut in half lengthwise and then cut crosswise into half moons about ⅛ inch thick
1	small red bell pepper, stemmed, seeded, and cut into ¼-inch dice
3	medium scallions, green parts only, sliced thin on the bias

1. Crack the eggs into a medium bowl. Add the salt, pepper, and milk. Whip with a fork until the streaks are gone and the color is pure yellow; stop beating while the bubbles are still large.

2. Heat the oil in a 10-inch nonstick skillet over medium-high heat until shimmering. Add the sausage and cook, stirring occasionally, until

slightly browned, about 1½ minutes. Add the bell pepper and continue to cook until the pepper softens slightly, about 1½ minutes. If necessary, remove excess fat from the pan; there should be no more than 1 tablespoon.

3. Pour the beaten eggs into the pan. With a wooden or heatproof rubber spatula, push the eggs from one side of the pan to the other, slowly and deliberately lifting and folding them as they form into curds, until they are nicely clumped into a single mound but remain shiny and wet, 1½ to 2 minutes. Serve immediately, sprinkled with scallions.

Scrambled Eggs with Ham and Swiss

SERVES 4

TIME: 15 MINUTES

If you use boiled rather than baked ham in this recipe, increase the cooking time in step 1 by a minute or so to cook off excess water. Try to get ham sliced about ⅛ inch thick at the deli counter.

8	large eggs
½	teaspoon salt
⅛	teaspoon ground black pepper
½	cup milk
2	teaspoons vegetable oil
6	ounces thickly sliced deli ham, cut into ½-inch dice
2	ounces Swiss cheese, shredded (about ½ cup)
2	tablespoons chopped fresh tarragon leaves

1. Crack the eggs into a medium bowl. Add the salt, pepper, and milk. Whip with a fork until the streaks are gone and the color is pure yellow; stop beating while the bubbles are still large.

2. Heat the oil in a 10-inch nonstick skillet over medium-high heat until shimmering. Add the ham and cook, stirring occasionally,

until lightly browned, about 2½ minutes.

3. Pour the beaten eggs into the pan. With a wooden or heatproof rubber spatula, push the eggs from one side of the pan to the other, slowly and deliberately lifting and folding them as they form into curds, until they are nicely clumped into a single mound but remain shiny and wet, 1½ to 2 minutes. Remove the pan from the heat and stir in the cheese and tarragon. Serve immediately.

Scrambled Eggs with Zucchini, Feta, and Mint

SERVES 4

TIME: 15 MINUTES

Cut the zucchini into small pieces so they release their liquid quickly.

8	large eggs
½	teaspoon salt
⅛	teaspoon ground black pepper
½	cup milk
1	tablespoon vegetable oil
1	medium zucchini, cut into ¼-inch dice
½	small onion, chopped fine
2½	ounces feta cheese, crumbled (about ½ cup)
1	tablespoon chopped fresh mint leaves

1. Crack the eggs into a medium bowl. Add the salt, pepper, and milk. Whip with a fork until the streaks are gone and the color is pure yellow; stop beating while the bubbles are still large.

2. Heat the oil in a 10-inch nonstick skillet over medium-high heat until shimmering. Add the zucchini and cook, stirring occasionally, until lightly browned and crisp-tender, about 4 minutes. Add the onion and continue to cook until it softens, about 1½ minutes.

3. Pour the beaten eggs into the pan. With a wooden or heatproof rubber spatula, push

the eggs from one side of the pan to the other, slowly and deliberately lifting and folding them as they form into curds, until they are nicely clumped into a single mound but remain shiny and wet, 1½ to 2 minutes. Remove the pan from the heat and stir in the cheese and mint. Serve immediately.

MIGAS

THE WORD MIGAS MEANS "CRUMBS" in Spanish. If you were to order migas in a restaurant in Spain, you would be served a dish of fried bread and ham, usually set on top of fried eggs. In Mexico, *migas* means something quite different. It is usually a combination of crushed tortillas and scrambled eggs cooked with onions, garlic, and chiles. A frugal dish created to stretch small amounts of protein to feed many people, the Mexican migas is easy to prepare and delicious.

While some of us had eaten migas before, many of us had questions about its proper preparation. We noticed that most recipes we found in our search were the same, except when it came to the tortillas. Some recipes called for fried corn tortillas (the kind you buy at the supermarket); others used stale dry tortillas. With the recipes in hand, we went to the kitchen to see which yielded the best migas.

The first recipes we tried were the ones that called for day-old or stale tortillas. The usual approach was to shallow-fry the tortillas and then add them to the eggs. While we certainly liked the flavor of these tortillas, we felt they made the eggs greasy and that their consistency was unpleasant and slightly chewy. Thinking these problems were the result of the chips being in contact with the eggs too long, we decided to add them to almost fully cooked eggs rather than adding

them to the pan at the beginning. While this alleviated some of the problems, we were still left with greasy eggs.

We shifted our focus to store-bought tortilla chips. We tried several brands of chips and liked the migas much better than we did those made with stale tortillas. Store-bought chips, especially the baked variety, didn't have the greasy flavor or the off-putting texture we had noted previously.

We then went on to develop the other flavors in the eggs. Onions and garlic were a given for their pungency. We also tried a variety of chiles and peppers. While tasters liked the mild flavors of Anaheim and poblano chiles, we had a hard time locating them at our local grocery store and felt it was better to go with widely available red bell pepper. To complement the sweet crunch of the red pepper, we added a jalapeño chile.

Many of the recipes we encountered called for adding tomatoes to the eggs while they cooked. We attempted this and liked the brightness they added to the dish. However, the tomatoes also made the eggs watery. Wanting to retain the tomato flavor and thinking of ways to do so, we realized that the ingredients we were adding were similar to the ingredients in a salsa. By increasing the amount of onion, garlic, and jalapeños in the recipe and adding lime juice, cilantro, and tomatoes, we made a quick salsa in the food processor. We let this salsa drain in a colander while we prepared the migas, thereby avoiding the wateriness that fresh tomatoes alone brought to the eggs. This salsa contributed a lot of flavor and freshness to the dish. With the addition of pepper Jack cheese for richness, we had a distinctive, satisfying dish that was easy to assemble.

Migas

SERVES 4

TIME: 25 MINUTES

This scrambled egg dish can be served by itself or with refried beans (page 110) for a satisfying dinner. Baked chips work better than fried chips.

1   small red onion, cut into ¼-inch dice (about 1 cup)

3   medium cloves garlic, minced or pressed through a garlic press (about 1 tablespoon)

1   medium jalapeño chile, stemmed, seeded, and minced (about 2 tablespoons)

2   tablespoons fresh cilantro leaves

2   teaspoons juice from 1 lime
    Salt

2   small tomatoes (about 1 pound), cored and cut into 8 pieces each

2   tablespoons vegetable oil

1   medium red bell pepper, stemmed, seeded, and cut into ¼-inch dice

6   large eggs, lightly beaten in a bowl

2   ounces baked tortilla chips, broken into ½-inch pieces (about 1 cup)
    Ground black pepper

2   ounces pepper Jack cheese, shredded (about ½ cup)

1. In a food processor fitted with a steel blade, pulse ¼ cup onion, 1 teaspoon garlic, 1 tablespoon chile, and the cilantro, lime juice, and ¼ teaspoon salt until finely minced, scraping down the sides of the bowl as necessary, about five 1-second pulses. Add the tomatoes and pulse until roughly chopped, about two 1-second pulses. Transfer the salsa to a fine-mesh sieve and set aside to drain.

2. Heat the oil in a 10-inch nonstick skillet over medium-high heat until shimmering. Add the bell pepper along with the remaining ¾ cup onion, 2 teaspoons garlic, and 1 tablespoon chile. Cook, stirring occasionally, until the peppers soften, 2 to 3 minutes.

3. Meanwhile, mix the eggs, tortilla chips, ¼ teaspoon salt, and a pinch of black pepper.

4. Pour the egg mixture into the pan with the vegetables. With a wooden or heatproof rubber spatula, push the eggs from one side of the pan to the other, slowly and deliberately lifting and folding them as they form into curds, until they are nicely clumped into a single mound but remain shiny and wet, 1½ to 2 minutes.

5. Remove the pan from the heat and stir in the cheese. Transfer the eggs to a serving platter or individual plates. Serve immediately, topped with the salsa.

OMELETS

OMELETS ARE A PERFECT CANDIDATE for a book about quick cooking. Within minutes, you can have a hot, satisfying meal that is welcome at breakfast, lunch, or dinner. In addition to being quick, omelets lend themselves to myriad interesting and flavorful filling combinations without much effort. But in all their simplicity, omelets can be disastrous. Having eaten plenty of overbrowned, tough, and watery omelets, we sought the best way to produce a soft, supple, and creamy omelet.

The major problem is overcooking. While browned eggs are good for a frittata, we felt the exterior of the omelet should remain unbrowned and moist. Normally, browning is the result of excessive heat or overcooking. In our initial testing, we too were guilty of overcooking our omelets. For this first round of tests, we used an 8-inch skillet to make a three-egg omelet. The small skillet made it impossible to cook the top side of the omelet without overcooking and browning the underside. We traded in our 8-inch pan for a 10-inch skillet. The larger pan worked much better. Because the omelet was thinner, we were able to cook the upper part without overcooking the bottom. But the exterior of the finished omelet was still a little too brown.

We attributed this excessive browning to the temperature of the burner. With our previous tests, we used a medium-high flame. Thinking that was too high, we tried both low heat and medium heat. Both these methods produced poor omelets. The cooking time was too long, and the eggs became tough and rubbery. Trying the opposite approach, we cooked the eggs at the highest setting on the stove. While this set the eggs almost at once, they also browned much too quickly. We then returned to medium-high heat, this time lowering the flame after the eggs set to finish the omelet. This method proved impractical because the omelet cooked so quickly. We then considered a method that allowed the residual heat of the pan to finish cooking the omelet off the heat. This turned out to be the ideal method; the leftover heat of the pan cooked the omelet to a perfect consistency without browning the exterior.

As for the fillings, the possibilities are endless. We did, however, identify in our trials several factors that affected the omelet. Because we were now using a larger pan, we noticed that if we used more than ¼ cup filling per omelet, the thin shell would break and the filling would ooze out of the omelet into the pan. We also realized that because the filling is added as the omelet is removed from the heat, it should be fully cooked beforehand. As for the cheese, we learned it was better to use a variety that melts easily and that it should be finely grated in order to melt in seconds.

The following omelets can be served with bread and a basic leafy salad from Chapter 2 to make a satisfying meal any time of the day. Although it's not too much work to make two omelets in succession in the same pan, if you

are feeding three or four people, we think a frittata (see the recipes on pages 354–356) is a better choice.

≈

Caramelized Onion, Bacon, and Blue Cheese Omelets
MAKES 2
TIME: 20 MINUTES

We tempered the assertiveness of the blue cheese in this recipe with a little bit of Monterey Jack, but if you prefer the fullest flavor, you can omit the Jack cheese and use 6 tablespoons blue. See the illustrations on page 351 for tips on making omelets.

2	slices bacon (about 2 ounces), cut crosswise into ¼-inch strips
½	medium onion, sliced thin
6	large eggs
	Salt and ground black pepper
1	tablespoon unsalted butter
4	tablespoons crumbled mild blue cheese
2	tablespoons finely grated Monterey Jack cheese

1. Fry the bacon in a 10-inch nonstick skillet over medium heat until crisp, about 6 minutes. With a slotted spoon, transfer the bacon to a paper towel–lined plate. Discard all but 1 tablespoon fat from the skillet. Set the skillet over medium heat and add the onion. Cook, stirring frequently, until softened and golden brown, about 4 minutes. Remove the paper towel from under the bacon and transfer the onion to the plate with the bacon; set aside until needed. Wipe the pan clean with paper towels.

2. Crack 3 eggs into each of two small bowls. Using a fork, beat ⅛ teaspoon salt and a pinch of pepper into each bowl of eggs until thoroughly combined.

3. Heat ½ tablespoon butter in the empty skillet over medium-high heat. When the

foaming subsides, pour in one bowl of beaten eggs. Cook until the edges begin to set, 2 to 3 seconds; then, with a heatproof rubber spatula, stir in a circular motion until slightly thickened, about 10 seconds. Use the spatula to pull the cooked edges toward the center and then tilt the pan to one side so any uncooked egg runs to the edge of the pan. Repeat until the omelet is just set but still moist on the surface, 20 to 25 seconds. Sprinkle 2 tablespoons blue cheese, 1 tablespoon Monterey Jack cheese, and half of the bacon-onion filling down the center of the omelet, perpendicular to the handle of the skillet.

4. Transfer the pan to a cool burner. Use a rubber spatula to fold the lower third (nearest you) of the omelet to the center; press gently with a spatula to secure the seams, maintaining the fold.

5. Run a spatula between the outer edge of the omelet and the pan to loosen. Jerk the pan sharply toward you a few times to slide the omelet up the far side of the pan. Jerk again so that 2 inches of unfolded edge folds over itself or use the spatula to fold the edge over. Invert the omelet onto a plate. Tidy the edges with the spatula.

6. Repeat steps 3, 4, and 5 with the remaining butter, eggs, cheeses, and filling. Serve immediately.

BUILDING BLOCK RECIPE

Cheese Omelets

MAKES 2

TIME: 10 MINUTES

Choose any finely grated cheese for this recipe, including cheddar, Monterey Jack, or Gruyère. If you want to add a filling with cooked vegetables or meat, use about ¼ cup per omelet.

6 large eggs
   Salt and ground black pepper
1 tablespoon unsalted butter
6 tablespoons finely grated cheese

1. Crack 3 eggs into each of two small bowls. Using a fork, beat ⅛ teaspoon salt and a pinch of pepper into each bowl of eggs until thoroughly combined.

2. Heat ½ tablespoon butter in a 10-inch nonstick skillet over medium-high heat. When the foaming subsides, pour in one bowl of beaten eggs. Cook until the edges begin to set, 2 to 3 seconds; then, with a heatproof rubber spatula, stir in a circular motion until slightly thickened, about 10 seconds. Use a spatula to pull the cooked edges toward the center, then tilt the pan to one side so any uncooked egg runs to the edge of the pan. Repeat until the omelet is just set but still moist on the surface, 20 to 25 seconds. Sprinkle 3 tablespoons cheese down the center of the omelet, perpendicular to the handle of the skillet.

3. Transfer the pan to a cool burner. Use a rubber spatula to fold the lower third (nearest you) of the omelet to the center; press gently with a spatula to secure the seams, maintaining the fold.

4. Run a spatula between the outer edge of the omelet and the pan to loosen. Jerk the pan sharply toward you a few times to slide the omelet up the far side of the pan. Jerk again so that 2 inches of unfolded edge folds over itself or use the spatula to fold the edge over. Invert the omelet onto a plate. Tidy the edges with the spatula.

5. Repeat steps 2, 3, and 4 with the remaining butter, eggs, and cheese. Serve immediately.

Mushroom, Fontina, and Oregano Omelets

MAKES 2

TIME: 20 MINUTES

Mushrooms contain a lot of water that must be cooked out before they are added to the omelet. See the illustrations below for tips on making omelets.

1	tablespoon vegetable oil
4	medium white mushrooms (about 2 ounces), cleaned and cut into ¼-inch-thick slices
1	medium shallot, minced (about 3 tablespoons)
½	teaspoon chopped fresh oregano leaves
	Salt and ground black pepper
6	large eggs
1	tablespoon unsalted butter
6	tablespoons finely grated fontina cheese

1. Heat the oil in a 10-inch nonstick skillet over medium heat until shimmering, about 2 minutes. Add the mushrooms and cook until softened and just beginning to color, about 3 minutes. Add the shallot and cook, stirring occasionally, until softened and lightly brown, about 3 minutes. Stir in the oregano and cook for 30 seconds. Season with salt and pepper to taste. Transfer the filling to a small bowl and set

PREPARING AN OMELET

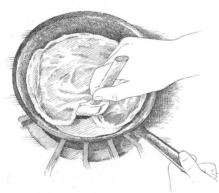

1. Pull the cooked eggs from the edges of the pan toward the center, tilting the pan so any uncooked egg runs to the pan's edges.

2. Transfer the pan to a cool burner. Fold the lower third of the eggs over the filling. Press the seam to secure.

3. Pull the pan sharply toward you so the omelet slides up the lip of the far edge of the pan.

4. Fold the far edge of the omelet toward the center. Press to secure the seam. Invert onto a plate.

351

aside until needed. Wipe the pan clean with paper towels.

2. Crack 3 eggs into each of two small bowls. Using a fork, beat ⅛ teaspoon salt and a pinch of pepper into each bowl of eggs until thoroughly combined.

3. Heat ½ tablespoon butter in the empty skillet over medium-high heat. When the foaming subsides, pour in one bowl of beaten eggs. Cook until the edges begin to set, 2 to 3 seconds; then, with a heatproof rubber spatula, stir in a circular motion until slightly thickened, about 10 seconds. Use the spatula to pull the cooked edges toward the center and then tilt the pan to one side so any uncooked egg runs to the edge of the pan. Repeat until the omelet is just set but still moist on the surface, 20 to 25 seconds. Sprinkle 3 tablespoons cheese and half of the mushroom filling down the center of the omelet, perpendicular to the handle of the skillet.

4. Transfer the pan to a cool burner. Use a rubber spatula to fold the lower third (nearest you) of the omelet to the center; press gently with a spatula to secure the seams, maintaining the fold.

5. Run a spatula between the outer edge of the omelet and the pan to loosen. Jerk the pan sharply toward you a few times to slide the omelet up the far side of the pan. Jerk again so that 2 inches of unfolded edge folds over itself or use the spatula to fold the edge over. Invert the omelet onto a plate. Tidy the edges with the spatula.

6. Repeat steps 3, 4, and 5 with the remaining butter, eggs, cheese, and filling. Serve immediately.

Sausage, Roasted Red Pepper, and Parmesan Omelets

MAKES 2

TIME: 20 MINUTES

Any type of sausage can be substituted for the Italian sausage in this recipe—just make sure to break it into small pieces (¼ inch or smaller) so it doesn't tear the omelet. See the illustrations on page 351 for tips on making omelets.

I	teaspoon vegetable oil
4	ounces sweet Italian sausage, removed from casings
2	ounces jarred roasted red peppers, drained and cut into ¼-inch dice (about ¼ cup)
	Salt and ground black pepper
6	large eggs
I	tablespoon unsalted butter
6	tablespoons finely grated Parmesan cheese

1. Heat the oil in a 10-inch nonstick skillet over medium heat until shimmering, about 2 minutes. Add the sausage and cook, breaking it into small pieces with the back of a spoon, until browned, about 5 minutes. With a slotted spoon, transfer the sausage to a paper towel–lined plate. Discard all but ½ tablespoon fat from the skillet. Set the skillet over medium heat and add the bell peppers. Cook, stirring frequently, until heated through, about 1 minute. Remove the paper towel from under the sausage and transfer the peppers to the plate with the sausage; set aside until needed. Wipe the pan clean with paper towels.

2. Crack 3 eggs into each of two small bowls. Using a fork, beat ⅛ teaspoon salt and a pinch of pepper into each bowl of eggs until thoroughly combined.

3. Heat ½ tablespoon butter in the empty skillet over medium-high heat. When the

foaming subsides, pour in one bowl of beaten eggs. Cook until the edges begin to set, 2 to 3 seconds; then, with a heatproof rubber spatula, stir in a circular motion until slightly thickened, about 10 seconds. Use a spatula to pull the cooked edges toward the center and then tilt the pan to one side so any uncooked egg runs to the edge of the pan. Repeat until the omelet is just set but still moist on the surface, 20 to 25 seconds. Sprinkle 3 tablespoons cheese and half of the sausage-pepper filling down the center of the omelet, perpendicular to the handle of the skillet.

4. Transfer the pan to a cool burner. Use a rubber spatula to fold the lower third (nearest you) of the omelet to the center; press gently with a spatula to secure the seams, maintaining the fold.

5. Run a spatula between the outer edge of the omelet and the pan to loosen. Jerk the pan sharply toward you a few times to slide the omelet up the far side of the pan. Jerk again so that 2 inches of unfolded edge folds over itself or use the spatula to fold the edge over. Invert the omelet onto a plate. Tidy the edges with the spatula.

6. Repeat steps 3, 4, and 5 with the remaining butter, eggs, cheese, and filling. Serve immediately.

MAKING A FRITTATA

Once the bottom of the frittata is firm, use a thin spatula to lift the edge closest to you. Tilt the skillet slightly toward you so the uncooked egg runs underneath. Return the skillet to a level position and swirl gently to distribute the uncooked egg.

FRITTATAS

FRITTATAS HAVE ALL THE GOOD characteristics of omelets without the finicky cooking technique. Italian in origin, frittatas incorporate more filling, making them more substantial than omelets. They are also more forgiving than omelets when it comes to cooking. In the time it takes to make two omelets, you can make a frittata that feeds four. However, frittatas are not foolproof. It took some testing to avoid the common pitfalls—typically toughness and dryness—and create a recipe that yielded a moist yet firm frittata every time.

The first issue we dealt with was pan size. Starting with six eggs, we made frittatas in skillets measuring 8 inches, 10 inches, and 12 inches. We found that the 10-inch pan was optimal. The frittata made with the 12-inch pan was too thin and ended up overcooked. The frittata made in the 8-inch pan took a little too long to cook, resulting in dry and tough edges. We then tried making the same frittata in both a traditional pan and a nonstick pan. While we found we could produce satisfactory frittatas in both pans, we had to use a lot more oil in the traditional pan to prevent sticking, making the resulting frittata slightly greasy. The 10-inch nonstick pan was the winner.

After several tests, we determined that about ¾ cup to 1 cup filling was enough for six eggs. Any more than that amount created problems with the frittata cooking evenly; any less and the frittata lacked substance. To keep the procedure simple, we wanted to sauté most of our fillings in the same pan as the frittata. Doing so would enable us, after sautéing, to simply pour the beaten eggs over the filling and proceed with shaping the frittata.

The methods for cooking the frittata fell into three camps: cooking the frittata fully on the stovetop, cooking the frittata fully in the oven, and starting the frittata on the stovetop and then finishing it in the oven. We first tried cooking the frittata fully on the stovetop, but no matter what we did, the underside always ended up tough and overcooked. Cooking the frittata fully in the oven proved problematic as well. We tried cooking at different temperatures and lengths of time, but the results were either too dry or unevenly cooked. A combination of the two turned out to work the best. Using this method, we cooked the frittata almost fully on the stove and then placed it in the oven and allowed the top to finish cooking. The resulting frittata was evenly cooked and firm without being too dry—exactly what we had been looking for.

These frittatas don't have to be eaten hot. They can be served at room temperature or even cold, so timing isn't an issue, as it is with omelets. Serve frittatas with potatoes, a vegetable side dish, and/or a leafy salad.

Frittata with Sun-Dried Tomatoes, Mozzarella, and Basil

SERVES 3 TO 4

TIME: 20 MINUTES

Blot the drained sun-dried tomatoes on paper towels to absorb excess oil.

1	tablespoon olive oil
½	small onion, chopped fine
¼	cup drained sun-dried tomatoes packed in oil, chopped fine
2	tablespoons chopped fresh basil leaves
⅓	cup finely diced fresh mozzarella cheese
¼	teaspoon salt
¼	teaspoon ground black pepper
6	large eggs, lightly beaten in a bowl

1. Adjust an oven rack to the upper-middle position and heat the oven to 350 degrees.
2. Heat the oil in a 10-inch nonstick, oven-proof skillet over medium heat until shimmering. Add the onion and sauté until softened, 3 to 4 minutes. Stir in the tomatoes and basil.
3. Meanwhile, stir the mozzarella, salt, and pepper into the eggs.
4. Pour the egg mixture into the skillet and stir it lightly with a fork until the eggs start to set. Once the bottom is firm, use a thin, nonmetallic spatula to lift the frittata edge closest to you. Tilt the skillet slightly toward you so the uncooked egg runs underneath (see the illustration on page 353). Return the skillet to the level position and swirl gently to evenly distribute the egg. Continue cooking about 40 seconds and then lift the edge again, repeating the process until the egg on top is no longer runny.
5. Transfer the skillet to the oven and bake until the frittata top is set and dry to the touch, 2 to 4 minutes; remove the frittata as soon as the top is just set.
6. Run a spatula around the skillet edge to loosen the frittata. Invert the frittata onto a serving plate. Serve warm, at room temperature, or chilled.

Frittata with Potatoes, Cheddar, and Thyme

SERVES 4

TIME: 25 MINUTES

If you have leftover potatoes, simply skip the first step and add 1 cup diced cooked potatoes in step 3.

2	medium red potatoes (8 ounces), scrubbed and cut into ½-inch dice
	Salt
1	tablespoon unsalted butter
½	small onion, chopped fine
2	teaspoons chopped fresh thyme leaves
⅓	cup grated cheddar cheese
¼	teaspoon ground black pepper
6	large eggs, lightly beaten in a bowl

1. Bring the potatoes, 2 cups water, and 1 teaspoon salt to a boil in a medium saucepan over high heat. Reduce the heat and simmer until the potatoes are just tender, about 6 minutes. Drain and set aside until needed.

2. Adjust an oven rack to the upper-middle position and heat the oven to 350 degrees.

3. Heat the butter in a 10-inch nonstick, ovenproof skillet over medium heat. When the foaming subsides, add the onion and sauté until softened, 3 to 4 minutes. Add the cooked potatoes and thyme and toss to coat with butter. Spread the potatoes in a single layer.

4. Meanwhile, stir the cheese, ¼ teaspoon salt, and the pepper into the eggs.

5. Pour the egg mixture into the skillet and stir it lightly with a fork until the eggs start to set. Once the bottom is firm, use a thin, nonmetallic spatula to lift the frittata edge closest to you. Tilt the skillet slightly toward you so the uncooked egg runs underneath (see the illustration on page 353). Return the skillet to the level position and swirl gently to evenly distribute the egg. Continue cooking about 40 seconds and then lift the edge again, repeating the process until the egg on top is no longer runny.

6. Transfer the skillet to the oven and bake until the frittata top is set and dry to the touch, 2 to 4 minutes; remove the frittata as

---

BUILDING BLOCK RECIPE

Parmesan-Herb Frittata

SERVES 3 TO 4

TIME: 20 MINUTES

Cheese and herbs are the simplest additions to a frittata.

1	tablespoon olive oil
½	small onion, chopped fine
2	tablespoons minced fresh herb leaves, such as parsley, basil, dill, tarragon, or mint
⅓	cup grated Parmesan cheese
¼	teaspoon salt
¼	teaspoon ground black pepper
6	large eggs, lightly beaten in a bowl

1. Adjust an oven rack to the upper-middle position and heat the oven to 350 degrees.

2. Heat the oil in a 10-inch nonstick, ovenproof skillet over medium heat until shimmering. Add the onion and sauté until softened, 3 to 4 minutes. Stir in the herbs.

3. Meanwhile, stir the cheese, salt, and pepper into the eggs.

4. Pour the egg mixture into the skillet and stir it lightly with a fork until the eggs start to set. Once the bottom is firm, use a thin, nonmetallic spatula to lift the frittata edge closest to you. Tilt the skillet slightly toward you so the uncooked egg runs underneath (see the illustration on page 353). Return the skillet to the level position and swirl gently to evenly distribute the egg. Continue cooking about 40 seconds and then lift the edge again, repeating the process until the egg on top is no longer runny.

5. Transfer the skillet to the oven and bake until the frittata top is set and dry to the touch, 2 to 4 minutes; remove the frittata as soon as the top is just set.

6. Run a spatula around the skillet edge to loosen the frittata. Invert the frittata onto a serving plate. Serve warm, at room temperature, or chilled.

soon as the top is just set.

7. Run a spatula around the skillet edge to loosen the frittata. Invert the frittata onto a serving plate. Serve warm, at room temperature, or chilled.

Frittata with Tomatoes, Corn, and Cilantro

SERVES 4

TIME: 20 MINUTES

Although the flavors in this frittata are not Italian, they work well with eggs. It is important to seed the tomatoes well. See page 125 for tips on seeding plum tomatoes.

I	tablespoon vegetable oil
3	medium scallions, whites sliced into thin rounds, greens sliced thin on the bias
4	plum tomatoes (about I pound), cored, halved, seeded, and cut into ¼-inch dice
½	cup frozen corn
2	tablespoons chopped fresh cilantro leaves
⅓	cup grated Monterey Jack cheese
¼	teaspoon salt
¼	teaspoon ground black pepper
6	large eggs, lightly beaten

1. Adjust an oven rack to the upper-middle position and heat the oven to 350 degrees.

2. Heat the oil in a 10-inch nonstick, oven-proof skillet over medium heat until shimmering. Add the scallion whites and sauté until softened, 1 to 2 minutes. Add the tomatoes, corn, and cilantro and toss to coat with the oil. Spread the vegetables in a single layer.

3. Meanwhile, stir the cheese, salt, and pepper into the eggs.

4. Pour the egg mixture into the skillet and stir it lightly with a fork until the eggs start to set. Once the bottom is firm, use a thin, non-metallic spatula to lift the frittata edge closest to you. Tilt the skillet slightly toward you so the uncooked egg runs underneath (see the illustration on page 353). Return the skillet to the level position and swirl gently to evenly distribute the egg. Continue cooking about 40 seconds and then lift the edge again, repeating the process until the egg on top is no longer runny.

5. Transfer the skillet to the oven and bake until the frittata top is set and dry to the touch, 2 to 4 minutes; remove the frittata as soon as the top is just set.

6. Run a spatula around the skillet edge to loosen the frittata. Invert the frittata onto a serving plate and garnish with the scallion greens. Serve warm, at room temperature, or chilled.

EGG SANDWICHES

WHO DOESN'T LIKE EGG SANDWICHES? You take rich, creamy eggs, top them with oozing cheese, and sandwich the cheesy eggs in a crusty English muffin. Add meat and you've got a quick meal that can be on the table in 20 minutes. While the process of making egg sandwiches may seem obvious, we found ways to improve upon this simple recipe.

Our first step in developing this recipe was to determine the best way to cook the eggs. Because most people wanted the richness of a runny yolk, we decided to try both poached and fried eggs. The fried eggs were preferred overwhelmingly, whereas the poached eggs were bland on their own. Having a foolproof method for fried eggs already developed by the test kitchen (see page 358), we could focus on the other issues.

A potential problem with egg sandwiches, especially if you are making more than two, is that simultaneously having all the components hot and fresh is difficult. You have to wait for the muffins to finish toasting while the eggs are in the pan overcooking. Alternatively, if you toast the muffins ahead of time, they are cold and dry by the time the eggs are cooked. To solve this timing problem, we enlisted the help of our broiler.

By using the broiler in conjunction with the stovetop, we found we could cook the components for our sandwiches quicker and more efficiently. Previously, we had always cooked the meat for our sandwiches in the pan in which we were frying the eggs. But because our technique for frying eggs used low heat, no matter how long we cooked the bacon, it would never brown in our pan. We avoided this problem by cooking the meat under the broiler. We now could brown the meat easily in a matter of minutes and didn't have to alter our technique for frying eggs.

The broiler also came in handy for toasting the muffins. Most people have a small two-slot toaster in their home, so toasting more than one or two items is a logistical nightmare. But, again, our broiler solved this problem. By placing the muffins on a baking sheet, we could toast all of them in the time it took to toast one muffin in a regular toaster. This technique also fit well with our

GETTING THE EGGS INTO THE PAN

Crack the eggs into two small bowls or cups and then let the eggs slide into the hot skillet simultaneously from opposite sides of the pan.

egg-frying method. In the time it took the eggs to cook, we could both toast the muffins and top them with cheese while they were hot. This meant that when the eggs were ready, the muffins were ready—and because both were piping hot, we had no problem with unmelted cheese.

Egg Sandwiches
MAKES 4
TIME: 20 MINUTES

For a more substantial meal, serve these sandwiches with hash browns (page 81). Havarti is especially buttery and works well in this dish. Other possible choices include cheddar and Monterey Jack cheese.

- 4 slices Canadian bacon (about 4 ounces)
- 4 English muffins, split in half
- 4 large eggs
- 1 tablespoon unsalted butter, cold
  Salt and ground black pepper
- 2 ounces Havarti cheese, finely grated (about ½ cup)

1. Adjust an oven rack so it is 6 inches away from the broiler element and heat the broiler. Place the bacon slices on a wire rack set on a rimmed baking sheet. Broil until browned around the edges, about 2 minutes. With tongs, turn over the bacon and brown the other side, about 2 minutes. Transfer the bacon to a plate and cover it with foil to keep warm. (Do not turn off the broiler.) Arrange the English muffin halves, split side up, on the empty rack and set aside.

2. Meanwhile, heat a 10-inch nonstick skillet over low heat for 5 minutes. While the pan is heating, crack 2 eggs each into two small cups or bowls. Add the butter to the skillet. When the foaming subsides (this should take about 1 minute; if the butter

357

browns in 1 minute, the pan is too hot), swirl to coat the pan.

3. Working quickly, pour one bowl of eggs into one side of the pan and the second bowl into the other side (see the illustration on page 357). Season with salt and pepper to taste. Cover and cook about 2½ minutes for runny yolks, 3 minutes for soft but set yolks,

and 3½ minutes for firmly set yolks.

4. While the eggs are cooking, toast the muffin halves under the broiler until deep golden. Remove the baking sheet from the oven and top each muffin half with 1 tablespoon cheese. Using a spatula, transfer 1 egg to each muffin bottom. Top with the bacon and the remaining muffin halves. Serve immediately.

BUILDING BLOCK RECIPE

Fried Eggs

SERVES 4

TIME: 10 MINUTES

A nonstick skillet is essential because it ensures an easy release of the eggs. Because burners vary, you may have to experiment with an egg or two before you determine the ideal setting for frying eggs on your stovetop. Follow the visual cues in the recipe and increase the heat if necessary. If you've just fried some bacon or happen to have bacon grease around, use it in place of the butter for really tasty fried eggs. Unlike butter, however, bacon grease will not go through visual changes you can use to gauge the pan's heat.

4   large eggs
1   tablespoon unsalted butter, cold
    Salt and ground black pepper

1. Heat a 10-inch nonstick skillet over low heat for 5 minutes. While the pan is heating, crack 2 eggs each into two small cups or bowls. Add the butter to the skillet. When the foaming subsides (this should take about 1 minute; if the butter browns in 1 minute, the pan is too hot), swirl to coat the pan.

2. Working quickly, pour one bowl of eggs into one side of the pan and the second bowl into the other side (see the illustration on page 357). Season with salt and pepper to taste. Cover and cook about 2½ minutes for runny yolks, 3 minutes for soft but set yolks, and 3½ minutes for firmly set yolks. Slide the eggs onto a plate and serve immediately.

13

MUFFINS, BISCUITS, AND SCONES

MUFFINS, BISCUITS, AND SCONES— all quick breads—can be quickly prepared (the batter or dough can usually be assembled in the time it takes to preheat the oven) and quickly baked. This sets them far apart from yeast breads, which must rise for hours. Quick breads contain chemical leaveners, such as baking powder and baking soda, which are speedy and reliable.

Several methods are used to assemble quick breads. The most common, often referred to as the *quick bread method*, calls for mixing wet and dry ingredients separately, pouring the wet into the dry, and then mixing them together as quickly as possible. Batters for pancakes, popovers, and many quick breads rely on this approach. It's the fastest approach and the one we've adopted for many of these recipes.

A second technique, often called the *creaming method* and more common to cake batters, starts with creaming butter and sugar until light and fluffy. Eggs and flavorings are beaten in and then the dry and liquid ingredients alternately added. Given that creaming starts with softened butter and softening butter is best accomplished by leaving wrapped sticks at room temperature for an hour or so, we've avoided this method in developing the recipes in this chapter.

A third method is the traditional way in which biscuit and pie dough is made—by cutting cold fat into the dry ingredients with fingertips, forks, a pastry blender, or the blade of a food processor. Once the mixture has achieved a texture like cornmeal, with pea-size flecks, liquid is added and quickly mixed in.

Banana Muffins

A BANANA MUFFIN IS UNLIKE THE more familiar banana bread. First, it's lighter, airier, and springier than a tight-crumbed banana bread. Second, it takes half as long to bake. Whereas a loaf of banana bread requires almost an hour to bake through, banana muffins need barely 25 minutes. Although we had never made banana muffins in the test kitchen, we had made plenty of banana bread, and we used our favorite recipe as a starting point.

Our favorite banana bread is ripe with flavor from three mashed bananas. It also contains yogurt and baking soda. This recipe relies on a simple mixing method—you mix together the dry ingredients, mash the bananas and mix them in with the wet ingredients, and then fold the two together.

When we simply divided this batter into 12 muffin cups, we felt the muffins were too solid and dense. Sure, they tasted delicious, but when you break apart a muffin, you expect to see an open grain, a light crumb, and a tender texture. To solve these problems, we added baking powder to the dry ingredients to help the baking soda provide extra lift. Although the baking powder did lighten the color of the muffins a bit, we didn't mind—it made them lighter and more cakey,

SAVING OVERRIPE BANANAS

Rather than throwing away overripe bananas, we save them until we have enough for making muffins. Place the peeled overripe banana in a zipper-lock plastic bag and freeze. Add more bananas to the bag as they overripen. When you are ready to bake with them, thaw the bananas on the counter until softened.

and tasters reacted favorably to both changes.

We also decided to use buttermilk instead of yogurt. In prior tests with our banana bread, we found that yogurt was preferable to milk, sour cream, and buttermilk. It added a nice tang to the banana bread and didn't cover the banana flavor. However, we wanted our muffins to be lighter, and we knew buttermilk was our ticket to a more open texture. Sure enough, muffins made with buttermilk were lighter than those made with yogurt, but they still had that pleasing acidic tang. Muffins made with milk were bland, and those made with sour cream were too rich.

Finally, we increased the sugar amount from ¾ cup to 1 cup because tasters wanted the muffins to be a bit sweeter than the almost-savory banana bread. Not quite cake and not quite bread, these muffins are happy to be in the middle.

Banana Muffins

MAKES 12 MUFFINS

TIME: 45 MINUTES
(INCLUDES 35 MINUTES BAKING
AND COOLING TIME)

If you like, fold 1¼ cups toasted and chopped walnuts into the finished batter.

2	cups (10 ounces) unbleached all-purpose flour
1	cup (7 ounces) sugar
1	teaspoon baking powder
½	teaspoon baking soda
½	teaspoon salt
3	very ripe, soft, darkly speckled large bananas, mashed well (about 1½ cups)
⅓	cup buttermilk
2	large eggs
6	tablespoons unsalted butter, melted and cooled slightly
1	teaspoon vanilla extract

1. Adjust an oven rack to the lower-middle position and heat the oven to 375 degrees. Spray a standard muffin tin with nonstick cooking spray.

2. Whisk together the flour, sugar, baking powder, baking soda, and salt in a large bowl until combined. Mix the mashed bananas, buttermilk, eggs, butter, and vanilla with a wooden spoon in a medium bowl. Lightly fold the banana mixture into the dry ingredients with a rubber spatula until just combined and the batter looks thick and chunky (do not overmix).

3. Use an ice cream scoop or a large spoon to drop the batter into the greased muffin tin. Bake until golden and a toothpick inserted into the center of a muffin comes out clean, 20 to 23 minutes, rotating the pan from front to back halfway through the baking time. Cool the muffins in the tin for 5 minutes and then transfer them to a wire rack and cool for 10 more minutes. Serve warm.

BRAN MUFFINS

ABOUT 5 YEARS AGO, WE DEVELOPED A recipe for bran muffins in the test kitchen. Although these muffins were tender and delicious (and much more refined in crumb and flavor than your standard tough and chewy bran muffin), the recipe called for 17 ingredients, including two types of flour, two kinds of leavener, two kinds of liquid, plus wheat bran, eggs, sugar, spices, flavorings, and raisins. The recipe also used the creaming method, which in itself is a lengthy process. We reviewed the recipe and found many ways to streamline it—by both eliminating ingredients and simplifying the mixing method.

First, we tackled the ingredients. We decided to forgo the ¼ cup whole-wheat flour the original recipe called for, replacing it with the same amount of all-purpose flour, which was already in the recipe. We also pared the list of spices from allspice, cinnamon, and nutmeg to just allspice. Without the whole-wheat flour, we found that too many spices covered up the now more delicate flavor of the bran in the muffin—which we kept the same as the original recipe, at 1½ cups.

We eliminated the molasses and vanilla extract but kept the dark brown sugar, which contributed plenty of molasses and caramel notes. Last, we decided not to use sour cream.

EQUIPMENT: Muffin Tins

The majority of muffin tins on the market are made of coated aluminum and are lightweight. We purchased two tins of this type as well as two heavy-gauge "professional" aluminum tins and one "air-cushioned" aluminum tin. Three had a nonstick coating. The tins ranged in price from $5 to $26.

We baked up two varieties of muffins to test the two things that really matter: browning and sticking. We wanted the muffins to brown uniformly and to be easily plucked from the tin. Corn muffins were ideal for the browning test, blueberry for the sticking test—no one wants a sweet, sticky berry to be left behind in the tin.

Browning ended up being the deciding factor in these tests. Sticking was not an issue as long as the tins were coated with cooking spray. The best tins browned the muffins evenly; the worst browned them on the top but left them pallid and underbaked on the bottom. As we observed in other bakeware tests, darker coated metals, which absorb heat, do the best job of browning baked goods. The air-cushioned tin produced pale muffins that were also small (the cushioning made for a smaller cup capacity, about ⅓ cup rather than the standard ½ cup).

We found the heavier-gauged aluminum tins to have no advantage; they are much more expensive than other tins, weigh twice as much, and do not produce superior muffins. Their heft may make them durable, but unless you bake commercially, the lightweight models will last a lifetime. The $5 Ekco Baker's Secret tin took top honors, besting tins that cost five times as much.

Although originally we thought that butter-milk and sour cream used in tandem created a more tender and moist muffin, when we substituted all buttermilk for the sour cream, we barely noticed a difference.

Once we got the ingredients down to a manageable number (10), we examined the mixing method. The recipe called for the creaming method, whereby softened butter and sugar are beaten in the bowl of a standing mixer; then the eggs are added (one at a time), and finally the dry and liquid ingredients are added to the batter in alternating turns. Instead, we decided to try the quick bread method, whereby liquid ingredients are combined, dry ingredients are whisked together, and then the two are mixed.

Because we wanted to use the quick bread mixing method, we needed to use a liquid fat. We didn't want to forfeit the richness butter contributed to the muffin, so instead of substituting oil, we melted it. Now it could easily be mixed with the other liquid ingredients.

After baking for about 22 minutes in a 375-degree oven, the muffins were done and ready to cool. The result? Tender, earthy, delicate, and rich-flavored, not to mention easy to make, these bran muffins may be healthful, but they sure don't taste like health food.

PORTIONING OUT MUFFIN BATTER

We use an ice cream scoop to distribute muffin batter evenly among the greased cups in a muffin tin. A large spoon can also be used, but it is a bit messier and not as precise.

Bran Muffins

MAKES 12 MUFFINS

TIME: 45 MINUTES
(INCLUDES ABOUT 35 MINUTES
BAKING AND COOLING TIME)

Bran muffins overbake in a flash. Muffins are baked through when they retract ever so slightly from the sides of the cups and the tops spring back very gently when touched (don't look for an active spring). The muffins are baked through even though a wooden toothpick withdraws from the center with a few moist crumbs clinging to it. For raisin bran muffins, add 1 cup raisins to the dry ingredients. You can also flavor these muffins with 1 cup dried cherries, dried cranberries, chopped dried apricots, or chopped prunes or ⅓ cup chopped crystallized ginger.

1½	cups (7½ ounces) unbleached all-purpose flour
1½	cups wheat bran
2	teaspoons baking powder
½	teaspoon baking soda
1	teaspoon ground allspice
½	teaspoon salt
2	large eggs
½	cup packed (3½ ounces) dark brown sugar
1¼	cups buttermilk
8	tablespoons (1 stick) unsalted butter, melted and cooled slightly

1. Adjust an oven rack to the lower-middle position and heat the oven to 375 degrees. Spray a standard muffin tin with nonstick cooking spray.

2. Whisk together the flour, bran, baking powder, baking soda, allspice, and salt in a medium bowl until combined. Whisk together the eggs, brown sugar, and buttermilk in a large bowl until combined. Add the melted butter and whisk vigorously until thick and homogeneous. Whisk in half of the dry ingredients

until the two begin to come together and then add the remaining dry ingredients and stir with a rubber spatula or wooden spoon until just combined (do not overmix).

3. Use an ice cream scoop or a large spoon to drop batter into the greased muffin tin. Bake until golden and a toothpick inserted into the center of a muffin comes out with just a few moist crumbs, 22 to 25 minutes, rotating the pan from front to back halfway through the baking time. Cool the muffins in the tin for 5 minutes and then transfer them to a wire rack and cool for 10 more minutes. Serve warm.

GINGERBREAD MUFFINS

WE LOVE TRADITIONAL GINGERBREAD, but it does take a long time to bake—upward of 45 minutes even when prepared in a small square baking pan. We wanted to develop a shorter method for creating delicious, pleasantly spicy gingerbread, so we decided to use a muffin tin instead.

To carry out our experiments, we needed a basic recipe. We could follow one of two routes: water-based gingerbread recipes or milk-based ones. After testing both, we chose a milk-based recipe because it tasted richer and baked up moister.

We next concentrated on finding the best type and blend of sweeteners. We tested gingerbread made with granulated sugar, light and dark brown sugar, honey, three types of molasses (light, dark, and blackstrap), corn syrup, and even maple syrup. At first, we thought molasses was an essential ingredient because tasters liked the combination of light molasses and granulated sugar. After more testing, we realized this combination is essential but these ingredients are not. For ease and speed, we chose to use just dark brown sugar, which is white sugar mixed with molasses (light brown sugar also contains molasses, but not as much as dark brown).

Next we looked at fat, eggs, and milk. Butter decisively won over vegetable oil (which produced flat-flavored muffins). Instead of creaming the butter, we decided to melt it. For moistness and lift, we chose to use two eggs in the gingerbread batter. When it came to the milk, buttermilk received our stamp of approval for its rich flavor and the tender crumb it produced. Finally, tasters voted for ginger, cinnamon, and allspice, rejecting more exotic and elaborate spice combinations.

We decided to mix the batter by hand—it seemed a waste of effort to pull out the standing mixer for such a simple throw-together recipe. We found it the best way to work out any lumps in the batter. The muffins did not toughen easily; however, excessive beating would eventually compromise the texture of baked muffins.

MEASURING FLOUR

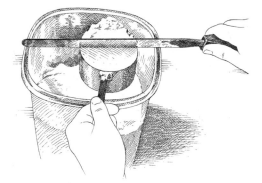

No matter the type or brand, we measure all flour by the dip-and-sweep method. Dip a metal or plastic dry measure into a bag or canister of flour so the cup overflows; then use the flat side of a knife or an icing spatula to level the flour, sweeping the excess back into the container. Short of weighing flour (which is what professional bakers do), this measuring method is your best guarantee of using the right amount of flour. Spooning the flour into the measuring cup aerates it, and you might end up with as much as 25 percent less flour by weight.

Gingerbread Muffins
MAKES 12 MUFFINS
TIME: 45 MINUTES
(INCLUDES 35 MINUTES BAKING
AND COOLING TIME)

If you like crystallized ginger, try this topping for the gingerbread muffins: 2 tablespoons crystallized ginger minced in the food processor with ¼ cup sugar. Sprinkle a little ginger sugar over each muffin before baking. The payoff is a crisp, slightly spicy muffin top.

2	cups (10 ounces) unbleached all-purpose flour
½	teaspoon baking soda
1	tablespoon ground ginger
2	teaspoons ground cinnamon
½	teaspoon ground allspice
½	teaspoon salt
2	large eggs
1½	cups packed (10½ ounces) dark brown sugar
1	cup buttermilk
8	tablespoons (1 stick) unsalted butter, melted and cooled slightly

1. Adjust an oven rack to the middle position and heat the oven to 375 degrees. Spray a standard muffin tin with nonstick cooking spray.

2. Whisk together the flour, baking soda, ginger, cinnamon, allspice, and salt in a medium bowl until combined. Whisk together the eggs, brown sugar, and buttermilk in a large bowl until combined. Add the melted butter and whisk vigorously until thick and homogeneous. Whisk in half of the dry ingredients until the two begin to come together and then add the remaining dry ingredients and stir with a rubber spatula or wooden spoon until just combined (do not overmix).

3. Use an ice cream scoop or a large spoon to drop the batter into the greased muffin tin.

Bake until golden and a toothpick inserted into the center of a muffin comes out clean, 18 to 22 minutes, rotating the pan from front to back halfway through the baking time. Cool the muffins in the tin for 5 minutes and then transfer them to a wire rack and cool for 10 more minutes. Serve warm.

PUMPKIN MUFFINS

DENSE BUT NOT BREADY AND LIGHT without being cakey, pumpkin muffins represent a true study in muffin balance. It's easy to go overboard with spices or sweeteners, but a good pumpkin muffin exhibits restraint. The one way in which a pumpkin muffin can genuinely tip the scales—and for the better—is in pumpkin flavor, which it should have in the extreme.

Because it is unreasonable for anyone to purchase a small sugar pumpkin, peel it, seed it, roast or steam it, and puree it to make muffins, we knew canned pumpkin would be the way to go. Although we have seen canned pumpkin in stores around the holidays, it can be hard to find at other times of the year—whereas pumpkin pie filling is always available. The drawback to pumpkin pie filling, however, is that it already contains sweetener and spices. Our pumpkin muffin recipe had to take this into account.

We started by mixing a couple of eggs, melted butter, sugar, milk, and pumpkin pie filling and then adding flour, baking powder, and salt. Into a greased muffin tin the batter went, and about 30 minutes later, out came the baked muffins. These muffins were far from perfect. First, they lacked flavor—not only pumpkin flavor but any flavor at all. Second, they were too dense; we needed to make them lighter.

To tackle the first problem, we decided to increase the amount of pumpkin pie filling from ½ cup to 1 cup. Next, we substituted 1 cup molasses-rich dark brown sugar for the plain white sugar. Finally, we bolstered the muffins' flavor with a dash of ground cloves, ginger, and cinnamon. But still the pumpkin flavor was thin. Once again, we upped the amount of pumpkin pie filling—this time to 1½ cups. Still, though, the pumpkin flavor was weak.

Because the batter could not hold any more pumpkin filling, we decided to switch tacks and figure out which ingredients in our recipe were deadening the pumpkin flavor. Could it be the milk? We reduced the amount of milk in the next test and, to our surprise, not only did the pumpkin muffins taste more like pumpkin, but they were lighter, airier, and more tender too! Because this test was so successful, we decided to test the muffins with no milk—or any other liquid ingredient—at all. These muffins were the lightest of all and had the strongest pumpkin flavor.

To further lift our muffins, we increased the baking powder from 1 teaspoon to 1 tablespoon. With all of that heavy pumpkin filling to counter, we knew the muffins would benefit from the baking powder's muscle. Spicy and sweet and light and pumpkiny, these muffins deserve to be eaten year-round.

EQUIPMENT: Muffin Papers
Do you need to line muffin tins with ruffled paper cups? To find out, we baked muffins with and without paper liners. Those baked in papers were shorter than those baked right in the cup, but they also had a more rounded, filled-out look. When peeling off the papers, though, we lost a good portion of the muffin. Muffin papers also kept the sides of the muffins from browning as nicely as those baked right in the cup. We prefer to grease muffin tins rather than use paper liners.

Pumpkin Muffins

MAKES 12 MUFFINS

TIME: 45 MINUTES
(INCLUDES 35 MINUTES BAKING
AND COOLING TIME)

*If you like, mix ¾ cup raisins into the dry ingre-
dients before adding them to the wet ingredients.
An equal amount of toasted walnuts, pecans, or
even pumpkin seeds (commonly sold as pepitas)
also makes a nice addition.*

1¾	cups (8¾ ounces) unbleached all-purpose flour
1	tablespoon baking powder
1	teaspoon ground cinnamon
½	teaspoon ground ginger
¼	teaspoon ground cloves
½	teaspoon salt
1	large egg
1	cup packed (7 ounces) dark brown sugar
1½	cups canned pumpkin pie filling
8	tablespoons (1 stick) unsalted butter, melted and cooled slightly

1. Adjust an oven rack to the middle position and heat the oven to 375 degrees. Spray a standard muffin tin with nonstick cooking spray.

2. Whisk together the flour, baking powder, cinnamon, ginger, cloves, and salt in a medium bowl until combined. Whisk together the egg and brown sugar in a large bowl until combined. Add the pumpkin pie filling to the egg mixture and whisk to combine. Add the butter and stir vigorously until thick and homogeneous. Add half of the dry ingredients to the pumpkin mixture and stir with a rubber spatula or wooden spoon until the two begin to come together; then add the remaining dry ingredients and stir until just combined (do not overmix).

3. Use an ice cream scoop or a large spoon

INGREDIENTS: Chemical Leaveners

Muffins, biscuits, and scones, as well as cookies and cakes, get their rise from chemical leaveners—baking soda and baking powder—rather than yeast. Chemical leavenings react with acids to produce carbon dioxide, the gas that causes these baked goods to rise.

To do its work, baking soda relies on an acid in the recipe, such as buttermilk or molasses. It's important to use the right amount of baking soda; use more than can be neutralized by the acidic ingredient and you'll end up with a metallic-tasting, coarse-crumbed muffin or cake.

Double-acting baking powder is made of baking soda (the single-acting ingredient), another rise ingredient (such as sodium aluminum sulfate and/or calcium phosphate), and cornstarch (a buffer to keep the ingredients separate in the can). Baking powder goes to work immediately when mixed with a liquid and gets a second lift when it hits the heat of an oven. Although most markets carry just one kind of baking soda, you do have a choice of baking powders, so we put four nationally available brands to the test.

Two brands, Davis and Clabber Girl, contain both sodium aluminum sulfate and calcium phosphate. Calumet contains both of these ingredients along with calcium sulfate, which according to the label "maintains leavening," while Rumford has just calcium phosphate. We wondered if these leaveners would perform differently. Also, some experts say baking powders with aluminum can give baked goods an off flavor. Is this true?

Based on our tests with a simple biscuit recipe containing just flour, baking powder, salt, and cream, you don't need to worry about finding a specific brand of baking powder when shopping. All four biscuits were nearly identical in appearance. A couple of sensitive tasters did notice a faint chemical taste in the biscuits made with Clabber Girl but admitted that if they hadn't been looking for it, they wouldn't have noticed it at all.

to drop the batter into the greased muffin tin. Bake until golden and a toothpick inserted into the center of a muffin comes out clean, 18 to 22 minutes, rotating the pan from front to back halfway through the baking time. Cool the muffins in the tin for 5 minutes and then transfer them to a wire rack and cool for 10 more minutes. Serve warm.

INGREDIENTS: Bleached versus Unbleached Flour

In the test kitchen, we always use unbleached all-purpose flour, and we call for this kind of flour in our recipes. Never use cake or bread flour in a recipe that calls for all-purpose flour, and it's best not to use bleached flour in recipes that call for unbleached. Here's why.

All-purpose flour is typically made from hard red winter wheat, soft red winter wheat, or a combination of the two. Hard winter wheat is about 10 to 13 percent protein; soft wheat is about 8 to 10 percent. Mixtures of the two wheats are somewhere between the extremes. You can actually feel this difference with your fingers; the hard wheat flours tend to have a subtle granular feel, while soft wheat flours feel fine but starchy, much like cornstarch.

High-protein bread flours (with a protein content of 12 to 13 percent) are generally recommended for yeasted products and other baked goods that require a lot of structural support. The reason is that the higher the protein level in a flour, the greater the potential for gluten formation. The sheets that gluten forms in dough are elastic enough to move with the gas released by yeast, yet sturdy enough to prevent that gas from escaping, so the dough doesn't deflate.

On the other hand, lower-protein cake flours (with a protein content of 8 to 9 percent) are recommended for chemically leavened baked goods. This is because baking powder and baking soda are quick leaveners. They lack the endurance of yeast, which can force the naturally resistant gluten sheets to expand. Gluten can overpower quick leaveners, causing the baked product to fall flat.

All-purpose flours (most have a protein content of 10 to 12 percent) are best for baking jobs where you want some structure but not too much—as in most cookies, quick breads, pie dough, and many cakes.

All all-purpose flours are not the same; some are bleached, and some are not. Technically, they all are. Carotenoid pigments in wheat lend a faint yellowish tint to freshly milled flour. But in a matter of about 12 weeks, these pigments oxidize, undergoing the same chemical process that turns a sliced apple brown. In this case, yellowish flour changes to a whiter hue (though not stark white). Early in the 20th century, as the natural bleaching process came to be understood, scientists identified methods to chemically expedite and intensify it. Typically, chemically bleached all-purpose flours are treated with either benzoyl peroxide or chlorine gas. The latter not only bleaches the flour but also alters the flour proteins, making them less inclined to form strong gluten.

Today, consumers prefer chemically bleached flour over unbleached because they associate the whiter color with higher quality. In our tests, some of the baked goods made with bleached flour were such a pure white they actually looked startlingly unnatural and "commercial" rather than homemade. We found that bleached flour can also give really simple baked goods, such as biscuits, an off flavor. Most bleached all-purpose flours tend to have less protein (about 10 percent) than unbleached all-purpose flour (closer to 11 or 11.5 percent). This difference in protein content can affect the way the flour absorbs liquid (higher-protein flours hold more liquid) and thus affect baked goods.

For all these reasons, when we say unbleached all-purpose flour, we mean it. As for specific brands, we tested nine leading all-purpose flours in a range of baked goods. Both King Arthur and Pillsbury unbleached flours regularly made for highly recommended baked goods, producing a more consistent range of preferred products than the other seven flours in the taste tests.

CORNMEAL BISCUITS

BISCUITS ARE THE QUINTESSENTIAL American quick bread. They are at home baked in a Dutch oven over a campfire as well as in the most expensive restaurant oven. Biscuits are also among the simplest of all breads to prepare, and our cream biscuits (see our book *American Classics*) are especially simple. We hoped to jazz up this recipe to make a tasty biscuit with cornmeal. We wanted something a bit heartier, with enough flavor to stand up to a robust pot of chili.

In our basic cream biscuit recipe, we use 2 cups flour, 1 teaspoon baking powder, 2 tablespoons sugar, and ½ teaspoon salt. The secret ingredient in these biscuits is the liquid—heavy cream, which makes the biscuits tender and light. Because this recipe contains no butter (which is usually cut into the dry ingredients by hand), the dough comes together in less than 5 minutes.

But to turn these cream biscuits into cornmeal biscuits, we had to institute some changes. In our first batch, we tried substituting ¼ cup cornmeal for ¼ cup flour, but these biscuits were weak in terms of corn flavor. Next, we increased the amount of the swap to ½ cup cornmeal for the flour. These biscuits had a lot of corn flavor but were too dense.

To solve this problem, we increased the amount of baking powder from 1 teaspoon to 1½ teaspoons. This change definitely improved the texture of the biscuits. They were much airier, and their flavor didn't suffer as we had feared (adding too much baking powder can give a metallic flavor to baked goods), as the cornmeal was pretty potent in its own right.

Our research on cream biscuits had shown that they rise more with a bit of kneading, so we kneaded the cornmeal biscuit dough for 30 seconds and then shaped the dough into a circle. We cut the dough circle into eight wedges and baked them for just under 20 minutes. Golden and corny in flavor, these biscuits are just the thing when you crave a taste of home cooking.

SHAPING BISCUITS AND SCONES

Rather than rolling out the dough, using a biscuit cutter, and then rerolling and cutting the scraps, use this quick method, which yields wedge-shaped biscuits.

1. Pat the dough on a lightly floured work surface into a rough 8-inch circle.

2. With a knife or a bench scraper, cut the dough into 8 wedges.

Cornmeal Biscuits

MAKES 8 BISCUITS

TIME: 35 MINUTES
(INCLUDES 20 MINUTES BAKING
AND COOLING TIME)

Bake the biscuits immediately after cutting them; letting them stand for any length of time can decrease the leavening power and thereby prevent the biscuits from rising properly in the oven. The biscuits are best eaten within 1 hour of baking.

1½	cups (7½ ounces) unbleached all-purpose flour
½	cup (2¾ ounces) yellow cornmeal
1½	teaspoons baking powder
2	teaspoons sugar
¾	teaspoon salt
1½	cups heavy cream

1. Adjust an oven rack to the upper-middle position and heat the oven to 425 degrees. Line a baking sheet with parchment paper.

2. Whisk together the flour, cornmeal, baking powder, sugar, and salt in a large bowl. Add the cream and stir with a wooden spoon until a dough forms, about 30 seconds. Transfer the dough to a lightly floured countertop and knead by hand for 30 seconds.

3. Following the illustrations on page 368, cut the dough into 8 wedges. Place the wedges on the parchment-lined baking sheet.

4. Bake until the biscuit tops are light brown, 15 to 18 minutes. Cool the biscuits on a wire rack for 5 minutes. Serve warm.

➤ VARIATIONS

Cornmeal Biscuits with Corn Kernels

This dough may be slightly stickier than the basic cornmeal biscuit recipe. Use kernels cut from 1 large ear or thawed frozen kernels. See photo of this recipe on page 160.

Follow the recipe for Cornmeal Biscuits, increasing the amount of flour to 1⅔ cups (8¼ ounces) and whisking ¾ cup corn kernels into the dry ingredients.

Cornmeal Biscuits with Cheddar and Jalapeños

Follow the recipe for Cornmeal Biscuits, whisking 2 tablespoons minced jalapeño chiles and ½ cup (2 ounces) sharp cheddar cheese cut into ¼-inch pieces into the dry ingredients. Increase the baking time to 18 to 20 minutes.

Cornmeal Biscuits with Fresh Herbs

Marjoram, rosemary, sage, and thyme all work well in these fragrant biscuits.

Follow the recipe for Cornmeal Biscuits, whisking 2 tablespoons minced fresh herbs into the dry ingredients.

Sweet Potato Biscuits

SWEET POTATO ROLLS HAVE AN EARTHY orange color and a sweet, tender crumb that complements everything on the holiday dinner table. Most sweet potato roll recipes call for yeast, which means softening the yeast in warm water, kneading the yeasted dough, rising, proofing, shaping, and baking. Realistically, who has this kind of time during holiday meal preparation? We wanted to create a sweet potato roll that could be made and baked in under an hour to better fit a busy holiday schedule. We figured a biscuit, rather than a yeasted roll, was our best bet.

We went through our biscuit recipes and found two possible models: Cornmeal Biscuits (left) and Cinnamon Buns (basically a quick biscuit made with buttermilk instead of cream and a couple of tablespoons of melted butter;

see page 375). To turn them into sweet potato biscuits, we added 1 cup mashed canned sweet potatoes to each recipe and judged the results. Neither was a winner.

The cornmeal biscuit recipe (we replaced the cornmeal with flour) enhanced with sweet potatoes produced biscuits that were leaden and flavorless. When sweet potatoes were added to the cinnamon bun recipe (sans cinnamon filling, of course), the result was even worse; these biscuits were leaden and flavorless *and* rubbery. We decided to go with the lesser of two evils and try to spin our cornmeal biscuit recipe into sweet potato biscuits.

First, we had to resolve the texture issue. In our next test, we upped the baking powder to 1 tablespoon to help lift the heavy sweet potato–enhanced dough. These biscuits were much lighter—and better. Because sweet potatoes contain so much moisture, we wanted to add just enough cream to moisten the dry ingredients and make a soft, workable dough. After several tests, we cut the amount of cream to just ¾ cup.

We also made changes to improve the flavor of the biscuits. First, we doubled the amount of salt to 1 teaspoon. Although this sounds like a lot—especially for only eight biscuits—the sweet potatoes seemed to suck it all away. For sugar, we tested granulated against light and dark brown sugar. Dark brown sugar produced an earthy-colored biscuit with a deep, molasses twang, and it became our sweetener of choice. However, it didn't resolve all of our flavor issues. We decided to see how the biscuits would taste with a little ground cinnamon added to the dry ingredients. This addition provided the warmth we were looking for. Tasters reacted even more positively when we also included a little freshly grated nutmeg.

But the biscuits still seemed somewhat dull. Then we had an idea: Would lightly cooking the sweet potatoes before adding them to the dry biscuit ingredients help? We had success using this method when we were developing our pumpkin pie recipe many years ago. We found that simply warming the pumpkin filling for a few minutes on the stovetop provided a rounder pumpkin flavor. We decided to warm the sweet potatoes along with the sugar and the spices in the microwave to save time. Sure enough, this intensified the sweet potato flavor in the biscuits.

We baked the biscuits in a 425-degree oven until they were slightly browned. It took a lot of willpower to hold back, but we concluded that a minimum 10-minute cooling period brought all of the flavors together nicely. Unlike our cream biscuits, which must be eaten within an hour of baking (because the dough contains no butter or oil, they go stale quickly), these biscuits stayed fresh for a surprisingly long time. The sweet potato's starches and high sugar content retained moisture well, and we enjoyed these biscuits up to 24 hours after we baked them.

❧

Sweet Potato Biscuits

MAKES 8 BISCUITS

TIME: 50 MINUTES
(INCLUDES 35 MINUTES BAKING
AND COOLING TIME)

Bake the biscuits immediately after cutting them; letting them stand for any length of time can decrease the leavening power and thereby prevent the biscuits from rising properly in the oven.

2   cups (10 ounces) unbleached all-purpose flour, plus ¼ cup for dusting the work surface
1   tablespoon baking powder
1   teaspoon salt
1   (15-ounce) can sweet potatoes in light syrup, drained

¼ cup packed (1¾ ounces) dark brown sugar
½ teaspoon ground cinnamon
⅛ teaspoon freshly grated nutmeg
¾ cup heavy cream

1. Adjust an oven rack to the middle position and heat the oven to 425 degrees. Line a baking sheet with parchment paper.

2. Whisk together 2 cups flour, the baking powder, and the salt in a large bowl.

3. Mash the sweet potatoes with a fork or potato masher in a microwave-safe bowl. Add the brown sugar, cinnamon, and nutmeg and stir with a wooden spoon or rubber spatula to combine. Microwave on high power until the sweet potatoes are warmed through and the sugar is completely dissolved, 2½ to 3 minutes. Stir to combine, add the cream, and whisk until somewhat smooth (there will be a few lumps) and homogeneous in color.

4. Add the sweet potato mixture to the dry ingredients and use a rubber spatula to combine. Transfer the dough to a work surface dusted with the remaining ¼ cup flour. Gently knead the dough by hand until it comes together (it will be sticky), about 1 minute.

EQUIPMENT: Digital Scales

Every serious cook needs an accurate scale for weighing fruits, vegetables, and meats. When making muffins, biscuits, cakes, and cookies, a scale is especially critical. Professional bakers know that measuring flour by volume can be problematic. A cup of flour can weigh between 4 and 6 ounces, depending on the type of flour, the humidity, whether or not it has been sifted, and the way it was put into the cup. Weight is a much more accurate way to measure flour.

Kitchen scales come in two basic types. Mechanical scales operate on a spring and lever system. When an item is placed on the scale, internal springs are compressed. The springs are attached to levers, which move a needle on the scale's display (a ruler with lines and numbers printed on a piece of paper and glued to the scale). The more the springs are compressed, the farther the needle moves along the ruler.

Electronic, or digital, scales have two plates that are clamped at a fixed distance. The bottom plate is stationary; the top plate is not. When food is placed on the platform attached to the top plate, the distance between the plates changes slightly. The movement of the top plate (no more than 1/1000 inch) causes a change in the flow of electricity through the scale's circuitry. This change is translated into a weight and expressed in numbers displayed on the face of the scale.

We tested ten electronic scales and nine mechanical scales. As a group, the electronic scales were vastly preferred. Their digital displays were much easier to read than the measures on most mechanical scales, where the lines on the ruler are so closely spaced it's impossible to nail down the precise weight within ½ ounce. Also, many mechanical scales weigh items only within a limited range—usually between 1 ounce and 5 pounds. What's the point of owning a scale that can't weigh a large chicken or roast? Most electronic scales handle items that weigh as much as 10 pounds and as little as ¼ ounce.

Among the electronic scales we tested, we found several features that make the difference between a good electronic scale and a great one. First, readability is a must. The displayed numbers should be large. Also, they should be steeply angled and as far from the weighing platform as possible. If the display is too close to the platform, the numbers can hide beneath the rim of a dinner plate or cake pan.

An automatic shut-off feature saves battery life, but this feature can be annoying, especially if the shut-off cycle kicks in at under 2 minutes. A scale that shuts off automatically after 5 minutes or more is easier to use.

A large weighing platform (which detaches for easy cleaning) is another plus. Last, we preferred electronic scales that display weight increments in decimals rather than fractions. The former are more accurate and easier to work with when scaling a recipe up or down.

5. Following the illustrations on page 368, cut the dough into 8 wedges. Place the wedges on the parchment-lined baking sheet.

6. Bake until the biscuit tops are light brown, 22 to 25 minutes. Cool the biscuits on a wire rack for 10 minutes. Serve warm.

➤ VARIATION

Sweet Potato Biscuits with Pecans

Follow the recipe for Sweet Potato Biscuits, adding ¾ cup toasted, chopped pecans to the dry ingredients.

CREAM SCONES

SCONES, THE QUINTESSENTIAL TEA cakes of the British Isles, were intended to be delicate, fluffy biscuits, which may come as a surprise to Americans. The clunky mounds of oven-baked sweetened dough that the British call *rock cakes* are often called *scones* in our coffee shops and bakeries. Unlike rock cakes, in which dough is dropped from a spoon onto a baking sheet, traditional scones are quickly rolled or patted out and cut into rounds or wedges. Our goal was to develop a scone that exemplified the traditional specimen: light, with a texture between cake and biscuit.

We began our testing with the flour. We constructed a composite recipe and then made one version with bread flour, one with all-purpose flour, and another with cake flour. The differences in outcome were astonishing. The scones made with bread flour were heavy and tough. Those made with all-purpose flour were lighter and much more flavorful. Cake flour produced scones that were doughy in the center, with a raw taste and poor texture. We found that for 2 cups flour, only 5 tablespoons butter were needed for a rich, light scone.

The choice of liquid can also profoundly affect the flavor of a scone. We tested various liquids and found that cream made scones that were tender yet still light. Scones made with milk were bland and dry. Buttermilk gave us scones with plenty of flavor, but they were too flaky and biscuitlike. Scones made with cream were more moist and flavorful than the others.

In traditional recipes, 1 or 2 tablespoons of sugar is enough to sweeten an entire batch of scones. American scones tend to be far sweeter than the British versions, which are usually sweetened with toppings such as jam. Americans seem to eat scones the way they eat muffins, with nothing more than a smear of butter. To accommodate the American sweet tooth, we decided to increase the sugar in our recipe to 3 tablespoons.

The quickest and easiest way we found to make these scones was in a food processor. We found the food processor more reliable than hand mixing, which can overheat the butter and soften it. To shape the scones, all we did was pat the dough into an 8-inch circle and then cut it into eight wedges.

Cream Scones

MAKES 8 SCONES

TIME: 40 MINUTES
(INCLUDES 25 MINUTES BAKING
AND COOLING TIME)

We find it easier to mix the scones in a food processor, but they may also be mixed by hand. Cut the butter into the dry ingredients with two knives or a pastry blender. Resist the urge to eat the scones hot out of the oven. Letting them cool for at least 10 minutes firms their texture.

2	cups (10 ounces) unbleached all-purpose flour
1	tablespoon baking powder
3	tablespoons sugar
½	teaspoon salt

5 tablespoons unsalted butter, chilled, cut
  into ¼-inch cubes

½ cup currants

1 cup heavy cream

1. Adjust an oven rack to the middle position and heat the oven to 425 degrees. Line a baking sheet with parchment paper.

2. Place the flour, baking powder, sugar, and salt in the workbowl of a food processor fitted with a steel blade. Pulse 6 times to combine.

3. Remove the cover from the workbowl and distribute the butter evenly over the dry ingredients. Cover and combine with twelve 1-second pulses. Add the currants and pulse one more time.

4. Remove the cover from the workbowl and pour the cream evenly over the dry ingredients. Pulse until the ingredients start to gather into moist pebbles, eight to ten 1-second pulses.

5. Transfer the dough and all dry, floury bits to a countertop and knead the dough by hand just until it comes together into a rough ball, about 5 to 10 seconds. Following the illustrations on page 368, pat the dough into an 8-inch circle and cut into 8 wedges. Place the wedges on the parchment-lined baking sheet.

6. Bake until the scone tops are light brown, 12 to 15 minutes. Cool the scones on a wire rack for at least 10 minutes. Serve warm.

➤ VARIATIONS

Glazed Scones

A light glaze of cream and sugar gives scones an attractive sheen and sweeter flavor.

Follow the recipe for Cream Scones, brushing the tops of the scones with 2 tablespoons heavy cream and then sprinkling them with 2 tablespoons sugar just before they go into the oven.

Oatmeal-Raisin Scones

We found that old-fashioned rolled oats produced the best oatmeal scones, with a flakier texture and more noticeable oat flavor than those made with quick-cooking oats.

Follow the recipe for Cream Scones, substituting 1 cup rolled oats for ½ cup flour. Replace the currants with ¾ cup raisins. Increase the sugar to 4 tablespoons and the butter to 6 tablespoons.

Ginger Scones

Follow the recipe for Cream Scones, substituting ½ cup chopped crystallized ginger for the currants.

Cranberry-Orange Scones

Follow the recipe for Cream Scones, adding 1 teaspoon grated orange zest with the butter and substituting ¾ cup dried cranberries for the currants.

CINNAMON BUNS

IT'S A SHAME THAT MAKING CINNAMON buns at home can try the patience of the most devoted cooks. Most recipes call for yeast, which means they also call for a lot of time and skill as well as a standing mixer (or powerful biceps). The alternative is to make cinnamon buns from a tube or a box, options that produce inferior buns whose flavor lies somewhere between chemicals and cardboard. Our aim was to put cinnamon buns back in the home kitchen in good time, sacrificing neither flavor nor fluffiness to speed. In short, we wanted great buns without the hassle.

We started with a tasting of our favorite yeasted cinnamon buns. With a soft and resilient texture and a bready, open crumb, the texture of these buns was top-notch, and the combination of cinnamon and yeast produced a grown-up flavor. Unfortunately, the start-to-finish time was nearly 5 hours. Now we knew what texture and flavor we wanted from cinnamon buns; we just wanted it quicker and easier.

To this end, the first decision we made was to work from recipes leavened with baking powder rather than yeast. The next step was to determine the best method for incorporating the fat into the other ingredients. First, we tried the classic mixing method of cutting cold butter into dry ingredients, as for pie dough. This method turned out cinnamon buns that were dense, flaky, and craggy rather than tender, light, and fluffy.

The next mixing method we tried called for combining melted butter with the liquid ingredients in a food processor and then adding the dry ingredients. While the food processor made the mixing process easier, the price was too high; the resulting dough was sticky and difficult to work with.

The last method we tried was a quick cream biscuit method, in which heavy cream is added to flour, sugar, baking powder, and salt. What makes this dough unusual is its complete lack of butter; it relies entirely on the heavy cream for tenderness and flavor. Still better, the dough can be mixed in a minute using just one bowl. This process was by far the fastest and easiest, and we wanted to go with it, but a few refinements were required before it produced really good cinnamon buns.

Our next inclination was to test whole or skim milk in place of heavy cream, but whole milk made the buns too heavy, whereas skim milk made them tough and bland. We increased the amount of baking powder to achieve lightness but ended up with metallic-tasting buns. We then tested buttermilk, a common ingredient in biscuit doughs, and had some success. (We also added ½ teaspoon baking soda to balance the acidity of the

buttermilk. Baking soda reacts with the acid in buttermilk to produce carbon dioxide gas, which causes lift.) The acid in the buttermilk gave the buns a more complex flavor and tenderized the gluten in the dough, making the interior airy and light.

But now the dough was too lean for our taste (owing to the buttermilk, which is made by adding acidic cultures to skim or lowfat milk). The solution was to add 2 tablespoons melted butter to the buttermilk. Just as we had hoped, the dough was tender, complex, and rich.

Whereas most recipes instruct bakers to roll out the dough, we found it easier to pat the dough into a rough rectangle, thus making the process even simpler. For the cinnamon-sugar filling, we decided on a union of brown sugar, white sugar, cinnamon, cloves, and salt. Before adding the filling, we brushed the dough with 2 tablespoons melted butter to help the filling cling to the dough. Because the cinnamon mixture was loose and dry, however, it still tended to fall away from the dough when the buns were cut and transferred to the baking pan. The easy solution was to also add 1 tablespoon melted butter to the filling ingredients.

To finish the buns, we tried a host of glazes, all based on a quick confectioners' sugar and water glaze, which is inherently pasty and grainy. After a few trials, we found a way to mask the graininess and pasty flavor by combining buttermilk and cream cheese, then sifting the confectioners' sugar over the paste (if the sugar is not sifted, the glaze is lumpy). This glaze was smooth, thick, and pleasantly tangy, although it does add another ingredient—cream cheese—to the shopping list.

As for the pan, we tried muffin tins, pie plates, cookie sheets, springform pans, glass baking dishes, and cake pans. In the end, we chose a 9-inch round nonstick cake pan with straight sides—the perfect size. We started baking at 425 degrees and got lucky the first time out. The buns baked in 25 minutes, rose and browned nicely, and were fully cooked.

Now the moment of truth had come. It was time for a blind tasting of our quick cinnamon buns head-to-head with our yeasted cinnamon buns. The quick buns got a quick nod of approval, with many tasters even preferring them to the more sophisticated and elegantly flavored yeasted buns. Best of all, these shortcut cinnamon buns can be on the table in less than an hour—a fact you may very well choose to keep to yourself.

~⊱⊰~

Fastest Cinnamon Buns

MAKES 8 BUNS
TIME: 55 MINUTES
(INCLUDES 30 MINUTES BAKING AND COOLING TIME)

Melted butter is used in both the filling and the dough and to grease the pan—it's easiest to melt the total amount (8 tablespoons) all at once in a heatproof measuring cup and then measure it as needed. The cream cheese makes the glaze thicker and less grainy, but it can be omitted. See the illustrations on page 376 for tips on making the buns.

CINNAMON BUNS

8	tablespoons unsalted butter, melted
¾	cup packed (5¼ ounces) dark brown sugar
6	tablespoons granulated sugar
2	teaspoons ground cinnamon
⅛	teaspoon ground cloves
⅛	teaspoon plus ½ teaspoon salt
2½	cups (12½ ounces) unbleached all-purpose flour, plus more for dusting the work surface
1¼	teaspoons baking powder
½	teaspoon baking soda
1¼	cups buttermilk

GLAZE

2	tablespoons cream cheese, softened
2	tablespoons buttermilk
1	cup (4 ounces) confectioners' sugar

1. FOR THE BUNS: Adjust an oven rack to the upper-middle position and heat the oven to 425 degrees. Brush a round 9-inch nonstick cake pan with 1 tablespoon butter. Spray a wire cooling rack with nonstick cooking spray.

2. Combine the brown sugar, 4 tablespoons granulated sugar, cinnamon, cloves, and ⅛ teaspoon salt in a small bowl. Add 1 tablespoon melted butter and stir with a fork or fingers until the mixture resembles wet sand; set the filling mixture aside.

3. Whisk together the flour, remaining 2 tablespoons sugar, baking powder, baking soda, and remaining ½ teaspoon salt in a large bowl. Whisk together the buttermilk and 2 tablespoons butter in a measuring cup. Add the liquid to the dry ingredients and stir with a wooden spoon until the liquid is absorbed (the dough will look shaggy), about 30 seconds. Transfer the dough to a lightly floured work surface and knead until just smooth and no longer shaggy, about 30 seconds.

4. Pat the dough with your hands into a 12 by 9-inch rectangle. Brush the dough with 2 tablespoons melted butter. Sprinkle the dough evenly with the brown sugar filling, leaving a ½-inch border. Press the filling firmly into the dough. Using a bench scraper or metal spatula, loosen the dough from the work surface. Starting at a long side, roll the dough, pressing lightly, to form a tight log. Pinch the seam to seal. Roll the log seam-side down and cut it evenly into 8 pieces. With your hand, slightly flatten each piece of dough to seal the open edges and keep the filling in place. Place 1 roll in the center of the prepared pan and then place

the remaining 7 rolls around the perimeter of the pan. Brush the rolls with the remaining 2 tablespoons butter.

5. Bake until the edges are golden brown, 23 to 25 minutes. Use an offset metal spatula to loosen the buns from the pan. Wearing oven mitts, place a large plate over the pan and invert the buns onto the plate. Place the greased cooling rack over the plate and invert the buns onto the rack. Cool about 5 minutes before glazing.

6. FOR THE GLAZE AND TO FINISH BUNS: While the buns are cooling, line a rimmed baking sheet with parchment paper (for easy cleanup); set the rack with the buns on the baking sheet. Whisk the cream cheese and buttermilk in a large bowl until thick and smooth (the mixture will look like cottage cheese at first). Sift the confectioners' sugar over the mixture and whisk until a smooth glaze forms, about 30 seconds. Spoon the glaze evenly over the buns; serve immediately.

MAKING CINNAMON BUNS

1. Pat the dough into a 12 by 9-inch rectangle and brush it with melted butter. Sprinkle the filling evenly over the dough, leaving a ½-inch border. Press the filling firmly into the dough.

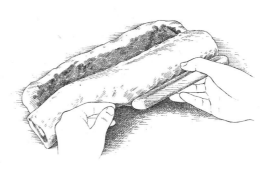

2. Using a bench scraper or metal spatula, loosen the dough from the work surface. Starting at a long side, roll the dough, pressing lightly, to form a tight log. Pinch the seam to seal.

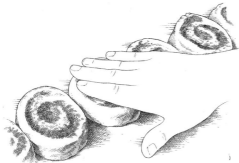

3. Roll the log seam-side down and cut it evenly into 8 pieces. With your hand, slightly flatten each piece of dough to seal the open edges and keep the filling in place.

4. Place 1 roll in the center of the prepared nonstick pan and place the remaining 7 rolls around the perimeter of the pan.

14

CAKES AND COOKIES

MOST COOKS DON'T THINK OF CAKES or even cookies as particularly quick. In addition to lengthy prep time, many cake and cookie recipes include long baking and cooling times. So how do you bake a cake or a batch of cookies and have them cooled and ready to serve in an hour or less?

Here are a couple of general principles to keep in mind. When it comes to cakes, try to bake individual cakes or jelly rolls, which require much less baking time than other cake recipes. Also, use the refrigerator or even the freezer to speed cooling times.

For cookies, it's key to make small batches. No matter how quickly the batter comes together, if you have to shape and bake batch after batch of cookies, the total cooking time is quite lengthy. Melted butter can be ready to use in just a couple of minutes. If a recipe calls for softened butter, use the microwave to hasten this process.

Finally, when baking any cake or cookie, be sure to heat the oven as soon as you walk into the kitchen.

INDIVIDUAL COFFEECAKES

NO MATTER HOW QUICKLY YOU CAN make a coffeecake batter, most recipes take upward of an hour to bake off the cake. We tried baking coffeecakes in a loaf pan, a glass pan, and a cake pan—to no avail. Because the batter is so dense and rich, it takes the heat a good, long time to reach the center of the cake. Tack on another 30 minutes or an hour to cool and you have a cake that took minutes to prepare but needed hours to bake and cool. Our mission was to find a way to make, bake, and cool coffeecake in less than an hour.

The problem was that we didn't want to sacrifice the richness of a coffeecake for time. We still wanted butter, eggs, and sour cream, but we needed to find a way for the heat to get to the center of the batter faster so the cake baked—and cooled—in less time. We thought about using a muffin tin to accomplish this task, but honestly, we weren't too thrilled with the idea of coffeecake muffins. However, because we never discard an idea before testing it, we tried the muffin tin anyway.

In a food processor, we followed the procedure for our favorite sour cream coffeecake and combined one third of the flour with half of the brown sugar and all of the granulated sugar. We set aside ¾ cup of this dry mixture for our streusel layer, adding to it cinnamon for depth and more brown sugar for moistness; we left out butter because we found that it made the filling pasty. To the remaining dry ingredients, we added the rest of the brown sugar and flour, plus the baking powder, baking soda, and salt. We pulsed cold butter into the dry ingredients and made a pebbly dry mixture, to which we added 3 eggs and ½ cup sour cream. After a few bursts in the food processor, the batter was ready to go into the muffin tins and turn into coffeecake.

We filled the muffin cups three quarters full and topped them with the streusel. Less than 30 minutes later, they were ready to come out of the oven. We inverted them onto a wire cooling rack. Then it hit us—serve the muffins upside down! This way, the muffins didn't look like muffins per se but rather like pretty little cakes, narrow at the neck and wide at the base. Now the problems were that the streusel was on the bottom of each cake and that those bottoms were round, causing the cakes to rock on the plate.

For our next test, we decreased the baking powder to just ½ teaspoon. This was the first time in memory that we *wanted* stout, flat-topped muffins. We also decided to layer the streusel into the middle of the muffin rather than sprinkling it over the top. These muffins were great. They had a flatter bottom than the first batch (although still slightly rounded, but with any less leavener the muffins were too dense), and the streusel core provided a nice contrast in both appearance and flavor to the muffin interior.

To really finish the muffins—we mean *cakes*—off right, we decided to make a quick confectioners' sugar icing and spoon it over the tops of the cakes. The glaze formed an opaque shell across the little cakes and dripped down the sides; the result looked nothing like muffins. What's the best thing about our coffeecake? You won't feel guilty about eating a whole one.

Individual Coffeecakes

MAKES 12 CAKES

TIME: 45 MINUTES
(INCLUDES 30 MINUTES BAKING
AND COOLING TIME)

Either dust the cakes with confectioners' sugar or glaze them with the super-simple confectioners' sugar icing (see variation). For chocolate chip coffeecakes, sprinkle about 10 semisweet chocolate morsels per cake over the streusel layer and then top with batter as described in the recipe. You can use toasted pecans or walnuts the same way.

1½	cups (7½ ounces) unbleached all-purpose flour
½	cup packed (3½ ounces) dark brown sugar
1	cup (7 ounces) granulated sugar
1	tablespoon ground cinnamon
½	teaspoon baking powder
¼	teaspoon baking soda
½	teaspoon salt
12	tablespoons (1½ sticks) unsalted butter, cold, cut into 1-inch cubes
3	large eggs
½	cup sour cream

1. Adjust an oven rack to the middle position and heat the oven to 350 degrees. Spray a standard muffin tin with nonstick cooking spray.

2. Combine ½ cup flour, ¼ cup brown sugar, and all of the granulated sugar in the workbowl of a food processor. Combine the mixture in five 1-second pulses. Remove ¾ cup of this mixture and place it in a medium bowl. Add to it the remaining ¼ cup brown sugar and the cinnamon, mix to combine, and set aside.

3. Add the remaining 1 cup flour to the mixture remaining in the food processor workbowl along with the baking powder, baking soda, and salt. Combine the mixture in five 1-second pulses. Scatter the butter over the dry ingredients and pulse until the mixture breaks down into small pebbly pieces that resemble wet sand, about ten 1-second pulses. Add the eggs and sour cream and process the mixture until it is well combined and thick, about eight 1-second pulses.

4. Place enough batter (about 2 tablespoons) into each muffin cup to cover the bottom surface of the cup but rise no more than

GLAZING COFFEECAKES

Spoon 2 teaspoons glaze on top of the upside-down cake (the narrow end will be facing up). Make an X in the glaze so that it runs down the sides of the cake in four places.

½ inch up the sides. Sprinkle about 1½ tablespoons streusel mixture over the batter and cover with an additional 1 to 2 tablespoons of batter, or enough to fill the cup three quarters full. Bake until light golden brown and until the cake feels firm but springs back when touched, 20 to 24 minutes, rotating the pan from front to back halfway through the baking time. Invert the cakes onto a wire rack and cool 5 minutes. Dust with confectioners' sugar or drizzle with Quick Confectioners' Sugar Icing (see variation). Serve immediately.

➤ VARIATION

Individual Coffeecakes with Quick Confectioners' Sugar Icing

Follow the recipe for Individual Coffeecakes. Place a sheet of parchment paper beneath the wire rack as the cakes cool. Whisk 1 cup (4 ounces) confectioners' sugar and 2 tablespoons water in a medium bowl until smooth. Spoon about 2 teaspoons glaze over each cake, forcing the glaze to run down the sides of the cake (see the illustration on page 379).

No-Bake Cheesecake

SWEET AND TANGY, WITH A TENDER graham cracker crust, cheesecake is an all-time favorite American dessert. Most recipes contain eggs to thicken the filling, meaning that the cheesecake needs to bake in an oven for around 1 hour—this is in addition to prep and cooling times, which, when added together, can push the total allotted time of making a cheesecake to many hours. We were convinced we could create a delicious cheesecake that didn't need to be baked and could therefore be made in about an hour from beginning to end.

We started by preparing a graham cracker crust. The crust had to be sturdy enough that a wedge of cheesecake could be cut and served completely intact—that is, without falling apart as the segment was transferred to a plate. In addition, the crust had to be easy to make and easy to press into a tart pan or pie plate. We combined flour and graham cracker crumbs with confectioners' sugar (the cornstarch in confectioners' sugar would provide tenderness), salt, and butter in the food processor. The first crust we made, with 8 tablespoons butter to about 1¾ cups dry ingredients, was too short—the ratio of fat to flour was too high—so the crust crumbled too easily. We decreased the butter to 6 tablespoons, but now we found the crust was too solid and hard. Seven tablespoons seemed to be the lucky number; it made a crust that was neither too stiff nor too loose.

For the filling, we began by beating cream cheese in a standing mixer and folding sweetened whipped cream into it, figuring the whipped cream could lighten the cheese much the way eggs lighten the texture in a conventional recipe. While the flavor was bright and fresh, it needed diversity and depth. In addition, even after 30 minutes of chilling in the refrigerator, the filling still was a little too loose to slice into neat wedges.

First, we decided to add lemon juice and salt to brighten the flavors of the filling. Next, we chose to add gelatin to help it set up. We divided the heavy cream we were using for the whipped cream, using ¼ cup to soften and dissolve the gelatin and the other ¼ cup to whip and lighten the cream cheese. After dissolving the gelatin, we added the warm cream back to the whipped cream and cream cheese mixture and whipped the two together for a couple of minutes. Then we added the filling to our cooled graham cracker crust.

Rather than placing the cheesecake in the refrigerator to cool, we chose to pop it into the freezer instead. In just 15 minutes, the filling had set. We removed a slice from the pan; both the filling and the crust remained intact. The filling was creamy and smooth, neither too heavy nor too light, and the crust offset the filling with a nice crunch. Top this cheesecake with fresh berries and a dusting of confectioners' sugar, and people will never guess that it took less than an hour to make from start to finish.

No-Bake Cheesecake Tart

SERVES 8

TIME: 1 HOUR
(INCLUDES 25 MINUTES COOLING
AND CHILLING TIME)

If you don't have a tart pan with a removable bottom, use a 9-inch glass pie plate instead. On their own, slices of this tart are a bit plain, but in 5 extra minutes you can top it with mixed berries and dust with confectioners' sugar (see the illustration on page 382).

CRUST

¾   cup (2¾ ounces) graham cracker crumbs (5 whole crackers, broken into rough pieces and processed in a food processor until uniformly fine)

⅔   cup (3⅓ ounces) unbleached all-purpose flour

⅓   cup (1⅓ ounces) confectioners' sugar

½   teaspoon salt

7   tablespoons unsalted butter, cold, cut into 1-inch pieces

FILLING

½   cup heavy cream

1½   teaspoons plain, unflavored gelatin

¼   cup (1¾ ounces) granulated sugar

8   ounces cream cheese

1   tablespoon juice from 1 lemon
    Pinch salt

1. FOR THE CRUST: Adjust an oven rack to the middle position and heat the oven to 350 degrees. Spray a 9- to 9½-inch tart pan with a removable bottom with nonstick cooking spray.

2. Pulse the graham cracker crumbs, flour, confectioners' sugar, and salt in a food processor workbowl fitted with a steel blade. Add the butter and process to blend, 8 to 10 seconds, and then pulse until the mixture is pale yellow and resembles coarse meal, about three 1-second pulses. Sprinkle the mixture into the prepared pan and press firmly with your fingers into an even layer over the entire pan bottom and up the sides. Bake the crust until golden brown, 18 to 20 minutes. Cool on a wire rack for 10 minutes.

3. FOR THE FILLING: While the crust is baking, pour ¼ cup cream into a glass measuring cup. Add the gelatin and whisk to combine; let stand for 5 minutes to hydrate the gelatin and then microwave on high power for 30 to 45 seconds or until the cream is bubbling and the gelatin is completely dissolved. Meanwhile, pour the remaining ¼ cup cream into the bowl of a standing mixer fitted with a whisk attachment. Add the sugar and beat at medium-high speed until the cream holds stiff peaks, 3 to 4 minutes. Add the cream cheese and beat at low speed until combined, about 30 seconds. Scrape the bottom and sides of the bowl well with a rubber spatula. Add the lemon juice and salt and beat at medium-low speed until combined, about 1 minute. Scrape the bowl again. Increase the speed to medium-high and beat for 3 minutes or until aerated and thoroughly combined. Add the dissolved gelatin mixture and beat for an additional 2 minutes to combine.

4. Pour the filling into the cooled crust and, using an offset or icing spatula, spread it evenly. Place the pan in the freezer on a flat surface, such as a rimmed baking sheet (be wary of the removable bottom; you don't

want the crust to pop out, which it may if it's resting on an uneven surface). Freeze until the filling sets, about 15 minutes. Slice and serve.

➤ VARIATIONS

Strawberry-Swirl Cheesecake Tart
Follow the recipe for No-Bake Cheesecake Tart through step 3. Place ¼ cup filling in a small bowl; pour the remaining filling into the crust and spread evenly as directed in step 4. Mix ¼ cup strawberry jam into the reserved filling. Place the strawberry mixture in a zipper-lock plastic bag and use scissors to snip a small opening from the corner of the bag. Squeeze the strawberry mixture onto the plain filling in a zigzag motion. Using a long wooden skewer or toothpick, swirl the strawberry filling into the plain filling, being careful not to touch the crust. Chill as directed. Decorate the top of the cheesecake with quartered strawberries and serve.

QUICK FRUIT GARNISH

Rather than painstakingly arranging mixed berries over the cheesecake, use this quick method. Place ½ pint blueberries, ½ pint blackberries, and 1 pint raspberries in a large plastic bag. Hold the bag closed with one hand and use the other to gently jostle the berries about to combine them. Open the bag and carefully empty the berries onto the cheesecake in an even layer. Use your finger to adjust the berries as necessary to cover the entire surface of the cheesecake. Dust the fruit with confectioners' sugar to finish.

Pumpkin-Swirl Cheesecake Tart
Follow the recipe for No-Bake Cheesecake Tart through step 3. Place ¼ cup filling in a small bowl; pour the remaining filling into the crust and spread evenly as directed in step 4. Mix ½ cup canned pumpkin pie filling into the reserved filling. Place the pumpkin mixture in a zipper-lock plastic bag and use scissors to snip a small opening from the corner of the bag. Squeeze the pumpkin mixture onto the plain filling in a zigzag motion. Using a long wooden skewer or toothpick, swirl the pumpkin filling into the plain filling, being careful not to touch the crust. Chill as directed. Serve with a dollop of whipped cream.

LEMON PUDDING CAKE

BASED ON RECIPES THAT DATE TO colonial times, pudding cakes have existed in their present form for hundreds of years. Unlike ordinary egg custards, pudding cakes contain a little flour and beaten egg whites. During baking, the beaten egg whites float to the top, creating a spongy, cakelike cap. Meanwhile, the remainder of the batter sinks to the bottom to make a puddinglike layer.

The acidity of citrus juices makes for especially good pudding cakes because the juice lightly clabbers the milk-based batter, causing it to thicken. The frothy upper layer becomes thick, stiff, and stable, and it puffs better than if no citrus juice is used. At the same time, the acidic juice undercuts the thickening power of the flour, making for a more tender custard.

We tried making pudding cakes with butter and even cream instead of milk but found that the added fat caused the whipped egg whites to collapse, making for a thin top.

Many pudding cake recipes call for placing the baking pan inside a roasting pan filled with hot water (which is called a water bath). This process is tedious, and we found it is unnecessary for a basic pudding cake with minimal fat. In and out of the oven in less than 45 minutes, it's no wonder why this cake has been around for so long. It's fast and delicious, and it is a cake and sauce all in one.

Lemon Pudding Cake

SERVES 4 TO 6

TIME: 1 HOUR

(INCLUDES 45 MINUTES BAKING AND COOLING TIME)

This cake comes out of the oven quite loose. The top is set and cakelike, but the bottom is softer, more like pudding. Fresh raspberries or strawberries are the perfect accompaniment to this cake. To quickly bring the eggs to room temperature, place them (still in their shells) in a bowl of warm water for 5 minutes.

1	tablespoon unsalted butter, softened
¾	cup (5¼ ounces) plus 2 tablespoons sugar
¼	cup (1 ounce) plain cake flour
¼	teaspoon salt
3	large eggs, separated, room temperature
1	cup milk
1	tablespoon grated zest plus ¼ cup juice from 2 medium lemons
½	teaspoon cream of tartar

1. Adjust an oven rack to the middle position and heat the oven to 325 degrees. Lightly grease a 9 by 9-inch glass baking pan with the softened butter.

2. Whisk together ¾ cup sugar, the flour, and the salt in a medium bowl. Beat the egg yolks, milk, lemon zest, and lemon juice together in a small bowl. Pour this mixture over the dry ingredients and blend well with a whisk.

3. In the bowl of a standing mixer, beat the egg whites at medium-high speed until they are foamy, about 30 seconds. Add the cream of tartar, raise the speed to high, and beat until the whites hold soft peaks, about 1½ minutes. Add the remaining 2 tablespoons sugar and beat until the egg whites hold a 2-inch peak, about 30 seconds. Using a whisk, fold the egg whites into the yolk mixture.

4. Pour the batter into the prepared baking dish. Bake until the center is set and springs back when gently pressed, about 35 minutes. Remove the pan from the oven and cool for 10 minutes. Spoon the cake (it will be soft) into bowls and serve warm.

VARIATION

Orange Pudding Cake

Follow the recipe for Lemon Pudding Cake, substituting 1 tablespoon orange zest for the lemon zest. Reduce the lemon juice to 2 tablespoons and add ¼ cup orange juice at the same time.

JELLY ROLL CAKE

WHY DON'T WE SEE MORE JELLY ROLL cakes served for dessert? Not only are they impressive-looking but they're easy to make. You don't have to worry about applying frosting perfectly because it's rolled up inside the cake. All you do is spread the filling onto the cake and roll it up. Determined to make a filled jelly roll cake that met our 1-hour, minimal-ingredient requirements for this book, we entered the test kitchen with the clock ticking.

Jelly roll cakes are traditionally made with sponge cakes—delicate cakes that take well to rolling. There are several kinds of sponge or foam cakes, so named because they depend on eggs (whole or separated) beaten to a foam to provide lift and structure. All the kinds use egg foam for structure, but they differ in two ways: whether fat (butter or milk) is added and whether the foam is made from whole eggs, egg whites, or a combination.

We started by making a classic American sponge cake, which includes no fat in the form of butter or milk and calls for eight beaten egg whites folded into four beaten egg yolks. The cake certainly was light, but it lacked flavor, and the texture was dry and a bit chewy. To solve these problems, we turned to a recipe for a hot-milk sponge cake, in which a small amount of melted

INGREDIENTS: Cake Flour

Two types of cake flour are sold in supermarkets: plain and self-rising. The latter contains leavener and salt and cannot be used in recipes calling for plain cake flour.

Bakers who use cake flour infrequently may not want to dedicate a separate canister for this flour. However, keeping the box of flour in the pantry for a prolonged period isn't a good idea, as bugs can work their way in. Here's how to avoid this problem and make measuring cake flour easier.

Open the box of cake flour, transfer the contents to a zipper-lock bag, and store the bag inside the original box so you know what's inside the bag. When you want to use the flour, it's easy to dip a measuring cup into the bag and sweep off the excess—something you can't do if the flour is stored in its original box.

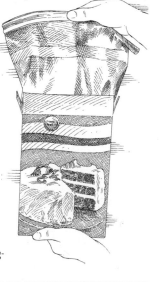

butter and hot milk are added to the whole-egg foam. This cake turned out much better on all counts. The added fat not only provided flavor but also tenderized the crumb. This particular recipe also used fewer eggs than our original sponge cake recipe.

We were now working with a master recipe that called for ¾ cup cake flour, 1 teaspoon baking powder, ¾ cup sugar, and 5 eggs. We started by separating out all five whites and found that the cake was too light, its insufficient structure resulting in a slightly sunken center. We then separated out and beat just three of the whites, and the resulting cake was excellent. When all-purpose flour was substituted for cake flour, the cake had more body and was a bit tougher than the version with cake flour. We then tried different proportions of the two flours, finally settling on a 2:1 ratio of cake flour to all-purpose flour.

We thought the baking powder might be optional, but it turned out to be essential to a properly risen cake. Although classic sponge cakes, with no added fat, do not require chemical leavening, in this sponge cake—given the addition of milk and melted butter combined with the relatively small amount of beaten egg whites in proportion to the flour—baking powder was necessary.

With our basic recipe in hand, we played with the order of the steps. Beating the whole-egg foam first and then the whites allowed the relatively fragile foam to deteriorate, producing less rise. We found that beating the whites first was vastly better. After much experimentation, we also found it best to fold together, all at the same time, the beaten whole eggs, the beaten whites, and the flour and then, once the mixture was about half mixed, to add the warm butter and milk. This eliminated the chance that the liquid would damage the egg foam and also made the temperature of the butter mixture less important than it was in other sponge cakes.

Determining when a sponge cake is properly cooked is a little more difficult than it is with a regular American layer cake. A sponge cake should provide some resistance and not feel as if one just touched the top of a soufflé. Another good test is color. The top of the cake should be a nice light brown, not pale golden or a dark, rich brown.

Up to this point, we were inverting the just-baked cake onto a tea towel dusted with confectioners' sugar and then rolling the cake and towel together into a jelly roll shape to cool. Although this is a common practice that reduces the risk of the cake cracking during rolling (the cake is more pliable when hot, and the tea towel prevents the cake from sticking to itself), we found that the towel was retaining too much heat, so cake was slow to cool. Instead, we decided to roll the cake with a sheet of parchment paper. This worked nicely; the cake didn't stick to itself or to the paper, and it cooled quickly. After 15 minutes, the cake was ready to be unrolled, filled, rolled again, and sliced into individual servings.

ASSEMBLING A JELLY ROLL CAKE

1. Starting from a short side, roll the cake—parchment and all—into a jelly roll shape. Cool for 15 minutes.

2. Unroll the cooled cake. Using an offset spatula, spread raspberry jam evenly over the surface of the cake, almost to the edges. Repeat with whipped cream (if using).

3. Roll the cake gently but snugly around the filling, carefully peeling off the parchment as you roll. Dust the top of the cake with confectioners' sugar, if desired.

4. Trim thin slices from both ends and then cut the cake into individual slices using an electric or serrated knife.

Jelly Roll Cake with Raspberry Jam

SERVES 12

TIME: 1 HOUR
(INCLUDES 25 MINUTES BAKING
AND COOLING TIME)

Just about any kind of jam or preserve is delicious in this simple sponge cake—from apricot preserves to orange marmalade. Fresh raspberries are a perfect accent to the cake filling—just place about ½ pint (6 ounces) fresh raspberries on top of the jam layer before rolling the cake. To quickly get the eggs to room temperature, place them in warm water for 5 minutes. The whites should be beaten to soft, billowy peaks. If beaten until stiff, they will be difficult to fold into the whole-egg mixture. See photo of this recipe on page 164.

½	cup (2 ounces) plain cake flour, plus more for dusting the pan
¼	cup (1¼ ounces) unbleached all-purpose flour
1	teaspoon baking powder
¼	teaspoon salt
3	tablespoons milk
2	tablespoons unsalted butter
½	teaspoon vanilla extract
5	large eggs, at room temperature
¾	cup (5¼ ounces) granulated sugar
	Confectioners' sugar for dusting
1	cup raspberry jam

1. Adjust the oven rack to the middle position and heat the oven to 350 degrees. Spray a 12 by 17½-inch rimmed jelly roll or half-sheet pan with nonstick spray, cover the pan bottom with parchment paper, and spray the parchment with nonstick cooking spray; dust the surface with plain cake flour and tap out the excess.

2. Whisk together the ½ cup plain cake flour and the all-purpose flour, baking powder, and salt in a medium bowl. Heat the milk and butter in a small saucepan over low heat until

the butter melts. Remove the pan from the heat and add the vanilla; cover and keep warm.

3. Separate 3 eggs, placing the whites in the bowl of a standing mixer. Combine the 3 yolks with the remaining 2 whole eggs in a separate bowl and set aside. Beat the whites at high speed with the whisk attachment until they are foamy. Gradually add 6 tablespoons sugar; continue to beat the whites to soft, moist peaks. Do not overbeat. Transfer the whites to a large bowl and reserve.

4. Transfer the yolk–whole egg mixture to the empty mixing bowl, add the remaining 6 tablespoons sugar, and beat, using the whisk attachment, at medium-high speed until the eggs are thick and are a pale yellow color, about 5 minutes. Transfer the beaten eggs to the bowl with the whipped whites. Sprinkle the flour mixture over the beaten eggs and whites and fold very gently 12 times with a large rubber spatula. Make a well in one side of the batter and pour the milk mixture into the bowl. Continue folding until no trace of flour remains and the whites and whole eggs are evenly mixed, about 8 additional strokes. Immediately pour the batter into the prepared pan and spread evenly with an offset spatula.

5. Bake until the cake top is light brown, feels firm, and springs back when touched, 10 to 12 minutes. Immediately upon removing the cake from the oven, run a knife around the edges of the pan to loosen it. Invert the pan onto a piece of parchment generously dusted with confectioners' sugar. Peel off the top layer of parchment and, following illustration 1 on page 385, roll the cake with the parchment from one short side to the other. Let the rolled cake cool for 15 minutes.

6. Following illustrations 2 through 4 on page 385, fill the cake with the jam and cut it into individual slices. Serve. (Cover any leftover cake with plastic and refrigerate; bring to room temperature before serving.)

➤ VARIATION

Jelly Roll Cake with Whipped Cream Filling

Follow the recipe for Jelly Roll Cake with Raspberry Jam. While the cake cools, beat 1 cup chilled heavy cream with ¼ cup confectioners' sugar in the bowl of a standing mixer at medium-high speed until medium-stiff peaks form, about 1½ minutes. After spreading the jam on the cake, spread the whipped cream evenly over the jam with an offset metal spatula. Roll the cake as instructed.

BANANA CAKE

BANANA CAKE COMES IN MANY guises—from Bundt pan creations to rectangular loaves studded with walnuts or raisins and spiced with cinnamon, cloves, or nutmeg. While there seems to be a banana cake to fit every occasion and every palate, we couldn't seem to find a recipe for one that could be baked, cooled, and frosted in under an hour—that is, until we decided to use a jelly roll or sheet pan.

Because the pan is shallow (a sheet pan is barely 1 inch deep), the heat can penetrate and cook the cake faster than if it were several inches deep. We decided that a simple sponge cake would probably fit our pan needs best. We were perplexed, however, about the presentation of the cake until we thought to cut the baked-off cake into quarters and then fill and stack the quarters as layers. We decided that we could leave the perimeter untouched and simply dust the top of the cake with confectioners' sugar. The cake would be delicate and light—different from the heavy, dowdy, dark banana cakes with which we were familiar.

Because we wanted a delicate crumb, we used the sponge cake that worked so well in our jelly roll cake recipe (page 386). We found that two super-ripe bananas, added to the beaten egg mixture, gave the cake a good banana flavor. We scraped the batter into a jelly roll pan, baked it for 10 minutes, inverted it onto a cutting board lined with

ASSEMBLING A BANANA CAKE

1. To anchor the first layer of the cake, spread a dab of cream filling in the center of a flat serving platter. Using a big, flat spatula, transfer a quarter of the cake from the parchment to the center of the platter.

2. Place one third of the cream filling in the center of the cake layer and spread it with an icing spatula, leaving a ½-inch border free of filling. Put the next two cake layers on top, spreading each with half of the remaining filling.

3. Put the fourth cake layer on top and dust the top of the cake with confectioners' sugar.

parchment, and cut it into quarters.

After cooling for 10 minutes, the cake was ready to be filled. But with what? Because the cake itself was so supple and dainty, we didn't want to fill it with a thick, sticky cake filling, nor did we want to invest the time needed to make a buttercream. We decided that a whipped cream filling with a banana added for texture and flavor would be perfect. After a simple dusting of confectioners' sugar to decorate the top, the cake was ready to be sliced and served. With a pure, unadulterated banana flavor and light-as-a-cloud texture, this banana cake floats above its peers.

Banana Cake

SERVES 8

TIME: I HOUR
(INCLUDES 25 MINUTES BAKING
AND COOLING TIME)

If you like, add 1 tablespoon banana liqueur to the whipped cream filling. Note that the bananas in the filling will discolor with time, so this cake is best served as soon as it is assembled.

BANANA CAKE

½	cup (2 ounces) plain cake flour, plus more for dusting the pan
¼	cup (1¼ ounces) unbleached all-purpose flour
I	teaspoon baking powder
¼	teaspoon salt
3	tablespoons milk
2	tablespoons unsalted butter
½	teaspoon vanilla extract
5	large eggs, room temperature
¾	cup (5¼ ounces) granulated sugar
2	very ripe bananas, peeled and broken into 8 pieces
	Confectioners' sugar for dusting

FILLING

I	cup heavy cream, chilled
¼	cup (1 ounce) confectioners' sugar
I	very ripe banana, peeled and broken into 4 pieces

1. FOR THE CAKE: Adjust the oven rack to the middle position and heat the oven to 350 degrees. Spray a 12 by 17½-inch rimmed jelly roll or half-sheet pan with nonstick spray, cover the pan bottom with parchment paper, and spray the parchment with nonstick cooking spray; dust the surface with plain cake flour and tap out the excess.

2. Whisk together ½ cup plain cake flour and the all-purpose flour, baking powder, and salt in a medium bowl. Heat the milk and butter in a small saucepan over low heat until the butter melts. Remove the pan from the heat and add the vanilla; cover and keep warm.

3. Separate 3 eggs, placing the whites in the bowl of a standing mixer. Combine the 3 yolks with the remaining 2 whole eggs in a separate bowl and set aside. Beat the whites at high speed with the whisk attachment until they are foamy. Gradually add 6 tablespoons sugar; continue to beat the whites to soft, moist peaks. Do not overbeat. Transfer the whites to a large bowl and reserve.

4. Transfer the yolk–whole egg mixture to the empty mixing bowl, add the remaining 6 tablespoons sugar, and beat, using the whisk attachment, at medium-high speed until the eggs are thick and are a pale yellow color, about 5 minutes. With the mixer running, add the bananas, 1 piece at a time, waiting 10 seconds after each addition. Transfer the egg-banana mixture to the bowl with the whipped whites. Sprinkle the flour mixture over the beaten eggs and whites and fold very gently 12 times with a large rubber spatula. Make a well in one side of the batter and pour the milk mixture into the bowl. Continue folding

until no trace of flour remains and the whites and whole eggs are evenly mixed, about 8 additional strokes. Immediately pour the batter into the prepared pan and spread evenly with an offset spatula.

5. Bake until the cake top is light brown, feels firm, and springs back when touched, 10 to 12 minutes. Immediately upon removing the cake from the oven, run a knife around the edges of the pan to loosen it. Invert the pan onto a parchment-lined cutting board generously dusted with confectioners' sugar. Peel off the top layer of parchment, cut the cake into 4 equal pieces, and cool for 10 minutes.

6. FOR THE FILLING: While the cake is cooling, place the cream and sugar in the bowl of a standing mixer fitted with a whisk attachment. Beat at medium-high speed until medium-stiff peaks form, 1½ minutes. Add the banana, 1 piece at a time, and beat until the cream holds stiff peaks, about 30 seconds longer.

7. Assemble and fill the cake following the illustrations on page 387. Cut the cake into slices using an electric knife or a serrated bread knife. (Cover any leftover cake with plastic and refrigerate; bring to room temperature before serving.)

➤ VARIATIONS

Banana Cake with Fresh Strawberries

Follow the recipe for Banana Cake. While the cake is cooling and before preparing the filling, hull and cut 6 ounces (about 12 medium) strawberries into ¼-inch slices and toss them in a medium bowl with 2 tablespoons sugar. Place about 15 strawberry slices on the first cake layer and then cover them with the cream filling. Fill and assemble the cake as directed, placing the remaining berries directly on top of the second and third cake layers.

Banana Cake with Cocoa or Chocolate Filling

Follow the recipe for Banana Cake. After placing the cream filling on each cake layer, dust it with cocoa powder or grate semisweet chocolate over it. Dust the top of the cake with cocoa powder and then with confectioners' sugar.

MACAROONS

WHEN WE BEGAN LOOKING AT RECIPES for coconut macaroons, we found that they varied widely. In addition to different kinds of coconut and coconut flavorings, recipes often called for one or more of a wide array of ingredients, including extracts such as vanilla or almond, salt, flour, sugar, sweetened condensed milk, and even an egg or two. We wanted a simple macaroon in which the coconut received the most attention and that took only minutes to make and cook.

Our initial recipe testing yielded interesting results. One batch of macaroons made with beaten egg whites led to a light, airy, meringue-style cookie, pleasantly delicate but lacking in coconut flavor and chew. Another macaroon with whole eggs, cream of coconut, and sugar was gooey and over the top in the sweetness department without so much as a hint of coconut. Still other batches of macaroons that had lots of coconut came out dense and completely dry.

The winner of the bunch was a simple egg-white macaroon made by beating together an egg white, vanilla extract, sugar, and salt and then combining this with sweetened coconut. The problem was that these macaroons were slightly sticky. In addition, the coconut flavor seemed to be slightly flat.

Our first solution to the texture problem

was to add more coconut to the batter, but these cookies turned out dense and dry, somewhat like one of our original trials. Next, we tried tossing the coconut with flour before adding the wet ingredients, but these cookies were hard, floury-tasting, and still a little dry. Then we came up with a great idea: tossing the coconut with cornstarch. The cornstarch not only soaked up the extra moisture in the cookie but, unlike gluten-rich flour, didn't toughen the macaroon. After one test, we knew this was the answer.

To solve the problem of less-than-intense coconut flavor, we just eliminated the vanilla. Now there was nothing to stand in the coconut's way. While some of us liked the extra hit of coconut that extract provided, others thought it was a bit too much. We decided to leave this addition to the cook's discretion.

Fast Macaroons

MAKES 10 LARGE COOKIES

TIME: 35 MINUTES

(INCLUDES 25 MINUTES BAKING
AND COOLING TIME)

Add ¼ teaspoon coconut extract to the liquid ingredients for a real hit of coconut flavor. This recipe easily doubles to make 20 cookies.

I	large egg white
⅓	cup (2⅓ ounces) sugar
⅛	teaspoon salt
1¼	cups (3¾ ounces) sweetened flaked coconut
2	tablespoons cornstarch

1. Adjust an oven rack to the middle position and heat the oven to 375 degrees. Line a baking sheet with parchment paper and lightly spray the parchment with nonstick cooking spray.

2. Whisk together the egg white, sugar, and salt in a small bowl. Toss the coconut and cornstarch together in a medium bowl, making sure to thoroughly coat the coconut with the cornstarch. Pour the liquid ingredients over the coconut mixture and mix with a rubber spatula until evenly moistened.

3. Drop heaping tablespoons of batter onto the parchment-lined baking sheet, spacing them about 1 inch apart. Form the cookies into loose haystacks with your fingertips, moistening your hands with water as necessary to prevent sticking.

4. Bake until light golden brown, 12 to 14 minutes, rotating the baking sheet front to back halfway through the baking time. Cool the macaroons on the baking sheet until slightly set, about 2 minutes. Using a metal spatula, transfer the macaroons to a wire cooling rack. Cool for 10 minutes and serve.

VARIATION

Chocolate-Dipped Macaroons

Follow the recipe for Fast Macaroons. While the macaroons are cooling, place 4 ounces semisweet chocolate morsels in microwave-safe bowl and microwave at 50 percent power for 1½ minutes. Stir the chocolate; if it is not completely melted, microwave it an additional 30 seconds at 50 percent power. Add 1 ounce semisweet chocolate morsels and stir until smooth. Holding a cooled macaroon by the pointed top, dip the bottom and ½ inch of the sides into the chocolate, scrape off the excess with your finger, and place on a baking sheet lined with parchment paper. Refrigerate until the chocolate sets, about 15 minutes.

CRANBERRY CORNMEAL COOKIES

CRAGGY AND RUSTIC, A CRANBERRY cornmeal cookie is big, hearty, and satisfying. Rich yellow from cornmeal and studded with little red cranberries, it is crisp on the outside, slightly chewy on the inside, and not too sweet—perfect with a giant mug of coffee or a cup of chamomile tea. Our goal was to create a cookie that needed no beating or softening of ingredients. We didn't want to have to turn on any appliance to make these comforting cookies; we wanted to make do with a couple of mixing bowls and a wooden spoon.

First, we decided to use vegetable oil in place of butter. This was because butter made the cookies taste too much like polenta; oil had a cleaner flavor that allowed the cornmeal's nutty flavor to come through. In addition, rather than having to melt the butter or cream it with sugar, with oil we just measured, poured, and mixed.

Without butter, the cookies needed more tenderizing action. Here is where eggs came into the picture. We mixed two eggs with the oil and then added this mixture to flour, cornmeal, baking powder, salt, and the dried cranberries. We shaped the cookies into rough, large balls to bring home that quaint, country feeling.

After baking and sampling the cookies, we felt something was missing: spunk. We decided orange zest would be the perfect addition, working well with both the cornmeal and the cranberries. One teaspoon proved just right. We also added light brown sugar for caramel sweetness. These finished cookies are crispy and chewy; their complex corn flavor is set off by the sweetness of the cranberries and brown sugar and the tartness of the orange zest.

Cranberry Cornmeal Cookies

MAKES 12 LARGE COOKIES

TIME: 45 MINUTES
(INCLUDES 35 MINUTES BAKING AND COOLING TIME)

If you like cookies with extra crunch, reduce the amount of dried cranberries to ½ cup and add ½ cup toasted, chopped pecans to the dry ingredients. You can substitute 2 tablespoons chopped candied orange peel for the orange zest.

1	cup (5 ounces) unbleached all-purpose flour
½	cup (2¾ ounces) yellow cornmeal
½	cup (3½ ounces) granulated sugar, plus ⅓ cup for rolling
¼	cup packed (1¾ ounces) light brown sugar
1	teaspoon baking powder
½	teaspoon salt
1	teaspoon grated zest from 1 orange
¾	cup dried cranberries
2	large eggs
¼	cup vegetable oil

1. Adjust an oven rack to the middle position and heat the oven to 375 degrees. Line a baking sheet with parchment paper and lightly spray the parchment with nonstick cooking spray.

2. Whisk together the flour, cornmeal, ½ cup granulated sugar, brown sugar, baking powder, and salt in a large bowl. Add the orange zest and whisk to combine. Add the cranberries and, using a rubber spatula, toss to combine. Whisk together the eggs and oil in a measuring cup. Pour the egg mixture over the dry ingredients and mix with a rubber spatula until evenly moistened.

3. Fill a small bowl with cold water and

place ⅓ cup sugar in an 8- or 9-inch cake pan. Dip your hands into the water and roll about 2 tablespoons of cookie dough into a rough ball. Drop the ball into the cake pan with the sugar and toss to coat. Place the formed, sugar-coated cookie on the prepared pan, leaving 1½ inches between balls. If your hands become too sticky, dip them into the water and shake away the excess.

4. Bake until the cookies are light golden brown, 18 to 20 minutes, rotating the baking sheet front to back halfway through the baking time. Cool the cookies on the baking sheet until slightly set, about 2 minutes. Using a metal spatula, transfer the cookies to a wire cooling rack. Cool for 15 minutes.

➤ VARIATION
Cranberry Cornmeal Cookies with Orange Essence

The orange zest in the sugar coating causes the sugar to become sticky and take on a light orange hue, giving the baked cookies a frosty look. These cookies will have a smooth top rather than a bumpy, rustic top like the basic recipe.

Follow the recipe for Cranberry Cornmeal

MEASURING BROWN SUGAR

For maximum accuracy, it's best to pack brown sugar into measuring cups. Use the next smaller cup to pack it down. For instance, if you need ½ cup packed brown sugar, use the bottom of the ⅓-cup measure to pack it down.

Cookies, omitting the orange zest from the dough. In the workbowl of a food processor, process ⅓ cup sugar and 1 teaspoon grated orange zest until pale orange, about 10 seconds; transfer the sugar to an 8- or 9-inch cake pan and set aside. After forming the cookie dough balls, drop them into the cake pan with the orange sugar and toss to coat. Place the balls on the prepared pan and bake as instructed.

BROWN SUGAR SHORTBREAD

TAKE SHORTBREAD, A SCOTTISH COOKIE, and give it a dose of Americana—namely pecans and brown sugar—and it is transformed into a nutty, buttery cookie with a hint of caramel flavor. The texture should be tender but crisp and sandy, with a slow melt-in-your-mouth character.

The recipes we researched for brown sugar shortbread ran the gamut. We made cookies similar to simple sugar cookies with pecans that were dropped onto a baking sheet; we baked basic roll-and-cut cookies made with cake flour; we sampled cookies made with vegetable oil and a combination of ground and chopped nuts; and we sliced cookies from a refrigerated cookie log. From these tests, we made a few quick conclusions. Cake flour was unnecessary; a tender cookie can be made with unbleached all-purpose flour, our kitchen standard. Oil does make for a sandy texture, but it falls short on flavor. We also learned that a dropped cookie doesn't have the neat, clean edges that shortbread should have. However, a rolled and refrigerated cookie takes too long to harden in the refrigerator (about 2 hours) before it is cold enough to be sliced into neat, round coins. We decided to throw out all of these ideas and develop a cookie dough that could be pressed without chilling into a jelly roll pan, baked, sliced, and served. This method would also yield cookies with the traditional square shortbread shape.

First, we needed to determine the amount and types of sugar to use. In a working recipe we assembled, we tried granulated sugar, light brown sugar, dark brown sugar, confectioners' sugar, and various combinations of each. Confectioners' sugar, with its small amount of cornstarch, had a noticeably tenderizing effect on the cookies. Too much, however, and the cookies turned pasty and gummy; just ¼ cup was perfect. Granulated sugar had little to offer in the way of flavor; dark brown sugar offered too much flavor. Light brown sugar, tinged with molasses, gave the cookies a gentle caramel flavor that complemented—not overwhelmed—the nuttiness of the pecans and richness of the butter.

To assemble the batter, we combined the nuts (tasters liked pecans best, but other nuts are good, too), flour, sugars, and salt in the workbowl of a food processor and then cut in the chilled butter until the mixture resembled coarse meal. We turned the mixture into the pan and used a metal measuring cup to smash

and push the dough into place. We lightly scored the cookies into squares and baked them for just shy of 20 minutes. When they came out of the oven, we cut through the perforations in the dough and then transferred the cookies to a wire cooling rack to finish cooling completely. We like confectioners' sugar dusted over the top.

❧

Brown Sugar Shortbread

MAKES 32 COOKIES

TIME: 1 HOUR
(INCLUDES 40 MINUTES BAKING
AND COOLING TIME)

You can substitute hazelnuts, peanuts, pine nuts, or walnuts for the pecans.

⅔	cup finely chopped pecans
1¾	cups (8¾ ounces) unbleached all-purpose flour
1	cup packed (7 ounces) light brown sugar
¼	cup (1 ounce) confectioners' sugar, plus more for dusting the cookies
½	teaspoon salt
8	tablespoons (1 stick) unsalted butter, chilled, cut into ½-inch pieces

MAKING SHORTBREAD COOKIES

1. Turn the dough into a greased 10 by 15-inch jelly roll pan and use the back of a sturdy 1-cup measuring cup to force the dough into the corners of the pan. Keep pressing the dough with the measuring cup until it is compact and level.

2. Use the back of a knife to score the dough, but do not cut all the way through it. Make 4 horizontal and 8 vertical markings to yield 32 squares. The shortbread is now ready to be baked.

1. Adjust an oven rack to the middle position and heat the oven to 350 degrees. Spray a 10 by 15-inch jelly roll pan with nonstick cooking spray.

2. Process the nuts, flour, brown sugar, confectioners' sugar, and salt in a food processor fitted with a steel blade until uniform, about 3 seconds. Sprinkle the butter evenly over the flour mixture and pulse until the mixture resembles a coarse cornmeal, about eighteen 1-second pulses. Dump the mixture into the prepared jelly roll pan. Following the illustrations on page 393, use a measuring cup to pack the dough into the pan and smooth it to create an even surface. Use the back of a knife to mark the dough into 32 squares.

3. Bake until deep nutty brown and fragrant, 15 to 18 minutes, rotating the pan front to back halfway through the baking time. Following the marks, use a knife to completely cut through the shortbread and make individual cookies. Cool the cookies in the pan for 10 minutes. Using the tip of a knife, pop the shortbread pieces out of the pan (a metal spatula can be used once the first couple of cookies are out) and transfer them to a wire cooling rack. Cool an additional 20 minutes. Sprinkle with confectioners' sugar and serve.

MICROWAVE BROWNIES

WE DON'T OFTEN USE MICROWAVES in the test kitchen. They come in handy for melting butter or chocolate and for heating cream, but for baking? The thought never really occurred to us—that is, until we thought about making super-fast brownies.

Thick and fudgy, brownies don't require the forced heat of an oven to rise; they stay pleasantly squat and flat. Unlike many bars and cookies, brownies don't really brown. In an oven, all you're basically doing is raising the temperature of the batter high enough to set the eggs and thereby create a solid chocolate mass. So why not try a microwave?

Using a microwave would require different ingredients than those in our ultimate brownie recipe, developed several years ago in the test kitchen. First, we replaced the chopped chocolate in the recipe with chocolate chips for the sake of convenience. We also decided to increase the cocoa powder from 3 tablespoons to 1 cup to pump up the chocolate flavor. We decreased the amount of flour in our conventional recipe, partly because we had to compensate for the increase in dry cocoa powder and partly because we didn't want the brownies to get too hard.

When it came time to microwave the brownies, we weren't sure how we would know the brownies were fully baked. The spring test—gently pressing the center to see if it bounces back—wouldn't work on these brownies until they were cooled because the tops were just too hot to depress without crumbs sticking to your fingers. The pulling-from-the-sides-of-the-pan cue didn't work either, as these brownies pretty much stay in place. We discovered that one traditional key still worked; a skewer or toothpick (or even a thin knife) should come out of the center of the pan without any raw batter clinging to it (it's OK if a cake crumb or two sticks to it, though). We also learned to tilt the pan; if the brownies slouch to the lower end, they need another minute in the microwave. If the brownies stay in place when tilted, they're ready to be cooled and eaten.

These brownies are moist and chocolatey. We bet no one will guess it took you just 15 minutes to make and bake your brownies—and that you never even turned on your oven.

Microwave Brownies

MAKES 9 LARGE BROWNIES

TIME: 25 MINUTES (INCLUDES 10 MINUTES COOLING TIME)

For mocha brownies, add 1 tablespoon instant espresso powder to the batter. For nut brownies, add ½ cup toasted, chopped walnuts to the batter along with the other dry ingredients. The brownies must be eaten warm; they turn rock hard after they cool completely.

3	large eggs
1½	cups (10½ ounces) sugar
8	tablespoons (1 stick) unsalted butter, melted
¾	cup (3¾ ounces) unbleached all-purpose flour
1	cup (4 ounces) cocoa powder
⅛	teaspoon salt
1	teaspoon vanilla extract
⅓	cup semisweet chocolate morsels

1. Spray an 8 by 8-inch microwave-safe baking dish with nonstick cooking spray.

2. Whisk together the eggs and sugar in a medium bowl. Slowly whisk in the butter. Stir in the flour, cocoa powder, and salt. Stir in the vanilla and chocolate morsels. With a spatula, scrape the batter into the prepared pan.

3. Microwave on high until a toothpick or skewer inserted into the center comes out clean, 5 to 7 minutes. You can tell the brownies need more time in the microwave if, when the pan is tilted, the brownies slouch to the lower side. Cool the brownies for 10 minutes, cut into squares, and serve warm.

➤ VARIATION

Frosted Microwave Brownies

Follow the recipe for Microwave Brownies, microwaving them for only 4 minutes. Remove the pan from the microwave and evenly sprinkle ½ cup semisweet chocolate morsels over the top of the brownies. Return the pan to the microwave and cook for an additional 1 to 3 minutes (or until a toothpick or skewer inserted into the center comes out clean). Remove the pan from the microwave and, using the back of a spoon, spread the softened chocolate morsels (they will not melt in the microwave) over the top of the brownies. Cool and cut into squares as directed.

TOFFEE BARS

TOFFEE BARS CAN BE MADE IN MANY ways. Some recipes call for a condensed milk topping that includes milk, eggs, and toffee. Others call for a topping of corn syrup, egg, sugar, and toffee, perhaps with almonds tossed in. Still others simply call for sprinkling chocolate chips over a hot crust, spreading them with the back of a spoon, and then sprinkling toffee chips over the warm chocolate. We found none of these methods produced quick, easy, and delicious toffee bars.

The problem with the first two methods is that they take too long. As the crust cooks, you make the filling and then bake the filling on top of the crust. By the time the bars come out of the oven and cool, you are far over the 1-hour time limit. The third method (with the chocolate chips) turned out decent toffee bars—but, even after 20 minutes of cooling in the freezer, the top chocolate layer was still wet.

However, as we tried variations of this third method out (all to no avail), we ended up developing quite a satisfying crust. We began by beating together softened butter with brown sugar, an egg, flour, and salt. We packed the somewhat crumbly mixture into a square baking pan and baked it at 375 degrees for just shy of 30 minutes. We concluded the egg was unnecessary; it produced a cakey crust. In addition, we found that a crust made entirely of brown sugar was too pliable.

Next, we tested a combination of half brown sugar and half granulated sugar, but the granulated sugar made the crust brittle and hard. Our last idea was to replace granulated sugar with confectioners' sugar. This worked beautifully because the cornstarch in the confectioners' sugar tenderized the crust while the sugar contributed sweetness.

With the crust patted into place, we still were grasping for ideas for the toffee topping. We liked the ease of sprinkling chocolate chips and chopped toffee over the cooked crust; we just wanted to improve on the

technique so the bar cookie wasn't so difficult to eat. Then we had the idea to create a topping made from the crust itself.

After patting about three quarters of the dry crust mixture into place, we sprinkled the toffee and chocolate chips over it; then we sprinkled the remaining dry crust mixture over the top. The bars turned golden brown in the oven, and when we tried one, we were really pleased. The sprinkling of dry ingredients over the top made the bar come together. It tasted great, looked pretty, and was easy to eat.

PARCHMENT SLING FOR BAR COOKIES

Lining baking pans with parchment (or foil greased with cooking spray) makes it easy to remove brownies and bars in a single piece. The baked dough can then be placed on a cutting board and neatly cut into squares.

1. Place 2 parchment sheets (each 8 inches wide and about 16 inches long) perpendicular to each other in the pan. Press the crust into the pan, making sure to push it into the corners.

2. After the bars are baked, use the overhanging parchment to remove the entire unit easily from the pan.

Toffee Bars

MAKES 9 LARGE BARS

TIME: I HOUR
(INCLUDES 45 MINUTES BAKING
AND CHILLING TIME)

Our preference is to use hard buttercrunch toffee. You can buy plain buttercrunch toffee, or you can use Skor candy bars, which are buttercrunch toffee covered with chocolate. To soften the butter quickly, cut it into 2-tablespoon chunks and microwave at 50 percent power for 10 seconds. Check the butter (it should yield to pressure but should not be melted or warm) and microwave for another 10 seconds, if necessary.

10	tablespoons unsalted butter, softened
1/3	cup packed (2 1/3 ounces) dark brown sugar
1/3	cup (1 1/3 ounces) confectioners' sugar
1 1/2	cups (7 1/2 ounces) unbleached all-purpose flour
1/2	teaspoon salt
6	ounces hard toffee or 4 Skor candy bars, chopped fine (about 2/3 cup)
1/4	cup semisweet chocolate morsels

1. Adjust an oven rack to the lower position and heat the oven to 375 degrees. Spray an 8

by 8-inch baking pan with nonstick cooking spray. Line the pan with 2 sheets of parchment paper (see illustration 1 on page 396).

2. In a standing mixer fitted with a paddle attachment, beat the butter, brown sugar, and confectioners' sugar at medium speed until fluffy, about 3 minutes, scraping down the sides of the bowl with a rubber spatula as needed. Add the flour and salt and beat at low speed until the mixture becomes sandy, with large pea-size bits, about 30 seconds.

3. Sprinkle 2¼ cups of the crumb mixture into the lined pan and press firmly with your fingers into an even layer that covers the entire pan bottom. Sprinkle the toffee and chocolate morsels over the crust and then sprinkle them with the remaining crumb mixture.

4. Bake until golden brown, 25 to 30 minutes. Use the parchment to gently lift the entire bar out of the pan (see illustration 2 on page 396). Place the toffee bar on a flat surface (such as a baking sheet or large platter) and freeze until cooled and firm, about 20 minutes. Transfer the bar to a cutting board, cut into 9 squares, and serve.

S'MORES BARS

THERE'S NO REASON TO SAVE THE joyful experience of eating a s'more for campfires. At least, not when making s'mores bars —with a graham cracker crust, chocolate filling, and marshmallow topping—is so easy.

Our first challenge was to determine the best ratio of graham crackers to flour and the amount, as well as the type, of sugar. We decided, after several taste tests, that equal parts graham cracker crumbs and flour yielded a crust that didn't taste enough like graham crackers. But we also didn't want to use too many graham cracker crumbs; we wanted the crust to retain a texture like shortbread. We

decided to increase the amount of graham cracker crumbs by just a couple of tablespoons. That was enough; now we had delicious graham cracker shortbread.

As for the sugar in the crust, brown sugar proved too rich for our tasters' palates, while granulated sugar produced a crust that was brittle and gritty. The best, most tender texture came from confectioners' sugar.

We used a standing mixer to cream softened butter and sugar and then added the dry ingredients. Then we tried using a food processor to cut cold butter into the dry ingredients as if making a pie dough. We decided that because of the proportion of flour to butter and the absence of liquid, the second method was better suited for this crust. Cutting the butter into the flour yielded a crumbly mixture that was easily pressed into the pan. Twenty minutes at 375 degrees transformed the raw crust into a golden brown base for the s'mores.

We tried many methods of marrying the chocolate and marshmallows to the graham cracker crust. First, we melted chocolate, poured it over the crust, and broiled marshmallows on top of the chocolate. This produced bars with an extremely hard chocolate layer. We tried making a ganache (from cream, chocolate, and butter) and folding the marshmallows into the ganache. This didn't work because the marshmallows formed a spongy layer that prevented the chocolate from adhering to the crust. The ganache filling was also too soft; we wanted something denser.

Next, we tried making a thicker ganache by decreasing the amount of cream and eliminating the butter. We poured it straight onto the crust and then gently pressed the marshmallows into the chocolate. We tried chilling the bars and serving them, but tasters agreed in one voice that s'mores bars aren't s'mores bars if the marshmallows are not toasted. The next time, after we poured the ganache on the crust, we put the bars under the broiler for 2 minutes. Toasty and browned, the bars were ready to be chilled.

Although the bars can be chilled in the refrigerator, we thought this approach would take too long—so we popped them into the freezer instead. Less than 30 minutes later, the chocolate had set and the crust had completely cooled. The s'mores bars were ready to be sliced and devoured.

S'mores Bars

MAKES 9 LARGE BARS

TIME: I HOUR (INCLUDES 45 MINUTES BAKING AND CHILLING TIME)

For easy removal, line the baking pan with two pieces of foil. The technique is similar to that used for the toffee bars (see the illustrations on page 396.) However, because these bars go under the broiler, you must use foil rather than parchment. Be sure to grease the foil with cooking spray to ensure easy removal.

CRUST

¾	cup (2¾ ounces) graham cracker crumbs (5 whole crackers, broken into rough pieces and processed in a food processor until uniformly fine)
⅔	cup (3⅓ ounces) unbleached all-purpose flour
⅓	cup (1⅓ ounces) confectioners' sugar
½	teaspoon salt
7	tablespoons unsalted butter, cold, cut into 1-inch pieces

FILLING

12	ounces semisweet chocolate morsels
⅓	cup heavy cream
2	cups miniature marshmallows

1. FOR THE CRUST: Adjust an oven rack to the middle position and heat the oven to 375 degrees. Spray an 8 by 8-inch baking pan with nonstick cooking spray. Fold two 16-inch pieces of foil lengthwise to measure 8 inches wide. Fit one sheet in the bottom of the greased pan, pushing it into the corners and up the sides of the pan (the overhang will help in removal of the baked bars). Perpendicular to the first sheet, fit the second sheet in the pan in the same manner. Spray the foil with nonstick cooking spray.

2. Pulse the graham cracker crumbs, flour, confectioners' sugar, and salt in a food processor workbowl fitted with a steel blade to combine. Add the butter and process to blend, 8 to 10 seconds, then pulse until the mixture is pale yellow and resembles coarse meal, about three 1-second pulses. Sprinkle the mixture into the lined pan and press firmly with your fingers into an even layer that covers the entire pan bottom. Bake the crust until golden brown, 18 to 20 minutes. Use the foil handles to gently lift the crust from the pan. Cool the crust on a wire rack for 10 minutes, then return it to the cooled baking pan with the foil handles in place.

3. FOR THE FILLING: While the crust is cooling, place the chocolate in a medium bowl. Bring the cream to a boil and pour it over the chocolate. Cover the bowl with plastic wrap and allow the chocolate to soften for 3 minutes. Whisk the chocolate until smooth. Pour the chocolate mixture over the cooled crust, using an offset spatula to spread it evenly.

4. Adjust an oven rack to the highest position and heat the broiler. Assemble the marshmallows in an even layer over the top of the chocolate, gently pressing them into place. Broil until lightly browned, 1 to 2 minutes. Chill in the freezer until firm, about 25 minutes. Pull the overhanging foil to remove the entire bar from the pan. Place the bar on a cutting board, cut it into 9 squares, and serve.

15

FRUIT DESSERTS

A BOWL OF PERFECTLY RIPE FRUIT IS often the best (and simplest) ending to a meal. However, on many occasions you want something more special than plain fruit. The recipes in this chapter demonstrate simple strategies for embellishing fruit quickly. Some of the recipes are extremely fast and require little or no cooking. Other recipes, including those for apple turnovers, blueberry cobbler, and *tarte Tatin,* show how to prepare favorite baked fruit desserts in far less time (and with far fewer ingredients) than conventional recipes require.

MANGOES WITH LIME AND GINGER

FRESH MANGOES FIND THEIR WAY into everything from smoothies to dessert sauces. We wanted to create a dessert where the mango was the star and not the sidekick. Because a fresh, ripe mango is so wonderful on its own, our goal was to embellish it without smothering its natural flavor.

Our first instinct was to just squeeze a little lime juice over mango spears, thinking that the acidity and tartness of the citrus would

PREPARING A MANGO

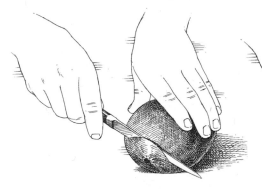

1. Remove a thin slice from one end of the mango so it sits flat on a work surface.

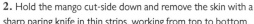

2. Hold the mango cut-side down and remove the skin with a sharp paring knife in thin strips, working from top to bottom.

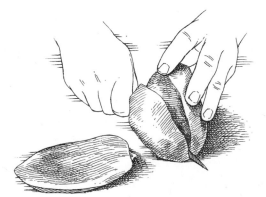

3. Cut down along the side of the flat pit to remove the flesh from one side of the mango. Do the same on the other side of the pit.

4. Trim around the pit to remove any remaining flesh. The mango flesh can now be chopped or sliced as desired.

nicely counter the sticky-sweet nature of the mango. Although the lime juice was nice, it was too tart. We toyed with the notion of adding sugar to the lime juice but discarded the idea for the time being; we didn't want the saccharine character of granulated sugar to obstruct the natural sugars in the mango.

Then we came up with an intriguing idea—pairing the mango and lime juice with minced crystallized ginger. Because crystallized ginger is coated with sugar, it would indirectly provide the mango with more sweetness; the ginger itself would supply a fiery, spicy kick. We minced the ginger and then sprinkled it over the lime juice–drizzled mango. The flavors were good but too intense. We decided to dissolve a couple of tablespoons of sugar in the lime juice to temper the bite of the ginger and lime. This sample was much better. The sugar-enhanced ginger was sweet and crunchy, and when we combined it with the tart lime and sweet mango, the trio was complete.

Fresh Mangoes with Lime and Sugared Ginger

SERVES 4 TO 6
TIME: 10 MINUTES

If you like, garnish the mangoes with thin slivers of lime zest.

2	tablespoons juice from 2 limes
2	tablespoons sugar
	Pinch salt
2	large ripe mangoes
1	ounce (about 10 pieces) crystallized ginger, minced

1. Stir the lime juice, sugar, and salt together in a small bowl until the sugar dissolves.

2. Following the illustrations on page 400, peel and cut the mangoes into ½-inch-wide strips (you should get about 15 strips per mango). Divide the mango strips among individual plates or small bowls.

3. Drizzle a little lime juice mixture over each serving of mango and then sprinkle with the ginger. Serve immediately.

➤ VARIATIONS

Fresh Papaya with Lime and Sugared Ginger

Follow the recipe for Fresh Mangoes with Lime and Sugared Ginger, replacing the mangoes with 1 ripe papaya, halved, seeded, and cut crosswise into 1½-inch-wide crescents.

Fresh Pineapple with Lime and Sugared Ginger

Follow the recipe for Fresh Mangoes with Lime and Sugared Ginger, replacing the mangoes with 1 ripe pineapple, quartered, peeled, cored, and cut into long spears (see the illustrations on page 404).

FIGS WITH BLUE CHEESE

FEW FRUITS CAN RIVAL A RIPE FIG. From its dewy, honeylike flavor to the slight snap of its seeds between your teeth, a fig is as close to perfection as a fruit can be—which is why it needs almost no doctoring to become a postdinner indulgence. Our goal was to further concentrate the figs' sweetness and then counter it with a salty, sharp, and tangy blue cheese such as Italian Gorgonzola or even a smoother blue like English Stilton.

First, we tried sautéing the figs. We reasoned this would be a fast method—just slice the figs in half, toss them in sugar, and sear them, face down, in melted butter for a couple of minutes. But this didn't work, for several reasons. First, the delicate sweetness of the fig was overcome by the fattiness of the butter. Sautéing in other fats—we tried vegetable and walnut oils—was no better; the oils' greasy mouthfeel suffocated the figs. In addition, the saccharine qualities of the granulated sugar were too pronounced, overcoming the fig's natural sweetness. A method that seemed to work better was to dip the exposed side of the halved fig in sugar. Just enough sugar clings to the fig to caramelize it without contributing an overpowering sweetness.

We dropped the sautéing method and opted to try broiling the figs. We placed the sugared halves face-up on a baking sheet and broiled them for just a couple of minutes. These figs were far superior to those made in the other trials. They were lush and juicy and sweet, with a thin crackling sheet of sugar that iced the surface.

We crumbled room-temperature Stilton over the just-broiled figs and were pleased with the sharp juxtaposition of flavors. Although crumbled blue cheese over the broiled fig was fantastic, we were curious to see what would happen if we broiled the cheese-topped fig. Just a half minute beneath the flame was all the little pebbles of cheese needed to weep ever so slightly into the center of the figs, creating a more refined and mellow flavor.

Brûléed Figs with Blue Cheese

SERVES 4 TO 6

TIME: 15 MINUTES

For a sharp contrast, top each fig with a morsel of blue cheese just before serving. For a smoother flavor, broil the cheese on top of the figs as directed in the recipe. If you like, you can place one toasted walnut half on top of each cheese-capped fig. Use the best-quality blue cheese; see page 32 for details

on our testing. We recommend serving the figs alongside a high-quality port and toasted walnuts.

¼ cup (1¾ ounces) sugar

1 pound (about 16) medium-ripe black figs, cut in half lengthwise

4 ounces high-quality blue cheese, crumbled into small nuggets (about 1 cup)

1. Adjust an oven rack to the highest position and preheat the broiler.

2. Place the sugar in a shallow bowl and dip the exposed surface of each fig into the sugar. Place the figs, sugar-side up, on a rimmed baking sheet.

3. Broil the figs until their surfaces begin to caramelize and the sugar begins to bubble around the edges, 3 to 5 minutes. (Make sure to watch the figs closely, as broilers vary.) Place a small nugget of cheese on each fig and broil for an additional 30 seconds. Remove the baking sheet from the broiler and transfer the figs to a platter. Serve immediately.

CARAMELIZED BANANAS

A BANANA IS A FAIRLY ORDINARY fruit—until you eat one that's been caramelized. It's warm and sweet, the color of honey. Paired with a buttery rum sauce, it is pure bliss. Because a medium-ripe banana is already tender and sweet, we knew we wouldn't have to work hard to coax out its natural sweetness even further.

First, we decided to cut the banana into four manageable pieces. We cut it in half crosswise and then cut each half again lengthwise. Under the broiler the four halves went. Out came shriveled and dried bananas that had hardly colored—clearly, our bananas needed a bit of help from fat and sugar. We brushed the cut side of each banana with melted butter and then dipped one sample cut-side down in granulated sugar and the other in dark brown sugar. After broiling, we decided that the granulated sugar version had a much cleaner flavor than the brown sugar. However, by the time the sugar turned golden, our banana had turned to mush. The heat of the broiler was just too intense for the delicate banana flesh.

We traded in our baking sheet for a nonstick skillet and tried again. This method worked perfectly. The bananas were golden on the curved side and caramelized on the sugared side. We removed the bananas from the pan and added dark brown sugar, rum, and cream. In just a couple of minutes, we had made a creamy rum sauce. We drizzled some over the browned bananas and took a bite; an ordinary banana never tasted so good.

Caramelized Bananas with Buttered–Rum Sauce

SERVES 4 TO 6

TIME: 10 MINUTES

Options for garnishing the caramelized bananas include toasted coconut, toasted and chopped peanuts, and chocolate shavings. Stirring ¼ teaspoon to ½ teaspoon grated fresh ginger into the sauce gives it a nice, gingery kick. The vanilla ice cream is not a must, but it does make the warm bananas more enticing.

4	bananas, peeled, cut in half widthwise and then lengthwise
2	tablespoons unsalted butter, melted
¼	cup (1¾ ounces) granulated sugar
¼	cup packed (1¾ ounces) dark brown sugar
1	tablespoon dark rum
¼	cup heavy cream
	Vanilla ice cream (optional)

1. Brush both sides of the banana pieces with the melted butter. Place the granulated sugar in a shallow bowl. Dip the cut side of the bananas into the sugar. Heat a 12-inch nonstick skillet over medium-high heat. Lay the bananas, sugar-side up, in the hot pan. Cook until lightly golden, about 1 minute. Using tongs, turn the bananas and cook until deep golden brown, 1 to 2 minutes. Transfer the bananas to a plate and set them aside.

2. Reduce the heat to medium and add the brown sugar and rum to the empty skillet. Cook until the sugar melts slightly, 15 to 20 seconds. Whisk in the cream and simmer until the sauce thickens, about 1 minute. Divide the bananas and sauce among individual bowls and top with a small scoop of ice cream and garnishes, if desired. Serve immediately.

GLAZED PINEAPPLE

SOME FOODS, SUCH AS SPICY INDIAN dishes and Thai curries, just don't pair well with traditional desserts like apple pie and chocolate cake. In these cases, we choose to serve fruit for dessert. Fruit is light, quick, and simple, and it counters heavily spiced foods with aplomb. The sweet and acidic qualities of pineapple seem to serve this purpose especially well. We decided, however, that we wanted to dress up plain pineapple a bit and make them more grand than just sliced fruit.

We first had to decide how to cut the pineapple. We found it easiest to lop off the leafy and base ends and then quarter the pineapple lengthwise, slice the fruit away from its rough jacket, and remove its four core pieces. We then sliced each quarter into long spears. This presentation was definitely more elegant than pineapple chunks or rounds.

We brushed each spear with melted butter and then pressed it into a bed of dark brown sugar to coat its surface. We broiled the pineapples for 8 minutes, turning them over halfway through. Although this sample was okay, it wasn't special. We turned to a pan for some help.

We melted the butter in a heavy-bottomed nonstick skillet, this time sprinkling the brown sugar over the butter rather than pressing it into the pineapple. We also added a couple of

PREPARING A PINEAPPLE

1. Start by trimming the ends of the pineapple so it sits flat on a work surface. Cut the pineapple through the ends into four quarters.

2. Lay each quarter, cut-side up, on a work surface and slide a knife between the skin and flesh to remove the skin.

3. Stand each peeled quarter on end and slice off the portion of the tough, light-colored core attached to the inside of the piece. The peeled and cored pineapple can now be sliced or diced as desired.

tablespoons of kirsch (cherry brandy) to provide a bit of a kick. After a few minutes of cooking on each side, our pineapple spears were golden and gorgeous. They still tasted sweet, but the sweetness wasn't flat; the brown sugar and kirsch had added layers of complexity. With a sprinkle of toasted coconut, this dessert graduated from the ranks of plain sliced fruit.

Brown Sugar and Kirsch–Glazed Pineapple with Coconut

SERVES 6 TO 8

TIME: 20 MINUTES

If you prefer, you may use dark rum in place of the kirsch. See the illustrations at left for tips on preparing the pineapple. To toast the coconut, place it on a baking sheet and bake at 350 degrees, stirring once or twice, until golden, 6 to 8 minutes.

4	tablespoons unsalted butter
¼	cup kirsch (cherry brandy)
½	cup packed (3½ ounces) dark brown sugar
I	ripe pineapple, quartered, peeled, cored, and cut lengthwise into ¾-inch-thick spears
½	cup sweetened flaked coconut, toasted

Melt the butter in a 12-inch heavy-bottomed nonstick skillet over medium-high heat. Add the kirsch and sprinkle the brown sugar evenly over the butter and liqueur. Cook until slightly thickened, about 1 minute. Lay the pineapple spears in the pan, reduce the heat to medium-low, and cook until deep golden brown, 3 to 4 minutes. Turn the pineapple spears and cook until deep golden and slightly browned on a second side, 3 to 4 minutes longer. Transfer the pineapple to a serving platter. Return the pan with the glaze to medium-high heat and simmer until thickened, about 1 minute. Pour the glaze over the pineapple and sprinkle with the toasted coconut. Serve immediately.

➤ VARIATION

Caramel and Kirsch–Glazed Pineapple with Coconut

Follow the recipe for Brown Sugar and Kirsch–Glazed Pineapple with Coconut. After removing the pineapple from the pan and thickening the glaze, whisk in ⅓ cup heavy cream and cook until the caramel sauce thickens, about 1 minute. You can either spoon the caramel over the pineapple and then sprinkle the spears with toasted coconut, or, for an especially attractive presentation, dip the spears into the caramel and then roll each one in the coconut.

INGREDIENTS: Pineapple

In the test kitchen, we wanted to know if all supermarket pineapples were equal. A survey of local supermarkets produced pineapple of two origins: Hawaii and Costa Rica (easily identifiable by their attached tags). The chosen pineapples (four from each growing region) were similar in ripeness. All yielded slightly when touched, were golden in color (green pineapples are underripe), and carried the familiar heady pineapple aroma. We tasted the fruit both straight up and in a smoothie recipe.

The fruit from Hawaii was astoundingly astringent. Tasters could only unpucker their mouths long enough to exclaim "bitter" and "sour." Smoothies made with this fruit were not terribly sour, but they were flavorless. The Costa Rican pineapples (sometimes labeled "extra-sweet" or "gold") triumphed in the tasting. Both straight up and in smoothies, this fruit was packed with an ultrasweet, honeylike flavor that one taster called "pumped-up pineapple." We're sure that bad Costa Rican pineapples are for sale as well as better Hawaiian fruit. But in our experience, it pays to check where that pineapple comes from—the source can make a big difference.

WHIPPED MASCARPONE CREAM WITH BERRIES

WHETHER WHIPPED INTO MASHED potatoes or made into a cheesecake, mascarpone cheese is known for its thick, velvety texture and rich flavor. We wondered, therefore, if mascarpone whipped with sugar could provide a creamy, more interesting alternative to plain whipped cream.

We started by whipping mascarpone and a couple of tablespoons of sugar in a standing mixer. Thick and pasty, this sample wasn't quite the concoction we had in mind. We added a couple of tablespoons of heavy cream to thin out the mascarpone and lemon zest to perk up the dense dairy flavor. This version curdled; it went straight into the trash.

We thought perhaps the lemon zest had curdled the mascarpone. We tried the recipe again, without the lemon zest, but the cheese and heavy cream mixture still curdled. Then we had the idea to whip the cream first and then blend it with the mascarpone. This worked much better; the mascarpone was lighter and airier—and, most important, didn't look like ricotta cheese after it was whipped. We then added the lemon zest to the whipped mascarpone cream, where it contributed a bright, fresh flavor we had missed.

We topped the whipped mascarpone cream with fresh fruit and tried it out. Plain fresh berries just weren't flavorful enough, so we tossed them with sugar and Marsala wine. We also decided to drizzle honey over the completed dessert. It was sweet and elegant, with a hint of sherrylike refinement.

Whipped Mascarpone Cream with Marsala and Berries

SERVES 6

TIME: 15 MINUTES

Super-ripe nectarines and peaches are also wonderful served alongside the whipped mascarpone cream. If you don't care for the sherrylike flavor of Marsala wine, you may use a white dessert wine, such as Muscat or Vin Santo, instead. The whipped mascarpone may be prepared up to 24 hours in advance.

1	cup heavy cream, chilled
½	cup (3½ ounces) plus 3 tablespoons sugar
8	ounces mascarpone cheese
1½	teaspoons grated zest from 1 lemon
3	cups mixed berries, such as blackberries, blueberries, raspberries, and strawberries (if using strawberries, hull and cut them into ¼-inch-thick slices)
2	tablespoons sweet Marsala wine
	Honey for drizzling

1. Place the cream and ½ cup sugar in a chilled bowl and beat at low speed until small bubbles form, about 30 seconds. Increase the speed to medium and continue beating until the beaters leave a trail, about 30 seconds. Increase the speed to high and continue beating until the cream forms stiff peaks, about 30 seconds. Transfer the whipped cream to a clean bowl. Place the mascarpone in the bowl used to whipped the cream (there's no need to clean the bowl) and beat it at medium speed until aerated and lightened, about 30 seconds. Add the reserved whipped cream and beat at medium speed until incorporated, about 30 seconds. Add the lemon zest and beat at medium speed for an additional 10 seconds. Transfer the whipped mascarpone cream to a medium bowl, cover with plastic wrap, and refrigerate until needed.

2. Stir together the berries, remaining 3 tablespoons sugar, and Marsala wine in a small bowl. Let the berries stand until the sugar dissolves, about 5 minutes.

3. To serve, spoon the whipped mascarpone cream into individual bowls and top with fruit. Drizzle honey to taste over each portion. Serve immediately.

CHOCOLATE FONDUE

DIPPING AN ENORMOUS RED STRAWBERRY into a pot of warm melted chocolate is guaranteed to make just about anybody happy. Making a chocolate fondue couldn't be simpler, but we found a few helpful tricks to improve the recipe.

We decided to make the fondue the same way we make chocolate ganache—by simply chopping the chocolate into fine bits, pouring steaming hot cream over it, letting the chocolate fade into the cream, and stirring the mixture before serving. We were positive that if we started with slightly more chocolate than cream, the result would be a thick, velvety chocolate sea into which we could dip our fruit.

Although the fondue was rich and thick, it looked dull and a little tightly wound, so we decided to add corn syrup. With the corn syrup, the fondue became satiny and retained a beautiful gloss. In less than 15 minutes, we had dessert in the fondue pot. Surrounded by strawberries, mandarin oranges, bananas, pineapples, marshmallows, and pound cake, we grabbed our fondue spears and dove into the chocolate pool.

Chocolate Fondue

SERVES 8 TO 10

TIME: 15 MINUTES

The chocolate fondue stays true to the flavor of the unmelted chocolate; therefore, we suggest using a chocolate you like straight from the package. Milk chocolate will produce a mild and sweet fondue, semisweet chocolate will bring a deeper and more bitter flavor to the fondue, and bittersweet chocolate will present a pronounced bitter and even slightly acidic flavor. If you'd like just a touch of bitterness in the fondue, you may combine milk and semisweet or bittersweet chocolates. We recommend about ¾ cup bread, cake, or fruit per person. The fruit may be prepared up to 4 hours and the bread and cake up to 1 hour ahead of time. You will need a real fondue pot (with heat source) to keep the chocolate mixture warm and fluid.

ACCOMPANIMENTS
(CHOOSE FROM THE FOLLOWING)

Angel food cake or pound cake, cut into 1-inch cubes

French bread or sourdough bread, cut into 1-inch cubes

4 **medium-ripe bananas, peeled and cut into 1-inch-thick rounds**

2 **medium mandarin oranges or tangelos, peeled and segmented**

1 **ripe pineapple, quartered, peeled, cored, and cut into 1-inch chunks (see the illustrations on page 404)**

1 **pint raspberries**

1 **quart strawberries, hulled (see the illustration on page 412)**

FONDUE

12 **ounces high-quality chocolate, chopped**

1⅓ **cups heavy cream**

Pinch salt

1 **tablespoon corn syrup**

1. Prepare the accompaniments and set them aside.

2. FOR THE FONDUE: Place the chocolate in a medium bowl. Bring the cream and salt to a boil in a small saucepan and pour the hot cream over the chocolate. Cover the bowl with plastic wrap and allow the chocolate to soften for 3 minutes. Whisk the chocolate until smooth, then add the corn syrup and whisk to incorporate. Transfer the mixture to a fondue pot, warm the pot over the Sterno flame for 5 minutes, and serve immediately with the desired accompaniments.

➤ VARIATIONS

Five-Spice Chocolate Fondue

Follow the recipe for Chocolate Fondue, adding 2 teaspoons ground cinnamon, 5 whole cloves, 1 teaspoon whole black peppercorns, 2 pieces star anise, and 1 (1-inch) piece peeled fresh ginger, cut in half, to the cream and salt mixture. Bring the cream, salt, and spices to a boil, cover, remove from the heat, and steep the spices in the cream for 10 minutes. Pour the cream through a fine-mesh strainer; discard the spices. Return the cream to the pan and bring it back to a simmer. Pour the infused cream over the chocolate and proceed as directed.

Chocolate–Orange Fondue

Follow the recipe for Chocolate Fondue, adding 1 tablespoon grated orange zest to the cream and salt mixture. Bring the cream, salt, and zest to a boil, cover, remove from the heat, and steep the zest in the cream for 10 minutes. Pour the cream through a fine-mesh strainer; discard the zest. Return the cream to the pan and bring it back to a simmer. Pour the infused cream over the chocolate. Add 2 tablespoons orange liqueur, such as Grand Marnier or Cointreau, with the corn syrup and proceed as directed.

Caramel-Rum Fondue

A CARAMEL-RUM FONDUE IS EASY TO put together, requires little preparation, and doesn't create a ton of dirty dishes. To develop a recipe, we first had to choose our fondue base—butterscotch sauce or caramel sauce. Although a butterscotch sauce made with brown sugar, butter, and cream is definitely quicker than a classic caramel sauce, the cloying, super-sweet flavor of a bowl of butterscotch wasn't something that we necessarily wanted to dip a chunk of fruit into. Instead, we decided to simplify a recipe for classic caramel sauce and transform it into fondue.

In the traditional recipe, sugar is added to a pan first, and then water is poured over the sugar. Next, a wet pastry brush is used to brush the sides of the pan free of sugar debris; even one sugar crystal that migrates into a cooking caramel from the side of a pot can cause a caramel sauce to seize and crystallize. We avoided this problem by adding the sugar to the water and not vice versa. This way, the sugar was wet by the time it touched the bottom of the pot, making stirring unnecessary. For extra insurance, we decided to cover the pot and set it over high heat to dissolve the sugar quickly and let the condensation from the lid flow down the sides of the pot to dissolve potentially pesky crystals.

Another problem with the standard caramel recipe is that you have to stir cream into the piping hot amber-colored sugar syrup. The hissing and bubbling that ensues can pose a risk to your safety as well as to the surface of your cooktop. Instead of adding the cream to the sugar syrup all at once, we added it in two batches. We added the first quarter of the cream to the sugar syrup and allowed its bubbling reaction to stir the cream for us. We added the rest of the cream and gave it a minute to mingle with the body of the sauce. Then, we whisked in the butter and rum—the ingredients that turn caramel sauce into fondue.

Straight from the pot, our caramel-rum fondue is too hot. Let it cool slightly and transfer it to a wide pot for dipping. Delicious and simple, caramel-rum fondue is great served with bananas, pineapple, strawberries— or even chunks of good French bread.

❧

Caramel-Rum Fondue
SERVES 8 TO 10
TIME: 45 MINUTES (INCLUDES 20 MINUTES OF COOLING TIME)

We recommend about ¾ cup bread, cake, or fruit (or a combination thereof) per person. The fruit may be prepared up to 4 hours and the bread and cake up to 1 hour ahead of time. A small dish of sweetened whipped cream is nice to serve alongside the fondue. You can also present small dishes with toppings like toasted flaked coconut, chocolate shavings, and toasted nuts into which people can roll their fondue-dipped items. A candy thermometer (or instant-read thermometer) can be used to monitor the progress of the caramel. However, if you cook the caramel in a light-colored pan (stainless steel is ideal), you can easily judge by color where the caramel is in the cooking process.

FONDUE

2	cups (14 ounces) sugar
1¼	cups heavy cream
	Pinch salt
2	tablespoons unsalted butter, cold
3	tablespoons dark rum

ACCOMPANIMENTS
(CHOOSE FROM THE FOLLOWING)
Angel food cake or pound cake, cut into
   1-inch cubes
French bread or sourdough bread, cut
   into 1-inch cubes

1 ripe pineapple, quartered, peeled, cored, and cut into 1-inch chunks (see the illustrations on page 404)
1 quart strawberries, hulled (see the illustration on page 412)
4 medium-ripe bananas, peeled and cut into 1-inch-thick rounds

1. FOR THE FONDUE: Pour ½ cup water into a 2-quart heavy-bottomed saucepan. Add the sugar to the center of the pot, avoiding getting granules of sugar on the sides. Cover the pot and bring to a boil over high heat. Uncover and continue to boil until the syrup is thick and straw-colored (300 degrees on an instant-read thermometer), about 15 minutes. Reduce the heat to medium and continue to cook until the sugar is deep amber (350 degrees), about 5 minutes longer. Meanwhile, when you reduce the heat under the sugar syrup, bring the cream and salt to a simmer in a small saucepan over high heat. (If the cream reaches a simmer before the syrup reaches 350 degrees, remove the cream from the heat.)

2. Remove the sugar syrup from the heat. Pour one quarter of the hot cream into the sugar syrup; let the bubbling subside. Add the remaining cream; let the bubbling subside. Whisk gently until smooth. Whisk in the butter and rum. Let cool for about 20 minutes; prepare the accompaniments. Transfer the warm fondue sauce to a bowl and serve immediately.

QUICK NECTARINE "TARTS"

THERE'S NOTHING QUICK ABOUT making a fruit tart. The dough must be made, chilled, rolled, and baked, which takes time. Then you have to prepare the tart filling and bake again. We wanted to create a quick version that can be prepared with the simplest ingredients: fresh fruit and sourdough bread. This kind of dessert has its roots in rustic Italian cooking. Although unconventional, these individual "tarts" still comprise a crust and a filling.

We decided to use nectarines for our testing because they bake more quickly than apples and pears and because they hold their shape well after being baked. First, we tried slicing the nectarines, tossing them with sugar, and then placing them on a slice of sourdough bread and roasting the two in the oven for about 25 minutes. The nectarines didn't fare too well in this trial—they shriveled and became a bit sour, losing their fresh juiciness; in addition, the bread tasted like a piece of toast rather than the base of a tart.

Next, we tried brushing the bread with melted butter before adding the nectarines, which we tossed in robust-flavored brown sugar rather than white. In addition, because we didn't really care for the effect roasting had on the nectarines, we decided to broil the tart instead. This version was much more promising—the nectarines retained their honeylike sweetness, which was accentuated by the brown sugar. Now it was time to perfect the bread.

For our next test, we decided to toast the bread first, brush it with melted butter, add a shower of sugar, and then top it with the nectarines. We were pleased with these results. The bread crust retained some crunch while soaking up sweetness from the sugar and the nectarine juices. The problem now was that after toasting and broiling, the bread crusts were a little singed. We lopped off the crusts and tried the tart one more time. Our final touch was a sprinkle of cinnamon sugar over the nectarines. Toasty and warm, sweet and spicy, juicy and crunchy, our nectarine "tart" proved a great alternative to the fancy French version.

Nectarine and Sourdough Bread "Tarts"

SERVES 8

TIME: 15 MINUTES

These "tarts" are similar to bruschetta, only instead of olive oil, garlic, and tomatoes, the bread is crusted with butter and sugar and then topped with fruit. You can also use 4 ripe peaches, 6 plums, or 1 pint fresh raspberries to make these tarts. Seedless red grapes are an unusual yet surprisingly delicious topping as well—just slice in half and place them, flat-side down, on the bread. If you like, dress up these desserts with a dollop of whipped cream or small scoop of vanilla ice cream.

2	tablespoons plus 4 teaspoons granulated sugar
¼	teaspoon ground cinnamon
4	ripe nectarines, halved and pitted, each half cut into 4 wedges
2	tablespoons dark brown sugar
4	thick slices sourdough bread, each about 8 inches long
3	tablespoons unsalted butter, melted

1. Adjust an oven rack to the upper-middle position and preheat the broiler.

2. Combine 2 tablespoons granulated sugar and the cinnamon in a small bowl; set aside. Toss the sliced nectarines with the brown sugar in another bowl.

3. Trim the crusts from the bread and cut each slice in half crosswise. Place the bread on a foil-lined baking sheet and toast under the broiler until golden, about 1 minute per side.

4. Brush one side of each slice of bread with about 1 teaspoon melted butter. Sprinkle the buttered side of the bread slices with the remaining 4 teaspoons granulated sugar. Arrange 4 nectarine slices on the buttered and sugared side of each slice of bread. Sprinkle the cinnamon sugar over the nectarines and broil until it has mostly dissolved and the edges of the bread are golden brown, about 2 minutes. (Make sure to watch the tarts closely, as broilers vary.) Serve immediately.

FRUIT NAPOLEONS

UNLESS YOU'RE WELL VERSED IN THE world of phyllo dough, it can be exasperating to work with. Although you don't have to make it from scratch, phyllo still threatens to dry out and tear if not handled properly. Because phyllo is sometimes used to make the pastry layers in a Napoleon, we wanted to find a substitute. Frozen commercial puff pastry was also a possibility, but we wondered if store-bought wonton wrappers could be used to make an even quicker (if somewhat unconventional) version of a fruit Napoleon.

We began by toasting our square wrappers on a sheet pan in the oven for just a couple of minutes until they were golden. Then we layered them with thinly sliced raw plums (we chose plums because they require so little preparation) and a tablespoon of whipped cream. While the result looked impressive, flavor and texture left a lot to be desired. The baked squares were hard and tough, and the plums weren't sweet enough on their own.

For our next test, we tried macerating the plums in sugar and ginger and brushing butter and a sprinkle of sugar on the wonton wrappers before baking. This produced more promising results—the plums had a lovely ginger flavor, and the Napoleon layers were slightly more tender. We highly approved of the sweetness and richness the butter-sugar duo brought forth. But still, the layers were a little too tough.

Instead of brushing the raw wrappers with butter before baking, we decided to reverse the order and brush butter on them afterward.

The butter sizzled into the hot golden squares and the sugar half dissolved, forming a crispy sheet across the top of the wrapper. We shingled plums across the surface, drizzled a little of the macerating liquid over the fruit, and added a sizable dollop of whipped cream. This towering triumph was created in 20 minutes.

Plum and Ginger Napoleons

SERVES 4

TIME: 25 MINUTES

If you like, sprinkle sliced and toasted almonds or finely ground pistachios over the final addition of whipped cream or even between the layers. Look for wonton wrappers in the refrigerator case at the supermarket, often near the tofu. Because the fruit is not cooked, it must be ripe and juicy.

2	medium ripe plums, halved and pitted, each half cut into 8 thin wedges
¼	teaspoon grated fresh ginger
2	tablespoons plus 2 teaspoons sugar
8	wonton wrappers
2	tablespoons unsalted butter, melted
1½	cups Whipped Cream (page 431)

GRATING GINGER

Instead of cutting a small chunk of ginger from a larger piece and trying to grate it, peel a small section of the large piece of ginger and grate the peeled portion, using the rest of the ginger as a handle to keep your fingers safely away from the grater.

1. Adjust an oven rack to the middle position and preheat the oven to 425 degrees. Combine the plums with the ginger and 2 tablespoons sugar in a medium bowl and set the bowl aside. Place the wonton wrappers on a parchment paper–lined baking sheet and bake until golden brown, 2 to 4 minutes. Remove the baking sheet from the oven and immediately brush the wrappers with the melted butter. Sprinkle ¼ teaspoon sugar over each baked wrapper. Set the wrappers aside to cool.

2. Set 1 baked wonton square on an individual serving plate, layer 4 plum wedges across it, and top with a dollop of whipped cream. Place a second wonton square over the whipped cream and layer 4 more plum wedges on top of it. Drizzle ¼ teaspoon of the plum syrup (the sugary juices that develop as a result of macerating the fruit) over the plums. Place a dollop of whipped cream on top. Repeat the process on 3 more plates. Serve immediately.

➤ VARIATIONS

Mango Napoleons
See page 400 for tips on handling mangoes.

Follow the recipe for Plum and Ginger Napoleons, substituting 1 cup finely chopped mango from 2 mangoes for the plums. Toss with the ginger and sugar as described above. Proceed as directed, spooning about 2 tablespoons chopped mango over each baked wonton square (4 tablespoons chopped mango for each Napoleon).

Strawberry Napoleons
Follow the recipe for Plum and Ginger Napoleons, substituting 2 cups strawberries for the plums and 6 fresh mint leaves for the ginger. Cut the strawberries into ¼-inch-thick slices and toss with the sugar. Bruise the mint leaves with the heel of a chef's knife and

macerate them with the strawberries. Once the baked wontons are ready to be layered with the fruit, discard the mint. Proceed as directed, spooning sliced strawberries over each baked wonton.

STRAWBERRY CRÊPES

STRAWBERRY CRÊPES ARE DELICIOUS—tender and soft, sweet and warm. But making crêpes doesn't exactly bring to mind a quick and easy endeavor. We wondered whether we could use refrigerated egg roll wrappers (usually found in the supermarket produce section near the tofu and bean sprouts) to make a quick fruit crêpe, thereby eliminating the hassle of making a crêpe batter, resting it (so the crêpes don't tear), cooking and flipping the crêpes, and then filling and rolling them.

First, we tried buttering the wrapper and filling the crêpe with freshly sliced strawberries. We then cooked the crêpes in a greased skillet. Although the crêpes cooked quickly, they were tough and chewy. In addition, the filling was unexciting, and the wrapper's flap opened during cooking. Next, we tried macerating the strawberries in sugar to encourage them to become juicy, and we eliminated buttering the wrapper. We also added jam to the strawberry filling, hoping it would stick the rolled crêpes shut as they cooked.

These tests proved successful. The crêpes stayed shut during cooking, and the wrappers were definitely more tender. The filling was sweeter and more flavorful. Our crêpes were pretty good imposters for the real thing—and they took just minutes to assemble and cook.

Whipped cream was too sweet to serve as a topping for these crêpes, but a mixture of heavy cream and sour cream (with a bit of sugar) whipped into creamy, tangy topping finished off this dish.

Strawberry Crêpes with Whipped Sour Cream Topping
SERVES 4
TIME: 20 MINUTES

If you like, you can replace the strawberries with blueberries or raspberries—or you can combine the three berries to make a three-berry crêpe. If using the liqueur in the crêpes, you might add 2 tablespoons of the same liqueur to the whipped sour cream topping. See the illustrations on page 413 for tips on assembling the crêpes.

WHIPPED SOUR CREAM
TOPPING
- ½ cup heavy cream, chilled
- ¼ cup sour cream
- 1 tablespoon sugar

STRAWBERRY CRÊPES
- 2 cups strawberries, hulled and cut into ¼-inch-thick slices
- 2 tablespoons strawberry jam
- 1 tablespoon sugar

HULLING STRAWBERRIES

Many strawberries have tough white cores that should be removed along with the leafy green top. If you don't own a strawberry huller, push a plastic drinking straw through the bottom of the berry and up to the leafy stem. The straw will remove the core as well as the leafy top.

1   tablespoon Grand Marnier or kirsch
    (cherry brandy) (optional)
8   egg roll wrappers
2   tablespoons unsalted butter

1. FOR THE TOPPING: Whip the heavy cream, sour cream, and sugar to medium-stiff peaks in the bowl of a standing mixer. Refrigerate the topping until needed.

2. FOR THE CRÊPES: Combine the strawberries, jam, sugar, and liqueur, if using, in a medium bowl and set aside until the sugar dissolves, about 5 minutes. Lay an egg roll wrapper on the work surface so a longer end faces you. Spoon 3 tablespoons berry filling across the bottom section of the egg roll wrapper, making sure the berries don't touch the edge of the wrapper. Starting at the end nearer you, roll the wrapper to form a tight cylinder with open ends. Repeat with the remaining wrappers and filling.

3. Melt 1 tablespoon butter in a heavy-bottomed nonstick 12-inch skillet over medium-high heat. When the foaming subsides, lay 4 crêpes, seam-side down, in the pan and cook until golden, 1 to 2 minutes. Using tongs, turn the crêpes over and brown on the other side, about 1 minute. Transfer the crêpes to 2 individual plates (2 crêpes per plate). Melt the remaining 1 tablespoon butter in the empty pan and cook the remaining 4 crêpes. Transfer those crêpes to 2 more plates and spoon a dollop of the sour cream mixture onto each plate. Serve immediately.

30-MINUTE TARTE TATIN

MAKING A TRUE TARTE TATIN IS A labor of love. First, you need to make the puff pastry, a multihour endeavor requiring dexterity with a rolling pin and a no-fear attitude toward incorporating hundreds of layers of butter within a single sheet of dough. Next, you put the apples into a hot heavy-bottomed pan to caramelize. Then you top the pastry with the browned apples and put the entire pan into the oven, where the apples will caramelize further, their juices

ASSEMBLING STRAWBERRY CRÊPES

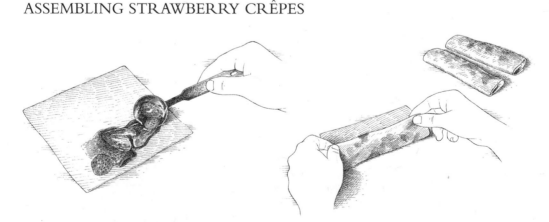

1. Place an egg roll wrapper on a work surface so a longer side faces you. Spoon 3 tablespoons berry filling across the bottom section of the egg roll wrapper, making sure the berries don't touch the edge of the wrapper.

2. Starting at the end nearest you, roll the wrapper to form a tight cylinder with open ends. Repeat with the remaining wrappers and filling.

bubbling into the dough as the pastry puffs like an inflatable pillow. With a pot holder in one hand and a plate in the other, fearless Tatin-makers invert the tart onto the plate. In a perfect world, the apples fall from the pan and perfectly nestle into the pastry.

If you think this process sounds stressful, you're right; it is. Not only do you have to worry about making puff pastry and caramelizing the apples in a pretty, concentric circle (so they retain an orderly look when they're inverted onto the pastry) but also the inverting process must be regarded with the rational fear of spitting-hot caramel dripping from the pan and down your arm.

Our goal was to whittle the Tatin process to a manageable affair. We wanted to retain the sticky-sweet flavor of caramelized apples and the flakiness of buttery puff pastry but didn't want to be chained to the kitchen for hours to do so. So we came up with an idea: Could the apples and puff pastry be made separately and then married just before serving? We thought this was worth a try.

We started by simplifying the puff pastry—rather than making it from scratch, we bought puff pastry from the grocery store. We popped it into the oven for about 12 minutes and took it out when it was golden and inflated. Easy enough.

We then focused on the apples, melting butter in a large pan, sprinkling in sugar, and laying quartered apples on top. We allowed the apples to caramelize for about 10 minutes, flipped them over, and browned the other side. We then removed the apples, piece by piece with tongs, and arranged them in pretty, over-lapping rows on the baked puff pastry square.

We spooned about three quarters of the leftover caramelized juices in the pan over the tart. To the remaining juices, we added a few tablespoons of the whipped sour cream topping served alongside the tart. This makes an instant caramel sauce that provides a nice tangy contrast to the tart's sweet, syrupy juices. In just 30 minutes, we created a faux Tatin that even Francophiles will like.

30-Minute Tarte Tatin

SERVES 6 TO 8

TIME: 30 MINUTES

Tarte Tatin is France's most famous apple tart, made here with several ingenious shortcuts. Bake the pastry while the apples are caramelizing. Stir some of the whipped sour cream topping into the caramelized apple juices left in the pan to make a caramel sauce. Dollop the remaining whipped sour cream topping over individual tart portions. See photo of this recipe on page 163.

PUFF PASTRY

1   sheet (9 by 9½ inches) frozen commercial puff pastry, thawed on the counter for 10 minutes

CARAMELIZED APPLES

8   tablespoons (1 stick) unsalted butter
¾   cup (5¼ ounces) sugar
2   pounds Granny Smith apples (6 medium or 4 large), peeled, quartered, and cored

WHIPPED SOUR CREAM TOPPING

1   cup heavy cream, chilled
½   cup sour cream
2   tablespoons liqueur (spiced rum, Calvados apple liqueur, or Grand Marnier orange liqueur) (optional)

1. FOR THE PASTRY: Adjust an oven rack to the middle position and heat the oven to 400 degrees. Line a rimmed baking sheet with parchment paper. Place the puff pastry on the parchment and bake until golden brown and puffed, 10 to 12 minutes. Using a wide

metal spatula, transfer the baked pastry shell to a cutting board or flat serving platter.

2. FOR THE APPLES: Meanwhile, melt the butter in a 12-inch heavy-bottomed skillet over high heat. Remove the pan from the heat and sprinkle evenly with the sugar. Place the apples in the skillet so they are all resting flat-side down. Return the skillet to high heat and cook until the juices in the pan turn a rich amber color, 10 to 12 minutes. Using tongs, turn the apples over to the other flat side. Continue to caramelize the apples for an additional 5 minutes.

3. FOR THE TOPPING: Whip the heavy cream and sour cream to soft peaks in the bowl of a standing mixer. Add the liqueur, if desired, and continue to whip to medium-stiff peaks.

4. TO ASSEMBLE: Using tongs, remove the apple slices from the pan one at a time and place in 3 overlapping horizontal rows on the baked pastry square. Spoon about three quarters of the pan juices over the apples (you can use a pastry brush to dab some of the liquid onto the edges of the pastry). Whisk 2 tablespoons whipped sour cream topping into the leftover liquid in the pan.

5. To serve, cut the tart in half vertically down the center and then horizontally into 3 or 4 rows (to serve 6 or 8, respectively). Transfer portions to individual plates and top each with a dollop of whipped sour cream and a drizzle of caramel sauce from the pan. Serve immediately.

➤ VARIATION

Tarte Tatin with Pears

Follow the recipe for 30-Minute Tarte Tatin, substituting 2 pounds Anjou or Bartlett pears (6 to 8 medium) for the apples. You may need to increase the caramelization time in step 2 to 15 minutes for the first side and 8 minutes for the second side. Poire Williams is the best liqueur to use in the whipped sour cream.

APPLE TURNOVERS

AN APPLE TURNOVER TAKES ONLY SECONDS to eat. The way the crust shatters when bitten into, its fragility and tenderness, prompts one to consume this treat as fast possible. What a shame it is, then, that making apple turnovers—even with a streamlined version of homemade puff pastry dough—takes hours. We were determined to find a quicker way to enjoy homemade apple turnovers.

We started with the filling. Although we tried more traditional methods of preparing the apples, such as dicing or slicing them into wedges, no method was as good, or as quick, as using a box grater. Grating apples on the box grater took only seconds. The thin ribbons of apple allowed the sugar and lemon juice tossed with them to permeate the entire filling rather than just coat its surface.

Homemade puff pastry is a delectable treat. It's buttery, with thousands of lithe layers; it's tender and golden. But it requires time and patience to roll and fold the butter-laden dough. Between rounds of rolling and folding, the dough must chill so the butter can resolidify; otherwise, it squirts out the sides. This takes more time. Taking all of this into consideration, we decided to turn our backs on homemade puff pastry and instead purchase frozen puff pastry at the supermarket.

Commercial puff pastry isn't as pretty, as buttery, or as delicious as homemade puff pastry, but the trade-off is that in just minutes (not hours), you can have your turnovers in the oven. However, we first needed to roll the dough a little thinner, to a thickness of about ⅛ inch.

To fill the turnovers, we decided to follow the method of making raviolis, whereby you place the apple filling in the center of a dough rectangle, fold the dough over, pinch the open seams shut, and then crimp the edges with the upturned tines of a fork. After 10 minutes of chill time in the refrigerator and 16 minutes baking in the oven, the turnovers were done and ready to cool. Turnovers in less than 1 hour are not only possible but tasty too.

Easy Apple Turnovers

MAKES 12 TURNOVERS

TIME: 60 MINUTES
(INCLUDES 40 MINUTES OF BAKING AND COOLING TIME)

This recipe makes 12 turnovers, or 6 to each sheet of puff pastry. We used Pepperidge Farm Puff Pastry Sheets, which come 2 sheets to a box. You can make these apple turnovers up to a day before baking. Store them on a parchment paper–lined baking sheet in the refrigerator; brush them with water and sprinkle with cinnamon sugar before baking. See the illustrations on page 417 for tips on assembling the turnovers.

APPLE FILLING

1½ pounds Granny Smith apples (3 large or 4 medium)
1½ cups (10½ ounces) sugar
1 tablespoon plus 1 teaspoon juice from 1 lemon
¼ teaspoon salt

PUFF PASTRY

2 sheets (9 by 9½ inches) frozen commercial puff pastry, thawed on the counter for 10 minutes

CINNAMON SUGAR

½ cup (3½ ounces) sugar
2 teaspoons ground cinnamon

1. Adjust an oven rack to the upper-middle position and heat the oven to 375 degrees. Line 2 rimmed baking sheets with parchment paper.

2. FOR THE FILLING: Peel the apples and grate them on the large holes of a box grater.

Combine the grated apples, sugar, lemon juice, and salt in a medium bowl.

3. FOR THE PASTRY: Unwrap the puff pastry and, using a rolling pin, roll each sheet on a floured work surface to an 11 by 9-inch rectangle about ⅛ inch thick. Using the back of a paring knife, gently make a vertical line down the center of the dough (you want to mark the dough without cutting through it). In the same way, mark each dough half into 3 horizontal sections, cutting all the way through the dough and forming 6 rectangles per sheet. Place 2 tablespoons grated apple filling (squeezed of excess liquid) in the center of each dough rectangle.

4. Fold one edge of the dough over to meet the original dividing line in the center of the dough; repeat with the other side (see illustration 2 on page 417). Press the edges to seal and, using your finger, make indentations between the rectangles. Use a paring knife to cut down the center of the dough (dividing the dough into 2 long halves with 3 filled rectangles on each half) and then to cut the filled rectangles away from one another. Press the edges to seal and then crimp the edges with the tines of a fork. Refrigerate the turnovers on the parchment-lined baking sheets for 10 minutes (or cover with plastic wrap and refrigerate up to 24 hours).

5. FOR THE CINNAMON SUGAR: Combine the sugar and cinnamon in a small bowl. Brush or mist the turnovers with water and sprinkle evenly with the cinnamon sugar. Bake until golden brown, 16 to 18 minutes. Using a wide metal spatula, transfer the turnovers to a wire rack to cool slightly, about 20 minutes. Serve warm.

BLUEBERRY COBBLER

A BLUEBERRY COBBLER ISN'T TIDY AND pretty. It doesn't get served on a precious dessert plate alongside a dainty silver fork. Blueberry cobbler gets served in a big bowl, with a spoon, topped with a craggy country-style biscuit—and if you're lucky, adorned with a heaping scoop of vanilla ice cream. It's eaten warm and with gusto.

Making a blueberry cobbler should retain some of these hedonistic qualities—throw the berries into a bowl, sweeten them, put that biscuit topping on, get the cobbler in and out of the oven as fast as possible, and set the cobbler on the table while it's still warm. Keeping these ideals in mind, we attacked our favorite recipe for blueberry cobbler (developed last year in the test kitchen) and looked for ways to streamline the recipe process.

We started with the blueberries. Instead of picking and sorting through fresh berries, we decided to opt for an easier solution: frozen berries. Not only are frozen blueberries far less expensive than fresh but also, because they're picked at their peak and individually quick-frozen, they're often sweeter. Rather

ASSEMBLING TURNOVERS

1. Roll each sheet of puff pastry to an 11 by 9-inch rectangle. Using the back of a paring knife, gently make a vertical line down the center of the dough (you want to mark the dough without cutting through it). In the same way, mark each dough sheet into 3 horizontal sections, cutting all the way through the dough.

2. Place 2 tablespoons grated apple filling (squeezed of excess liquid) in the center of each dough rectangle. Fold one edge of the dough over to meet the original dividing line in the center of the dough; repeat with the other side.

3. Press the edges to seal and, using your finger, make indentations between the rectangles.

4. Use a paring knife to cut down the center of the dough (dividing the dough into 2 long halves with 3 filled rectangles on each half) and then to cut the filled rectangles away from one another. Press the edges to seal and, using the tines of a fork, crimp the edges.

than defrosting them at room temperature, we placed the frozen blueberries in a deep-dish pie plate and microwaved them on high power for 5 minutes.

In our classic recipe for blueberry cobbler, we reduce the blueberry juices until syrupy and thick, which takes about 10 minutes, then return the reduced juices to the sugar-coated berries. The fruit component of the cobbler goes into the oven for 30 minutes so the fruit is steaming hot before the biscuit topping is added. We found that if the topping is added to cold fruit, the cobbler biscuits have a hard time baking through and remain somewhat doughy at their bottoms.

For our fast version, we decided to eliminate reducing the blueberry juices on the stovetop altogether and instead opted to use less of the blueberry juices, which are strained from the defrosted blueberries. We added lemon juice and cornstarch to the berry juices and then put the resulting dark purple juices with the sugar-tossed berries into the pie

plate. Rather than baking them for 30 minutes, we just popped the blueberries into the microwave for another 5-minute zap. The berries were now piping hot and ready for the biscuits in 10 minutes rather than the 60 minutes this process took in our original recipe.

The biscuit dough in our favorite cobbler recipe was already pretty quick. Rather than making rolled biscuits by cutting cold butter into the dry ingredients (as in a pie dough), our recipe calls for drop biscuits. Simply mix the dry ingredients, mix the wet ingredients, and then combine the two. For extra insurance against soggy-bottomed biscuits, we decided to increase the amount of flour in the recipe by ¼ cup. We broke off eight knobby pieces of biscuit dough to top the berries. With a final sprinkle of sugar over the dough, the cobbler went into the oven just 15 minutes after we had stepped into the kitchen—and in under an hour, the cobbler was baked, cooled, and ready to be devoured.

INGREDIENTS: Frozen Blueberries

Just how good are frozen berries, and are all brands and types the same? To find out, we baked up cobblers with five brands of frozen berries as well as fresh berries, both locally picked and those picked in South America and shipped to American markets in the off-season. While the cobbler made with locally grown fresh berries was best, we were surprised at how good the cobblers made with frozen berries tasted. We were particularly impressed with those made with frozen wild berries, which are smaller and more flavorful than regular cultivated blueberries. They were far superior to (and a lot cheaper than) the South American berries, which are the standard supermarket choice for many months of the year. In addition, frozen berries do not need to be washed or picked over to remove stems. They are our first choice for a quick cobbler.

Blueberry Cobbler

SERVES 8

TIME: 50 MINUTES
(INCLUDES 35 MINUTES OF BAKING
AND COOLING TIME)

You can save time by mixing the dry ingredients while the berries are defrosting in the microwave. Add the liquid ingredients to the dry while the berries are in the microwave for the second time. If you like, add ⅛ teaspoon ground cinnamon to the sugar topping sprinkled over the biscuits just before they go into the oven. Serve with vanilla ice cream. For information about frozen berries, see the left column. See photo of this recipe on page 165.

FILLING

36 ounces (about 6 cups) frozen blueberries (preferably wild)

½ cup (3½ ounces) sugar

1½ teaspoons grated zest plus 1 tablespoon
   juice from 1 lemon
1 tablespoon cornstarch

BISCUIT TOPPING
1¼ cups (6¼ ounces) unbleached
   all-purpose flour
2 tablespoons yellow cornmeal
¼ cup (1¾ ounces) sugar, plus 2 teaspoons
   for sprinkling
2 teaspoons baking powder
¼ teaspoon baking soda
¼ teaspoon salt
4 tablespoons unsalted butter, melted
⅓ cup buttermilk
½ teaspoon vanilla extract

1. Adjust an oven rack to the lower-middle position and heat the oven to 425 degrees.

2. FOR THE FILLING: Place the frozen berries in a 9½-inch deep-dish glass pie plate. Microwave the berries on high power, stirring once, until thawed and the juices are running, about 5 minutes. Drain the berries in a colander set over a bowl to catch the juices and then return the berries to the pie plate. Add the sugar and lemon zest to the berries and gently stir to combine. To ¾ cup berry juices, add the lemon juice and cornstarch and then vigorously whisk to remove any cornstarch lumps; discard the remaining berry juices. Add the thickened liquid to the berries, cover the pie plate with plastic wrap, cut vents in the plastic wrap with a paring knife, and microwave the berries on high, stirring once, until hot and bubbling, about 5 minutes.

3. FOR THE TOPPING: Whisk the flour, cornmeal, ¼ cup sugar, baking powder, baking soda, and salt in a large bowl to combine. Whisk together the melted butter, buttermilk, and vanilla in a small bowl. One minute before the blueberries come out of the microwave (for the second time), add the wet ingredients to the dry ingredients and stir with a rubber spatula until just combined and no dry pockets remain.

4. TO ASSEMBLE AND BAKE: Remove the berries from the microwave and discard the plastic wrap. Pinch off 8 equal-size pieces of biscuit dough and place them on the hot berry filling, spacing the biscuits at least ½ inch apart (they should not touch). Sprinkle each mound of dough with a portion of the remaining 2 teaspoons sugar. Place the pie plate on a rimmed baking sheet and bake until the filling is bubbling and the biscuits are golden brown on top and cooked through, 15 to 18 minutes. Cool the cobbler on a wire rack for 20 minutes; serve warm.

➤ VARIATION
Blueberry Cobbler with Gingered Biscuits
Follow the recipe for Blueberry Cobbler, adding 3 tablespoons minced crystallized ginger to the flour mixture in step 3.

CHERRY CLAFOUTI
ORIGINALLY FROM THE LIMOUSIN region of France, clafouti is a rustic crustless custard made with fresh cherries and loads of eggs and milk. It's baked in the oven and served warm or at room temperature, often with no garnish other than a quick dusting of confectioners' sugar.

We researched clafouti recipes and decided to take the easy road—just place the liquid and then the dry ingredients in a blender and mix for about 1 minute, and then pour the batter over the cherries and bake until the custard puffs. Because the method was so simple, we saw no reason to choose ingredients, like whole fresh cherries, that would complicate the recipe. Rather than stand over the sink pitting ¾ pound cherries, we decided to use pitted frozen or jarred cherries instead.

For a rich, eggy custard that was firm enough to hold its own but not turn rubbery, we chose to use 6 whole eggs. We also opted for a mix of whole milk and cream, finding that the combination provided the nicest texture. Leaner custards, made with just milk, tasted hollow. With just a squeeze of lemon juice and a pinch of salt, the flavors came together. After 40 minutes in the oven, the clafouti had puffed like a soufflé—with half the effort.

~≫~

Cherry Clafouti

SERVES 8 TO 10

TIME: 1 HOUR (INCLUDES
45 MINUTES OF BAKING
AND COOLING TIME)

Clafouti can be served warm or at room temperature. You can substitute sugar-tossed apricots, nectarines, peaches, plums, or raspberries for the cherries. Do not use sweet cherries in this recipe; we particularly like jarred Morello cherries, an especially flavorful sour variety.

1	tablespoon unsalted butter, melted
1½	cups (about 12 ounces) jarred sour cherries, drained of juices, or 1½ cups frozen sour cherries, thawed
6	large eggs
1	cup milk
⅔	cup heavy cream
1	teaspoon juice from 1 lemon
1	cup (7 ounces) sugar
½	cup (2½ ounces) unbleached all-purpose flour
⅛	teaspoon salt
	Confectioners' sugar for dusting

1. Adjust an oven rack to the middle position and preheat the oven to 350 degrees. Brush a 9½-inch glass pie plate with the melted butter and place the cherries in a single layer in the plate.

2. Add the eggs, milk, cream, and lemon juice and then the sugar, flour, and salt to a blender jar. Blend the batter for 1 minute and then pour it over the cherries. Bake until the top is browned and puffed, 35 to 45 minutes. Cool the pie plate on a rack for at least 10 minutes. Dust with confectioners' sugar, cut into wedges, and serve.

16

ICE CREAM DESSERTS AND PUDDINGS

THIS CHAPTER FOCUSES ON SO-called spoon desserts, including puddings and ice cream sundaes. The pudding recipes we've chosen to highlight are somewhat exotic. Yes, we've included our recipe for quick chocolate mousse, but we've also added an Indian recipe for semolina pudding with dried fruit and nuts as well as English sticky toffee pudding.

Our ice cream recipes include several sundaes, which are as American as apple pie—maybe even more so, as they were actually invented in this country just before the dawn of the 20th century. The precise origins of the ice cream sundae are a bit murky. Several sources cite 19th-century prohibitions against the drinking of soda water on Sunday. With popular ice cream sodas out of bounds, ice cream parlors started serving sauces and other toppings with ice cream instead. The most popular sundae is, of course, the hot fudge sundae, but we've also included a recipe for butterscotch sundaes. This chapter also includes several simple sauces for ice cream, including warm cherry sauce and raspberry sauce.

KEEPING ICE CREAM FRESH

Leftover ice cream can lose its fresh taste, and ice crystals can ruin its texture. To slow this process, cover the portion remaining in the carton with heavy-duty plastic wrap, pressing the wrap directly onto the surface of the ice cream.

AFFOGATO

SERIOUSLY SIMPLE, AFFOGATO, WHICH means "drowned" in Italian, consists of a scoop of vanilla ice cream in a bowl or a parfait glass with a shot of espresso poured over it. The ice cream melts into the hot espresso, providing a hot-cold, bitter-sweet, acidic-creamy sensation.

The trick to making a good affogato is to use a high-quality ice cream with lots of butterfat and a low overrun (see page 426 for more information on overrun). Butterfat gives the ice cream a creamy, rich mouthfeel. A low overrun means the ice cream didn't have a lot of air pumped into it during churning. Because the ice cream has fewer air pockets and a higher density, it is slower to melt, prolonging your enjoyment of affogato. When affogato is made with a fluffy, high-overrun ice cream, we found it melts too quickly.

To dress up this quick dessert, add a shot of Armagnac, coffee liqueur, or cognac to the espresso-drenched ice cream. Italian cookies are another traditional embellishment.

Affogato

SERVES 4

TIME: 10 MINUTES

Affogato is best made tableside. Bring out the ice cream in individual dishes, with the espresso on the side. Let individuals pour their own espresso over the ice cream and eat immediately. Ultrathin pizzelle wafers (sold in Italian markets and many gourmet stores) are nice served alongside the affogato. See page 423 for information about our ice cream tasting.

1	pint high-quality vanilla ice cream
4	(2-ounce) servings espresso, freshly brewed and still hot
4	(1-ounce) servings Armagnac, coffee liqueur, or cognac (optional)

INGREDIENTS: Vanilla Ice Cream

We wondered if the many brands of vanilla ice cream on the market were very different from one another. To find out, we gathered 20 tasters to sample eight leading national brands of vanilla ice cream, made in what's known as the French, or custard, style, with egg yolks.

Many ice cream manufacturers add stabilizers—most often carrageenan gum or guar gum—to prevent *heat shock*, an industry term for the degradation in texture caused by the partial melting and refreezing that occurs when ice cream is subjected to extreme temperature changes during transit to the supermarket or when an ice cream case goes through its self-defrosting cycle. Gum additives stabilize ice cream by trapping water in the frozen mass and slowing the growth of ice crystals during melting and refreezing. We thought the presence of stabilizers might affect the test results. To our surprise, this was not the case. The top two brands in our tasting, Edy's Dreamery and Double Rainbow, use stabilizers.

We also expected the nature of the ice creams' vanilla flavor—artificial or natural—would affect the outcome of the test. Again, we were a bit surprised with the results. Blue Bell was the only brand in the tasting that contained artificial vanilla flavor, and it rated smack-dab in the middle, thus negating any link between natural flavor and superior flavor. In fact, tasters took greater issue with several brands made with real vanilla extract—including Häagen-Dazs, Ben and Jerry's, and Edy's Grand—for tasting "artificial" and "boozy." To help explain this odd result, we contacted Bruce Tharp, an independent ice cream consultant based in Wayne, Pennsylvania. He explained that the perceived artificial and alcohol flavors are often caused by the quantity of vanilla extract added to the ice cream—that is, the more extract, the more likely one is to taste the alcohol. Although it's impossible to confirm this theory (manufacturers won't release their recipes to the public), it was clear that the absence of stabilizers and the use of natural flavorings were not reliable indicators of quality.

Next up was the issue of butterfat, which contributes to smooth texture, rich flavor, and structure. Of the ice creams we tasted, butterfat content ranged from 10 to 16 percent and, in general, the higher the butterfat content, the higher the ice cream rated. Our two top-rated ice creams had butterfat contents of 14.5 percent (Edy's Dreamery) and 15 percent (Double Rainbow). The two lowest-rated brands had butterfat contents of 10 to 12 percent and 13 percent.

All commercial ice cream makers also add air to the mix. The air is called *overrun*—and without it, the ice cream would look more like an ice cube. While the top two ice creams had low overruns of 21 and 26 percent, our third favorite had a whopping overrun of 93.5 percent. Furthermore, the two last-place ice creams had very different overruns—26 percent and 100 percent, 100 percent being the legal limit). Our conclusion? In general, low overrun is preferable, although butterfat content is a better measure of quality.

The last component we researched was emulsifiers, such as mono- and diglycerides, which are used to control the behavior of fat in ice cream by keeping it from separating from the ice cream mass. Emulsifiers give an ice cream rigidity and strength. The only ice cream in our tasting with emulsifiers was also the least favored sample: Edy's Grand. So, according to our taste test, it seems that emulsifiers are not desirable.

The winner of our tasting, as mentioned above, was Edy's Dreamery, with Double Rainbow coming in second and Breyers third. The real news, however, was the poor showing of the two best-known premium brands, Häagen-Dazs and Ben and Jerry's, which rated fourth and seventh, respectively, out of the eight brands sampled.

THE BEST VANILLA ICE CREAMS

Edy's Dreamery Vanilla (left) was the favorite of our tasters. Double Rainbow French Vanilla (middle) came in second, and Breyers French Vanilla (right) was third.

Scoop the ice cream into individual bowls or parfait glasses (about ½ cup per serving). Bring the bowls of ice cream to the table, along with individual servings of espresso and liqueur, if using, in demitasse cups or shot glasses. Pour the espresso and the liqueur, if using, over the ice cream. Serve immediately.

VANILLA ICE CREAM WITH WARM CHERRY SAUCE

WHO NEEDS A CHERRY PIE WHEN YOU can make a cherry sauce in a fraction of the time? Served with vanilla ice cream, it's got all of the cherry flavor of pie à la mode without the bother of a pie crust.

We started our testing with a warm Bing cherry sauce we had developed in the test kitchen some years ago. With 1 pound fresh cherries, brandy, sugar, corn syrup, almond extract, and lemon juice, the sauce was sweet, tangy, and slightly acidic. The brandy gave it warmth, and the almond extract gave it depth. It was delicious and easy—except that it took more than 15 minutes to pit all of those cherries. We wanted to try using pitted jarred or frozen cherries instead.

We decided to test jarred sour cherries as well as frozen sour cherries and frozen sweet cherries in a cherry sauce face-off. We drained the jarred cherries, reserving their liquid (a sweet, somewhat thin syrup) to use in place of the corn syrup. To the frozen cherries, we did nothing but defrost them. All three samples were cooked with sugar and brandy—the two frozen cherries with corn syrup as well—and then a cornstarch slurry was added. The sauces were brought back to a boil, and into the pot went the lemon juice and the almond extract.

After about 10 minutes, when the sauces had sufficient time to cool and thicken, we sampled them side by side. The sauce with the jarred sour cherries tasted cleaner and more cherrylike than the frozen sour cherry sauce with the corn syrup. The frozen sweet cherry sauce with corn syrup was bland and listless in comparison with the other two. When paired with vanilla ice cream, however, the differences among the sauces became less substantial. Although the sauce made with the jarred sour cherries still tasted best, all three cherry products yielded sauces good enough to spoon over ice cream.

Vanilla Ice Cream with Warm Cherry Sauce

SERVES 4

TIME: 20 MINUTES

We prefer jarred sour cherries in a light cherry syrup to frozen sour or sweet cherries. Use the microwave to thaw the frozen cherries, if using them. If you can find jarred sour cherries (not maraschino cherries), use the liquid they're packed in instead of corn syrup in the recipe for a much more natural and cherrylike flavor in your sauce. For some crunch, slivered, toasted almonds can be scattered over the ice cream and sauce.

6   ounces jarred sour cherries, drained, juices reserved, or 6 ounces frozen sour or sweet cherries, thawed

¼   cup (1¾ ounces) sugar

2   tablespoons light corn syrup or reserved cherry juices

2   tablespoons brandy
    Pinch salt

1   teaspoon cornstarch

½   teaspoon juice from 1 lemon
    Several drops almond extract (optional)

1   pint vanilla ice cream

¼   cup slivered almonds, toasted (optional)

1. Bring the cherries, sugar, corn syrup or reserved cherry juices, brandy, and salt to a boil in a medium saucepan. Reduce the heat and simmer, stirring occasionally, until the sauce thickens slightly, about 8 minutes.

2. Remove the pan from the heat. Stir the cornstarch and 1 tablespoon water together in a small bowl. Add the cornstarch mixture to the sauce and stir until incorporated.

3. Return the pan to the heat and bring the sauce back to a boil. Simmer, stirring constantly, until the sauce thickens, about 1 minute.

4. Remove the pan from the heat and stir in the lemon juice and almond extract, if using. (The sauce may be refrigerated in an airtight container for several days. It will thicken as it cools. Reheat the sauce in a microwave or double boiler.)

5. To serve, scoop the ice cream into individual bowls (about ½ cup per bowl). Spoon warm cherry sauce over each portion and sprinkle with the toasted almonds, if using. Serve immediately.

Vanilla Ice Cream with Peaches and Raspberry Sauce

IT'S RARE TO DINE AT A RESTAURANT and not see raspberry sauce (also called Melba sauce, named after the Australian opera singer Dame Nellie Melba) listed on the dessert menu. Raspberry sauce is delicious paired with creamy desserts (like ice cream or custard), and it is incredibly easy to prepare—simply mix raspberries with sugar, put it over a flame, and, once the sugar dissolves and the raspberries liquefy, strain the sauce and serve.

Rather than expensive fresh raspberries, we

decided to use frozen. After just a couple of minutes on the stove, the raspberries broke down into a brilliant fuchsia sea. All we had to do was add a bit of acid to brighten the other flavors and strain the sauce so no pesky seeds would mar its smooth texture. When you taste this simple sauce spooned over vanilla ice cream and served alongside fat summer peaches, you'll be singing its praises too.

Vanilla Ice Cream with Peaches and Raspberry Sauce

SERVES 4

TIME: 10 MINUTES

To really bring out the sweetness of the peaches, toss them with 2 teaspoons sugar or 1 teaspoon honey and let them sit while you make the raspberry sauce.

6	ounces frozen raspberries
¼	cup sugar
1½	teaspoons juice from 1 lemon
1	pint vanilla ice cream
4	ripe peaches, halved, pitted, and each half cut into 4 slices

1. Place the raspberries and sugar in a small saucepan. Cook, stirring constantly, over medium heat until the sugar dissolves and the berries soften, 3 to 4 minutes.

2. Remove the pan from the heat and stir in the lemon juice. Transfer the sauce to a fine-mesh strainer set over a small bowl. Press on the solids to extract as much liquid as possible. Discard the seeds. (The raspberry sauce can be refrigerated in an airtight container for several days. Reheat before using.)

3. To serve, divide the sliced peaches among individual bowls and top with ice cream (about ½ cup per bowl). Pour raspberry sauce over each portion and serve immediately.

➤ VARIATIONS

Vanilla Ice Cream with Peaches and Basil-Raspberry Sauce

This sauce is also nice served over lemon sorbet.

Follow the recipe for Vanilla Ice Cream with Peaches and Raspberry Sauce, adding 12 roughly chopped fresh basil leaves to the sauce after it has cooked for 2 minutes. Cover the pan, remove it from the heat, and allow the basil to steep with the raspberries for 10 minutes. Strain the sauce and proceed as directed.

Vanilla Ice Cream with Peaches and Raspberry-Ginger-Lime Sauce

This sauce is also excellent served over coconut ice cream.

Follow the recipe for Vanilla Ice Cream with Peaches and Raspberry Sauce, adding 1½ teaspoons roughly chopped fresh ginger to the sauce after it has cooked for 2 minutes. Cover the pan, remove it from the heat, and allow the ginger to steep with the raspberries for 10 minutes. Replace the lemon juice with lime juice. Strain the sauce and proceed as directed.

CRYSTALLIZED GINGER ICE CREAM WITH BITTERSWEET CHOCOLATE SAUCE

MAKING A HOMEMADE ICE CREAM dessert doesn't have to take all day. Rather than making a custard base, taking the time to freeze it in an ice cream machine, and then letting it harden in the freezer, all you need to do is visit your grocery store. We figured that by purchasing high-quality vanilla ice cream and folding in spicy-sweet crystallized ginger, we could make "homemade" ginger ice cream in a half hour. Then we thought to top it with

a 5-minute bittersweet chocolate sauce. The result: a dessert that tasted much more interesting than plain old store-bought ice cream and that required little more work.

Before we could stir in the crystallized ginger, we had to find a way to soften the vanilla ice cream. We tried letting it soften in the refrigerator, but this took too long. Next, we tried softening it at room temperature, but this also took too long. Next, we decided to slice the ice cream into smaller slabs and let the pieces sit at room temperature. While this was faster than both of the previous tests, it still took more than half an hour to convince rock-hard vanilla ice cream to soften enough to add the ginger.

We were about to give up when we decided to try a radical idea: to place the ice cream in a hot-water bath. We filled a large

WHY SOME ICE CREAMS MELT FASTER THAN OTHERS

All ice cream, even homemade, contains air that is beaten in during the churning process. Commercial ice cream manufacturers pump in air, which they call *overrun*. Ice cream with more air and a high overrun (left photo) melts fairly quickly. Ice cream with less air and a low overrun (right photo) melts more slowly. In our taste test, some panelists liked fluffier ice cream with a high overrun. However, when making affogato (page 422), you must use a low-overrun super-premium ice cream that melts slowly.

bowl with hot water and then placed the slabs of ice cream in another bowl that easily nested within the bowl filled with water. In just 5 minutes, our ice cream was soft enough to mix with the ginger.

Although we thought about pulsing the ginger in a food processor, we decided we didn't want the ginger to be a uniform size; rather, we wanted small and large chunks to be revealed in the ice cream. An ounce of chopped crystallized ginger was enough to flavor a pint of ice cream.

Next, we went on to the chocolate sauce. More refined than slow, sticky hot

EQUIPMENT: Ice Cream Scoops

We've all struggled with an intractable pint of rock-hard ice cream. That's where a good ice cream scoop comes in handy; it can release even hard-frozen ice cream from bondage. We gathered ten readily available scoops and dipped our way through 20 pints of vanilla ice cream to find the best. We tested three basic types of scoop: classic, mechanical-release (or spring-loaded), and spade shaped. Prices ranged from $3.99 to $22.

Classic ice cream scoops sport a thick handle and curved bowl. They can be used by lefties and righties with equal comfort. There are a few variations on the theme; of the four classic scoops we purchased, one had a pointed "beak" scoop, another offered a "comfort grip" rubber handle, and another contained a self-defrosting liquid. Testers were unanimous in assigning first place—in both its own category and overall—to the Zeroll Classic Ice Cream Scoop ($22). Its thick handle was comfortable for large and small hands, and its nonstick coating and self-defrosting liquid (which responds to heat from the user's hand) contributed to perfect release, leaving only traces of melted ice cream inside the scoop. The defrosting fluid and the elegantly curved bowl allowed the scoop to take purchase immediately, curling a perfect scoop with minimal effort. Only one caveat: Don't run this scoop through the dishwasher, as it will lose its magical defrosting properties.

Coming in second among the other classic scoops tested was the Oxo Beak Scoop ($11.99). The beak point dug into ice cream with ease, and the ice cream curled up nicely. Our only minor quibble was the short handle, which forced testers with larger hands to choke up close to the head. If price is a concern, you might consider this model.

Mechanical-release scoops come in various sizes and operate with a spring-loaded, squeezable handle (or thumb trigger) that connects to a curved steel lever inside the scoop. When the handle or lever is released, the ice cream pops out in a perfectly round ball. Although we frequently use a mechanical-release scoop to measure even portions of cookie dough and muffin batter, we found this type less than ideal when it came to ice cream. The scoops are designed for right-handed users only, and their thin, straight-edged handles were distinctly uncomfortable when considerable pressure was applied. Of the four models we tested, none was worthy of recommendation.

Spades, with their flat, paddle-type heads, are useful when you need to scoop a lot of ice cream quickly—say, for an ice cream cake or sandwiches—but they are too big to fit into pint containers. If you make frozen desserts frequently or need to work your way through multiple gallon-size containers of ice cream, a spade might be for you. Our preferred model, made by the same manufacturer as our overall winning scoop, is the Zeroll Nonstick Ice Cream Spade ($19.60).

THE BEST ICE CREAM SCOOPS

The Zeroll Classic Ice Cream Scoop (left) was the favorite model tested. If you need to scoop a lot of ice cream for an ice cream cake, you might consider the Zeroll Nonstick Ice Cream Spade (right), but this tool is too big to fit into pint containers.

fudge, chocolate sauce has a pure, complex, potent chocolate flavor tempered by a gentle sweetness. It should pour with ease and cling with a glossy sheen.

We started with a recipe we had developed several years ago in the test kitchen. Instead of the usual sugar, this recipe calls for corn syrup, which gives the sauce a shiny, lacquered finish and keeps it fluid when poured over cold ice cream. This sauce was so quick and easy that we found little to do to make it even faster. The only change we made was to use chocolate morsels instead of bits hand-chopped from a block.

INGREDIENTS: Chocolate Chips

Are all chocolate chips the same? To find out, we tested seven brands. Chips have a lower cocoa butter content than chocolate bars, which keeps them from becoming too liquid when baked. Often the cocoa butter is replaced by sugar, which is why we found many chocolate chips in our tasting quite sweet. We also found that the chips we liked best straight out of the bag tasted best in cookies. Nestlé, Guittard, Ghirardelli, and Tropical Source (a brand sold in natural food stores) all received high marks. The chips that excelled were noted for a balance of bitterness, sweetness, and smoothness—and, as we discovered, these chips hold a few curious secrets.

On the spectrum of chocolates, chips are generally considered at the least refined end. The most refined chocolate is coating chocolate, also known as *couverture*, an extremely glossy chocolate found mainly in specialty candy-making shops and used by pastry chefs in various confections. Chocolate chips lack the fluidity necessary to meet the technical demands of the work turned out by pastry chefs, such as molds and truffles and even the seemingly simple chocolate-dipped strawberry. For example, a bowl of melted couverture pours out smoothly, like cream, but a bowl of melted chips slides sluggishly, like glue. High viscosity and low fluidity are what make the chip shape possible. When squeezed through a nozzle onto a moving belt in the factory, the chocolate quickly sets up into a pert morsel rather than collapsing into a small blob.

The chip that rated second in our tasting defied the unspoken standard for chip shape. Guittard grinds and blends its chip chocolate in the same way it does its couverture. This helps develop the flavor. The tradeoff, however, is that the chip is too fluid to hold the typical tightly pointed shape. Even so, some of our tasters liked the large size and unorthodox disk shape of the chip in a thick, chewy cookie. The shape does not, however, work well in a thin, crisp cookie.

The top-rated chip, Tropical Source, did showcase the typical pointed shape, but, like the Guittard chip, it had an unusually high cocoa butter content. The average chip is 27 percent cocoa butter, but both Guittard and Tropical Source chips contain 30 percent. Cocoa butter is renowned for providing the melt-in-your-mouth lusciousness of chocolate. Because it is costly, though, most chocolate chip manufacturers limit cocoa butter content. Tasters typically had to agitate chips between their tongue and the roof of their mouth or even bite into some to break them down. Guittard and Tropical Source stood out because they melted more smoothly than the rest.

Finally, what about the classic Nestlé Toll House Morsels? These chips taste good and are ultragooey. They received good ratings from tasters but did not have as much chocolate punch as the top-rated brands.

THE BEST CHOCOLATE CHIPS

Tropical Source Semisweet Chocolate Chips (left) received top marks for their "velvety" mouthfeel and complex flavor. These chips are sold in natural food markets and many supermarkets. Guittard Super Cookie Chips (right) also received high marks. These two brands have more cocoa butter (and more flavor) than other chips.

Crystallized Ginger Ice Cream with Bittersweet Chocolate Sauce

SERVES 4

TIME: 30 MINUTES (INCLUDES 20 MINUTES CHILLING TIME)

For an even faster version of this dessert, scoop the ice cream from the pint (or quart) while it is still hard and then roll it in the crystallized ginger. Serve with the bittersweet chocolate sauce poured over the top. You can follow this recipe and replace the crystallized ginger with toasted coconut, toasted almonds or hazelnuts, chopped caramel turtles or other candy bars, or candied orange peel to make other customized ice cream flavors. You should make this dessert the day you plan to eat it; because you are thawing and refreezing the ice cream, it will be more prone to freezer burn if it sits in the freezer for more than 24 hours.

CRYSTALLIZED GINGER ICE CREAM

1	pint vanilla ice cream
1	ounce (about 2½ tablespoons) crystallized ginger, chopped

CHOCOLATE SAUCE

½	cup plus 2 tablespoons heavy cream
2	tablespoons light corn syrup
2	tablespoons unsalted butter
	Pinch salt
4	ounces (⅔ cup) semisweet chocolate morsels

1. FOR THE ICE CREAM: Place 4 cups hot tap water in a large bowl. Remove the lid from the ice cream container and place the pint on its side on a cutting board. With a serrated knife, slice the ice cream into 4 rounds. Peel away and discard the cardboard container. Place the ice cream rounds in a second large bowl and set this bowl inside of the bowl filled with hot water. Let the ice cream sit in the water bath until soft enough for you to mix in the crystallized ginger, about 5 minutes.

2. Remove the bowl with the ice cream from the water bath and, using a rubber spatula, quickly stir in the ginger. Pack the ice cream into a medium bowl, lay plastic wrap directly on top of the surface of the ice cream, and cover the top of the bowl tightly with another layer of plastic wrap. Place in the freezer until the ice cream is firm, 20 to 30 minutes.

3. FOR THE CHOCOLATE SAUCE: While the ice cream is rehardening in the freezer, bring ½ cup heavy cream plus the corn syrup, butter, and salt to a boil in a small saucepan over medium-high heat. Off the heat, add the chocolate morsels while gently swirling the saucepan. Cover the pan and let stand until the chocolate is melted, about 5 minutes. Uncover and whisk gently until combined. If necessary, adjust the consistency by heating the remaining cream and stirring it in.

4. To serve, scoop the ice cream into individual bowls (about ½ cup per bowl). Spoon chocolate sauce over each portion and serve immediately.

HOT FUDGE SUNDAES

THE QUEEN OF CHOCOLATE SAUCES, hot fudge sauce should be lush and complex. Commercial hot fudge sauces, while readily available, are overly sweet, lack chocolate flavor, and contain stabilizers or preservatives. We wanted to develop a master recipe for a smooth, rich sauce with an intense chocolate impact. The sauce had to be thick and turn chewy over ice cream. Because ice cream is relatively sweet, we thought the sauce itself should be minimally so.

Although we had tried a number of hot

429

fudge sauces, we kept coming back to the same one developed in the test kitchen several years ago. This recipe uses both semisweet chocolate and Dutch-processed cocoa to build layers of chocolate intensity. To make the sauce, you melt chocolate and butter in a double boiler and then whisk in sifted cocoa powder. Next, you bring cream, sugar, corn syrup, salt, and a tablespoon of water to a boil. You add vanilla extract to the cream mixture and combine the liquids—and you're done.

Although we liked the flavor, we wanted to change two things about the method. First, we didn't want to have to chop chocolate, so we decided to use semisweet chocolate chips instead. Second, we didn't want to have to melt the butter and chocolate separately in a double boiler. Instead, we opted to add the butter and chocolate to the hot cream mixture after the sugar had dissolved. The heat from the cream melted the butter and chocolate in less than 2 minutes. Given how thick and rich the sauce is, it's no wonder that hot fudge sundae is an everlasting favorite.

Classic Hot Fudge Sundaes

SERVES 4

TIME: 20 MINUTES

Add 2 tablespoons instant espresso powder for a mocha-hot fudge sauce. Chopped nuts, whipped cream, and a cherry are all you need for true sundae indulgence. For maximum flavor, toast the nuts in a skillet over medium heat just until fragrant. Jimmies (also known as sprinkles), crushed Oreos, chopped peanut butter cups, and vanilla wafers also make nice garnishes.

HOT FUDGE SAUCE

- 2 tablespoons sifted Dutch-process cocoa powder
- 6 tablespoons heavy cream
- 3 tablespoons light corn syrup
- 1/3 cup (2 1/3 ounces) sugar
- Pinch salt
- 5 ounces (3/4 cup) semisweet chocolate morsels
- 1 1/2 tablespoons unsalted butter, cut into pieces
- 1/2 teaspoon vanilla extract

WHIPPING CREAM TO SOFT AND STIFF PEAKS

SOFT PEAKS
Cream whipped to soft peaks droops slightly from the ends of the beaters or whisk.

STIFF PEAKS
Cream whipped to stiff peaks clings tightly to the ends of the beaters or whisk and holds its shape.

1   pint vanilla ice cream

2   cups Whipped Cream (below)

¼   cup nuts (almonds, peanuts, pecans, and/or walnuts), toasted and chopped

4   maraschino cherries (optional)

1. TO MAKE THE SAUCE: Whisk the cocoa and 2 tablespoons hot tap water together in a heavy-bottomed medium saucepan until the cocoa dissolves. Whisk in the cream, corn syrup, sugar, and salt. Bring to a boil and then reduce the heat to medium-low, whisking constantly to keep the sauce from boiling over, until the sugar is dissolved, about 2 minutes.

2. Remove the pan from the heat and add the chocolate morsels, butter, and vanilla. Let sit for 2 minutes and then stir to combine. (The sauce may be refrigerated in an airtight container for several weeks. It will thicken slightly as it cools. Reheat the sauce gently in a microwave or double boiler.)

3. TO ASSEMBLE THE SUNDAES: Scoop the ice cream into individual bowls or parfait glasses (about ½ cup per serving). Top each portion with about ¼ cup hot fudge sauce and ½ cup whipped cream. To finish, sprinkle with toasted nuts and, if using, place a cherry on top.

Whipped Cream

MAKES ABOUT 2 CUPS

TIME: 5 MINUTES

For maximum volume and best flavor, use pasteurized rather than ultrapasteurized heavy cream. It contains fewer stabilizers and is exposed to less heat during processing. In taste tests, we found that pasteurized cream (often organic creams are processed this way) also tastes better than ultrapasteurized cream. When you think the cream is almost properly whipped, you may want to switch from an electric mixer to a whisk for greater control. Cream can go from properly whipped to overwhipped in a matter of seconds. If the cream becomes granular and looks curdled, you've beaten it too long and must start over with a new batch of cream.

1   cup heavy cream, preferably pasteurized, chilled

1   tablespoon sugar

½   teaspoon vanilla extract

1. Chill a deep bowl and the beaters of an electric mixer by filling the bowl with ice water, dropping the beaters in, and letting the bowl stand on the counter for several minutes. When the bowl and beaters are well chilled, dump out the ice water and dry thoroughly.

2. Add the cream, sugar, and vanilla to the chilled bowl. Beat at low speed until small bubbles form, about 30 seconds. Increase the speed to medium and continue beating until the beaters leave a trail, about 30 seconds. Increase the speed to high and continue beating until the cream is smooth, thick, and nearly doubled in volume, about 20 seconds for soft peaks or about 30 seconds for stiff peaks (see the illustrations on page 430), as desired. If necessary, finish beating with a whisk to adjust consistency. Serve immediately or spoon into a fine sieve set over a measuring cup, cover with plastic wrap, and refrigerate for up to 8 hours.

BUTTERSCOTCH SUNDAES

CARAMEL SAUCE IS TO GOLD AS butterscotch is to gold-plated. Although not as luxurious as the real thing, butterscotch is a pretty good impostor. When making a caramel sauce, you have to caramelize sugar, raise its temperature above 350 degrees, add cream, and cool it down. The whole process can take almost 30 minutes. Making oh-so-sweet butterscotch sauce takes just a few minutes, and there's no need to heat the mixture much beyond the boiling point.

We began our search with a recipe developed several years ago in the test kitchen. For this recipe, sugar, corn syrup, butter, and salt were melted together and simmered for about 10 minutes or until the mixture reached 280 degrees. Then cream and vanilla were added and the sauce cooled. Although this procedure is not difficult, we were pretty sure we could shorten it. What we didn't want to sacrifice, though, was flavor. This sauce was buttery, glossy, rich, and thick.

To begin testing, we melted butter and dark brown sugar together. When the sugar had completely dissolved, we added the cream. This version, which took half the time, was cloyingly sweet. We replaced the dark brown sugar with light brown sugar and added a pinch of salt and some vanilla extract. Delicious, yes, but glossy, no. So into the pot we poured 1 teaspoon corn syrup. Now the sauce was rich and

MAKING CHOCOLATE SHAVINGS

Start with a block of high-quality bittersweet or semisweet chocolate. It's easier to cut shavings from a slightly warmed piece of chocolate. To accomplish this, warm the block of chocolate by sweeping a hair dryer over it, taking care not to melt the chocolate. Holding a paring knife at a 45-degree angle against the chocolate, carefully scrape toward you, anchoring the block with your other hand.

thick and glossy. Pouring it over vanilla ice cream and adding whipped cream, toasted peanuts, shaved chocolate, and the requisite cherry, we had a 24-karat winner.

Butterscotch Sundaes

SERVES 4

TIME: 20 MINUTES

If you like, substitute 1½ teaspoons dark rum for the vanilla extract. Toasted cashews or macadamia nuts paired with toasted coconut are nice strewn over the butterscotch sauce. Toast the nuts and coconut on a baking sheet in a 350-degree oven until fragrant, 6 to 8 minutes. Toasted peanuts and chocolate shavings make for a delicious turtle sundae. For a classic presentation, use a star tip to pipe the whipped cream onto the sundae and top it with a cherry.

BUTTERSCOTCH SAUCE

4	tablespoons unsalted butter
½	cup packed (3½ ounces) light brown sugar
¼	cup heavy cream
1	teaspoon light corn syrup
½	teaspoon vanilla extract

1	pint vanilla ice cream
2	cups Whipped Cream (page 431)
¼	cup toasted nuts, toasted sweetened flaked coconut, and/or chocolate shavings (see the illustration at left)
4	maraschino cherries (optional)

1. Place the butter and brown sugar in a medium-size heavy-bottomed saucepan over medium heat. Cook, stirring often, until the sugar melts, 2 to 3 minutes.

2. Remove the pan from the heat and slowly stir in the cream until the sauce is smooth. Stir in the corn syrup and vanilla. The sauce will thicken as it cools. Serve warm or at room temperature. (The butterscotch sauce can be refrigerated in an airtight container for

several weeks. Reheat in a microwave or double boiler.)

3. **TO ASSEMBLE THE SUNDAES:** Scoop the ice cream into individual bowls or parfait glasses (about ½ cup per portion). Top each serving with about ¼ cup butterscotch sauce and ½ cup whipped cream. Sprinkle with toasted nuts, toasted coconut, or chocolate shavings. If using, finish by placing a cherry on top.

WAFFLES WITH ICE CREAM

THE SQUARE HONEYCOMBED SURFACE of a waffle makes it the perfect "dish" on which to serve a giant scoop of ice cream. As the ice cream melts into the boxy cups, it seeps into the core of the waffle, creating a sweet dessert that's similar to bread pudding. But it takes a special waffle to hold up to heavy, sweet, wet ice cream. We wanted our waffle to remain somewhat crisp around the edges, even after the ice cream had begun to melt. From past tests, we knew this would be a challenge; most waffles turn soggy under melting ice cream.

For light waffles with a crunchy exterior and fluffy interior, we have found that it is best to treat the egg yolks and egg whites separately. The yolks are mixed with the rest of the liquid ingredients in the recipe (like milk and vanilla), and the whites are whipped on their own and then folded into the batter just before cooking. Unfortunately, this is a tedious process that dirties many bowls, spatulas, and whisks. We vetoed it and decided to find a way to make waffles in just one bowl—and with no whipping required.

We decided to try the food processor to make the batter. Into the workbowl we put a couple of eggs along with melted butter, milk, and vanilla. We mixed these ingredients and then added our dry ingredients, which included flour, sugar, and baking powder. While these waffles were certainly easy, they had many problems. First, they were too heavy. Second, they were too greasy. And third, they were not crunchy enough.

To address the first two problems, we decided to halve the butter and double the baking powder. The smaller amount of butter would eliminate the grease issue, and the increase in baking powder would provide the waffles the lift they weren't getting from whipped egg whites. We also decided to try sprinkling sugar directly onto the waffle iron before pouring in the batter. We hoped the sugar would stay hard and granular, yielding a crunchy coating.

To our delight, all of our solutions worked beautifully. We had tall waffles that fought the wetness of the ice cream and stayed crisp. These waffles didn't become too heavy with the melted ice cream's weight, either. Best of all, they were made in a food processor in just minutes. We also found that while plain waffles are a delicious base for ice cream, it's easy to make waffles with more interesting flavors, too.

~

Waffles with Ice Cream

SERVES 6

TIME: 20 MINUTES

If you don't have a food processor, you can make these waffles in a blender. To slightly alter their flavor, add 2 teaspoons lemon zest or 1 tablespoon finely ground crystallized ginger (pulsed in a food processor with 1 teaspoon sugar) directly to the batter. Another idea is to roll the scoops of ice cream in cocoa powder, cinnamon sugar, or toasted coconut. A little maple syrup drizzled over the ice cream is a perfect complement to this dessert dish. You can also make toaster waffles out of leftover batter: Undercook the waffles a bit, cool them on a wire rack, wrap them in a plastic bag, and freeze—then pop them straight into the toaster as you like for a quick dessert. Note that the sugar sprinkled onto the waffle iron hardens as it cools, so you'll want to clean the waffle iron while it's still hot. Sprinkle a little water on the warm grids and brush out the sugar with a bristle brush.

1¼	cups (6¼ ounces) unbleached all-purpose flour
½	cup (3½ ounces) plus 1 tablespoon sugar
2	teaspoons baking powder
½	teaspoon salt
4	tablespoons unsalted butter
3	large eggs
1	cup milk
1	teaspoon vanilla extract
1½	pints vanilla ice cream

1. Heat a waffle iron. Whisk together the flour, ½ cup sugar, baking powder, and salt in a medium bowl. In a glass measuring cup, melt the butter in the microwave. In the bowl of a food processor fitted with a steel blade, combine the melted butter, eggs, milk, and vanilla and process until smooth, about 5 seconds.

2. Add the dry ingredients and pulse to combine, about five 1-second pulses. Transfer the mixture to a large bowl.

3. Sprinkle about ½ teaspoon sugar over the waffle iron (if your waffle iron makes 2 waffles at a time, sprinkle ½ teaspoon sugar over each side). Using a ladle, spread an appropriate amount of batter onto the hot waffle iron. Following the manufacturer's instructions, cook the waffle(s) until golden brown, about 5 minutes. Transfer the waffle(s) to individual plates and top each with a scoop or two of ice cream. Serve immediately. (If you prefer, you can keep the waffles warm on a wire rack in a 200-degree oven for up to 10 minutes and then top all the waffles with ice cream at the same time.)

➤ VARIATIONS

Double Chocolate Waffles

These waffles are especially good with mint chocolate chip ice cream.

Follow the recipe for Waffles with Ice Cream, adding ¼ cup cocoa powder to the dry ingredients and melting ½ cup semisweet chocolate morsels with the butter.

Gingerbread Waffles

Ginger or pumpkin ice cream (if you can find it) is nice here, as is plain old vanilla.

Follow the recipe for Waffles with Ice Cream, substituting ½ cup dark brown sugar for the ½ cup granulated sugar and adding 2 teaspoons ground cinnamon, 2 teaspoons ground ginger, 1 teaspoon ground cloves, 1 teaspoon ground allspice, and 1 teaspoon ground nutmeg to the dry ingredients. Add 2 tablespoons molasses to the liquid ingredients.

Brown Sugar–Pecan Waffles

Cinnamon or butter pecan ice cream is a perfect match for these waffles.

Follow the recipe for Waffles with Ice Cream, substituting ½ cup dark brown sugar for the ½ cup granulated sugar and adding ½ cup toasted whole pecans to the workbowl of the food processor with the dry ingredients.

30-MINUTE CHOCOLATE MOUSSE

CHOCOLATE MOUSSE SERVED IN AN elegant dessert cup or in crystal stemware will never go out of fashion. Its smooth texture and rich, creamy flavor sate even the most zealous chocolate fiend's appetite. But classic recipes, with their raw eggs, have fallen out of favor, as egg yolks and whites should be heated to kill harmful bacteria. Therefore, modern mousse recipes require the cook to whip the egg yolks over a water bath to bring them up to temperature. Once the egg yolks are at a safe temperature, they must be whipped until they cool. The whites are treated in the same way and then folded into the rest of the mixture.

As you can imagine, the entire process is, well, a bit of a process. We wondered if we could create a faux mousse—one that retained the richness and creaminess of classic *mousse au chocolat* but bypassed all of that egg whipping.

We started with a recipe for ganache, which is essentially hot cream poured over chopped chocolate with a couple of tablespoons of butter added for thickness and gloss. The softened butter, chocolate, and cream are whipped in a food processor until smooth and then chilled until the mixture hardens. Typically, ganache is used as a filling for truffles or as a cake filling or frosting. But we had a different idea in mind. We wanted to fold whipped cream into the not-quite-set ganache.

We chilled the ganache until it reached the consistency of soft frosting. Then, we whipped cream with sugar and vanilla and beat it into the ganache. This "mousse" was an excellent impostor—rich and smooth and creamy. Best of all, it was ready to eat in less than 30 minutes.

⇥✦

30-Minute Chocolate Mousse

SERVES 6

TIME: 30 MINUTES (INCLUDES 15 MINUTES COOLING TIME)

If you like, add 2 tablespoons brandy, coffee liqueur, or cognac to the ganache as it is being whipped in the food processor. If the finished mousse is refrigerated for more than 15 minutes before serving, it will lose its creamy texture and turn stiff and crumbly. A better idea is to make the ganache ahead of time (it can be stored in the refrigerator for up to 1 week), leave it at room temperature (or over a water bath) until it reaches the consistency of soft frosting, and then add it to the whipped cream as instructed in the recipe. Serve the mousse with a dollop of whipped cream on top. Add chocolate shavings (see page 432), sliced strawberries, or whole raspberries, if you like. See photo of this recipe on page 166.

¾	cup heavy cream
	Pinch salt
6	ounces high-quality semisweet or bittersweet chocolate, chopped
3	tablespoons unsalted butter, chilled
1	teaspoon vanilla extract
2	cups Whipped Cream (page 431), refrigerated in the bowl of a standing mixer

1. Microwave the cream and salt in a measuring cup on high power until bubbling, about 1½ minutes. (Alternatively, bring the mixture to a simmer in a small saucepan over medium-high heat.)

2. Place the chocolate in the bowl of a food processor fitted with a steel blade. With the machine running, gradually pour the hot cream mixture through the feed tube and process until smooth, about 1 minute. With the machine still running, add the butter, 1 tablespoon at a time, and process until smooth, about 2 minutes. Add the vanilla and continue to process until smooth and thickened, 1 to 2 minutes longer. Transfer the ganache to a medium bowl and refrigerate until it has the consistency of soft frosting, about 15 minutes.

3. Remove ½ cup whipped cream from the bowl and reserve it for a garnish. Scrape the chilled ganache into the bowl with the remaining whipped cream. Using the whisk attachment, beat the ganache into the cream at medium-high speed until smooth, about 30 seconds. Scrape down the sides of the bowl

with a rubber spatula to make sure no pockets of whipped cream remain. Spoon the mousse into glasses, garnish with a dollop of plain whipped cream, and serve immediately.

Semolina Pudding with Cashews and Raisins

SEMOLINA PUDDING IS A DELICIOUS Indian dessert made by toasting semolina flour (which is also used to make fresh pasta) in melted butter (many recipes call for *ghee*, or clarified butter, but we think regular unsalted butter is just fine) and then adding scalding hot milk infused with sugar and spices. At the very end, toasted nuts and dried fruit are stirred into the thick, porridgelike pudding. Although traditional recipes call for chilling the pudding and cutting it into squares, we like it warm so the texture is creamy rather than firm.

What makes this pudding unusual and quick to make is that it contains no eggs. This meant we wouldn't have to worry about baking the pudding—or, for that matter, even making a custard base to bring the eggs up to a safe temperature. For the same reason, we knew the ratio of butter to milk to semolina would be crucial to achieving a creamy pudding.

We examined the ratios of butter and milk in a few recipes for the pudding. First, we tried using twice as much milk as butter and adding equal amounts of butter and semolina. This produced a pudding that was somewhat dry. We decided to increase the amount of milk to help ensure a creamy pudding consistency and to decrease the amount of butter to reduce the grease factor. This version was perfect— luscious and creamy.

Almost every recipe for semolina pudding includes cardamom as a main flavoring. We thought the exotic flavor of the cardamom paired nicely with the earthiness of the semolina. But the pudding needed more depth, and for this we chose ground cinnamon. Salt rounded out the flavors. For crunch and sweetness, we chose to add toasted cashews and chopped raisins to the pudding.

Semolina Pudding with Cashews and Raisins

SERVES 8

TIME: 20 MINUTES

For maximum flavor, toast the nuts in a small skillet over medium heat just until fragrant.

8	tablespoons (1 stick) unsalted butter
1 ½	cups (about 7 ounces) semolina
4	cups milk
1	cup (7 ounces) sugar
1	teaspoon ground cardamom
¾	teaspoon ground cinnamon
¼	teaspoon salt
1	cup unsalted cashews, toasted and chopped
½	cup raisins, chopped
1	cup heavy cream

1. Melt 4 tablespoons butter in a large heavy-bottomed saucepan or Dutch oven over medium heat. Add the semolina and stir with a wooden spoon until the mixture looks like wet sand, about 1 minute. Continue to cook the semolina, stirring occasionally, until fragrant and lightly colored, 5 to 7 minutes.

2. While the semolina is toasting, bring the remaining 4 tablespoons butter, milk, sugar, cardamom, cinnamon, and salt to a boil in a large saucepan. Once the semolina is lightly toasted, add about one quarter of the liquid to the semolina (the liquid will hiss and sizzle as it hits the dry, hot

semolina) and quickly whisk, breaking up any clumps. Add another one quarter of the liquid and whisk; repeat twice more until all the liquid is incorporated and the semolina looks like a thick porridge. Cook the semolina pudding, stirring constantly, until it thickens considerably, 2 to 4 minutes. Stir in the nuts and raisins.

3. Divide the pudding among individual bowls, drizzle each with 2 tablespoons heavy cream, and serve immediately.

➤ VARIATIONS

Semolina Pudding with Cashews, Dates, and Coconut

Follow the recipe for Semolina Pudding with Cashews and Raisins, substituting ½ cup chopped dates for the raisins and adding 1 cup toasted sweetened flaked coconut to the pudding along with the cashews and dates.

Semolina Pudding with Apricots, Pistachios, and Saffron

Follow the recipe for Semolina Pudding with Cashews and Raisins, substituting 1 teaspoon crumbled saffron threads for the cinnamon, 1 cup chopped pistachios for the cashews, and ½ cup chopped apricots for the raisins.

STICKY TOFFEE PUDDING

NOT QUITE A CREAMY PUDDING AND not quite a spongy cake, English sticky toffee pudding (made from eggs, sugar, flour, and dates and glazed with butterscotch sauce) is a unique dessert. Like a pudding, its consistency is creamy and rich, but like a cake, it can be cut into squares and served on a plate with a fork. Not for the sugar-sensitive, sticky toffee pudding packs an intense hit of sweetness in each bite.

After some initial research, we found most recipes started the same way. First, dates (either whole or chopped) were soaked and softened in a combination of boiling water and baking soda. Next, the butter and sugar were creamed together, eggs added, and the liquid date mixture and the dry flour mixture introduced into the butter mixture in alternating additions. The batter bakes for about half an hour and then a butterscotch sauce is poured over the top. At this point, the cake is either cooled or put back into the oven to meld the hot, sticky sauce to the sweet cake.

We decided to streamline this already simple dessert even further. First, we tried using a food processor to make the batter. Because dates left whole simply sank to the bottom of the cake, we knew we would have to chop them first, and it made sense to use a food processor to chop the dates efficiently. So they wouldn't stick to the bowl or the blade, we decided to pulse the dates and the sugar together. To this sandy mixture, we added water (we decided to use warm water to help soften the dates), a couple of eggs, and vanilla extract. After a quick blend, it was time to add the flour. We tried adding the dry ingredients to the food processor but found that mixing the flour into the batter by hand produced a more tender cake. The cake then went into the oven for a short stay, after which we pierced the top with a toothpick many times over and then covered the cake with a satiny butterscotch sauce.

We unanimously preferred putting the cake back into the oven for a couple of minutes to allow the sweet sauce to seep into the cake rather than just pouring the sauce over the cake and serving it as is. With its intensely sweet glaze, its yielding interior crumb, and its dense, creamy mouthfeel, sticky toffee pudding combines the best of both the cake and pudding worlds in one dessert.

Sticky Toffee Pudding

SERVES 8 TO 10

TIME: 60 MINUTES
(INCLUDES 45 MINUTES BAKING
AND COOLING TIME)

Instead of pouring all of the butterscotch sauce over the top of the cake, you can reserve half of it to serve alongside the baked cake. The cake will keep for up to 3 days if covered with plastic wrap and refrigerated. Use the microwave to reheat a chilled slice before serving.

PUDDING

4	tablespoons unsalted butter, melted, plus 1 tablespoon, softened, for greasing the pan
1¼	cups (6¼ ounces) unbleached all-purpose flour
½	teaspoon baking powder
½	teaspoon salt
1	cup (6 ounces) pitted dates
1	cup (7 ounces) sugar
2	large eggs
1¼	cups warm water
1	teaspoon vanilla extract

SAUCE

8	tablespoons unsalted butter
1	cup packed (7 ounces) light brown sugar
⅔	cup heavy cream
2	tablespoons brandy or rum (optional)

Vanilla ice cream or Whipped Cream
(page 431)

1. FOR THE PUDDING: Adjust an oven rack to the middle position and heat the oven to 350 degrees. Grease an 8 by 8-inch baking pan with 1 tablespoon softened butter.

2. Whisk together the flour, baking powder, and salt in a medium bowl. In the workbowl of a food processor fitted with a steel blade, combine the dates and sugar in three 1-second pulses. Add the eggs, warm water, and vanilla to the date mixture and process until smooth, about 5 seconds. With the food processor running, pour the melted butter through the feed tube in a steady stream. Transfer the mixture to a large bowl.

3. Add one third of the flour mixture to the bowl with the egg mixture; whisk gently to combine. Add the remaining flour mixture to the egg mixture in 2 more additions, whisking just to incorporate. Pour the batter into the prepared pan.

4. Bake, rotating the pan halfway through the baking time, until the center of the cake bounces back when lightly pressed with your finger, 25 to 30 minutes.

5. FOR THE SAUCE: While the cake is baking, melt the butter in a medium saucepan over medium-high heat. Reduce the heat to medium and whisk in the brown sugar. Continue to cook, stirring occasionally, until the sugar is completely dissolved and the mixture looks puffy, 4 to 5 minutes. Whisk in the cream and brandy or rum, if using, and simmer for 3 minutes. The sauce should develop a frothy head. (If the sauce climbs too close to the lip of the saucepan, reduce the heat to low.) Remove the pan from the heat.

6. After the cake has baked for 25 to 30 minutes, remove it from the oven and poke many holes in the top with a toothpick. Pour the sauce over the cake and evenly distribute it using a rubber spatula. Return the pan to the oven and bake for 5 minutes. Cool the baking pan on a wire rack for 10 to 15 minutes. Cut the warm pudding into squares and serve with vanilla ice cream or whipped cream.

INDEX

NOTE: PAGE NUMBERS IN *ITALICS* REFER TO COLOR PHOTOGRAPHS.